EDWARD ALBEE

CASEBOOKS ON MODERN DRAMATISTS
Kimball King, *General Editor*

PETER SHAFFER
A Casebook
edited by C. J. Gianakaras

SIMON GRAY
A Casebook
edited by Katherine H. Burkman

JOHN ARDEN AND MARGARETTA D'ARCY
A Casebook
edited by Jonathan Wike

AUGUST WILSON
A Casebook
edited by Marilyn Elkins

JOHN OSBORNE
A Casebook
edited by Patricia D. Denison

ARNOLD WESKER
A Casebook
edited by Reade W. Dornan

DAVID HARE
A Casebook
edited by Hersh Zeifman

MARSHA NORMAN
A Casebook
edited by Linda Ginter Brown

BRIAN FRIEL
A Casebook
edited by William Kerwin

NEIL SIMON
A Casebook
edited by Gary Konas

TERRENCE MCNALLY
A Casebook
edited by Toby Silverman Zinman

STEPHEN SONDHEIM
A Casebook
edited by Joanne Gordon

HORTON FOOTE
A Casebook
edited by Gerald C. Wood

SAMUEL BECKETT
A Casebook
edited by Jennifer M. Jeffers

WENDY WASSERSTEIN
A Casebook
edited by Claudia Barnett

WOODY ALLEN
A Casebook
edited by Kimball King

MODERN DRAMATISTS
A Casebook of Major British, Irish, and American Playwrights
edited by Kimball King

PINTER AT 70
A Casebook
edited by Lois Gordon

TENNESSEE WILLIAMS
A Casebook
edited by Robert F. Gross

JOE ORTON
A Casebook
edited by Francesca Coppa

BETH HENLEY
A Casebook
edited by Julia A. Fesmire

EDWARD ALBEE
A Casebook
edited by Bruce J. Mann

EDWARD ALBEE
A CASEBOOK

EDITED BY
BRUCE J. MANN

Routledge
New York and London

Published in 2003 by
Routledge
29 West 35th Street
New York, NY 10001
www.routledge-ny.com

Published in Great Britain by
Routledge
11 New Fetter Lane
London EC4P 4EE
www.routledge.co.uk

Library of Congress Cataloging-in-Publication Data

Edward Albee : a casebook / edited by Bruce J. Mann.
    p. cm. —(Casebooks on modern dramatists ; v. 29)
Includes bibliographical references and index.
ISBN 0-8153-3165-7 (acid-free paper)
1. Albee, Edward, 1928—Criticism and interpretation. I. Mann, Bruce J., 1952- II. Series.

PS3551.L25 Z655   2003
812'.54—dc21

                                                   2002011279

For Kappa

Contents

General Editor's Note

KIMBALL KING

As Bruce Mann notes in his introduction, this casebook grows out of the revival of Edward Albee's plays and the need to reconsider his achievement. According to critics, Albee has written at least four major plays, *The Zoo Story, Who's Afraid of Virginia Woolf?*, *A Delicate Balance*, and *Three Tall Women* and others, including *Tiny Alice*, *Box* and *Quotations from Chairman Mao Tse-Tung*, *All Over*, *Seascape*, and *The Lady from Dubuque*, that demand a second look. This casebook offers new essays on all four major plays and reconsiderations of *Box* and *Quotations from Chairman Mao Tse-Tung*, *All Over*, and *The Lady from Dubuque*. In addition, there are studies of less well-known Albee works; among them, *Malcolm*, his adaptation of James Purdy's novel, *The Man Who Had Three Arms*, *Marriage Play*, and *Fragments*. Also included is an interview with the playwright. In the interview we learn to appreciate even more Albee's achievements as a writer, director, teacher, and intellectual influence on modern life. It should also be noted that in 2002, Albee received a Tony award for his latest play, *The Goat, or Who Is Sylvia?*, written too recently to be analyzed in this volume.

Bruce Mann, who is writing a book-length study of late-life-style in American plays, has gathered a talented group of literary scholars to comment on one of the twentieth century's leading American playwrights. Professor Mann is chair of the Department of English at Oakland University in Rochester, Michigan. At Oakland he was awarded the university's Teaching Excellence Award in 1991 and the Judd Family Faculty Achievement Award in 1999. He has also served as a dramaturg for Oakland University's professional theater company, Meadow Brook Theatre, and he has published articles and given conference presentations on O'Neill, Williams, Miller, Pinter, Shepard, and Churchill. His most recent contribution, "Memories and Muses: *Vieux Carre* and *Something Cloudy, Something Clear*," appears in *Tennessee Williams: A Casebook* (2001), edited by Robert Gross, also published by Routledge in the Casebook Series.

Chronology

1928	Born March 12 in Washington, D.C. Adopted by Reed A. and Frances Cotter Albee of Larchmont, New York. Named Edward Franklin Albee III, after his adoptive grandfather, co-owner of four hundred vaudeville theaters across the country (the Keith-Albee circuit).
1940	Enrolls in Lawrenceville Academy, New Jersey, and is dismissed during the second year for not attending classes.
1943	Attends Valley Forge Military Academy, Pennsylvania, and is dismissed during second year.
1944	Enrolls in the Choate School, Wallingford, Connecticut. Begins writing and receives encouragement from his teachers.
1946	Graduates from Choate. Attends Trinity College, Hartford, Connecticut, and is dismissed after three semesters for attendance problems and refusal to attend chapel.
1949	Leaves home. Moves to Greenwich Village and works at various jobs, including messenger for Western Union. Supported by small inheritance from his paternal grandmother. Continues to write.
1958	Writes *The Zoo Story*.
1959	Attends world premiere of *The Zoo Story*, Schiller Theatre, Berlin, Germany. Albee's play, which receives excellent reviews, is paired with Samuel Beckett's *Krapp's Last Tape*.
1960	*The Zoo Story* opens at the Provincetown Playhouse, New York. *The Sandbox* produced at the Jazz Gallery, New York. *The Death of Bessie Smith* staged at Schlosspark Theater, Berlin. *Fam and Yam* produced at the White Barn, Westport, Connecticut, and later at the Theatre de Lys, New York.
1961	*The American Dream* staged at the York Playhouse, New York. Directs *The Zoo Story* (off-Broadway and tour).

1962   *Who's Afraid of Virginia Woolf?* produced at the Billy Rose The-
        ater, New York, and receives the Drama Critics Circle Award, a
        Tony Award, and other prizes. It runs for 644 performances. Albee
        directs *The American Dream* (off-Broadway and tour).

1963   Creates the Playwrights Unit, with Richard Barr and Clinton
        Wilder, to encourage new playwrights. About one hundred plays
        are presented at the workshops, including works by Lanford Wil-
        son, Sam Shepard, Adrienne Kennedy, Terrence McNally, Amiri
        Baraka, and John Guare. *The Ballad of the Sad Café*, an adaptation
        of the novella by Carson McCullers, produced at the Martin Beck
        Theater, New York. Albee travels with John Steinbeck to the Soviet
        Union.

1964   *Tiny Alice* opens at the Billy Rose Theater, New York, and later
        wins the New York Drama Critics Award and a Tony Award.

1966   *Malcolm*, an adaptation of James Purdy's novel, opens at the Schu-
        bert Theater, New York. Film of *Who's Afraid of Virginia Woolf?*
        released, with Elizabeth Taylor, Richard Burton, George Segal, and
        Sandy Dennis in the cast. *A Delicate Balance* produced at the Mar-
        tin Beck Theater, New York. It runs for 132 performances and later
        wins the Pulitzer Prize.

1967   *Everything in the Garden*, an adaptation of a Giles Cooper play,
        opens at the Plymouth Theater, New York.

1968   *Box* and *Quotations from Chairman Mao Tse-Tung* staged at Stu-
        dio Arena Theater, Buffalo, New York, and in September at the
        Billy Rose Theater, New York.

1971   *All Over* opens at the Martin Beck Theater, New York, directed by
        John Gielgud and starring Jessica Tandy and Colleen Dewhurst.

1972   *All Over* produced by the Royal Shakespeare Company, London.

1973   *A Delicate Balance* filmed by Tony Richardson for the American
        Film Theater series, with Katharine Hepburn, Paul Scofield, Lee
        Remick, Joseph Cotten, and Kate Reid.

1975   Directs *Seascape* at the Schubert Theater, New York, which later
        earns Albee his second Pulitzer Prize.

1976   *Listening* broadcast on BBC Radio Three, London. Albee directs
        Broadway revival of *Who's Afraid of Virginia Woolf?* with Colleen
        Dewhurst and Ben Gazzara. The Hartford Stage Company produc-
        tion of *All Over* is broadcast on "Theatre in America," the public
        television series. *Counting the Ways* premieres at the National The-
        ater, London.

1977   *Counting the Ways* and *Listening* produced by Hartford Stage
        Company, Connecticut.

1980   *The Lady from Dubuque* opens at the Morosco Theater, New York,
        and closes after twelve performances. Albee receives a Gold Medal

in Drama from the American Academy and Institute of Arts and Letters.

1981   *Lolita*, an adaptation of Vladimir Nabokov's novel, produced at the Brooks Atkinson Theater, New York.

1982   *The Man Who Had Three Arms* produced at Goodman Theater, Chicago.

1983   *The Man Who Had Three Arms* opens at Lyceum Theater, New York, and closes after sixteen performances. *Finding the Sun* staged at the University of Northern Colorado, Greeley.

1985   Directs one-act plays by David Mamet, Lanford Wilson, and Sam Shepard at English Theater, Vienna.

1987   Directs world premiere of *Marriage Play* at English Theater, Vienna.

1988   Named Distinguished Professor of Drama at the University of Houston.

1989   Albee's adoptive mother, Frances Cotter Albee, dies. Albee directs revival of *Who's Afraid of Virginia Woolf?* with Glenda Jackson and John Lithgow, in Los Angeles.

1991   Directs *Krapp's Last Tape* and *Ohio Impromptu* by Samuel Beckett for Alley Theater, Houston. Directs world premiere of *Three Tall Women* at Vienna's English Theatre. Directs American premiere of *Marriage Play* at Alley Theatre, Houston, and McCarter Theatre, Princeton, New Jersey.

1992   Directs world premiere of *The Lorca Play* at the Houston International Festival. American premiere of *Three Tall Women* at River Arts Repertory, Woodstock, New York.

1993   Directs world premiere of *Fragments* at Ensemble Theater of Cincinnati, Ohio. Signature Theater Company, New York City, produces *Counting the Ways*, *Listening*, and *Marriage Play*. Albee directs *Happy Days* by Samuel Beckett for Alley Theater, Houston.

1994   *Three Tall Women* opens in New York at the Vineyard Theatre—with Myra Carter, Marian Seldes, and Jordan Baker—and later moves to the Promenade Theatre, winning Albee his third Pulitzer Prize for Drama and also the Drama Critics Circle Award, the Lucille Lortel Award, and the Outer Critics Circle Award. The London production, with Maggie Smith, wins an Evening Standard Award. Albee directs *Sand*, an evening of his one-acts—*Box*, *The Sandbox*, and *Finding the Sun*—at Signature Theater Company, New York. *Fragments* also produced by Signature. Albee wins an Obie Award for Sustained Achievement in the theatre.

1996   *A Delicate Balance* revived on Broadway, with Rosemary Harris, George Grizzard, and Elaine Stritch. Albee receives Kennedy Center Honors in Washington, D.C. *Who's Afraid of Virginia Woolf?*

produced at Almeida Theatre, London, with Diana Rigg and David Suchet.

1997   *Tiny Alice* revived at Hartford Stage, with Richard Thomas as Julian. Albee receives the Common Wealth Award in Wilmington, Delaware. Revival of *A Delicate Balance* in London.

1998   *The Play about the Baby* premieres at London's Almeida Theatre.

1999   Mel Gussow's biography, *Edward Albee: A Singular Journey*, published.

2000   Directs American premiere of *The Play about the Baby* at Alley Theatre, Houston.

2001   *The Play about the Baby* opens Off-Broadway. *Who's Afraid of Virginia Woolf?* produced at Canada's Stratford Festival.

2002   *The Goat, or Who Is Sylvia?* opens in March and receives 2002 Tony Award for Best Play. Also wins New York Drama Critics Circle Award, Drama Desk Award, and Outer Critics Circle Award, all for Best Play.

Introduction

BRUCE J. MANN

This has been a good time for Edward Albee. At long last, he is receiving the recognition he deserves for his many contributions to the American theater. During the past decade, he has collected his third Pulitzer Prize for *Three Tall Women*, and important revivals have been mounted in New York and London of *Who's Afraid of Virginia Woolf?* and *A Delicate Balance*. In 1996, Kennedy Center honors were conferred upon Albee. Three years later, Mel Gussow's biography of the playwright was published, and in 2002, Albee won the Tony Award for Best Play for *The Goat, or Who Is Sylvia?* Through it all, Albee has not missed a step, continuing to teach, direct, and write new plays.

After more than a decade of critical neglect, Albee returned to the spotlight with the stunning success of *Three Tall Women* in 1994. This play about his adoptive mother opened our eyes again to Albee's inimitable virtues: his vaunted wit, his mix of darkness and light (like Rachmaninoff *and* Satie), his innovative use of dramatic space, his focus on the American family and its ills, his brilliant use of language (from the gentle to the vitriolic), and his fearless search for meaning. Watching the award-winning New York production, directed by Lawrence Sacharow, I realized that *Three Tall Women*, with its autobiographical revelations, was a summing-up of sorts, a play that cast new light on all of Albee's other plays. It made me return to them to reexamine their dramatic worlds.

This casebook grows out of the Albee revival and the need to reconsider his achievement, which is significant. According to his biographer, Mel Gussow, Albee "has written at least four major plays (*The Zoo Story*, *Who's Afraid of Virginia Woolf?*, *A Delicate Balance*, and *Three Tall Women*), others (*Tiny Alice*, *Box* and *Quotations from Chairman Mao Tse-Tung*, *All Over*, *Seascape*, and *The Lady from Dubuque*) that demand a second look, and one-acts that remain models of their kind" (17). This casebook offers new essays

1

on all four major plays and reconsiderations of *Box* and *Quotations from Chairman Mao Tse-Tung*, *All Over*, and *The Lady from Dubuque*. In addition, studies of less well-known Albee works are included, among them, *Malcolm*, his adaptation of James Purdy's novel; *The Man Who Had Three Arms*; *Marriage Play*, and *Fragments*. An interview with the playwright is also included.

Three Tall Women is given special attention. Framing the other essays are commentaries on this seminal drama. In "*Three Tall Women*: Return to the Muses," I argue that *Three Tall Women* belongs to the same genre of autobiographical plays as Eugene O'Neill's *Long Day's Journey into Night* and Tennessee Williams's *Something Cloudy, Something Clear*. At midlife or later, a crisis impelled these playwrights to revisit—in drama—the people, events, and forces that first shaped them—their mother muses, including literary ones. The experience is a kind of rebirth, because they emerge with a more expansive perspective on their lives. Complicating Albee's return to his formative events is his troubled relationship with his mother; but, in an imaginative, dramatic landscape filled with echoes of Beckett, Chekhov, and Pirandello, Albee reconnects with his mother, and after an epiphany, frees himself from her hurtfulness.

Anne Paolucci, the dean of American Albee critics, provides a survey of the playwright's career in "Edward Albee: A Retrospective (and Beyond)." For many of us, Paolucci's pioneering work, *From Tension to Tonic: The Plays of Edward Albee*, provided the first map of Albee's challenging world. In her essay in this volume, she reviews Albee's initial reception, and then charts his achievements as a playwright of greatness, "a consummate artist who knows both his craft and his own true voice." Noting his ties to post–World War II European theater, she nevertheless finds strong correspondences between Albee's plays and those of Luigi Pirandello, and she illustrates her points with an extended analysis of Albee's 1982 play, *The Man Who Had Three Arms*. In this difficult work, Paolucci locates strategies reminiscent of Pirandello's *Each in His Own Way* and *Tonight We Improvise*. Paolucci writes that Albee "dismissed the literal message of the political and social realism of the forties, fifties, and sixties as subjects for drama and gave the American theater new content and form, portraying our postexistential tensions on a stage swept bare of standard conventions."

In her essay, "Absurdly American: Rediscovering the Representation of Violence in *The Zoo Story*," Lisa Siefker Bailey argues that Albee's celebrated drama is more an American play than an absurdist one (as it is often labeled). Focusing on Jerry's determination to educate Peter and invoking Richard Slotkin's *Regeneration through Violence*, Siefker shows how Albee metatheatrically connects with his audience. She describes the play as timeless and time-bound, emerging from the alienation felt by many in American culture during the 1950s. But Jerry's battle for connection with Peter transcends the times, leaving Peter and the audience with an indelible image of American violence that cannot be ignored, a Derridean trace, a non-event that is a disturbing reality nonetheless, one that keeps echoing in our minds.

Lincoln Konkle identifies Albee as an American Jeremiah in " 'Good, Better, Best, Bested': The Failure of American Typology in *Who's Afraid of Virginia Woolf?*" Konkle reads Albee's best-known play as a jeremiad that records our regressive tendencies while urging us to do better. The playwright, as prophet figure, wants us to reverse our moral decline and improve our sense of values. Konkle's analysis of the typology of seventeenth–century New England Puritans explains how the playwright's characters risk a kind of death-in-life by choosing to remain "types," and not evolve further. Konkle also points out how George functions as the teacher he is, in reality, to encourage the others—Honey, Martha, and Nick—to learn and grow. Transformation comes in the final act, for the characters as well as the audience of this jeremiad, which sees that regeneration is possible, that we can mature as individuals and work together to carry on America's errand into the wilderness.

In "Like Father, Like Son: The Ciphermale in *A Delicate Balance* and *Malcolm*," Robert F. Gross explores the nature and consequences of two melancholic male figures. Gross creates the term "ciphermale" to describe Tobias and Malcolm, both of whom are "characterological blanks." Neither has sufficiently mourned the loss of a male family member; Tobias has lost Teddy, his son, while Malcolm's father has disappeared. As a result, both have become passive, withdrawn, and obsessed with their melancholia. Gross shows how ciphermales alter the dynamics of the dramatic world, moving drama away from the conventional model of psychological depth introduced by Eugene O'Neill. Albee uses Tobias to reveal unresolved tensions in middle-class America during the 1960s; Malcolm emerges as a more difficult case of irreparable loss. Gross probes the father/son dyad in both plays in detail, finding it a site that opens into an abyss. At the same time, Albee's use of the ciphermale opens the theater to a new sense of space, far beyond the well-made play and toward the postmodern.

Rakesh H. Solomon provides a behind-the-scenes look at Edward Albee in another of his roles, director. His essay, "Forging Text into Theatre: Edward Albee Directs *Box* and *Quotations from Chairman Mao Tse-Tung*," developed from his extensive documentation of rehearsals for a 1978–1979 production of these plays. Interviewing the playwright and watching him interact with the cast members, Solomon recorded Albee's rationale behind movement, word emphasis, and linkage of speeches, for example, all of which illuminate the texture and meaning of these elusive, apocalyptic dramas. Albee's comments are wide-ranging, from his own approach to writing a play, for example, to the distinction he makes between his plays of exterior and interior action. Albee emerges as a collaborative director with clear ideas about realizing his play onstage. He also has a phenomenal memory; according to Solomon: "Without director's promptbook or script, he accurately recalls not only every line and stage direction but even minute details of textual emphasis and punctuation."

Emily Rosenbaum explores gender roles in "A Demystified Mystique: *All Over* and the Fall of the Cult of True Womanhood." Rosenbaum focuses on The Wife, whose unhappiness is evident as she lives out her dying husband's final hours at home, along with The Mistress, The Doctor, family members, and friends. The Wife has internalized nineteenth-century ideals of "True Womanhood," as defined by Barbara Welter, and Rosenbaum argues that she now finds her duties taken over by others or emptied of meaning. From The Wife's memories, we learn about her expectations and how these were subverted over time, leaving her angry and with no apparent role to fill. *All Over* reveals the persistence of "True Womanhood" ideals into the 1970s in America, and how these lead to tragic disappointment for The Wife, since her authority has been usurped, by The Doctor and Mistress, for example. Identified only with her husband, she has nowhere to turn when he dies.

In *"The Lady from Dubuque*: Into the Labyrinth," Ronald F. Rapin studies one of Albee's most challenging plays. He argues that, in great measure, the medium in this play is also the message. Albee creates a Borges-like maze with his plot structure that continually frustrates the reader/audience member. The "veiled riddling" of the first act, with its game of Twenty Questions and its textual dead-ends, creates tension and disorientation that expresses the characters' failed search for happiness, fulfillment, and self-identity. The second act adds to the labyrinthine complexity with the arrival of two mysterious older characters. Rapin suggests that Act Two is Sam's nightmarish response to all that has happened, especially his wife's fatal illness. Thus, what is being expressed, and communicated to us, is his "helplessness, the physical and mental restraints which immobilize Sam." Represented onstage is the condition Beckett referred to as "the suffering of being" (qtd. in Esslin, 38), which draws everyone into its subconscious labyrinth, if they choose to follow it and deal with it.

Norma Jenckes, in "Postmodernist Tensions in Albee's Recent Work," finds evidence of a struggle between modernist values and the valueless nature of postmodernism. Studying *Marriage Play*, *Fragments*, and *Three Tall Women*, Jenckes notes how all three undermine traditional dramatic conventions. In *Marriage Play*, a husband calls attention to his entrance as a character in a play and even repeats it. *Fragments* dispenses with causality, unfolding as a series of monologues by the unnamed characters. In *Three Tall Women*, a woman is divided into three different characters that represent her in youth, middle age, and old age. Drawing on Jameson, Lyotard, Wollen, and other theorists, Jenckes uncovers these plays' postmodern strategies.

However, she also finds that Albee continues to search for meaning amid the valueless, postmodern landscape; hence, he "remains a high modernist."

The final essay returns to *Three Tall Women*, but with a difference. Director Lawrence Sacharow recounts the story of bringing the play to life onstage, first in Woodstock, New York, and then in New York City. Sacharow's work with Albee—the casting process, rehearsals, the exploration of subtext, the blocking—is described and the decisions explained, shedding light on the text and revealing how the stage images communicate its meaning. Sacharow is aware of the play's autobiographical content and recounts the time, in rehearsal, when Albee himself played the Young Man, energizing the cast. Nevertheless, Sacharow approaches *Three Tall Women* as a drama of universal appeal and impact, with moments that remind him of Greek drama. Reading his essay, one discovers the collaborative nature of theater and the complexity of staging a new play. As audiences discovered, this production offered a deeply layered experience, one filled with nuance, color, and music.

The casebook ends with an interview of Albee, conducted by myself. The playwright comments on many subjects: some of his most recent plays, including *Three Tall Women* and *The Lorca Play*; his fascination with engaging an audience; a new play he is composing; the musical quality of his writing; his thoughts about other playwrights, including Thornton Wilder, and his concerns about critics; the state of American theatre; and the development of young playwrights. Like the articles in this collection, the interview reveals the playwright's agile mind and articulate expression. As he speaks, we sense his devotion to his craft, and also how much he has achieved as a playwright, director, teacher, and intellect—an artist still determined to make us look at ourselves, our nation, and our world in a critical way, so that we choose to participate in the betterment of life.

Works Cited

Esslin, Martin. *The Theatre of the Absurd*. Rev. ed. Garden City, N.Y.: Doubleday Anchor Books, 1969.
Gussow, Mel. *Edward Albee: A Singular Journey*. N.Y.: Simon & Schuster, 1999.

1

Three Tall Women: Return to the Muses

BRUCE J. MANN

Three Tall Women (1994) brought new life to Edward Albee. After more than a decade of critical neglect, Albee received his best reviews ever for this remarkable autobiographical drama. Reviewers were fascinated by its inventive design and its main character, a daunting elderly woman modeled on the playwright's adoptive mother. The play immediately revived interest in Albee's work and earned the playwright, then in his sixties, a third Pulitzer Prize. In this article, I explore why Albee wrote *Three Tall Women*, and what motivated him to dramatize the life of his mother. I argue that, while the play itself renewed his career, the act of writing it brought another kind of renewal—internal self-renewal for Albee.

Academic critics have paid little attention to *Three Tall Women*. Only two articles focus on it, and one commentator is dismissive.[1] Neither critic identifies the type of play Albee has written, which is crucial to its analysis. *Three Tall Women* belongs to a series of autobiographical dramas, written by playwrights in midlife or later, that includes *Long Day's Journey into Night* (1941) by Eugene O'Neill and *Something Cloudy, Something Clear* (1981) by Tennessee Williams.[2] Something impels each dramatist to look back to his earliest influences, his muses—the figures, events, and authors that first shaped and inspired him as a writer. He finds them in a realm, deep in his mind, where he stores his formative memories—some of them painful—and this realm becomes the play's setting. What we see on stage is really a mental landscape at the roots of his imagination where his sense of self was born.

This explains the intensely self-reflective nature of these plays. Each playwright's muses fill the dramatic world. At every turn, we encounter someone or something that influenced the playwright and, subsequently, found its way into his plays. In *Long Day's Journey*, O'Neill recalls his tormented family—his mother, father, brother, and younger self—the prototypes for so many of his characters, and he also evokes his literary muses. By means of echoes and allusions, we sense the presence of Strindberg, Chekhov, Shakespeare, Synge, Dowson, Baudelaire, Nietzsche, and even Fechter's *The Count of Monte Cristo*, the melodrama in which O'Neill's father acted. In *Something Cloudy, Something Clear*, Williams recalls his love affair in Provincetown four decades earlier with Kip, a dancer, who inspired his theme of a lost, ideal love. Woven into the play are unmistakable strands of Rilke and Williams's beloved muse, Hart Crane. The effect of these personal references is astonishing, like a window opening into the playwright's inner world.

The effect in *Three Tall Women* is similar, but still different. The play contains the same resonance as O'Neill and Williams' plays, but has a less elegiac tone and more energy. Albee is not writing a final statement like *Long Day's Journey* and *Something Cloudy, Something Clear*. His mission is to renew his sense of self, and to do this, he must revisit his muses and reconnect with them. That is why Albee writes about his mother, a larger-than-life figure, whom he portrays as being alternately domineering, childish, funny, and venomous. A difficult woman who seemed unable to love her son, she was Albee's primary muse—or "anti-muse," as one commentator dubs her (Gussow, *Singular*, 18)—negatively inspiring many of his characters and his lifelong war against shallow, entrenched American values and attitudes. Watching her in *Three Tall Women*, we cannot help but think of steely Agnes in *A Delicate Balance*, the wife in *All Over*, and the mothers in *The American Dream*, *The Sandbox*, and *The Lady from Dubuque* (see Brantley 1, 22). Other important muses in *Three Tall Women*, who are discussed but remain unseen, include Albee's adoptive father (the "penguin"), his aunt, and his grandmother, who contributed to such characters as Tobias and Claire in *A Delicate Balance*, the complacent Peter in *The Zoo Story*, and Grandma and Daddy in *The American Dream*.

Also evident in *Three Tall Women* are Albee's literary muses. He seems to take enormous pleasure in alluding to the works of dramatists who influenced him and shaped his imagination. Albee's love of Samuel Beckett shows in innumerable ways. At times, his main character sounds like Winnie, the garrulous woman buried in a mound in Beckett's *Happy Days*. *Krapp's Last Tape* can also be detected; both plays use the situation of a lonely, older figure sifting through memories. As she asks whether her son will come today, Albee's elderly mother reminds us of Beckett's *Waiting for Godot*. The ghostly quality of Albee's second act, with the three characters representing his mother at different stages of life, suggests Luigi Pirandello's *Six Characters in Search of an Author*, as do some of the ferocious speeches. Noel Coward's *Blithe Spirit* is also echoed; there is more than a touch of Coward's humor and elegant language here. At times, I also hear the voice of Amy, the aristocratic and controlling matriarch in T. S. Eliot's *The Family Reunion*. Albee's title, *Three Tall Women*, reminds us of Anton Chekhov's *Three*

Sisters, and the final tableau, with the women holding hands, mirrors the ending of Chekhov's play, as well. At other times, *Three Tall Women* calls to mind such works as Jean Genet's *The Maids*, a three-character drama in which two housemaids plot against their wealthy mistress; Eugene Ionesco's *Exit the King*, which focuses on a figure unprepared for death; Thornton Wilder's *Our Town*; and works by O'Neill and Williams.

For Albee, O'Neill, and Williams, returning to their muses is not a nostalgic act. I believe it is motivated by a crisis of identity related to aging. Kathleen Woodward has named it "the mirror stage of old age" (109), after Lacan's mirror stage of infancy; however, the crisis appears to occur in either middle or late adulthood. In the mirror one day, we discover a jarring image of the older person we have become, which we cannot reconcile with the image of the younger self we think we are. This self-division fosters a sense of the Freudian uncanny, according to Woodward (104). But for an artist, this crisis can be more disturbing, even terrifying. Suddenly, he has become an older Other, separated and even estranged from his younger self. Unsure of his identity, he feels lost, lonely, and abandoned, an emotional orphan cut off from his "mother," the nurturing powers that gave him his sense of self. For the older Albee, the experience must have rekindled disturbing anxieties, because he is himself an orphan.

How is this crisis resolved? Writing in "The Orphan Archetype," Rose-Emily Rothenberg argues that orphans exploring their own identity should relive the trauma of separation in order to bring out their pain and face the reality of their loss (192). Then, they need to build a stronger "autonomous" self by creatively reconnecting with the mother at her "archetypal source," the unconscious, to tap into nurturing forces there (192–3). This is what the aging Albee does to overcome his crisis. As early as *The Man Who Had Three Arms* (1982), Albee seems to be dealing with the anguish caused by his divided self. The main character reflects the playwright in crisis; he is a celebrity confused about his identity, desperately and angrily lecturing a group about his having grown a third arm, which has since disappeared. In *Three Tall Women*, Albee takes the next step, shaping a new, inclusive self by creatively reconnecting with his mother and his literary muses, powers that gave him his initial sense of identity.

But this is not easily done. The whole matter is complicated by Albee's troubled relationship with his mother. Frances Cotter Albee was a tall, demanding, wealthy socialite who did not understand her son. Her conservative views and hollow values fueled his rebellion. She all but threw him out of the house when he was about twenty years old, and they remained apart for some two decades, after which he initiated their reunion, coming to visit her and take her out to dinner, for example. Even then, she remained unforgiving. About her final years, he said: "I was a very dutiful and good son. But she never quite approved of me or forgave me for walking out. When she died she almost completely cut me out of her will" (see Gussow, "States-man," C22). Given their sad history, how can the playwright reconnect with his mother and renew his sense of self?[3]

In *Three Tall Women*, Albee solves the problem. He uses the play to understand his mother, thereby freeing himself from her hurtful treatment. This liberation allows him to develop a stronger "autonomous" self and resolve his crisis. He creates a character in her image—an imperious, vain, and fragile figure in her nineties—and in the first act, he looks at her from the outside. In the second act, he transforms the actresses into his mother's younger, middle-aged, and older selves so he can explore why she became such a bitter woman. This imaginative approach helps him creatively recon-nect with her, and after he relives the shattering scene when she orders him to leave, he experiences a renewing epiphany. During the play, as Albee learns more and more about his mother and what motivated her, he takes away her power to hurt him. At the same time, his own sense of self strengthens, because he can see where he came from and how these events contributed to his development as an individual and a writer.

The play unfolds in an elegant bedroom. Albee names his main character only "A," and we find her in the company of her thoughtful caregiver ("B") and a young female attorney ("C"), who is visiting. Almost at once, we real-ize A is a handful; she rivets our attention. While she looks frail, she is arro-gant, combative, and self-consumed. She finds fault with everyone and relishes their imagined comeuppances: "Don't you talk to me that way!" (6); "Oh, she'll learn" (22); "You all want something . . ."(20); "None of it's true! You're lying!" (31); "It hasn't happened to you yet? You wait!" (47). She is also racist, anti-Semitic, and homophobic, using such expressions as "a real smart little Jew" and "none of those uppity niggers" (37, 46). Her vanity is breathtaking; she shaves a year off her age ("I'm ninety-one") and holds court like royalty in her room. In her mind, she is the only one who matters. Everyone else has failed, let her down, or is out to get her. Her former friends broke their "contract" with her by dying (41). Her employees are stealing from her. Her son's visits are infrequent. Since she cannot have her way, she will spite them all.

Nevertheless, as monstrous as she is, A has our commiseration. At ninety-two, she is deteriorating, physically and mentally. Time has taken a heavy toll on her, and we are inclined to sympathize. In the face of her infir-mities, her tenacity is amazing; she will not give in. For example, she suffers from incontinence, and several times must pad off with her walker to the bathroom to avoid an incident; she "won't have" "a diaper," according to B (12). She also suffers from osteoporosis and a broken arm that has never healed; the arm should be amputated, but she refuses and endures excruciat-ing pain. Memory lapses afflict her, as well, along with uncontrollable spells of weeping:

A: (*To B; tearful again.*) Why can't I remember anything?
B: I think you remember everything; I think you just can't bring it to mind all the time.
A: (*Quieting.*) Yes? Is that it?
B: Of course!
A: I remember everything?
B: Somewhere in there.
A: (*Laughs.*) My gracious! (*To C.*) I remember everything!
C: Gracious. That must be a burden. (51–2)

Her isolation also elicits some sympathy. As she shares memories with the other women, we realize how alone A is. Her way of life is gone—big houses, riding at her stables, clubs for the well-heeled, servants and chauffeurs, vacationing at a resort with the likes of Norma Shearer and Irving Thalberg. She has outlasted her husband and what friends she had. Now only her son is left; but while she yearns for his visits, she is vindictive about him: "He never comes to see me and when he does he never stays. (*A sudden shift in tone to hatred.*) *I'll* fix him; I'll fix *all* of 'em" (19).

Helping us respond to A are the other characters, B and C. They serve a choral function, providing commentary on A. However, Albee also designs them almost as stand-ins for his two selves, divided by the mirror stage crisis. C represents his youthful attitude toward his mother, while B represents the attitude Albee's mature self would like to have. In the New York production, Marian Seldes, who played B, found that thinking of Albee helped her play the character; she even costumed herself in colors and fabrics she remembered the playwright wearing (Seldes, 26). While C expresses shocked disapproval of A, B works hard to keep the seas calm:

A: . . . You don't think *any*thing's funny, do you?
C: Oh, yes; I'm just trying to decide what I think's really the most hilarious—unpaid bills, anti-Semitism, senility, or . . .
B: Now, now. Play in your own league, huh? (40)

Throughout the play, B often resorts to such phrases as "Let her alone" (41), "Well . . . what does it matter?" (3), and "And so it goes" (11). She knows everything that C knows about A's dreadful behavior and beliefs, but she remains suitably detached, above it all, and accepting. Devoted to her charge, self-effacing, inventive, and wise, she is the perfect caregiver. (Is she inspired by Albee's own Nanny Church from childhood?) Again and again, for example, she supports A's son, telling A that he does care about her and is a good son in an attempt to alter A's spitefulness. Her vantage point is just right, and she has a rounded of vision that C lacks:

B: What *are* you, *twenty* something? Haven't you figured it out yet? (*Demonstrates.*) You take the breath in . . . you let it out. The first one you take in you're upside down and they slap you into it. The last one . . . well, the last one you let it all out . . . and that's it. You start . . . and then you stop. Don't be so soft. I'd like to see children learn it—have a six-year-old say, I'm dying and know what it means.

C: You're horrible!

B: Start in young; make 'em aware they've got only a little time. Make 'em aware they're dying from the minute they're alive.

C: Awful!

B: Grow up! Do *you* know it? Do *you* know you're dying? (13–14)

Her words are vintage Albee, with a touch of Beckett; but this is because B has the perspective that the older Albee wants to have—on life and on his mother.

If he is to achieve it, Albee must resolve his crisis. In the second act of *Three Tall Women*, Albee does what Rothenberg argues is necessary: he creatively reconnects with his mother. Thus far, the older Albee really has only observed A. But since she suffers a debilitating stroke at the end of the first act, Albee must now imagine her life himself. In a bold move, he decides to transform C, B, and A into representations of A in youth, middle age, and old age, and he has them meet in A's bedroom. As these spirits interact and ask questions (the experience is not unlike Pirandello's *Six Characters in Search of an Author*), each learns what will happen to her or how she has changed over time. Watching them, the older Albee finally understands his mother, including what made her unable to love him, or anyone. At the end, after he relives her tragic rejection of him, he feels her negative power over him fall away.

Let me describe the characters in Act Two. C is tall, young, and beautiful; she is also naïve, headstrong, and selfish. At twenty-six, she works as a mannequin, modeling clothes at a dress shop, and she is on the lookout for the right man. She expects happiness and is repelled by what B and A tell her. "I will not become . . . *that!*" she screams, pointing at A (69). At age fifty-two, B is sarcastic and angry. Life has not turned out the way she expected; she has had to fight on too many fronts—her husband's affairs, his jealous in-laws, her rebellious son. She remains embattled and furious. As for A, she is more together than in Act One, and when she walks on stage as her metaphysical character, the audience is surprised, because we think A is still in bed after her stroke (she is, or rather a life mask of her is). A's spitefulness takes time to rise, but after discussing her dwindling resources, her husband's fatal cancer, and her mother's hatred for her, she condemns her son and her other selves with terrifying wrath.

Working through the histories of these women, we understand what happened to Albee's mother. She began her adult years with high expectations for happiness, but what finally mattered most was social position and mate-rial comfort. She meets her husband-to-be at age twenty-eight. "The man of my dreams?" asks C (78), since she has not yet seen him, but B and C fail to answer in the affirmative:

C: (*Timid again.*) What's he like?
B: (*Expansive.*) Well . . . he's short, and he has one eye, and he's a great
        dancer—'cept he keeps running into things, the eye, you know—and he
        sings like a dream! A lovely tenor—and he's funny! God, he's funny! (83)

C cannot understand why she would marry anyone like this, but B points to a pragmatic reason. "The penguin," her derisory name for him, is also rich, or about to become rich. B makes clear that it becomes a loveless marriage, that her husband is weak and that she must fight continuous, unpleasant "battles" with her in-laws:

> the mother who "just doesn't like you" for no good reason except her
> daughter hates you, fears you and hates you—*envies* and therefore hates
> you—dumpy, stupid, whining little bitch! Just *doesn't* like you—maybe in
> part because she senses the old man's got the letch for you and besides, no
> girl's good enough for the penguin, not *her* penguin; the first two sure
> weren't and this one's not going to be either. (95)

Over time, too, her husband had affairs, and she had one, too, with the groom (and then she fired him). Still, it infuriates her that her husband betrayed her, and once when she was incapacitated in a riding accident, she worried, in the words of B, "Who he's doing it with; who's he got cornered in what corner, what hallway, who he's poking his little dick into" (99). But there was never consideration of divorce, since she says she had "a good deal" with the pen-guin and would not want to jeopardize her place (94).

This shows us, and the older Albee, that his mother is someone rooted in "stance," a term coined by James P. Driscoll. Motivating her is an abiding con-cern for her social identity; she cannot see beyond it and does not realize that this limits her and makes her unhappy. In a discussion of Shakespearean char-acters, Driscoll describes those in "stance" as hardened, selfish types who live in narrow worlds. Without a larger vision, they risk becoming inflexible, pride-fully egotistical, and selfish, all characteristics of Albee's mother. What drives them is the arrogant and childish belief that they can control the world, an atti-tude that will inevitably lead to disappointment and defeat. On the other hand, according to Driscoll, characters in "metastance," such as Prospero, have the ability to step back from their social identity and see everything in a much larger context (155–61). They cultivate self-knowledge and accept tragedy, death, evil, and loss as parts of life; characters in stance hold desperately to their limited perspective and fear death, tragedy, and loss. In Act One, B is in metastance; she recognizes, for example, that death is something to be aware of, and not feared, so that we appreciate what little time we have. In Act Two, however, these three tall women are obviously in stance—clinging to social identity, materialistic, hardened, selfish, and egotistical.

In the middle of this act, Albee stages a coup de théâtre; he brings his younger self on stage. B informs C that they have children: "We have one; we have a boy" (89). To our surprise, a young man, representative of Albee about the time he left home, appears and moves toward A's bed to comfort her. C is fascinated. But B moves to scream right in his face, at full volume: "Get out of my house!" (89). The Young Man, existing in his more realistic dimension, does not hear her; he remains mute. However, this moment is electrifying for the audience, which looks on in disbelief, and also for the older Albee. Watching B, he relives a painful memory, and in so doing, he finds himself again. In an instant, more than three decades after it happened, the older playwright sees his birth as a writer. Here is the wound that made him write so many characters resembling his mother—Agnes, Mommy, the wife in *All Over*, and others—and so many plays designed to make us look at ourselves and how we treat others—*The Zoo Story*, *The American Dream*, *The Sandbox*, *The Death of Bessie Smith*, *Who's Afraid of Virginia Woolf?*, *All Over*, *Everything in the Garden*, and more. His impatience with complacency and fossilized values, his impulse to make the world better, and many of his other themes pour out of this wound. The older Albee is catapulted into a new perspective; in effect, he reviews his career, sees all that he has accomplished, and realizes he has grown far beyond the young man on stage.

The wounding moment continues with B explaining to C, in a lacerating monologue, why she was unhappy and why she took this attitude toward her son:

> and then try to raise that?! (*Points to him.*) That?! gets himself thrown out of every school he can find, even one or two we haven't sent him to, sense he hates you, catch him doing it with your niece-in-law *and* your nephew-in-law the same week?! Start reading the letters he's getting from—how do they call it—older friends?—telling him how to outwit *you*, how to survive living with his awful family; tell him you'll brain him with the fucking crystal ashtray if he doesn't stop getting letters, doesn't stop saying anything, doesn't stop . . . just . . . doesn't . . . stop? (95)

This is followed by more rejection, when A looks at him and cruelly tells him about a premonition she had about his finding her dead in a hospital and having no feelings for her. Even though he cannot hear her, the young man "*shudders*," as if he felt the wave of her disapproval (106). Finally, after A's monologue, C announces she will not allow herself to "become" A, and A responds defiantly: "Oh? Yes? You *deny* me? . . . Well, that's all right: I deny you too; I deny you all" (107). She denies the figures on stage, one by one and then all of them collectively, in a sweeping denunciation that makes everything almost too much to bear.

Suddenly, at the darkest moment in the play, Albee resolves his crisis. He experiences an epiphany and follows it with three upbeat speeches—one each, by C, B, and A. I will discuss these later; but, for now, what has happened? I believe that Albee, having learned what motivated his mother—her rootedness in "stance," her desire to control him—relives her painful rejection of him and realizes that he must let it go. His reasoning is something like this: It happened. It was unforgivable. I don't want it to hurt me anymore. I will move on. Like B in Act One, the older Albee assumes the perspective of metastance. He can be more detached, accepting, and understanding of his mother and her hurtfulness. He knows now that she took his rebelliousness, homosexuality, and political views as insults, because of her "stance," and she could never grow out of her embattled world. But he can, and does, at the end of the play.

The epiphany begins with A, sounding almost like Emily in *Our Town*, asking: "*Is* it like this? What about the happy times . . . the *happiest* moments?" (107). Her monologue, about the ever-hopeful condition of living as a young person, hardly sounds like C at all. Nor does B's speech, also addressed to the audience, which argues that middle age is the best: "Standing up here right on top of the middle of it *has* to be happiest time. I mean, it's the only time you get a three-hundred-and-sixty-degree view—see in all directions. Wow! What a view!" (108–9). Elderly A finally comes forward, and she, too, is transformed. For her, the "happiest moment" is also now: "Coming to the end of it, I think, when all the waves cause the greatest woes to subside, leaving breathing space, time to concentrate on the greatest woe of all—that blessed one—the end of it" (109). She also discusses how interesting it is to live at her stage of life, but her mind wanders, and she begs our indulgence: "I mean, give a girl a break!" (110). Then, for the final tableau, all three women come together and hold hands.

The three women have become emblems of renewal, Albee's renewal. Everything we see and hear at the end of the play expresses the feelings of the older Albee himself. A, B, and C, for example, are themselves transformed and renewed because they reflect Albee's internal renewal. The dark forces of A, B, and C are no longer haunting him and causing him anguish; he has let those forces go, and he is left with figures that speak of happiness and living life now, in the moment (the word "now" occurs seven times in the three speeches). Just as he has been able to rise above it all, so have A, B, and C; they no longer speak of petty things, but of seeing life as if from great heights ("Wow! What a view!"). They have a new perspective on things, and so does the playwright. They accept evil, death, and tragic events with equanimity (even young C), and they find everything—even bad things—so "*interesting*" (108). Their speeches soar, clearing the air and carrying us to a higher level. At the end of their monologues, when A, B, and C hold hands, A speaks of "the happiest moment. When it's all done. When we stop. When we can stop" (110). Is she speaking of death, as it appears, or of the end of the pain between the playwright and his mother? Whatever the case, it is all over now, and he can move on with his life, a renewed man and artist.

The final tableau is reminiscent of the ending of Chekhov's *Three Sisters*, when Olga puts her arms around Masha and Irena. Albee's ending is more positive, although it is still shadowed by the earlier tragic events, giving it a complex resonance, like a Chekhov play. As we have seen, this is not the only echo of a favorite literary muse in *Three Tall Women*. While I have concentrated on Albee's mother muse, I have not meant to neglect the literary muses that fill its dramatic world by means of echoes and allusions. We recall how Albee alludes to Pirandello's *Six Characters* in the second act and how the three not-so-blithe spirits also suggest Coward. The first act has a structure similar to Ionesco's *Exit the King*, with King Bérenger, unwilling to face death, being advised by his two wives: Marie, who encourages his illusions, and Marguerite, who sounds more like B. Earlier, we cited other allusions— direct or otherwise—to Albee's favorite muse, Samuel Beckett, and Genet's *The Maids*, Wilder's *Our Town*, and Eliot's *The Family Reunion*. B's use of the world "letch" also echoes tenacious Maggie in Tennessee Williams's *Cat on a Hot Tin Roof*, and Eugene O'Neill seems echoed in B's dismissal of her son, "He *never* belonged" (92). With so many examples, it is clear that Albee intended to evoke his literary muses, just as O'Neill and Williams did in *Long Day's Journey* and *Something Cloudy, Something Clear*.

Why? Because they helped shape his sense of self, too. If this paper focuses more on Albee's mother muse, it is not because she is more important, but rather, because Albee found it more difficult to reconnect with her. He had no trouble reconnecting with his beloved literary muses. In a 1996 interview with Carol Rosen, Albee explained their importance to him in revealing terms:

ROSEN: Did any established artists help you early on?
ALBEE: Help? Well, yes. I received a great deal of help from Chekhov and Pirandello and Beckett, and those folk [laughs]. I got a lot of help from them, sure. A great deal.
ROSEN: But they didn't take you in.
ALBEE: In a way they did, yes. They took me in, and nurtured me and nourished me. (29)

Albee writes *Three Tall Women*, in part, to acknowledge this debt. Not only does he want to come to terms with his mother, he also wishes to thank his literary muses. After he left home, his muses served as caregivers, surrogate parents who nurtured him as a writer and gave him the nourishment he was otherwise unable to get as he developed his own distinctive voice. Is it any wonder, then, that during the interview at the end of this casebook, Albee refers to himself as Beckett's "adopted child"?

By returning to his early influences in *Three Tall Women*, Albee is reborn, overcoming his mirror stage crisis. It is a crisis we all must face, and if we also hope to be renewed, we need to study Albee's play, along with the other autobiographical dramas written by O'Neill and Williams. These plays show us that the crisis appears as a kind of death, threatening to overwhelm us; to battle it, we must return to our origins, which means revisiting memories charged with indescribable and often painful feelings. But if we do this, we gain immeasurably, because we grow into our older selves. In their plays, O'Neill, Williams, and Albee integrate the past into their own sense of self, transforming their muses into ancestors who teach them about themselves, just as we will need to do. O'Neill reconciles with his haunted family. Williams reconciles with his first love and forgives himself. Albee, in this luminous play, draws on his literary muses to understand his mother and is reborn into metastance.

Notes

1. Hutchings argues that *Three Tall Women* is derivative of Samuel Beckett and Albee's own *All Over*. Staub finds "the enthymeme of death" in the play. Roudané analyzes the play briefly in his survey of American drama since 1960. Perhaps the best critical treatment of *Three Tall Women* is Lahr's lengthy review in the *New Yorker*.

2. For more on this genre, see my article, "Memories and Muses: *Vieux Carré* and *Something Cloudy, Something Clear*," in *Tennessee Williams: A Casebook*, edited by Robert F. Gross (New York: Routledge, 2001) 139–52.

3. In his introduction to *Three Tall Women*, Albee discusses his adoptive mother as the play's subject: "I knew I did not want to write a revenge piece—could not honestly do so, for I felt no need for revenge. We had managed to make each other very unhappy over the years, but I was past all that, though I think she was not." The best source for information on Albee's mother is Gussow's biography.

Works Cited

Albee, Edward. *The Man Who Had Three Arms. Selected Plays of Edward Albee.* Garden City, N.Y.: Nelson Doubleday, 1987. 417–70.

———. *Three Tall Women*. New York: Dutton, 1995.

Beckett, Samuel. *Happy Days*. New York: Grove, 1961.

———. *Krapp's Last Tape*. New York: Grove, 1960.

———. *Waiting for Godot*. New York: Grove, 1954.

Brantley, Ben. "Albee's Tigers, Albee's Women." *New York Times* April 21, 1996, sec. 2:1+.

Chekhov, Anton. *Three Sisters. Five Plays*. Trans. Ronald Hingley. Oxford: Oxford University Press, 1977. 169–237.

Coward, Noel. *Blithe Spirit. Three Plays*. New York: Vintage, 1999. 7–109.

Driscoll, James P. *Identity in Shakespearean Drama*. London and Toronto: Associated University Presses, 1983.

Eliot, T. S. *The Family Reunion*. New York: Harcourt, Brace & World, 1939.

Gussow, Mel. *Edward Albee: A Singular Journey*. New York: Simon & Schuster, 1999.

———. "Edward Albee, Elder Statesman, Is in a State of Professional Reprise." *New York Times,* December 1, 1993: C17+.

Hutchings, William. "*All Over* Again: Edward Albee's *Three Tall Women* and the Later Beckett Plays." *Text and Presentation*. Lanham, MD: University Press of America, 1996. 30–33.

Ionesco, Eugène. *Exit the King*. New York: Grove, 1963.

Lahr, John. "Sons and Mothers." *New Yorker* May 16, 1994: 102–15.

O'Neill, Eugene. *Long Day's Journey into Night*. New Haven: Yale University Press, 1989.

Pirandello, Luigi. *Six Characters in Search of an Author. Naked Masks*. Ed. Eric Bentley. New York: Dutton, 1952. 211–76.

Rosen, Carol. "Writers and Their Work: Edward Albee." *Dramatists Guild Quarterly* (Autumn 1996): 27–39.

Rothenberg, Rose-Emily. "The Orphan Archetype." *Psychological Perspectives* 14 (1983): 181–94.

Roudané, Matthew C. *American Drama since 1960: A Critical History*. New York: Twayne, 1996.

Seldes, Marian. "Albee and Me." *American Theatre*, September 1996: 22+.

Staub, August W. "Public and Private Thought: The Enthymeme of Death in Albee's *Three Tall Women.*" *Journal of Dramatic Theory and Criticism* 12.1 (1997): 149–58.

Wilder, Thornton. *Our Town*. 1938. New York: Harper & Row, 1985.

Williams, Tennessee. *Something Cloudy, Something Clear*. New York: New Directions, 1995.

Woodward, Kathleen. "The Mirror Stage of Old Age." *Memory and Desire: Aging—Literature—Psychoanalysis*. Eds. Kathleen Woodward and Murray M. Schwartz. Bloomington: Indiana University Press, 1986. 97–113.

2
Edward Albee:
A Retrospective (and Beyond)

ANNE PAOLUCCI

In his essay "Tradition and the Individual Talent," T. S. Eliot explains what happens when a new writer comes on the scene. If his irrepressible urge to express what has not been said that way before is to be recognized, eventually, as part of the acknowledged literary experience already in place, that urge or "individual talent" must batter its way into the established canon. If that happens, writes Eliot, all that has gone before is altered, howsoever slightly. Every writer starts by discovering his own vision, his own voice, his own form and language. In Goethe's words: "Art is arrogance." But is that arrogance worth preserving in and for itself? Should innovation, no matter how assertive, be treasured as part of our literary history? Eliot, who never shied away from the hard questions, tells us that we should look for greatness in the delicate balance of "strong local flavour" and "unconscious universality" ("American Literature," 54). Does Edward Albee pass that test? Can we say, after more than four decades, that his work has indeed battered its way into the established theater canon?

The Critics

Albee's first Broadway play, *Who's Afraid of Virginia Woolf?* (1962), was a hit both on stage and in the film version that featured Elizabeth Taylor and Richard Burton. Its recognizable setting and characters lulled both critics and audiences into welcoming it as an exciting frenetic enactment of a reality they could relate to—an exaggerated version of quarrels couples do have in real life, often saying things they do not mean, especially with a few drinks in them. The play's eccentricities—like cryptic references to a son who doesn't exist—were easily absorbed in the excitement of personal revelations fueled by too much booze and articulated in a cacophony of unrelenting vitriolic exchanges. Everybody loved it. Whatever else the play had to offer went unnoticed.

18

Understandably, the plays that followed were seen as a departure from, even a betrayal of, that early success. Critical confusion prevailed, and audiences were frustrated. Ben Brantley of the *New York Times* correctly reminds us that, thirty-six years after the opening of *Who's Afraid of Virginia Woolf?*, "garlanded in [its] success . . . [Albee was] thrust onto cultural heights that have not been visited since by an American playwright" (E1). The plays that followed would provoke the "nasty, protracted lynching of Mr. Albee which would continue for a good two decades." That "lynching" began two years later, in 1964, with *Tiny Alice* ("a crucifixion of sorts"): "many critics and theatergoers felt they had been handed a custom-made hammer and set of nails to use on its author":

> What was this self-important, pretentious gobbledygook that Mr. Albee was trying to put over? Even respectful reviews expressed irritation and puzzlement over the bizarre, verbally dense and sexually lurid allegory about a man (played by John Gielgud) in search of God; others went straight for the jugular in alarmingly personal terms, describing the work with phrases like "homosexual nightmare." (E1)

In the light of such criticism, Albee's remark that he learns "a lot more from other playwrights" than from "most critics" has a certain relevance (qtd. in Rosen, 30).

Clearly, both critics and audiences were unprepared for the plays that followed. In a cultural milieu still uneducated in the new stage conventions of Pirandello, Beckett, and Ionesco, Albee's open-ended, often "unresolved," plays, his paradoxes and repetitions, and his fractured language appeared arbitrary, tentative. American critics, not ready to shift their sights to accommodate the new theater, and without a new critical language to deal with it, were harsh and impatient. Against the critical guidelines that had served for *Who's Afraid of Virginia Woolf?*, the new plays were found wanting. Elizabeth Hardwick, reviewing the first production of *A Delicate Balance* for the *New York Review*, called it "dull," "old fashioned," set in a "more or less timeless Scarsdale." The dialogue "has a fleshless vehemence," that suggests "so much unmotivated heavy breathing"; the overall effect is "repetitive and amateurish" (5). For Walter Kerr, the play failed "because Mr. Albee has not got the particular kind of poetry he was after, because he has used theoretical words to describe a theoretical situation instead of using intensely practical words to show how impractical words are."[1]

By the time *All Over* appeared in 1971, reviews, though still mixed, had begun to reflect growing awareness of Albee's talent and skill. At one end of the spectrum we find Douglas Watt writing: "Albee deliberately set down an almost completely static creation in the hope—a lost one, in my opinion—of moving us by the power of words alone." Actually, what we have, he explains, are "sculptured speeches written in a self-conscious literary style and dotted with obscure contradictions. . . . People are zombies, their talk rings false." The play is "frozen right from the start," a "ludicrous," "empty," and "pretentious work." At the other end of the spectrum we have William A. Raidy telling us that it is the dialogue that makes the play "fascinating, chilling, unsettling . . . eloquent drama." Albee's art, he concludes, is "simply to put the puzzle forth" and "he has done it with brilliance." Walter Kerr once again comes down hard: the play was "detached [and] noncommittal . . . a man in the room is dying," but the "non-quite mourners are already dead." In the same vein, *Tiny Alice* was "an essay and an exercise when it might have been an experience"—something "out of a very young philosopher's notebook."

Seascape (1975), too, drew mixed reviews, ranging from Clive Barnes's description of the play as a "major dramatic event . . . leaner, sparer, and simpler" to John Simon's description of it as a "simpleminded allegory," "quivering inaction," a "piece of flotsam washed ashore near Albee's Montauk home," the kind of playwriting that "should have been put out of its misery sooner, while it still preserved a shred of dignity."

But with *Three Tall Women*, not only did Albee win a third Pulitzer Prize, the critics too seem to have reached a consensus with respect to his talent and his well-deserved place in the American theater. Even John Simon finally came around. But by this time the American theater had become aware, at least of the impact on the American stage, of those major European playwrights who had fashioned an exciting, new kind of drama called "Theater of the Absurd."

The Audiences

Even a brief summary of the response of American critics to Albee's plays shows the experts confused, often falling back on dogmatic pronouncements that simply could not do justice to his new plays. Audience reaction, for the most part, followed the lead of the critics. Albee's early plays were incomprehensible for most theatergoers, except for those few who recognized, in his more realistic plays, a kind of scrim that served to prepare the stage for something else. *Tiny Alice* was the litmus test. The opening of the play is soon seen as an outer shell rather abruptly discarded for an interior that is an unmistakable Dantesque metaphor. Judged against *Who's Afraid of Virginia Woolf?*, plays like *The Lady from Dubuque*, *Marriage Play*, *Listening*, and *Tiny Alice* simply did not measure up. For audiences used to more traditional stage action, and without the hysterical distractions of *Who's Afraid of Virginia Woolf?*, Albee's genial innovations often went unnoticed, especially the musical cadences and variations of the language—what many who are familiar with his work have come to regard as Albee's signature. Caught in a moment of unrelieved crisis, reacting to major events in a variety of orchestrated voices, Albee's characters did not follow the usual pattern. The experience of such plays for most audiences was disconcerting.

Scholars, too, for the most part, held back. If they tried to apply the familiar Aristotelian categories to this new kind of theater, the keener ones soon discovered that the results were anything but encouraging. Within those guidelines, Albee did not fare too well. His plays had little plot, his stage action was cyclical and often without resolution, his characters seemed voices rather than personalities. His genial use of language, his greatest contribution to the American contemporary stage, went virtually unnoticed. Few students of drama could find a way to shift their critical focus in order to accommodate plays whose themes were other than social or political commentary and more subtle. It was much easier to continue teaching Arthur Miller, Tennessee Williams, and Eugene O'Neill.

Today, after four decades, most critics, audiences, and scholars have come to recognize Albee as a major American playwright. He brings home the best of the post–World War II European theater that Beckett and Ionesco refashioned, in the wake of Pirandello's revolutionary experiments. I have often compared Albee to Pirandello, who also had to batter his way into prominence, and enjoyed his first success outside of Italy. Albee is the true heir of Pirandello in his ability to lure audiences with a realism that is a prelude and a promise.

Pirandello and Albee

I have said, more than once, that my discovery of Albee's theater and continued interest in it is due, to a very large extent, to my long-standing appreciation of Pirandello's works. In referring to Pirandello, I have never meant to suggest anything derivative about Albee's plays, or any deliberate effort on his part to try out some of the innovations that Pirandello introduced on the post–World War II European stage. For me, correspondences surfaced easily and persuasively. The results were illuminating, often exciting. They still are.

Pirandello came to theater with an already-established reputation as an author of novels and short stories. After a brief interlude writing plays for the well-known Sicilian actor, Angelo Musco, he suddenly produced, in 1921, the first of a series of plays that revolutionized the twentieth-century stage: *Six Characters in Search of an Author*. That play and the others that followed—as Robert Brustein has pointed out—influenced every dramatist after him in some way (316).

There was nothing to prepare European audiences for the open-ended action of *Six Characters*, or for protagonists who are a series of superimposed, fragmented roles. Together with *Each In His Own Way* (1924) and *Tonight We Improvise* (1930), *Six Characters* explores the relationship between actors and their roles, the actors and the audience, actors and script, director and actors, audience and actors—dramatizing the stage experience itself. In Italy, *Six Characters* was badly received but the Paris production of the Pitoeffs was a huge success. The European theater would never be the same again.

Almost half a century ago, Eric Bentley gave this penetrating assessment of the playwright who, in 1934, had received the Nobel Prize in Literature but was still relatively unknown in America:

> Ostensibly Pirandello's plays and novels are about the relativity of truth, multiple personality, and the different levels of reality. But it is neither these subjects nor—precisely—his treatment of them that constitutes Pirandello's individuality. . . . The novelist Franz Kafka was long neglected because his work also gave the impression of philosophic obsession and willful eccentricity. Then another and deeper Kafka was discovered. Another and deeper Pirandello awaits discovery. (148)

Other and deeper Pirandellos have indeed been discovered since Bentley wrote those lines. Today, most critics agree with Robert Brustein that Pirandello is indeed "the most seminal dramatist of our time," and that his most original achievement can be defined as "the dramatization of the very act of creation" (316). In Pirandello's characters, Brustein writes, we see the living signatures of his artistry, "being both his product and his process" (316). Like Shakespeare, Pirandello emerges more and more as a source of "infinite variety," but also a total theater man who reshaped the stage in new and exciting ways for our time.

What Albee drew from Pirandello and made his own, according to Brustein, was the "approach to the conflict of truth and illusion" (316). From the beginning of his career, it was clear that Albee had struck a rich vein in the challenging new medium mapped out by Pirandello, and others. His focus from the outset was on moments of crisis, "rites of passage": marriage, death; separation; the inevitable change of human relationships; the search for a secret sharer and the anguish of isolation. These elusive mysteries are at the heart of Albee's dramatic art. Like Pirandello, whose central subject throughout remained the intricacies and contradictions of the human soul, Albee explores every facet of the struggle for control over the external events and forces that impact each of us, every day of our lives. The early abstractions of *The American Dream* were softened into allegorical transparencies in *Tiny Alice*. Violent death, first explored against the socio-racial background of the sixties in *The Death of Bessie Smith*, was presented as a biblical reading in *The Zoo Story*. His multilayered dramatic style is clearly in evidence as a modern parable in *Seascape*, as a religious parody in *Tiny Alice*, and as a brilliant exegesis of ordinary events (including a mass for the dead), in *Who's Afraid of Virginia Woolf?*

The Plays

The Zoo Story was that rare thing: a flawless first play. There was nothing tentative or uncertain about it. Albee had found his dramatic style with impressive ease. Later plays simply proved the point. The emotional dissonances of *Who's Afraid of Virginia Woolf?*, the transparent religious allegory of the Chinese-box mansion that houses some kind of eternity in *Tiny Alice*, the fractured language and musical reverberations of *Box* and *Quotations from Chairman Mao*, *A Delicate Balance*, and *The Man Who Had Three Arms*, and the aria-like exchanges of *Marriage Play, Listening*, and *Three Tall Women* are already present in *The Zoo Story*. We recognize also in this short play what will become one of Albee's favorite stage devices: the use of narrative to enhance dramatic movement. Tobias's obsessive reminiscing about the cat he loved and destroyed (*A Delicate Balance*), the extended story of the imaginary son (*Who's Afraid of Virginia Woolf?*), the autobiographical monologues (*Box* and *Quotations from Chairman Mao*), the long, virtually uninterrupted monologue account of events that changed a man's life (*The Man Who Had Three Arms*)—all of this comes out of that first memorable description of the landlady's dog in *The Zoo Story*.

There is ample evidence in that first play of what Robert Brustein attributed to Pirandello, a fusion of product and process. *The Zoo Story*, like so many of Pirandello's innovative works, is an open-ended experience into which audiences (as well as critics and scholars) are gently prodded. Religious resonance rises out of a chance encounter in Central Park; revelation is the end result of frustrated, inadequate communication; the end product is a kind of crucifixion, a theme brilliantly revisited in a cathedral-like setting in *Tiny Alice*. The very names of the two protagonists, Jerry and Peter, have biblical overtones and the park bench might indeed be a church pew, where strangers share in a parody of the sacrifice of the Mass: a genial device superbly orchestrated in *Who's Afraid of Virginia Woolf?* What Albee has managed to do in this, his first play, is dramatize an ecstatic experience on familiar emotional territory. One cannot help thinking of Pirandello's short play in this context, *The Man with the Flower in His Mouth*.

Seascape jolts us into an Aesopian encounter. A dull, bleak *now* is shattered by a primeval *then*. A couple is relaxing on the beach. They indulge in Ionesco-type banalities until, suddenly, two "lizards" appear. Their emergence from the sea, where all life begins, not to mention the fact that they talk, is a signal (or should be) that we must shift focus. Like children who crave bedtime stories, the man and woman are drawn into the fantasy. The newcomers are full of questions. Things that are obvious to most humans (and to the audience, by extension) have to be explained as though for the first time ever. The strangers from the sea need to touch, smell, experience a reality new to them. Their simple wonder reminds us of innocence lost, of the encrustations of habit that must be scraped away to reveal what is truly worthwhile. We are encouraged to a new reading of a habitual "text." The creatures who display human attributes are a mirror image of an emotional landscape turned *inscape*. They help us recapture truths buried under the layers of our daily accommodations to life. Their curiosity strips away human conventions prescribed by society, accepted but not necessarily understood. They remind us, in almost childlike terms, of what is really important in life: simplicity, wonder, that Pirandellian need to see consciousness or awareness of the world around us as only the beginning of an essential movement from self-consciousness to identity, and to see that movement as an ongoing process, an ever-changing equation that tells us, at any one moment, who we are, in ourselves and with respect to others. In Albee's juxtaposition of fantasy and reality, the search for identity finds natural comic expression, very like the exchanges that lead to comic (but also profound) self-discoveries in Ionesco's *The Bald Soprano*, or the comic aspects of some of the most bitter encounters in Dante's *Inferno*.

In his usual fashion, Albee has mapped a journey into the interior through what appears to be a fixed point. Striking back at some of his harder-to-please critical colleagues, Clive Barnes had (with a touch of noblesse oblige) hit it right: the play settles inside us, taking on the colors of our chameleon existence. The high-tension confrontations of earlier plays are reduced to a simple but provocative question, the terms of which contain complex psychological phenomena. Time and space are compressed into a point of no dimension through which images of the things around us are restructured, as indeed our eyes restructure for us the picture of the world upside down, right side up. In this process, in which reality is turned into its opposite, comedy is funny but also protective.

Albee does not spell out solutions. Like Pirandello, he leads us to the edge of fresh insights. He dramatizes the phoenix life-in-death struggle that is always a new threshold of self-awareness. Pirandello often used mirror images to dramatize the stripping of our many masks. In *Seascape*, Albee gives us paired characters in parallel but reversible situations: one couple is settled into familiar routines; the other assaults the edges of the conventional with fairy-tale incongruity. In the reversal, the wall of consciousness separating self from self becomes a scrim. The lizards are the crazy, Pirandellian mirrors that show us the infinite distortions of the self as it struggles with the paradoxes of so-called reality.

Pirandellian correspondences are particularly compelling in Albee's *The Man Who Had Three Arms*. Anyone familiar with Pirandello's theater plays—especially *Each in His Own Way* and *Tonight We Improvise*—will at once recognize the characteristically Pirandellian layering of roles and open-ended conclusion in Albee's tour-de-force.

The protagonist of *The Man Who Had Three Arms* has taken on a double role as public speaker addressing an audience that is the very theater audience watching the play. His task, it soon becomes evident, is to shatter our complacency, drag us into the limelight as it were, and force us self-consciously to recognize our own version of "the emperor's new clothes" syndrome. In this Pirandellian setting, the audience becomes part of the dramatic action and is identified by the speaker on stage with all those who have crossed his path. The immediate action on stage spills out into our own collective self-consciousness, forcing us into a dual role: an audience playing a role within the action itself and the objective theater audience watching the play unfold at a distance. The Hosts (Man and Woman) who introduce the evening's speaker (Himself) and monitor the evening's activities also serve as intermediaries and anticipate the audience's reactions.

The situation recapped for us at the beginning of the play, as the Hosts open the proceedings and introduce Himself, is certainly funny enough. When their early and best choices (a Nobel Prize winner included) for the society's 231st meeting could not make the speaking engagement, the Host committee reached down into the barrel and came up with Himself, whose only claim to notoriety was the fact that he had made headlines and enjoyed intense media attention for a short while—with all the immediate rewards that come with newsworthy eccentricity—by having suddenly developed a third arm. The drawing power of such perverse qualifications seems to have justified the choice made by the host committee. The show goes on. But it soon becomes evident that Himself is undergoing an emotional crisis right there on stage, and that the Hosts cannot easily control him. What was meant to be the usual formal lecture, a social and cultural evening, turns into an escalating, virulent attack on the public and the media.

At first, the speaker simply describes the situation, his being there. He reviews his story. What first seemed the answer to all prayers, and what brought him fame and money, soon became a nightmare as the third arm began to wither and finally disappear. All of this is relayed in a series of manic-depressive reversals, attacks and apologies, a fugue-like recounting in which the Hosts (sitting on stage) and the audience are used as a sounding board by the speaker. As he moves from one vivid moment of his transformation to another, Himself weaves other tales and insights into the central story, and his listeners (on and off the stage) take on—in his eyes—a variety of attitudes to which he responds in different voices and moods. His listeners soon become targets, real or imagined: the public at large with its morbid curiosity, greedy agents and unscrupulous press representatives, unsupportive wives and children, dinner speakers with their pseudocultural platitudes, members of committees (like the Hosts seated on the stage) who organize such evenings and always compromise with bland dishes and weak drinks (if any) at the dinners that precede such a lecture, and the critics and promoters of "best-sellers," the arbiters of so-called taste and intelligence. No one is spared. In short, the protagonist's life story with its brief moment of glory and the bitter disappointments that followed is reviewed in an emotional replay that is both attractive and repellent. Like the catharsis of pity and fear, the morbidity of the third arm *distances* the audience from Himself, while his near-hysterical account of the reversals endured *draws* the audience to him through some kind of empathy. More interesting, this catharsis is pursued throughout the play on two levels since, as we know, the audience is playing a double role.

The action in *The Man Who Had Three Arms* is constantly interrupted by the guest speaker (Himself), who steps out of his role to share his frustrations with those on the other side of the footlights—in the same way as the "Director" and "actors" in *Tonight We Improvise*, and the "actors" in *Each in His Own Way*. In Albee's play, Himself turns out to be a Hinkfuss as well, for he provides the cues for his hosts to take on other scripted roles as his story unfolds.

From another side, Albee's play is, like Pirandello's *Each in His Own Way*, a devastating exposure of intellectual and literary sham among professed academic experts, lecture-circuit authors and speakers, high-visibility personalities who have made a career of trumpeting their esoteric specialties, and, of course, theater critics and critics generally. The tirades of the guest speaker against those who have undermined him resemble, in many ways, the exchanges of the critics during the intermissions of *Each in His Own Way*. In that play, Pirandello moves the action into the lobby of the theater, where a number of "critics" take on the job of demolishing Pirandello's work even before the play is over. Albee's play is a similar extension of the dramatic action, a direct exchange or confrontation with the audience—the stage itself serving as a podium from which to startle us into Pirandellian awareness. *The Man Who Had Three Arms* is a manic monologue against the excesses of pseudointellectualism and cultural platitudes. I am sure Albee had as much fun debunking critics and media people in this play as Pirandello had in pitting his detractors against his supporters in the heated "Intermission" debates of *Each in His Own Way*.

If this play is a Pirandellian tour-de-force, it is also a tour-de-force for the actor playing the role of Himself. Like the woman in *Quotations from Chairman Mao*, the protagonist in *The Man Who Had Three Arms* holds the stage virtually alone in what turns out to be a long dramatic monologue. (Albee, by the way, considers *Quotations* one of his best works, and the reason may well be the challenge—successfully redeemed in his opinion, and mine too—of transforming the third voice of poetry [the dramatic voice] into the first voice [lyric].) The audience is treated to an entire life story, oases of emotional highs and dark introspective moments of despair, an Eisensteinian superimposition of moods held together and beautifully balanced by the sometimes confident, sometimes strident voice of the main character. Like Pirandello's *Enrico IV*, *The Man Who Had Three Arms* redefines the purpose and soul of drama as a series of states of mind, masks, shards of experience mirroring the anguish and joys of the spirit, a search for meaning that can only raise new questions.

The Man Who Had Three Arms is also a funny play, but its humor is inextricably bound with the pathos of the human condition. The laughter we experience as we watch the antics of the speaker and listen to his exaggerated claims is tempered by the recognition of those traits in ourselves. Pirandello's genial definition of humor as the "sentimento del contrario," an awareness of the built-in paradox in things, applies here. The humor of *The Man Who Had Three Arms* is fused with anger, hysteria, and bitterness we all can relate to, in a world indifferent to our individual sensibilities.

The critics, not accustomed to this kind of play, tore it apart. More precisely, they recognized in it (as we said earlier) a bitter tirade against their inadequacies. The playwright himself noted in 1985 that, of all his plays, *The Man Who Had Three Arms* "is the one for which I received the most enthusiastic and favorable response from people in the arts—my peers" (qtd. in Kolin, 204). Ironically, the play is perfectly accessible for most audiences. It resembles, in many ways, *Who's Afraid of Virginia Woolf?*, and has the same kind of effect.

Woman opens the evening's program by telling the assembled audience about the difficulties of locating a speaker. She rambles on about their letter of invitation to a Doctor Tomlinson, an eminent zoologist and Nobel Prize winner, who in the course of his work, they just learned, had "fallen into an Andean crevasse" over a year ago (424). When found, the body was in an advanced state of decomposition, identified only through dental records and a locket containing a photograph of the late Doctor Tomlinson himself and another of a large pig. Their next choice, a Doctor Fischman, an internationally famous plastic surgeon, was arrested for malpractice the day before, in Mexico, where he lived. We are almost ready for the introduction of the evening's speaker, but not before we are given a long, detailed account of the progress of a suit the host group members have brought against Cheesecake Company and Tante Marie Quiche for ptomaine poisoning suffered after eating their quiche Lorraine at the last annual July 4th membership picnic. Finally, the speaker is introduced.

This typical Albee narrative is a vivid preview of things to come. The speaker begins by picking up some of the things Woman has reported, thus establishing a rapport with the audience in a similarly rambling fashion. As he gets into his own narrative, the speaker assumes the mannerisms and inflections of people who have figured in his story, creating a "play-within-a-play" effect, a strategic layering of personalities and voices that heightens the dramatic effect and also suggests a kaleidoscopic epiphany. In effect the entire play is a dramatic narrative, a superbly orchestrated cacophony of voices, the illusion of dissonance adding to the overall grand effect. In some ways, we are reminded of a Milhaud opera in which the possibilities of, say, the alto are strained almost beyond the potential of that kind of voice within a musical structure that threatens traditional harmony.

Himself, in other words, is many others selves, as well. His pyrotechnic verbal displays (reminiscent of the exchanges between George and Martha in *Who's Afraid of Virginia Woolf?*) give us access to an entire world. Here are some of the glimpses of that world:

> Look, fucking yourself cross-eyed is a mound of fun, and no mistake about it. Even when *I* was a pup, out in puppyland, there were those girls who took a lineup of the local boys easy as beaten biscuits. (440)

> I don't like my salad first, but I am in a minority these days, this land. . . . I was somewhere in the Midwest once when they served coffee as soon as we sat down to table—and they drank it! My hosts and hostesses, smiling and sipping while all I wanted was another gin, which come to think of it . . . ? (441)

> this one came to the press conference all prepared, not homework-wise, but. . . . opinioned. The article was already written; all she wanted was my assent, my agreement to the dismemberment. (443)

> Well, then, sit there and cross your eyes for fifteen minutes or so. *I'm* going to have an intermission—a gin, and a pee, and a quiet cry—two sobs and a gulp and a freshet of tears in a corner somewhere. (445)

In Act Two, Man and Woman become more directly involved with the speaker, commenting on his outbursts, filling in the blanks, and, at one point, as though called into his play by some silent cue, taking their place near the speaker and becoming part of the dramatization of the discovery of the third arm. The scene is effective both in itself and as the telescoping of a past moment that is translated into an immediate present when, at the end, the same two hosts discover a new growth beginning on the speaker's back. The cycle is complete.

Woman also takes on the part of the speaker's wife in a venomous exchange in which hidden motives surface on both sides as husband and wife lash out against one another; Man, in turn, assumes the character of the Colonel, identified earlier as the speaker's agent. The play ends with an interruption that is also an open-ended resolution. What has already transpired and has been so eloquently described and recounted for us will assuredly be played again in a series of new variations.

In spite of all the apparent digressions and the shattered continuity of the narrative as it turns into recriminations, accusations, and shouting matches, there is nothing in this play that is not relevant or pertinent to the central focus of the action. Himself's candid remarks about the mediocre meal he was served earlier in the evening, his mounting obsession for gin (which occasions the intermission, in beautifully Pirandellian fashion), and all the seemingly arbitrary intrusions relate the insufficiencies and weaknesses of the immediate audience and hosts with the human failings of the world at large, the world that helped destroy the speaker. The superimposition of narrative and stage is a happy medium for interweaving present actions and intentions into the larger spectrum of past motives and deeds. Nothing is marginal or accidental. Everything is part of a complex and paradoxical dramatic design held together, as in Pirandello's *Enrico IV*, by a man who has taken on the role of protagonist, director, script writer, revisionist historian reshaping the past in his own voice and image, and chief judge of all who have come into his life. Himself is indeed a splendid reincarnation of the seemingly mad emperor of Pirandello's masterpiece.

In reviewing Albee's work, one can distinguish at least three distinct stage formats. The first and perhaps most striking is the illusory realism of plays like *Who's Afraid of Virginia Woolf?*, *Tiny Alice*, *A Delicate Balance*, *The Lady from Dubuque*, *Three Tall Women*, and *The Zoo Story*. The second and more experimental format can be described as a kaleidoscopic monologue, a series of flashes into the past brought into the present (*Box* and *Quotations from Chairman Mao*, *The Man Who Had Three Arms*). The third suggests art transcending itself, what Vivian Mercier has termed a *non-play*. Albee's *Fragments* seems to fit this third category. It can best be appreciated as a "cantata," a series of voices skimming the impersonal surface of things for permanence, order, and continuity.

In *Fragments*, the seemingly static action forces the audience into a keener awareness of language and attitudes. The "characters" are identified simply by symbols—M for Man, W for Woman; 1, 2, 3, etc. The play opens and ends with a kind of game in which the participants think up proverbs. Act One contains a number of segments, beyond the quick exchanges of the opening just described: "Poem," "Celebrity Auction," "Dream Theatre," "Knife Grinders," "A Visit to the Doctor," "Food Fight," "Harry's Funeral," and "Two Boxes." Act Two opens with a brief preface, followed by "The Hustler," "Sunday in the Park," "Helping," "Shoplifting," "Talking to Plants," "Lillian Gish," and "Getting Old." The play ends with a brief return to coining "proverbs," giving it an obvious, though not necessarily essential, frame. The Albee trademark of dramatic narrative is the substance of "The Hustler" and reminds us of the striking narratives in *The Zoo Story* and *A Delicate Balance*. A good deal of the dialogue is casual banter, not particularly memorable except that it strikes some familiar chord in all of us. "Talking to Plants" is the kind of obsessive chatter we, too, indulge in at some time or other.

Fragments could be described, in fact, as a dramatic reading of the Sunday *Times*. The "players" comment on theater arts, on items in the news, current events, on common routines, on just about anything that could come up in casual conversation or in the privacy of one's own brooding. The "dialogue" is reminiscent of the exchanges of Ionesco's faceless couples in *The Bald Soprano*.

Conclusion

As that excellent craftsman, Ezra Pound, tells us: the function of the poet is to "make it new." Albee has done just that. He dismissed the literal message of the political and social realism of the forties, fifties, and sixties as subjects for drama, and gave the American theater new content and form, portraying our postexistential tensions on a stage swept bare of standard conventions. Like Picasso in painting, he restructured our experience of the world. In the process, he prodded our sensibilities in startling new ways, articulating the human dilemma in the fragmented language of imperfect beings. Albee meets Eliot's definition of greatness for having brought to our national theater that magic combination that is the unmistakable sign of greatness in literature: "strong local flavour" and "unconscious universality." And he has done so with the fine instinct of the consummate artist who knows both his craft and his own true voice.

Note

1. For reviews of *A Delicate Balance, All Over,* and *Seascape,* see *New York Theatre Critics' Reviews* (1966, 1971, and 1975) and *The New York Times Theater Reviews.*

Works Cited

Albee, Edward. *The Man Who Had Three Arms. Selected Plays of Edward Albee.* Garden City, N.Y.: Nelson Doubleday, 1987. 417–70.

Bentley, Eric. *The Playwright as Thinker: A Study of Drama in Modern Times.* 1946. New York: Harcourt, Brace, 1967.

Brantley, Ben. "Pursuing a Woman, a Fortune, and God." *New York Times,* June 10, 1998: E1+.

Brustein, Robert. *The Theatre of Revolt.* Boston: Little, Brown, 1964.

Eliot, T. S. "American Literature and the American Language." *To Criticize the Critic, and Other Writings.* Lincoln: University of Nebraska Press, 1992. 43–60.

———. "Tradition and the Individual Talent." *Selected Essays.* 3rd ed. London: Faber and Faber, 1953. 13–22.

Hardwick, Elizabeth. Rev. of *A Delicate Balance. New York Review,* October 20, 1966: 4–5.

Kolin, Philip C. *Conversations with Edward Albee.* Jackson: University Press of Mississippi, 1988.

Pirandello, Luigi. *Six Characters in Search of an Author. Naked Masks.* New York: Dutton, 1952. 211–76.

Rosen, Carol. "Writers and Their Work: Edward Albee." *Dramatists Guild Quarterly* (Autumn 1996): 27–39.

3

Absurdly American: Rediscovering the Representation of Violence in *The Zoo Story*

LISA M. SIEFKER BAILEY

Since the premiere of *The Zoo Story* in 1959, the drama's violent ending has shocked audiences. In this intense one-act play, Albee presents, with the precision of a diamond cutter, the exposition and violent denouement of two strangers' conversation in New York's Central Park. Each turn of the dialogue brings the two men closer to each other and to an understanding of human relationships. Some elements in the play, however, such as the men's chance meeting and their conversation, which touches on themes of fragmentation, alienation, and isolation, have prompted reviewers and critics to read it as an absurdist drama. Mary Castiglie Anderson calls *The Zoo Story* "an example of absurdist and nihilist theater" (93). Charles Lyons places the play "within the genre classification of the absurd . . . because it assumes the absurdity, the chaos, of the human condition and its essential loneliness" (qtd. in Bigsby, 15). Anne Paolucci compares *The Zoo Story* to Sartre's *No Exit* (43).

Insofar as Jerry, Albee's alienated protagonist, tries to makes sense of a senseless world, *The Zoo Story* may belong in the category of the Theatre of the Absurd. Martin Esslin, in *The Theatre of the Absurd*, finds aspects of the play, particularly Jerry's "inability to establish genuine contact with a dog, let alone a human being," corresponding with the kind of interactions found in Harold Pinter's plays (267). But while granting that *The Zoo Story* contains absurdist tones and moods, Esslin argues that Albee's play ultimately fails as an absurdist drama:

> the effect of this brilliant one-act duologue between Jerry, the outcast, and Peter, the conformist bourgeois, is marred by its melodramatic climax; when Jerry provokes Peter into drawing a knife and then impales himself on it, the plight of the schizophrenic outcast is turned into an act of sentimentality, especially as the victim expires in touching solicitude and fellow-feeling for his involuntary murderer. (267)

Esslin is correct: the play does not end on an absurdist note. The audience is not left with a feeling of senselessness of purpose or the absurdity of life.[1] Instead, I would argue that the characters and the audience are left with a story full of purpose and meaning. From the beginning, Jerry hopes that he can make a difference, that his actions can create some kind of change. With such desire, the ending is not sentimental at all, but rooted in its time and place.

The Zoo Story takes place in 1958, and the play's mood reflects the cultural ethos of the 1950s. Albee is writing social criticism in the Cold War era, a time in America's history when Ozzie and Harriet made the domestic ideal look easy amid the threat of nuclear war. This split has become a hallmark of the 1950s. Uncomfortable subjects like communism, (homo)sexuality, contraception, women's equality, segregation, civil rights, and cancer—if they were not mentioned—seemingly could be ignored. America refused to confront such issues directly. Disturbing subjects remained hidden; the dominant culture felt it could disregard them. Nevertheless, when the media reported findings and events—think of the McCarthy hearings, the Kinsey Report, Brown vs. Board of Education—the public could not ignore controversies, but was forced to face them. Thus, while images presented by entertainment television, on family comedies like *I Love Lucy*, *Leave it to Beaver*, or *Father Knows Best*, fostered the idea that the American suburban lifestyle made people happy, the real world did not reflect these idealistic family portraits. The more society felt pressured to live up to television's impossible standards, the more people began to examine their inner desires and values.

The poetry of Allen Ginsberg, the plays of Tennessee Williams, and the novels of Jack Kerouac revealed discontentment with American cultural development. Jerry's attitude, bizarre as it initially appears, grows out of the cultural dissatisfaction felt by those who asked deeper questions. Like so many voices suppressed and ignored by 1950s attitudes, Jerry has a desire to tell his own story. He wants to give voice to the people of his stratum whose bypassed histories seem lost in the fast-paced tumult of society. With his isolation and painful sense of alienation, Jerry wants his story to make a difference; he wants to earn his marginalized story a memorable place in the larger narrative of society. The entire play involves Jerry's attempts at storytelling; Albee entitles it *The Zoo Story* to emphasize this. If Jerry's story can somehow become real in another's mind, Jerry can help end the alienation.

In the play, Jerry's goal is to make meaningful contact with another human being. His behavior with Peter parallels his experiment with the dog. At the conclusion of the play, if Jerry could miraculously live, like the dog lived, Peter and he could be "friends"; Jerry could "see what our new relationship might come to" (33). In an interview, Albee admits, "I suppose the dog story in *The Zoo Story*, to a certain extent, is a microcosm of the play by the fact that people are not communicating, ultimately failing and trying and failing" (qtd. in Sullivan, 184). Jerry wants to initiate communication with someone, so he begins his attempts with the dog. As he explains, "if you can't deal with people, you have to make a start somewhere. WITH ANI-MALS!" (34). He then draws on what he has learned from the dog to attempt communication with a human being. But it is Jerry's numbed society that forces him to select a violent act, like the extreme action he took with the dog, to provoke a response. The final image of Jerry's brutal death does communicate with Peter and the audience, and this intense desire on Jerry's part to accomplish connection keeps this play out of the realm of the Theatre of the Absurd. With its hope for change, *The Zoo Story* presents itself as an American play.

Albee's message recognizes humanity's potential to progress beyond its isolated condition. Matthew Roudané finds in *The Zoo Story* "the potential for regeneration, a source of optimism which underlies the overtly aggressive text and performance" (42–3). According to Roudané, Jerry experiences "a degree of religious fulfillment by giving his life" (43). My reading moves beyond religious sentiment and places the play in a more specifically American context. Jerry's death does much more than martyr him as a Christ-figure. Albee uses the savage final tableau to force a kind of American optimism on *The Zoo Story*'s characters and their audience. The communication accomplished through Jerry's violent death follows an American tradition identified by Richard Slotkin in his exploration of American myth, *Regeneration through Violence*. Slotkin identifies a "frontier psychology" running through American literature. His study identifies patterns of violence in American literature and culture: "The first colonists saw in America an opportunity to regenerate their fortunes, their spirits, and the power of their church and nation; but the means to that regeneration ultimately became the means of violence, and the myth of regeneration through violence became the structuring metaphor of the American experience" (5). Albee's play participates in this tradition.

Jerry's frontier is Central Park. Here he opposes the establishment. His vigilante experiment breaks through the boundaries of civilized communication and proves that people, when confronted with an outrage, can alter their compartmentalized, zoo-like condition. With his experiments in communication, Jerry discovers that society's structure, "this humiliating excuse for a jail" (35), has the potential for regeneration by virtue of its inhabitants' animalistic capacity to respond to vicious acts. Roudané indicates that the "regenerative spirit of *The Zoo Story* is not limited to the actors; Albee also directs the benevolent hostility of the play toward the audience" (43). However, the effect on the audience is greater than has heretofore been observed. Just as in Slotkin's myth of regeneration through violence, Albee allows Jerry to commit an unthinkable act in his desperate effort to communicate with someone else. Albee uses the shock of this unacceptable violence to instill in his audience the idealistically American call to action to change the world for the better.

If Jerry can begin to defeat the monstrous isolation endured by his genera-tion, Jerry becomes an heroic player in the war for change. Jerry's role as hero, in the Aristotelian sense of the word, encompasses his tragic flaw.[2] Jerry's desire to play this role ironically becomes what destroys him. To fulfill the vic-tor's role, he must die, and his realization of this fact at the zoo precipitates the actions that necessitate his murder/suicide. Jerry has been interpreted as play-ing the hero in the Christian tradition.[3] But whether or not Jerry draws on the Christian myth of Jesus' martyrdom and victory through crucifixion is less important than the regenerative response his death creates. The significance lies in the reaction to his death: only through something so violent can he achieve a place worthy of remembrance. While Jerry's heroic regeneration comes through a typically American act of violence, Jerry does not care what kind of hero he is, as long as he communicates something valid enough to earn a place in history, even if that history is only one night's segment on the news or one article in tomorrow's papers. In this 1950s world, the media offers Jerry his best chance of being immortalized as something real. Without transference of his story from his own private isolation into the media shared by others in the public realm, Jerry's narrative will remain alienated and unremembered.

As information technology developed, the media has increasingly recorded American history. Historian David Halberstam writes that "the fifties were captured in black and white, most often by still photographers; by contrast, the decade that followed was, more often than not, caught in liv-ing color on tape or film" (ix). In Jerry, Albee creates a character who partic-ipates in this cultural phenomenon. He desires photographs in his empty frames as if those pictures would confirm his identity, his place in history. Jerry does not feel he fits into his own family annals, and his inability to cre-ate that sense of private history inspires him to try to create a different kind of story, one that might be remembered in visual images beyond his isolated space. Jerry's consciousness of America's growing reliance on television reflects the cultural movement of the consumption of events in the 1950s. "People now expected to *see* events, not merely read about or hear about them. At the same time, the line between what happened in real life and what people saw on television began to merge" (Halberstam, 195). The media, especially television, provided a kind of privileged space for stories, which became more real and meaningful to people through visual images. From television, Americans at home heard vivid stores of events they did not phys-ically participate in. Americans learned to create their own dramas, their own heroes, their own stories, because the repetition of those stories gave them a sense of permanence, allowed them to become real. Jerry's awareness of the power of the media creates in him a desire to tell a story dramatic enough to become newsworthy.

Jerry walks "northerly" in search of an actor to fill the role in the drama he has created to be performed as the zoo story. When he first encounters Peter, Jerry effectually interviews him for the part. Jerry wants to cast a bourgeois mainstream persona. Peter works nicely, as Jerry notes, "Who better than a nice married man with two daughters and . . . uh . . . a dog?" (17). Peter's wife, two daughters, and two parakeets are close enough to the standard Jerry seeks to cast in his drama. (The flat, social stereotypes that Peter and Jerry represent have also misled critics to read this play as Absurdist.) Peter represents suburbia. He is part of established society, in which he resides conventionally and respectably. Jerry dwells elsewhere. He inhabits part of the underworld, where he resists and subverts the norm. Halberstam provides an historian's view of this social split:

> During the course of the fifties, as younger people and segments of society who did not believe they had a fair share became empowered, pressure inevitably began to build against the entrenched political and social hierarchy. But one did not lightly challenge a system that seemed, on the whole, to be working so well. Some social critics, irritated by the generally quiescent attitude and the boundless appetite for consumerism, described a "silent" generation. Others were made uneasy by the degree of conformity around them, as if the middle-class living standard had been delivered in an obvious trade-off for blind acceptance of the status quo. (xi)

Albee's characters fit into the paradigm Halberstam describes. Jerry wants to find a way to bridge the gap between his underworld and Peter's middle-class world.

Peter functions as a cog in the system of consumerism, a man who contributes to the standard of society. Jerry, on the other hand, exists on the margins of society. His "laughably small room" exists surrounded by other tenement living quarters inhabited by characters as unique and outcast as Jerry: a colored queen, a Puerto Rican family, and someone else who is marginalized even a step further than the others in the building. He explains, and "in the other front room, there's somebody living there, but I don't know who it is. I've never seen who it is. Never. Never ever" (22). Jerry's life outside the mainstream "doesn't sound like a very nice place" to Peter, who lives in an easily definable and average apartment in the East 70s.

Jerry desires to tell the story of what happened at the zoo, the story of the dog, the story of his family to someone outside his realm. If these stories can be told and consumed by an audience, then Jerry can escape his grotesque isolation. Albee's strategy mirrors Jerry's tactics. He entitles his play *The Zoo Story* and uses the drama to tell the story of society's alienation. Jerry carries with him a need to tell stories in the same way he keeps the picture frames empty in his apartment. If he can just fill the need, fill the frames, he can make a connection that will overshadow the alienation of his existence. After hearing Jerry list his odd possessions, Peter asks, "About those empty picture frames . . . ?" To which Jerry answers: "I don't see why they need any explanation at all. Isn't it clear? I don't have any pictures of anyone to put in them" (23). Jerry's answer does not make sense to Peter, as he surely could have pictures of his parents or his aunt in those frames if he so desired. He tells Peter the story of his mother's "adulterous turn," which ended with her death, and his father's subsequent two-week drinking celebration, which resulted in his being "slapped in front of a somewhat moving city omnibus" (24). With both parents dead before he was twelve, he moved in with his aunt who died "on the afternoon of [his] high school graduation" (24). He concludes these memories: "But that was a long time ago, and I have no feeling about any of it that I care to admit to myself. Perhaps you can see, though, why good old Mom and good old Pop are frameless" (24).

Jerry also tells Peter stories of his sex life. The first summarizes his philandering: "And let's see now; what's the point of having a girl's picture, especially in two frames? I have two picture frames, you remember. I never see the pretty little ladies more than once, and most of them wouldn't be caught in the same room with a camera" (25). His encounters with "the little ladies" are about only the physical sex act, not about remembering or connecting to the women in emotional, spiritual, or intellectual ways, so Jerry does not put their pictures in the frames. When his physical connection with one of them ends, the relationship is over and has served its purpose. His casual sexual encounters do not rate a monumental frame. Jerry also tells Peter the story of his eleven-day "h-o-m-o-s-e-x-u-a-l" relationship with the park superintendent's son, which occurred when he was fifteen. The way Jerry avoids using the word, "homosexual," but must spell it out for Peter, indicates his shame in participating in acts of same-sex desire.[4] This relationship appears to be the most meaningful partnership he has experienced, but he has closeted it and disallows himself to display it in picture frames at home. When Peter responds to these stories with an unfinished comment, "It seems perfectly simple to me . . . ," Jerry overreacts: "Look! Are you going to tell me to get married and have parakeets?" (25). With traditional American boldness, Jerry territorializes from the margins. Jerry's paranoia charges out to face off with Peter, whose wife and daughters and parakeets provide familiar mainstream images easily framed, displayed, and presented to the world. Peter does not have episodes like these or sexual rendezvous to hide; Peter conforms.

Jerry has no images of people he desires to fill the empty frames, because he does not want to be reminded of the past. Jerry wants to create a memorable story in the present. Jerry does not care which story he tells, as long as he has an audience. His opening line declares as much. He states, "I've been to the zoo" (12). When Peter "*doesn't notice*," Jerry repeats his sentence twice, with force: "I said, I've been to the zoo. MISTER, I'VE

BEEN TO THE ZOO!" (12). Peter, not sure that this stranger is addressing him, does not know how to respond. Jerry opens the play by finding an audience and telling that audience a story, the story he conceived at the zoo. Until he relates this zoo story to someone, his actions remain unaccountable; they are not "real." The narrative of the events, the characters, the staging of the "plot" of the zoo story do not exist until Jerry tells the story by acting it out.

That Peter the individual becomes a murderer is coincidence. However, Jerry has known about his own death since he anticipated it at the zoo. He begins conversing with Peter in order to create a scenario that he has planned to end with his death. Thus, the play is not absurdist, because Jerry ultimately controls it. He has arrived at his purpose at the zoo and tells the story to Peter to end his narrative with the conclusion he discovered there. Ultimately, Peter is not the only audience for Jerry's story; Peter also simultaneously plays a part in the story that the audience witnesses at the theatre. Albee metatheatrically tells the story to the audience as Jerry tells it to Peter. Jerry indicates this plan when Peter questions Jerry's behavior, and Jerry replies: "I'll start walking around in a little while, and eventually I'll sit down. (*Recalling*) Wait until you see the expression on his face" (19). Jerry's "you" addresses the theatre audience; Jerry's "his" refers to Peter's face. Jerry's zoo story moves from the microcosmic world in Central Park to the larger audience of the play, which will come to understand Jerry's intent to manipulate the way the zoo story becomes historicized.

As we have said, in order to bring a sense of reality to his story, Jerry must find an audience for his tale. Jerry wants to be noticed. He wants to narrate the scene. He wants to create the history of the events he sees. He wants to be a part of those events that count; and, ultimately, he wants to exert his control over those events. He plays Horatio and Hamlet and Claudius and Gertrude all at the same time: he tells the story, thinks about the story, plots the story, and acts out the story simultaneously.[5] Jerry experiments with his roles in each of his microstories as he tests Peter. He describes the landlady: "she has some foul parody of sexual desire. And I, Peter, I am the object of her sweaty lust" (28). Jerry explains how he has learned that he can control her with stories:

> But I have found a way to keep her off. When she talks to me, when she presses herself to my body and mumbles about her room and how I should come there, I merely say: but, Love; wasn't yesterday enough for you, and the day before? Then she puzzles, she makes slits of her eyes, she sways a little, and then, Peter . . . and it is at this moment that I think I might be doing some good in that tormented house . . . a simple-minded smile begins to form on her unthinkable face, and she giggles and groans as she thinks about yesterday and the day before; as she believes and relives what never happened. (28)

Jerry fends off the landlady's advances by planting stories of their sexual trysts in her mind. Through the power of Jerry's suggestion, the landlady surmises a memory of their imaginary love-making, which satisfies her lust. By concocting the story of their relationship in her mind, Jerry has deflected her advances and allowed her to reproduce them in her memory. Jerry has learned that the story of something that never happened can eliminate the need for it to happen. Jerry's power lies in convincing the landlady to believe in the story; the act need not take place if only she wills it in her imagination. Jerry creates what Jacques Derrida would define as pure trace or *differance*, which "does not depend on any sensible plenitude, audible or visible, phonic or graphic. It is, on the contrary, the condition of such a plenitude" (62). By creating the non-event of their intimacy, Jerry subdues her advances. Whether or not the relationship exists in reality does not matter, for both opponents win. Encouraging her to repeat the story protects Jerry from the landlady's propositions and satisfies her urges. The existence of the story makes the event real to the landlady, and that is enough to empower both parties.

Like the landlady, Peter cannot help but be fascinated with Jerry's vivid stories. "It's so . . . unthinkable. I find it hard to believe that people such as that really *are*" (28). Peter's bourgeois existence is so far removed from the world Jerry inhabits, that Peter can hardly imagine it. Ontologically, Jerry's world did not exist for Peter until Jerry told him about it. Jerry himself is not real to Peter until he makes himself known through the stories he tells. Jerry nudges Peter's discomfort: "(*Lightly mocking*) It's for reading about, isn't it?" (28). Peter replies, "Yes." Jerry continues, "And fact is better left to fiction" (29). If Peter can keep the uncomfortable and alarming facts of the world at bay, then he will not have to deal with things that might threaten, scare, hurt, or change his environment. Peter, a reader, even makes his living in publishing. Jerry saw Peter's signifying book when he initially approached the man on the bench. Jerry selects an audience who would absorb a story. He then uses a series of shorter stories to prepare his audience for the story of the dog: "Because after I tell you about the dog, so you know what then? Then . . . then I'll tell you about what happened at the zoo" (29). Carefully and calculatedly, Jerry focuses on the execution of his plan. Peter begins to feel Jerry's exertion of control: "You're . . . you're full of stories, aren't you?" (29). Peter's discomfort lies in being caught unawares, and in his surprise at how intensely Jerry presents the stories he tells. Jerry's interruption of Peter's Sunday ritual of reading in Central Park escalates from a conversation with a stranger to a clash of two very different worlds.

Jerry expects their collision to edify their positions, as he explains in his story of the dog, which he uses as a sort of experiment. "We have to know the effect of our actions," he explains (33). He has told stories of his family and his lovers and his acquaintances, but none of these stories has had any real consequences. He does not feel the stories he has told so far have been significant in his life, except, perhaps the story of the park superintendent's son. Even in that story, which he would like to believe means that he was "very much in love," he admits that he was in love "maybe just with sex" (25). In the dog story, however, Jerry works on a relationship that starts out as an irritation and builds to a severe passion. In fact, it resulted in the most meaningful experience of his life so far. His relationship with the dog distills his desire to make contact with a human being.

Jerry builds his language to convince his audience that he has experienced heightened passion. Jerry rambles on and on in what Anne Paolucci calls his "compulsion to talk" (41), and the turning points in the plot are punctuated by Peter's reactions. "I decided: First, I'll kill the dog with kindness, and if that doesn't work . . . I'll just kill him" (31). This radical jump to violence earns a reaction from Jerry's audience. Peter *"winces"* (31). His sympathy for the dog and disgust at Jerry's idea is premature, and Jerry directs him to wait before he responds: "Don't react, Peter; just listen" (31). Jerry then describes the way he fed the dog six hamburgers a day for six days until he decided he could not overcome the dog's "antipathy" (31). He moves to his next step just as he said he would: "So, I decided to kill the dog" (32). Again, Peter reacts; he *"raises a hand in protest,"* but Jerry refuses to heed Peter's gesture.

Jerry explains to Peter how much must be at stake to make a difference. He uses words one might choose to describe the longings of a would-be lover: "I was heart-shatteringly anxious to see my friend again" (33). Jerry claims to have achieved love. He says, "Now, here is what I wanted to happen: I loved the dog now, and I wanted him to love me. I had tried to love, and I had tried to kill, and both had been unsuccessful by themselves" (34). Jerry explains that "neither kindness nor cruelty by themselves, independent of each other, creates any effect beyond themselves; and I have learned that the two combined, together, at the same time, are the teaching emotion" (35–6). In the end, Jerry and the dog are back in their respective places, like the animals held by society's constructs in their cages at the zoo. "We neither love nor hurt because we do not try to reach each other" (36). They, like people in general, retreat to their designated places in society. They have, however, reached a kind of truce: "Whenever the dog and I see each other we both stop where we are. We regard each other with a mixture of sadness and suspicion, and then we feign indifference. We walk past each other safely; we have an understanding. It's very sad, but you'll have to admit that it is an understanding" (35). While Jerry's attempts at contact with the dog "failed," they make a difference in their relationship. The dog and Jerry are no longer isolated from one another; they must "feign" their alienation. They have generated a history between them that they must pretend to forget. They repress what they know to ignore the battle that has connected them.

Until Jerry challenged the dog and all but killed him, Jerry felt that "animals are indifferent to me . . . like people (*he smiles slightly*) . . . most of the time" (30). By fighting a death-battle with the dog, Jerry has created a new relationship with the dog. He tells Peter the story of the dog to impress upon Peter the vital importance of such contact. He also wants to impress upon him the extremity of violence that his environment forced him to use to make such contact. Peter, however, cannot understand. "I don't know what I was thinking about;" says Jerry, "of course you don't understand. (*In a monotone, wearily*) I don't live in your block; I'm not married to two parakeets, or whatever your setup is" (37). Jerry realizes what he already learned at the zoo: Peter cannot understand his story only through hearing it; he must experience it through acting it out in a sensational drama. Jerry's comic incongruity underscores how little he understands Peter's milieu, just as Peter cannot relate to Jerry's circumstances.

Peter and Jerry describe their positions to one another, but they are the only two characters who actually exist in the world of the play. They are opposites, yet they reflect one another. Like kindness and cruelty in the story of Jerry and the dog, the meanings of their positions become clear through their opposition. Just as was the case in the story of the dog, the reaction to the experience of their meeting will be what makes their encounter real. Jerry discovered this truth in his lessons from both the landlady and the dog. As he began telling the story of the dog, he indicated as much: "What I am going to tell you has something to do with how sometimes it's necessary to go a long distance out of the way in order to come back a short distance correctly; or, maybe I only think it has something to do with that. But, it's why I went to the zoo today, and why I walked north . . . northerly, rather . . . until I came here" (30). The event he has planned belongs in the range of the unworldly, the unbelievable, the unthinkable. Yet, the telling and dramatizing of it will make it real. The news reports will record it, and Peter's memory will relive it. The significance of what happened at the zoo is that Jerry determined the final act of his own drama. His subsequent onslaught of Peter casts and acts out an event significant enough to result in coverage on the evening news. Jerry tells Peter, "You'll read about it in the papers tomorrow, if you don't see it on your TV tonight" (15). Jerry wants to control (to direct) the outcome (the final scene) of his life. Jerry does not desire to harm Peter or his family, but he wants to "know" the end of the story. If he could, Jerry would play all the parts in his drama. He'd kill himself, but his suicide would not be remarkable enough to create much, if any, narrative in the media. Murder has a chance of making the news.

Jerry wants to tell the story that the oppressor kills him. He does not want Peter the individual to be blamed. In fact, he makes special efforts to ensure that Peter gets away unseen, that he does not leave his book as evidence. This caring action, what Esslin calls "fellow-feeling," illustrates

Jerry's larger-than-life purpose. Jerry does not want Peter to be victimized; he wants to tell the story of humanity's victimization. In his biography of Albee, Mel Gussow writes that in one of the playwright's letters, "he said that Peter was the key to the audience's response: 'I find as a general rule, the audience identifies completely with Peter and is taught as he is and is attacked as he is' " (131). Peter, a representative of the dominant hegemonic society, provides Jerry, and Albee, with a tool to teach the members of the theatre-going audience how to begin thinking in new ways about themselves and the construction of their world.

Neither Jerry nor Albee wants to promote violence or destruction; but, typical of the America Slotkin identified, it takes violent extremes to gain regenerative results. The violence of their encounter elevates the action of the zoo story to newsworthy, and, thereby, "real." Anything less would remain marginalized, outside recorded history, contained in an isolated space like the animals in their cages at the zoo. Albee's stage direction for Jerry to open his story of the dog "As if reading from a huge billboard" sets an overemphatic hyped media-style stage for Jerry's tale. When he finishes telling Peter the story of the dog, Jerry is disappointed in his story's lack of media sensation-alism. Jerry scoffs at his narrative impotence: "Do you think I could sell that story to *Reader's Digest* and make a couple of hundred bucks for *The Most Unforgettable Character I Ever Met*? Huh?" (36). Peter offers no answer to this question not only because, as he explains in the play, he is confused, but because there is no chance Jerry could sell this story that has so little main-stream thought or "human interest" to the editors of the pages of *Reader's Digest*, a popular magazine designed to appeal to millions of people. With the zoo story, however, Jerry has the potential to place his work on media's pages and screens. Jerry's goal is to create *"The Most Unforgettable Charac-ter I Ever Met"* by introducing himself to Peter in the action of the zoo story. In order to make his story memorable, he must create an event so dramatic that Peter will find Jerry *"Unforgettable."* By enacting the events he brain-stormed at the zoo, Jerry will begin, through Peter, to have his story enter into the mainstream of society and touch lives in the retelling of it in the media.

Jerry's language indicates as much just before he battles Peter for the bench: "but, you know, as they say on TV all the time—you know" (46). When Jerry attacks Peter, he cries, "Now you pick up that knife and you fight with me. You fight for your self-respect; you fight for that goddamned bench" (46). As Jerry reclines, impaled, dying on the bench, he explains the method behind his seeming madness, "and now you know what you'll see in your TV, and the face I told you about ... you remember ... the face I told you about ... my face, the face you see right now" (48). If Jerry's story does not make it to the news, he knows at least he will be remembered by Peter, who will have to tell the story to himself as he attempts to deal with it. In the same way that he affected the landlady by controlling the stories she understood in her mind, Jerry controls the story of Peter's life by adding this heinous scene to it. Without the extreme violence, Peter would remain isolated. Instead, Peter wins Jerry's admission: "you're not really a vegetable; it's all right, you're an animal" (49). Following in the mythic tradition identified by Slotkin, Jerry has forced Peter to connect with him. The event has given Jerry faith in others. He has the relief of knowing that humanity has the potential for connection. He has connected with someone and feels the mythic hope of violently won regeneration.

Peter will not be able to erase this event from his mind. He will have to face Jerry whenever he relives the memory of killing him. The barbaric violence of his act makes it unforgettable. A nonviolent encounter would not have created a haunting repetition in Peter's mind; Jerry and Peter would have gone back to their respective cages in society's invisible zoo. There might have been a change in Jerry's understanding, like the change after his engagement with the dog. But to make an indelible impression on Peter, Jerry had to create an unforgettable event. The violence of the event is the key to why Peter will forever be plagued by it. Peter plays the part of the empty picture frame—like those waiting for personal histories in Jerry's room—which Jerry selects to hold and display the zoo story. Whether Peter's guilt results from murder or listening does not matter, because his memory of killing Jerry results in Derridian *differance*. Peter shares with a Jerry a violent history that becomes pure trace, but no less real. Peter's shock at the murderous act he has passively committed also translates to the audience that, in turn, holds Peter's experience, the *differance*, in its own memory.

This metatheatrical shock effect fulfills Jerry's and Albee's purpose. Jerry will be forever linked to Peter by the image of his dying face. Not only has Jerry succeeded in implanting his story in Peter's memory, but Albee has used *The Zoo Story* to duplicate the experience in the minds of his audience. Jerry's zoo story mirrors Albee's drama. Albee needs to make a connection with his audience, and—just as Jerry's landlady interprets their love affair as real and relives it as she desires—Albee has tantalized his audience with a story that has, through its dramatic violence, become a disturbing non-event for the audience. Was it real? The effect of Jerry's death ripples out into the memory of the audience, another victim of its *differance*. *The Zoo Story* will be remembered, historicized, reenacted, traced by them. Absurd as it may initially appear, Jerry's death expands to communicate the relentlessly American tale of what happened at the zoo, in the park, and at the theater.

Notes

1. See Way for another explanation of how *The Zoo Story* ultimately fails as Theatre of the Absurd. Like Esslin, Way argues that the play falls apart as an absurdist attempt when Jerry dies, because the events of the play then become rational, explainable, and naturalistic.

2. For a reading of *The Zoo Story* in the vein of Greek tragedy, see Amacher, especially 41–2.
3. For detailed interpretations of the play's Christian symbolism, see Paolucci, *From Tension to Tonic*, 36–44, and Zimbardo. Paolucci writes about the Biblical overtones of the play and reads the dog story as a parable. Zimbardo sees Jerry as a Christ figure.
4. See Kostelanetz for an interpretation of Jerry's interactions with Peter as an "unsuccessful homosexual pass."
5. See Paolucci's "Albee and the Re-Structuring of the Modern Stage" for a detailed interpretation of Hamlet as Jerry's predecessor.

Works Cited

Albee, Edward. *The American Dream* and *The Zoo Story: Two Plays by Edward Albee*. New York: Plume, 1997.

Amacher, Richard E. *Edward Albee*. Rev. ed. Boston: Twayne, 1982.

Anderson, Mary Castiglie. "Ritual and Initiation in *The Zoo Story*." In *Edward Albee: An Interview and Essays*. Ed. Julian N. Wasserman. Houston: University of St. Thomas Press, 1983. 93–108.

Bigsby, C. W. E. *Albee*. 1969. Chip's Bookshop, 1978.

Derrida, Jacques. *Of Grammatology*. Baltimore: Johns Hopkins University Press, 1974.

Esslin, Martin. *The Theatre of the Absurd*. Rev. ed. Garden City, N.Y.: Anchor, 1969.

Gussow, Mel. *Edward Albee: A Singular Journey*. New York: Simon and Schuster, 1999.

Halberstam, David. *The Fifties*. New York: Villard, 1993.

Kostelanetz, Richard. "The Art of Total No." *Contact* 4 (1963): 62–70.

Paolucci, Anne. "Albee and the Restructuring of the Modern Stage." *Studies in American Drama, 1945–Present* 1 (1986): 3–23.

———. *From Tension to Tonic: The Plays of Edward Albee*. Carbondale: Southern Illinois University Press, 1972.

Roudané, Matthew C. *Understanding Edward Albee*. Columbia: University of South Carolina Press, 1987.

Slotkin, Richard. *Regeneration through Violence: The Mythology of the American Frontier, 1600–1860*. Middletown, Conn.: Wesleyan University Press, 1973.

Sullivan, Kathy. "Albee at Notre Dame." *Conversations with Edward Albee*. Ed. Phillip C. Kolin. Jackson: University Press of Mississippi, 1988. 184–93.

Way, Brian. "*The American Dream* and *The Zoo Story*." *American Theatre*. Stratford-Upon-Avon Studies 10 (1967): 189–208.

Zimbardo, Rose. "Symbolism and Naturalism in Edward Albee's *The Zoo Story*." *Twentieth Century Literature* 8 (1962): 10–17.

4

"Good, Better, Best, Bested": The Failure of American Typology in *Who's Afraid of Virginia Woolf?*

LINCOLN KONKLE

Early in *Who's Afraid of Virginia Woolf?* George tells Nick, "Dashed hopes, and good intentions. Good, better, best, bested. How do you like that for a declension, young man? Eh?" (32). George repeats himself to see if Nick gets his pun on "declension" in the grammatical sense and in the sense of a decline. Ostensibly, George is describing his own career at the college, but his witty declension is one of many expressions in Edward Albee's first full-length play of a more universal theme of decline or entropy, and the particular decline of the United States from its promising beginning as a democratic society that valued individualism and liberty above all to a conformist, materialistic society that values "success" above all.

Virtually every article or book chapter that analyzes *Who's Afraid of Virginia Woolf?* has explicated or acknowledged this national theme, but what has not been understood fully is that Albee's response to the social decline of the United States is in the particular form of the *American* jeremiad.[1] Furthermore, George, as the Jeremiah figure in the play, does not merely lament the current state of affairs, but rather, like the seventeenth-century New England Puritan ministers who first formulated the American jeremiad, he also affirms the earliest individualistic ideals of our country, and urges the next generation, as represented by Nick and Honey, to recommence the "errand into the wilderness"; that is, to renew the social evolution of America.[2]

As I have asserted elsewhere,[3] virtually every one of Albee's plays can be read as an American jeremiad, which Sacvan Bercovitch has called "a nationwide ritual of progress [that] contributed to the success of the republic" (*The American Jeremiad*, xiv–xv).[4] Like Jerry in *The Zoo Story*,[5] Grandma in *The American Dream* and *The Sandbox*,[6] Claire in *A Delicate Balance*, "Voice" in *Box*, and other characters from Albee's plays, George perceives the United States (represented by individuals, families, and Western civilization as a whole) in moral crisis, so he "preaches" to his congregation of three, rhetorically and dramatically enacting the American jeremiad.[7] But another vestige of New England Puritanism, reflected in the "good, better, best, bested" line, and that underlies Albee's criticism of American history, is typology. Because typology is a complex subject, an explanation of some length is necessary.

One of the most important aspects of New England Puritanism relevant to the evolution of American culture, in general, and American literature, in particular, is typology, and only in the past three decades have early American literature scholars fully understood the radical or extended typology of seventeenth-century New England Puritans.[8] Typology was originally a biblical hermeneutic that allowed theologians to conjoin similarities of character, event, or language between the Old Testament and New Testament in a sequential relationship of type, (prototype) and antitype (the realization, completion). For example, Moses freeing the Israelites from the bondage of slavery in Egypt was seen as a type (a foreshadowing) of Christ, the antitype, leading humankind out of the bondage of sin in this life. In short, the New Testament antitypes are more perfect realizations of the Old Testament types. Thus, as a structural paradigm, typology—whether applied to the Old and New Testaments, American history, literature, or an individual's life—is both cyclical and linear, both archetypal and progressive.

The Puritans employed typology as the basis for a providential interpretation of history, which led them to a protonationalist ideology, and ultimately became an integral part of their literary aesthetic.[9] The New England Puritans were not the only Christians to make use of typology in this way; however, as explained by Emory Elliott in "From Father to Son: The Evolution of Typology in Puritan New England,"

> What makes the function of typology in early American thought and writing unusual, if not unique, is, however, that the special experiences of the New England Puritans seem to have provided a remarkable continuous analogy of biblical events: Thus, in the imaginations of seventeenth-century American preachers and writers, typological interpretations of scripture provided a basis for shaping a powerful cultural vision. (204–05)

Thus applying hermeneutic to history, the New England Puritans could make a much stronger case than could English Puritans that they were God's *new* chosen people instructed to cross a *new* "Red Sea" in order to escape persecution and to inherit the "Promised Land." In other words, the New England Puritans believed that they were the antitypal fulfillment of the type of God's chosen people, the Old Testament Israelites. As Bercovitch explains in his analysis of Cotton Mather's biography of John Winthrop in *Magnalia Christi Americana*, " 'Nehemias Americanus' proclaims the forward movement of redemptive history. As the representative of theocracy, the Hebrew

stands not with but behind the Puritan" (*Puritan Origins*, 55). This identification with the Old Testament is found in the sermons, the histories, and even
the spiritual autobiographies and conversion narratives of the seventeenth
century. In fact, many New England Puritans believed that the divine plan of
history had progressed to the point that they were literally laying the foundations of the New Jerusalem in which Christ would rule during the millennium, as prophesied in the Book of Revelation: "This developmental pattern
of progressively clearer dispensations provided the basis upon which New
England Puritans claimed their covenant community as God's chosen succes-
sor to Israel and voiced their latter-day millennial prophecies" (Rowe, 49).

By no means am I arguing that Albee consciously appropriated the Puritan rhetoric of crisis or other Puritan codes, structures, and paradigms that I
find traces of in his plays. As Karl Keller says of another writer influenced by
the "New England Mind," "We do not need to think that Emerson *believed* in
the assumptions behind typology, for it was *already* the frame of his mind.
Typology was not what he thought about but the way he thought about things
in general" (285 n., emphasis added). That is, typology and other vestiges of
New England Puritanism were instilled in Albee as part of the American culture he was exposed to as a child attending church and boarding schools in
the Northeast and specifically New England, as well as in the classic American literature he read in school and on his own.[10] He was further influenced
by the cultural legacy of Puritanism within the works of two other American
dramatists, Tennessee Williams and Thornton Wilder, especially.[11]

In his role as an American Jeremiah, Edward Albee examines the issue
of history-as-progress from a variety of perspectives: generational, national,
technological, aesthetic, political, and evolutionary.[12] Though Albee gives little space in his dramatic jeremiads to explicitly affirming America, this does
not mean he is unpatriotic or a Marxist; on the contrary, as one scholar
expresses it, "Albee's usual rage against America is a lover's rage against the
beloved's failure to live up to his best self, not an enemy's basic disgust with
his opponent" (Hopkins, 81–2).[13] In fact, Albee apparently believes in the
progressive liberal values associated with America, in particular, in the nineteenth and first half of the twentieth centuries, as he can be found to assert
straightforwardly on occasion: "We are nowhere near utopia anywhere on
this planet but I do believe in the perfectibility of society. So I'm an optimist,
I suppose" (Bigsby, *Critical Introduction*, 279). Albee believes in the ideal of
progress, then, but he is not a "cosmic optimist" like the Puritans,[14] who
believed that progress had taken place and was ongoing because their view of
history was typological and providential. As will be evident in the following
analysis of *Who's Afraid of Virginia Woolf?*, Albee reads American history
not as progressive but as regressive or, in Puritan terms, as an inverted typology in which representative American characters demonstrate that we have
become types rather than antitypes of the founders.[15]

Though *Who's Afraid of Virginia Woolf?* appears more realistic than Albee's one-act satire on contemporary America, *The American Dream*, a few scholars have observed that the longer play is not realistic, that its characters are just as much caricatures or types (in the common usage) as those in the one-act play. That is, Martha is a domineering wife like Mommy, George is an "ineffectual" husband like Daddy, and together they "mutilate" their imaginary son as cruelly as Mommy and Daddy did their adopted son. Furthermore, George and Martha's son, as a fiction, is as insubstantial as the vacuous Young Man, Mommy and Daddy's new "adopted" son in *The American Dream*, and Nick is a more fleshed-out version of the Young Man (also called "the American Dream" by Grandma) in the earlier one-act, as several critics have noted.[16] This intertextual analogy between *Who's Afraid of Virginia Woolf?* and *The American Dream* is underscored when Martha calls herself Mommy (15), Nick is addressed as Young Man (32), and George is called Grandma (116).

However, although few critics and scholars would argue that the characters in the one-acts are one-dimensional stereotypes, Albee insists that "all [his] characters are real people, real three-dimensional people—or lizards—they're all real" (Albee, personal interview). One way to make sense out of this statement is to recognize that in Albee's estimation, his characters represent people who have become types; their one-dimensional appearance is their reality in all three dimensions. In typological terms, instead of the antitypal fulfillment, the concrete realization of the founders, modern Americans have reduced themselves to types, becoming less individualistic and more abstract. "Well, I'm a type," says the Young Man in *The American Dream* (113); in *A Delicate Balance* Agnes observes, "We become allegorical, my darling Tobias, as we grow older. The individuality we hold so dearly sinks into crotchet; we see ourselves repeated by those we bring into it all, either by mirror or rejection, honor or fault" (*The Plays*, 216). In *Who's Afraid of Virginia Woolf?* George and Martha are "a couple of middle-age types" (92) and they, along with Nick and Honey, are "college-type types" (139). Martha refers to George and Nick as "you two types" (101), Nick says to George, "It's you sneaky types worry me the most" (111), and George refers to Honey as "a wifey little type" and Honey and Nick together as "teensie little types" when they were children (142). What is particularly damning about this reduction from three-dimensional individual to one-dimensional type is that, as Baxandall says of *Tiny Alice*'s male characters, but which applies as well to most of Albee's representations of contemporary Americans: "Though they are well educated, their personalities are determined by their social roles and they have no names but their functions. These men have in a sense chosen to be types rather than individuals" (24).

That Albee is practicing something like a national rather than a biblical typology in *Who's Afraid of Virginia Woolf?* is indicated by his explanation of naming George and Martha after George and Martha Washington: "[It is] not its most important point, but certainly contained within the play [is] an attempt to examine the success or failure of American revolutionary principles" (qtd. in Kolin, 58). Although Albee seems to assume that those principles originate in the eighteenth rather than the seventeenth century, and elsewhere he is more ambivalent about the integrity of the revolution of 1776,[17] in writing *Who's Afraid of Virginia Woolf?* he connected with an even older ideology: not only the rhetoric of the jeremiad, but a broader swath of the Puritan ethos itself was a factor in the revolution and the continuity of Puritanism in American culture.[18]

However, the continuity of Puritanism in America has also had its downside: "It is possible, for instance, to trace the unique American attitude toward 'success' to roots in our Puritan past, to see this ideology as a secularization of the Protestant ethic" (Porter, 17). Albee would appear to be referring to the materialistic corruption of religion by the American dream in George's allegory of Nick and Honey in the "Get-the-Guests" game: "She was a money baggage among other things. . . . Godly money ripped from the golden teeth of the unfaithful, a pragmatic extension of the big dream" (145). Furthermore, Stenz says, "Like the earlier plays, *Who's Afraid of Virginia Woolf?* is a castigation of a society obsessed with the mystique of success or the appearance of it" (44). Nick, as the representative of the next generation American in *Who's Afraid of Virginia Woolf?*, exhibits this attitude, as Paolucci notes: "For George, money means compromise; for Nick, it is the one sure sign of success" (50).

It is a familiar argument that Benjamin Franklin is partially responsible for the secularization of Puritan spiritual progress into the Protestant work ethic in the eighteenth century; as Westbrook notes (192), Ben Franklin himself was raised Calvinist. However, it was the nineteenth century when Calvinist beliefs were conflated with capitalism so that economic progress was presumed to be as certain as the Puritans' belief that human history was providentially determined:

> Carnegie's faith in the inevitability of progress—"all is well since all grows better"—suggests another common ground shared by social Darwinism and early American Calvinism. Though Carnegie doubtless felt that the tendency for all to grow better was worldwide, he took the United States as the bellwether of progress, as indeed did many other Americans of the nineteenth century. (Westbrook, 128)

The danger in both Calvinistic and capitalistic or naturalistic ideology is the atrophy of individual volition and responsibility: "The problem of the freedom of the will was as central to Puritan discussion as it was to that of the scientific determinists and their opponents in the nineteenth and twentieth centuries" (Westbrook, 119).[19] Though Calvinism was deterministic in the sense of God's predestination of who was elect and reprobate, saved and damned, each person still had free will to do as he or she pleased. In other words, although God had predetermined who was elect, it was up to the individual to live his or her life in such a manner as to gain assurance that he or she was one of the elect. "The pursuit of happiness" is one of the God-given rights cited in the "Declaration of Independence"; thus, American history should have taken the form of a progressive incarnation of revolutionary principles of individual liberty and opportunity. Instead, we seemed to have fallen victim to presumption and passivity: "History and evolution were deemed to be on America's side [by Whitman, Theodore Roosevelt, and other American optimists]; one need only flow along with the natural course of events and America's dominance would be assured" (Westbrook, 130). Indeed, a subtle yet pervasive legacy of New England Puritanism in modern American culture is a national optimism and assurance based upon the presumption that progress is always ongoing and for the benefit of all.[20]

This is precisely the attitude that Edward Albee thinks has led to our decline, as Porter says: "The convention that is being attacked finally in *Who's Afraid of Virginia Woolf?* is the notion that we can expect salvation from without" (245). George, who is an academic historian, concludes that Nick is making this mistake of presumption: "Everything's going to work out anyway, because the timetable's history, right?" (116). In other words, where the responsibility once lay with individual choice, commitment, and effort—what used to be the meaning of the American Dream—now hope is invested in a historical inevitability guaranteed by a system that will regulate society and its growth. At some point, this typology-based national self-assurance mutated into arrogance: "The typological structure applied, in the early American mind, wherever there was a situation involving partial and total fulfillment. In time the structure of types turned faith in Christ into national and personal egocentrism" (Keller, 276–77). Nick's personal egocentrism is most apparent at the beginning of Act Three. Despite his having admitted to marrying Honey in part for her father's wealth, and having just for all intents and purposes committed adultery, he has the audacity to respond to Martha's "Relax; sink into it; you're no better than anybody else," with "I think I am" (188).

Indeed, early in *Who's Afraid of Virginia Woolf?* Nick shows every indication of embodying the American Dream: he was a boy genius (earned his Master's degree in his teens), an All-American athlete (quarterback and boxer), and now is a promising researcher and teacher. As Roudané says, "Nick will be successful, Albee implies, because of the young scientist's a priori belief in the myth of the American Dream" (78). However, in the game " 'Get the Guests," George's characterization of the young scientist casts doubts on Nick's impressive curriculum vitae, at least as a teacher: "Blondie was in disguise, really, all got up as a teacher" (144), which implies that he thinks Nick is more interested in his genetic research. But if that is the case, the question arises, why is Nick working at what appears to be a small liberal arts college? If he got his master's at nineteen and ten years later was beginning a job not at a research institution like M.I.T. but at this small liberal arts college, then Nick has not lived up to his early promise any more than George has. Perhaps that accounts for George's attempt to reach/teach Nick: he can empathize. If George and Martha have been married twenty-three years (153), and they were married after he came to the college, then George's age of forty-six means he also must have gotten his advanced degrees at a young age, suggesting that he, too, was a prodigy whose early potential is unrealized. That Albee means this theme of unfulfilled promise to apply to a broad context is suggested by Martha's comment in Act Three at her unsuccessful attempt at sex with Nick: "Oh my, there is sometimes some very nice potential, but, oh, my! My, my, my. But that's how it is in civilized society" (189). Albee's point, if not Martha's, is that civilized society has potential, but it does not perform up to that potential.

While it may have seemed ironic, then, that Albee named Nick after Nikita Krushchev,[21] the comparison to the leader of a socialist and totalitarian government is appropriate to the dramatization of Albee's criticism that the United States has fallen away from its individualistic and progressive ideals. That is, Nick represents inverted typology not merely as an incarnation of the American dream or the all-American hero type; as a genetics researcher, he also signifies the regression from antitype back to type developed as a system and ideology itself. The point of George's running attack on the genetic engineering research Nick is engaged in is that the propagation of the race will become mechanical with the end result that the species will be reduced to a uniform type:

> This young man is working on a system whereby chromosomes can be altered . . . the genetic makeup of a sperm cell changed, reordered . . . *to* order, actually . . . for hair and eye color, stature, potency . . . I imagine . . . hairiness, features, health . . . and *mind*. Most important. . . . Mind. All imbalances will be corrected, sifted out. . . . We will have a race of men . . . test-tube-bred . . . incubator-born . . . superb and sublime. . . . *But!* Everyone will tend to be rather the same. . . . Alike. Everyone . . . and I'm sure I'm not wrong here . . . will tend to look like this young man *here*. (65)

But what really concerns George is the cultural ramifications of such a system:

> I suspect we will not have music, much painting, but we will have a civilization of men, smooth, blond, and right at the middleweight limit . . . a race of scientists and mathematicians, each dedicated to and working for the greater glory of the super-civilization. . . . There will be a certain . . .

> loss of liberty, I imagine, as a result of this experiment . . . but diversity will
> no longer be the goal. Cultures and races will eventually vanish . . . the ants
> will take over the world. (66–7)

In George's thinking, technological progress runs counter to social and moral progress; Albee would articulate this view of technology again in *Box* and *Quotations from Chairman Mao Tse-Tung*.[22]

Thus, Nick's genetic engineering project, though well intentioned perhaps, poses a threat to an American society founded upon individualism. However, Albee does not criticize the current generation alone; as Bigsby says, George and Martha "embody the fate of the American dream which has moved progressively further away from the supposed liberalism of those revolutionary principles. . . . Nick and Honey . . . are themselves a warning of the next stage of decline" (*Critical Introduction,* 266, 267). At times, George and Martha behave quite childishly, even to the point of using baby-talk, for example in the first act when Martha says, "I'm firsty" (16) and in the last act when George says, "Weally?" (197) and "No climb stairs with Georgie?" (207). Because they couldn't have children, they became children themselves. Martha and George have regressed to childhood, and the next generation, Nick and Honey, do not look any more promising, as George says: "I don't know what the younger generation's coming to" (172).

But so much has been made of Martha's self-delusion—about their son and the purgative effect the evening has upon her and what that will mean for her relationship with George—that comparatively little attention has been paid to the significance of Nick and Honey and the potentially positive effect of the night's events upon them.[23] While Albee uses George and Martha to represent their generation's part in the decline of America, at the same time he has George evoke a golden age of American principles, as suggested by Roudané's description of him: "George, the torchbearer for past history. . . . George, a Thoreauvian surveyor of human history" (79). That is, George is the jeremiad voice in *Who's Afraid of Virginia Woolf?*, trying to inspire the new generation to recommit themselves to the American ideals of individualism, liberty, and self-actualization, as well as to values of community, communication, and shared morality that can then enact rather than enforce social progress. In other words, George, a type of the father of the nation, attempts to convince Nick, a type of what the nation has become, to father the antitypal fulfillment of American revolutionary principles.

What is hardly ever acknowledged in discussions of *Who's Afraid of Virginia Woolf?* is that George is a teacher. In Act One Martha asks him, "You imitating one of your students?" (18), who perhaps have functioned as George's surrogate children over the years. The first nonironic or nonflippant thing George says to Nick is, "What made you decide to be a teacher?" (31). He later asks Nick, "Do you believe that people learn nothing from history? Not that there is nothing to learn, mind you, but that people learn nothing? I am in the History Department" (37). Then George offers Nick another version of the "good, better, best, bested" declension: "I am a Doctor. A.B. . . . M.A. . . . PH.D. . . . ABMAPHID! Abmaphid has been variously described as a wasting disease of the frontal lobes and as a wonder drug. It is actually both" (37). Yet for all his pessimism, George still tries to teach others, as in the third act when he prompts Martha, as if she were a student in his classroom: "All right, Martha; your recitation, please" (217), and through her recitation, like any encouraging teacher, he helps her when she is struggling or stating the "wrong answer," and approves her self-correction: "Ah . . . yes. Better" (217). Granted, earlier in Act Three, George slaps Martha before the game begins to rouse her, saying, "I want a little life in you, baby" (208). But this action recalls Jerry slapping Peter near the end of *The Zoo Story* in an attempt to muse him from his "vegetative" state to at least the "animal" level. There is also a verbal intertextuality with Jerry's speech when he realizes that an extreme solution is necessary to get through to Peter: "So be it!" (*The Zoo Story*, 47). When Martha proclaims Nick a "stud" rather than a "houseboy," George also says, "(*With great, sad relief*) So be it" (202). Nick accurately describes both George's and Jerry's intentions, although he rejects George's offer to help:

GEORGE: I've tried to . . . to reach you . . . to . . .
NICK: (*Contemptuously*) . . . make contact?
GEORGE: Yes.
NICK   (*Still*) . . . communicate?
GEORGE: Yes. Exactly.
NICK: . . . UP YOURS! (116)

In fact, as Albee's stage directions suggest, George is trying to be "Like a father" (115) to Nick. This de facto adoption is George's attempt to overcome his biological sterility, the nation's social sterility. Unfortunate as his and Martha's barrenness is, even worse, Albee suggests, would be to make that condition the social norm by means of genetic engineering. Thus George attacks Nick's research with an image straight out of *Brave New World*:

A certain amount of regulation will be necessary . . . uh . . . for the experiment to succeed. A certain number of sperm tubes will have to be cut. . . . Millions upon millions of them . . . millions of tiny little slicing operations that will leave just the smallest scar, on the underside of the scrotum but which will assure the sterility of the imperfect . . . the ugly, the stupid . . . the . . . unfit. (66)

Nick's acquiescence to Martha's seduction suggests that George's characterization of genetic engineering as mass production of human reproduction is really a large-scale version of Nick's stud fantasy to be "a personal screwing machine" (69) and to "plow a few pertinent wives" (112). Nick claims that this is only George's depiction of him, but he demonstrates that he cares about his stud image when he begs Martha to tell George he is not a "houseboy," which in George and Martha's code signifies someone who could not perform sexually. As George says in response to Nick's promise to be what George says he is, "You are already . . . you just don't know it" (150). Thus Nick's vision of scientific virility, of state-controlled mass reproduction, may be interpreted as the equivalent of George and Martha's imaginary child on a more ambitious scale: a substitute for Nick and Honey's own childlessness.

But it is not Nick, finally, who must be persuaded to reject personal sterility or barrenness, for it is Honey who has been preventing conception: "How do you make your secret little murders stud-boy doesn't know about, hunh? Pills? PILLS? You got a secret supply of pills? Or what? Apple jelly? WILL POWER?" (177). Nick's hesitant, evasive responses to George's inquiries about his and Honey's family plans indicate that he does not realize what Honey is doing, and that he thinks she may be unable to have children, but perhaps fears he is the one who is sterile. George tells Honey, "When people can't abide things as they are, when they can't abide the present, they do one of two things . . . either they . . . either they turn to a contemplation of the past, as I have done, or they set about to . . . alter the future" (178), which is what George understands Nick to be attempting to do, though not in a way that will renew the progress of American ideals. He then tells her, "And you, you simpering bitch . . . you don't want *children*" (178). George's harsh attack reveals his frustration that he cannot directly alter the future by raising children of his own because he is sterile, whereas Honey only chooses to be sterile. George knows that Nick is, in theory, agreeable to having children, "But you *are* going to have kids . . . anyway. In spite of history" (40), so it is Honey who must be converted, which George succeeds in doing during the last game of the evening, "Bringing Up Baby."

The title of this climactic game suggests growth, learning, and progress, but ironically George brings him up in order to "kill" him. Thus, the title of the game is a pun on the stock phrase for raising a child and a synonym for Martha's mentioning the "you know what" to Honey, breaking George's rule to never talk about their imaginary child to others. The title may have yet a third application: since both George and Martha have, throughout the play, used "baby" as a casual term of address to Nick and Honey, the bringing up—in the sense of raising a child—might refer to what George will accomplish with the child-like Honey or both Nick and Honey: to raise them, educate them, propel them into a new maturity. George even refers to them as children before the game begins: "Here come the tots" (209) and after it is all over: "Home to bed, children, it's way past your bedtime" (238). Thus

"Bringing up Baby" is, in effect, a bedtime story, complete with moral.

George's moral initiates the real transformation during the "exorcism" in Act Three: Honey's conversion to wanting a child. As George prompts Martha into what is evidently an invented memory of their son's life from birth to adolescence, though no less impassioned for being fictional, Honey listens and is demonstrably moved:

HONEY: (*Suddenly*; *almost tearfully*) I want a child.
NICK: Honey. . . .
HONEY: (*More forcefully*) I want a child! (222–3)

George's challenge to her, "On principle?"—that is, in the abstract like Martha—evokes a more concrete expression of her new desire: "(*In tears*) I want a child. I want a baby" (223). George's next line—"There; you see? I knew she'd shift"—while ostensibly in reference to Martha's resumption of her narrative, indicates the transformation in Honey, as well.

Though this would seem to make the subsequent "killing off" of the imaginary son unnecessary, it must be remembered that Honey knows what George is doing; she witnessed his inspiration for the idea earlier, pleaded with him then not to do it, and pleads again as he is about to announce to Martha that they received a telegram informing them that their son is dead. Only with Honey's foreknowledge could the exorcism have the effect upon her that it does. By being made to realize the pathos of George and Martha, who are unable to have a child, and the tragedy of the death even of an imaginary child, Honey seems to have connected with a motherly instinct that had previously been repressed or perhaps transferred to Nick. When Honey, intent on Martha's narration, tells George to "Be still!" he replies, "Sorry . . . mother" (223) in mockery, but clearly she is empathizing with Martha's desire for a child.

This is not to say that Albee is advocating biological reproduction and, subsequently, parenthood as a miracle cure for the corruption of American society; sterility and fertility are simply metaphors for social stagnation and progress, respectively. George's solution, rather, is closer to a religious one, which has always been part of American ideology: George and Martha's son is sacrificed (crucified) that Nick and Honey's son (children, that is) may live—biologically and spiritually. As Paolucci and others have pointed out, George and Martha's son is associated with Christ, his death with the crucifixion:

> Martha's "son"—invisible but real—is the most striking paradox of the play. He is the imagination made flesh—or, more precisely, the "word" made flesh, for Martha and George have brought him into the world as talk,

as a game between them, in which he arbitrates, comforts, gives strength to his parents. He is clarity, insight, parable. If one were disposed to take on the burden of polysemous reading, one might trace some interesting religious analogies such as the "lamb" and the "tree" against which the boy met his death, and the "porcupine" which he tried to avoid, like the crown of thorns in the story of Christ. (59)

Paolucci also notes "hints of a virgin birth" (60), and the parody of the Eucharist in George's eating the telegram (61). Albee himself has admitted, "I begin to suspect that I put an awful lot more Christian symbolism in my plays than I was consciously aware of" (Rutenberg, 112). Perhaps, then, Albee is suggesting that the Christian value of self-sacrifice is the only way to resurrect our American dream of "liberty and justice for all."[24]

Such a hopeful reading would seem to fly in the face of the pessimistic tone of most of George's comments on history, American history in particular. Most of his references to the direction of history are downward; for example, he laments "this whole sinking world" (72), and he expresses a typology of literary cities or places that are associated with death, fantasy, sin, God's wrath, and conquest: "And this . . . (*With a handsweep taking in not only the room, the house, but the whole countryside*) . . . this is your heart's content—Illyria . . . Penguin Island . . . Gomorrah. . . . You think you're going to be happy here in New Carthage, eh?" (40). In certain of George's speeches in the play, history appears to be not merely entropic but fatalistic, as when George reads from *The Decline of the West*; "And the west, encumbered by crippling alliances and burdened with a morality too rigid to accommodate itself to the swing of events, must . . . eventually . . . fall" (174). George first laughs ruefully, perhaps realizing that the passage also applies to him personally, then, enraged, he throws the book at the doorbell chimes. That action could signify George's (or Albee's) rejection of the prediction of the West's fall. Not that he denies there is a point of no return, but he won't admit that he or the West has reached that point. In response to Martha's request to light her cigarette, he says, ". . . [M]an can put up with only so much without he descends a rung or two on the old evolutionary ladder . . . (*Now a quick aside to* Nick) . . . which is up your line . . . (*Then back to* Martha) . . . sinks, Martha, and it's a funny ladder . . . you can't reverse yourself . . . start back up once you're descending" (51). The point here, though, is that George refuses to light her cigarette because that would be, to him, a step in the wrong direction, would lead to irreversible decline, thus implying that he has not yet reached the point of no return.

Though decline, destruction, death and metaphorical crucifixions seem to dominate George's worldview, he believes in the possibility of resurrection as well, as demonstrated by his argument with Martha that the moon has come back up:

MARTHA:	There is no moon; the moon went down.
GEORGE:	There is a moon; the moon is up. . . .
MARTHA:	There is no goddamn moon. . . .
GEORGE:	Martha, I do not pick flowers in the blink. I have never robbed a hothouse without there is a light from heaven.
MARTHA:	There is no moon; the moon went down.
GEORGE:	That may very well be, Chastity; the moon may very well have gone down . . . but it came back up. (198–99)

In fact, *Who's Afraid of Virginia Woolf?* ends early Sunday morning with the rising of the *sun*, which has been explicitly and implicitly punned with *son* throughout the play. The religious-mythic imagery attached to George and Martha's son might also suggest that a more authentic Christianity or other religion or ideology may be resurrected out of the ashes of the hypocritical (Honey's father) or Calvinistic (Martha's father) manifestations of God in American culture.[25]

Ultimately, George acknowledges that history is open-ended, and may be evolutionary, even eschatological, as suggested in the following lament spoken as if from an omniscient perspective, almost as though by God:

> You take the trouble to construct a civilization . . . to . . . to build a society, based on the principles of . . . of principle . . . you endeavor to make communicable sense out of natural order, morality out of the unnatural disorder of man's mind . . . you make government and art, and realize that they are, must be, both the same . . . you bring things to the saddest of all points . . . to the point where there *is* something to lose . . . then all at once, through all the music, through all the sensible sounds of men building, attempting, comes the *Dies Irae*. And what is it? What does the trumpet sound? Up yours. (117)[26]

The narration ends disappointingly, a more straightforward expression of George's witty declension, "Good, Better, Best, Bested," yet his disappointment stems from his awareness that America had been making progress at one time. That is, the trumpet is supposed to sound an affirmative note.[27] However, there is nothing in *Who's Afraid of Virginia Woolf?* to prove irrefutably that the outcome is predetermined. George's stated reason for opposing Nick's genetic project indicates that he affirms free will even if it means having to endure a Hitler:

> History . . . will lose its glorious variety and unpredictability. I, and with me the . . . the surprise, the multiplicity, the sea-changing rhythm of . . . history, will be eliminated. There will be order and constancy . . . and I am unalterably opposed to it. I will not give up Berlin! (67)

Even Honey shows she is self-aware enough to imply that she has free will; when George sarcastically says, "It's just some things you can't remember . . . huhn?" she corrects him: "*Don't* remember; not *can't* " (211).

Scholarly readings of the end of *Who's Afraid of Virginia Woolf?* suggesting that there will be a rejuvenation of George and Martha's marriage have been based mostly upon Albee's stage direction, "*A hint of communion in this*" (238) when they respond to Nick's assumption that George was sterile: "You couldn't have . . . any?" But there may also be an invigoration of Nick and Honey's relationship; that is, perhaps Nick has been affected positively by the night's events as well Honey. Twice in the closing scene Nick says, "Oh my God" (231, 232), recalling Peter's cry and Jerry's dying words in *The Zoo Story*. Perhaps, then, George has reached Nick after all; as they begin to exit, Nick starts to apologize: "I'd like to . . ." but George cuts him off with a final "Good night" (238). One can read this either as Nick's attempt to repair the damage he has done, which might also damage his chances for advancement at the college, or as a sincere moment of self-realization, promising a change. His reaching his hand out to Honey (238) could also be played tenderly by the actor, suggesting that Nick and Honey's relationship may develop real intimacy that will probably result in a child, since Honey now wants one.

Thus, Albee's examination of American history as the progress of American revolutionary principles that have their origins at least partially in the theology, ideology, and aesthetics of the New England Puritans shows America to be retreating from the errand into the wilderness, to be less and less a New Israel or even the new democratic nation the United States was in 1776. People have become types; they even seem to believe in an ideology of types or conformity rather than of individualism. Yet Albee does not express a fatalistic view, as do the Theatre of the Absurd playwrights, nor must his assertion of self-determination have been inspired solely by European existentialism. Albee might not necessarily reject the Puritan belief in a providentially determined progress of human history because it did not abrogate personal responsibility for individuals to do their part in the history of their own lives. Twenty years after the debut of *Who's Afraid of Virginia Woolf?* Albee had another of his representative American characters—this one named Sam (as in Uncle?)—say, "Everything is reversible" (*The Lady from Dubuque*, 65), but it does not depend upon historical inevitability; rather, as Albee brilliantly dramatizes in *Who's Afraid of Virginia Woolf?*, it is up to us, first as individuals and perhaps then collectively as a free people, to halt the moral decline and continue the errand into the future.

Notes

1. Albee has frequently been read in the context of the European Theatre of the Absurd; however, he is so self-consciously an *American* dramatist (cf. *Fam*

and Yam) that the influence of his native tradition needs to be taken more into account.

2. "Errand into the Wilderness" is the title that Perry Miller, the preeminent scholar of American Puritanism in the 1950s and 1960s, gave to a collection of his essays on the Puritans. Miller took his title from the title of a Puritan election sermon, delivered by Samuel Danforth on May 11, 1670, "A Brief Recognition of New England's Errand into the Wilderness," which alluded to the Puritans' belief that God had sent them into the wilderness (America) to advance Christianity and prepare for the second coming of Christ and the establishment of New Jerusalem in New England.

3. See my "American Jeremiah: Edward Albee as Judgment Day Prophet in *The Lady From Dubuque*," or for a more in-depth analysis of Albee as an American Jeremiah, the chapter of that title in my "Errand into the Theatrical Wilderness: The Puritan Narrative Tradition in the Plays of Wilder, Williams, and Albee."

4. Bercovitch uses the term "ritual" in the sense employed by anthropologist Victor Turner and New Historicist literary critics: an active agent in the conservation or revolution of a society at any given point in its development. See Victor Turner's *Dramas, Fields, and Metaphors: Symbolic Action in Human Society.* See also Bercovitch's *The American Jeremiad*, Elliott's "The Puritan Roots of American Whig Rhetoric," and David Minter's "The Puritan Jeremiad as Literary Form" in Bercovitch, *The American Puritan Imagination.*

5. In his didactic intention, Jerry not only suggests Jesus of the New Testament but, as a few critics have noted, Jeremiah of the Old Testament. See Baxandall (26), Cohn (9), and Weales (45).

6. By allowing Grandma to step out from the wings and utter a brief epilogue at the end of *The American Dream*, Albee is "invoking the American past in order to attack the vacuity of the American present" (Bigsby, *Critical Introduction*, 263), which is close to the rhetorical strategy of the jeremiad. The complete pattern is most concisely expressed by Elliott in "New England Puritan Literature": "Taking their texts from Jeremiah and Isaiah, these orations followed—and reinscribed—a rhetorical formula that included recalling the courage and piety of the founders, lamenting recent and present ills, and crying out for a return to the original conduct and zeal" (257).

7. This didactic intention was present in Albee's earliest, uncompleted attempts at playwriting, which are archived at the New York Public Library at Lincoln Center. In his reading of these manuscripts, Bigsby denotes the theme of "the necessity to reconstruct a moral existence, to recuperate the biblical virtues of an America which has betrayed its values and lost its purpose" (*Critical Introduction*, 255), again, sounding very much like the American jeremiad.

8. See, for example, Bercovitch, *Typology and Early American Literature*, Miner, and Rowe.

9. As Bercovitch says about New England preacher and poet Edward Taylor, "Taylor fuses typology and poetry, transforms hermeneutic into aesthetic" (*Typology and Early American Literature*, 6).

10. Choate, the private preparatory school in Connecticut from which Albee graduated, was imbued with the Puritan ethos, as Albee himself confirmed in

expressed in an amalgam of religious and political terms. In so recasting the Puritan vision, the leaders of the Revolution played an important part in the process of transmission in which we may discover the continuity of American Puritanism and nineteenth-century American thought and writing. They preserved the Puritan vision of the city on the hill and the garden in the wilderness and refined the Puritan idiom for use by later orators and politicians. It is to this recognizable transmission of Puritan habits of thought and psychological response that such writers as Hawthorne, Melville, Twain, and James reacted, and that continues to fascinate American writers in our own century" ("Puritan Roots," 109).

19. The two systems of belief are not that different in form: "Far from being mutually exclusive, then, orthodox Calvinism and orthodox Darwinism tend almost to fortify one another" (Westbrook, 121).

20. "The reservoir of types provided the sustaining power of a God-sanctioned myth, one which placed the Puritan migration and each saint's spiritual journey within providential history and millennial revelation. Those imaginative visions of America's grand destiny resonate today, even in a world significantly altered from the theocracy of the Massachusetts Bay Colony" (Rowe, 64).

21. As widely reported in readings of *Who's Afraid of Virginia Woolf?*; see, for example, Roudané (80).

22. Voice alludes to the nuclear age, "Seven hundred million babies dead in half the time it takes, took, to knead the dough to make a proper load" (*The Plays*, 272), suggesting that technological progress has only served to bring us to the brink of destruction.

23. Of the few exceptions, see, for example, Stenz (53), Otten (191), Herr, and Sisko.

24. Roudané says, "Albee would not want to push the religious dimension of the play too far. . . . Still, Albee's script radiates a sense of redemption and secular salvation" (107). See also Bigsby, *Critical Introduction* (270).

25. As Cohn noted, "The offstage fathers of Martha and Honey are seen as god-figures" (26). Nick explains that Honey's father was a "man of the Lord" called by God at age six. George implies that in the manner of an Elmer Gantry, Honey's father's traveling salvation show was a scam; Nick's denial that he grew wealthy on "God's money" (108) is unconvincing. Of Martha's father, George says, "He's a god, we all know that" (26) and Martha admits that she revered him: "Jesus, I admired that guy! I worshipped him . . . I absolutely worshipped him. I still do" (77). Albee has George describe him as "a great big white mouse" with "that great shock of white hair, and those little beady red eyes" (75); a similar characterization of God—"the mouse in the model"—appears in Albee's next play, *Tiny Alice*, which is more explicitly concerned with religious issues.

26. Relevant to the discussion of the treatment of history, Cohn says, "Albee reaches out beyond America into a metaphysical examination of the nature of love, which may be a metaphor for civilization. Concealing eschatology beneath the surface psychology, however, Albee's play is limited by its camouflage" (25–6). See also Weales (45), Paolucci (45), Hirsch (30), and Bloom (7).

an interview with this author, and also is documented in Peter Prescott's b
about Choate. The typological rhetoric of the New England Puritans
alive and well in the chapel jeremiads delivered by Choate headmaster S
mour St. John, the son of the headmaster at the time Albee was there.
example, in response to the disruption in the school during the 1967 to 1
year, St. John told the student body, "Like Nehemiah rebuilding the wall
Jerusalem, we are doing a great work and we cannot come down" (342). A
all American jeremiads, St. John concluded with a recommitment to progr
"We shall keep our school moving forward" (342).

11. "Two of the most affecting moments that I remember having in the Amer
theater when I was formative—though I'm still formative—really forma
came from Thornton's plays . . . I remember being enormously affected
them [*Our Town* and *The Skin of Our Teeth*]" (Albee, personal interview).
more on Wilder and Williams' influence upon Albee, see my "Errand into
Theatrical Wilderness."

12. In a 1975 interview, Albee said that *Seascape* is about "whether or not ev
tion has taken place," and when asked if he thought we were growing
responded, "I don't share the view that we're on our way up, anyway" (K
117), citing pollution and the potential for nuclear annihilation.

13. That Albee does not subscribe to communist doctrine is evident in Bigs
analysis in *Collection of Critical Essays* (157–63) of the undermining
Mao's speeches in *Quotations from Chairman Mao Tse-Tung*.

14. This was Perry Miller's term for the Puritan purview, countering the t
tional characterization of the Puritan vision as pessimistic, foreboding.

15. Gary M. Ciuba makes a similar argument, though from an evolutionary p
of view: "The play itself is a headlong descent of man. Albee's chara
have regressed, given up their humanity to go at each other like be
devolved in Darwin's way of thinking" (74). However, in his focus or
older and younger generations, Ciuba contrasts *Who's Afraid of Virg
Woolf?* to *Seascape*, arguing that in the earlier play there is only a Darwi
battle between generations, while in the later play there is coopera
between generations to promote evolution. My contention is that George
tries to promote evolution or progress in the younger generation represe
by Nick and Honey.

16. See Stavrou (59), Roudané (76), Bigsby (*Collection of Critical Essays,*
Schneider (71), and Clurman (78).

17. In one interview, he says, "We are supposed to be a revolutionary society.
reason for our existence, however, was an economic revolution, rather th
revolution for freedom as we all like to pretend. It was caused by an up
middle class trying to get richer—like many revolutions. We've had a co
uing revolution from the first one to the social revolution of 1932. If w
become static and stagnant, we may indeed have lost our value as a soci
(Kolin, 161). Even in this cynical comment on the revolution, he impli
affirms a conceptualization of American society as having been progres
until recently.

18. As Elliott says, "The American Revolution may be seen as a political G
Awakening in which the people were reconverted to their national miss

27. Readings of *Who's Afraid of Virginia Woolf?* have noted "apocalyptic undercurrents of the play" (Roudané 94); see also Cohn (25–6), Amacher (91), and Evans (118).

Works Cited

Albee, Edward. *The American Dream and The Zoo Story.* New York: Signet, 1961.
———.*The Lady from Dubuque.* New York: Atheneum, 1980.
———. Personal interview. 24 May 1990.
———. *The Plays.* 4 vols. New York: Atheneum, 1981–82.
———. *Who's Afraid of Virginia Woolf?* 1962. New York: Signet, 1983.
Amacher, Richard E. *Edward Albee.* Rev. ed. Boston: Twayne: 1982.
Baxandall, Lee. "The Theatre of Edward Albee." *Tulane Drama Review* 9 (1965): 1940.
Bercovitch, Sacvan. *The American Jeremiad.* Madison: University of Wisconsin Press, 1978.
———, ed. *The American Puritan Imagination.* Cambridge: Cambridge University Press, 1974.
———, *The Puritan Origins of the American Self.* New Haven: Yale University Press, 1975.
———, ed. *Typology and Early American Literature.* Amherst: University of Massachusetts Press, 1972.
Bigsby., C. W. E., ed. *Edward Albee: A Collection of Critical Essays.* Twentieth Century Views series. Englewood Cliffs, N.J. Prentice-Hall, 1975.
———. *A Critical Introduction to Twentieth-Century American Drama.* 3 vols. Cambridge: Cambridge University Press, 1984.
Bloom, Harold. ed. *Edward Albee: Modern Critical Views.* New Haven, Conn.: Chelsea House, 1987.
Ciuba, Gary M. "Albee's Descent of Man: Generational Conflict and Evolutionary Change." *Mid-Hudson Language Studies* 6 (1983): 73–9.
Clurman, Harold. "Who's Afraid of Virginia Woolf?" *Edward Albee.* Ed. Bigsby. 76–79.
Cohn, Ruby. *Edward Albee.* Pamphlets on American Writers, No. 77. Minneapolis: University of Minnesota Press, 1969.
Elliott, Emory. "From Father to Son: The Evolution of Typology in Puritan New England." *Literary Uses of Typology.* Ed. Miner. 204–27.
———. "New England Puritan Literature." *The Cambridge History of American Literature, Vol. I: 1590–1820.* Ed. Sacvan Bercovitch. Cambridge: Cambridge University Press, 1994. 169–306.
———, ed. *Puritan Influences in American Literature.* Illinois Studies in Language and Literature 65. Urbana: University of Illinois Press, 1979.
———. "The Puritan Roots of American Whig Rhetoric." *Puritan Influences in American Literature.* Ed. Elliott. 107–27.
Evans, Arthur. "Love, History, and Edward Albee." *Renascence* 19 (1967): 115–18, 131.
Herr, Denise Dick. "The Tophet at New Carthage: Setting in *Who's Afraid of Virginia Woolf?*" *English Language Notes* 33.1 (September 1995): 63–71.

Hirsch, Foster. *Who's Afraid of Edward Albee?* Berkeley, Calif.: Creative Arts Book, 1978.

Hopkins, Anthony. "Conventional Albee: *Box and Quotations from Chairman Mao Tse-Tung.*" *Edward Albee.* Ed. Bloom. 75–82.

Keller, Karl. "Alephs, Zahirs, and the Triumph of Ambiguity: Typology in Nineteenth-Century American Literature." *Literary Uses of Topology.* Ed. Miner. 274–302.

Kolin, Philip C., ed. *Conversations with Edward Albee.* Jackson: University Press of Mississippi, 1988.

Konkle, Lincoln. "American Jeremiah: Edward Albee as Judgment Day Prophet in *The Lady from Dubuque.*" *American Drama* 7.1 (Fall 1997): 30–49.

———. "Errand into the Theatrical Wilderness: The Puritan Narrative Tradition in the Plays of Wilder, Williams, and Albee." Diss. University of Wisconsin-Madison, 1991.

McCarthy, Gerry. *Edward Albee.* New York: St. Martin's, 1987.

Miller, Perry. *Errand into the Wilderness.* Cambridge: Harvard University Press, 1956.

Miner, Earl, ed. *Literary Uses of Typology from the Late Middle Ages to the Present.* Princeton: Princeton University Press, 1977.

Otten, Terry. *After Innocence: Visions of the Fall in Modern Literature.* Pittsburgh: University of Pittsburgh Press, 1982.

Paolucci, Anne. *From Tension to Tonic: The Plays of Edward Albee.* Carbondale: Southern Illinois University Press, 1972.

Porter, Thomas E. *Myth and Modern American Drama.* Detroit: Wayne State University Press, 1969.

Prescott, Peter S. *A World of Our Own: Notes on Life and Learning at a Boys' Preparatory School.* New York: Coward-McCann, 1970.

Roudané, Matthew C. *Who's Afraid of Virginia Woolf?: Necessary Fictions, Terrifying Realities.* Twayne's Masterwork Studies No. 34. Boston: Twayne, 1990.

Rowe, Karen E. "Prophetic Visions: Typology and Colonial American Poetry." *Puritan Poets and Poetics.* Ed. White. 47–66.

Rutenberg, Michael E. *Edward Albee: Playwright in Protest.* New York: Avon, 1969.

Schneider, Alan. "Reality Is Not Enough: An Interview with Alan Schneider." *Edward Albee.* Ed. Bigsby. 69–75.

Sisko, Nancy J. "Comic Strategies in *The Tempest* and *Who's Afraid of Virginia Woolf?*" *English Language Notes* 28.4 (June 1991): 63–7.

Stavrou, C. N. "Albee in Wonderland." *Southwest Review* 60 (1975): 46–61.

Stenz, Anita Marie. *Edward Albee: The Poet of Loss.* The Hague: Mouton, 1978.

Turner, Victor. *Dramas, Fields, and Metaphors: Symbolic Action in Human Society.* Ithaca: Cornell University Press, 1967.

Weales. Gerald. "Edward Albee: Don't Make Waves." *Edward Albee.* Ed. Bloom. 29–50.

Westbrook, Perry D. *Free Will and Determination in American Literature.* Cranbury, N.J. Associated University Presses, 1979.

White, Peter, ed. *Puritan Poets and Poetics: Seventeenth Century American Poetry in Theory and Practice.* University Park & London: Pennsylvania State University Press, 1985.

5

Like Father, Like Son: The Ciphermale in *A Delicate Balance* and *Malcolm*

ROBERT F. GROSS

> The Father and I are one.
> (*JOHN* 10:30)

I

A fifteen-year-old, expensively dressed boy seated on a bench, completely unaware of what he should do next, now that his father has mysteriously disappeared; a middle-aged man in an expensive suburban home, who has withdrawn from life following the death of his son. These two figures, drawn respectively from Edward Albee's plays *Malcolm* and *A Delicate Balance* are complementary—Malcolm, the deserted son, and Tobias, the bereft father. Both plays, first produced on Broadway in 1966, dramatize the experiences of male protagonists who exhibit a pronounced passivity that arises from loss.

Father has lost son; son has lost father. Neither one, however, is undergoing the process of mourning, in which the sense of loss is slowly and painfully assimilated. Rather, both Tobias and Malcolm have been unable to relinquish their emotional investment in a lost family member. They have come to identify with the loss and have become melancholics.

In "Mourning and Melancholia," Sigmund Freud describes the major features of melancholia:

> a profoundly painful dejection, cessation of interest in the outside world, loss of the capacity to love, inhibition of all activity, and a lowering of the self-regarding feelings to a degree that finds utterance in self-reproaches and self-revilings. . . . (74)

On the face of it, the Freudian melancholic makes for an unsatisfactory protagonist. Marked by an inhibition of activity, this figure negates the principle of action that has dominated Western drama since Aristotle. While the traditional dramatic protagonist moves the plot forward through an engagement with the world, the melancholic, suffering from disengagement, has no interest in anything but the stasis of loss. Even such notable tragic melancholics as Electra and Hamlet only take on theatrical vitality when the call to action and engagement, in the form of revenge, displaces their inaction.

But neither Malcolm nor Tobias are called to revenge, or are even shaken out of their fundamental passivity. Indeed, although both are undeniably the structural centers of their respective plays, they tend to be upstaged by characters around them who are flashier, wittier, more eccentric, passionate, and active. The actor who plays Tobias has been given a challenging role, but it is hard for him to compete for attention with the brilliantly battling sister act of Agnes and Claire. Malcolm, whose dramatic energy lies somewhere between Lewis Carroll's Alice and his Dormouse, cannot hope to draw focus from the vivid grotesques who squabble for possession of him. Both *Malcolm* and *A Delicate Balance* thus share a dramaturgical peculiarity as dramas centered about fundamentally undramatic characters. In both cases, the effect of this structural oddity is to situate absence, in the form of a dramatic figure, at a privileged place in the dramatic structure. I will call these characterological blanks "ciphermales"—males who are strangely isolated within their plays, largely passive and fixated in their melancholia, and fundamentally opposed to the traditional masculine heroes of activity and agency. The characterology of the ciphermale, his effect on dramatic structure and meaning, and his place in the dynamics of gender and sexuality in mid-'60s American culture is the terrain I have set out to explore.

II

Although *Malcolm* opened on Broadway nine months before *A Delicate Balance*, I will turn to the later play first, since the impasse in the later play, both more dramaturgically conservative and undeniably more commercially and critically successful, establishes a context for the understanding of the earlier, less well-known and more idiosyncratic work.

A Delicate Balance takes the familiar genre of the domestic drama and turns it into an investigation of the boundaries of the domestic realm and the transgression of those boundaries. While already eccentric, the suburban household of Tobias, his wife Agnes, and his sister-in-law Claire braces itself for the return of daughter Julia, fresh from the collapse of her fourth marriage. But it is not prepared for the sudden appearance of Harry and Edna, neighbors and long-time friends, on their doorstep. Harry and Edna are shaken with a severe and sudden bout of existential terror, and ask to be taken in. The couple's desperate request violates the segregated domestic order of post–World War II American suburbia, in which the appropriate household unit is defined by kinship. The primacy of kin over even the tightest extrafamilial bonds is dramatized to show the ultimate superficiality of extrafamilial relationships in a society that has determinedly organized itself according to the nuclear family. The crisis of the play becomes whether or not Harry and Edna will be allowed to stay, and the rigid limitations of suburban life reassert themselves against the threat.

Tobias and Agnes's household was once the epitome of Cold War American suburban life; it boasted a prosperous father with a career, a suitably domestic mother, a son, and a daughter. But some years ago, the son, Teddy, died, leaving the family in emotional disarray. Agnes remembers it as "an unreal time" (101):

> Ah, the things I doubted then: that I was loved—that *I* loved, for that matter!—that Teddy had ever lived at all—my mind, you see. That Julia would be with us long. I think I thought that Tobias was unfaithful to me then. (102)

For most of the family, life has gone on. Julia has grown older, and embarked on her series of disastrous marriages. Claire (whose time of arrival in the household is never made clear) has wandered through various stages of alcoholism and recovery, only to find her way back repeatedly to the bottle. Agnes has continued to do her best to impose order on her somewhat disorderly ménage. Only Tobias has never recovered from Teddy's death, living as an exile within his own home:

AGNES: (*Sweet; sad*) Well, my darling, you are not young now, and you do not live at home.
TOBIAS: (*Sad question*) Where do I live?
AGNES: (*An answer of sorts*) The dark sadness. Yes? (129)

Ignoring Agnes's desire to conceive another child, he began to withdraw from her before ejaculation, and eventually made the unilateral decision to cease marital relations altogether, taking to his "own sweet room," as Agnes puts it (138). Rejecting both physical intimacy and procreation, retiring from his career, becoming a "cipher" (63) in his daughter's life, he has withdrawn from the role of suburban patriarch, taking on the ineffectual and slightly ridiculous role of "squire, parading about in jodhpurs and confusing the gardener" (18).

On the surface, it might seem that Tobias's melancholic self-exile from the role of patriarch might be greeted with relief by his martinet wife, but Agnes reveals that the truth of the situation is quite different. Tobias's melancholia has been imposed upon her, and she has been forced to live with its consequences. When faced with the challenge of Harry and Edna's visit,

Agnes insists that Tobias emerge from his passivity and reassume his patriarchal role.

And yet Agnes's insistence places Tobias in a situation rife with contradictions. He does not actively accept his role as patriarch, but is placed there by his wife. In other words, he somewhat passively assumes the active role. Moreover, Agnes explains that his passive, melancholic role has had the active result of dominating their marriage for years; nothing has been so powerful as his decision to be absent. Once Tobias accepts the responsibility for dealing with Harry and Edna, however, his decision is twice repudiated—first by Agnes, who believes that their friends pose a serious threat to the family by staying, and then by Harry, who, even before hearing Tobias's invitation, has already decided to leave. Tobias's courageous and unconventional resolve to redefine the boundaries of the domestic realm is ruthlessly undercut, and he is left at the play's end in silence, morning cocktail in hand, as Agnes has the last word.[1]

Tobias's melancholic position in the household is not presented as a unique situation, but as representative. Albee generalizes from his protagonist's situation out to all modern American men. Agnes sees women as more complex beings than men, whose sole interests are money and death—"making ends meet until they meet the end" (64), as opposed to the rich, interpersonal realm of female existence. To be a male, according to this description, is to be the melancholic cog in a capitalist machine.

Later, Agnes shares with amusement the observations of a psychiatrist that the gender roles in America are reversing. This leads her to indulge in a series of verbal whimsicalities that end with her becoming Julia's "father," and Tobias being metamorphosed into Julia's "mother."

This amusing rhetorical role-reversal points in two directions. On the one hand, it works subversively as an entertainingly camp moment of genderfuck, in which traditional notions of male and female identity are confused. On the other hand, it reinforces certain conservative concerns about the American family throughout the Cold War. The constellation of absent father, domineering mother, and emotionally confused children was not only a commonplace of popular culture during the period—such films as *Psycho* (1960), *The Manchurian Candidate* (1962), and *The Fall of the Roman Empire* (1964) immediately spring to mind as examples—but was tantamount to dogma in psychological and childbearing literature of the age. Psychoanalyst Irving Bieber's highly influential 1962 study, *Homosexuality*, fostered the widespread misapprehension of male homosexuality as commonly the result of overcontrolling mothers and of hostile or detached fathers (Lewes, 206–10). Insufficient fathering, it was believed, could easily result in the development of "sissies," who would be vulnerable to perversion, homosexuality, and manipulation by communists (May, 146–47).[2] Among leftists, the weakening of the patriarch was also seen as a salient feature of contemporary American culture, one which weakened the psychological formation of the individual. Herbert Marcuse described the patriarch in decline:

> His authority as transmitter of wealth, skills, experiences, is greatly reduced; he has less to offer, and therefore less to prohibit. The progressive father is a most unsuitable enemy and a most unsuitable "ideal"—but so is any father who no longer shapes the child's economic, emotional, and intellectual future. (97)

These broadly felt anxieties about the weakening patriarchy in the family resonate most strongly in the allusions to Teddy's sexual orientation. When Julia says that she still misses her first husband, Charlie, who is homosexual, because he reminds her of what her dead brother might have grown up to be, Tobias is instantly defensive:

TOBIAS: (*Quiet anger and sorrow*) Your brother would not have grown up to be a fag.
JULIA: (*Bitter smile*) Who is to say?
TOBIAS: (*Hard look*) I! (65)

That Charlie may well have been a substitute for Teddy not only for Julia, but for her parents as well, is implied by Tobias's admission that he and his wife railroaded Julia into marrying Charlie. Despite Tobias's homophobic reaction, the linkage of Teddy with homosexuality lingers. The household, with its detached father and dominant mother, is haunted by a spectral homosexuality.

Seen from this angle, Tobias's relationship with his friend Harry takes on a different color. While it would be incorrect to characterize the relationship as overtly homosexual, it is clear that Tobias's friendship is both his deepest relationship to anyone outside his now female family, and his strongest bond to a living male. Early in the play, Claire challenges Tobias about the nature of his friendship, wondering if he really has anything in common with his "very best friend" (19). The subsequent action of the play puts his friendship to the test. Tobias admits that he does not particularly care for Edna, and that his invitation to the couple to share his home is based on his friendship for Harry. It is as if the melancholia induced by Teddy's death can be assuaged only by the introduction of another male into the household, whether through Julia's spouse, Charlie, or Tobias's friend, Harry.

The fundamental conflict of *A Delicate Balance*, then, becomes one of female domesticity versus male intimacy. Agnes, the representative of female domesticity, sees the claims of male intimacy as a "plague"(151) and urges her husband to repudiate it. Harry preempts Tobias's invitation by rejecting the prospect out of hand, and never answering his friend's desperate entreaty. The distance between suburban homes becomes the distance between men, tainted by the hidden fear of homosexuality—the fear that makes male intimacy impossible.

This gendered conflict is obscured by Albee's introduction of a somewhat clumsy articulation of existentialist thematics. The experience of existential anguish that sends Harry and Edna scurrying to their friends' house is the most schematic and least developed element in the entire drama. It is asserted rather than dramatically embodied. The borrowings from Albert Camus, the motifs of silence, terror, and plague, seem pasted on the dramatic action with a sophomoric earnestness in what is otherwise a very insightful and sophisticated play. It is as if Harry, in the midst of reading his French (45), had hysterically overreacted to a passage in Camus's *The Stranger* or *The Plague*.

This clumsy eruption of allegory obscures the play's anguished exploration of male intimacy in '60s suburbia. The perceived threat of male homosexuality, although central to Tobias's dilemma, is moved to the margins, just as homosexual males are carefully kept offstage, in the figures of Teddy and Charlie. If one part of Albee is Tobias, looking for male intimacy to fill a melancholic absence, another part of him is Agnes, who succeeds in containing the action within the heteronormative limitations of Cold War domestic drama. Yet the motifs of silence, terror, and plague have the effect of taking the melancholic absence occasioned in Tobias by Teddy's death and letting it spread, like a miasma, through the suburban landscape. The personal, psychological dilemma is thus connected to the social and existential levels.

Superficially, there is no immediate justification for the references to male homosexuality in *A Delicate Balance*. Further investigation, however, shows that the physical intimacy between males repeatedly returns to the margins as what has been repressed out of the Harry-Tobias friendship, and what Albee is trying to exclude, Agnes-like, from the play's world. The "plague" is nothing less than the displacement of homosexual impulses, both feared and desired. It sends Tobias back, after years of absence, to his wife's bedroom, although even then only the outward form of heterosexuality succeeds in reasserting itself.

In another bedroom in the house, Harry came to Edna's bed, where she flattered his sense of heterosexuality, letting him "think I . . . wanted to make love" (163). There Harry asks, "like a little boy" ' (163), "Do they love us?" (163). This reappearance of the specter of Teddy, in the body of middle-aged Harry, is swiftly regulated. His desire for love outside of the constraints of marriage is answered by his wife, Edna, who substitutes for love a stringent reciprocity—Agnes and Tobias love them, she observes, as much as they love Agnes and Tobias. When a law of balance replaces love, Harry can only acquiesce in his own rejection, just as he imagines he would reject Tobias if the roles were reversed. By rigorously projecting himself onto the Other, the fear of transgression linked to love between men polices itself. The heterosexual bedroom becomes the locus of social control.

In *A Delicate Balance*, Albee adopts the form and trappings of domestic drama and rewrites it, undermining the strength of the patriarchal figure, which has been the genre's primary locus of order since its initial formation in the late eighteenth century.[3] He undermines the patriarch, not by moving him to the periphery of the action, as Clifford Odets did in *Awake and Sing*, nor by removing him from the stage altogether as Tennessee Williams had done in *The Glass Menagerie*. Instead, Albee keeps the patriarch at the center of the play's structure, but in a passive and feminized position, effaced by his own melancholy. The result is a play that is at once progressive for its time, in its awareness of the limitations imposed on male relations by a rigidly heteronormative and homophobic society, and conservative in its containment of its characters within those heteronormative and homophobic limitations. As such, it is representative of white, middle-class anxiety in the late 1960s. It registers a cultural moment in which the limitations of both Cold War ideology and the nuclear family were being more keenly felt and widely discussed. It saw the rise of second-wave feminism, as reflected in Betty Friedan's 1963 trailblazing bestseller, *The Feminine Mystique*. But it still slightly preceded the emergence of a radical gay rejection of the status quo, most forcefully expressed in the Stonewall riots of 1969. *A Delicate Balance* manifests a deep discontent and yearning, but is timid in the force and clarity of its critique. It embodies a society in which heterosexuality is being problematized, but gay identity has not quite come into its own in a strong, public voice.

III

Albee's *Malcolm*, a dramatization of James Purdy's fascinating 1959 novel of the same name, is not constrained by the decorum of Cold War suburban mores or by the closed form of domestic drama, so evident in *A Delicate Balance*. *Malcolm* can be described best as a "postdomestic" drama. It begins with its pubescent protagonist perched on a bench outside the hotel in which he lives, abandoned by his father, and quite at a loss as to what he should do next. In Malcolm's world, the competing claims of family and long-time friends are nonexistent; he has no such ties, save a somewhat vague memory of a father. Rather than the severely drawn boundaries of suburban domesticity, the play's episodic structure follows the meanderings of a protagonist without purpose. The episodic structure may, at times, suggest a quest narrative or bildungsroman, but Malcolm seems singularly unaffected by experience. Both Purdy's novel and Albee's play suggest the adventures of Candide, Justine, Alice, and Serena Blandish—all innocent sojourners thrust by chance into a vivid and even grotesque world that seems to have amazingly little effect on their innocence.

In this postdomestic world, strictures against male homosexuality are suspended. Indeed, the world is permeated with a gay ethos. Malcolm's aimless existence on the park bench is transformed when he makes the acquaintance of a waspish astrologer with exotic social connections, an eccentric gentleman with the phallic name, Mr. Cox. Cox has no reservations about asking whether or not young Malcolm has sprouted pubic hair, and, when the answer is "yes," begins to send him off to a succession of bizarre married couples: Kermit, who considers himself the oldest man in the world, and his slatternly wife, Laureen; the bohemian artist Eloisa and her ex-convict, homosexual husband, Jerome; and the incredibly rich and promiscuous Girard Girard, and his frequently drunken wife, Madame Girard. Given these examples of matrimony, it is not surprising that Malcolm quickly comes to the conclusion, "Married love is the strangest thing of all" (26).

Both men and women take an immediate, even obsessive interest in the visiting youth, and Malcolm effortlessly drifts along with their plans for him. Even by '90s standards, *Malcolm* is incredibly blasé about the introduction of a minor to homosexual relationships with adults—virginity is clearly not an issue here. When Madame Girard delicately asks if he has been *used* at Eloisa Brace's house and hostel for jazz musicians, Malcolm explains, "Well it *is* a little crowded when it comes to bedtime, and I suppose I've . . ." only to be cut off by Madame Girard, who is obsessed with having Malcolm for herself (75). Innocence and sexual experience are not mutually exclusive. Indeed, Malcolm goes to an early grave, the victim of alcohol and "a violent protracted excess of sexual intercourse" (134), without any noticeable change in attitude.

Passive and feminized, Malcolm circulates in the market. He becomes a friend for Kermit, a sexual partner for Jerome, a painter's model for Eloisa, a potential son for Girard Girard, and a husband for Melba, a sexually voracious jazz singer. He is manipulated, propositioned, and sold like "a white slave or something" (86), and yet never seems to be able to summon up any indignation. A true man without qualities, this adolescent ciphermale resists representation. When Eloisa paints Malcolm's portrait, Cox appraises the result: "It doesn't look exactly like *him*—or he doesn't look exactly like *it*. . . . Maybe it's a picture of what he used to be . . . or what he's becoming" (69). In the wake of his father's disappearance, Malcolm has only one concept to anchor his understanding of the world—loss:

> THE WHOLE WORLD IS FLYING APART!! The . . . the whole world is. . . . Have . . . have I done this? Is . . . is this because of me? I've been polite and honest, and . . . I've *tried*. I don't understand the world. No, I don't understand it at all. I feel that thing, father. . . . Loss. Loss . . . father? (80)

In this passage, the words "father" and "loss" become the two poles of a closed, chiastic system, one that is incapable of alteration. Even on his deathbed, Malcolm's last words are reflections on his father and loss.

Rather than immersing himself in the painful temporality of the mourning process, Malcolm remains in the isolated stasis of melancholia, and suspended in a relationless present. He is doomed to be a "contemporary," as Gus calls him (90), existing outside of history. This contemporaneity is a form of emptiness; Malcolm cannot find out what he is a contemporary *of* (90).

The only passion detected in Malcolm is his melancholic fixation on his absent father. When Madame Girard opines that no one believes in the existence of Malcolm's father, the indignant adolescent responds: "That's . . . that's . . . blasphemy . . . or, a thing above it!" (33–4). Malcolm's belief in that primal relationship goes beyond religious faith. Indeed, it is more absolute than can be described or imagined. It is a faith that accepts no substitutes; once severed, it cannot be replaced. Girard Girard offers to take the place of Malcolm's father, only to be rebuffed:

GIRARD GIRARD: (*So gentle*) That is all we ask. Come spend the summer with us; be our son.

MALCOLM: Be *like* your son, sir.

GIRARD GIRARD: (*As he prepares to leave the set*; *wistfully*) Between simile and metaphor lies all the sadness in the world, Malcolm. (48)

Malcolm's fixation on his absent father leads to a climactic encounter in a men's room, in which Malcolm accosts a man he believes to be his father, only to be accused of solicitation and violently rejected. Soon after this mishap, Malcolm begins to decline. The doctor may diagnose the causes as alcoholism and sexual hyperaesthesia, but the progression of the plot implies that behind those immediate causes was the more devastating experience of paternal rejection.

In the gay ethos of both novel and play, this climactic scene of misrecognition has decidedly sexual overtones. Malcolm follows a strange man into a restroom, touches him, asks if he has been rejected because of his heterosexual union, and is accused of solicitation. Purdy takes the sexual underscoring even further in Malcolm's subsequent conversation with Melba:

> "With my fame and money," Melba told him, "and your special gift, blow your father," and she motioned for him to sip her drink.
>
> "Blow my father!" Malcolm echoed, and then hearing his own voice, his jaw dropped slowly.
>
> "Say, kiddy are you all right?" Melba said, somewhat concerned.
>
> "Blow my father!" Malcolm said.
>
> "Don't say that again," Melba adjured him, and her mouth set. (Purdy, *Malcolm*, 185)

Melba, acting from her own narcissistic sense of plenitude and heterosexual privilege, behaves like a more vulgar version of Edna or Agnes, and rejects her consort's movement toward a male relationship that threatens her marriage. But her dismissive imperative, "blow," carries other, more transgressive possibilities. Malcolm, his jaw dropping open, whether in shock or in mental contemplation of paternal fellatio, repeats the phrase. With repetition, the phrase increasingly takes on a meaning that subverts Melba's intent, and she silences the utterance. Sexuality between father and son, seen by society as transgressive of the rules of kinship, gender, and age, comes to its most powerful expression in this passage.

The passage above does not appear in Albee's play, and indeed, the entire sequence containing the failed recognition of the father and its aftermath is hurried in his adaptation, leaving it less resonant, and giving the conclusion of the play less weight and finality. Perhaps Albee, working in the far more conservative forum of Broadway theater, was more cautious and prone to self-censorship in his handling of this transgressive material. I cannot help but wonder if relatively slight alterations to Albee's *Malcolm*, written in the freer atmosphere of today's theater, might give the adaptation an emotional power equal to Purdy's novel, and greater success on the contemporary stage. As it stands, the adaptation requires some referencing back to the novel to restore its power and inner coherence.

In more standard narratives of the Cold War period, it would be easy to assimilate both the novel and the play to the concerns about absent fathers and homosexual sons that were discussed in relation to *A Delicate Balance*. The interpretation would go like this: Malcolm, deserted by his father, becomes a "sissy," easily manipulated by neurotics and perverts. Eroticizing the absent father, he falls into sordid and delusional behavior, and never matures. Neither Purdy nor Albee, however, indulge in that sort of psychologizing or moralizing.[4] Actions are rarely given motivational justification or subjected to judgment. Thomas Lorch's definition of the novel's ontological vision can apply easily to the play, as well: "*Malcolm* depicts characters variously deficient in being encircling an absolute metaphysical blank" (211). That metaphysical void renders psychological and moral judgments impossible; the reader is left with no more foundation for judgment and understanding than the protagonist has. We are led to read as ciphermales, alienated and emotionally removed.

Lorch's reading is insightful, but like an existentialist reading of *A Delicate Balance*, it reads absence as a metaphysical absolute, somehow detached from the structures of gender and sexuality in the work. Blankness in *Malcolm* is given its strongest expression in the opaque character of its protagonist, and that blankness is tied to the inexplicable absence of his father. This absence is so powerful that it leads characters to wonder if Malcolm even had a father—an absence that would make Malcolm himself an impossibility. Unlike the death of Teddy in *A Delicate Balance*, which is realistically grounded, Malcolm's nameless father becomes increasingly detached from any grounding, and begins to approach allegory. Growing increasingly powerful as the object of loss and decreasingly believable as a palpable figure, the fatal, humiliating encounter in the restroom becomes the inevitable result of a loss that cannot be repaired.

After this encounter, Malcolm's deterioration is swift. Purdy repeatedly identifies his malady as "melancholy" (189), and Albee dramatizes that melancholy in Malcolm's anguished reflections on loss. But while Purdy's Malcolm is able to transmute loss into literary activity—"three hundred pages of manuscript" (195)—Albee's youthful protagonist lapses into silence, with no written legacy left behind to communicate his experience. Of the two Malcolms, Albee's is more completely effaced.

IV

Tobias and Malcolm both suffer melancholia from the destruction of the father/son dyad. In neither case do we see an Oedipal configuration. The relationship between Teddy and Tobias does not triangulate to include Agnes, and there is no reference to Malcolm's mother anywhere in the play. The result is an image of the father/son relationship that runs counter to that presented by Jacques Lacan. Lacan begins with the child (in this case, son) caught up in the imaginary, held by the image of the mother, and the arrival of the father institutes the symbolic, which contains language, law, and the incest prohibition.[5] In Albee, it is the father/son relationship that stands for a primal emotional plenitude prior to the trauma of separation. Moreover, in complete contradiction to the Freudian and Lacanian models, the father can be as traumatized by the separation as the son. It is clear that Albee's dynamic has little, if anything to do with the Freudian tradition. He operates, rather, in the realm of the male homoimaginary.

I have coined the term "male homoimaginary" elsewhere to describe a mythical state of male intimacy that exists before the imposition of the symbolic (Gross, 19–21). In the homoimaginary, males are unaware of differences in sexual orientation, and feel no need to scrutinize their relationships. There is no love that dare not speak its name, for there is no imperative to endow male relationships with names. The male homoimaginary appears throughout Western culture in a wide-range of texts, from Leontes and Polixenes' idyllic boyhood in *The Winter's Tale* to Brick and Skipper's football days in *Cat on a Hot Tin Roof*. It can be found in boy's adventure stories, as well as gay pornographic fiction, with its blissfully unreflective societies of cowboys, sailors, truckers, and pirates. It can function either as gay utopia, or as a mystification of homosexuality for those who want to have indulgent, male, erotic fantasies without having to admit their homosexual component.

As seen in the examples above, the homoimaginary is usually config-
ured in terms of peers. Albee's construction of a father/son homoimaginary is
potentially more subversive, since it simultaneously transgresses the boundaries male/male, parent/child, and adult/minor. Moreover, it threatens to
revise the most sacred homoimaginary myth in Western culture, that of the
intimacy between God the Father and God the Son. Drawing on many
expressions in the Gospel of John, Christian myth and theological specula-
tion has hinged on "the only Son, who is nearest to his father's heart" (*John*
1:18) who declares "the Father is in me and I am in the Father" (*John* 10:38).
From the early Father of the Church, the divine Father/Son dyad was investigated in all its ontological intimacy. For Tertullian, the Son is a substance
emitted by the Father; for Athanasius, "All that is said of the Father is also to
be said of the Son, except that the Son is Son, and not Father" (Lonergan,
47). The minimal difference between Father and Son, always threatening to
lapse into heretical lack of differentiation, creates the central romance of
Christianity in all of its ardor and cruelty.[6] As a result, fathers searching for
sons, and sons for fathers, almost inevitably takes on theological overtones in
Christian cultures; every abandoned son echoes Golgotha.

While the father/son homoimaginary remains scandalously central to
Christianity—and must be finessed, using the symbolic's notions of law, obe-
dience, and duty—it is repressed altogether with Freud's mythology of social
beginnings, as related in *Totem and Taboo*. In this quintessential myth of heterosexual patriarchy, the primal father is exclusively heterosexual, and has
control over all women. The sons identify with the primal father's desire and
kill him to have access to his harem. Obviously, an interdiction against
homosexuality obscurely precedes the beginning of myth. Otherwise, what
would keep the father from having sexual access to his sons as well as his
daughters? And what would have kept some sons from desiring, rather than
merely identifying with, the father's virility? In this myth, Freud assumes
that for a man to be a father, he must have channeled all his libidinous energy
into heterosexuality; that there is nothing that can escape the black hole of
compulsory heterosexuality.[7] The interdiction of homosexuality constructs
gender difference as the ultimate form of difference, and subordinates all
other modes of difference, including class, age, race and ethnicity, as secondary (Warner, 199–200). The image of the male homoimaginary is indifferent to any primal, heterosexual edict: "we knew not/The doctrine of
ill-doing, nor dream'd/That any did" (*Winter's Tale*, 1.i.69–71). In the
father/son homoimaginary, there is a fatherhood before law, language, and
heterosexuality.

The ciphermale emerges in the wreckage of the father/son dyad's
destruction, leaving a fundamental, irremediable melancholia within the
male. The reason for the destruction remains obscure. Unlike the Lacanian
model, it is not imposed by the parent of the opposite sex upon the child.

Teddy dies; Malcolm's dad disappears. It is tempting to speculate that the introduction of the symbolic, with its taboos against incest and homosexuality, ruptures the homoimaginary idyll. That would help to account for Harry's avoidance of Tobias's offer, for Tobias's insistence that Teddy would not have been a "fag," and for Malcolm's devastating rejection by his "father." This implies that it is homophobia, not death, that destroys the homoimaginary and compels melancholia. But Albee's construction of a myth of the father/son homoimaginary is elliptical, and the scene of its destruction is veiled. What is clear in each of these Albee plays, however, is that two males were once one, and now the one left behind is something less than that.

Malcolm and *A Delicate Balance* are generated in the space created between father and son, an unbridgeable abyss opened up by the destruction of the homoimaginary. The space is one of melancholia and longing, and is maintained by homophobia. Albee condemns both the fatherless son and the sonless father to life imprisonment, ciphermales who suffer solitary confinement within separate plays.

V

The placing of the ciphermale at the center of both *Malcolm* and *A Delicate Balance* has two very important sets of implications: one for the presentation of gender, another for the understanding of character.

The ciphermale rejects the assumptions of activity, agency, order, and presence associated with the traditional, masculine protagonist in Western drama. His loss resists recuperation into masculinity. In the space left open by his melancholia, strong female characters emerge, like Agnes, Claire, Eloisa, and Madame Girard. Not only does Agnes's playful consideration of a massive gender switch in society become a dramatic possibility, as the linkage between male and masculine is severed, but the whole molar opposition of masculine and feminine begins to disintegrate into smaller, more subtle psychological movements that defy dichotomization. Albee's protagonists are involved in a process called by Gilles Deleuze and Felix Guattari 'becoming-woman,' "carrying the indeterminacy, movement, and paradox of the female stereotype past the point at which it is recuperable by the socius" (Massumi, 87). Instead of fulfilling the limitations of normative masculinity, they reach out (Tobias tentatively, Malcolm more strongly) toward the traditionally feminine position of greater indeterminacy and paradox. "To be" in Agnes's words, "a wife; a mother; a lover; a homemaker; a nurse; a hostess, an agitator, a pacifier, a truth-teller, a deceiver" (57), is to explore a realm of fragmentation, paradox, masquerade, and multiplicity.

This "becoming-woman" in turn requires a new dramaturgy. While Eugene O'Neill was instrumental in introducing a new psychological depth to an American public that was learning to prize depth in character over surface,

Albee begins to resist depth with his ciphermales.[8] A blank has, after all, no depth. In place of in-depth psychological portraiture, the ciphermale is a collage of impulses, both diffident and passionate, that cannot be explained by references to a psychological case history. In Tobias's desperate entreaty to Harry, and in Malcolm's passionate eruptions of language to his absent, perhaps nonexistent father, Albee approaches the irrational eruptions and collage-characters of Richard Foreman's ontological theatre. Emotions no longer need to be carefully prepared through a structure of given circumstances and Stanislavskian superobjectives—they can break out in bursts of contradiction. When Teddy dies, and Malcolm's father disappears, the door opens on an absence that can replace molar oppositions with molecular swirls of movement and plays of mysteriously fluctuating intensities. The oppositional grids of the well-made play are dissolving before our eyes in *Malcolm* and *A Delicate Balance*, opening Deleuzean spaces not only for Albee's later works, like *All Over*, *Marriage Play*, and *Finding the Sun*, but for a number of postmodern theater artists. It is good to remember that, just as *Malcolm* and *A Delicate Balance* predate the Stonewall riots, they also predate the first production of Richard Foreman's Ontological-Hysteric theatre by about the same interval:

> Within you and your lover, for instance, a myriad of Brownian movements circulate. If you can make yourself small enough to follow the Brownian movement of my plays, you might discover the same Brownian movement at work in those monolithic shapes that seem to block you from the happy ending you hope awaits you at the end of your various involvements. (Foreman, 27–28)

In both *A Delicate Balance* and *Malcolm*, the spaces of melancholy open onto the spaces of the postmodern.

Notes

My thanks to James Gulledge for his comments on this essay.

1. The ambiguous tone of *A Delicate Balance*'s conclusion has proved a challenge to critics. For an affirmative, somewhat feminist interpretation, see Nilsen. For a less hopeful reading, see Kolin.
2. See Rogin for further analysis of the family in Cold War ideology.
3. See Hart, especially 1–24, for an examination of the patriarchal dynamics at the basis of domestic tragedy.
4. This is not to say, however, that Purdy's critics have been able to resist homophobic judgments about the novel. See Herr's comments on Purdy's totally "gratuitous" homosexual references (24–5), and Schwarzchild's oddly moralistic reading of the novel.
5. The literature on Lacan's concepts of the imaginary and symbolic is vast. For a particularly clear and intelligent introduction, see Ragland-Sullivan, especially

chapter 5. Gerland, providing an explanation that is concise and illustrated with examples from Ibsen, is particularly useful to the student of drama.

6. See Moore's provocative questions concerning the role of the Father in the crucifixion: "What if the divine Emperor were still in a state of undress despite all the determined efforts of his theological tailors? Most embarrassing of all, what if the denuded Emperor were even discovered to be in a state of arousal as he allows the soldiers to violate the naked body of his Son?" (12).

7. For a similar reading of heterosexist presumptions in Freud, see Butler, 64.

8. For O'Neill and the development of a drama of depth psychology, see Pfister.

Works Cited

Albee, Edward. *A Delicate Balance*. New York: Atheneum, 1966.

———. *Malcolm*. New York: Atheneum, 1966.

Butler, Judith. *Gender Trouble: Feminism and the Subversion of Identity*. New York: Routledge, 1990.

Foreman, Richard. *Unbalancing Acts: Foundations for a Theater*. New York: Pantheon, 1992.

Freud, Sigmund. "Mourning and Melancholia." *Standard Edition of the Complete Psychological Works of Sigmund Freud*. Trans. James Strachey, Anna Freud, et al. Vol. 14. London: Hogarth Press, 1957. 73–88.

Gerland, Oliver. "The Lacanian Imaginary in Ibsen's *Pillars of Society* and *The Wild Duck*." *Comparative Drama* 24 (1990–91): 342–62.

Gross, Robert F. "The Pleasures of Brick: Eros and the Gay Spectator in *Cat on a Hot Tin Roof*." *The Journal of American Drama and Theatre* 9 (Winter 1997): 11–25.

Hart, Gail C. *Tragedy in Paradise: Family and Gender Politics in German Bourgeois Tragedy, 1750–1850*. Columbia: Camden House, 1996.

Herr, Paul. "The Small, Sad World of James Purdy." *Chicago Review* 14 (1960–61): 19–25.

The Jerusalem Bible. Ed. Alexander Jones. Reader's Edition. Garden City N.Y.: Doubleday, 1968.

Kolin, Philip C. "The Ending of Edward Albee's *A Delicate Balance* and *Agamemnon*." *Notes on Contemporary Literature* 21 (1991): 3–5.

Lewes, Kenneth. *The Psychoanalytic Theory of Male Homosexuality*. New York: Simon and Schuster, 1988.

Lonergan, Bernard. *The Way to Nicea: The Dialectical Development of Trinitarian Theology*. Trans. Conn O'Donovan. Philadelphia: Westminster Press, 1976.

Lorch, Thomas M. "Purdy's *Malcolm*: A Unique Vision of Radical Emptiness." *Wisconsin Studies in Contemporary Literature* 6 (1965): 204–213.

Marcuse, Herbert. *Eros and Civilization: A Philosophical Inquiry into Freud*. Boston: Beacon Press, 1966.

Massumi, Brian. *A User's Guide to "Capitalism and Schizophrenia": Deviations from Deleuze and Guattari*. Cambridge: MIT Press, 1992.

May, Elaine Tyler. *Homeward Bound: American Families in the Cold War Era*. New York: Basic Books, 1988.

Moore, Stephen D. *God's Gym: Divine Male Bodies of the Bible*. New York: Routledge, 1996.

Nilsen, Helge Normann. "Responsibility, Adulthood, and the Void: A Comment on Edward Albee's *A Delicate Balance*." *Neophilologus* 73 (1989): 150–57.

Pfister, Joel. *Staging Depth*: *Eugene O'Neill and the Politics of Psychological Discourse*. Chapel Hill: University of North Carolina Press, 1995.

Purdy, James. *Malcolm*. London: Serpent's Tail, 1994.

Ragland-Sullivan, Ellie. *Jacques Lacan and the Philosophy of Psychoanalysis*. Urbana: University of Illinois Press, 1986.

Rogin, Michael Paul. "Kiss Me Deadly: Communism, Motherhood, and Cold War Movies." In *Ronald Reagan, The Movie*: *and Other Episodes in Political Demonology*. Berkeley: University of California Press, 1987.

Schwarzschild, Bettina. "The Forsaken: An Interpretive Essay on James Purdy's *Malcolm*." *The Texas Quarterly* 10 (1967): 170–77.

Shakespeare, William. *The Winter's Tale*. Ed. J. H. P. Patford. London: Methuen, 1963.

Warner, Michael. "Homo-Narcissism; or, Heterosexuality." In *Engendering Men*: *The Question of Male Feminist Criticism*. Ed. Joseph A. Boone and Michael Cadden. New York: Routledge, 1990. 190–315.

6

Forging Text into Theatre: Edward Albee Directs *Box* and *Quotations from Chairman Mao Tse-Tung*

RAKESH H. SOLOMON

As early as 1968, less than a decade into Edward Albee's career, the *New York Times* pointed out that unlike other playwrights—whether young or well established—Albee had wrested control of almost all of the key areas of the staging of his own plays. Vigorously exercising the prerogative ensured for playwrights by the Dramatists' Guild standard contract, Albee, from the beginning of his career, has been actively involved in most aspects of the production of his own work, from the choice of director, designers, and cast—including understudies—to the specifics of settings, costumes, properties, and lighting. During the 1980 Broadway rehearsals of *The Lady from Dubuque* that I observed, for example, Albee's preference for a simple set and minimal properties frequently prevailed over director Alan Schneider's desire to introduce small set pieces and properties to convey a lived-in feeling or to illustrate information. Beyond substantially influencing first productions of his plays staged by other directors, from the start Albee has also regularly and with growing frequency taken complete charge as director of his own plays. Barely two years after his first play, *The Zoo Story* (1959), was produced in Berlin, Albee directed a professional production of the play. He has since directed professional productions—revivals or premieres—of nearly all his original plays, including the Broadway premieres of *The American Dream* (1968), *Seascape* (1975), and *The Man Who Had Three Arms* (1983), and the Broadway revival of *Who's Afraid of Virginia Woolf?* (1976). In view of his nearly four decades of practical experience in the American theater as playwright and director, Albee's rehearsal work invites close scrutiny. In this essay, I focus on this major American playwright's staging of two of his most innovative but insufficiently analyzed plays, *Box* and *Quotations from Chairman Mao Tse-Tung* (1968).

    Box—a play without an onstage actor—and *Quotations from Chairman Mao Tse-Tung*—a play without dialogue—remain the high-water marks of

Albee's experimental dramaturgy. In *Box*, an offstage female voice meditates on the decline in craft and art, and on the corruption and sense of loss in life, while the outline of a cube dominates a bare stage. Into this scene, *Quotations from Chairman Mao Tse-Tung* introduces four characters on board an ocean liner, three of whom speak intercutting monologues while the fourth remains silent. Intermittently, the disembodied Voice from *Box* breaks in. At the end of *Quotations from Chairman Mao Tse-Tung*, with characters and cube still on stage, brief ruminations from *Box* form a reprise. (Originally, *Box* was replayed in its entirety and the plays called *Box-Mao-Box*, as at their first public performance on March 6, 1968 at the Studio Arena Theatre in Buffalo, New York.[1]) Although written as two independent works, *Box* and *Quotations from Chairman Mao Tse-Tung* "are more effective performed enmeshed," Albee wrote in his program note for their Broadway premiere on September 30, 1968 at the Billy Rose Theatre.[2]

Maintaining that view, a decade later Albee staged the two plays together.[3] I will examine his rehearsal work for these productions to show how he forged his written texts into complex stage performances. Albee argues, "I try to make [a text] work most effectively as a stage piece, as closely as I can to the way I see it working in my head when I write it, and that's something no other director can do."[4] Given such a goal, an examination of Albee's comments and decisions during his staging of *Box* and *Quotations from Chairman Mao Tse-Tung* offer crucial and concrete evidence about how he had originally envisioned his texts and what aural, visual, and kinetic life he created for them in performance. Moreover, it provides insights into the interpretation and dramaturgy of these plays, and, more broadly, reveals how rehearsals *complete* a script through the myriad semiological constituents of performance.

I draw on my first-hand documentation of the rehearsals of *Box* and *Quotations from Chairman Mao Tse-Tung*; rehearsals of several other Albee-directed plays, such as his earliest works, *The American Dream* and *The Zoo Story*; his most celebrated drama, *Who's Afraid of Virginia Woolf?*; and his recent New York and London success, *Three Tall Women*, which won him his third Pulitzer Prize.[5] For each production, I usually attend all rehearsals, record staging details in a production book, photograph some rehearsal and performance scenes, copy the stage manager's production book, and tape interviews with Albee and his actors, designers, and stage manager.

Textual Revisions and Directorial Preparation

Albee chooses not to make any changes in his scripts *prior* to rehearsals, although he may depart later from his original text and introduce new performance elements. When preparing for a revival, Albee believes that the text has already been trimmed sufficiently during rehearsals of its first production directed by him or others.[6] Moreover, he also believes that his texts are "tightly constructed," because he typically keeps a play in his head for a long time in order to mentally "rewrite" it before actually putting it down on paper.[7] During his "three months at the typewriter to write a play," he makes "revisions on each page at the end of each day's work"; later, while doing "an entire second draft," he revises again. In view of these earlier revisions, any additional alteration of lines or business in his revivals, Albee insists, must emerge from work during rehearsals: "Why would I make a theoretical cut when in a rehearsal I can make a practical one?"[8]

Not all playwright-directors share this attitude. George Bernard Shaw often made prerehearsal changes when staging revivals of his plays. As codirector of the 1921 revival of *Heartbreak House*, Shaw deleted over sixty lines from the third act of the 1919 version; for Max Reinhardt's 1906 production of *Caesar and Cleopatra*, the dramatist advised dropping the entire lighthouse act (Act 3) from the 1898 original.[9]

Albee also differs from other author-directors like Shaw and Samuel Beckett in choosing not to compose a director's notebook when staging his own plays. "I keep everything in my head," he explains, "I've got a pretty good idea of the way I want the play to look and the way I want the play to sound."[10] Shaw instead insisted on a promptbook that specified in words and diagrams, "every entry, movement, rising and sitting, disposal of hat and umbrella."[11] Beckett's meticulously handwritten director's notebooks—one eighty-five pages long, another in two volumes—detailed rehearsal scene divisions and matters requiring special work, from physical staging to philosophical patterning.[12] While Albee, too, prepares to focus on specific scenes and problems, he sees no need for transcription: "I've merely got to try to remember what was in my head."[13] Without director's promptbook or script, he accurately recalls not only every line and stage direction, but even minute details of textual emphasis and punctuation.

Beyond familiarity with word, emphasis, or punctuation, Albee as the author claims a "special insight" regarding what a "play is about" and regarding "the concepts he wanted to write into it."[14] Analyses of similar matters are what directors traditionally commit to their notebooks. Elia Kazan jotted down such conceptual planning in his notebooks, defining directing as "half-conceptual, the core of it—you get into what the events mean, what you're trying to express," and half "just work."[15] "The producer's business, when faced either with a new script or . . . old," Tyrone Guthrie insisted, "is first of all to decide what it is about."[16] "The first thing I write on the blank pages of my production notebook," Alan Schneider emphasized, is "what the play is 'about,' as well as what its tone or texture should be. . . . [This] is the director's main concern—and contribution."[17] As the author, Albee considers preparing such a director's notebook unnecessary.

Albee does believe, however, that as a director, his "job is to plot out [his] work very carefully."[18] He makes an overall plan and a schedule of what he will rehearse each day, but he likes to be sufficiently open to allow "for improvising, for a certain amount of on-the-spot intuitive directing."[19] Thus, despite this daily schedule, he is prepared "to be flexible enough to revise the schedule every day," as determined by the progress of his work with the actors.[20] Notwithstanding any prerehearsal planning, however, Albee wants to have flexibility as a director "to surprise [himself] with new solutions," as he did during his staging of *Box* and *Quotations from Mao Tse-Tung*.[21]

Texts into Theater

Albee introduced *Box* and *Mao Tse-Tung* to his cast, as director and actors sat in chairs arranged in a circle on the stage.[22] "No one really interacts with anybody in *Mao Tse-Tung*," Albee began; "when connections do occur, these are completely accidental, though very carefully arranged by the playwright." The play is "very fragmented—everyone is exceedingly concerned with himself." Albee further suggested both *Box* and *Mao Tse-Tung* "flow with a sea rhythm"; in both, the Voice from *Box* should be "a bit autumnal, very gentle."

As is usual with Albee, following the brief remarks, he asked the cast to read the plays aloud, while he listened without interrupting. Unusually for a first reading, however, this one displayed emotional intensity as well as a close approximation of the characterizations desired by the playwright. Toward the end of *Box*, Patricia Kilgarriff as Voice dissolved in tears, while Eileen Burns as the Long-Winded Lady trembled with sadness through most of *Mao Tse-Tung*. Three weeks later, Albee still marveled how some of these actors had "*become*" his characters to a degree unprecedented at initial rehearsals.[23] Albee's admiration for this reading suggests that, notwithstanding *Box* and *Mao Tse-Tung*'s nonrepresentational nature, the playwright intends them to have a strong emotional impact. Not surprisingly, then, Albee recalled with satisfaction how a young man, "quivering with rage," accosted him backstage during *Mao Tse-Tung*'s opening performance.[24] The playwright mimicked the playgoer: "'I walked out! . . . How—how dare you sub—subject me to—to a woman saying things like that! I mean, she's so sad and so awful!' "[25] Albee regards the outburst as a vindication of his directorial strategy. Moreover, such an emotional staging, on the one hand, supports critics like Anne Paolucci who argue that, although *Mao Tse-Tung* is the "most far-fetched of his allegorical compositions," it evokes "intensely *human* feeling," and on the other, debunks those who assume Albee's stylistic and formal experimentation necessarily leads to merely cerebral theatre.[26]

Albee shed light on his original authorial intent, as he guided the performers toward an accurate representation of his text, as well as subtext. Early in *Box*, the Voice comments with a "tiny laugh," "Nature abhors, among so many, so much else . . . amongst so much, us, itself, they say, vacuum" (5). Albee explained the appropriate tone—"a little schoolmarmish"—

and the meaning—"Nature abhors three things: 1: Us; 2: Itself; 3: Vacuum." During the subsequent lament about the death of seven hundred million babies, corruption, the spilling of milk, and art that hurts, the Voice unexpectedly shifts to "So much . . . flies. A billion birds at once, black net skimming the ocean . . . blown by the wind, but going straight . . . in a direction. Order!" (5–7). For this switch, Albee offered a simple, practical reason— "Suddenly you see the birds"—and a revealing subtextual reading—"You're trying to talk of the saddest of all things, but the wonder of the flying birds keeps breaking in."

Probably in view of *Box* and *Mao Tse-Tung*'s experimental form and his cast's relative unfamiliarity with the subject matter, Albee provided other unusually explicit comments on textual meaning. A little after first sighting the birds, the speaker in *Box* exclaims, "There! More! A thousand, and one below them, moving fast in the opposite way!" (8). Helping the Voice achieve a mixed mood of happy admiration tinged with anxiety, Albee explained, "Although you appreciate the order, you're full of wonder about the one bird going in the opposite direction—the only remains of humanism in our society; you're grateful for it, but also worried that it is going in the opposite direction." After a *"two-second silence"* following this speech, the Voice remembers, "What was it used to frighten me? Bell buoys and sea gulls; the *sound* of them, at night, in a fog, when I was very young" (8). Although she recalls things that made her afraid, Albee urged "a child-like eagerness" and an "emotional, not clinical quality." Clarified the playwright-director: "You're sort of enthusiastic about what used to frighten you *then*—that is so much better than what frightens you *now*."

More frequently than the Voice, the Long-Winded Lady talks of the past. Albee elucidated one of her reminiscences about falling off an ocean liner. The Long-Winded Lady remembers, "And me up here, up *there*—this one? No—and being burned! In that—" (41). Albee explained what her lines mean: "On this deck? On this boat? Or the other one?—She doesn't know on which boat it happened." On another occasion the Long-Winded Lady summoned up a long-past conversation, "Death! Yes, my husband would say. . . . Bishop Berkeley will be wrong" (47). Albee revealed the implication of the reference to the eighteenth-century clergyman and philosopher: "Nothing exists unless you're aware of it, said Bishop Berkeley; since you aren't aware of death, death does not exist—only dying exists." As a director, Albee provided these insights into authorial intent and subtextual import in order to help his actors grasp and convey the surface, as well as the subsurface, life of his dramas.

As a dramatist, however, Albee shrinks from commenting on such matters. Asked what effects on the audience he had contemplated when creating *Box* and *Mao Tse-Tung*'s unusual dramatic structure, Albee answered, "I don't remember, [but] I was aware that I was making a fairly complex experiment."[27]

He did explain the genesis of these plays. Albee first wrote *Box*, then he "decided to write a play with Chairman Mao in it"; later, he wrote the Long-Winded Lady's part—"as one entire speech."[28] After selecting quotations from Chairman Mao and clipping them, he "discovered this poem," which he put into quatrains, just as he "clip[ped] the Long-Winded Lady's speech into arias." Finally, Albee arranged the approximately one hundred and fifty cards into what he "ultimately thought was a proper order."

Beyond such comments, Albee's directorial decisions illuminated his dramaturgy—what determined the "proper order." From the first rehearsal, Albee insisted that the speeches, although disconnected, were "very carefully fragmented." A passage early in the play provides an example:

LONG-WINDED LADY:	You never know until it's happened to you.
VOICE, FROM *BOX*:	Many arts: all craft now . . . and going further.
CHAIRMAN MAO:	Our country and all the other socialist countries want peace; so do the peoples of all the countries of the world. The only ones who crave war and do not want peace are certain monopoly capitalist groups in a handful of imperialist countries which depend on aggression for their profits.
LONG-WINDED LADY:	*Do* you.
VOICE, FROM *BOX*:	Box.
CHAIRMAN MAO:	Who are our enemies? Who are our friends?
LONG-WINDED LADY:	*Do* you. (29–30)

Albee asked Stephen Rowe, as Chairman Mao, to carefully enunciate the two "do's" in his speech, to the point of slightly stressing them. The director then ensured strong emphasis on the Long-Winded Lady's first "*Do*," aurally suggesting a connection between the two speeches. Thus the Long-Winded Lady seemed to ask Chairman Mao, "*Do* you want peace?" or "*Do* you depend on aggression for profits?" Albee also explained that "the Long-Winded Lady's second '*Do* you' is an extension of the first," and demanded an "identical" delivery, thereby reinforcing the impression of the Lady's questioning Chairman Mao. On one level, of course, the Long-Winded Lady's words simply dovetailed into her previous speech as: "You never know until it's happened to you. . . . *Do* you." But Albee's staging clarified his original intent of ironically subverting Chairman Mao's political certitude with the Long-Winded Lady's questioning uncertainty.

Both dramaturgically and directorially, in addition, Albee wished to avoid too heavy-handed a connection. Consequently, he eschewed interrogation points, which also explains his statement appended to the published text: "There are one or two seeming questions that I have left the question mark off of" (16). As Albee staged the scene, the Long-Winded Lady did not look toward Chairman Mao during her questions. While Chairman Mao remained upstage and left of the cube, the Long-Winded Lady stood at the cube's downstage right corner, facing out. Since she looked directly into the auditorium, the staging also implied the possibility that those questions were being addressed to the audience, as well.

The directing revealed several other instances of Albee's dramaturgic strategy of encouraging connections between juxtaposed but apparently unrelated speeches. For example, speaking of Hitler and the reactionary rulers of Russia, China, and Japan, Chairman Mao ends with, "As we know, they were all overthrown" (34). In the speech that follows, the Long-Winded Lady exclaims, "All that falling," recalling her own fall, but a subject mentioned two speeches ago. Albee linked the Long-Winded Lady's comment to Chairman Mao's in order to undercut his political gloating with her deep, personal feeling: the director instructed her to cut in with unusual speed and shake her head in sadness, as if over the historical events. This staging corroborated the connection suggested by Ruby Cohn in "Albee's Box and Ours," and by C. W. E. Bigsby in "*Box* and *Quotations from Chairman Mao Tse-Tung*: Albee's Diptych."[29]

Although pointing out such linkages remained a crucial directorial concern in a play crafted out of juxtaposed speeches, Albee also labored to theatricalize a text largely without traditional stage interaction. He encouraged Chairman Mao to incorporate some "characteristically Chinese mannerisms," bowing, for example, before and after certain long addresses. Urging him to imitate the historical Mao, as well, Albee cited documentaries, posters, and photographs of the Chinese leader to point out that Mao typically "appears to be doing one of three things—standing, gesturing, or applauding." During certain sections, in addition, the director suggested specific actions. Following the speech, "Communism is at once a complete system of proletarian ideology and a new social system . . . sweeping the world with the momentum of an avalanche and the force of a thunderbolt," Albee told Mao to turn away from the audience and "take the stance of a person in thought, with one hand behind your back" (20). On "People of the world, be courageous, dare to fight . . . ," he asked him to cross centerstage right and raise his arm like a leader addressing a crowd (69). A few times Albee directed him to lean against an upstage pole of the cube as if resting, or to hold an upstage railing as if looking out from aboard a ship.

In dramatizing his original vision of the title character as "basically factual and ironic," Albee also undercut the realism of Mao's gestures, demeanor and costumes—Communist Chinese gray button-up suit and black shoes—with theatrical double masks. Over a mask that resembled Chairman Mao's face, the actor held another, identical mask attached to a stick. From time to time, such as before beginning a series of addresses, Chairman Mao—who speaks only to the audience—would face or walk towards the audience, lower the outer mask and hold it behind his back. After that set of speeches, he would replace it and turn away, usually to an upstage railing. Besides theatricalizing the text, the mask within the mask suggested the possibility of more similar-looking faces underneath—"a joke about a box-within-in-a-box and Chinese duplicity," confirmed Albee.[30]

To further enliven the character in performance, Albee devised many new moves for Chairman Mao—departing from his text's opening stage direction which states "*He may wander about the set a little, but, for the most part, he should keep his place by the railing*" (13). During one eight-line monologue, "Riding roughshod everywhere, U.S. imperialism has made itself the enemy of the people . . . ," Mao began a cross from an upstage center location behind the cube, slowly strolled diagonally across to the down right corner of the stage, and sat on his heels in dramatic proximity to the audience (25–26). "Do the Judy Garland bit!" commented Albee during one of Mao's briefer homilies: he directed him to come from behind the Old Woman at stage left, walk straight to the stage edge, step down, push himself back up to sit on the stage with his feet dangling, and proclaim, "All reactionaries are paper tigers . . ." (33). When Mao stresses how imperialists always "make trouble, fail, make trouble again, fail again. . . . This is a Marxist law," Albee instructed him to step right on to the auditorium floor and traverse the length of the orchestra (37). For his next speech, "When we say 'imperialism is ferocious' . . . [t]his is another Marxist law," Mao climbed on to the center steps connecting stage to auditorium and spoke as if from a podium (37). After his address—and as the Long-Winded Lady began her lines—Mao bowed, put the hand-held mask to his face, stepped back on stage, and traveled all the way back to the right rail.

In a parallel and simultaneous movement stage left, the Long-Winded Lady sauntered from the cube's upstage pole to its downstage one—achieving a stronger position during her speech. Just as he did for Mao, Albee created new gestures and movement for the Long-Winded Lady, whose movements ranged throughout the cube in his production. Again, he modified his own stage direction: "*She should, I think, stay pretty much to her deck chair*"(13). When the Voice from *Box* speaks for the first time in *Quotations from Mao Tse-Tung*, Albee directed the Long-Winded Lady to react by rising slowly from her chair, remain standing—lost in thought for a moment—and then begin her lines by turning toward the Minister to indicate that she is addressing him. As her speech recalls her standing by the rail of an ocean liner, Albee suggested she stroll diagonally across to the downstage right pole and mime holding and moving along a rail, at the cube's downstage edge. When asked about his departure from his text to create several new moves for Chairman Mao and the Long-Winded Lady, Albee stressed that he had controlled those and reaffirmed his essential dramaturgical goal of restricting stage movement in certain kinds of plays:

"If your play is basically interior action, then you have less physical movement."[31] Clarifying further, he confessed, "I don't like movement to get in
the way, especially with plays that are fairly complex in their ideas, plays
like *Listening* and *Quotations from Chairman Mao Tse-Tung.*" In other
plays, like *The Zoo Story* and *Who's Afraid of Virginia Woolf?*, when "you
have exterior action mostly, then, of course, you have a great deal of physical movement."

Whether a play's action is more interior or exterior, Albee frequently
advises actors to mime an activity referred to in the dialogue. Such directions
help to theatricalize the narrative elements in a speech, as well as help actors
concretize their character's reality for themselves and for the audience.
"Show us all the things you mention in the lines," Albee told the Long-
Winded Lady, as she began another walk from her deck chair to the front
edge of the cube during the following speech:

LONG-WINDED LADY: But if you've been sitting on a chair, that is what you
                      do: you put down the Trollope or James or sometimes
                      Hardy, throw off the rug, and slightly unsteady from
                      suddenly up from horizontal . . . you walk to the
                      thing . . . the railing. It's that simple. You look for a
                      bit, smell, sniff, really; you look down to make sure
                      it's moving, and then you think shall you take a turn,
                      and you usually do not . . . (58)

Guiding her to physicalize the recalled action, Albee skillfully re-created on
stage the crucial moments before the Long-Winded Lady's brush with death.
He urged similar action during several speeches, and at one stage, he encouraged her, "Do this as often as you can."

In the same way, during each of the three references by the Voice to a net
of flying birds, Albee instructed all four characters, "Look up in the sky—no
matter what direction you're facing—and follow the movement of the birds a
little." Each character's observing a different area of the sky contributed variety and individuality to their similar action. At the same time, this staging
stressed the thematic point that although in a group, each character was so
locked in his or her individual consciousness as to perceive the same event
idiosyncratically.

Albee also specified other gestures for the Minister, played by James
Knobeloch, and for the Old Woman, played by Catherine Bruno. He
directed both to continue their respective activities, and not freeze, during
other characters' monologues. Placing Knobeloch in a desk chair right of
center stage, Albee gave him a pair of spectacles and a book, besides the
text's tobacco pouch, pipe, and matches, and instructed him to keep busy
with them throughout. To convey "professional solicitude," Albee referred

Knobeloch to the play's original stage directions: the Minister *"must try to pay close attention to the Long-Winded Lady . . . nod, shake his head, cluck, put an arm tentatively out, etc."* (14) Although he must also *"doze off from time to time,"* it should be momentary, the director clarified, "or we'll fall asleep!" (14).

While Albee encouraged Knobeloch to respond as often as possible, he warned him against extreme reactions, such as the thigh slapping and loud laughter indulged in by Richard Barr, the playwright's long-time producer, when he played the part in Spoleto. In addition, Albee did not allow the Minister to move out of his chair, just as he restricted the Old Woman to her downstage left suitcase. In their case—in contrast to that of Chairman Mao and the Long-Winded Lady—Albee preferred to follow the text's original directions: the Minister *"stays in his deck chair,"* and the Old Woman *"should stay in one place"* (14).

As the first public performance neared, Albee made a few final changes—again approaching his creations pragmatically. "When I write a play," he explained, "maybe I'm attempting something that's impossible, but when I direct a play I've written, my job as a director is to make everything possible."[32] Since some actors felt insecure because they were not yet line-perfect, Albee decided, "Let's make a virtue of it!" and improvised new props. He reasoned that each character could habitually carry a book in a play in which two of the three talking characters only speak in quotations from books, and the third spends most of her time reading books. (Albee had already given a book to the nonspeaking Minister.) But Albee also had the stage manager paste each character's lines in each book. Thus, completely in character, if necessary, Chairman Mao could read from a collection of his own sayings—Albee gave him his personal copy of Chairman Mao's Little Red Book, what he termed "the real *Quotations From Chairman Mao Tse-Tung*"—and the Old Woman could read from her beloved book of Will Carleton poems. Since the Long-Winded Lady immerses herself in Trollope, James, and Hardy on her voyages, she could just as fittingly glance at a book. Although without practical use for the silent actor, a copy of the Bible became an emblem of the clergyman's profession. Albee's new props thus provided his actors a sense of security, enabled them to develop new bits of business, and visually underscored character traits.

Albee also decided to play the haunting clarinet dirge from his early play, *The Sandbox*, at the beginning of *Box*, as well as throughout the post–*Mao Tse-Tung* "Reprise" from *Box*, evoking a profound feeling of loss and heightening the play's apocalyptic atmosphere. Through the introduction of such props and music, new gestures and theatrical movement, textual and subtextual underscoring, Albee translated *Box* and *Quotations from Chairman Mao Tse-Tung* from script into vibrant performance.

Conclusion

Albee's comments and decisions, as detailed in this discussion, delineate an authorial vision for *Box* and *Quotations from Chairman Mao Tse-Tung* in ways that his playscripts can only approximate. Providing a performance component hitherto missing from the scholarship on these plays, this essay also preserves a record of a crucial but evanescent process and presents stage-derived insights into the meaning of the play. Particulars about scenes, characters, and lines, in addition, suggest practical solutions to staging problems, especially useful for other directors and actors, and testify to playwright-director Albee's skill in creating compelling theater. The account of his rehearsal deliberations, moreover, reveals the thinking of an eminent dramatist at work on his own plays, and the way he articulates his concerns offers a glimpse into his artistic and personal sensibility. Above all, without suggesting any naive intentionalism, Albee's views on *Box* and *Quotations from Chairman Mao Tse-Tung*, and their effective realization on stage, constitute crucial evidence about his dramaturgic and directorial aesthetic, an aesthetic honed during a lifetime of spirited and distinguished participation in the American theater.

Notes

1. See Martin Gottfried, "Theatre: 'Box' and 'Mao'," *Women's Wear Daily*, 1 October 1968, and Walter Kerr, "Mao—But What Message?" *New York Times* March 17, 1968, sec. 2:1.
2. Reprinted as "Introduction" in Edward Albee, *Box* and *Quotations from Chairman Mao Tse-Tung: Two Inter-related Plays* (New York: Atheneum, 1969), ix–xi. All subsequent page references to these plays, including Albee's "Introduction" and "General Comments," appear within parentheses in my text.
3. Albee directed *Box* and *Quotations from Chairman Mao Tse-Tung* as part of a three-evening program of eight of his plays for a limited run in New York City and a tour of the United States and five other countries from Fall 1978 to Spring 1979.
4. Personal interview with Albee, September 14, 1978.
5. All rehearsal information and quotations of Albee's directorial comments come from my own firsthand record of the staging process from August 14 to September 14, 1978.
6. Personal interview with Albee, September 14, 1978.
7. Information and quotations for this and the next two sentences come from Albee, interviewed in "Edward Albee Talks About: What Does A Playwright Do?" *New York Theatre Review*, October 1978, 10.
8. Personal interview with Albee, September 14, 1978.
9. See Dukore, 39, 59, 61, 189.
10. Personal interview with Albee, September 14, 1978.

11. Shaw's letter to Siegfried Trebitsch, December 10, 1902, Berg Collection, New York Public Library; quoted in Dukore, 29.

12. Cohn 230–79. For a thorough analysis of Beckett's prerehearsal preparation see McMillan and Fehsenfeld.

13. Personal interview with Albee, September 14, 1978.

14. Mitchell Freedman, "He Knows the Author, But . . ." *Newsday*, October 21, 1978, 9.

15. Quoted in Ciment, 175.

16. Guthrie, 245.

17. Schneider, "What Does A Director Do?" *New York Theatre Review*, 16.

18. Albee, quoted in Daniel Stern, "I Want My Intent Clear," *New York Times* March 28, 1976, sec. 2:1.

19. Albee, quoted in Stern.

20. Personal interview with Albee, September 14, 1978.

21. Albee, quoted in Stern.

22. During the rehearsals and interviews, Albee customarily abbreviated the longer title as *Mao Tse-Tung*; critics, in contrast, use *Quotations*. Each of the five critical volumes on Albee with a chapter or article on this play uses this abbreviation: see Bigsby, Mayberry, Hayman, Paolucci, and Stenz.

23. Personal interview with Albee, September 14, 1978.

24. Ibid.

25. Ibid.

26. Paolucci, 127.

27. Information and quotations in this paragraph come from the personal interview with Albee, September 14, 1978.

28. Nearly two decades later, he published this untruncated speech as "Monologue of the Long-Winded Lady," in Edward Albee, *Selected Plays of Edward Albee* (Garden City, N.J.: Doubleday, 1987), 293–304.

29. See Cohn, "Albee's Box and Ours," *Modern Drama* 14.2 (September 1971), 141–2, and Bigsby, 159.

30. Personal interview with Albee, September 14, 1978.

31. This and the next two quotations are from my personal interview with Albee, September 14, 1978.

32. Ibid.

Works Cited

Albee, Edward. *Box* and *Quotations from Chairman Mao Tse-Tung*. New York: Atheneum, 1969.

———. *Selected Plays of Edward Albee*. Garden City, N.J.: Doubleday, 1987.

Bigsby, C. W. E. "*Box* and *Quotations from Chairman Mao Tse-Tung*: Albee's Diptych." *Edward Albee: A Collection of Critical Essays*. Ed. Bigsby. Englewood Cliffs, N.J.: Prentice-Hall, 1975. 151–64.

Ciment, Michel. *Kazan on Kazan*. New York: Viking, 1974.

Cohn, Ruby. *Just Play: Beckett's Theatre*. Princeton: Princeton UP, 1980.

———. "Albee's Box and Ours." *Modern Drama* 14.2 (September 1971): 141–42.

Dukore, Bernard F. *Bernard Shaw, Director*. Seattle: University of Washington Press, 1971.

Guthrie, Tyrone. "An Audience of One." *Directors on Directing: A Source Book of the Modern Theater*. New York: Macmillan, 1976.

Hayman, Ronald. *Edward Albee*. London: Heinemann, 1971.

Mayberry, Robert. "Dissonance in a Chinese Box: Edward Albee's *Box* and *Quotations from Chairman Mao Tse-Tung*." *Edward Albee: Planned Wilderness*. Ed. Patricia de da Fuente. Edinburg, Tex.: Pan American University, 1980.

McMillan, Dougald and Martha Fehsenfeld. *Beckett in the Theatre*. London: Calder, 1988.

Paolucci, Anne. *From Tension to Tonic: The Plays of Edward Albee*. Carbondale: Southern Illinois University Press, 1972.

Stenz, Anita Maria. *Edward Albee: The Poet of Loss*. Studies in American Literature 32. The Hague: Mouton, 1978.

7

A Demystified Mystique: *All Over* and the Fall of the Cult of True Womanhood

EMILY ROSENBAUM

A life of constant inaction, bodily and mental,—the friction of ceaseless ennui and discontent, united to the ordinary weakness which attended the period of maternity,—in course of a few years changed the blooming young belle into a yellow faded, sickly woman . . .

UNCLE TOM'S CABIN (243)

Maybe that's how we keep the nineteenth century going for ourselves: pretend it exists . . .

THE MISTRESS IN *ALL OVER*

In 1966, Barbara Welter looked back on American women of a century before and tried to explain their lives and their writings. Her work began a discussion of what she named "The Cult of True Womanhood." In the decades since, debates have raged over the consequences of this cult of domesticity. What was its real effect on everyday life? Did it gain power for women? Did it debase women? Did women debase themselves? What is certain is that, just as the cult of domesticity had a powerful effect in its own time, the debate over the cult of domesticity has had strong implications for Welter's time.

The concept is simple: "The attributes of True Womanhood, by which a woman judged herself and was judged by her husband, her neighbors and her society, could be divided into four cardinal virtues—piety, purity, submissiveness and domesticity." These were not merely attributes for which a woman strove; they were woman herself. "Without them, whether there was fame, achievement or wealth, all was ashes. With them she was promised happiness and power" (21). As Welter explains it, women writers embraced and propagated the notion that American women were bastions of virtue. Womanhood came to hold great power within the very limited sphere of the home because women were so crucial to the maintenance of morality.

Nowhere was woman more important than at the sickbed. "Nursing the sick, particularly sick males, not only made a woman feel useful and accomplished, but increased her influence" (33). The women thrived in the role of nurse because there they were useful, loving, and, most importantly, in charge. They took control of the nursing, the death, and the mourning (Welter, 32–3; Douglas, 207). At the beginning and end of life, women were crucial and powerful.

Five years after Welter's seminal article, Edward Albee's *All Over* was produced on Broadway. The play, like much of Albee's work, explores issues of dying, living, and control. In this play, only the man is dying, but The Wife is not really living, and the two main women characters are struggling for control. Unlike women in the mid-nineteenth century, The Wife cannot automatically assume that she has dominion over the family and the deathbed. *All Over* demonstrates the aimlessness of many mid-twentieth-century women and the bitterness that arose due to their frustrated search for purpose. Womanhood no longer had a clear, albeit idealized, definition, and Albee focuses on the resulting chaos in women's roles.

Albee almost completely disregards the ineffectual men in the play. In *All Over*, unlike *The Lady from Dubuque*, the dying person is not visible, much less alert and a part of the action. His bed looms on the stage, but he is important only in that he has defined the lives of those around him. As a result, Albee refers to the characters only in terms of their relationships to the dying man. The Wife's definition, in particular, suffered vast changes as her relationship to the dying man developed.

Early on, according to The Wife, the relationship seemed idyllic. She keeps reminding everyone of "the little girl I was when he came to me" (18). She was pure and innocent, as was their relationship, with "no summer lovemaking" such as The Mistress describes (104). Her relationship with her soon-to-be husband was not passionate or sexual. He simply made her feel young and "comfortable" (104). When she was young, then, The Wife was a perfect candidate for Welter's "true woman."

A "true woman" hands herself over to her husband's control, and he is to protect her and keep her safe (Welter, 28–30). Sexuality, Welter explains, is to be downplayed in a successful marriage (67–8). The Wife insists that, in their courting, she and her husband did just that. There was no corrupting sexuality, just a young girl and a protecting man. The Wife is careful to define her early role in keeping with the formula encouraged in the mid-nineteenth century.

Of course, The Wife is not living in 1840. It is clear, however, that the notion of a "true woman" was still compelling in the 1960s and 1970s. By the time Albee wrote *All Over*, feminist theorists were fascinated with the falsity of the cult of domesticity in the same way that their nineteenth-century counterparts assumed its truth. Frustrated with the way the cult of sentimentality limited women, Ann Douglas wrote her scathing study, *The Feminization of American Culture*, in 1977. Douglas criticizes nineteenth-century women writers and ministers for selfishly promoting their own weakness as admirable without adding much to the society. "The triumph of the 'feminizing,' sentimental forces that would generate mass culture," Douglas laments, "redefined and perhaps limited the possibilities for change in American society" (13). Douglas reveals a concern not only with ministers and women writers of the mid-nineteenth century, but with the limitations their cult placed upon the women to follow them.

Douglas's frustration makes sense. In mid-twentieth-century American society, domesticity was no longer respected, but women had no other role for themselves. In her groundbreaking work, Betty Friedan explains what happened:

> The feminists had destroyed the old image of woman, but they could not erase the hostility, the prejudice, the discrimination that still remained. Nor could they paint the new image of what women might become when they grew up under conditions that no longer made them inferior to men, dependent, passive, incapable of thought or decision. (100)

In the aftermath of the suffrage movement, women lost the respect accorded to their work in the home, but they did not seek a new role. In fact, they tried to slide backward, into what Friedan calls "the feminine mystique." This mystique is quite similar to a woman's role under the cult of domesticity, except that the married woman of the twentieth century is supposed to revel in her own sexuality. The Wife has lost her sexual role to The Mistress, a factor that serves to underscore her total failure as a woman.

Certainly, the Wife has failed. She came into the marriage pure and submissive, of which she is quite proud. As a Wife, what else could be expected? As she points out to The Mistress, she "function[s] as a wife" while The Mistress does not (85). The nineteenth-century definition of the "true woman" still holds power, but the twentieth-century woman, despite her early potential, can no longer succeed in the role. In explaining the difference between herself and The Mistress, The Wife says, "I would always be a wife and mother, a symbol of stability rather than refuge" (85). For the nineteenth-century woman, a wife was both stability and refuge, a place men could go so they "would not go elsewhere in search of a good time" (Welter, 31). In *All Over*, the role has been split, and The Mistress takes much of the power a nineteenth-century wife would have had.

The Wife cannot claim any of the virtues of a "true woman." She has lost her purity in an affair with The Best Friend. She is at times apathetic, but certainly not submissive. Far from pious, she has raised a daughter who scoffs at religion (68). As for the greatest role a "true woman" can fulfill,

The Wife is anything but domestic. Her relations with her children are disastrous, and she makes a point of telling her daughter that she is a stranger (78). This failure would not be an issue but that The Wife still wants to claim the rights held by a nineteenth-century "true woman," even as she fails to fulfill any of the qualifications.

In trying to take control of her husband's death, The Wife asserts her rights as a wife. "I will have my way," she explains. "Not a question of faith, or a repugnance; merely an act of will" (79). In the nineteenth century, women had control over such issues as a continuation of their function as domestic angels. In the twentieth century, watching a loved one die is a matter of power: "you may lose your husband while he is alive, but when he is not, then he is yours again" (92). This may seem a drastic change from the early ideals, but Ann Douglas explains that the cult of femininity, and interest in death, is always a play for power.

As Douglas describes it, the cult of femininity was not about real virtues, but about their appearance. Women (and ministers) had lost any true function in their society and had become weak and narcissistic. In order to draw attention to themselves, they overplayed sentiment and then declared themselves the experts on it. Through consolation literature, and in all matters of death, "the minister and the mother become at last the only genuine authorities" (203), and "death widened rather than limited the . . . maternal sphere of influence" (207). Far from truly feeling sadness, Douglas implies, these women used sadness to give some authority to their flaccid lives.

In *All Over*, The Wife tries to claim her foremothers' authority over death, but she cannot sustain the show. In the twentieth century, women have lost this power and doctors have gained it. The Doctor reminds the gathered characters, "I'm rather like a priest: you have me for limits, for birth and dying, *and* for the minor cuts and scratches in between" (25). While The Doctor has dominion over more than The Wife does, for the important things people call the younger doctors. The old way of doing things is no longer viable, and just like The Wife, The Doctor has been replaced by a younger model. The reason his functions sound so limited is because they are exactly the limited moments in which women used to gain authority: birth, dying, and maintenance of the family. The characters demonstrate the same contempt for the effeminized Doctor that Douglas demonstrates for the nineteenth-century minister who gains power when he "accommodates and imitates" the women to whom the "modern age . . . would belong" (117). Just like those ministers, The Doctor trades his strength for some of the power that accompanies womanhood, but he now has a humiliatingly limited role due to his feminization. In the characters' responses to The Doctor, Albee portrays the mid-twentieth-century societal contempt for all things "feminine" that drives Douglas to condemn nineteenth-century ministers.

In The Wife's desperate attempts to decide how her husband's remains
will be disposed of, she hopes to reclaim some of the authority that used to be
attached to femininity and womanhood. That authority has eroded as The
Wife has given up the sentimentality by which it was gained. She continually
belittles her son for the emotion he purports to feel. The nineteenth-century
woman promoted mourning as a boost to her sphere of influence, but the
twentieth-century Wife scoffs, "you find a BATHROOM . . . *MOVING?*"
(80). In the end, she tries to declare her right to mourn, but she does not
couch it in the selfless terms of the "true woman." Her right to mourn is
purely selfish; she is unhappy. The Wife is claiming a right to satisfaction
based on her rights as a wife. What she does not understand is that she has
abdicated those rights, earned by the "true women," because she exemplifies
none of the virtues.

In mocking The Son's tears, The Wife shows contempt, much like Douglas's, for the sentimentality that earned women domestic power. Indeed, as
Jane Tompkins points out in her response to Douglas, "the tears and redemption that they signify belong to a conception of the world that is now generally regarded as naive and unrealistic" (132). This is the crux of the issue.
Welter named the nineteenth-century "cult of true womanhood" in 1966, and
eleven years later, Douglas criticized this cult as "sentimentalist self-
absorption, a commercialization of the inner life" (255)—in other words, as
weak and meaningless. In 1985, Tompkins responded, explaining that this
sentimentality is actually a clever way women gained power in a male world.
"Instead of rejecting the culture's value system outright, they appropriated it
for their own use, subjecting the beliefs and customs that had molded them to
a series of transformations that allowed them both to fulfill and transcend
their appointed roles" (161). Into the midst of all this, Albee wrote The Wife,
a woman who still wants the privileges of wifehood without understanding
the source of such rights.

What *All Over* shows is that the "cult of womanhood" debate is not only
about the nineteenth-century woman, but also about her twentieth-century
descendant. Welter, Douglas, and Tompkins are not only debating whether
the sentimentalists believed what they wrote or whether they were strong
women for writing it. They are reacting to a society in which sentimentality
is no longer valued, but a woman has yet to find a satisfactory new role for
herself. The Wife is this woman. Her entire identity is built around her husband, yet he has not been a part of her life in years. She hopes to reclaim her
status as a wife, but eventually abdicates even her claims to her husband's
remains with a resigned, "Do what you want with him" (94). She can only
define who she will be after her husband's death in terms of what she will not
do; she will not remarry. In the end, all she knows is that she is unhappy.

The Wife's dream indicates her frustration over her role. She goes to the
store looking for a very domestic item, "a kind of thread, a brand that isn't

manufactured anymore" (75). In fact, that brand of domesticity is no longer manufactured. When she goes back in the store room, "it was not at all what I'd expected," just as her marriage was not (75). Instead, she finds canned goods and prepared foods. Rather than finding the old brand of domesticity, she finds that the role of food preparation has been usurped by manufacturers, as have so many of a woman's roles, and that this environment is of no use to her. Rather than finding a use for the canned goods and developing a new role for herself, she instead returns to her childhood living room. Here, she is back in an environment in which her role is clear, before she realized that the modern world is "not a help" to her (75). This frustration and confusion is precisely what Friedan saw in a world in which a woman's sentimental importance had faded while her function within the marketplace was rising with painful slowness.

The Mistress explains how the traditional woman's role is now only fodder for a good joke. She makes up a tale about her parents, in which her father cannot see to drive anymore but her mother will not take control. When The Best Friend and The Daughter offer suggestions of ways such a woman could take control, The Mistress explains that her mother is so passive because "she loves him, you see" (45). The Mistress initially seems to be advocating a passive and supportive womanhood. When the whole crowd, except the angry Daughter, breaks up into laughter, The Mistress acknowledges she was just making up stories. Such a dutiful woman is laughable, especially to The Wife, who cannot control her giggling.

Friedan, writing about the women of the 1950s and early 1960s, recognized the impact of the cult of domesticity on her own time. "The identity crisis of American women began a century ago," Friedan acknowledges, "as more and more of the work important to the world, more and more of the work that used their human abilities and through which they were able to find self-realization, was taken from them" (334). The Wife is the product of more than one hundred years of this identity crisis. She has no role left in the home, but she has no place else to go. At first, she wonders what she will feel when the man who has defined her dies. Her cry at the end of the play, however, is the cry of "the problem that has no name" that Friedan pointed out eight years earlier. She cannot explain or fix it; all she can do is repeat, "I'm unhappy" (110).

Most troubling about *All Over*, however, is the unhappiness The Wife's uselessness promises for the next generation. Friedan comments at length on the way that frustrated, unfulfilled women encroach upon their children's development. Like many of the women described in *The Feminine Mystique*, The Wife once "would have killed for my children" (102), but now is bitter toward them. In response, The Daughter is in an unhealthy, abusive relationship, simply for the sake of the guilt such a relationship will cause for her mother (62). If there is no role for a woman in society, as *All Over* demonstrates, all that seems to be left is to turn on other women or on herself.

In *All Over*, Edward Albee dramatizes the dilemma that American womanhood began to face in the late 1960s and early 1970s. Now that women had dismissed the sentimentality by which they were for so long defined, who were they? The Wife and Mistress both understand that the scenario suggested by the line "she'd rather sit there with him and see things his way" (45) is "not true" (48) and no longer an option. What they do not know is what they are to do now that the cult of domesticity is "all over."

Works Cited

Albee, Edward. *All Over*. New York: Atheneum, 1971.
Douglas, Ann. *The Feminization of American Culture*. New York: Doubleday, 1977.
Friedan, Betty. *The Feminine Mystique*. 10th Anniversary Edition. New York: Norton, 1974.
Stowe, Harriet Beecher. *Uncle Tom's Cabin*. 1852. New York: Penguin, 1986.
Tompkins, Jane P. *Sensational Designs: The Cultural Work of American Fiction, 1790–1860*. New York: Oxford University Press, 1985.
Welter, Barbara. *Dimity Convictions: The American Woman in the Nineteenth Century*. Athens: Ohio University Press, 1976.

8

The Lady from Dubuque: Into the Labyrinth

RONALD F. RAPIN

Since plot unfolds continuously on stage, and since there is no opportunity for "instant replay" of a given scene during live theater, dramatic dialogue is often kept simple, constrained, and easy to follow. An audience must be able to comprehend the actions and motivations of the characters onstage without taking too much time pondering or analyzing, lest they find themselves left behind by the dramatic action, which, of course, proceeds whether they are keeping up with it or not. A live audience does not have the luxury of re-reading a paragraph, for example, as the reader of a novel does, and neither do they have the privilege of reflecting too long on the symbolism, structure, or any other facet of the drama they are viewing at that moment.

But what happens when a drama is dense, abstract, and multifaceted? What if the very complexity of the work is precisely that which gives it its dramatic integrity and aesthetic value? Edward Albee's *The Lady from Dubuque* is one such play. It is highly innovative, but it almost takes an "explication of text" to appreciate its artistic merit. Any attempt to comprehend this drama must include an effort to analyze its complex dramatic structure that Albee, in turn, utilizes as a metaphor for the labyrinthine plot itself.

Act One: The Maze

The play opens with three couples on stage, and they are playing, each with a greater or lesser degree of enthusiasm, a game of Twenty Questions. This "guessing game" is used by Albee as a pretext for the planting of larger, more serious philosophical issues in the work as a whole. In fact, the question "Who am I?" repeated over and over by one of the main characters, Sam, at the beginning of Act One, is ostensibly only a question regarding the game of of Twenty Questions. Repeated time and again as it is in the first act, it takes on a desperate tone, and begins to represent, quite obviously, an existential quest for self-discovery. It soon becomes painfully clear—due in large part to the allusions made by the six characters in their own ways—that none of them has been able to answer that all important question "Who am I?" and hence, each finds him or herself locked into a frustrated and cynical search for the fulfillment and happiness that they lack in their personal lives.

Albee emphasizes the thematic search for self-identity by utilizing a confusing, mazelike dialogue, thereby incorporating the theme of a search into the very structure of the text. By supplying a terse and disjointed dialogue between the characters (comparable to and, one will undoubtedly note, reminiscent of that found in *Who's Afraid Of Virginia Woolf?*), he creates the same sense of frustration and disorientation in his audience—or readers—that his characters portray in the work. He often leaves allusions that the characters make either unexplained or contradicted, and in so doing, leads the audience or reader into a series of textual traps, or dead ends, from which they must then retrace their intellectual steps much in the same way that they would be obliged to retrace real steps were they attempting to escape from a labyrinth.

As already mentioned, six characters are onstage when the curtain opens. Jo and Sam are a married couple, Lucinda and Edgar are married, but, while Fred and Carol are a couple, they are not married. The predominant ambiance among the six characters is one of tedium and a certain grogginess due to the lateness of the hour (near midnight) and the characters having been drinking. Since Albee breaks down the traditional barrier between the cast and the audience, each viewer is also led into this slightly inebriated and tedious ambiance along with the characters onstage, who often speak directly to them. Both acts of *The Lady from Dubuque* unfold in Sam and Jo's home.

Despite the fact that the six characters are playing a game, the tone of the first act is tense and the dialogue sardonic. The intense discomfort the audience feels stems from the fact that, as the game of Twenty Questions is played, each character is also alternately intercalating personal observations and opinions concerning the other characters—and it is, in fact, from these observations that we keep running into the textual blind alleys so reminiscent of those in a maze.

The first dead end in the verbal maze occurs when Jo, very casually, states that she is dying, amidst the twenty questions being asked by the other characters. It is not so much the statement itself that is puzzling: "Your name is Sam, and this is your house, and I am your wife, and I am dying. . . ." (7), but rather, it is the reaction of Sam, her husband, that seems so inappropriate: "Don't, Jo. (*To the others.*) Come on, gang. Who am I?" (7). His response seems to be an admonition that she should not bring up the subject (and hence, one supposes, ruin the game, or spoil their guests' evening, or both); and it is decidedly not the reaction one would expect from the husband of a wife who is dying. But it is left ultimately unexplained, and the audience, who at this point is still trying to discern the thread of a storyline, is simply left to search for the dramatic cohesion on its own.

The next blind alley occurs almost immediately when Sam and Jo have a verbal altercation concerning her mother (a subject that grows in importance as the drama progresses). This first allusion to the mother is somewhat cryptic:

JO: (*Glum*) At least you had a *mother*.
SAM: (*Curiously annoyed*) Oh, come on, Jo!
JO: (*Undaunted*) WELL . . .
SAM: You've got a perfectly good mother!
JO: (*Clearly this is a private argument*) Yeah? Where is she? Where the hell is she?
SAM: (*Spits it out*) "In the hour of your need?" (17–18)

This exchange is puzzling for two reasons: We realize that the two of them have been arguing about Jo's mother for some time (since it is clearly "*a private argument*") and that Albee is not allowing us full access to it; we are also troubled by the satirical tone in Sam's voice—"In the hour of your need." Again, the audience intuits the tension but does not understand its source. And why, exactly, is Sam "*curiously annoyed*"? At this point, each reader/audience member must puzzle out these things alone.

Sam then supplies a description of Jo's mother, which, while seemingly not important at this juncture, will become so during the second act:

The lady leaves something to be desired. She's tiny, thin as a rail, blue eyes—darting furtive blue eyes— . . . pale hair, tinted pink, balding a little; you know; the way women do, when they do. We don't see her much. We don't like her; I don't like her. (20)

The next puzzling exchange occurs between Fred and Jo, when Fred says, "You be careful now; I'm still pretending to be pleasant, but these social events are wearing on a man," to which Jo responds, "Mmmmmmm: what a pity they're compulsory" (23). But exactly why attendance at these soirees is "compulsory" is never explained, and in light of the fact that all six of these characters seem to be miserable throughout (there is an almost continuous undercurrent of bickering and sniping among them), the audience wonders why they are obligated to be there—out of guilt, pity, or compassion for Jo, who is "dying"? It is one more in a series of unanswered textual riddles Albee creates for us.

Consider the observations of Robert Scholes concerning the nature of "riddle" itself:

Riddling . . . focuses on the ability of the riddler to veil his knowledge and
of the decipherer to unravel this linguistic veil. . . . the riddle directs attention to language itself, its potential for semantic duplicity, its ability to convey meaning and to hide it, simultaneously. (45)

It is precisely this type of linguistic "veil," to which Scholes refers, that
Albee manipulates with such dexterity in *The Lady from Dubuque*. He forces
the reader/audience member to search continuously for the true meaning or
the messages that lie beneath or behind each of the characters' lines. And, as
with most of Albee's dramas, things are never quite what they appear to be.
In fact, this veiled riddling creates the mounting tension—a strange mixture
of vertigo and disorientation—that comes to characterize this remarkable
play.

The next somewhat cryptic remark occurs when Fred says, "I'd think
twice about having another drink if I were you, Edgar. My God, all the things
that could happen? They coulda put poison in the ice cubes" (25). One has
the feeling that Fred has said this facetiously, but still, the allusion to their
hosts wishing their guests ill is troubling enough. What makes it even more
vexing is the fact that it is left dangling completely out of context and unexplained; we keep searching for clues to make the drama coalesce and cohere,
but we search in vain. Our inability to resolve matters causes the maddening
effect that the playwright has obviously willed us to experience.

One of the most disconcerting episodes in the first act involves Sam and
Carol, who apparently, while out of the room together, conspire to pretend
that Sam has taken some sexual liberties with her in the other room—and for
a husband whose wife is "dying," this seems more sadistic than funny.
Although the other characters manage to feign amusement with a forced
laugh or two, we, in the audience, are not laughing—we are, rather, left trying to fathom the reason for this cruel joke at Jo's expense. And so, once
again, we have been led into another dead end in the textual maze of this
play.

The six characters are not terribly satisfied with their lives. Jo, who is
strong-willed, finds herself in a weakened and dependent state due to the
mysterious disease that afflicts her. Her husband, Sam, is powerless to help
ease her suffering. Fred has been married three times before and is contem-
plating asking Carol to be his fourth wife. Carol, we discover, is unhappy
because she is always treated as though she is a "bimbo" (28). Lucinda, a former college friend of Jo's, is both hurt and baffled by Jo's cruel barbs, many
targeted specifically at her, and Edgar, her husband, suffers because the others do not think highly of their marriage for reasons never really explained.
In fact, at one point Edgar says to Sam, "People don't cry at *our* house! People don't come over and visit *us* and go away sobbing!" Sam responds: "No!
They go away laughing! Behind your back, of course, but laughing!" (57).

Implied during this heated exchange is that the scorn to which Sam alludes has something to do with Edgar and Lucinda's marriage, yet we never find out the real reason. The closest we come to discovering what is bothering Edgar is when he says to Sam, "I decided a long time ago that the fact I love Lucinda gives her all the virtue she needs—if there's any lack to begin with" (58). Hence, one more obscure twist in the dialogue, and one more riddle for the audience to solve.

Toward the end of Act One, Edgar has an emotional exchange with Jo because he is concerned that Lucinda has been hurt by Jo's insults. He asks her to apologize and points out that Lucinda is in as much emotional pain as Jo has physical pain:

> We get outside, Jo, and we start across the lawn, and she plops right down and she starts crying, right there. She says she can't take it anymore, Jo, the way you go at her; the way you make such terrible fun of her in front of everybody! She says it was all right until you got sick but now you're sick you mean it in a different way, and it's breaking her heart. (*She howls.*) Don't do that, Jo; I'm trying to *tell* you. Lucinda's down there on the lawn, and she's pulling up tufts of grass and throwing 'em around. . . . So I think you better get down there and help her—apologize or what—in spite of your pain, because she's in pain down there, too, and she didn't cause yours. (52)

As Edgar is speaking, Jo howls, and if it is a howl like the one she has just let out moments before, it is "*a sound of intense agony and protest at the same time. It is not very loud, but profound*" (51). Then why does Edgar respond to the howl with such an unfeeling, almost absurd request, "Don't do that, Jo?" And once more, we find ourselves lost in the labyrinthine text that conceals at least as much as it conveys.

As the act ends, the other two couples have left the party, and Jo has suffered a painful attack from her illness. Sam carries her up the flight of stairs, and they disappear into their bedroom. But after a brief pause, with the stage empty, suddenly, and completely out of nowhere, appear two mysterious characters, Elizabeth and Oscar, who "*enter the set from one side, from without the set.*" Elizabeth speaks, "Is she alive? Are we here in time? (*The sound of Jo's scream from upstairs. . . .*) Ah yes! Well, then; we *are* in time" (73). And a few seconds later, the curtain falls.

Act Two: The Nightmare

One cannot fail to notice that the second act is more absurdist in nature than the first, and unless one recognizes that a fundamental shift has taken place in the nature of the play, one cannot completely realize what is happening. Act One is vintage Albee—curt dialogue, bitter exchanges of barbs and insults, collective angst and ennui. The mazelike dialogue made the first act a challenge to follow; however, in the second act, the irrational and oneiric qualities with which it is imbued take the play to another, more profound level.

I would like to posit that Act Two is an attempt to depict Sam's subconscious reaction, his nightmare response, if you will, to the previous night's soiree. If the first act is a "textual maze," through which Albee leads the characters into dead ends and blind alleys, then Act Two is the onieric equivalent. The audience is equally, if not more, disoriented, but it is because we now become witnesses to Sam's free-flowing, irrational nightmare.

Consider the observations of Arturo Fallico, in *Art and Existentialism*:

> In both the art and the dream phenomenon there is clearly exhibited a consciousness which works freely or spontaneously to produce or enact self-contained presentations. . . . In the dream as in art, life and the world are projects founded on a spontaneity which sustains them in being. Things do not have to appear or to happen as the theoretical and practical consciousness requires. Time can move backward, forward, or not at all; spatial orderings are determined by spontaneous feeling and imagination alone. In art as in dreaming, we can "die" and "live again" many times over, even within a single dream or single play, as the case may be. (33)

The second act is characterized by this very lack of structure and "spontaneity" to which Fallico refers, and this naturally makes the play somewhat difficult to comprehend. However, if it is seen in the context of Sam's nightmare, his reaction to the previous night's soiree, *The Lady from Dubuque* not only begins to make sense, but becomes an experience of rich nuance and great complexity.

In the stage directions at the beginning of the play, Elizabeth is described as "*a stylish, elegant, handsome woman; splendid for whatever her age*," and Oscar is described as, "*an elegant, thin black man; 50 or so.*" And as mentioned above, Elizabeth and Oscar appear for a few brief seconds at the end of the previous act. They are still in Sam and Jo's house when Act Two begins, and it is Sam who first encounters them as he comes down to breakfast "the next morning." He does not recognize them, and is amazed that they are in his house at all. He asks, "*Who are you?*" and then repeats the question over and over, sometimes uneasily, sometimes angrily, since the two strangers appear to be making themselves completely at home—while totally uninvited—in his kitchen (74–7). The parallelism of his question, "Who are you?" should not go unnoticed, since it was Sam who opened the first act by repeating over and over again, "Who am I? Who am I?" In this case, the repetition of the question serves to heighten the tension in Sam's nightmare—and to draw us in, as well—as he demands to know who these two strangers are invading his home/dream.

When Elizabeth and Oscar finally deign to answer Sam's question, after numerous attempts to change the subject, Elizabeth claims that she is "Jo's mother." But in light of Sam's description of Jo's mother given during the game of Twenty Questions, Elizabeth, the "stylish, splendid, handsome woman," bears no resemblance to the woman ("She's tiny, thin as a rail, . . . —pale hair, tinted pink, balding") Sam described in Act 1. In his response to Elizabeth, Sam insists: "You are *not* Jo's mother" (91). Later, he repeats this assertion and adds, "You are not Jo's mother, you have never been on a farm, Jo was not raised on a farm, you are not from Dubuque; you are not a relative, and this black man is not a friend" (93). But since the question of identity was so important in Act One, we are not surprised that it continues to be a principal concern. At one point, Elizabeth and Sam have an exchange that sums up the confusion of identities:

ELIZABETH: In the outskirts of Dubuque, on the farm, when I was growing up—back there, back then—I learned, with all the pigs and chickens and the endless sameness everywhere you looked, or thought, back there I learned—though I doubt I knew I was learning it—that all of the values were relative save one . . . "Who am I?" All the rest is semantics—liberty, dignity, possession. (*She leans forward; only to Sam now.*) There's only one that matters: "Who *am* I?"

SAM: (*simple*) I don't *know* who I am.

ELIZABETH: Then how can you possibly know who I am? (151–2)

In Act Two, the maze becomes more tangled—reflecting as it does Sam's nightmare. Jo and Sam's friends from the night before all reappear, unannounced, uninvited, and out of the blue, such as characters do in dreams. Jo, who appeared at least verbally very strong, if not physically, is now portrayed as weak and almost childlike in her docility. She does not even possess the strength to challenge Elizabeth when she claims to be her mother. What has happened to the strong, bitter, sniping Jo we saw last night? It must be Sam's dream that we are witnessing, Sam's nightmare that we, too, are experiencing. At one point, Fred even ties Sam up:

OSCAR: Hold him for me. Hold him (*Fred and Edgar each grab one of Sam's arms. Oscar touches Sam on the neck and he is instantly unconscious.*)

OSCAR: Ease him down. (*Sam, unconscious, slips to the floor.*)

EDGAR: How did you do that? (*Fred ties Sam's hands behind him with his belt.*)

FRED: . . . I tied him up.

OSCAR: You did!? So you did. Those are splendid knots. Really first rate. He must be *very* grateful to you. (120–21)

Oscar touches Sam on the neck and he is instantly unconscious? How else can this second act be understood if not in terms of Sam's expressionistic nightmare? Even though Elizabeth is not Jo's mother, she *is* Jo's mother. Naturally, since this is really Sam's dream. Act Two is subconscious in nature, a series of "unrelated objects and fortuitous encounters" in the Surrealists' sense and in the spirit of the irrational. The helplessness, the physical and mental restraints that immobilize Sam in real life are shared, in turn, by the audience as the dramatic action draws to a close.

The play ends with no one escaping the thematic/textual web that Albee has so skillfully created. It is a play one should read with care to experience its insights. Only then can it be appreciated for the innovative dramatic achievement it most definitely is.

Works Cited

Albee, Edward. *The Lady from Dubuque*. New York: Atheneum, 1980.

Fallico, Arturo B. *Art and Existentialism*. Englewood Cliffs, N.J.: Prentice-Hall, 1962.

Scholes, Robert. *Structuralism in Literature: An Introduction*. New Haven, Conn.: Yale University Press, 1974.

9
Postmodernist Tensions in Albee's Recent Plays

NORMA JENCKES

Three recent plays of Edward Albee—*Marriage Play, Fragments,* and *Three Tall Women*—demonstrate that Albee has moved into that realm of discourse some critics have labeled postmodernist. In terms of their displays of self-reflexivity, shifting values, parody, and pastiche, these three plays exhibit an invigorating tension between the self-ironizing value shifts of postmodernism and the old "sincere" values of modernism (Lyotard, *Postmodern Condition,* 71).

To turn an old bromide on its head, one might say that postmodernists know the valuelessness of everything and the cost of nothing. Armed with the insights of existentialism and steadied by the chastening example of Samuel Beckett, Albee has long known the valuelessness of many things, and in these recent plays he has extended the range of valuelessness. However—and this is where the Puritan moralist in Albee remains recognizably present in these newest works—Albee cannot forget the cost of anything. His plays cast a cold glance and tally relentlessly the staggering human cost of the heartlessness that he depicts so elegantly. *Marriage Play* begins at that moment in a long-standing marriage in which a husband announces his decision to leave an unsuspecting wife. *Fragments* bookends eight characters' seemingly random reminiscences in aphorisms, and *Three Tall Women* presents three figures who construct themselves as three different characters in the first act—lawyer, caregiver, invalid—and by the end of the second act discover themselves to be three depictions of the same woman at different ages. In these works, Edward Albee has taken up the aesthetic agenda of Samuel Beckett. However, he goes beyond Beckett to question the originating myth of authentic experience (see Geis, 33).

A recalcitrant postmodernist, Albee writes to break the grip of the two tricksters, memory and desire, that mordantly pick open the scabs that time has fashioned over all the old wounds. Opening and bloodying afresh the place where desire first struck, they make all things dubious, refuse all certainties, undermine any stability of self, and ridicule the very possibility of the persistence of identity. In the new works, Albee dramatizes how a continuous and consistent self gives way to a constantly shape-shifting subject. Who is that masked stranger? C'est moi.

In *Marriage Play*, the struggle between modernist values and postmodernist valuelessness receives a domestic color. Questions of value have always been vexed ones for Albee. His plays have not created spaces where we keep our comfortable assumptions intact; they have been iconoclastic. In *Marriage Play*, he subjects all of the interactions to an intensification of their ludic and staged qualities. The play is thoroughly self-reflexive. It takes a dramatic convention, like the entrance, and stages and restages it like takes and outtakes from an exasperatingly tedious film process. The first scene forces the husband Jack to enter several times, for example. "I think I'll come in again," he says, only to discover that he is not getting the reaction he wants from his wife; he decides to go out and enter again: "I'll try it once again; I'll give you one more chance!" (10).

Everything is scripted. Jack begins to tell repeatedly the story of the epiphany that he had at his desk that afternoon that led him to decide to leave his wife: "You look up one day from your desk; you are sitting there in your usual manner, doing your usual things—and they are neither boring nor exciting. . . ." (6). When Jack asks his wife if she "knows the feeling," she almost immediately constructs a parody of his existential moment that mocks and denies any feeling:

> I look up one day from my stove. I am standing there in my usual manner, doing my usual things—and they are neither boring nor exciting. . . . I look up from my familiar burners and am startled by the object that has been my refrigerator for fifteen years. (8)

Here Albee enlists the ideas of repetition and the banality of the quotidian that the great existentialists like Ionesco, Pirandello, and Beckett used to explore the absurdity of existence in order to display the emptiness of both form and its content.

Albee embeds the conflict between modernism and postmodernism in his two characters; they personify the paradigmatic shift that they are living through. In a sense they bring the theoretical discussion home. As a postmodernist, the wife derides the clichés and borrowed expressions that her husband must use to propound his great insight. She knows that these are old and shoddy wares from the performative world (see Watt, 76–81). The pervasiveness of cliché and the interpenetration of ideas from film and the theatre in daily life—ideas of entrance, exit, final scene, epiphany, thrilling tones, curtain speech—these notions shape our human intercourse and vitiate any possibility of "spontaneity." In fact, spontaneity is thoroughly ironized and suspect like the old modernist values of sincerity or authenticity. Style is all, and it's nothing but a trick of the trade.

Postmodernist gestures from the art world are dramatized in *Marriage Play*. Peter Wollen, in *Raiding the Ice-Box*, describes Andy Warhol's collecting and hoarding activities as foregrounding nonselectivity as an aesthetic principle. Wollen sees Warhol's hoarded, unedited tapes of his interminable conversations as a celebration of impartial accumulation (54). Thus, Warhol exemplifies one large gesture of postmodern culture; it acts as a clearinghouse for the teeming images acquired from the past and from the global present—from innumerable and indiscriminate sources. In this sense, Albee fashions Gillian, the wife in *Marriage Play*, as a postmodern artist with her creation of *The Book of Days*.

Albee's invention of *The Book of Days*, an ur-text within the playtext, is itself a postmodernist gesture and a concretization of the primary conflict. Gillian is absorbed in perusing her homemade book when her husband enters with the news of his decision to leave her. What is the book? It is, in Gillian's words, "a set of notations. . . . Every time we have made love I have notated it here; I have commented on it—duration, positions, time of day, necessity, degrees of enjoyability, snatches of conversation, the weather." She has in their "[t]hirty years of marriage" catalogued "nearly three thousand . . . events" (12).

There is, of course, elegantly compacted in this aid to memory and recall, if not relighting of desire, an homage to Beckett's use of the tapes in *Krapp's Last Tape*. But Albee has taken the device much further and given it a decidedly postmodern frisson. When, at her husband's insistence, Gillian reads a few of the entries, we are given several things: first, a tiny flashback effortlessly included in the present action. But also, each of the entries, when read aloud, is pounced on by the husband and pronounced to be in the style of a certain literary master. One, he thinks, is like Hemingway, and it is: "Sunday morning, late, warm for the season, coffee on the bedside table, the papers all over; sex hangs in the air—like a moisture, and you know it will happen and you know it will be good and it does and it is" (13). Another reminds him of James and another of Lawrence. *The Book of Days* has brought onstage, in an amazingly concise form, the total archive of Western literary culture like a giant warehouse wherein we can find and use eclectically all of the hard-won styles and insights of the mighty dead. Here we have, with a vengeance, the commodification of culture that Frederic Jameson finds in the postmodernist art of late capitalism (272).

Pastiche of styles adds an alluring surface shimmer to *Marriage Play*, dazzling in performance. The device of *The Book of Days* brilliantly reinterrogates the old question Sartre raises in *Existentialism and Human Emotions* (43). What happens with accumulation? Do all the seconds, minutes, hours, days, weeks, months, and years add up to anything that we can call a life? Or are they nothing more than a heap of sand particles? Is the whole ever even equal to the sum of its parts? Is there a whole at all? Jack and Gillian have climbed that hill to fetch that pail of water almost three thousand times, and now Jack has walked in the door to announce his imminent departure. What is to be believed about their connection; where does meaning reside? Sartrean questions of authenticity and bad faith take a postmodernist turn. As Jameson, in *Marxism and Form*, brilliantly explicates, "the peculiar force of Sartre's dramatization of the problem comes from his instinctive feeling for the form which the illusion of being takes for the middle class: namely, regret and remorse" (277). The modernist husband, caught in the illusion of being, is thus filled with regret and remorse while the postmodernist wife eclectically catalogues the discontinuous, fragmented moments of their mutual bad faith.

The fact that the question of meaning still erupts so powerfully in recent Albee plays is a tribute to the persistence of his high modernist concerns. In his discussion of the simulacrum, Jean Baudrillard has discussed postmodernism as an empty term chosen to designate what is really empty (152–53). Albee is never empty of meaning; but he is haunted by the emptiness and the emptied-out lives that he perceives all around him. He uses his plays to wonder aloud if any sense of fullness or meaning is not a false comfort that he must interrogate. Albee's play questions that last resort of the post-Enlightenment, Candide-like world: cultivate your garden. In a kind of exquisite irony, it is Gillian who proffers this old solution to her fleeing husband: "You put in a garden every year; you always have; it's hopeless every year—everything: the garden, going on, everything. You put in a garden; you do it every year. It is . . . what you do" (40). She promises that *"Something will come up."* When she extends this perennial promise of the cyclical, natural world, she echoes the words of the Beckettian paradoxical ending: "I can't go on. I'll go on." In response, Jack doggedly repeats the words of his opening line; "I'm leaving you." This time Gillian receives them with gentle reaffirmation, "I know; I know you are" (40). The leaving has become not the thrashing about of a man in a midlife crisis, but the universal leaving of all mortal things. The simply stated and accepted fact of death stops the play—without value or meaning—the simple fact of stopping.

On that indeterminate, valueless, but solemn coda, we turn to the next play, *Fragments*. A commissioned work, in the published "Author's Note" Albee ironically labeled it "A Sit-Around" in response to critical complaints: "an unnerving number of critics (not audiences, I hasten to add) have declared that it isn't a play as they understand the term, and, therefore, it can't *be* one" (3). Amazingly, even in the last decade of the twentieth century, a playwright still had to answer to the same type of literal critics Bernard Shaw thought to have silenced a century earlier.

Fragments refuses the conventions of the well-made play; for example, it rejects causality. In a series of monologues supposedly drawn from the memories of the unnamed characters, the play proceeds by groupings of anecdotes. Sometimes the power of the storytelling takes over—as in the hilarious and sad description of trying to bury an immense, frozen dog carcass with an outstretched tail that makes the dog too long for the hole. Or the sexually explicit memory that illustrates an enviable claim: "People want me; people have *always* wanted me" (36). These words begin the second act's extended tale of a boy who excited lust in all who saw him from infancy on, and holds the audience by its voyeuristic narrative drive. When finished, the truth or sincerity of a story often is undermined by one of the listeners who immediately begins to parody the intensity or tone of the teller—"When I was a baby, people couldn't keep their hands off me"—or sometimes by the teller himself (41).

The sequence of speeches onstage both begs and provokes questions of causation and meaning, but fails to provide any discernible and expected dramatic build. We wonder if these are fragments of an unwritten autobiography, pieces of unfinished plays, or stories overheard from the playwright's notebook. In fact, in Mel Gussow's biography of Albee, specific stories, such as the one about the frozen dog, emerge as events from the playwright's life (350).

Accustomed as we are now to post-Brechtian techniques of presenting short, separate scenes that force the audience to discover connections, our minds exert a tremendous amount of effort to find significance in these stories and give coherent identities to the unnamed actors who tell them. However, the struggle for verbal coherence collapses under the pressure of one character's simple request for nonverbal reassurance. Near the end of the piece, an older man discloses an unsatisfied desire to touch and be touched. One by one, in answer to his need, the actors perform a kind of ritual of touching. The stage action suddenly becomes emblematic of all the things left unsaid between people, or unable to be said. We have heard the stories, not unlike our own, that they tell each other about their experiences, but then we see all of them as maneuvers for connection or distance. Man 4 finally enunciates the subtext of longing for connection underneath all conversations and entertaining words: "Sometimes I wonder why we all go through our lives without touching one another very much. Everyone I know who's died I know I haven't touched enough, no matter how much I have—or been touched enough by them." (55) With this, Albee risks the bathetic to insist on the never-enough quality of human intimacy. Viewed in the light of this stage action, somehow all the pet stories and animal stories become a kind of surrogate touching; the great thing about animals is that they let us touch them—they seem to want it, and welcome it, without rebuke or rejection.

Albee risked derision in this piece, as he had in earlier ones like *Box-Mao-Box*, *Tiny Alice*, and *The Man Who Had Three Arms*. When he takes such giant risks, he often suffers a setback in his commercial advancement, but he makes an artistic gain. To this extent, he could be credited with taking up the project that Jean-Francois Lyotard outlined: "A postmodern artist or writer is in the position of a philosopher: the text he writes, the work he produces are not in principle governed by preestablished rules, and they cannot be judged according to a determining judgment, by applying familiar categories to the text or to the work. Those rules and categories are what the work of art itself is looking for. The artist and the writer, then, are working without rules in order to formulate the rules of what *will have been done*" ("Answering," 149).

Many commentators have shunned the heterogeneity and profound discontinuities of the postmodernist work of art, no longer unified or organic, but now a virtual grab-bag or lumber room of disjoined subsystems and random raw materials and impulses of all kinds. Actually, it seems as if Albee sat down to write just such an exemplary, postmodernist performance piece when he composed *Fragments*. The playtext could be a parodic, postmodern illustration of the conclusion of T. S. Eliot's modernist classic, *The Waste Land*: "These fragments I have shored against my ruins" (50). A textbook amalgam of the elements of the postmodern, like a collection of outtakes from other plays and perhaps from the playwright's creative notebook, *Fragments* begins and ends in the recitation of proverbs, which shed no light but seem a kind of pseudowisdom culminating in the last one, which sounds nonsensical: "Dunder do gally the beans" (56).

The play moves from one monologue to another of various characters who, more or less in an unmotivated manner, are moved to tell some story. Topics flow down a meandering narrative stream from pets to pet burials to cremations to aging movie stars to travel reminiscence to sexual memoir to performance anecdote—and it all ends in the request of one man to be touched and each of the seven other actors fulfilling his request. In performance, the play effects an amazing catharsis at that moment as the audience sees onstage one human being admit that he is alone and needs more contact, ask for that holding, and receive it from all present. The wisdom found here is not unlike that expressed in the endings of *Marriage Play* and *Three Tall Women*:

MAN 4:   I'm pretty sure—(*Pause*) that there is a way to get through it—so long as you know there's doom right from the beginning; that there is a time, which is limited, and woe if you waste it; that there are no guarantees of anything—and that while we may not be responsible for everything that *does* happen to us, we certainly are for everything that *doesn't*; that since we're conscious, we have to be aware of both the awful futility of it and the amazing wonder. Participate, I suppose.

MAN 3:   (*Some sarcasm*) Let me write this down. (55)

That speech and the sarcastic rejoinder demonstrate the uneasiness of Albee's method in *Fragments*. He has earnest, existential truths that he still wants to enunciate, but he has learned that they will not wash in the late 1990s environment of relativism and disdain. So he places the modernist speech in one character's mouth, but then instantly undercuts it with the post-modernist denigration of another character. This is one way of demonstrating continuing modernist and postmodernist tensions.

Deborah Geis has identified monologue as one of the defining elements of postmodern theatrics. The term "postmodernism" has been used to delineate both a recurring trend within the history of cultural movements and a historical movement (i.e., after modernism) taking place in the present. The process of describing the aesthetic of postmodernism is a complicated one, for postmodernism itself is to some degree resistant to the "aesthetizing" quality of modernism (31). The postmodern subject—that is, the split, multiple, or contradictory "I"—is also a decentered one, and so the notion of "character" is no longer holistic (35). The eight voices of *Fragments* may be, in this sense, multiple expressions of such a decentered, split, and contradictory "I."

Attacking the unified subject, Albee achieves a quiet demolition of traditional aspects of character in *Three Tall Women*. He shows the self as discontinuous, ignorant, and contradictory, with no sense of an intact, psychic interiority. In the person of a woman at three different ages of her life, he puts three actors onstage in the second act who do not know and cannot comprehend how they connect to each other. Neither of the younger ones can accept that the older one is what they have or will become. They are literally three different women, and they poignantly portray the discontinuities of experience, the bewilderment of identity and the inevitability of decay. Pirandello was one of the earliest dramatists, in *Henry IV*, to show the disruptions of personality due to the erasures of time and memory. He used the idea of madness and amnesia to explain the radical disjunctions of manifestations of the self over time. Albee refuses the excuses of psychosis; instead, he forces us to look at the unaware and ahistorical self of everywoman at three different times.

Three Tall Women is self-reflexive in its insistence on reducing character to plot; the women are abstractions of the Aristotelian dictum of the need for a beginning, middle, and end. They are also the unadmitted and inadmissible contradictions and about-faces of everyone's life and experience. The women are unnamed; their different speeches are indicated by the simple letters A, B, and C. The three women characterize the three parts of a plot and show both the inevitability and the discontinuity of the story of anyone's life. C, the youngest, cannot imagine becoming A or B; B refuses to imagine that she will soon be A, and A can barely remember ever being B or C. In the opening exchange, they argue about how old A is. C, who is only twenty-six, thinks that a year makes a difference, and she insists that it matters over the middle-aged B's insistence that "It doesn't matter." Albee presents the problems of nursing the incontinent aged woman who refuses diapers; he gives that thankless nursing task to the fifty-two-year-old self. She also has to explain the routine to the young self, who, when left alone, asks herself the rueful question, "Why can't I be nice?" (11).

Who could be or should be "nice" in this savage scenario of decay that existence has prepared for all? She can't be nice; she can only be appalled by the specter of her future which, like some modern-day, twisted Cassandra, she is doomed both to see and yet not herself believe. None of us believes in our own dissolution, much as we rationally know it is certain. To the overly fastidious and detached young C, B acts as a transition and translator of the future to the past with her insistence in the first act that "It's downhill from sixteen on! For all of us!" (13). We can hear in B's remarks a kind of fury at being the middle man on this passage; she can't stand the ignorance of her younger self of the harsh realities:

> Haven't you figured it out yet? (*Demonstrates*) You take the breath in . . . you let it out. The first one you take in you're upside down and they slap you into it. The last one . . . well, the last one you let it all out . . . and that's it. You start . . . and then you stop. Don't be so soft. I'd like to see children learn it— have a six-year-old say, I'm dying and know what it means. (13)

The parodic element looms large in this play. Who would not laugh at the consternation of a person if an older and younger self were suddenly to appear in the same room and challenge her? Such an apparition would not only challenge her present-day self-image, but also contradict her memories of her past and short-circuit her fantasies of her future. We might find another's discomfort humorous, but for ourselves it would be an experience fraught with dread and pathos. The youngest self insists, "There's *nothing* the matter with me," and is answered by the middle-aged self, "Well . . . you just *wait* " (18). Who has not enunciated that covert curse either silently or aloud when faced with some particularly arrogant example of smug youth with its sense of perfection and imperviousness to time?

Like an omniscient narrator or the traditional idea of God, the oldest woman holds all the cards of knowledge and experience. She knows what will happen to B and C because it has already happened to her. But knowing does no good: she can tell B and C about all sorts of future events, about their marriage, for instance, and about osteoporosis, but that telling neither makes those things happen nor means that they can prevent them from happening. The knowledge is useless. It is common; we all know that marriages and spines collapse, but that does not mean that we can stiffen ours with that fore-knowledge. We can only add dread of the future to our already teeming cata-logue of woes. Albee's play destabilizes any sense of individual will and power; everything is in the hands of time. He captures that terrible qualitative leap of action: that until something has happened, it might not; it is in the future, and then as soon as it does happen, it is too late; it is in the past. He vitiates that narrow moment of human will and agency to the split-second "nows" that flash by so quickly that we cannot act effectively in them. This torrent of now flows by and changes forever the "we" that would act into another being that the young "us" would not even recognize.

Albee, unlike O'Neill in *Long Day's Journey into Night*, does not present the entrance of the husband into a woman's life as a kind of finale of "am." If A knows all because she has endured all, she is also unreliable because she cannot recall all. She cannot, for example, remember which of her husband's eyes is glass. B comforts A when she weeps at this lapse of memory: "I think you remember everything; I think you just can't bring it to mind all the time" (51). The mirror of experience that shaped the personality has shattered, and it can be apprehended only one shard at a time. This is the fearful comfort of Albee's play.

The refusal of moral judgment, which has been growing in each of the three plays, becomes absolute in this play for the first time in Albee's work. On the evidence of his earlier work, Lincoln Konkle has characterized Albee as a contemporary Jeremiah (30), but here Albee suspends the harsh assignment of blame and withholds judgment. Instead, moral values shift constantly in *Three Tall Women*, and we see time as a terrible leveler. Even the silent, maligned visiting son casts no aspersions on the three visions of the woman who was his mother. She is granted that grace that a son can so rarely give his own mother, a life before him and an erotic life with her husband and lovers.

One of the central memories that A recalls, B cannot really contradict, and C has not yet experienced is of a night when her husband approaches her. Both are naked, and he has an erection and a diamond bracelet, hanging on his penis, which she may take if she sucks his penis. When she refuses—"I could *never* do that" (56)—he loses his erection and lets the bracelet drop into her lap with the words "Keep it." Here, we have a perfect concretization of the cash nexus in marriage and the poverty of the erotic imagination of both lovers. Later on, when C learns that she will be unfaithful to her husband and he to her, she asks, "Why would I marry him if I'm going to cheat on *him*?" (82). Again we are forced to see our lives as a kind of parody of plot: If I tell you how it comes out, that doesn't mean that you will not want to read the book. No one believes the dire outcome will be the end of her book. As much as we know about the certainty of the death of erotic love in marriage or the frequency of marital infidelity, the fact that none of us marries with that in mind does not prevent it from happening, and the certainty that it is going to happen does not stop people from marrying. Does the certainty that we will all die stop most of us from living? We act in that brief, sunny lull while the clouds of probability gather over us.

Three Tall Women is a painful play, unflinching. Some things cannot be told so close up, and Albee draws us into the hellish inner circle of human subjectivity and denial that tries to separate our selves from the statistical norm, and expects our lives to be exceptional. We contemplate the contradictions of all of our cherished beliefs and the futility of will and human desire in the face of statistics and probability. At one shattering moment in the second act, the youngest asks, "How did we change? How did I change?" (92). The silent, rejected son can only stroke the aged mother's face in response. Later she vows "I . . . will . . . not . . . become . . . you. I will *not*. I . . . I deny *you*" (107). It is like the silent promises children make to themselves—"I'll never be like my parents"—a vow they think they have honored until the day they hear themselves shouting at a child.

Albee ends the play in a parody of subjective self-satisfaction. Each character insists, after this display of misery, that she is happy and living precisely at the happiest time of her life. The youngest, C, says that youth is best because she has everything before her: "my best times—what is it? happiest?—haven't happened yet. They're to *come*"(107). B calls her silly and insists that middle age is the best: "This must be the happiest time: half of being adult done, the rest ahead of me . . . it's the only time you get a three-hundred-and-sixty-degree view—see in all directions. Wow! What a view!" (108–9). Albee dramatizes the way that, to the very last breath drawn, a bubble of ego and narcissism cocoons the soul from the terrible knowledge of its own impotency and extinction. Even the stroke-ridden, almost dead A ends the play by insisting that dying is best, "That's the happiest moment. When it's all done. When we stop. When we can stop" (110).

Writing on the cusp of the twenty-first century, Albee is still clearing new ground. He has become a recalcitrant postmodernist. His artistic honesty compels him to chronicle the increasing emptiness of our time and place, and against his own moral grain, he is forced to raise questions not of meaning, but of the lack of meaning. He does not know where to lay the blame, and again he makes a reluctant postmodernist gesture of refusing to assign it. The questions of fidelity and infidelity in both *Marriage Play* and *Three Tall Women* are examined and then dismissed as mutual and strangely irrelevant.

Albee understands the profound core of boyishness in men that only dies with them. Characteristically, in these recent plays, his women lead the men through the experience to a confrontation with extinction. Death dwarfs the questions that preoccupy our lives. Then in a mighty flip, we see that finally death is a dwarf—that those experiences are all we have. *The Book of Days*. In an extraordinary summation in the last few moments of *Marriage Play*, Jack displays his sense of the doom of love and life:

> We come to the moment we understand that no matter what we have done—
> forget *not* done, forget the . . . avoiders!—no matter what we have done, no

matter how satisfying, how brave, how . . . "good," no matter what, *or where, or* with whom, we come to the moment we understand that nothing has made any difference. We stare into the dark and know that nothing is enough, *has* been enough, *could* be enough, that there is *no way* not to have . . . wasted the light; that the failure is built into us, that the greatest awareness gives to the greatest dark. That I'm going to lose you, for example—*have* lost you—no more, no less than fingers slipping from each other, that I'm going to lose *me, have* lost me—the light . . . losing the light. (38)

Gillian answers, "Oh, poor darling. You know it, too. Then why rush it?"

This dazzling moment onstage strikes with the force of its Shakespearean comic wisdom, echoing as it does Sonnet 73, "That time of year thou mayst in me behold," the advice of the last line: "To love that well which we must leave 'ere long." So we leave Jack and Gillian sitting quietly, facing mutual and separate leavings.

Terry Eagleton insists, in his essay "Capitalism, Modernism, and Postmodernism," that modernism "obstinately refuses to abandon the struggle for meaning" (132). To this extent, Albee remains a high modernist. There is a contradiction in his work that drives it and makes it extremely interesting and timely: Caught up in the struggle to make sense of a world that feels increasingly senseless. As an artist, he must be true to his postmodernist experience of the performative nature of all—even, one might say, especially—the most intimate aspects of existence that have been inscribed with the commodity ideas of performance. Although unacceptable to his moral standards, this commodified simulacrum is inescapable in his lived experience.

Albee has progressively emptied out the traditional markers of meaning in his work, from *Tiny Alice* to *Fragments*. However, the idea of meaning, the hope of meaning, a nostalgia for meaning, continue to exert an implacable force on his imagination. Albee is at the cutting edge of contemporary writing, wherein he participates in, personifies, and yet regrets the crisis of representation. Albee cannot abandon the search for truth, even though he can no longer imagine what truth would look like. He has had to jettison the old maps and guidebooks as corrupt and damaged.

Postmodernism would presume that if all the old maps are defective, the search is to be dismissed as defective, too. One stubborn, moral remnant Albee cannot abandon: He still thinks there is some truth to be uncovered. Even when it turns out there is not, the gesture of uncovering remains an authentic, necessary move.

Throughout his writing career Albee has been, like Beckett, part of the reaction against modernism that is inside modernism. Jameson raises an interesting question about the ways postmodernism could be contestatory:

There is some agreement that the older modernism functioned against its society in ways which are variously described as critical, negative, contestatory, subversive, oppositional and the like. Can anything of the sort be affirmed about postmodernism and its social moment? ("Postmodernism and Consumer Society," 179)

Albee's three later plays raise similar questions and betray their uneasiness with the total relativism of postmodernism. Albee translates the struggle between modernism and postmodernism into his plots and characters: these plays are about that conflict, and also about the contest within the postmodernist moment for a new moment beyond itself. The river of cultural production in any decade can never be so thoroughly channeled that we cannot distinguish eddies, currents, even side streams that give the torrent its dynamism, interest, and force. They remind us of the opposing forces inside everything. We used to call that dialectics. Whatever we label it, that struggle toward the new energizes Albee's latest work.

Works Cited

Albee, Edward. *Fragments*. New York: Dramatists Play Service, 1995.
———. *Marriage Play*. New York: Dramatists Play Service, 1995.
———. *Three Tall Women*. New York: Dutton, 1995.
Baudrillard, Jean. From "Simulacra and Simulations." *Modernism/Postmodernism*. Ed. Peter Brooker. London: Longman, 1992. 151–62.
Eagleton, Terry. "Capitalism, Modernism and Postmodernism." *Against the Grain*. London: Verso, 1986. 131–47.
Eliot, T. S. *The Complete Poems and Plays*. New York: Harcourt, Brace, Jovanovich, 1971.
Geis, Deborah R. *Postmodern Theatric[k]s*. Ann Arbor: University of Michigan Press, 1993.
Gussow, Mel. *Edward Albee: A Singular Journey*. New York: Simon & Schuster, 1999.
Jameson, Frederic. *Marxism and Form: Twentieth Century Dialectical Theories of Literature*. Princeton: Princeton University Press, 1971.
———. "Postmodernism and Consumer Society." *Modernism/Postmodernism*. Ed. Peter Brooker. London: Longman, 1992. 163–79.
———. *Postmodernism, or The Cultural Logic of Late Capitalism*. Durham, N.C.: Duke University Press, 1991.
Konkle, Lincoln. "American Jeremiah: Edward Albee as Judgement Day Prophet in *The Lady From Dubuque*." *American Drama* 7.1 (Fall 1997): 30–49.
Lyotard, Jean Francois. "Answering the Question: What is Postmodernism?" *Modernism/Postmodernism*. Ed. Peter Brooker. London: Longman, 1992. 139–50.
———. *The Postmodern Condition: A Report on Knowledge*. Trans. Geoff Bennington and Brian Massumi. Minneapolis: University of Minnesota Press, 1984.
Sartre, Jean Paul. *Existentialism and Human Emotions*. New York: Philosophical Library, 1957.
Watt, Stephen. *Postmodern/Drama*. Ann Arbor: University of Michigan Press, 1998.
Wollen, Peter. *Raiding the Icebox: Reflections on Twentieth Century Culture*. Bloomington: Indiana University Press, 1993.

10
Directing *Three Tall Women*

LAWRENCE SACHAROW

As a college student, I saw Edward Albee's *The Zoo Story* and fell in love with what I call a "language of humanity." This language expanded the dimension of character and story to embrace the spontaneity of unfettered behavior truly in the moment. The dialogue crackled with rawness, reality, and a musicality that engaged the heart and mind in a quest for the small and large issues of existence. The experience was a *cri de coeur* that shook me to the roots of my young, theatrical soul—looking for north where, as Jerry says, "sometimes it's necessary to go a long distance out of the way in order to come back a short distance correctly" (30). Edward captured the existential angst of defining oneself with a Zen-like purity, using a pure "language of humanity" that elevated us out of naturalism and into transcendent realism: the power of poetry in a human dimension reaching for the God of catharsis. This was the kind of work I wanted to direct, and it inspired my choices of material to direct for the rest of my career.

Many years later, in the summer of 1991, I am in Woodstock, New York, where I am founding Artistic Director of River Arts Repertory, a summer regional theater devoted to presenting new plays, the classics, and international festivals. A colleague has just returned from Vienna after seeing the English language production of *Three Tall Women*, and he is raving about this extraordinary new Albee play. I immediately fall in love with the title and cannot stop imagining what this title could embrace as a play. I know I have to see this script and feel a rush of excitement at sending a letter to the playwright. Several weeks later, a postcard comes from Mr. Albee with a cryptic but intriguing response that says to "stay in touch." Little do I know that this will become one of the most rewarding playwright/director relationships I have known.

A few months later, when planning for the 1992 season begins, I ask to see a script and shortly receive one in the mail. I cannot put it down. The language takes my breath away. The story moves in dimensions outside of time and into an imaginative realm that poses great mysteries. I have always been attracted to material that stimulates a journey of discovery into the unknown. This script is a symphony of riches, and I know I must work on this play to discover the theatrical language that will bring it to life. I arrange a meeting with Mr. Albee at his loft in Tribeca, my first meeting with the author to whom I feel a profound indebtedness for having influenced my theatrical life. We meet and speak about the play, the theater at large, and my enthusiasm to do *Three Tall Women* in Woodstock that summer. Edward agrees, and the journey begins.

At our next meeting, I ask Edward what the play means to him, and he says, "I guess it's about a woman we don't like very much in Act One and get to like a little better in Act Two." Having lived with the language of Edward's plays for so many years, I intuitively understand what he says. It is my job as director to communicate in actors' language what the play is about and plumb the script for all of its levels of meaning. The simplicity of Edward's statement gives me delicious clues and freedom of imagination to get to what the author intends. Edward is very clear that the characters of B and C are different people in Act One, as the caretaker and lawyer of A, than they are as younger versions of A in Act Two. The creation of those different characters in Act 2 results in one of the most extraordinary *coups de théâtre* of our time.

When we speak about casting, one of the first names that comes up is Marian Seldes, whom we both admire. Edward mentions Myra Carter, whose work I do not know. Myra played the role of A in Vienna under Edward's direction and he asks me to see her when we hold auditions. We audition Marian Seldes first and she reads the parts of A and B. After the audition, we ask Marian if she would consider either role and she graciously agrees to play whatever we ask of her. Marian and Edward worked together in the original production of *A Delicate Balance*, and it is my first experience of the loyalty people who have worked with him in the past feel toward Edward. He is so real, his work so penetratingly honest, that a bond gets established between people who embrace Edward and his work without the usual social mask. There is an unspoken loyalty that develops and does not go away.

The process of auditioning when working on a new script allows the director to learn a great deal about character. We hear many people read the different parts and I get a much stronger sense of the direction of the play. Discussions with Edward after auditions are very useful as he expresses why an actress may be right or wrong for the parts, and in some cases, why someone may be right for either the Act One or Act Two character but not for both. These parts demand great range and versatility from actors who can work with language and rhythm and create solid, rooted characters.

Edward is not there the day I audition Myra Carter since he knows her very well. Myra reads one of the A monologues and I am mesmerized. When we then talk afterwards, I have the eerie feeling I am talking to the character, not just an actress. Myra has known Edward for a long time and knew Edward's mother, as well. The auditioning process has just deepened and crossed over into another realm in which biography and art join to make something bigger. There is no doubt that Myra Carter must play the role of A. During auditions for the role of C, we meet Jordan Baker. Jordan is an intelligent actress who is able to play the broad range needed for both characters, the young lawyer in Act One and the young version of A in Act Two.

Edward and I finalize the casting, and we agree on Myra Carter as A, Marian Seldes as B, and Jordan Baker as C. We cast Michael Rhodes, who lives near Woodstock, in the role of The Boy. I am learning that Edward likes to be involved in the entire process of realizing his play onstage and is able to express his preferences through a creative dialogue that discusses my point of view and reasons for choices. As a young director, I worked in the 1960s theatre movement at the Cafe Cino, Cafe La MaMa, and Judson Poets Theatre. This was a golden age of theatrical exploration with artists engaged in constant dialogue and discovery. I was living in Greenwich Village, and the dialogue would spill over into coffee houses and late night bars with work explorations between writers, dancers, actors, painters, and composers. It was a time when the work of art was foremost and one's life was centered on the discovery of the work. Albee was very much an influence at that time, and the dialogue we create around *Three Tall Women* brings me back to the excitement of that period.

In our preproduction discussions about set, costumes, and casting, there is a strong guiding principle inherent in the play that Edward clearly expresses. Choices flow naturally from the play. The costumes in Act One define the characters in their roles of rich elderly woman, middle-aged caretaker, and young lawyer. In Act Two, A is ninety-one (or is it ninety-two?), B becomes A at fifty-two, and C becomes A at twenty-six. Some simple arithmetic begins to set the characters of B and C in their time periods. The costumes need to suggest B living in the period of the 1950s and C living in the period of the 1920s. The costumes also suggest a unity of character through the choice of fabric, but an individuality of character in the choice of color. At the Vineyard Theatre, the costume designer, Muriel Stockdale, introduces the women all wearing pearls, which also serves to unify the characters. The set designer for the Woodstock production is James Noone and we both work closely with Edward to evolve the design of the set, which will be used for both the New York City productions and the touring company.

We are about to start rehearsals in Woodstock where the cast will live for the next six weeks. I have a phone conversation with Edward to set some guidelines for our process. We agree to talk through our thoughts together and have a united point of view with the actors. Edward will come to Woodstock for the first reading and then leave for a week or so until the first run-through.

The evening before our first rehearsal, I have a dinner at my house with Edward, the cast, and Garson Kanin, who is staying in Woodstock with his wife, Marian Seldes. Edward arrives early and immediately picks up my three-year-old daughter Nina and plays with her. I am cooking dinner and he goes into my wife Michele's painting studio to look at her work. As a major art collector and curator of painting exhibits, Edward engages Michele in penetrating conversation about her work. Edward later joins me at the stove as dinner is being prepared, smelling the food and suggesting ingredients. When the cast arrives for dinner, we have a champagne toast to launch the project. I am overcome with awe at my forthcoming collaboration with the man whose play *The Zoo Story* changed my life. We have a wonderful evening as we bask in the presence of two great writers.

The next day, at the reading, I hear the full play for the first time. The musicality of the language stands out, and I am inspired to work on a movement plan that is simple, yet musical like the language. We don't talk much about the play afterward. Edward is very complimentary toward the cast and leaves us feeling confident about having the right company. Edward will go back to New York with a promise to return for our first run-through. Garson tells Edward he will have rewritten the play by then so "not to worry." We all laugh and say fond farewells.

We spend the next several days reading the script and I break the play into acting sections. We spend a lot of time reading each section, discussing the subtext, and reading each section again. We are developing a strong sense of the subtext and we start discussing character background. How long has B been the caretaker of A, why does she stay with her, what does the young lawyer C want to accomplish, and so on. We begin to create our story for the subtext. Myra Carter is very helpful as she has already done the play in Vienna and has known Edward and his mother. I hear more from Myra about the biographical material the play is based on than from Edward. I make it a point not to ask Edward what his adoptive mother was like. We always talk about the play as the characters he wrote. I find that very useful as it allows us more imaginative freedom to create these people as three-dimensional characters. It helps us probe and discover the play and find what is universal to all of us. If we were only to work on creating the characters as they had been in real life, we would risk the possibility of subjective interpretations that can be reductive.

After several days at the table we start to work on our feet. The subtext frees the actors to work with the musicality of the writing to deepen character. I develop a staging pattern that follows the music of the words. Since there are mostly three actors on stage all the time, and the focus keeps shifting, the blocking starts to become a constantly changing series of triangles. This allows two of the actors to look at a third and immediately change the focus. The change of focus follows through in the energy present in the actor's body, and as the body shifts, the energy changes in the line of focus one wants to emphasize. The first impulse of characters B and C is to move quickly with the words. I ask them to move slowly in Act One as we are in a situation where there is nothing else to do except wait to see if A will help the young lawyer C achieve her goals of letting her take over the finances. B is used to waiting in her job, and Marian develops a wonderful physical sense of patience, timelessness and caring for A that embraces and frames the stories A tells about her past, wonderful journeys into the realm of inner thought and memory. Slowly we begin to feel there is no beginning or end to time as we travel into the past of A and back to the present of the room. Jordan as C slowly enters that world and becomes part of the space that feels like suspended time as A probes her past.

It is exhilarating to penetrate Act One. The movement pattern that develops continues to open up new possibilities of discovery for the characters and adds to the subtext. The rhythm of the text and movement now gives us more information about the physical world of the play that adds another dimension to the situation and story. Playing the rhythm gives us deeper clues that live in the actor's body and deepen the subtext.

At the end of Act One, A has a stroke and ends up in bed. At the beginning of Act Two, there is a dummy figure in the bed with a face mask of A. B and C enter in different costumes as younger versions of A. They talk about whether her death will be quick or not, and then A enters after two pages of dialogue. When the audience does not know the play, there is a great shock of surprise when A enters because they think she is in the bed. We make the physical choice to have A move in a more agile way than in Act One and not to have the physical trouble with her arm. This means the character is not bound by the constraints of her body. We could say that the three characters were also in the world of "out of body," therefore existing in their own time. This choice allows for a free emotional exchange between the characters and makes the characters more grounded. While doing the table work on the subtext, once again we all made very strong, concrete choices about these characters that were different for B and C than for their Act One characters. C has to answer many questions about her twenty-six-year-old self and her future goals, while B plumbs the depths of this character at fifty-two. B delves into what kind of life she has now, the relationship with the rest of the family that A mentions, how she copes with her husband's infidelity, and why she does. We discover what a strong survivor she is and how she stays in the world of intention. This becomes an important factor in the playing of Act Two as the three characters don't back off when they challenge each other. We penetrate their individual psyches with the power of the rhythm of the language and eliminate all acting that is reactive. The characters have to continually play their own intention fully, even in the face of harsh confrontation. The movement grows again from the subtext and rhythm of the language. Since the script clearly says that they are now one character at three different ages, there is no need to copy gestures or emblematize any physical choices that show they are one person. It would only reemphasize a point made clearly and strongly in the text and simplify the characters. We work in the opposite direction of making strong individual, physical choices for each character in order to deepen who they are at those ages.

One of the themes of the play is how different we are at different ages in our life. The play reveals the journey we take toward aging and death, and the characters examine their lives in vivid, three-dimensional tall depth. We have to chart clearly what A does not know because it is her future and what B does not know in the future that A has lived after age fifty-two, while B and A both know more than C about the future up to B's current age.

In Act Two, the choice is made to move slightly faster than Act One, as the characters are all in the same moment of time waiting for A's death. It's almost like close relatives waiting in the hospital room of a family member on her deathbed. They tell the story of the life she lived. Since they are also the person in the deathbed, they live the story of the life as they tell it. The space still accommodates the idea of triangles, but there is more group movement, especially when they are in the part of the story that all three have lived, up to age twenty-six. They sit in closer groups when there is a keen interest in learning more about the future from A, or when A and B discuss their common past. The movements also reflect the tension or lack of tension in the dialogue. They can sit comfortably near each other when they are having a mutual, fond memory. They split apart, and usually go back to triangles when they are having a confrontation. At one point, they are all comfortably sitting around one chair when they remember meeting their husband for the first time. Sitting in one group in one corner of the stage creates a vacuum of space around them. Suddenly, the Young Man walks in from the opposite side, and it is a startling event. The entrance of the Young Man has always surprised me, as it surprised Edward when he was writing the play and the Young Man appeared in his imagination.

When the Young Man walks in, he is in real time from the end of Act One when A had her stroke, but he is also in his early twenties, not older, as he would have been when A had her stroke and died. We now have several layers of time onstage together: the present time of A at age ninety-one having a stroke, the presence of A at twenty-six and fifty-two, and the Young Man coming to see his mother at an earlier age than his true age at the time, and whom C is seeing for the first time as her future son. The Young Man sits next to the bed and stays in his own time, without seeing or hearing A, B, and C. They have tremendous freedom to talk about him and to him without getting a reaction from him. This structure is complex and intriguing and allows the characters to deepen their memories about their relationship with the son.

I think it is brilliant playwriting to have the son not talk. We have a ritual exorcism going on, with the characters freely expressing their deepest emotions and going through them on their journey toward catharsis and final human acceptance of the inevitably of one's own death. If the son were to talk, they would not have to deal with their personal emotions. They express and purge themselves in front of the son who is silent and attentive to his dying mother. The sympathy we feel for the characters comes from experiencing their bravery in traveling that deep and painful road.

After almost two weeks of rehearsal, Edward returns to Woodstock. We are all nervous and excited to see him again. After the run-through, Edward and I have an interesting discussion about choices and how to clarify the play. Edward always asks the reasons for making a choice and weighs in his own mind whether it supports the play. He is very clear when it does not, and I learn a lot more about his intentions with the characters. He likes Act Two but expresses reservations about Act One. I know what needs to be done to clarify the characters and action. Although the play is very personal, as it is based on Edward's mother, I never sense his personal connections. The play is its own entity, his work that he has entrusted to us and that we lovingly care for.

After my note session with Edward, he says goodbye to the actors and is very complimentary about their work. Edward shows a great generosity of spirit to all of us. This is the beginning of a note process between author and director that will go on for the next four years. I work to find the right language to communicate to the actors. The cast is quite extraordinary in their understanding of how immediately to grasp changes in intention and character, and they contribute greatly by adding their own insights. Marian and Myra have worked on Albee plays in the past and have an intuitive understanding of unlocking the rhythm of the language to clarify the intentions of the character. Jordan very quickly finds her way and makes a strong contribution in evolving the movement pattern for her character. Michael Rhodes brings a vital presence sitting by the side of the bed, and we evolve a series of small movements that shift his body in conjunction with the rhythm and content of the dialogue flashing around him.

As we move into the third week of rehearsal, the actors are very present in their bodies with the inner weight of their characters. It is a joy to work with a text that has such a rhythm. Beckett and Pinter are the only other contemporary playwrights I know whose work has that intuitive sense of rhythm that defines the theatrical event. Each of these writers has a unique voice, demanding a different rehearsal process differing greatly in content, but each gives you the joy of the richness of language with clues in the text that unlock the play for performance.

Edward will return to Woodstock at the end of the third week of rehearsal and will stay for the dress rehearsals and opening. We have our first run-through for the staff of the theater and a few friends before Edward returns. This is always an interesting time because you never know how the first audience will respond to your work. At the end of the run-through, the small group of people sit stunned in silence, with some people crying. I could feel the tension increase when the Young Man enters and I also feel very moved by the drama of that relationship and the purging that goes on. My associate artistic director, Michael Cristofer, suggests that we only need to run the form and it will continue to deepen.

There is a catharsis in this play that is like Greek drama. Indeed, when A goes to the Young Man near the end of Act Two to vent her anger, there is a mythic dimension to the event. This speech and the speech by A at the end of Act One when she is in bed, and before she has her stroke, I liken to the character of Clytemnestra railing against Agamemnon for sacrificing their daughter Iphigenia. The text has that awesome power, and both Myra, and later Marian when she takes over the role of A, capture the full dimension of that ancient, primal scream for vengeance. Edward has written a drama that is based on his adoptive mother but is bigger than his own subjective relationship. This is a universal human play about the rupture of family relationships and the mythic need for purging emotions. On the journey of life that changes at different ages, we all share the human inevitability of facing our own death one day. At the end of the play, there are three exquisite monologues summing up each character's view at her particular age. When A finishes her last monologue, the actors join hands, take a deep breath, and exhale together before the last word of the play, "When we can [*breath*] stop" (110), I feel the characters are unified by the honesty of their emotional journey. A classic catharsis has occurred in not holding back the honesty that unifies them in accepting the inevitability of death. When we have true knowledge of our mortality, it heightens our awareness of the importance of how we live our daily life.

Our next run-through is for Edward and again we have a note session that heightens our awareness of what to work on. Adjustments are made on character choices and subtext for the next week as we move into dress rehearsals and final performances. Edward is very pleased with the production and the strong and skillful work of the actors. After several performances in Woodstock, word of mouth spreads and the run quickly sells out. The audience knows this is a major, new Albee play. Edward stays through opening night and our theatre owner, Sally Grossman, has a wonderful opening night party. We say our farewells to Edward at a company breakfast the next day.

Edward comes back several times during the run and we make plans to bring the production to New York City. Over a year later, we all agree to open the play at the Vineyard Theatre. The artistic director, Doug Aibel, is a great fan of the script and the company from Woodstock begins a four-week rehearsal process fifteen months after the last Woodstock performance. This allows the actors to continue to investigate the richness of the play, and it is a luxury to go back into rehearsal with a great play. The Vineyard space is three-quarter round, and modifications are made in the original proscenium blocking to adjust to the new space. Edward comes to crucial run-throughs before we open and again is a very helpful collaborator on clarifying and deepening character interpretation. He makes some minor textual changes. The Vineyard staff creates a warm and nourishing working environment.

The play opens to excellent reviews and audience reception. This is clearly a landmark theatrical event. The distinguished producer, Liz McCann, who loved the play when she saw it in Woodstock, comes to see the play again. We are sitting in the lobby after the performance and Liz says she would like to move the production for an extended off-Broadway run. She creates a first-rate producing team with Daryl Roth and Jeffrey Ash, the most brilliant and supportive team of producers I have ever worked with. They rent the Promenade Theatre and the production opens there two weeks after it closes at the Vineyard. We have one week to adjust the staging back to a proscenium space. Each rehearsal process feels like we are moving deeper and deeper into the world of the play. *Three Tall Women* runs for two years in New York, wins the Pulitzer Prize among many other awards, and recoups its investment in record time.

It is difficult to sustain the freshness of performance in a long run. I try to get to the theatre at least twice a month and give notes to the actors. Edward comes periodically and we always discuss the play and what needs to be tightened. This ritual has become a part of my life that I look forward to. It is fascinating to engage continually in a dialogue with Edward about the nuance of performances in an extended run. Toward the end of the second year it is difficult for Myra Carter to sustain the herculean performance she has rendered as A, and she decides to leave. Jordan Baker also decides to leave for other work she is offered. We offer Marian Seldes the role of A, and cast Christina Rouner in the role of C. Several different women play the role of B, including Joan van Ark, Frances Conroy, and Michael Learned who is with the play when it closes at the Promenade. It is wonderful to work with Marian on the role of A as we search to reinvent the character.

The producers arrange a national tour that will start at the Colonial Theatre in Boston and go to the Kennedy Center, The Mark Taper Forum, and theaters in many American cities. We rehearse two weeks in New York before the tour, and it is a real chance to work on the play again with Marian as A, Michael as B, and Christina as C. Michael Rhodes joins us as the Young Man again and Mark Wright, the stage manager of *Virginia Woolf*, becomes an important member of the company. At one run-through for Edward and the producers, Michael Rhodes is not available to play the Young Man. I ask Edward if he would sit in the chair as the Young Man for that run-through and he agrees. It provides a shock of energy for the cast to say those lines to

Edward sitting in the chair. Edward is so generous and giving with his spirit, and we feel blessed to be taking this play across the country.

We all go to Boston, stay there for the run, and work on the new performances. Garson Kanin is my nightly date as we sit together and I take notes on the performances. Edward and I confer after each performance and I give notes to the actors. The cast grows in stature and the play once again assumes its awesome power. Marian rises to new heights in what I call the Clytemnestra monologues, and she plays that image very strongly. The play travels around the country for the next two years and is brilliantly received. Edward and I meet in each city for the dress rehearsal and first few performances. The partnership and collaboration is something I treasure in my life.

Working on an Edward Albee play for me is like working on a play by Chekhov, Shakespeare, or Beckett. One never feels finished. The depth and scope of the text, the humanity of characters, the awesome penetration of the psychological with the spiritual, allow for endless investigation. I never tire of working on each production we have undertaken over the years. I was recently a guest at the Moscow Art Theatre with another play of mine and it was exhilarating to be part of that tradition. I had always imagined what it would be like to have Chekhov in rehearsals while working on one of his great plays. Working with an author of genius like Edward Albee, and collaborating with great actors, makes the play come alive in a special way for all of us. I imagine the inspiration the Moscow Art Theatre received from Chekhov is like the gift we have received from Edward Albee in *Three Tall Women*. That gift is timeless, classical drama that enriches us all with a "language of humanity."

Works Cited

Albee, Edward. *Three Tall Women*. New York: Dutton, 1995.
———. *The American Dream and The Zoo Story: Two Plays by Edward Albee*. New York: Signet, 1961.

11
Interview with Edward Albee

INTERVIEW BY BRUCE J. MANN

In April 1999, Edward Albee met with me for several hours to discuss his most recent work and other subjects. Our setting was the University of Houston campus, where Albee is a distinguished professor, teaching playwriting and dramatic literature each spring. What follows is an edited version of our interview.

MANN: You have said, "All my plays are about people missing the boat, closing down too young, coming to the end of their lives with regret at things not done." What interests you about these kinds of dramatic characters?

ALBEE: I guess that's a fairly general description of what the majority of my plays are about. There are some, like *The Death of Bessie Smith* and a few others, that are not about that. It must be a combination of two things—instructive to myself that I don't fall into a trap of wasting my life, and also the fact that I think it's one of the most terrible things that could happen to anyone: to come to the end of a life or close to the end and realize that one hasn't participated and there is nothing to be done about it. Also, I think there is a third thing.

I find the passivity of American society constantly growing, getting more dangerous, the fact that less than half the people vote, two-thirds of the people don't know the names of their senators and representatives. Three-quarters of the people, when they were asked—Would you give up the Bill of Rights for some security?—said "Sure." The drift toward religious autocracy in this country, a sort of curious kind of polite fascism that is generally in our society, is very troubling, and I think if people spent more time informing themselves about what it is to be alive and the responsibilities of it and the responsibilities of democracy, we'd be a lot better off. Plus the fact that our college and university students are totally politically uninvolved, which is very dangerous for a democracy—a whole variety of things.

MANN: I am reminded of the girl in *Listening* who says, "we do not have to live, you know, unless we wish to. The greatest sin, no matter what they tell you, the greatest sin in living is doing it badly—stupidly, as if you weren't really alive."

ALBEE: I like that. That's good.

MANN: In many of your plays, characters are faced with a deep fear of something. For example, Martha at the end of *Who's Afraid of Virginia Woolf?*, Peter in *The Zoo Story*, the characters in *A Delicate Balance*, A in *Three Tall Women*. What are they afraid of?

ALBEE: Well, first of all, anybody who doesn't carry a certain amount of existentialist angst with them throughout their lives is either a dumb brute or, by choice, insensitive. We must have it; we have to have it. If you think of yourself and the world around you, you must participate in that. You have to have these anxieties and these fears, especially if you come to the conclusion that you're going to go through it only once. The opiate of religion carries a lot of people right to the end, and maybe even right through the end, without even considering what they've not done; but without the opiate of religion, then one is out there.

MANN: What you call existentialist angst/fear seems related to the kind of menace we see in Pinter's plays and the void in Beckett's plays, but yours is different.

ALBEE: We all come from that period in French thought between 1919 and 1947. . . .

MANN: But as you trace, in your plays, the landscapes of fear and anxiety, aren't you somewhat different in encouraging us to do something about it?

ALBEE: It's interesting. . . . I've said often and I'm convinced of it: one of the things that may have put the idea of being a playwright in my head was seeing the world premiere of *The Iceman Cometh* in 1947, where O'Neill postulates that you must have "pipe dreams," falsity, in order to survive. And I'm convinced that *Who's Afraid of Virginia Woolf?* is probably written in part to argue against that theory. It's okay to have false illusions as long as you know they are false. . . .

We [Beckett, Pinter, Albee] all come from the same source, but mind you, we come from different societies, different times, and different cultures. I was adopted into a privileged, WASP class in the United States. Beckett was middle-class Irish, Harold was East-End British, Jewish. . . . So while I think there are probably . . . three or four themes that really should predominate the thought of any creative artist in any particular period, we all express it very differently and approach it very differently.

MANN: And we should celebrate the difference.

ALBEE: Well, that too, of course—though we're all Beckett's children.

MANN: You mention Beckett and Chekhov often in interviews.

ALBEE: I wonder if it isn't, in part, the music—the musical quality of their writings . . . the fact that they are writing chamber music at the same time they write plays. . . . One of the things I tell my students is that to be a playwright is to be a composer, and that you must be able to hear precisely. What a great playwright O'Neill would have been if he hadn't had a tin ear, for example. What a much better playwright. . . . And Beckett and Chekhov had two of the best ears; they heard more intelligently, clearly, and precisely than other playwrights, and their work is very closely related to classical music. Now I wanted to be a composer when I was a kid, and I never got there. So, I always think when I'm writing a play, I'm writing a piece of chamber music.

MANN: So the sounds guide you as much as the ideas?

ALBEE: Well, there has to be sound. There has to be sense to the sound. . . . The fact that I do hear very precisely and hear a kind of musical quality and rhythm to my characters as they are speaking—that allies me to Beckett and Chekhov.

MANN: And to some extent Pinter?

ALBEE: Well, yes, I say. We're all Beckett's children. Harold is probably more noticeably influenced by Beckett than I am. . . . I might be an adopted child.

MANN: Still on the music question, do you mean structurally, as well?

ALBEE: Structurally, and also the rhythms and the sound. When I'm writing a play, I hear it and see it as a performed piece on stage. . . . That's another thing the playwright should be able to do: he should be able to punctuate his score, if you will, as precisely as any composer notates his. I mean the difference between a dotted eighth note and an eighth note is the same as the difference between a semicolon and a period. A playwright has got to be able to use all of the devices of language to make his point. . . . I think it's nice to have a firm grounding in painting and sculpture, but the grounding in classical music is much more important. Drama is a heard experience, much more than a seeing experience.

MANN: That's an interesting point. I'm not sure all playwrights would agree with you.

ALBEE: Well, no, of course not. And I don't want anybody to agree with me unless they understand what I'm after; but you can take a blind person to a play, and they can understand what happens throughout the play. [Y]ou take a blind person to a movie, and there's practically nothing they're going to get. You take a deaf person to a movie, they get it.

MANN: Going back to a point you made earlier, a contributor to our collection calls you an "American Jeremiah" figure, because your plays show how we, as Americans, have fallen short of our ideals.

ALBEE: Anybody who is a creative writer—most of us don't admit it—but everybody who is a writer is trying to change society and the world to our point of view or to show people where they have failed, according to our standards and our lives. Everybody is writing corrective work; there is no point in doing it if it is merely decorative. . . .

MANN: You have found problems with America's values at least since the late 1950s, and in the preface to one of your plays, you called those values "artificial." You seem disturbed that American values haven't improved as the century ends.

ALBEE: We're supposed to be a peacefully evolving revolutionary society, but we seem to have lost sight of what we're up to. We seem to have hit a kind of stasis, which is very troubling.

MANN: And your outlook is not particularly positive on this as the millennium ends?

ALBEE: As Beckett said: If I weren't an optimist, I wouldn't write.

MANN: You have been celebrated for your language, which is soaked in nuance and very expressive, precise, musical, and often humorous. Why is language so important to you in the dramatic experience?

ALBEE: It all has to do with the artifice of playwriting. Another thing I tell my students is that, in the most naturalistic play, you do not write the way people talk. You select, you make sense out of, you make comprehensible the way people talk. People do not talk that way; they're not as coherent in real life as they are in one's plays. You also try to levitate a little bit off the ground with naturalism, and this leads to a kind of organization of sound, an organizational sense of speech that is removed from naturalism to begin with.

MANN: So even naturalism is artificial?

ALBEE: Oh, yes. Sure.

MANN: You also use humor devastatingly.

ALBEE: Well, I don't know whether *I* do. My characters are quite often funny.

MANN: Why humor when so many of your themes are dark?

ALBEE: Laughter in the dark. [Like] another favorite writer of mine, Nabokov, and Jorge Luis Borges. . . .

MANN: The decade of the '90s has been a very busy one for you.

ALBEE: One has busy decades. . . .

MANN: Among other plays, you have had productions of *The Lorca Play*, *Three Tall Women*, and *The Play about the Baby*. . . .

ALBEE: Probably *The Goat* will be finished in the nineties—*The Goat*, with the subtitle, *or Who Is Sylvia?*

MANN: *Who Is Sylvia?* Sounds a little pastoral.

ALBEE: Well, it is [laughter]. In a very odd way, it is. The goat is called Sylvia.

MANN: The goat is a character?

ALBEE: Hmm. Double-meaning, of course.

MANN: Somewhat like a lizard?

ALBEE: No, more goat-like, actually, and played by a goat.

MANN: A non-speaking part, I assume?

ALBEE: We don't know.

MANN: We don't know? So this is in process?

ALBEE: I'm writing it down on paper.

MANN: Let me circle back on the decade, if I can. *The Play about the Baby* is your most recent production.

ALBEE: Which you saw in London?

MANN: Yes, at the Almeida, which is a remarkable theater.

ALBEE: Yes, a nice theater, isn't it?

MANN: Were you pleased with the production?

ALBEE: Very much. I was amazed. Of course, most of my plays seem to be written in the Bermuda Triangle. They're neither American nor British nor European, or they don't seem to be. . . . But when I saw the rehearsals, it didn't seem like, "Oh, this is an English version of my play." I had to change a couple of words, not many. . . . But it struck me as being the play I had written. This happens with a lot of my plays. When they are done in England, they don't seem to be British productions, necessarily. It seems to be the way I wrote the play. But when I have them done in America, it seems to be the way I wrote the play. . . . This may have something to do with my language and the music that we were talking about, that it works just as well in Britain and in the United States.

MANN: This was a very detailed production, and the Almeida seems noted for that. Why don't we have more theatres like the Almeida in America? Where they do classic and cutting-edge work, as well.

ALBEE: Because they're not quite as concerned with commerce, the Almeida Theatre. They're not quite as concerned with the pound as we are with the dollar, even with our so-called regional theaters. . . .

MANN: Why did you give the play that title—*The Play about the Baby*? Is there some irony?

ALBEE: Isn't that what it is? *The Zoo Story* is about the story of the zoo. *The Death of Bessie Smith* is about the death of Bessie Smith. A lot of times you just be very specific. *Marriage Play* is a play about marriage. I try to be very specific.

MANN: Perfectly straightforward.

ALBEE: Some titles are not straightforward.

MANN: Some critics are anxious to see *The Play about the Baby* as another version of *Who's Afraid of Virginia Woolf?*, and it's really quite different.

ALBEE: Totally different.

MANN: It seems to me, even if you acknowledge some parallels. . . .

ALBEE: There are four characters: two older characters, two younger characters. The younger characters in *The Play about the Baby* have a baby. Nobody in *Who's Afraid of Virginia Woolf?* has a baby. . . .

MANN: *The Play about the Baby* has qualities, at times, of a folktale or overtones of *Il Trovatore* and gypsies and stealing babies; but there still are social and political overtones that are disturbing. Am I reading too much into that?

ALBEE: I'd like to think not.

MANN: Because it seems to me that one of the odd aspects of modern life is how much we are encouraged not to believe what we should.

ALBEE: True. If you want to find a close analogy to another one of my plays, you have to go back to *The Lady from Dubuque*.

MANN: Where we also have two visitors.

ALBEE: Both plays raise the question—I guess, equally—as to reality being determined by our needs. They both raise that question.

MANN: In both *The Play about the Baby* and *Three Tall Women*, characters at times directly address the audience.

ALBEE: This happens in many of my plays.

MANN: In one performance of *The Play about the Baby*, Alan Howard actually provoked audience response at the beginning of the second act.

ALBEE: Very nice. . . . Some plays I'm perfectly happy having the audience being a voyeur, but not when I do the others, because it interests me to break down the fourth wall, to make experiments. Look, for example, what I did in *Counting the Ways*. Not only do the characters talk to the audience, but at one point the actors talk to the audience as themselves and then go back talking to the audience as characters. This stuff is great fun to do. One loves being a magician, a juggler . . . levitating and juggling. It's great fun. And also, there are some plays, like *Who's Afraid of Virginia Woolf?*; I wouldn't dream of having anyone talk to the audience in that. It gives the illusion of being a completely naturalistic play, observing all the proper time barriers and everything. . . . [Still,] I don't think audiences should be allowed to be disinvolved. . . . Naturalism can involve. It really can. I've always thought that all of Sam Beckett's plays were naturalistic.

MANN: Women buried in mounds.

ALBEE: Yes, of course. It's a metaphor, but there's nothing that happens in that play that isn't real.

MANN: It's true. In reality we're all sinking.

ALBEE: If *Godot* were set in a living room, no one would have any problems with it. *Krapp's Last Tape*, which I've directed, is the most naturalistic play imaginable. . . . Anyway, I don't think an audience should be allowed to be disengaged. I used to annoy [critic] Walter Kerr greatly whenever I broke the fourth wall convention because he loathed being seen as a member of the audience and being spoken to and involved in that way.

MANN: The sixties must have been difficult for him.

ALBEE: Very difficult. You really could not trust Walter much, even up as far as Pirandello.

MANN: This points to a problem in our theater; our critics have certain limitations.

MANN: Most critics are hired to tell people whether they want to see something or not, not whether they *should* see it. It's a fundamental problem.

MANN: How do we go about changing that?

ALBEE: No critic who runs counter, long enough and hard enough, to the readership's desire will keep his job.

MANN: Which makes it difficult for us ever to see a change. . . .

ALBEE: That's true, especially as the economics of the theater get more and more crippling.

MANN: Which is sad. . . .

ALBEE: It's very sad; it's corrupting, but there's not much to be done about it. The only thing you can do is re-educate your audience, which is the responsibility of university theatre and regional theatre. I don't hold out much hope, but. . . . I'm going to teaching a course next fall—not this fall, next fall—in New York with young students, teaching them how to be a real dramatic critic rather than a reviewer. These are kids, and I'm going to take them to see previews of plays, especially off-Broadway plays, and make them write reviews and communicate their feelings about the play to other people, and then show them the reviews. Show them how the reviewers so often go wrong in what they do.

MANN: You have complained that critics' reviews don't help you as a play-wright very often.

ALBEE: I wish I learned more about my craft as a playwright from critics. I learn, unfortunately, mostly how long my play will run and whether I am on the up or the downswing trend. I wish I learned more about my craft. I learn more about my craft in certain technical areas by watching an audience. I learn more, by watching an audience that has not read reviews, whether I'm communicating the way I thought I was communicating. . . .

MANN: With *Three Tall Women*, you earned your third Pulitzer Prize and also the Drama Critics Circle Award, the Lucille Lortel Award, and the Outer Critics' Circle Award. Were you surprised by its success?

ALBEE: Probably. I was odd boy out there for a long time. It was sort of interesting to have it happen. Surprised? Well, what does surprise mean? Startled? Yes. Surprised? No, since I realized it was a good play. But I've written a lot of good plays that I thought were crucified.

MANN: Did this experience make you feel somewhat vindicated because of the way some of the critics had treated you?

ALBEE: No, they should have just been fairer to some of the other plays. It pointed that up.

MANN: And *Three Tall Women* has opened the way to new productions of other works and a reappraisal of plays we had not seen in some time. . . . To my mind, this play is your most musical. Like a chamber trio, it is a play of voices. I noticed that in the New York production, especially at the end, the three voices were both similar and had different timbres, the older one more chanted, the middle one realistic, the younger one almost like a dream.

ALBEE: That's the way it is with those periods of age for those three people. Also, they had become the same person again.

MANN: Can you discuss the ending? I feel very good about the ending. The women are holding hands, and they have lovely monologues of reflection; but right before that, they've been saying terrible things to each other.

ALBEE: The genesis of what happened at the end of the play—though nobody really sees it—is the fugue at the end of *Don Giovanni*. . . .

MANN: And that was the inspiration?

ALBEE: I think that was the musical inspiration for it, yes, and the structural inspiration.

MANN: The New York production was stunning.

ALBEE: Wasn't Myra Carter extraordinary?

MANN: She was able to shift so quickly in the role.

ALBEE: It drove her crazy. She's a very sweet, foul-mouthed lady. . . . Remarks in rehearsal like, "How the fuck do you expect me to start crying without any motivation three pages in and then stop again? How the fuck do you expect me to do that?" "Because you're a great actress. Now shut the fuck up and do it," I would say to her.

MANN: But that's very difficult. I've seen productions where this is boo-hooed.

ALBEE: Sometimes I regret that I don't write easier characters, or characters easier to act. It would make for a lot better productions.

MANN: Throughout *Three Tall Women*, there are echoes of many of your earlier plays. *All Over, The American Dream, The Zoo Story, A Delicate Balance*—I mean where do we stop?

ALBEE: They're all by the same guy; they're the same mind.

MANN: Is the play so reflective because in some ways you were going back to formative times?

ALBEE: Well, it was interesting, having observed that woman far more intimately and for a far longer time than I had ever had any desire to. Ultimately, I developed an amazing objectivity about her, which was very interesting to me, which allowed me to not write a revenge play, not write a rage piece, but to turn her into a wonderful fictional character.

MANN: It seems a nice thing to do to give A the second act, having her look at her life.

ALBEE: It wasn't my idea. It was the play's idea. I make a distinction there between me and the play. I'm sort of a carrier of the play, to a large extent. . . . The play has certain rights, prerogatives, and destinations that I try not to interfere with.

MANN: And you have to go with that?

ALBEE: For example, I didn't even know the Boy was going to come on stage until I wrote a line, "the Boy enters." I didn't know he was coming on stage.

MANN: That's one of two stunning entrances in the second act, and I think after the first entrance, we don't expect another.

ALBEE: But there he was. . . . One of the funs of writing: Gee, I didn't know I was going to do that! Isn't that interesting?

MANN: Another play written during this past decade, but very different in form, is *The Lorca Play*. Isn't this your first about an historical figure?

ALBEE: No, *The Death of Bessie Smith*.

MANN: Why Lorca?

ALBEE: I was sitting down here in Houston a number of years ago, and I got a call from the Houston Festival, which every year celebrates some sister city somewhere and another culture. And they said we'd like to commission a play. I said: Well, you know, I don't mind being commissioned since I'm writing a play anyway, and I give whoever commissioned the play the first performance; but I don't take subjects. And they said we don't really want to limit you, if you think you could write a play about any aspect that you would like of Spanish history or culture. I said, that is limiting but I'll think about it.

And then I decided why don't I write a play about García Lorca, because I found lots of very, very interesting parallels between what happened to Lorca, and the reasons that it happened to him, and a lot of stuff that I'm afraid is going on in the United States now. I mean, Lorca had a lot of very good reasons to be killed. He's an intellectual, he was politically leftist, he was a creative artist, and he was gay. Four very good reasons to kill some-body in the United States, or to silence people in both countries. And so I thought there were some interesting parallels there.

MANN: And you traveled to Spain to do research?

ALBEE: I'd never been to Spain; I'd been resisting going to Spain until around this time. I didn't want to do that. Isn't that bizarre, though? I don't like Communism either, but I used to go to Russia or the Soviet Union all the time. But I wouldn't go to Spain. I don't understand that. It doesn't make any sense to me. I would not go to fascist societies, but I would go to Communist fascist societies that I disliked just as much. I'd never been to Spain, and I thought since I was going to write a play about somebody who knew so much of the soil, I had to spend a lot of time down in southern Spain where Lorca lived. And I had to spend a lot of time down there to get a sense of it physi-cally, and the people, and I also had to go to Madrid to talk to what was left of the Lorca family.

MANN: So you met with them?

ALBEE: I met with the younger sister, the only one left alive who knew Lorca. And she wasn't much help. . . . Every single question, Lorca was just like everybody else. Nothing stood out, nothing special about him. So obvi-ously the image of Lorca that the Lorca family wants to perpetuate is of somebody with absolutely no distinguishing features whatever. . . . And cer-tainly, of course, Lorca gay? Are you crazy? Of course not. . . .

MANN: Is the play somewhat Brechtian?

ALBEE: Oh, it's a pageant! Thirty-seven actors. . . .

MANN: Given the economics of theater, how are we going to see it?

ALBEE: We'll have to bring it down to about twenty. I can do that. I'll have more doubling. . . . There are some characters I have to have in there: Lorca as an adult and a boy, Lorca's mother, Lorca's maid who raised him. I have to have Franco in there, the Catholic Church, de Falla. I have to have Dali.

MANN: So it is more episodic?

ALBEE: It is. It just takes us through his whole life, from when he's a child until he's executed by that firing squad. I also have a narrator. . . .

MANN: Switching subjects now. You've known many great artists. Would you discuss three of them and their effect on you and your work? Thornton Wilder, John Steinbeck, and Tennessee Williams.

ALBEE: There are moments in two of Thornton Wilder's plays that practically bring me to emotional collapse whenever I think about them. In *The Skin of Our Teeth*, when at the height of the storm, Mrs. Antrobus finally calls her son by his correct name, "Cain! Cain!" Such a brilliant, sad, terrifying moment. . . . And in *Our Town*, when Emily has come back and her father calls down the stairs, "Where's my girl? Where's my birthday girl?" Any playwright that can do that is a playwright we should listen to and pay some attention to. I can't understand why he's not considered "up there."

And there's another piece of literature, and I'm convinced now that all three of these have to do with my adoption, although I don't like to think of it that way. [It's] in the text of "Knoxville: Summer 1915" [the preface to James Agee's *A Death in the Family*], and it's about a very young child with his family on the lawn. . . . Read the text and go through it. I break up every time. . . .

But Wilder, yes, I didn't like everything he wrote. I didn't like his novels very much, but there are moments in a number of his plays that are astonishing. And he made experiments, very quiet experiments. . . .

MANN: You must have seen some of those productions?

ALBEE: Oh, sure, I did.

MANN: And you do tell a wonderful story about Wilder.

ALBEE: Well, it's true. He'd read my poetry and tell me to be a playwright, to save poetry from me.

MANN: John Steinbeck.

ALBEE: He and I were good friends. . . . We'd gotten to know each other, and when he was invited by the Soviet government as part of a cultural exchange program to spend a month in the USSR and a month in a satellite country, he was asked to bring a young American with him. And he liked my work, and we liked each other, so he chose me. We got to know each other very well during that trip. We were there when Kennedy was assassinated. And then we just fell into knowing each other rather well.

I liked his mind; I didn't like all the conclusions he'd come to about a lot of things, and I didn't greatly admire all of his writing; there's some of it I thought was truth-telling. And I didn't like the way he was being treated, especially after he got the Nobel Prize. They just started lashing out at him; he didn't deserve it as much as Pearl Buck did, they said. You hate to see a guy hurt that way. I liked him. He was a truth-teller, an honest man, told the truth as he saw it. And we just liked each other.

MANN: And you dedicated *A Delicate Balance* to him.

ALBEE: And Tennessee. Well, heavens. You get somebody that good, you admire them a lot, right?

MANN: Were you friends as early as the point that you put some of his lines in *Virginia Woolf?*

ALBEE: Oh, yeah, sure. I put some things in *Who's Afraid of Virginia Woolf?* so that when Tennessee came to see it, he'd be amused.

MANN: And he was.

ALBEE: Yes, he was. We never became intimate friends, but good acquaintances. When he started drugging and drinking too much, there was not much communication possible. . . .

MANN: Can you comment on the state of American theater today? Several years ago you were quite concerned about the Broadway scene and even a certain commercialism off-Broadway. Are you still concerned?

ALBEE: I still am, yes. I'm trying to think of how many worthwhile American plays originate on Broadway. Practically none. A lot of British imports come over, and now Irish imports, too; but good, serious American plays originating on Broadway?

MANN: Well, there are so few plays on Broadway.

ALBEE: So, why should there be any American ones?

MANN: Are there opportunities for young playwrights?

ALBEE: Yes, but they are further afield. There are regional theaters who'll take a chance on a young playwright; some of the smaller theaters in the major cities will take a chance on a young playwright. It's not the most congenial environment anywhere for the craft of playwriting. You must remember, playwriting is a minority experience. It's not participated in the way movies and television are. But then again, junk novels are much more popular than serious ones. And who reads poetry? Three people?

MANN: Do we nurture our playwrights?

ALBEE: Of course not. No, certainly not. You know ... the National Endowment of the Arts gives grants to theaters; let's give grants to the playwrights. Ninety percent of the time the grant is to the theater, not to the playwright. We don't nourish our creative artists very much.

MANN: In addition to writing, you have done many other things in the theater. How do teaching and directing figure into your work?

ALBEE: They all teach me about each other. Directing teaches me more about writing, working with actors, seeing about what works rather than what works theoretically. Teaching—the way I teach, which is fifteen different playwrights each year—every play they write has different problems and different solutions. . . . I know how to do the survey course of twentieth-century drama. I can do that. But it bores the hell out of me. This is not quite as academic, and I enjoy it. I find all those things relate to each other and help. . . .

MANN: Can you teach playwriting?

ALBEE: No. You can't teach somebody how to be a playwright. You can teach people how other people wrote plays, and they can do a fairly good imitation, but of the one hundred and fifty scripts I get, maybe a hundred of them are good or bad imitations of other people's work. These people are not really playwrights; they're not original; they don't have an original thought in their heads. But if somebody is a playwright and is making fascinating mistakes but doesn't quite know how to do it yet, then you can be helpful. But a person has to be a playwright and has to have a playwright's way of thinking—a playwright's mind, which is different from the novelist's mind, et cetera, et cetera.

MANN: You have been very generous in helping young playwrights during your career. What motivates that?

ALBEE: Common sense. Don't we want a world filled with functioning playwrights?

MANN: So there is a sense of responsibility to the art?

ALBEE: I don't know if it's responsibility. I think it's what one should do. It's another thing one should do. It may be a terrible thing. It may not be the right thing to do. Maybe the world would be a much better place without a surfeit of playwrights. But I'd like to take the chance and see.

Contributors

Robert F. Gross is Director of Theater and Professor of English and Comparative Literature at Hobart and William Smith Colleges. He is the author of *Words Heard and Overheard* and *S. N. Behrman: A Research and Production Sourcebook*. He has published articles on a variety of playwrights, including Henrik Ibsen, August Strindberg, Gerhart Hauptmann, Terence Rattigan, Wendy Wasserstein, and Normand Chaurette.

Norma Jenckes teaches dramatic literature and playwriting at the University of Cincinnati. The founding editor of *American Drama*, she has published many articles on modern and contemporary British, Irish, and American drama. She is director of the Helen Weinberger Center for the Study of Drama and Playwriting.

Lincoln Konkle is Associate Professor at The College of New Jersey, where he teaches courses in dramatic literature and creative writing. He has published articles on Edward Taylor, William Vaughn Moody, Thornton Wilder, Tennessee Williams, Edward Albee, J. B. Priestley, and Christine Brooke-Rose. He is currently at work on a book about Thornton Wilder's drama and fiction.

Bruce J. Mann is Associate Professor and Chair of the English Department at Oakland University in Rochester, Michigan. He teaches drama and modern literature and has served as a dramaturg for the university's Meadow Brook Theatre. He has published articles on Tennessee Williams, Eugene O'Neill, Arthur Miller, and Sam Shepard.

Anne Paolucci is the author of *From Tension to Tonic: The Plays of Edward Albee*. She is former chairperson of the Board of Trustees of the City University of New York and retired professor of English at St. John's University. She is President of the Council on National

Literatures, a nonprofit educational foundation. She has written dozens of books, articles, and reviews covering a spectrum of interests: dramatic theory, Hegel, the Theatre of the Absurd, Luigi Pirandello, Shakespeare, and Dante. She is an award-winning playwright and poet and also writes fiction.

Ronald F. Rapin is Associate Professor of Spanish at Oakland University in Rochester, Michigan. He specializes in twentieth-century Spanish literature and has published on Juan Benet and Luis Martín Santos. His interest in the works of Edward Albee is due in large part to Albee's self-declared interests in Hispanic writers such as Federico García Lorca, Julio Cortázar, and Jorge Luis Borges.

Emily Rosenbaum is a graduate student at the University of North Carolina at Chapel Hill. Her areas of research include American Studies, gender studies, performance, and the family, particularly in American drama.

Lawrence Sacharow is Chair of the Theater Department at Fordham University. He is also founding artistic director of River Arts Repertory in Woodstock, New York, where he has directed American premieres of new works by Edward Albee, Michael Cristofer, Derek Walcott, Richard Nelson, and numerous other writers. In addition to Chekhov's *The Seagull* with Joanne Woodward, he has directed more than fifty plays, including works by Beckett, Shepard, and Kroetz, at La MaMa, Hudson Guild, the Mark Taper Forum, Circle in the Square, and other theaters.

Lisa M. Siefker Bailey is Adjunct Assistant Professor of English at Franklin College in Indiana. She has taught a wide variety of courses, including drama, for Middle Tennessee State University and Indiana University. She has presented papers at the Comparative Drama Conference and the Tennessee Williams Scholars' Conference. Her current research focuses on representations of culture in American plays.

Rakesh H. Solomon, Associate Professor of Theater and Drama at Indiana University in Bloomington, is the author of *Albee in Performance: The Playwright as Director*, forthcoming from Indiana University Press. His articles on Albee and other contemporary American and British playwrights, as well as on colonial and postcolonial Indian theater, have appeared in *Theatre Survey, Theatre Journal, TDR: The Drama Review, Journal of Performance Studies, American Drama, Forum for Modern Language Studies, Religion and Theatre*, and *Alan Ayckbourn: A Casebook*. A recipient of NEH and American Institute of Indian Studies fellowships, he is currently completing a monograph titled *Culture, Politics, and Performance in Colonial India, 1753–1947*.

Index

THE ECOLOGY AND
MANAGEMENT OF
AQUATIC-TERRESTRIAL
ECOTONES

MAN AND THE BIOSPHERE SERIES

Series Editor: J.N.R. Jeffers

VOLUME 4

THE ECOLOGY AND MANAGEMENT OF AQUATIC-TERRESTRIAL ECOTONES

Edited by
R.J. Naiman and H. Décamps

PUBLISHED BY

PARIS

AND

The Parthenon Publishing Group
International Publishers in Science, Technology & Education

Published in 1990 by the United Nations Educational, Scientific and Cultural
Organization.
7 Place de Fontenoy, 75700 Paris, France—Unesco ISBN 9-231026-68-2

and

The Parthenon Publishing Group Limited
Casterton Hall, Carnforth,
Lancs LA6 2LA, UK—ISBN 1-85070-271-3

and

The Parthenon Publishing Group Inc.
120 Mill Road, Park Ridge
New Jersey, NJ, USA—ISBN 0-929858-25-5

Typeset by Lasertext, Stretford, Manchester
Printed and bound in Great Britain by
The Cromwell Press Limited, Broughton Gifford, Melksham, Wiltshire

British Library Cataloguing in Publication Data

Ecology and management of aquatic – terrestrial ecotones.
 1. Ecotones
 I. Naiman, Robert J.   II. Décamps, Henri   III. Series 574.524

 ISBN 1-85070-271-3
 ISBN 0-929858-25-5 U.S.
 ISBN 9-231026-68-2 France

Library of Congress Cataloging-in-Publication Data

Ecology and management of aquatic-terrestrial ecotones/edited by
 Robert J. Naiman and Henri Décamps.
  p.   cm. — (MAB); v. 4)
 Includes bibliographical references.
 ISBN 0-929858-25-5 (Parthenon)
 1. Ecotones. 2. Coastal ecology. 3. Coastal zone management.
 I. Naiman, Robert J. II. Décamps, Henri, III. Series: MAB (Series) : 4.
 QH541.5.C65E268 1990   90-30174
 574.5′2632—dc20   CIP

SERIES PREFACE

Unesco's Man and the Biosphere Programme

Improving scientific understanding of natural and social processes relating to man's interactions with his environment, providing information useful to decision making on resource use, promoting the conservation of genetic diversity as an integral part of land management, enjoining the efforts of scientists, policymakers, and local people in problem-solving ventures, mobilizing resources for field activities, strengthening of regional cooperative frameworks. These are some of the generic characteristics of Unesco's Man and the Biosphere Programme.

Unesco has a long history of concern with environmental matters, dating back to the fledgling days of the organization. Its first Director General was biologist Julian Huxley, and among the earliest accomplishments was a collaborative venture with the French Government which led to the creation in 1948 of the International Union for the Conservation of Nature and Natural Resources. About the same time, the Arid Zone Research Programme was launched, and throughout the 1950s and 1960s this programme promoted an integrated approach to natural resources management in the arid and semi-arid regions of the world. There followed a number of other environmental science programmes in such fields as hydrology, marine sciences, earth sciences, and the natural heritage, and these continue to provide a solid focus for Unesco's concern with the human environment and its natural resources.

The Man and the Biosphere (MAB) Programme was launched by Unesco in the early 1970s. It is a nationally based, international programme of research, training, demonstration, and information diffusion. The overall aim is to contribute to efforts for providing the scientific basis and trained personnel needed to deal with problems of rational utilization and conservation of resources and resource systems, and problems of human settlements. MAB emphasizes research for solving problems: it thus involves research by interdisciplinary teams on the interactions between ecological

v

and social systems; field training; and applying a systems approach to understanding the relationships between the natural and human components of development and environmental management.

MAB is a decentralized programme with field projects and training activities in all regions of the world. These are carried out by scientists and technicians from universities, academies of sciences, national research laboratories, and other research and development institutions, under the auspices of more than a hundred MAB National Committees. Activities are undertaken in cooperation with a range of international governmental and non-governmental organizations.

Further information on the MAB Programme is contained in *A Practical Guide to MAB, Man Belongs to the Earth*, a biennial report, a twice-yearly newsletter *InfoMAB*, MAB technical notes, and various other publications. All are available from the MAB Secretariat in Paris.

Man and the Biosphere Book Series

The Man and the Biosphere Series has been launched with the aim of communicating some of the results generated by the MAB Programme to a wider audience than the existing Unesco series of technical notes and state-of-knowledge reports. The series is aimed primarily at upper level university students, scientists, and resource managers, who are not necessarily specialists in ecology. The books will not normally be suitable for undergraduate text books but rather will provide additional resource material in the form of case studies based on primary data collection and written by the researchers involved; global and regional syntheses of comparative research conducted in several sites or countries; and state-of-the-art assessments of knowledge or methodological approaches based on scientific meetings, commissioned reports or panels of experts.

The series will span a range of environmental and natural resource issues. Currently available, in press or in preparation, are reviews on such topics as control of eutrophication in lakes and reservoirs, sustainable development and environmental management in small islands, reproductive ecology of tropical forest plants, the role of land/inland water ecotones in landscape management and restoration, ecological research and management in alpine regions, structure and function of a nutrient-stressed Amazonian ecosystem, assessment and control of non-point source pollution, research for improved land use in arid northern Kenya.

The Editor-in-Chief of the series is John Jeffers, until recently Director of the Institute of Terrestrial Ecology in the United Kingdom, who has been associated with MAB since its inception. He is supported by an Editorial Advisory Board of internationally-renowned scientists from different regions of the world and from different disciplinary backgrounds:

E.G. Bonkoungou (Burkina Faso), Gonzalo Halffter (Mexico), Otto Lange (Federal Republic of Germany), Li Wenhau (China), Gilbert Long (France), Ian Noble (Australia), P.S. Ramakrishnan (India), Vladimir Sokolov (USSR) and Anne Whyte (Canada). Bernd von Droste and Malcolm Hadley of Unesco's Division of Ecological Sciences are *ex officio* members of the board.

A publishing rhythm of three to four books per year is envisaged. Books in the series will be published initially in English, but special arrangements will be sought with different publishers for other language versions on a case-by-case basis.

CONTENTS

LIST OF CONTRIBUTORS

Eric Chauvet
Centre d'Ecologie des Ressources
  Renouvelables, C.N.R.S.
29, rue Jeanne Marvig
31055 Toulouse
Cédex, France

Henri Décamps
Centre d'Ecologie des Ressources
  Renouvelables, C.N.R.S.
29, rue Jeanne Marvig
31055 Toulouse
Cédex, France

Brigitte Desaigues
Université de Paris 1
12 place du Panthéon
75005 Paris
France

Marie-José Dole-Olivier
Hydrobiologie et Ecologie Souterraines
  U.R.A./C.N.R.S.
367 "Ecologie des Eaux Douces"
Université Lyon 143
bd du 11 Novembre 1918
69622 Villeurbanne
Cédex, France

Eliane Fustec
Centre d'Ecologie des Ressources
  Renouvelables, C.N.R.S.
29, rue Jeanne Marvig
31055 Toulouse
Cédex, France

Janine Gibert
Hydrobiologie et Ecologie Souterraines
  U.R.A./C.N.R.S.
367 "Ecologie des Eaux Douces"
Université de Lyon 143
bd du 11 Novembre 1918
69622 Villeurbanne
Cédex, France

Brij Gopal
School of Environmental Sciences
Jawaharlal Nehru University
New Mehrauli Road
New Delhi, 110 067
India

Marjorie M. Holland
Ecological Society of America
9650 Rockville Pike
Bethesda
Maryland 20814
USA

Pierre Marmonier
Hydrobiologie et Ecologie Souterraines
  U.R.A./C.N.R.S.
367 "Ecologie des Eaux Douces"
Université de Lyon 143
bd du 11 Novembre 1918
69622 Villeurbanne
Cédex, France

Robert J. Naiman
Center for Streamside Studies, AR-10
University of Washington
Seattle
Washington 98195
USA

William E. Odum
Department of Environmental Sciences
University of Virginia
Charlottesville
Virginia 22903
USA

Geoffrey E. Petts
Department of Geography
University of Technology
Loughborough
LE11 3TU
United Kingdom

xv

Ewa Pieczyńska
Department of Hydrobiology
Zoological Institute
University of Warsaw
Nowy Swiat 67 00-046
Warszawa
Poland

Gilles Pinay
Centre d'Ecologie des Ressources
    Renouvelables, C.N.R.S.
29, rue Jeanne Marvig
31055 Toulouse
Cédex, France

Paul G. Risser
University of New Mexico
Albuquerque
New Mexico 87131
USA

Jukka Salo
Department of Biology
University of Turku
SF-20500 Turku
Finland

Herman H. Shugart
Environmental Sciences Department
The University of Virginia
Charlottesville
Virginia 22903
USA

Frederick J. Swanson
U.S. Forest Service
Forest Sciences Laboratory
3200 Jefferson Way
Corvallis
Oregon 97311
USA

Philippe Vervier
Hydrobiologie et Ecologie Souterraines
    U.R.A./C.N.R.S.
367 "Ecologie des Eaux Douces"
Université Lyon 143
bd du 11 Novembre 1918
69622 Villeurbanne
Cédex, France

Dennis F. Whigham
Smithsonian Environmental Research
    Center
Box 28
Edgewater
Maryland 21037
USA

Robert C. Wissmar
Center for Streamside Studies, AR-10
University of Washington
Seattle
Washington 98195
USA

CHAPTER 1

TOWARDS AN ECOTONE PERSPECTIVE

Henri Décamps and Robert J. Naiman

ABSTRACT

In preface to this volume we present a brief summary of the origin of the conference held in Sopron, Hungary, on aquatic terrestrial ecotones. We also discuss the development of the interest in ecotones as it has appeared in freshwater and landscape ecology.

INTRODUCTION

This volume represents the first publication on the dynamics of ecotones associated with continental waters. Recent research has shown that ecotones play an important role in regulating the flow of materials and information across landscapes (Wiens *et al.* 1985, Naiman *et al.* 1988a). It is clear that, from a fundamental point of view, this role has numerous practical applications. Thus, having recognised the value of ecotones, we must now learn to utilise them for the management of continental waters. For example, can they be used as filter zones against nonpoint source pollution? Or can ecotones provide resistance to drought under a changing climate regime?

We must still, especially for rivers but also for all the other types of continental waters, document and understand their dynamics over various spatial and temporal scales. The dynamic nature of ecotones is particularly evident when land-inland water boundaries are considered. In fact, these latter ecotones constitute an important key towards understanding the shifting mosaic of river and lake landscapes. Despite this, little is known about land-inland water ecotones. In many instances, we are just beginning to glimpse answers to questions such as: What is, or is not, an ecotone? What are the characteristics of ecotones that can be recognised and manipulated?

Satisfactory responses to these questions can be achieved only from a perspective that considers the concept of multiple and shifting scales of space and time. The choice of scale is critical, since it permits identification of the ecotones. Consider, for example, that certain landscapes are organised as imbricated mosaics that are more or less connected. Ecotones on this landscape may be found from fine scales, such as differences between microclimates at the stream edge, to those of large and complex wetlands or riparian forests forming boundaries between terrestrial and aquatic ecosystems.

Yet, for each of these extreme scales and those in between, it must be clearly understood that an ecotone is not simply a boundary or an edge. The concept of an ecotone assumes the existence of active interactions between two or more ecosystems (or patches), with the appearance of mechanisms that do not exist in either of the adjacent ecosystems (Holland 1988). Further, even though the dynamics of ecosystems are essentially stabilised by feedback mechanisms, the dynamics of ecotones are inherently variable in space and time. This fundamental characteristic is supported by interactions within and between adjacent systems. Within-system interactions are strong within ecosystems and weaker in ecotones. Conversely, between-system interactions are weak within ecosystems and strong within ecotones. As the area of the ecotone increases, the likelihood of positive feedback increases and ecosystem properties emerge.

Historically, the ecotone concept has evolved since the beginning of the century. Clements (1905) envisaged the ecotone as a zone of tension where the dominant species of adjacent communities reached their limits, whereas Leopold (1933) saw it as a zone of transition particularly rich in the number of species. His idea of an 'edge effect' remains well known. Yet, subsequent research, more directly focussed on the functioning of diverse ecosystems, largely avoided questions of spatial variability, and therefore avoided the edges or boundaries constituting the ecotones.

However, two parallel developments over the past 15 years resulted in a re-examination of the ecotone concept:

1. In freshwater ecology, researchers began to realise that the well-being of continental waters depends largely on their terrestrial environment. Three Baldi Lectures organised by Societas Internationalis Limnologiae have addressed this question: "The Stream and Its Valley" (Hynes 1975), "Beyond the Shoreline: A Watershed Ecosystem Approach" (Likens 1984), and "Terrestrial-Aquatic Interactions" (Wetzel 1990).

2. In landscape ecology, researchers evaluating spatial heterogeneity had to modify their approach to fundamental questions, notably those concerned with the consequences of disturbance (Pickett and White 1985). Because of this, numerous studies are now oriented towards interactions and exchanges across heterogeneous landscapes, influences of heterogeneity on biotic and abiotic processes, and management of that heterogeneity (Risser 1985). These processes are now being examined

in research projects directed at continental waters (i.e., Johnston and Naiman 1987, Pringle *et al.* 1988, Décamps *et al.* 1988).

These two parallel developments strongly influenced the direction of the Man and Biosphere-5 (MAB-5) program at the United Nations Educational, Scientific and Cultural Organization (Unesco). In April 1986 a meeting was held in Toulouse, France, on Land Use Impacts on Aquatic Ecosystems: The Use of Scientific Information. Jointly sponsored by MAB-Unesco and the Programme Interdisciplinaire de Recherche sur l'Environnement (PIREN) of the Centre National de la Recherche Scientifique (CNRS), the workshop was organised into four sessions covering the use of scientific information, the impact of land use on the export rates of nutrients, urban areas, and riparian systems and wetlands (Lauga *et al.* 1988). One important outcome of this meeting was the recognition of the crucial role of ecotones in regulating transient biochemical processes and the character of the landscape mosaic. Participants at the meeting proposed that the role of ecotones, their management, and restoration should become a major focus of MAB research (Naiman *et al.* 1988b).

In January 1987, an informal technical consultation between the Scientific Committee on Problems of the Environment (SCOPE) and MAB was held in Paris on the concept of ecotones (Di Castri *et al.* 1988). A definition of ecotones was developed based on operational concerns: An ecotone is a zone of transition between adjacent ecological systems, having a set of characteristics uniquely defined by space and time scales and by the strength of interactions between adjacent ecological systems (Holland 1988). As part of this consultation, Naiman *et al.* (1988b) addressed the scientific focus of an international research programme specifically examining ecotones occurring at the aquatic-terrestrial interface. These ecotones include riparian forests, marginal wetlands, littoral lake zones, floodplain lakes and forests, and areas of significant groundwater-surface water exchange. Questions being examined are of practical interest. They include the resilience and resistance of ecotones to various classes of human disturbances, the means by which ecotones may be restored after disturbances, and the development of landscape management guidelines designed to take advantage of the ecologically valuable properties of ecotones.

These discussions underscored the necessity of establishing a state of knowledge concerning land-inland water ecotones. This became the goal of the MAB-5 symposium held in Sopron, Hungary, in May 1988. Ten of the plenary lectures presented at the workshop are assembled in this volume.

The contents of this volume provide an up-to-date evaluation of aquatic-terrestrial ecotones. P.G. Risser addresses the general ecological importance of land-water ecotones, emphasising their dynamic nature, unique properties, and their special relationship to adjacent resource patches. H.H.

Shugart considers various ecological models that could be used to examine ecotone structure and dynamics, and defines ecotones within the context of ecosystems. J. Salo addresses external processes influencing the origin and maintenance of aquatic-terrestrial ecotones, especially those related to hydrologic and geomorphic factors. R.C. Wissmar and F. Swanson document several cases in which geomorphology and hydrology act to influence ecotone dynamics in North America. W.E. Odum explores the influences of internal processes on the maintenance of ecotones, relating them to larger-scale external influences. E. Pieczyńska examines the special characteristics and importance of ecotones associated with lakes. G. Pinay, H. Décamps, E. Chauvet, and E. Fustec consider the characteristics and dynamics of fluvial ecotones, stressing system variability over wide spatial and temporal scales. M.M. Holland, D.F. Whigham, and B. Gopal offer a similar synthesis for wetland ecotones, including the range of natural functions they provide for humans. J. Gibert, M.J. Dole-Olivier, P. Marmonier, and P. Vervier give an insightful review of ecotones associated with the hydrologic system below the earth's surface. G.E. Petts examines the application of ecotones to aquatic landscape management, stressing the best practical environmental option for different scales. B. Desaigues discusses the socio-economic value of ecotones, reviewing several approaches to the issue. Finally, R.J. Naiman and H. Décamps summarise key points related to the structure and dynamics of aquatic-terrestrial ecotones, identifying new areas for research and application, and some of the approaches required to attain those goals.

This volume does not pretend to describe completely the dynamics of aquatic-terrestrial ecotones. It should be considered only a point of departure for future studies. Current research is still in the initial stages. However, there are three points to consider that have already emerged from the initial synthesis. The first is to note that there may be a clear distinction between the concepts of an ecotone and an ecosystem, and that it is not possible to apply the same methods of study and modelling to both of them. The second consideration, for both ecotones and their adjacent ecosystems (or patches), is the overwhelming importance of choosing appropriate spatial and temporal scales for study.

Finally, the third consideration, which we hope is clearly communicated in this volume, is that we are not promoting an ecotone 'perspective' so much as a landscape perspective for ecological research. It is this approach that will be found in the chapters of this book.

ACKNOWLEDGEMENTS

We thank F. Fournier, J.N.R. Jeffers, and M. Hadley for their enthusiasm and support for this project. Financial assistance was provided by the Unesco Man and the Biosphere Programme, the Centre National de la

Recherche Scientifique (France), the United States Man and the Biosphere Program (U.S. State Department), Programme l'Homme et la Biosphère (France), and the United States National Science Foundation (BSR 87-22852). All of the articles in this volume were evaluated by anonymous reviewers and the technical editing was accomplished by Leila Charbonneau and Beverly Anderson of the University of Washington Institute of Forest Resources and Kate O'Laughlin of the University's Center for Streamside Studies. This assistance is greatly appreciated.

Special appreciation is extended to our Hungarian colleagues for hosting the symposium in the beautiful city of Sopron. Their efforts in making arrangements and in providing logistical support will be long remembered by all those who attended.

LITERATURE CITED

Clements, F.E. 1905. Research methods in ecology. University Publishing Company, Lincoln, Nebraska, USA.

Décamps, H., M. Fortuné, F. Gazelle, and G. Pautou. 1988. Historical influence of man on the riparian dynamics of a fluvial landscape. Landscape Ecology 1:163-173.

Di Castri, F., A.J. Hansen, and M.M. Holland (editors). 1988. A new look at ecotones: emerging international projects on landscape boundaries. Biology International, Special Issue 17:1-163.

Holland, M.M. (compiler). 1988. SCOPE/MAB technical consultations on landscape boundaries: report of a SCOPE/MAB workshop on ecotones. Biology International, Special Issue 17: 47-106.

Hynes, H.B.N. 1975. The stream and its valley. Verhandlungen Internationale Vereinigung Limnologie 19:1-15.

Johnston, C.A., and R.J. Naiman. 1987. Boundary dynamics at the aquatic-terrestrial interface: the influence of beaver and geomorphology. Landscape Ecology 1:47-57.

Lauga, J., H. Décamps, and M.M. Holland (editors). 1988. Land use impacts on aquatic ecosystems: the use of scientific information. Académie de Toulouse, Toulouse, France.

Leopold, A. 1933. Game management. Charles Scribner's Sons, New York, New York, USA.

Likens, G.E. 1984. Beyond the shoreline: a watershed ecosystem approach. Verhandlungen Internationale Vereinigung Limnologie 22:1-22.

Naiman, R.J., H. Décamps, J. Pastor, and C.A. Johnston. 1988a. The potential importance of boundaries to fluvial ecosystems. Journal of the North American Benthological Society 7:289-306.

Naiman, R.J., M.M. Holland, H. Décamps, and P.G. Risser. 1988b. A new UNESCO programme: research and management of land/inland water ecotones. Biology International, Special Issue 17:107-136.

Pickett, S.T.A., and P.S. White (editors). 1985. The ecology of natural disturbance and patch dynamics. Academic Press, Orlando, Florida, USA.

Pringle, C.M., R.J. Naiman, G. Bretschko, J.R. Karr, M.W. Oswood, J.R. Webster, R.L. Welcomme, and M.J. Winterbourn. 1988. Patch dynamics in lotic systems: the stream as a mosaic. Journal of the North American Benthological Society 7:503-524.

Risser, P.G. (compiler). 1985. Spatial and temporal variability of biospheric and geospheric processes: research needed to determine interactions with global environmental change. The International Council of Scientific Unions Press, Paris, France.

Wetzel, R.G. 1990. Land–water interface: metabolic and limnological regulators. Verhandlungen Internationale Vereiningung Limnologie, *in press*.

Wiens, J.A., C.S. Crawford, and J.R. Gosz. 1985. Boundary dynamics: a conceptual framework for studying landscape ecosystems. Oikos 45:421-427.

Key words: Ecotone, freshwater ecology, landscape ecology.

CHAPTER 2

THE ECOLOGICAL IMPORTANCE OF LAND-WATER ECOTONES

Paul G. Risser

ABSTRACT

The idea of transitional zones, or ecotones, between ecological units has existed for several decades. Recently this concept has been enriched by recognising that ecotones (1) are not simply static zones where two communities join but are dynamic, change over time, and have unique properties and (2) must be understood in the spatial and temporal context of the adjacent ecological units. Because ecotones usually represent relatively steep gradients in abiotic and biotic variables, these ecological systems permit testing of ecological ideas such as mechanisms contributing to biodiversity and controls on the flow of materials across the landscape.

INTRODUCTION

For decades, ecologists, wildlife managers, geographers, and other scientists and land managers have been interested in the spatial transitions from one biological community to another. But these interests have not resulted in a common conceptual framework for describing the fundamental structural characteristics or the ecological processes in these geographical transition zones. More recently, attention has been expanded to include ecological processes that occur across the landscape but are mediated by these transition zones.

The 'ecotone' concept has been in the scientific literature for some time, generally defined as the transitional zone between vegetation types, and frequently including the notion that ecotones contain abiotic and biotic components found in one or both of the adjacent biological communities (e.g., Weaver 1960). This definition, though adequate for many purposes, fails to incorporate two important ideas explicitly. First, an ecotone is no longer regarded as a simple, static zone where two communities join, but rather a dynamic zone changing through time and possessing properties of its own. Second, ecotones are no longer considered only as entities, isolated from the landscape level processes. Ecotones are now considered integral parts of the landscape, deriving some properties from their position in the landscape and the resulting landscape level processes. With these newer and broader ideas, the following definition is more appropriate (Holland 1988): an ecotone is a zone of transition between adjacent ecological systems, having a set of characteristics uniquely defined by space and time scales and by the strength of the interactions between adjacent ecological systems.

Notice that in this definition the ecotone has specific properties but is also partly defined by its relationships with adjacent ecological systems. By using the term *ecological systems*, the definition is made scale independent, although ecological processes may be scale dependent. Therefore, an ecotone might occur between ecological systems at a broad spatial scale (e.g. boundaries between continental biomes) or at a fine scale, such as the transition between two specific biological communities (e.g. a wetland and an adjacent upland forest). In addition, the ecotone concept is useful as an abstract framework for organising the descriptive characteristics and properties of ecotones in general.

CHANGING ECOLOGICAL APPROACHES TO THE STUDY OF ECOTONES

The changes in analytical approaches to studying ecotones have paralleled the expansion of the definition of ecotones. From the wildlife management perspective, ecotones or edges have long been described in terms of their habitat value (Whitney and Davis 1986). These traits include combinations of food and cover or pathways for animal movement between habitat types. Ecologists have viewed ecotones as interesting for several reasons, among them as locations with a relatively high biological diversity, as communities that support certain sets of species such as 'edge' bird species, or as communities that have high biological productivity (Ovington *et al.* 1963). Agriculturists recognise ecotones adjacent to croplands as sources of agricultural pests or even as sources of predators on those pests (Risser *et al.* 1984). And rangeland managers have viewed ecotones as localities of relatively high forage production, but also as sources of water loss via evapotranspiration in riparian situations (Hubbard 1977).

While these views retain validity, more recent studies focus on the dynamic aspects of ecotones, and the landscape level processes that involve ecotones and adjacent ecological units. Before these studies are discussed, a few illustrations of the changing nature of analytical approaches might prove useful. Early studies described bird species characteristic of ecotones and then identified certain bird species as 'edge' species or 'interior' species.

The ecotone was described as having a certain number or percentage of bird species characteristic of the ecotone habitat. More recent investigations focus on the flow of birds across ecotones and adjacent communities. Similarly, earlier studies described the high organic matter content and greater number of soil organisms in ecotones, while recent interest has focussed on the pathways for movement of organic material and nutrients into and out of riparian ecotones. Also, as remote sensing and other data management techniques have become more readily available, there have been more complete pictorial and mathematical descriptions of ecotonal patterns over broad spatial scales. Thus, these new directions of investigation involve advancements in the concept of the ecotone, applications of improved technologies, and an increased appreciation of the importance of ecotones as functional components of the biosphere.

Although many approaches could have been adopted for this chapter, the chosen one seeks to identify the issues to be discussed in this volume and to provide a context for the subject of ecotones. The role of ecotones in supporting biologically diverse communities and the ways in which ecotones affect the flow of materials across the landscape are perhaps the two most important research topics of this discussion. In addition, it will be recognised that, in both an experimental and a conceptual sense, ecotones will serve as fertile grounds for future theoretical development. Ecotones will also increasingly be the focus of landscape management imperatives as natural and human pressure on the integrity of the biosphere continues. Thus, this chapter is designed to introduce these topics and so stimulate ideas, many of which may be addressed in the subsequent chapters.

BIODIVERSITY

From early discussions of wildlife habitat, 'edges' have been known to harbour a rich assemblage of species. More recently, studies on ecotones around small woodlots have focussed on general principles about the ecotonal characteristics useful in predicting the consequences to faunal populations (Askins *et al.* 1987, Blake and Karr 1987, Lynch and Whigman 1984, Scott *et al.* 1987, Wilcove 1985). For example, the size of the woodlot, and therefore the proportion of edge, can be correlated with the bird species complement that favours these transitional communities (Blake and Karr 1987). These studies (e.g. Wilcove 1985) also demonstrate that, along with the structural characteristics of the ecotones themselves, the interactions of the species in the adjacent ecological units are important (e.g. nest parasitism from birds inhabiting adjacent human-dominated systems). Thus, these ecotonal characteristics regulate community composition and population dynamics. The effects of landscape configuration on the distribution and abundance of plant and animal populations have also been described in landscape ecology publications such as Forman and Godron (1986) and

Urban *et al.* (1987).

Within the United States, riparian habitat (i.e. habitat along stream channels) supports some of the richest terrestrial vertebrate faunas in the arid southwestern United States (Carothers *et al.* 1974, Brown *et al.* 1977, Hubbard 1977, Ohmart and Anderson 1982, Szaro 1980). Szaro and Jakle (1985) compared the bird communities in central Arizona within an ecotone between a desert stream course (wash) and the adjacent upland communities. They demonstrated the usual pattern that the density of birds was highest at the edge between the upland and the streambed. The ultimate emphasis of the study, however, was to determine the percentage contribution of bird species to each of the vegetation types along a continuum including upland, riparian forest, and adjacent desert wash. The riparian bird community was a significant distribution source, contributing 23 to 33% of the birds found in the adjacent desert washes and 7 to 15% of the birds of the adjacent desert upland. Conversely, the desert bird community contributed only 1.0 to 1.5% of the birds found in the riparian community.

Changes in ecotones can significantly affect the diversity of adjacent ecological communities. For example, there were 95% fewer birds and 32% fewer species on agricultural lands along the Sacramento River, California, USA, from which the adjacent riparian vegetation had been removed, compared with agricultural lands in association with riparian vegetation (Hehnke and Stone 1978).

Most studies on riparian ecotones have been directed towards either large or small mammal habitats, and bird species. However, other parts of the fauna are also affected by the presence and condition of ecotones. For example, removal of near-stream vegetation in upstream areas can significantly reduce invertebrate and fish production as a result of loss of allochthonous (terrestrial) energy inputs into adjacent streams (Karr and Schlosser 1978). Thus, ecotones affect the presence of organisms ranging from large mammals to small invertebrates. These relationships are caused by characteristics of the ecotones themselves, and by interactions between the ecotones and adjacent ecological systems.

FLOWS OF WATER, NUTRIENTS, AND MATERIALS

Riparian forests can affect the flow of water, nutrients, and other materials from uplands into streams (e.g., Lowrance *et al.* 1983, 1984a; Omernik *et al.* 1981), Schlosser and Karr 1981, Verry and Timmons 1982). In a representative study, Lowrance *et al.* (1984c) considered a 1568 ha watershed of the Little River on the Georgia (USA) coastal plain. On the basis of inputs and the amount retained, the riparian forest captured significant portions of N, Ca, P, and Mg (Table 2.1). Of these materials, N is uniquely complicated, since fluxes can occur through diffusion from leaf surfaces, N fixation, NH_4-N volatilisation from soils, denitrification, and production

10

Table 2.1 Nutrient retention in the riparian forest of a Georgia (USA) coastal plain watershed. From Lowrance *et al.* (1984b)

Nutrient	Input (Output + Storage) $kg \cdot ha^{-1} \cdot yr^{-1}$	Percent Retained
Nitrogen	44.5	68
Phosphorus	2.1	30
Calcium	18.5	39
Magnesium	1.6	23
Potassium	17.4	6
Chlorine	7.9	7

of N_2O during nitrification. In the Little River watershed, gaseous losses were more important than gaseous inputs; N fixation within the riparian forest was less than either precipitation or streamflow inputs, and denitrification was more than twice the streamflow N loads. Riparian forest soil offered conditions conductive to denitrification: high organic matter, seasonal waterlogging, and large inputs of NO_3 via subsurface flow. Also, in these young forests (average age, 22-35 yr), vegetation accrual of nitrogen exceeded the total input from precipitation and subsurface flow. Observations in this study did not include surface flow, thus the budgets overestimate nutrient deficits and would be more nearly balanced if surface flows had been measured. Since riparian forests are repositories for sediment, and this sediment, along with buried organic debris, contains immobilised nutrients, this system would be balanced only over much longer periods (decades to centuries). As a consequence, periodic harvesting of trees would be necessary to maintain younger forests capable of a net uptake of nutrients (Lowrance *et al.* 1984b, c, 1985).

Riparian sources of dissolved organic matter include leaching from riparian vegetation, from decomposing litter in the floodplain, from soils, and from plants in the stream. Geomorphic changes in the stream, and in the soils of the watershed along the stream course, alter both the riparian vegetation and the assemblage of primary producers in the stream (Likens and Bormann 1974). Changes in the species of riparian plants influence the potential diversity of organic molecules leached from the vegetation. Potential diversity in the dissolved organic matter is thought to be highest in the headwaters of most streams (Vannote *et al.* 1980). It is clear that ecotones, especially riparian forests, contain longitudinal and vertical gradients in organic matter processing, and moreover that 'metabolic processes' of ecotones will be important if we are to understand the roles of ecotones in the sequestering and movements of materials across the landscape.

In the tall-grass prairie ecosystem, consisting of a broad grassland with riparian or gallery forests along the stream, McArthur and Marzolf (1986,

1987) found variable seasonal patterns in the dynamics of dissolved organic carbon. Leachates from grasses disappeared rapidly from stream water flowing through *in situ* chambers at upstream sites in grassland reaches. The reverse observation, uptake of leachates from trees, revealed that the dissolved organic carbon disappeared rapidly from chambers placed in the forested reaches, but bacteria in the grassland reaches did not utilise tree leachate as rapidly. Obviously, organic matter processing within ecotones is a significant influence on both the ecotone itself and the biotic components of the adjacent stream. Thus, the flow across ecotones in general, not only into streams, is influenced by the characteristics of the ecotones and the processes that connect ecotones to the adjacent landscape units.

USING ECOTONES TO TEST IDEAS

Ecotones may be particularly appropriate for testing new ecological ideas because of the intensity of interacting processes. Ecotones may have both longitudinal and lateral gradients, and be characterised by locations where species are at the periphery of their range or where their presence depends on a delicate balance of biotic and abiotic factors. In the following paragraphs, a few of these ideas are discussed briefly as an introduction to the use of ecotones to test ecological ideas.

Understanding local species diversity requires considering not just local processes of ecotones but also the matrix of processes on broader spatial and longer temporal-historical scales within which the community or ecotone is embedded (Ricklefs 1987). Ecological data must match the spatial and temporal scales of processes that influence the properties of ecological systems. Understanding ecotones, and especially their biodiversity, will thus require knowledge of the biotic dynamics at the next higher spatial scale of the region (Allen and Starr 1983, O'Neill *et al.* 1986).

The issue of measuring processes at different spatial and temporal scales is important for many ecological studies, but is particularly apparent in the investigation of ecotones whose very definition depends on the designation of scale. Individual small-scale processes on tributaries may become inconsequential if ecotones are defined at broader spatial scales such as the boundaries between biomes. In addition to the issue of spatial scale of definition, there is the confounding necessity to extrapolate small-scale measurements to larger-scale processes. This extrapolation requires models that comprehend the important processes and the characteristics of those processes that permit reasonable extrapolations. Denitrification, for example, can be measured only on small locations, so such models are required to explore just how this process is related to the ecotonal characteristics.

Invasions, and the ecotonal characteristics that permit and perpetuate invasions, may be important to animals (Kroodsma 1984) as well as plants (Risser *et al.* 1984). An extension of the invasion dynamics is the manner

12

in which riparian habitat is invaded after reconstruction. As one example, a reconstructed southwestern riparian habitat was more rapidly invaded by birds than herpetofauna, probably because of the isolation rather than the lack of essential habitat features (Szaro and Belfit 1986). This reinforces the realisation that ecotones must be managed in the context of the landscape and that reinvasion rates may provide information necessary for understanding and managing ecotones.

The river continuum concept and its subsequent modifications (Statzner and Higler 1985, Vannote *et al.* 1980), and the focus on resetting physical and biological processes in serial discontinuities (Ward and Stanford 1983), have provided an interesting and quite useful framework for examining the longitudinal differentiation of ecological processes along a stream or river. These concepts involve inputs from the adjacent landscape, for example, as a source of organic material and shading. Indeed, this concept has provided a theoretical basis for several studies concerning organic matter processing in streams (e.g. Elwood *et al.* 1983, Mulholland *et al.* 1985). Of particular importance to this volume is the possibility that similar conceptual frameworks can be developed for ecotones. It may be, for example, that riparian ecotones process organic material in such a way that respiratory quotients can be calculated, or that longitudinal gradients of nutrient or organic matter processing can be described in a way similar to the stream continuum concept. The forthcoming paper by Junk *et al.* (1989) demonstrates not only the power of such an approach but also the importance of considering both the temporal and spatial dimensions of ecotones along large rivers where the adjacent floodplains consist of well-developed riparian forests.

Classification has very practical applications, and there have been several attempts at classifying ecotones (Frissell *et al.* 1986, Wiens *et al.* 1985). Hughes *et al.* (1987) used cluster analysis to demonstrate the use of river basins and aquatic ecoregions (patterns of land-surface form, soil, land use, and potential natural vegetation) to explain ichthyogeographic regions in Oregon. A similar approach was taken in Ohio (Larsen *et al.* 1986). The classifications may be quite useful, since the descriptive attributes are those that can be measured, and in some cases manipulated. However, in the future, classifications may be more appropriately built around functional characteristics (e.g. discontinuities in carbon processing rates or conductance of nutrients such as nitrogen and phosphorus). Indeed, data sets for geographical information systems now frequently contain mapped buffers or ecotones; future generations of these data bases either will have ecotonal functional characteristics as mapped attributes or will include simulation models to describe and ultimately classify ecotones.

An idea receiving increasing attention is that ecotones may be sensitive indicators of global change. Early studies on the grasslands of the Great Plains in North America (Weaver and Albertson 1936) noted the effects of drought not only on individual plant species but on the boundaries between the short-grass steppe and the mixed and tall-grass prairies. If species are near the periphery of their range, and consequently under stress, these ecotonal communities may be among the first to respond to a changing climate. If, because the abiotic and biotic processes in an ecotone are balanced in a tenuous way, or if species from adjacent systems are restrained by minimal forces from invading an ecotone, small changes in the global environment may cause rapid responses in the ecotone. Thus, a significant research challenge for the future involves testing the idea of whether ecotones, or characteristics of ecotones, are valuable as indicators of changes in the global environment. These changes may involve conventional measures such as species composition or rate of nutrient cycling. In addition, there are other potential measures of sensitivity to global change (e.g. rate of energy transfers such as the energy processes in hydrologic transformation, changes in a α-diversity across the landscape, or mathematical distributions of measurable parameters that might be more sensitive, for example, than simple changes in density).

MANAGEMENT OF LAND

In a practical sense, riverine riparian ecosystems are defined as the composite of terrestrial subsystems spanning from the apparent bank of stream channels in medial positions of valley bottoms to the lower edge of upland positions. The definition excludes permanently flooded aquatic areas (Platts *et al.* 1987). A useful working definition of riparian soils is a collection of polypedons distinguished by characteristics indicative of saturation by groundwater during a significant period of the growing season within the rooting depth of the native vegetation (Platts *et al.* 1987). Managing this biological complex of soils, plants, and animals involves a broad array of data sets and managerial objectives. As such, the complexity of riparian ecosystems may require cooperation of several professional disciplines in evaluating the system and designing management structures (DeBano and Heede 1987).

Management of ecotones also requires the application of new knowledge as described in the preceding sections. The challenge is even greater because most management strategies have focussed on specific habitats, not on boundaries between habitats. In response to these needs, the United States Forest Service Intermountain Research Station has established a new Riparian Stream Ecology and Management research work unit based at Boise, Idaho. The purpose is to use a multidisciplinary team to improve the understanding of riparian and stream habitats and improve methods of managing them for conservation of resources and production of livestock, wildlife, and fish (Prouty 1987). Until a few years ago, the primary concern about the riparian zone in the relatively arid areas of North America was the role of streamside vegetation (phreatophytes) in water loss from streams. Now the interest is much broader; for example, ecotones provide forage for domestic animals and represent important habitat for approximately four-fifths of the wildlife species in eastern Oregon (Elmore and Beschta 1987).

Current understanding of riparian ecotones requires an appreciation of the driving physical processes. In an arid or semi-arid aggrading channel and a rising water table, the hydrologic consequence may outweigh the increased loss of water by evapotranspiration: more water is stored during wet seasons, and slow release of water may allow a stream to flow during the driest summers (Elmore and Beschta 1987). Recovery in grazed semi-arid riparian areas can be extremely rapid along low gradient streams that traverse alluvial valleys where streams carry substantial loads of silt during high flows. In practice, however, there are many jeopardies to riparian vegetation, such as changing climatic and precipitation patterns, more frequent flooding, patterns altered by beaver, heavy streamside grazing, improper use of upland watersheds or adjacent slopes, road construction close to channels, and so forth.

Because the riparian components of fish and wildlife habitat can often be manipulated quite quickly, it is often less costly and much easier to immediately benefit a fishery through riparian rehabilitation than through other stream enhancement activities such as the use of artificial channel flow modification structures (Anderson and Ohmart 1985). Rehabilitation procedures require an understanding of the entire ecotonal structure (Minshall 1988) but can take advantage of successional processes that accumulate organic matter and develop vegetation for cover and as a food source.

On broad regional scales, management of ecotones may need to recognise that riparian forests of different hydrologic positions can differ in nutrient retention (Brinson *et al.* 1984, Mitsch *et al.* 1979). A particularly valuable study was conducted in an eastern Illinois agricultural watershed consisting of a small stream embedded in a 1300 km² landscape dominated by croplands. Some stream boundaries contained riparian forests, but these forests were more prevalent in the lower portions of the watershed. The authors measured soluble reactive phosphorus and nitrate-nitrogen in the streams during the year and throughout the watershed. Using a geographic information system, they correlated these nutrient concentrations to characteristics of the watershed, specifically with the following parameters: total square kilometres in the watershed of the sampling station, ratio of urban to agricultural land, and ratio of forested to agricultural land (Osborne and Wiley 1988). Urbanisation rather than agriculture was the major factor controlling soluble reactive phosphorus in the stream throughout the year, and urbanisation explained the majority of the variance in stream nitrogen concentrations during more than half of the year.

Although the Illinois study focusses on the hierarchical characteristics of the watershed, given our knowledge of the role of riparian forests in retaining nutrients (Anderson and Ohmart 1985), it is surprising that the ratio of forested land to agricultural land was not a more important variable in predicting nutrient concentrations in the stream. Osborne and Wiley (1988) suggest that the diminished importance may have been because most of the riparian forest was limited to the lower portions of the watershed and because of the overwhelming importance of urbanisation in determining the phosphorus dynamics. Riparian forests cannot influence nutrients from are point sources, such as municipal treatment plants, nor can these forests influence in any significant way nutrients that enter the surface waters upstream.

There are several lessons from this study that are important for land management. First, most of the nonpoint loading of nutrients to the streams comes during major precipitation peaks and from agricultural sources. However, these loadings depend on agricultural practices, and throughout the year the urban point and nonpoint inputs are more important. Second, the riparian forests can be significant in controlling the nutrients moving into the stream. However, these forests have little effect if they are limited to only parts of the watershed, and cannot influence point sources that bypass the riparian vegetation. Third, the study demonstrates the importance of developing management studies based on year-round measurements and which include the entire watershed (Osborne and Wiley 1988).

Riparian forests frequently occupy steep slopes or flood-prone areas unsuitable for urban development or agriculture. Thus, the conditions precluding development indirectly reduce the nutrient loading of streams by industry and agriculture. Rather than reducing the loading after deposition, riparian areas represent conditions that make loading unlikely. Riparian areas may directly interfere with other potential land uses, and thereby regulate to some extent the connectedness and dominance of other land uses.

Peterjohn and Correll (1984), along with others (Bormann and Likens 1979, Brinson *et al.* 1985, Foster and Fritz 1987, Omernik *et al.* 1981, Whigham *et al.* 1986), recognised the power of using watersheds to examine the role of ecotones in nutrient dynamics. Their study, however, demonstrates an important point concerning the use of information about ecotones in managing the environment. Here, the riparian forest captured nutrients; in fact, the greatest proportion of nutrients were captured within the first 50 m of the forest. This leads to the idea that it may be possible to develop simple regression models or even Redfield-like molecular ratios (C:N:P 106:16:1 for maximum phytoplankton growth) for managing ecotones (Redfield 1958). Currently, the data base is inadequate for building these relatively simple models for management purposes, but future research efforts could remedy this deficiency.

In the area of resource management, more emphasis has been placed on gathering information than on effective and efficient use of available information for decision making and problem solving. Expert systems might be particularly valuable as (1) integrated expert systems, which link management models with natural resource models, (2) intelligent geographic information systems, which permit interpretation of relations within and among landscape data themes, and (3) artificial intelligence (AI) modelling of animal behaviour in relation to the environment (Coulson *et al.* 1987). The limitations are that the rules that are the way of representing knowledge in virtually all expert systems are not well suited to providing advice for problems involving natural systems, and that management in itself is a broad-based problem. A useful strategy may be to separate the 'deep knowledge' theory associated with scientific systems from surface rules for managing those systems. The application of these techniques may be particularly amenable to land-water ecotone management where much of the underlying scientific information is known and the management objectives can be defined.

CONCLUSIONS

There has been no attempt in this paper to further refine the explicit definition of an ecotone. Rather, the concept of a functional boundary or transition zone between ecological systems has been explored in the context of several classes of ecological phenomena. Biodiversity (i.e. the number of species) is often relatively high in ecotones. This biodiversity is caused by several processes both within the ecotone itself and because of its proximity and functional ties to the adjacent ecological systems. For similar reasons, the genetic diversity may also be high in these transitional zones, especially where the ecotones coincide with the extremities of species' distributions.

Certainly, high biological diversity of ecotones is an important attribute, but more recent investigations have focussed on the way that ecotones affect the characteristics of adjacent ecological systems – for example, as sources of species or genetic diversity. Future investigations will concentrate on the ecotone not as an isolated and distinct entity but as an integral component of the landscape.

Water, nutrients, and various materials move across the landscape, transported by animals, wind, subsurface and surface hydrologic flows, and via various human activities. Several studies at the landscape level have demonstrated that ecotones play important roles in controlling these flows. Nutrients, water, and sediment are either retained or their movement retarded in riparian forests. Yet the actual mechanisms are not known (e.g. whether nitrogen is lost by denitrification, immobilised by micro-organisms, or taken up by terrestrial vegetation). Furthermore, the seasonal dynamics and the geomorphic influences have not been described in a sufficient number of ecological situations to permit reasonable generalisations.

Whether or not ecotones are sensitive indicators of widespread changes, such as global warming, is not known. One could hypothesise that ecotones consist of delicate balances of biotic and abiotic patterns, and thus changes in the global environment will tip the balance in favour of one ecological system with the consequent change in the ecotone. However, there are too few data to permit a general conclusion on this subject.

Ecotones have played a significant role in the development and sustenance of humans. Today, ecotones possess many practical values (e.g. critical habitats, sources of agricultural pests and their predators, and as controls of nutrient and water flow). Management of these transitional areas requires a fundamental understanding of the underlying ecological processes coupled with the knowledge to anticipate just how various management strategies will affect those processes. While there are current management efforts in place that focus on ecotones, additional trials and experiments will be required before general management guidelines can be developed. Furthermore, basic experiments and field observations will be necessary from a wide variety of ecotones, especially those in the tropics, to determine the generality of ecological processes and the most appropriate management strategies and procedures.

LITERATURE CITED

Allen, T.F.H., and T.B. Starr. 1981. Hierarchy: perspectives for ecological complexity. University of Chicago Press, Chicago, Illinois, USA.

Anderson, B.W., and R.D. Ohmart. 1985. Riparian revegetation as a mitigating process in stream and river restoration. Pages 41-80 *in* J. Gore, editor. The restoration of rivers and streams. Butterworth Publishers, Boston, Massachusetts, USA.

Askins, R.A., M.J. Philbrick, and D.S. Sugeno. 1987. Relationship between the regional abundance of forest and the composition of forest bird communities. Biological Conservation 39:129-152.

Blake, J.G., and J.R. Karr. 1987. Breeding birds of isolated woodlots: area and habitat relationships. Ecology 68:1724-1734.

Bormann, F.H., and G.E. Likens. 1979. Pattern and process in a forested ecosystem. Springer-Verlag, New York, New York, USA.

Brinson, M.M., H.D. Bradshaw, and M.N. Jones. 1985. Transitions in forested wetlands along gradients of salinity and hydroperiod. Journal of the Elisha Mitchell Scientific Society 101:76-94.

Brinson, M.M., H.D. Bradshaw, and E.S. Kane. 1984. Nutrient assimilative capacity of an alluvial floodplain swamp. Journal of Applied Ecology 21:1041-1057.

Brown, D.E., C.H. Lowe, and J.F. Hausler. 1977. Southwestern riparian communities: their biotic importance and management in Arizona. Pages 201-211 *in* R.R. Johnson and O.A. Jones, editors. Proceedings of the Symposium, on Importance, Preservation and Management of Riparian Habitat. General Technical Report RM-43, United States Forest Service, Rocky Mountain Forest and Range Experiment Station, Fort Collins, Colorado, USA.

Carothers, S.W., R.R. Johnson, and S.W. Aitchison. 1974. Population structure and social organization of southwestern riparian birds. American Zoologist 14:97-108.

Coulson, R.N., L.J. Folse, and D.K. Loh. 1987. Artificial intelligence and natural resource management. Science 237:262-267.

DeBano, L.F., and R.H. Heede. 1987. Enhancement of riparian ecosystems with channel structures. Water Resources Bulletin 23:463-470.

Elmore, W., and R.L. Beschta. 1987. Riparian areas: perceptions in management. Rangelands 9:260-265.

Elwood, J.W., J.D. Newbold, R.V. O'Neill, and H. Van Winkle. 1983. Resource spiralling: an operational paradigm for analyzing lotic ecosystems. Pages 3-27 *in* T.D. Fontaine III and S.M. Bartell, editors. Dynamics of lotic ecosystems. Ann Arbor Science, Ann Arbor, Michigan, USA.

Forman, R.T.T., and M. Godron. 1986. Landscape ecology. John Wiley and Sons, New York, New York, USA.

Foster, D.R., and S.C. Fritz. 1987. Mire development, pool formation and landscape processes on patterned fens in Dalarna, central Sweden. Journal of Ecology 75:409-437.

Frissell, C.A., W.J. Liss, C.E. Warren, and M.D. Hurley. 1986. A hierarchical framework for stream habitat classification: viewing streams in a watershed context. Environmental Management 10:199-214.

Hehnke, M., and C.P. Stone. 1978. Value of riparian vegetation to avian populations along the Sacramento River system. Pages 228-235 *in* R.R. Johnson and J.F. McCormick, editors. Strategies for protection and management of floodplain wetlands and other riparian ecosystems. General Technical Report WO-12, United States Forest Service, Washington, D.C., USA.

Holland, M.M. (compiler). 1988. SCOPE/MAB technical consultations on landscape boundaries: report of a SCOPE/MAB workshop on ecotones. Biology International, Special Issue 17:47-106.

Hubbard, J.P. 1977. Importance of riparian ecosystems: biotic considerations. Pages 14-18 *in* R.R. Johnson and O.A. Jones, editors. Proceedings of the Symposium on Importance, Preservation and Management of Riparian Habitat. General Technical Report RM-43, United States Forest Service, Rocky Mountain Forest and Range Experiment Station, Fort Collins, Colorado, USA.

Hughes, R.M., E. Rexstad, and C.E. Bond. 1987. The relationship of aquatic ecoregions, river basins and physiographic provinces to the ichthyogeographic regions of Oregon. Copeia 2:423-432.

Junk, W.G., P.B. Bayley and R.E. Sparks. 1989. The flood pulse concept in river-flooding systems. Canadian Journal of Fisheries and Aquatic Sciences Special Publication 106: 110-127.

Karr, J.R., and I.J. Schlosser. 1978. Water resources and the land-water interface. Science 201:229-234.

Kroodsma, R.L. 1984. Ecological factors associated with degrees of edge effect in breeding birds. Journal of Wildlife Management 48:418-425.

Larsen, D.P., J.M. Omernik, R.M. Hughes, C.M. Rohm, T.R. Whittier, A.J. Kinney, A.L. Gallant, and D. Dudley. 1986. Correspondence between spatial patterns in fish assemblages in Ohio stream and aquatic ecoregions. Environmental Management 10:815-828.

Likens, G.E., and F.H. Bormann. 1974. Linkages between terrestrial and aquatic ecosystems. BioScience 24:447-456.

Lowrance, R., R. Leonard, and J. Sheridan. 1985. Managing riparian ecosystems to control non-point pollution. Journal of Soil and Water Conservation 40:87-91.

Lowrance, R., R.L. Todd, and L.E. Asmussen. 1983. Waterborne nutrient budgets for the riparian zone in an agricultural watershed. Agricultural Ecosytems Environment 10:371-384.

Lowrance, R., R.L. Todd, and L.E. Asmussen. 1984a. Nutrient cycling in an agricultural watershed: I. Phreatic movement. Journal of Environmental Quality 22:27.

Lowrance, R., R.L. Todd, and L.E. Asmussen. 1984b. Nutrient cycling in an agricultural watershed: II. Streamflow and artificial drainage. Journal of Environmental Quality 13:27-32.

Lowrance, R., R. Todd, J. Fair, Jr., O. Hendrickson, Jr., R. Leonard, and L. Asmussen. 1984c. Riparian forests as nutrient filters in agricultural watersheds. BioScience 34:374-377.

Lynch, J.F., and D.F. Whigham. 1984. Effects of forest fragmentation on breeding bird

19

communities in Maryland, USA. Biological Conservation 28:287-324.

McArthur, J.V., and G.R. Marzolf. 1986. Interactions of the bacterial assemblages of a prairie stream with dissolved organic carbon from riparian vegetation. Hydrobiologia 134:193-199.

McArthur, J.V., and G.R. Marzolf. 1987. Changes in soluble nutrients of prairie riparian vegetation during decomposition on a floodplain. American Midland Naturalist 117:26-34.

Minshall, G.W. 1988. Stream ecosystem theory: a global perspective. Journal of the North American Benthological Society 7:263-288.

Mitsch, W.J., C.L. Dorge, and J.R. Wiemhof. 1979. Ecosystem dynamics and a phosphorus budget of an alluvial cypress swamp in southern Illinois. Ecology 60:1116-1124.

Mulholland, P.J., J.D. Newbold, J.W. Elwood, L.A. Ferren, and J.R. Webster. 1985. Phosphorus spiralling in a woodland stream: seasonal variations. Ecology 66:1012-1023.

Ohmart, R.D., and B. Anderson. 1982. North American desert riparian ecosystems. Pages 433-479 *in* G.L. Bender, editor. Reference handbook on the deserts of North America. Greenwood Press, Westport, Connecticut, USA.

Omernik, J.M., A.R. Abernathy, and L.M. Male. 1981. Stream nutrient levels and proximity of agricultural and forest land to streams: some relationships. Journal of Soil and Water Conservation 36:227-231.

O'Neill, R.V., D.L. DeAngelis, J.B. Waide, and T.F.H. Allen. 1986. A hierarchical concept of ecosystems. Princeton University Press, Princeton, New Jersey, USA.

Osborne, L.L., and M.J. Wiley. 1988. Empirical relationships between land use/cover and stream water quality in an agricultural watershed. Journal of Environmental Management 26:9-27.

Ovington, J.D., D. Heitkamp, and D.B. Lawrence. 1963. Plant biomass and productivity of prairie, savanna, oakwood, and maize field ecosystems in central Minnesota. Ecology 44:52-63.

Peterjohn, W.T., and D.L. Correll. 1984. Nutrient dynamics in an agricultural watershed: observations on the role of a riparian forest. Ecology 65:1466-1475.

Platts, W.S., C. Armour, G.D. Booth, M. Bryant, J.L. Bufford, P. Cuplin, S. Jensen, G.W. Lienkaemper, J.R. Sedell, and J.S. Tuhy. 1987. Methods for evaluating riparian habitats with applications to management. General Technical Report INT-221, United States Forest Service, Intermountain Forest and Range Experiment Station, Ogden, Utah, USA.

Prouty, M. 1987. A riparian research program. Rangelands 9:271-272.

Redfield, A.C. 1958. The biological control of chemical factors in the environment. American Scientist 46:205-222.

Ricklefs, R.E. 1987. Community diversity: relative roles of local and regional processes. Science 235:167-171.

Risser, P.G., J.R. Karr, and R.T. Forman. 1984. Landscape ecology: directions and approaches. Illinois Natural History Survey, Special Publication Number 2, Champaign, Illinois, USA.

Schlosser, I.J., and J.R. Karr. 1981. Water quality in agricultural watersheds: impact of riparian vegetation during base flow. Water Resources Bulletin 17:233-240.

Scott, J.M., B. Csuti, J.D. Jacobi, and J.E. Estes. 1987. Species richness. BioScience 37:872-788.

Statzner, B., and B. Higler. 1985. Questions and comments on the river continuum concept. Canadian Journal of Fisheries and Aquatic Sciences 42:1038-1044.

Szaro, R.C. 1980. Factors influencing bird populations in southwestern riparian forests. Pages 403-418 *in* R.M. DeGraaf, editor. Workshop Proceedings, Management of Western Forests and Grasslands for Nongame Birds. General Technical Report INT-86, United States Forest Service, Intermountain Forest and Range Experiment Station, Ogden, Utah, USA.

Szaro, R.C., and S.C. Belfit. 1986. Herpetofauna use of a desert riparian island and its adjacent scrub habitat. Journal of Wildlife Management 50:752-761.

Szaro, R.C., and M.D. Jakle. 1985. Avian use of a desert riparian island and its adjacent scrub habitat. Condor 87:511-519.

Urban, D.L., R.V. O'Neill, and H.H. Shugart, Jr. 1987. Landscape ecology. BioScience 37:119-127.

Vannote, R.L., G.W. Minshall, K.W. Cummins, J.R. Sedell, and C.E. Cushing. 1980. The river continuum concept. Canadian Journal of Fisheries and Aquatic Sciences 37:130-137.

Verry, E.S., and D.R. Timmons. 1982. Waterborne nutrient flow through an upland-peatland watershed in Minnesota. Ecology 63:1456-1467.

Ward, J.V., and J.A. Stanford. 1983. The serial discontinuity concept of lotic ecosystems. Pages 29-42 *in* T.D. Fontaine III and S.M. Bartell, editors. Dynamics of lotic ecosystems. Ann Arbor Science, Ann Arbor, Michigan, USA.

Weaver, J.E. 1960. Flood plain vegetation of the central Missouri Valley and contacts of woodland with prairie. Ecological Monographs 30:37-64.

Weaver, J.E., and F.W. Albertson. 1936. Effects of the great drought on the prairies of Iowa, Nebraska, and Kansas. Ecology 17:567-639.

Whigham, D.F., C. Chitterling, B. Palmer, and J. O'Neill. 1986. Modification of runoff from upland watersheds: the influence of a diverse riparian ecosystem. Pages 305-332 *in* D.L. Correll, editor. Watershed research perspectives. Smithsonian Institution Press, Washington, D.C., USA.

Whitney, G.G., and W.C. Davis. 1986. From primitive woods to cultivated woodlots: Thoreau and the forest history of Concord, Massachusetts. Journal of Forest History 30:70-81.

Wiens, J.A., C.S. Crawford, and J.R. Gosz. 1985. Boundary dynamics: a conceptual framework for studying landscape ecosystems. Oikos 45:421-427.

Wilcove, D.S. 1985. Nest predation in forest tracts and the decline of migratory songbirds. Ecology 66:1211-1214.

Key words: Biodiversity, ecotone concept, management, material flows.

CHAPTER 3

ECOLOGICAL MODELS AND THE ECOTONE

Herman H. Shugart

ABSTRACT

The ecosystem concept, as originally proposed by Tansley, emphasised the ecosystem as a 'system of definition' rather than a tangible physical entity. If the ecotone is a boundary between ecosystems, then one is presented with an incongruity: the ecosystem is seen as arbitrary and unbounded, and the ecotone concept stresses bounds and boundaries. This chapter takes a pragmatic approach to categorising ecotones with respect to the causes of discontinuities in ecological variables of interest. This categorisation includes internal and external control of these causes. The discussions are based on considerations arising from attempts to develop computer models of ecotones.

INTRODUCTION

In a classic paper written by Tansley in 1935, the term *ecosystem* was defined as an arbitrary system with respect to both its spatial extent and the phenomena considered:

> But the more fundamental conception is, as it seems to me, the whole *system* (in the sense of physics), including not only the organism-complex, but also the whole complex of physical factors forming what we call the environment of the biome – the habitat factors in the widest sense. Though the organisms may claim our primary interest, when we are trying to think fundamentally we cannot separate them from their special environment, with which they form one physical system.
>
> It is the systems so formed which, from the point of view of the ecologist, are the basic units of nature on the face of the earth.... These *ecosystems*, as we may call them, are of the most various kinds and sizes. They form one category of the multitudinous physical

systems of the universe, which range from the universe as a whole down to the atom.

In this quotation (p. 299), which incidentally contains the first use of the word *ecosystem* in the English language, Tansley stressed that ecosystems are of various kinds and sizes. He viewed this relative arbitrariness as a necessary step in formulating an ecological science on a par with physics and other more established sciences. The value of the ecosystem as an abstract concept has been proven in the 50 years since Tansley coined the term.

If one applies a Tansleyan view of the ecosystem to ecotones, however, one confronts certain difficulties: ecotones are generally thought of as boundaries between systems (Hansen *et al.* 1988a,b); if the systems are arbitrary, the positions of the boundaries are also arbitrary. Thus, the fundamental concepts on which ecosystem sciences are built are at odds with a static view of an ecotone between systems. Depending on our view of the ecosystems involved, the ecotones or boundaries could be whatever positions we happen to assign to them. There is an interesting incongruity: the ecosystem is seen as arbitrary and unbounded and the ecotone concept stresses bounds and boundaries (McCoy *et al.* 1986).

This difference undoubtedly encourages debate and semantic arguments between scientists interested in ecotones and ecosystems. I would suggest that we take a rather pragmatic approach to the problem of understanding ecotones by defining them as obvious discontinuities between ecological systems. While this definition might not completely satisfy everyone, it does allow us to discuss the influences that might cause such boundaries to be maintained over long periods. The most obvious ecotones in terrestrial systems involve transitions from systems dominated by one life form to systems dominated by another (McCoy *et al.* 1986, Wiens *et al.* 1985), such as transitions from prairie to forest along continental moisture gradients (Carpenter 1935), along timberlines (Armand 1985, Payette and Filion 1985), or from field to woodlot in an agricultural landscape (Forman and Godron 1986, Wiens *et al.* 1985, Burgess and Sharpe 1981). The feature that marks these ecotones is that they are easily perceived by the observer, in part because of the change in the stature of the plants affected by the transition.

Of course, this is a simplified view of what an ecotone is, and one that is highly dependent on contrast between the different elements making up the landscape in its definition. This degree of contrast is, of course, highly dependent on the observer and the variables used by the observer to categorise the landscape elements (Urban *et al.* 1987). For example, a mangrove forest bordering the sea would appear to the naked eye to be a sharp ecotone between a body of salt water and a forest of a very peculiar kind of tree. But, from the point of view of a small fish or shrimp using the mangrove as a nesting ground and living in the open ocean, the mangrove forest is simply a resting place in a more-or-less saltwater environment. Thus, what to the human observer might seem to be a sharp boundary would appear to the crustacean observer to be no boundary at all.

The observer-dependent nature of ecotones does not invalidate the usefulness of the ecotone concept, if the pitfalls of arbitrariness in their definition are avoided. An essential feature of any ecotone is a discontinuity or rapid change in some observable environmental variable. Thus, in the example above, in which a mangrove system was characterised as relatively unbounded from the point of view of shrimp, a boundary with respect to one or more observable variables still exists.

The body of mathematical theory for dealing with discontinuous change in observable variables is quite large (Levin 1976, 1978; Levin and Paine 1974). It is also a rich field of current investigation in mathematics (Okubo 1980). Some of this work probably has direct application in understanding ecotone boundaries (Sprugel 1976, van Leeuwen 1966, van der Maarel 1976). My intention in this chapter is to try to categorise ecotones in a functional way that would allow us to draw from this body of mathematical literature.

EXOGENOUS AND AUTONOMOUS CONTROLS OF ECOTONE FORMATION

A boundary in nature may be created by discontinuities in the external influences controlling the ecological systems or by discontinuities in the internal working of the systems themselves. This distinction tempts one to categorise ecotones as either endogenously or exogenously created or maintained. Endogenous and exogenous control of succession was put forward as a concept in the early 1920s (Tansley 1929) and essentially abandoned by Tansley, its originator, in the same paper in which he coined the term *ecosystems* (Tansley 1935). Rather than characterising systems solely as created by exogenous or autonomous influences, a more fruitful approach is to investigate the interaction of these influences in the formation of sharp boundaries between ecological systems.

Fig. 3.1 illustrates a spectrum of equilibrium system responses to values of environmental gradient. In Fig. 3.1A, the environmental response to changes in the gradient is smooth and linear. In Fig. 3.1B, the response shows an abrupt break, perhaps due to a threshold response in one of the components making up the ecological system. In Fig. 3.1C, the response has a twist, or a bending back. In this situation, the response to the system can have two stable equilibrium states. In these cases, the state of the ecological system with respect to a given value of the environmental conditions driving it depends on the history of the system with respect to the environmental conditions. This is a class of behaviour called hysteresis.

25

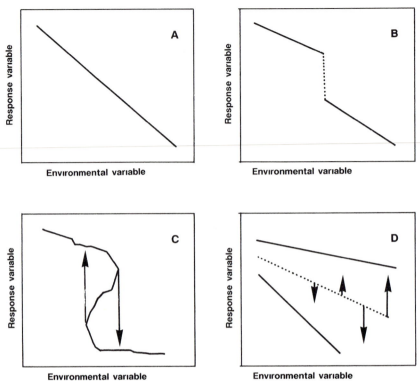

Figure 3.1 Ecosystem response to an environmental variable. (A) Case in which the response of the ecosystem is smooth with respect to the environmental variable. (B) Case in which the response is discontinuous. (C) Case in which the response is folded and results in hysteresis. (D) Case in which the system can have multiple responses

Hysteresis has been discussed in several recent papers in the mathematical field called catastrophe theory. In Fig. 3.1D, the system has two stable states with respect to the environmental gradient and can be pushed by internal interactions to take on one or the other.

The responses shown can be thought of as a continuum of responses of the system to the environmental variable. The linear response shown in Fig. 3.1A is bent to form the threshold response in Fig. 3.1B, which is, in turn, contorted to an even greater degree to produce hysteretic behaviour shown in Fig. 3.1C. The zone of multiple states in Fig. 3.1C could, in fact, be considered to be the multiple-state case in Fig. 3.1D. Thus, the various responses shown in Fig. 3.1 grade into one another depending on internal ecosystem responses, which presumably change the shape of the response curve to produce the variety of curves seen in Fig. 3.1. The shape of the curve is controlled to some degree by the autonomous internal features of the ecosystem.

The environmental gradient itself can be continuous, discontinuous, or interrupted to form a variety of patterns. Thus, an interaction between the environmental gradient and the response of the ecological system (that is, an interaction of autonomous and exogenous factors) controls the nature and pattern of the ecotones produced. These examples may seem simple or even trivial, but they are capable of being exercised to produce a rich range of patterns in space. In the next section, this range of patterns is discussed in more detail.

SMOOTH RESPONSES TO ENVIRONMENTAL GRADIENTS

When the response from the ecological system to changes in the driving environmental gradient is relatively smooth (such as shown in Fig. 3.1A), the creation of an ecotone is dependent on relatively abrupt changes in the quantitative value of the environmental gradient (Forman and Gordon 1986). It appears that many of the ecotones we see in nature are, in fact, of this type. The boundary between field and forest depends on whether or not plants are harvested. Boundaries between systems, one of which has been exposed to wildfire and the other has not, are (or can be) created by discontinuities in the fundamental driving gradient (fire history) to which the ecosystem has a relatively smooth response. The list of ecotones maintained by physical factors is large (Ghiselin 1977), and these cases are treated in greater detail by other articles in this volume.

Even when the response of an ecological system to changes in the environmental variable is smooth, we can still obtain a rich array of patterns in the structure of the boundaries themselves (Leak and Graber 1974). For example, in Fig. 3.2 we have two different ecotones, each created in a system having essentially a smooth response to the environmental driving variables. In Fig. 3.2A, the interaction between the vegetation and the environment causes a slight change in the environmental variable, and the ecotone is shown advancing from a forest into a grassland. This is producing several structural changes (Ranney 1978): the trees farthest back in the system have cantilevered limbs reaching out to the edge; there are small shrubs; and there may well be certain species that can compete with the grasses and the trees only in this ecotone phase. Many animals have evolved to utilise these sorts of ecotonal habitats; often they are totally dependent on ecotones, or at least on living in environments with mixtures of different habitat types. In Fig. 3.2B, we see a fixed edge – in this case fixed by a fence with agricultural crops on one side. This sharp discontinuity produces several structural features characteristic of the edge. Trees alongside the fence have long branches cantilevered into the field, and they have a geometry totally different from that of trees in closed canopy forest. The tendency for trees to be broad at the edge of the fence creates a hiatus (about one canopy in diameter) in the presence of large trees back from the edge. Thus, there is a spatial ordering of tree positions determined by the edge. When trees die

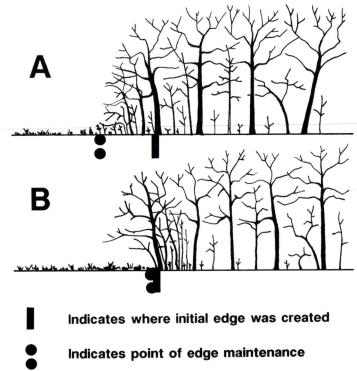

I   **Indicates where initial edge was created**

●
●   **Indicates point of edge maintenance**
●

Figure 3.2 Two common structures found at the edges between forests and fields. From Ranney (1978)

and fall out of such a fixed edge, they leave a scalloped appearance that eventually fills (Forman and Godron 1986). Vines and shrubs that are able to tolerate the conditions caused by maintaining the edge tend to prosper in such a fixed edge (Harper *et al.* 1970, Harper 1977).

Even though the responses to the environment pictured in Fig. 3.2 are smooth and uncomplicated, we see that the result, either in a transient case (Fig. 3.2A) or in a nontransient case (Fig. 3.2B), is diversity in structural form. These structural features can, in some cases, support animals and plants found nowhere else in the ecosystems lying on either side of the boundary (Wales 1972, Galli *et al.* 1976). The simple example shown in Fig. 3.1A of a smooth ecosystem response to an environmental gradient should not be considered a trivial case in any sense. The combination of transient behaviour and variable geometrics of the vegetation can create a rich array of microhabitats and microsite features. Furthermore, certain organisms are adapted or preadapted to the unique situations found in such edges (Johnson 1947). For example, in the fixed edges of many agricultural-forest interfaces, the flora has a strong component of plants with avian dispersed seed, because these edges are popular perch spots for birds. The presence of the ecotone itself can amplify the advantages of certain life history strategies over others (Grime 1979), so that there is a change in the fundamental nature of the ecosystem compositionally as well as structurally.

THRESHOLD RESPONSES

Ecological systems can change abruptly along the smooth environmental gradients. Such responses can have their origins at many different organisational levels. For example, one may see an abrupt gradient response when a physiological tolerance of some sort has been exceeded along the gradient, and in some cases these transitions can be fairly rapid. Typical examples are salinity gradients, temperature gradients, gradients involving a toxic material in the soil, or gradients in the availability of moisture, oxygen, or other essential resources. In other cases, abrupt responses can have origins in the interactions and species populations. In terrestrial plant populations, there can be rapid changes in the biological responses when the environment shifts the competitive advantage from one species to another. In these cases, the threshold response can be a complicated result of both physiological and competitive interactions. In these cases, and in threshold responses in general, experimentation is often necessary to determine if the threshold is a product of the internal system dynamics or of a fundamental physiological rule. One common protocol, the sort used in terrestrial communities, is to transplant seed material to different environments to try to get an idea of the ecological amplitude of the species in the absence of competition. Indeed, transplant experiments have proven valuable in interpreting gradient responses in plant communities at a larger scale.

It is often difficult to determine, even in amplifications of experimental protocols, whether these apparent boundaries caused by thresholdlike responses are continuous or discontinuous functions. In general, the experimental methods are such that they are performed at a qualitative level, or at least in a relatively small set of environments. Such experiments simply do not have the resolution to determine the continuity of the response function such as the one shown in Fig. 3.1B.

Regardless of the difficulties in determining the details of threshold responses creating ecotones, these responses can create internally generated boundaries between ecological systems that are under strong autonomous or internal control (Odum 1990). If the ecosystem response is a threshold response or a thresholdlike response, the ecotone occurrence depends on the values of the environmental gradient. In the case of threshold response it is possible for ecotonal situations to occur over large areas if the conditions of the environmental variables associated with an abrupt transition occur frequently.

The smooth response discussed earlier and the threshold response are related in the sense that they are both single-value responses to the environmental gradient. In a sense, the relative arbitrariness of scaling of many environmental gradients could make it difficult to determine whether a response was smooth or threshold. The experimental protocols needed to distinguish discontinuous responses from smooth, abrupt responses are not available. In a practical sense, the differences between smooth and threshold responses are, in part, a matter of scale and perception, given our current ability to test for these sorts of responses.

HYSTERETIC RESPONSES AND IMPLICATIONS OF THE CATASTROPHE THEORY

In Fig. 3.1C, we have a case that is experimentally different from either the smooth or the threshold response. This dynamic response is quantitatively different from the two in terms of the environmental variables, but it can be derived from the other two responses by an increased bending of the curve of the response variable as a function of the environmental gradient. If these ecosystem responses were to be described by a system of differential equations, the smooth responses would tend to be dominated by first-order terms and the thresholdlike responses would have significant quadratic terms in the equations. To obtain a response curve such as shown in Fig. 3.1C requires a significant cubic term in the equation for ecosystem response as a function of the environmental gradient. It is these higher-order terms (cubic or greater) that produce the behaviour that will be described below. These higher-order terms are often omitted when statistical techniques are used to try to fit ecosystem responses to the environmental gradient.

In the case of a hysteretic response, there is a range over which the response function folds back. In this range, there is a possibility of two different responses, depending on the history of the changes in the enviromental variable. The response curves in Fig. 3.1 are based on an assumption that the ecosystem response is a dynamic response to the environmental variable and is the equilibrium case.

As an example of what a hysteretic response might look like in nature, let us consider a stochastic computer model result. In this case (Fig. 3.3) the FORET model, a forest stand simulation model, was used in theoretical exercises in which two species, *Fagus grandifolia* (American beech) and *Liriodendron tulipifera* (yellow poplar), were allowed to compete against each other as an environmental condition (growing degree days) varied slowly over several thousand years. Fig. 3.3 shows the percentage of *Liriodendron* in the stand under these different environmental conditions. Since the model simulates only two species, the percentage of *Fagus* is the difference between 100% and the percentage of *Liriodendron*. There is an apparently hysteretic response in the behaviour of the model under a

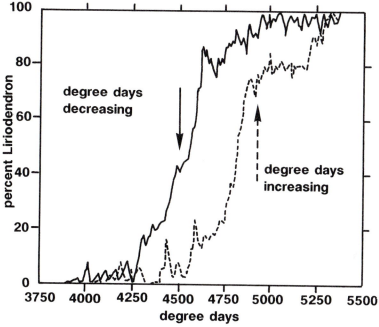

Figure 3.3 Percentage of total stand biomass that is attributable to *Liriodendron tulipifera* in a two-species mixture with *Fagus grandifolia* under gradually changing degree-day (F day) values. Each curve is the mean value of five simulated 1/12-ha stands as the annual degree-day value is increased (dashed line) or decreased (solid line) between 3800 and 5300 (2111 and 2944°C day) at the rate of 0.2 degree day/yr. Reprinted from Shugart *et al.* (1980)

simulated warming or cooling that arises from the differences in stand structure when *Fagus* or *Liriodendron* dominate the stand.

When the stand is dominated by *Fagus* under cooler conditions, the life history attributes of *Fagus* lead to a mixed-age forest. *Fagus* is a shade-tolerant species, capable of regenerating under forest conditions and not requiring gaps for its regeneration habit. In the *Fagus*-dominated forest, the forest comprises trees of all ages and sizes, with an increase in regeneration and growth of subordinate trees when a canopy tree is eliminated. *Liriodendron*, a shade-intolerant species, is planted every year in the simulated cases, but the trees are shaded out as seedlings by the relatively dense canopy.

If one warms the *Fagus* forest very slowly, eventually a point occurs at which conditions are sufficiently favourable for *Liriodendron* growth that the *Liriodendron* seedlings can grow through the gaps created by the death of a large tree before the subordinate trees can grow to close the gap. When this occurs, *Liriodendron* becomes the dominant species in the stand because of its taller stature. *Liriodendron* approaches 100% in the warming degree-

31

day condition. The structure of forest becomes even-aged and the dynamics are cohort-driven.

After a large *Liriodendron* tree dies in the *Liriodendron*-dominated forest, a cohort of *Liriodendron* seedlings becomes established and grows as a virtually even-aged stand, the trees of which compete with one another until, after about 200 yr, a single tree comes to dominate the stand. This tree suppresses both *Liriodendron* and *Fagus* trees at a relatively small size. When this large tree eventually dies, it creates a large canopy opening and a second opportunity for *Liriodendron* and *Fagus* seedlings to compete for canopy dominance. Under relatively warm conditions, *Liriodendron* will always win this race, since its growth rate is superior to that of *Fagus*. Thus, at the extreme ends of this climatic spectrum, one has two very different forest dynamics: a mixed-age dynamic with tree replacement and growth, and a second dynamic feature gap-phase replacement with the death of large trees creating large regeneration events. Both of these dynamics, once installed at a site, tend to be self-sustaining. For this reason, a *Fagus* forest, under warming conditions, tends to remain *Fagus* even into a climatic condition at which, were the forest *Liriodendron*, it would remain *Liriodendron*. Thus, in the intermediate range of growing degree days shown in Fig. 3.3, either forest can persist depending on the history of conditions antecedent to the generation of the forest structure.

If one imagined the x-axis of growing degree days as being a climatic gradient, such as a continental gradient from north to south or an elevational gradient from the top to the bottom of a mountain, the implication would be that there should be a rapid change from *Fagus* to *Liriodendron* at some point. The sharp discontinuity would be at one position or another, depending on whether or not the gradient has been exposed to a climatic warming or cooling.

Such an ecotonal boundary is generated by internal conditions involving feedback between the species of trees involved (Hansen and Walker 1985). The ecotone is generated by autonomous factors. The position of the ecotone depends on historical, or exogenous, conditions. Thus, the understanding of the location of an ecotone, in the case of hysteretic ecological responses to environmental gradients, is history dependent and requires a knowledge of both exogenous forces, particularly the past history of the environmental driving variable, and the nature of the internal variables.

Ecotones of this sort have several unusual features. For example, if one altered the ecotone in the range where two stable states are possible by some external human pertubation, the system could change from the stable state to the other, and this change would be either irreversible or difficult to reverse. Often environmental management involves monitoring for change in response to some human pertubation and then ameliorating the human pertubation when change is observed. In ecotonal areas created by hysteretic responses, such a management strategy might serve only to

32

change the system from one state to another. Once change is observable, a hysteretically responding system may already be moving towards the alternate state. Land use planning in systems with hysteretic responses requires an understanding of fundamental system dynamics. Simple monitoring schemes cannot guarantee that the ecosystem will always remain in a desired configuration.

For systems having the potential of multiple stable states across a long range of environmental driving variables (Fig. 3.1D), the comments made with respect to hysteretic systems in the range in which they have multiple stable states also pertain. Such systems would be difficult to manage, and would be capable of having abrupt transitions subsequently maintained internally at arbitrary points along environmental gradients. Experimental protocols for determining whether or not systems have, in fact, two stable states would seem straightforward. These protocols would involve a demonstration that, under equivalent environmental conditions, a given ecosystem can be manifested in two very different ways.

Unfortunately, in large natural systems, the ability to control environmental variables is rarely such that any two places replicate one another with any degree of exactness. Also, the biological response is typically subject to considerable sample variation. For this reason, although the experimental protocols for determining the multiple stable states of the system are relatively straightforward, the ability to conduct such experiments is limited. Recognising that demonstration of multiple stable states in nature is normally subject to data-related difficulties, it is interesting to note that this result often springs from ecological models, particularly models involving competition among sessile organisms.

ECOTONES AND NON-EQUILIBRIUM SYSTEMS

The examples treated to this point involve systems that seek an equilibrium – in some cases multiple equilibria – in response to a given set of environmental conditions. It has been illustrated that a fairly interesting array of ecotone or discontinuous responses can be produced either by discontinuities in the environmental variables or by internal discontinuities generated in the ecosystems themselves (DeAngelis *et al.* 1986, Okubo 1980). Another more complex, but very interesting, approach involves creating discontinuities in nature in nonequilibrium systems (Turing 1952, Okubo 1978, Mimura 1980). The behaviour of systems of this sort is often erratic or chaotic. Such systems have been the focus of considerable recent theoretical ecological work, particularly with regard to population oscillations (Addicott *et al.* 1989). The same fundamental dynamics that produce chaotic behaviour in the demography of populations can be used to generate patterns for spatial dimensions, particularly when the population dynamics are coupled with diffusionlike equations (Okubo 1980). What is involved here, in the simplest case, might be a population dynamic that was locally chaotic, and that spread across a landscape by diffusion processes – with areas of high population density moving to areas of lower density. It is interesting that this class of mathematics can generate geometric patterns with apparent coherence, even in cases where the patterns are not manifested by any change in the underlying environmental gradients (see Bullock 1976, DeAngelis *et al.* 1986).

CONCLUDING REMARKS

The overall goal of this chapter has been to discuss the ecotone concept as it is related to ecological modelling. The principal conclusion from this discussion is that one valuable contribution of ecological modelling for ecotone studies is in helping define ecotones in the context of ecosystems.

The classic view of the ecosystem (Tansley's originally definition quoted at the beginning of this chapter) does not easily accommodate the 'ecotone' idea for two fundamental reasons. First, the term *ecosystem* was coined as an alternative to the organismic view of the community, which Tansley explicitly considered an abused term in vegetation science. An ecotone might be a boundary between communities, if one takes a view of the community similar to that generally attributed to Clements (1916) and championed by John Phillips (see the July 1935 issue of *Ecology* dedicated to H.C. Cowles for position papers from most of the antagonists in this now classic ecological debate). However, this point of view is a step away from the view of the originators of the ecosystem concept. Second, given that an ecosystem, as originally defined by Tansley, is what systems scientists refer to today as a 'system of definition' or 'system of interest,' if the ecotone had some unique properties (and the other papers in this volume indicate that it does), it follows that the ecotone would become the system of definition, or the ecosystem *sensu stricta*.

The aim of this paper is not to dwell on the niceties of definitions from 50 years ago. Rather, it is important to note the recent work with ecological models and the development of mathematics, which is better able to treat the dynamics of abrupt change in dynamic systems. This gives considerable power to treat systems displaying discontinuous changes along smooth gradients in a manner that is both rigorous and does not fundamentally conflict with the ecosystem concept.

ACKNOWLEDGEMENTS

I thank John Paster, Robert J. Naiman, Dean L. Urban, and an anonymous reviewer for several helpful comments and advice during the development of this manuscript. This research was supported in part by the United States National Aeronautics and Space Administration (Grant NAG-5-

1018) and the United States National Science Foundation (Grant BSR 87-02333).

LITERATURE CITED

Addicott, J.F., J.M. Aho, M.F. Antolin, D.K. Padilla, J.S. Richardson, and D.A. Doluk. 1989. Ecological neighborhoods: scaling environmental patterns. Oikos, *in press.*

Armand, A.D. 1985. The change of vegetation near the timberline. Inter-Nord 17:59-62.

Bullock, S.H. 1976. Consequences of limited seed dispersal within simulated annual populations. Oecologia 24:247-256.

Burgess, R.L., and D.M. Sharpe (editors). 1981. Forest island dynamics in man-dominated landscapes. Springer-Verlag, New York, New York, USA.

Carpenter, J.R. 1935. Fluctuations in biotic communities. I. Prairie-forest ecotone of central Illinois. Ecology 16:203-212.

Clements, F.E. 1916. Plant succession: an analysis of the development of vegetation. Publication 242, Carnegie Institute of Washington, Washington, D.C., USA.

De Angelis, D.L., W.M. Post, and C.C. Travis. 1986. Positive feedback in natural systems. Springer-Verlag, New York, New York, USA.

Forman, R.T.T., and M. Godron. 1986. Landscape ecology. John Wiley and Sons, New York, USA.

Galli, A.E., C.F. Leck, and R.T.T. Forman. 1976. Avian distribution patterns in forest islands of different sizes in central New Jersey. Auk 93:356-364.

Ghiselin, J. 1977. Analyzing ecotones to predict biotic productivity. Environmental Management 1:235-238.

Grime, J.P. 1979. Plant strategies and vegetarian processes. Wiley, Chichester, UK and New York, USA.

Hansen, A.J., F. di Castri, and R.J. Naiman. 1988a. Ecotones: what and why? Biology International, Special Issue 17:9-46.

Hansen, A.J., F. di Castri, and P.G. Risser. 1988b. A new SCOPE project. Ecotones in a changing environment: the theory and management of landscape boundaries. Biology International, Special Issue 17:137-163.

Hansen, A.J., and B.H. Walker. 1985. The dynamic landscape: perturbations, biotic response, biotic patterns. South African Institute of Ecology Bulletin 4:5-14.

Harper, J.L. 1977. Population biology of plants. Academic Press, New York, USA.

Harper, J.L., P.H. Lovell, and K.G. Moore. 1970. The shapes and sizes of seeds. Annual Review of Ecology and Systematics 1:327-356.

Johnson, V.R. 1947. Breeding birds of the forest edge in Illinois. Condor 49:45-53.

Leak, W.B., and R.E. Graber. 1974. A method for detecting migration of forest vegetation. Ecology 55:1425-1427.

Levin, S.A. 1976. Population dynamic models in heterogeneous environments. Annual Review of Ecology and Systematics 7:287-310.

Levin, S.A. 1978. Pattern formation in ecological communities. Pages 433-465 in J.H. Steele, editor. Spatial pattern in plankton communities. Plenum, New York, USA.

Levin, S.A., and R.T. Paine. 1974. Disturbance, patch formation and community structure. Proceedings of the National Academy of Sciences, USA 71:2744-2747.

McCoy, E.D., S.S. Bell, and K. Walters. 1986. Identifying biotic boundaries along environmental gradients. Ecology 67:749-759.

Mimura, M. 1980. Asymptotic behavior of a parabolic system related to a planktonic prey and predator system. SIAM Journal on Applied Mathematics 37:499-512.

Odum, W.E. 1990. Internal processes influencing the maintenance of ecotones, *this volume.*

Okubo, A. 1978. Horizontal dispersion and critical scales for phytoplankton patches. Pages 21-42 in J.H. Steele, editor. Spatial pattern in plankton communities. Plenum, New York, USA.

Okubo, A. 1980. Diffusion and ecological problems: mathematical models. Springer-Verlag, New York, USA.

Payette, S., and L. Filion. 1985. White spruce expansion at the tree line and recent climatic change. Canadian Journal of Forest Research 15:241-251.

Ranney, J.W. 1978. Edges of forest islands: structure, composition, and importance to regional forest dynamics. Dissertation. University of Tennesee, Knoxville, Tennessee, USA.

Shugart, H.H., Jr., W.R. Emanuel, D.C. West, and D.L. DeAngelis. 1980. Environmental gradients in a simulation model of a beech-yellow-poplar stand. Mathematical Biosciences 50:163-170.

Sprugel, D.G. 1976. Dynamic structure of wave-generated *Abies balsamea* forests in the northeastern United States. Journal of Ecology 64:889-911.

Tansley, A.G. 1929. Succession: the concept and its values. Proceedings of the International Congress of Plant Science, 1926:677-686.

Tansley, A.G. 1935. The use and abuse of vegetational concepts and terms. Ecology 16:284-307.

Turing, A.M. 1952. The chemical basis of morphogenesis. Philosophical Transactions of the Royal Society, London 237:37-72.

Urban, D.L., R.V. O'Neill, and H.H. Shugart, Jr. 1987. Landscape ecology. BioScience 37:119-127.

van de Maarel, E. 1976. On the establishment of plant community boundaries. Berichte der Deutschen Botanischen Gesellschaft 89:415-443.

van Leeuwen, C.G. 1966. A relation theoretical approach to pattern and process in vegetation. Wentia 15:25-46.

Wales, B.A. 1972. Vegetation analysis of north and south edges in a mature oak-hickory forest. Ecological Monographs 42:451-471.

Wiens, J.A., C.S. Crawford, and J.R. Gosz. 1985. Boundary dynamics: a conceptual framework for studying landscape ecosystems. Oikos 45:421-427.

Key words: Boundaries, catastrophe theory, ecological models, ecosystem theory, ecotone concept.

CHAPTER 4

EXTERNAL PROCESSES INFLUENCING ORIGIN AND MAINTENANCE OF INLAND WATER-LAND ECOTONES

Jukka Salo

ABSTRACT

Inland water-land ecotones result from physical and biotic interactions. In this chapter, the geomorphic influences contributing to the origin, maintenance, and persistence of these ecotones are surveyed, with special reference to large river systems and tropical lowlands. Spatiotemporal classification of basic geomorphic processes and their biological correlatives is discussed in the context of landscape ecology. The Amazon River basin is presented as an example of an environment characterised by Quaternary fluvially induced site turnover.

INTRODUCTION

Landscape ecology, by introducing new concepts to describe the heterogeneity of landscapes, is rapidly becoming a key approach to studying biotic diversity, species dynamics, nutrient redistribution, and energy flow models (Forman and Godron 1986, Hill 1987, Westoby 1987, Risser 1987). The division of landscape elements into patches, corridors (strips), and background matrix (Forman and Godron 1984) has helped establish some new basic ways of understanding the dynamics of species turnover rates and ecosystem stability (see Pickett and White 1985). However, landscape ecology lacks a general theoretical core that could structure the field and lead in a more predictive manner to basic concepts (Westoby 1987). The crucial problem in the landscape ecology approach is the lack of experimental studies linking the environmental matrix at various scales to the observed ecological patterns. This holds true especially in continuous continental environments characterised by 'non-island' biogeography. Although there is a two-decade tradition of applying island biogeography concepts (*sensu*

MacArthur and Wilson 1967) to continental features, the result has not been satisfying (Wiens *et al.* 1986). This encourages new approaches.

The failure of simplistic island biogeography models to deal with patchy continental environments has arisen partly from the poor documentation of the physical setting, especially the geomorphology of these patches. Landscape ecology brings, at least, the demand of positioning natural landscape patches and ecotones into spatial and temporal scales (i.e. hierarchies; see Di Castri and Hadley 1988) and surveying the observed biotic patterns in relation to this scaling.

Patch dynamics, as referred to by Thompson (1978), has been the dominant concept in a wide array of recent ecosystem studies related to landscape ecology (Pickett and White 1985, Hill 1987). Ecological patch dynamics are related to effects of natural perturbance or human-induced disturbance on landscape patches. The relevant questions are those dealing with the frequency, severity, intensity, and predictability of the perturbance pattern (Pickett and White 1985). A concept similar to patch dynamics is the *shifting mosaic* (Bormann and Likens 1979, Naiman *et al.* 1988, Pringle *et al.* 1988)

The patch dynamics approach traditionally has been used in terrestrial and marine environments, while freshwater environments have received less emphasis (West *et al.* 1981). This is quite a biassed application, since the inland water-terrestrial patch dynamics often offer a more complicated and rapidly changing scheme than marine and terrestrial environments provide. Only relatively recent studies along undisturbed fluvial corridors have taken the opportunity to monitor ecosystem changes caused by external physical factors creating and disturbing patches, and modifying the dividing ecotone zones (Nanson and Beach 1977, Neill and Deegan 1986, Kalliola and Puhakka 1988). Historically, the pioneering studies on fluvial dynamics have mostly been carried out on sites in managed river systems like the Mississippi (Chamberlin and Salisbury 1909, Fisk 1944, 1947; Winkley 1977, Miall 1978). The data on environmental parameters important from the standpoint of landscape ecology are still rudimentary for such important river systems as the Amazon, Orinoco, Congo, and Nile (Miall 1978).

The need to study natural river and lacustrine environments, with regard to biotic behaviour, has been obvious since it was recognized that some of the world's richest species assemblages are found in tropical lowlands. These regions are characterised by high precipitation, active fluvial patch dynamics, and a shifting network of ecotones (Colinvaux *et al.* 1985, Salo *et al.* 1986, Räsänen *et al.* 1987). The findings are in strong contrast with the earlier view that stability *per se* brings diversity into the ecosystem.

Holland (1988) defined an ecotone as a 'zone of transition between adjacent ecological systems, having a set of characteristics uniquely defined by space and time scales and by the strength of interactions between adjacent ecological systems'. The importance of freshwater ecotones and

38

patch formation along the fluvial corridor was realised quite early (Cajander 1903), and their significance in maintaining between- and within-habitat biotic diversity has become evident in an array of environments (e.g. Farjon and Bogaers 1985, Frissell *et al.* 1986). However, it is difficult to make clear distinctions between the patch dynamics concept and the concept of ecotones: they are closely linked. The dynamics of either entity inevitably affect the other.

Naiman *et al.* (1988) give two alternatives for classifying ecotones bordering patches. The first is to classify them according to their origin and maintenance. The second possibility is to classify identifiable ecotones functionally in a hierarchy using relative temporal and spatial scales. This chapter attempts to develop a hierarchial setting to monitor the geomorphic processes affecting the origin and maintenance of the inland water-land ecotones and landscape patches, especially those along fluvial corridors.

ENVIRONMENTS CREATING INLAND-FRESHWATER ECOTONES: SCALING AND CLASSIFICATION

The main processes creating inland-freshwater ecotones in fluvial environments are largely related to erosion and the accumulation and reworking of sediment along the fluvial corridor. Deposited sediments undergo biogenic and pedogenic processing for extended periods (Lewin 1978). Several recent biogeographic works have demonstrated that the shifting mosaic structure of fluvial landscapes is a key factor in understanding their floristic patterns (Farjon and Bogaers 1985, Walker *et al.* 1986, Kalliola and Puhakka 1988). However, the areal and time scales within which the fluvial landscape processes operate are much wider than has been recognised by ecologists. These processes range from annual sediment movements to continental-scale tectonic events. Their classification relative to landscape ecology and population biology is virtually lacking (but see Allen and Starr 1982, Frissell *et al.* 1986), despite the long tradition in classifying fluvial sedimentary structures (Beerbower 1964, Allen 1965, Jackson 1975, Lewin 1978, Reineck and Singh 1980).

Di Castri and Hadley (1988) recently pointed out the necessity of scaling considerations with respect to monitoring change in biological communities composed of patches of varying size and change intensity, and suggest that the use of a multilevel scaling approach (Delcourt *et al.* 1983, Meentemeyer and Box 1987). The approach has been applied successfully to analyses of forest disturbance (Delcourt *et al.* 1983, Delcourt and Delcourt 1987, Urban *et al.* 1987) and population responses to patchy environments based on modelling (Wiens 1976, Allen and Starr 1982).

The ecotone concept is strongly related to geomorphic processes creating border zones between freshwater bodies and dry land. These geomorphic border zones can be classified on the basis of their spatial arrangement, their rate of emergence, and their persistence.

Using Murphy's (1967) basic division of the earth's surface, geomorphic processes in freshwater-land patch dynamics can be identified as net erosion, equilibrium, and net deposition events (Selley 1982; Table 4.1). The fundamental external factors behind these events are related, in most cases, to plate tectonics and subsequent processes of orogeny and formation of depositional basins. Furthermore, within these processes, it is possible to apply a classification adopted from landscape ecology which is related to the spatiotemporal dynamics of land patches created by sedimentary processes in environments with net deposition (Fig. 4.1, Table 4.2).

Megaform processes of the terrestrial relief (plate tectonics, eustatic uplift, and climate change) affect biotic evolution by creating water-land ecotones and patches that persist long enough ($> 10^4$ yr) to promote biological differentiation. These megaform border zones are well documented, especially along the dynamic forelands of mountain ridges with active Quaternary orogeny. These sites are characterised by reliefs of net erosion and deposition in direct contact with each other. In the central and eastern Amazon basin, this ecotone is known as the border zone between flooded (*várzea*) and the nonflooded (*terra firme*) forest. These two environments have strong floristic and faunistic separation (Erwin 1983, Balslev *et al.* 1987). The *várzea-terra firme* ecotone of Amazon lowlands may have also contributed to biotic differentation through Neogene eustatic oscillation from a shifting mosaic of large land and water patches (Erwin and Adis 1982).

Macroform processes, the large river-basin changes, primarily affect areas of net deposition in the basin. These changes result from changes in processes such as the hydrologic regime, catchment properties, floodplain

Table 4.1 Large-scale landscape division according to sedimentary status. Modified from Murphy (1967, 1968) and Selley (1982)

SEDIMENTARY ENVIRONMENTS OF NET EROSION. These are usually terrestrial and are largely found on the mountainous areas of the world. Weathering is often intensive and erosion is rapid. Ecotones are formed locally through sedimentation (predominantly glacial, mud flow, and flash flood processes). Because of renewed erosion, the deposits are ephemeral and there is minor soil profile development on either bedrock or sediment.

SEDIMENTARY ENVIRONMENTS OF EQUILIBRIUM. The equilibrium surfaces of the earth, both marine and terrestrial, stay for long periods as neither sites of erosion nor yet of deposition. These environments often experience intense chemical alteration of the substrate with laterite and bauxite horizons. On land, environments of equilibrium are represented by the great peneplains of the continental interiors (King 1962) like central Africa, the southern Amazon basin, and the northern Orinoco llanos.

SEDIMENTARY ENVIRONMENTS OF NET DEPOSITION. The inland environments under the influence of water subject to net deposition are largely those of lake, glacial, and fluvial environments (Reineck and Singh 1980). They are of more importance to the concept of ecotone formation because they are preserved as the geological record.

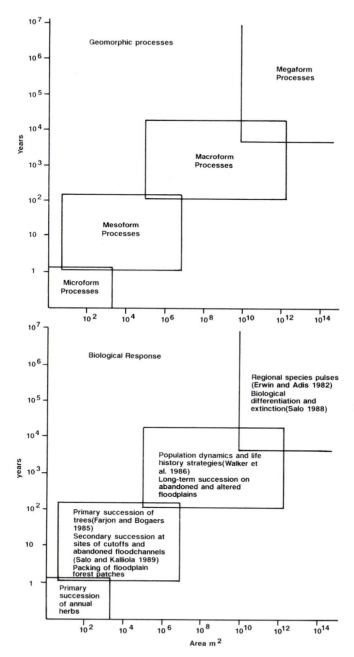

Figure 4.1 Fluvial geomorphic processes and their tentative biotic correlatives arranged in a spatiotemporal scale (Lewin 1978, Urban *et al.* 1987, Salo and Räsänen 1989)

41

Table 4.2 Selected landscape processes and geomorphic structure creating inland water-land ecotones and patches (following patch classification of Lewin 1978, Reineck and Singh 1980). The biotic responses of the processes are presented schematically in Fig. 4.1

Physical Process	Landscape Process	Landforms
MEGAFORM PROCESSES (> 10⁴ yr)		
Plate Tectonics		
Orogeny	Evolution of catchment basins	Drainage network
Volcanism	Mudflows	Alluvial fans
Foreland dynamics	Regional lowland denudation	Pediplains, peneplains
	Drainage reversals	Abandoned floodplains
	Tilting	Terraces, blocked valley lakes
Basinal infilling	Floodplain macroform change (Lewin 1978)	Aggrading fluvial environments
Climatic Change		
Quaternary oscillation	Polar ice-cap oscillation	Glacial and interglacial deposit structures (glacial deposits, eskers, kames, glacial deltas and lakes, sandur deposits)
	Regional denudation changes following precipitation alterations between glacial maxima and interglacials	Convexo-concave relief morphology in lowlands, drainage incisions
Eustatic Change		
Lower sea levels	Channel incision	Vertical ecotones along deepened river valleys
Rising sea levels	Floodplain widening	Lateral ecotones along aggrading floodplains, blocked-valley lakes
MACROFORM PROCESSES (10²-10⁴ yr)		
Floodplain changes	Change in width, slope, relief, etc.	Flood basin patch mosaic
Channel evolution	Alteration in channel pattern, sinuosity scale, form regularity; avulsions, entrenchment	Straight, meandering, anastomozing, and braided channels
MESOFORM PROCESSES (1-10² yr)		
Shear stress	Undercutting of banks	Cutbank facies
Sediment deposition	Deposition of lag-load	Longitudinal and transverse bars, point bars, and channel bars
	Deposition of suspension sediment	Overbank sediments, levees, crevasse splays
Channel processes	Change in channel width and depth, pool formation, cutoffs	Cutoff lakes, sloughs, backswamps
MICROFORM PROCESSES (< 1 yr)		
Activity changes	Annual flood regime, water flow	Plain beds, ripples, dunes, current lineations, flute marks, silt-clay deposits, shrinkage cracks, etc.

42

geometry, and channel characteristics (Lewin 1978). Macroform processes are strong edaphic factors with the potential to modify the life history strategies of floodplain communities. This is especially apparent in humid tropical lowlands and in polar latitudes where floodplain conditions are subject to abrupt changes from the unconsolidated nature of the substrate (Erwin and Adis 1982, Junk 1984, Walker *et al.* 1986).

Mesoform processes have their major biological impact on colonising strategies, on the primary succession and the zonation of woody angiosperms on the newly created depositional patches (Gill 1972), and on the secondary succession of depositional sites associated with meandering rivers, cutoffs, and former riverbeds (Donselaar 1961, Fonda 1974, Nanson and Beach 1977, Walker *et al.* 1986). Analyses of recent satellite imagery show that up to 12% of the Peruvian Amazon lowlands (area > 550,000 km²) is at present under the influence of mesoform fluvial changes (Salo *et al.* 1986) and that a major part of the area has gone through several mesoform change cycles during the Neogene (Räsänen *et al.* 1987).

Microform processes, the smallest-scale fluvially induced processes, take place generally during the annual environmental regime of the fluvial system. The microform processes generate short-lived edaphic patches and thus promote colonising dynamics of the annual herbs (Ware and Penfound 1949, Nilsson 1981, Hupp and Osterkamp 1985, Seidenschwartz 1986).

MEGAFORM PROCESSES: LONG-TERM EVOLUTION OF LOWLAND SEDIMENTARY RELIEFS

Basins and basinal filling

Lowland sedimentary basins are environments where the most intense, dynamic formations of the inland water-land ecotone complexes, especially aggrading floodplains and fluviolacustrine environments, are present (Reineck and Singh 1980). These environments show the complete continuum of geomorphic processes described in the previous section. Examples of intense hydrologic basin evolution include sites like the present Beni, Ucayali, and Pastaza-Marañon basins in the Andean foreland area, Peru and Bolivia (Räsänen *et al.* 1987); the Indian-Pakistan (Siwalik group) Himalayan forelands (Halstead and Nandu 1973); and the fossilised Kootenai Formation in the Rocky Mountains, USA (DeCelles 1986).

The mode of filling in subsiding basins differs according to whether the basin is undefaced by syndepositional surface faults when faulting takes place at deep crustal levels, or when the faults have actually reached the surface (Selley 1982; Table 4.3). The mode of filling largely determines the nature of the macro-mesoform ecotones separating water and land.

1. Intracratonic basins are found within modern continental margins, but their depositional history often shows marks of former marine

Table 4.3 A classification of sedimentary basins. Modified from Selley (1982)

Basin Type	Origin	Subdivision	Inland Basin Examples	Reference
Basins	Cratonic suite: associated with crustal stability	Intracratonic	Michigan basin, USA	Cohee and Landes (1958)
		Epicratonic	Niger delta, Nigeria	Burke (1972)
Troughs	Geosynclinal suite: associated with zones of crustal subduction	Miogeosyncline	Central Amazon basin, Brazil	Räsänen *et al.* (1987)
		Eugeosyncline	Ucayali basin, Peru	Räsänen *et al.* (1987)
		Molasse	Central Alps, Switzerland, Italy, Germany	Bernoulli *et al.* (1974)
Rifts	Drift suite: associated with zones of crustal spreading	Intracratonic	Rhine Valley, Germany	Illies (1970)
		Intercratonic	Gabon basin, Gulf of Guinea	Brink (1974)

connections. This is demonstrated by the Baltic Sea, which, during the late Pleistocene-Holocene, experienced several shifts between marine, brackish, and lacustrine environments.

2. Epicratonic basins lie on the edge of the continental crust. They are often embayed and open towards the adjacent ocean basin. The long-term filling of epicratonic basins is characterised by prisms of terrigenous clastics which have been deposited in a range of sedimentary environments, with the dominance of alluvial deposits on the landward sides. The depositional history of the coastal Atacama Desert, Chile, follows this scheme, which created a characteristic mosaic of present-day and fossilised ecotones during the Neogene (Krissek *et al.* 1980).

3. Geosynclines, as defined by Aubouin (1965), are linear tectonised sedimentary troughs. They show a complex morphology and a regular sequence of structural evolution, sedimentary facies, and igneous activity (Selley 1982). The geosynclines can be divided into several tectonomorphic zones such as a miogeosynclinal furrow (=fore-deep), a miogeanticlinal furrow, and a eugeosynclinal furrow (=main active and unstable trough). The eugeosyncline is separated from the oceanic basin by the eugeanticline, which often is an arc of islands with volcanos.

The geosyncline evolution is the driving force for a wide array of fluvial dynamics along the most active foreland zone with tectonics. A good example of this development is the modern river dynamics along the Cordillera Oriental in Bolivia and Peru (Putzer 1984), and the paleoenvironments of the Rocky Mountain forelands in North America (Bird 1988).

4. Rifts are formed at locations of crustal separation and are thus opposite phenomena to the geosyncline development. They are located along long fault-bounded troughs in various tectonic settings and show corresponding diversity of sediment fill (Selley 1982). Because of their origin, the majority of rifts having intercratonic location are thus strictly marine. Examples of the inland intracratonic rifts are Lake Baikal (USSR), the German Rhine Valley, and the east African Rift Valley. The intracontinental rifts become filled with continental fluviolacustrine deposits originating from the faulted basin margins. The igneous activity characterising young rift formation contributes lavas and volcaniclastic detritus to the basin fill.

Neotectonics

The long-term evolution of the hydrologic setting and the facies evolution of sedimentary basins are controlled by the tectonic setting of the basin. This setting contributes to further mega- and mesoform processes that structure the relief (Summerfield 1986, 1987). Late Cenozoic neotectonic activity has been shown to cause drainage network changes, especially in the foreland basins (Summerfield 1985, Hancock and Williams 1986, Gregory and Schumm 1987), and to create dramatic ecotones separating old denudational reliefs from the recently introduced depositional environments (Table 4.4).

Stoneley (1969) presented three basic causes for tectonic subsidence which are the essential prerequisites for the accumulation of thick sedimentary sequences and the subsequent modification of macro- and mesoform ecotones. These sequences are predominantly the results of deposition along fluvial corridors and alluvial fans:

1. Subcrustal displacement of the mantle causes compressional warping or down-dragging of the crust, which leads to geosynclinal sedimentation along the mountain ridge foreland zones of subduction (Khobzi *et al.* 1980).

2. Sedimentation is initiated by those changes in the mantle which cause foundering and subsidence of the crust, as in the case of intracratonic basins.

3. The weight of the sediment itself may cause isostatic depression of the crust, which is common along continental margins where the ocean basin forms an infilling depression (Drake *et al.* 1968).

The difficulty of detecting the control of neotectonic activity on drainage pattern is well known (see discussion in Beerbower 1964, Gregory and Schumm 1987). Erratic subsidence of basins bounded by active faults may cause repeated regrading of floodplains, thus generating thick piles of

Table 4.4 Examples of neotectonics investigations related to origin of large-scale freshwater-land ecotones. Modified from Summerfield (1987)

Type of Geomorphic Evidence	Location	Reference
Experimental; stream pattern	Mississippi, USA	Gregory and Schumm (1987)
Unidirectional channel migration, river terraces	Acre Province, Brazil	RADAMBRASIL (1977)
Channel diversions, river terraces	Madre de Dios and Ucayali provinces, Peru	Räsänen et al. (1987)
Scarp analysis, discordant land surfaces, drainage anomalies	Arizona, USA	Morrison (1985)
Offset stream channels, diverted glaciers	Tibetan Plateau, China	Chang et al. (1986)
Uplifted and deformed erosion surfaces, drainage asymmetry, floodplain evolution, terrace heights	Nicoya Peninsula, Costa Rica	Hare and Gardner (1985)
Fault scarp degradation, stream profile adjustment, escarpment retreat	Basin and range/Colorado Plateau boundary, Arizona, USA	Mayer (1985)
River terraces	Cape Fear Arch, North Carolina, USA	Markevich (1985)
River terraces, alluvial fans, river long profiles	China	Han (1985)
Offset stream channels	Shensi (Shaanxi) Province, China	Peltzer et al. (1985)
Offset stream channels	Yunnan Province, China	Allen et al. (1984)

alluvium with upward-fining cyclothems (Mitchell and Reading 1978, Selley 1982). These cyclothems are a further source for both lateral and vertical ecotone formation as the denudation process incises these sediments (Fig. 4.2).

The sedimentary structure of all basin types is characterised by this fining-upward sequence of the alluvium (Cotter 1978, McLean and Jerzykei-wicz 1978), a sequence that is also implicit in the sedimentary model of laterally migrating channels.

Beerbower (1964) was the first to suggest that it is not necessary to invoke external processes (i.e., tectonics, eustatics) as the cause of repeated

Figure 4.2 An erosional bank along the Tambopata River, southeastern Peruvian Amazon, showing cyclothem structure in an uplifted *terra firme* rain forest relief. On the top of a consolidated base (1), four upward-fining fluvial cyclothems (2-5) can be observed

alluvial cycles and the subsequent cyclothems. They can result from the lateral migration of a river channel across its floodplain coupled with a gradual isostatic adjustment of the basin floor in response to the weight of the sediment (McLean and Jerzykeiwicz 1978, Selley 1982). Allocyclic control would suggest the individual cyclothems to be basinwide if they are the result of external climatic or tectonic causes. Cyclothems due to channel migration, interrupted by cutoffs and channel inversions, should be a really more restricted.

Climatic and eustatic change

In addition to tectonic processes, other causes for the observed fining-upward cyclothems that promote formation of vertical ecotones along fluvial corridors include eustatic sea-level fluctuations, autocyclic control of the corridor, and precipitation cycles. Four fining-up cycles are present in the Quaternary alluvium of the Mississippi River valley, USA, and they correlate with eustatic sea-level changes during the Quaternary glaciations (Turnbull *et al.* 1950). Also the lower Amazon River terraces show evidence of late Quaternary eustatic sea-level fluctuations (Irion 1984, Klammer 1984). These river terraces create a sequence of land patches with between-site age heterogeneity of 10^3-10^4 yr. This causes the age heterogeneity between the terraces to resemble that created by neotectonic change.

Late Pleistocene climatic oscillations have been suggested as the cause for large-scale modifications of large river systems like the Congo and the Amazon (Garner 1974, Haffer 1987). Generally dryer than at present, the Pleistocene climate promoted deep incision of river channels into their floodplain sediments (Tricart 1975, Sioli 1984, Whitmore and Prance 1987). This incision was a major source of recycled floodplain sediments for the fluvial corridor during the Pleistocene. The infilling of deeply incised Pleistocene river valleys during the Holocene from rising sea levels and increased precipitation over large continental areas created by an abrupt ecotone between older river valley sediments and the newly deposited Holocene floodplain sediments (Klammer 1984). Today, in cases where the suspended sediment load of rivers is low, instead of base-level reaching floodplains, blocked-valley lakes (*rias fluviales*) are forming on the sites of ancient Pleistocene river valleys (Irion 1982).

MACROFORM PROCESSES: CHANGES IN LARGE RIVER SYSTEMS

Channel processes

Channel banks are inherently unstable because of the erosive power (shear stress) of the current. Instability varies according to river order, river stage, and local geomorphology (Schumm 1977, Pinay *et al.* 1990). The classical river stage concept divides the river system into three categories: (1) young: predominantly erosional in mountainous regions; (2) mature: foreland and lowland areas where the system is characterised by the formation of floodplains with lateral accretion deposits (e.g. bars); and (3) old: coastal regions with joining river systems and a braided channel network. In most cases, the within-floodplain depositional patch mosaic is best developed along upper reaches of the natural river system because of homogenous flooding along the lower reaches of the fluvial corridor. In depositional environments channel instability and subsequent packing of fluvial deposits are greatest in rapidly subsiding foreland basin sites where rivers flow predominantly through their own unconsolidated deposits.

Channel types

Braided channels. Braided channel subsystems are characterised by a network of constantly shifting, low sinuosity, anastomosing water courses (Selley 1982). Modern braided river systems are predominantly found on alluvial fans in semi-arid and arid climates, along many mountain foreland areas (also in the tropics), and along the outwash plains of ice caps and glaciers. The main channel of a braided river is divided into many subchannels. Channel bars of the braided rivers are mostly composed of gravelly material or stones. The flood cycle is often ephemeral because of the location close to mountains. The floods have large amplitude, and during peak floods the channel bars and islands are often totally submerged.

The basic influence directing channel evolution towards the braided pattern is the effect of excessive sediment load. Continuous formation of channel bars causes thalwegs to repeatedly diverge until they connect with another subchannel course. Often there is no terrain to collect overbank sediments; however, the fine-grained suspended load can be deposited in abandoned channels and in the pools of active channels when the floods end (Doeglas 1962).

Meandering channels. Meandering channels are generally found along low gradient rivers. These rivers have a high suspended load-bedload ratio, cohesive bank material, and relatively steady discharge (Reineck and Singh 1980). Material eroded from the outer bank is deposited on the point bar of the next downstream meander. The helicoidal flow pattern results from an elevated water surface making contact against the concave bank. Meander bars (point bars) are bedload sediment accumulations developed on the convex side of each bend forming a topographic high in the channel (Reineck and Singh 1980).

Anastomosing channels. Many large rivers like the Amazon show lack of channel competition along their middle and lower reaches. This leads to the channel pattern defined by Schumm (1977) as anastomosing. This channel form results from a strong flood regime and a dominance of suspension sediments over bedload sediments (Reineck and Singh 1980).

MESOFORM PROCESSES: FLOODPLAIN CHANGES

A fluvial depositional environment has physical, chemical, and geomorphic aspects that together form the *facies* (Reineck and Singh 1980). The facies is defined as the sum of all primary characteristics of a sedimentary unit (Teichert 1958, Krumbein and Sloss 1963). Processes that form the facies fall predominantly into the categories of meso- and microform change. In many cases, the facies can be considered equivalent to a landscape patch. In sedimentology, the facies is often used to distinguish various successional units on the basis of the dominant character of the deposit (e.g. colour, bedding characteristics, fossils). Other means of determining the facies are to use known processes of sedimentation (e.g. fluvial, lacustrine facies) or to apply the broad setting of the sedimentary basin (molasse facies, Reineck and Singh 1980).

There has been a rapid expansion of literature characterising depositional processes along the fluvial corridor (for reviews see Leopold *et al.* 1964, Allen 1965, Gregory 1977, Schumm 1977, Miall 1978, Reading 1978, Collinson and Lewin 1983, Richards 1987). Fluvial dynamics create patches varying from < 1 m² to tens of thousands of square kilometres. The turnover rate of terrestrial patches is rapid compared with most changes in lacustrine environments.

The primary fluvial process linked with channel migration is shear stress. As water flows round a bend, the current velocity increases on the outer edge of the curve and decreases on the inner edge. This leads to increased shear stress on the outer bank, forming a subvertical bank. On the inner part of the meander, a slackening of shear stress initiates sedimentation of the bedload, leading to the formation of a gently sloping point bar. Cross-bedding takes place along the channel bed through formation of subaqueous dunes which migrate downcurrent.

Channel migration creates a characteristic sequence of sedimentary deposits. Well-developed floodplains commonly show one or more sets of cyclothems (Fig. 4.2), which are characterised by a fining-upward sequence. In its simplest form, the cyclothemic sequence may reflect a progressive lateral decline in current velocity from the channel floor across the point bar up to the inner bank of the meander. In some cases, the fining-up cyclothem sequence is a result of deposition of overbank sediments, and thus evidence for a larger-scale channel alteration cycle with cutoff formation and inversions. Vertical fining of grain size will not be present if the source of sediments did not contain a broad enough spectrum of grain sizes.

River level fluctuation also results in levee formation as floodwater flows over the channel bank onto the floodplain. As current velocity diminishes with increasing distance from the channel, the deposited sediment size decreases. The levees separate the channel from low-lying flood basins on either side of the alluvial plain, causing backswamp formation on both sides of the channel.

Extrachannel floodplain processes

The patchy structure of the extrachannel floodplain relief is the result of sedimentation of channel and overbank deposits. They are often referred to as deposits of lateral and vertical accretion (Wolman and Leopold 1957). It is possible to distinguish channel, natural levee, and backswamp deposits in the floodplain. In a floodplain of a meandering river, cutoffs and loop compounds leave a complex scroll plain (Hickin and Nansen 1975). Migration of the point bar may form a series of low ridges separated by troughs in a 'ridge and swale' surface of meander scrolls (Morisawa 1985). Furthermore, the floodplains of meandering rivers are also characterised by levees and flood basins, chutes, sloughs, and crevasse splays (Kessel *et al.* 1974, Morisawa 1985). The low-lying inner deep that marks the fill between original bar and inside bank may be occupied by a slough or chute, or by a crescent lake, or in its later stages by a backswamp. The higher central axis of the bar remains as a low ridge or scroll (Morisawa 1985). A series of point bar swales, which are often formed within meanders of aggrading rivers, may subsequently form contemporaneous sites for overbank deposition of fine-grained sediments. A few of them function as a scouring chute channel during floods and may have a longer life span than other slowly infilling meander depressions (Lewin 1978).

Meander loops

The development of a sequence of meander loops forms the basic process behind extrachannel floodplain patch diversity. In meandering rivers, the present floodplain undergoes cycles of complete lateral erosion. Sequential succession of developing loops proceeds undisturbed until the migrating river channel cuts the meander from a different angle and starts to form a new loop close to the old one. The migration of the channel course creates a mosaic of uneven-aged loops within the present meander plain according to the repetitive nature of river dynamics.

Formation of cutoff lakes

Cutoffs (former channels), of which the most common types are the chute and neck cutoffs (Hooke 1984), form the second major source for extrachannel patches. Lewis and Lewin (1983) identify five types of cutoff: chute, neck, mobile bar, multiloop chute, and multiloop neck. Cutoff types range from the breaching of very narrow necks on single meander loops (Mosley 1975) to much longer flood chutes developed across point bar complexes (Handy 1972), and to channels that abandon whole groups of individual meander loops (Kuleimina 1973).

Cutoff lakes may be arranged according to their infilling and overgrowth states; these successions are situated in different combinations. The heterogeneity inside the oxbow lakes is formed with different kinds of infilling processes; the coarsest sediments normally are deposited at the neck of the lake. In both or in other limbs of the cutoff channel, changing floods create small escape channels for floodwaters which characteristically aggregate levees on both sides of the canal.

Backswamps

Along aggrading floodplains, flooding and overbank sedimentation may later modify the mosaic structure of the extrachannel floodplain by destroying the ridge-swale topography of the abandoned meander loops and by creating backswamp areas. Also, annual floods form a layer of overbank sediments above the patches of the extrachannel floodplain.

LANDSCAPE ECOLOGY OF THE AMAZON BASIN: FLUVIAL ECOTONES

The Amazon drainage basin, with areal cover exceeding 6×10^6 km^2, forms the largest and most complicated river system ever known (Fig. 4.3, Table 4.5). Although the depositional history of the Quaternary of the intercratonic Amazon basin is still under debate (see Sombroek 1966, Irion 1984), the western and central Amazon basin shows clear marks of fluvial activity, with shifting aggrading and degrading landscapes (Klammer 1984). Because of the large area and the largely undisturbed fluvial setting, the Amazon provides an environment where most features recorded in fluvial geomorphology are present. The Amazon also has the highest biotic diversity measures in the world for various terrestrial communities (Terborgh 1983, Gentry 1988). However, understanding of the landscape ecology of the Amazon is still rudimentary, especially outside Brazilian territory.

The conceptual framework applied in many studies of tropical Amazon lowland biota is often adopted from other tropical environments, and therefore neglects the patchy landscape pattern and ecotones that characterise the area. The ecotone concept may help to give a more realistic view about the edaphic control of both aquatic and terrestrial communities, which here are exceptionally closely linked. The newly emerging view of the patchy fluvially induced forest structure of the area has only become evident since the development of remote sensing methods (e.g. Brazilian Radambras project, Landsat TM images). The crucial role of fluvial dynamics in the formation of distinct forest types has also been recognised

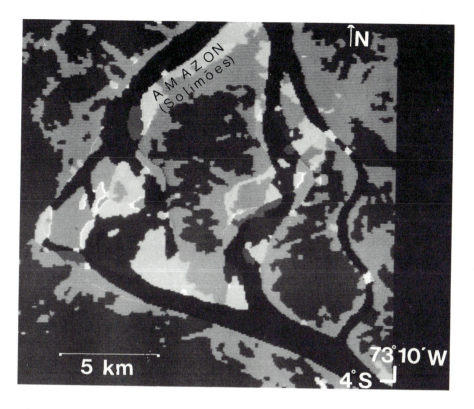

Figure 4.3 A bitemporal (1979-83) Landsat MSS image showing channel migration of an anastomosing Amazon River close to Iquitos, northern Peruvian Amazon, and the subsequent forest succession. The colour classes in the image represent change classes that combine the information of vegetation cover and channel position in the years 1979 and 1983 (Salo *et al.*, unpublished data)

by those providing classification perspectives for the lowland Amazon forest (Encarnación 1985).

Long-term landscape evolution of the Western Amazon Basin

The modern Amazon lowland alluvial relief is characteristically divided into two domains following the ecotone line between the nonflooded denudational relief (*terra firme*) and the permanently or temporally flooded floodplains (*várzea*). This ecotone has been shown to be an important zone segregating two floristically different types of broad-leaved rain forests (Balslev *et al.* 1987). In the upper Amazon basin, where floodplain processes are rapid, the ecotone is also a demarcation line between regeneration mechanisms of the rain forest. The forest regeneration in the *terra firme*

Table 4.5 Channel migration in Iquitos, along the Amazon River (Solimões), Peruvian Amazon, based on bitemporal Landsat MSS imagery proccesion. Two images (1979, 1983) are joined to demonstrate the patches created by channel migration during the surveyed period (Salo *et al.*, unpublished data)

Colour	Formation	Vegetation* 1979	Vegetation* 1983	Land or Water 1979	Land or Water 1983
	Well-drained soils				
Dark green	(*terra firme*)	+	+	L	L
Brown green	Poorly drained soils (*várzea*)	+	+	L	L
Dark blue (black)	Channel	−	−	W	W
Light blue	Channel migration area	+	−	L	W
Violet	Channel bar	−	−	L	W
Red	Bar 1	−	−	W	L
Yellow	Bar 2	−	+	W	L
Green	Bar 3	+	+	L	L

*Plus (+) indicates vegetation is present; minus (−) indicates vegetation is absent

relief is predominantly through senescence of individual canopy trees (light gap regeneration; Hartshorn 1980). Various fluvial processes like channel migration, extreme floods, and floodwater-induced undercutting of trees form important additional forest regeneration mechanisms in the floodplains (Salo and Kalliola 1989). The *terra firme-várzea* community separation has also been demonstrated for various animal groups (Erwin and Adis 1982, Erwin 1983).

The Quaternary Amazon deposition evolution was first initiated by a widespread syntectonic fluvial aggradation, induced by Andean uplift (Räsänen *et al.* 1987). This sequence was followed by further foreland fractioning, which triggered the erosional and depositional processes characterising the modern rain forest area. Related geodynamic processes have simultaneously functioned in a wide foreland area along the Cordillera Oriental from Venezuela to Bolivia (Pflafker 1964, Khobzi *et al.* 1980, Lowrie *et al.* 1981).

In the modern lowland area, the ecotone separating landscape patches with the widest age difference is formed on the border of the *terra firme* relief and the four major structural infilling basins: Pastaza-Marañon, Ucayali, Acre, and Madre de Dios-Beni. Similar basinal areas have probably been more common in the past, and also involved in the depositional history of the central Brazilian Amazon. The central parts of the Peruvian Pastaza-Marañon basin form the largest known ponded inland foreland basin, with modern fluvial aggradation by the Marañon, Huallaga, and Ucayali rivers. The aggradation is due to elevation of base level, either by active rise of the flanks of the basin in the eastern side or by greater relative subsidence in the basin.

The non-flooded lowland Amazon relief

The present *terra firme* relief of the western and central Amazon basin is of fluvial origin, deposited in a floodplain environment resembling the modern aggradational floodplains of the basinal areas of the Peruvian and Bolivian lowland Amazon (Räsänen *et al.* 1987).

The modern western Amazon *terra firme* is well known for its great biological diversity. This diversity results from substantial local neoendemism in woody angiosperms (Prance 1982), great between-habitat diversity (Gentry 1982), and extremely great α-diversity measures in trees (up to 300 species/ha, Gentry 1988).

Many of the modern biogeographic works still consider the *terra firme* relief to be of Miocene age (e.g. Haffer 1987), although there are no data on this backed by absolute dating techniques. Also, the fluvial origin of the *terra firme* that covers the majority of the Amazon forest has been unclear, and edaphic between-site differences or ecotones have not been searched specifically. The suggested old age of the *terra firme* rain forest bed would inherently suggest that tropical weathering processes have homogenised the forest bed lithological structure. This, in turn, would result in a relatively homogenous substrate with little between-site variance in nutrient or texture composition.

Recently, the western Amazon *terra firme* forest bed has been tentatively shown to be Quaternary by depositional origin (Räsänen *et al.* 1987). This would suggest that weathering has not destroyed all the primary structures present in the forest bed texture and that an edaphic patch dynamics approach would be welcome in order to examine factors creating the observed patchy forest structure.

The original primary sedimentation structure of Amazon *terra firme*, with its various fluvial facies, is well preserved at certain sites (Fig. 4.2). When the surface erosion (denudation) incises into these sediments, the fluvial sediment structures are exposed and provide a complex set of ecotones and patches for the colonisation processes of forest trees. At present, there are no data showing the size distribution of edaphic *terra firme* patches in the Amazon, but they can tentatively be claimed to follow the patch size and distribution of floodplain sedimentary structures. These structures would comprise the complete continuum of fluvial deposits, ranging from microform components such as ripples, silt-clay deposits, and current lineations to larger meso- and macroform structures such as cutoff-lake sediment patches, terraces, and abandoned floodplains. Gentry (1988) has shown that four 1-ha *terra firme* plots in Iquitos, Peru, located at distances from a few kilometres up to 80 km from each other, have a low floristic similarity comparable to differences between *várzea* and *terra firme* sites (Balslev *et al.* 1987). Despite the apparent geomorphic similarity of these sites, and their belonging to the *terra firme* category, they are all located at various terrace levels that have been formed through relocation of river channels induced by neotectonic change or autochthonous floodplain change.

The floodplain processes and ecotone structures

The Lower and Middle Amazon River has a slower rate of channel migration that the Upper Amazon River (Sternberg 1960, Mertes 1985). The Peruvian reaches of the Amazon, Marañon, and Ucayali rivers have not been subject to channel process studies until recently (Salo *et al.* 1986). The observation that the *terra firme* relief of the region has a fluvial origin brings additional interest to the understanding of modern macro- and mesoform deposition processes that provide an analogue for the evolution of the Amazon landscape.

The Amazon white-water rivers, which are characterised by high loads of Andean origin and recirculating suspended and bedload sediments, first take a braided channel pattern (e.g. rivers Alto Madre de Dios, Marañon, and Napo, in Peru and Ecuador) but become meandering channels at an elevation of about 350 m. The channel form of the largest rivers then becomes anastomosing at lower altitudes. The change is often induced by neotectonic alteration of the relief, as is probably the case for the Amazon River in the vicinity of Iquitos, Peru (Dumont *et al.* 1988).

The meandering and anastomozing sections of rivers in the upper Amazon basin often show extreme rates of lateral migration creating fast-shifting environments of mesoform patches, which are colonised by primary successional trees and annual herbs (Salo and Kalliola 1989). Mertes (1985) has documented a provisional channel migration rate up to 400 m/yr in the border area of Brazil and Peru, based on analysis of old river maps. Salo *et al.* (unpublished data) have documented, by using bitemporal Landsat MSS images (Fig. 4.3), that in some meandering and anastomosing stretches of the Ucayali and Amazon (Solimões) rivers in Peru, the lateral migration exceeds one kilometre during the years 1979-83. The resulting shifting successional forest mosaic shows a sequential successional pattern along the meandering Ucayali River and a patchy, nonpredictable pattern along the anastomosing sequence of the Amazon River (site in Fig. 4.3).

The channel migration process is the principal initiation process for floodplain forest turnover and subsequent succession. The mesoform fluvial patch packing further modifies the floodplain geomorphology, resulting in an overwhelmingly diverse and patchy forest structure, as shown at a site along the Ucayali River, central Peruvian Amazon (Fig. 4.4). The macroform processes, effecting a readjustment of complete floodplains, are also present (at the site presented in Fig. 4.4) by a tectonically induced avulsion of the Ucayali River and the subsequent formation of a new floodplain and complicated successional development of the forest community on the site of the abandoned floodplain.

The fluvial landscape presented in Fig. 4.3 will develop to a *terra firme* relief through future tectonic basin evolution. The terrace levels on the eastern margin of the image show existing evolutionary phases of terraces towards the denudated pattern.

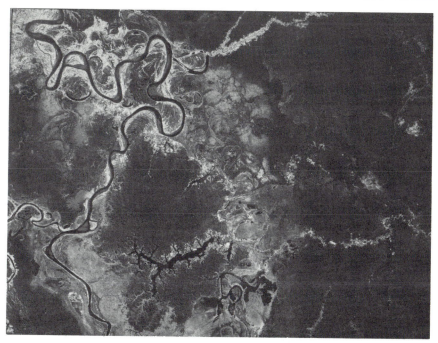

Figure 4.4   A Landsat TM image (A) of a site in Pucallpa, central Peruvian Amazon, showing floodplain ecotone formation, induced by fluvial dynamics and an avulsion, the result of a tectonic change. The image is developed from a principal component transformation using data from Landsat path 6, row 66QX, July 1985 (channels 2, 3, 4, 5, and 7). The ecotones and ecotone forming processes are described in B (overleaf) (1) present Ucayali River channel and floodplain; (2) abandoned Ucayali River floodplain; (3) well-developed scroll-swale topography in the mature floodplain; (4) developing meanders within the new floodplain; (5) infilling cutoff lake (originated 1944); (6) backswamps, permanently and temporally inundated; (7) abandoned floodplain mosaic; (8) inundated abandoned floodplain, blocked by newly formed tributary levees; (9) new floodplain of Tamaya River, avulsion induced by tilting; (10) blocked-valley lakes (*rias fluviales*), formed on sites of former river valleys; (11) overbank deposits, infilling old dissected relief; (12) crevasse; (13) flash flood zone; (14) terraces; (15) dissected terrace level; and (16) abandoned channels of Pachitea River

The processes described here, ranging from megaform change induced by plate tectonics to microform changes at sites of contemporary plant colonisation, have together resulted in the vastly complex shifting mosaic of the Amazon basin. It is probable that the influences of these landscape processes on the biota range from biologic evolution and extinction to local patch colonisation dynamics. It remains to be seen whether the observed contact zones between certain well-studied animal groups like birds (Haffer 1987, Haffer and Fitzpatrick 1985) and Nymphalid butterflies (Brown 1987) follow some of the ecotonal zones created by fluvial dynamics and relief evolution.

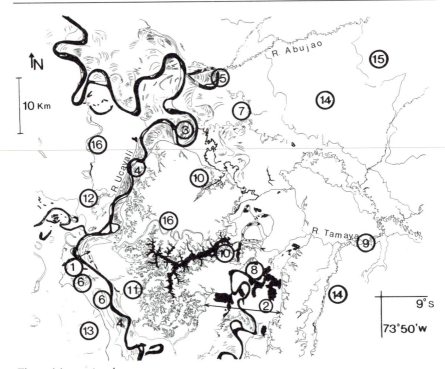

Figure 4.4 *continued*

CONCLUSIONS

Landscape analyses of fluvial landforms pose various questions on the nature of ecological communities living on these landform patches. Although geomorphic methods, especially sideways looking airborne radar (SLAR) and Landsat and SPOT colour composite image processing, can reveal patchy structures created by fluvial processes, the role of these patches in the ecological theatre often remains obscure. The lack of data on this subject is largely due to the paucity of undisturbed fluvial environments in the industrialised world. The patchy floodplain structure is the first to disappear after management efforts are targeted to the floodplain environment. However, it is clear that much of the biotic diversity present, especially in the tropics, either results from or depends on the presence of fluvial patches.

ACKNOWLEDGEMENTS

I thank Risto Kalliola, Maarit Puhakka, Matti Räsänen, Marjut Rajasilta, and Ron Neller for fruitful discussions on the theme. This work has been supported by the University of Turku Amazon project, funded by FINNIDA and the Academy of Finland.

LITERATURE CITED

Allen, C.R., A.R. Gillespie, Y. Han, K.E. Sieh, B. Zhang, and C. Zhu. 1984. Red River and associated faults, Yunnan province, China: Quaternary geology, slip rates and seismic hazard. Geological Society of America Bulletin 95:686-700.

Allen, J.R.L. 1965. A review of the origin and characteristics of recent alluvial sediments. Sedimentology 5:89-191.

Allen, T.F.H. and T.B. Starr. 1982. Hierarchy: perspectives for ecological complexity. University of Chicago Press, Chicago, Illinois, USA.

Aubouin, J. 1965. Geosynclines. Elsevier, Amsterdam, The Netherlands.

Balslev, H., J. Luteyn, B. Øllgaard, and L.B. Holm-Nielsen. 1987. Composition and structure of adjacent unflooded and floodplain forest in Amazonian Ecuador. Opera Botanica 92:37-57.

Beerbower, J.R. 1964. Cyclothems and cyclic depositional mechanisms in alluvial plain sedimentation. Bulletin of Kansas University Geological Survey 169:35-42.

Bernoulli, D., H.P. Laubscher, R. Trumpy, and K. Wenk. 1974. Central Alps and Jura Mountains. Pages 85-108 *in* Mesozoic-Cenozoic orogenic belts. Geological Society of London, Special Publications 4.

Bird, P. 1988. Formation of the Rocky Mountains, Western United States: A continuum computer model. Science 239:1501-1507.

Bormann, F.H., and G.E. Likens. 1979. Pattern and process in a forested ecosystem. Springer-Verlag, New York, USA.

Brink, A.H. 1974. Petroleum geology of Gabon basin. Bulletin of the American Association of Petroleum Geologists 58:216-235.

Brown, K.S., Jr. 1987. Biogeography and evolution of Neotropical butterflies. Pages 66-104 *in* T.C. Whitmore and G.T. Prance, editors. Biogeography and Quaternary history in tropical America. Clarendon Press, Oxford, England.

Burke, K. 1972. Longshore drift, submarine canyons, and submarine fans in development of Niger Delta. Bulletin of the American Association of Petroleum Geologists 56:1975-1983.

Cajander, A.K. 1903. Beiträge zur kenntnis der Vegetation der Alluvionen des Unteren Lena-Thalens. Dissertation. Drückerei der Finnischen Litteratur Gesellschaft, Helsingfors, Finland.

Chamberlin, T.C., and R.D. Salisbury. 1909. Geology: processes and their results. John Murray, London, England.

Chang, C. *et al.* (27 authors) 1986. Preliminary conclusions of the Royal Society and Academia Sinica 1985 geotraverse of Tibet. Nature 323:501-507.

Cohee, G.V., and K.K. Landes. 1958. Oil in the Michigan basin. Pages 473-493 *in* L.G. Weeks, editor. The habitat of oil. American Association of Petroleum Geologists, Tulsa, Oklahoma, USA.

Colinvaux, P.A., M.C. Miller, K.B. Liu, M. Steinitz-Kannan, and I. Frost. 1985. Discovery of permanent Amazon lakes and hydraulic disturbance in the upper Amazon Basin. Nature 313:42-45.

Collinson, J.D., and J. Lewin (editors). 1983. Modern and ancient fluvial systems. Special Publication Number 6, International Association of Sedimentologists. Blackwell Scientific Publications, Oxford, England.

Cotter, E. 1978. The evolution of fluvial style, with special reference to the central Appalachian paleozoic. Pages 361-383 in A.D. Miall, editor. Fluvial sedimentology. Canadian Society of Petroleum Geologists, Calgary, Alberta, Canada.

DeCelles, P.G. 1986. Sedimentation in a tectonically partitioned, nonmarine foreland basin: the lower Cretaceous Kootenai Formation, Southwestern Montana. Geological Society of America Bulletin 97:911-931.

Delcourt, H.R., P.A. Delcourt, and T. Webb. 1983. Dynamic plant ecology: the spectrum of vegetational change in space and time. Quaternary Science Reviews 1:153-175.

Delcourt, P.A., and H.R. Delcourt. 1987. Long-term forest dynamics of the temperate zone: a case study of late-Quaternary forest in Eastern North America. Springer-Verlag, New York, USA.

Di Castri, F., and M. Hadley. 1988. Enhancing the credibility of ecology: interacting along and across hierarchical scales. GeoJournal 17(1):5-35.

Doeglas, D.J. 1962. The structure of sedimentary deposits of braided rivers. Sedimentology 1:167-190.

Donselaar, J. van. 1961. On the vegetation of former river beds in the Netherlands. Wentia 5:112-162.

Drake, C.L., J.I. Ewing, and H. Stokand. 1968. The continental margin of the United States. Canadian Journal of Earth Sciences 5:99-110.

Dumont, J.F., S. Lamotte and M. Fournier. 1988. Neotectónica del Acro de Iquitos (Jenaro Herrara, Peru). Boletin de la Sociedad Geologica del Peru 77:7-18.

Encarnación, F. 1985. Introduction a la flora y vegetación de la Amazonia peruana: estado actual de los estudios, medio natural y ensayo de una clave de determinación de las formaciones vegetales en la llanura amazónica. Candollea 40:237-252.

Erwin, T.L. 1983. Beetles and other insects of tropical forest canopies at Manaus, Brazil, sampled by insecticidal fogging. Pages 59-75 *in* S.L. Sutton, T.C. Whitmore, and A.C. Chadwick, editors. Tropical rain forest: ecology and management. Blackwell Scientific Publications, Oxford, England.

Erwin, T.L., and J. Adis. 1982. Amazonian inundation forests: their role as short-term refuges and generators of species richness and taxon pulses. Pages 358-371 *in* G.T. Prance, editor. Biological diversification in the tropics. Columbia University Press, New York, USA.

Farjon, A., and P. Bogaers. 1985. Vegetation zonation and primary succession along the Porcupine River in interior Alaska. Phytocoenologia 13:465-504.

Fisk, H.N. 1944. Geological investigation of the alluvial valley of the lower Mississippi River. Mississippi River Commission, Vicksburg, Mississippi, USA.

Fisk, H.N. 1947. Fine-grained alluvial deposits and their effects on Mississippi River activity. War Department Corps of Engineers, Mississipppi River Commission, Vicksburg, Mississippi, USA.

Fonda, R.W. 1974. Forest succession in relation to river terrace development in Olympic National Park, Washington. Ecology 55:927-942.

Forman, R.T.T., and M. Godron. 1984. Landscape ecology principles and landscape function. Pages 4-15 *in* J. Brandt and P. Agger, editors. Proceedings of the First International Seminar on Methodology in Landscape Ecological Research and Planning. Volume 5. Roskilde Universitetsforlag GeoRuc, Roskilde, Denmark.

Forman, R.T.T. 1986. Landscape ecology. John Wiley and Sons, New York, USA.

Frissell, C.A., W.J. Liss, C.E. Warren, and M.D. Hurley. 1986. A hierarchial framework for stream habitat classification: viewing streams in a watershed context. Environmental Management 10:199-214.

Garner, H.F. 1974. The origin of landscapes. Blackwell, Oxford, England.

Gentry, A. 1982. Patterns of Neotropical plant species diversity. Pages 1-84 *in* M.K. Hecht, B. Wallace, and G.T. Prance, editors. Evolutionary biology 15. Plenum, New York, USA.

Gentry, A. 1988. Tree species richness of upper Amazonian forests. Proceedings of the National Academy of Sciences, USA 85:156-159.

Gill, D. 1972. The point bar environment in the Mackenzie River delta. Canadian Journal of Earth Sciences 9:1382-1393.

Gregory, D.I., and S.A. Schumm. 1987. The effect of active tectonics on alluvial river morphology. Pages 41-68 *in* K. Richards, editor. River channels. The Institute of British Geographers Special Publications Series 18. Blackwell, Oxford, England.

Gregory, K.J. (editor). 1977. River channel changes. Wiley, Chichester, England.

Haffer, J. 1987. Quaternary history of tropical America. Pages 1-18 *in* T.C. Whitmore and G.T. Prance, editors. Biogeography and Quaternary history in tropical America. Clarendon Press, Oxford, England.

Haffer, J., and J.W. Fitzpatrick. 1985. Geographic variation in some Amazonian forest birds. Ornithological Monographs 36:147-168.

Halstead, L.B., and A.C. Nandu. 1973. Environment of deposition of the Pinjor Formation Upper Siwaliks, near Chandigarh. Bulletin of the India Geological Association 6(1):63-70.

Han, M. 1985. Tectonic geomorphology and its application to earthquake prediction in China. Pages 367-386 *in* M. Morisawa and J.T. Hack, editors. Tectonic geomorphology. Allen and Unwin, Boston, Massachusetts, USA.

Hancock, P.L., and G.D. Williams. 1986. Neotectonics. Journal of the Geological Society, London 143:325-326.

Handy, R.L. 1972. Alluvial cut-off dating from subsequent growth of a meander. Geological Society of America Bulletin 83:475-480.

Hare, P.W., and T.W. Gardner. 1985. Geomorphic indicators of vertical neotectonism along converging plate margins, Nicoya Peninsula, Costa Rica. Pages 75-104 *in* M. Morisawa and J.T. Hack, editors. Tectonic geomorphology. Allen and Unwin, Boston, Massachusetts, USA.

Hartshorn, G. 1980. Neotropical forest dynamics. Biotropica 12:23-30.

Hickin, E.J., and G.C. Nanson. 1975. The character of channel migration on the Beatton River, northeast British Columbia, Canada. Geological Society of America Bulletin 86:487-494.

Hill, A.R. 1987. Ecosystem stability: some recent perspectives. Progress in Physical Geography 11:315-333.

Holland, M.M. (compiler). 1988. SCOPE/MAB technical consultations on landscape boundaries: report of a SCOPE/MAB workshop on ecotones. Biology International, Special Issue 17:47-106.

Hooke, J.M. 1984. Changes in river meanders: a review of techniques and results of analyses. Progress in Physical Geography 8:473-508.

Hupp, C.R., and W.R. Osterkamp. 1985. Bottomland vegetation distribution along Passage Creek, Virginia, in relation to fluvial landforms. Ecology 66:670-681.

Illies, J.H. 1970. Graben tectonics are related to crust-mantle interaction. Pages 4-27 *in* J.H. Illies and E. St. Müller, editors. Graben problems. Schweizerbartsche Verlagsbuchhandlung, Stuttgart, West Germany.

Irion, G. 1982. Minerological and geochemical contribution to climatic history in central Amazonia during Quaternary times. Tropical Ecology 23:76-85.

Irion, G. 1984. Sedimentation and sediments of Amazonian rivers and evolution of the Amazonian landscape since Pliocene times. Pages 201-214 *in* H. Sioli, editor. The Amazon: limnology and landscape ecology of a mighty tropical river and its basin. Dr. W. Junk, Dordrecht, The Netherlands; Boston, Massachusetts, USA; and Lancaster, England.

Jackson, R.G., II. 1975. Hierarchical attributes and a unifying model of bedforms composed of cohesionless material and produced by shearing flow. Geological Society of America Bulletin 86:1523-1533.

Junk, W.J. 1984. Ecology of *várzea*, floodplain of Amazon whitewater rivers. Pages 215-243 *in* H. Sioli, editor. The Amazon: limnology and landscape ecology of a mighty tropical river and its basin. Dr. W. Junk, Dordrecht, The Netherlands; Boston, Massachusetts, USA; and Lancaster, England.

Kalliola, R., and M. Puhakka. 1988. River dynamics and vegetation mosaicism: a case study of the River Kamajohka, northernmost Finland. Journal of Biogeography 15:703-719.

Kessel, R.H., K.C. Dunne, R.C. McDonald, and K.R. Allison. 1974. Lateral erosion and overbank deposition on the Mississippi River in Louisiana caused by 1973 flooding. Geology 2:461-464.

Khobzi, J., S. Kroonenberg, P. Faivre, and A. Weeda. 1980. Aspectos geomorphologicos de la Amazonia y Orinoquia Colombianas. Revista CIAF (Bogotá) 5:97-126.

King, L.C. 1962. Morphology of the earth. Oliver and Boyd, Edinburgh, Scotland.

Klammer, G. 1984. The relief of the extra-Andean Amazon basin. Pages 47-83 *in* H. Sioli, editor. The Amazon: limnology and landscape ecology of a mighty tropical river and its basin. Dr. W. Junk, Dordrecht, The Netherlands; Boston, Massachusetts, USA; and Lancaster, England.

Krissek, L.A., K.F. Scheidegger, and L.D. Kulm. 1980. Surface sediments of the Peru-Chile continental margin and the Nazca Plate. Geological Society of America Bulletin 91:321-331.

Krumbein, W.C., and L.L. Sloss. 1963. Stratigraphy and sedimentation. Second edition. W.H. Freeman, San Francisco, California, USA.

Kuleimina, N.M. 1973. Some characteristics of the process of incomplete meandering of the channel of the upper Ob River. Soviet Hydrology 6:562-565.

Leopold, L.B., M.G. Wolman, and J.P. Miller. 1964. Fluvial processes in geomorphology. W.H. Freeman, San Francisco, California, USA.

Lewin, J. 1978. Floodplain geomorphology. Progress in Physical Geography 2:408-437.

Lewis, G.W., and J. Lewin. 1983. Alluvial cutoffs in Wales and the Borderlands. Pages 145-

154 *in* J.D. Collinson and J. Lewin, editors. Modern and ancient fluvial systems. Blackwell, Oxford, England.

Lowrie, A., S.A. Cureau, and A. Sarria. 1981. Basement faults and uplift in the Colombian Llanos. Zeitschrift für Geomorphologie, Supplement 40:1-11.

MacArthur, R.H., and E.O. Wilson. 1967. The theory of island biogeography. Princeton University Press, Princeton, New Jersey, USA.

Markevich, H.W. 1985. Geomorphic evidence for Pliocene-Pleistocene uplift in the area of the Cape Fear Arch, North Carolina. Pages 279-297 *in* M. Morisawa and J.T. Hack, editors. Tectonic geomorphology. Allen and Unwin, Boston, Massachusetts, USA.

Mayer, L. 1985. Tectonic geomorphology of the basin and range Colorado Plateau boundary in Arizona. Pages 235-259 *in* M. Morisawa and J.T. Hack, editors. Tectonic geomorphology. Allen and Unwin, Boston, Massachusetts, USA.

McLean, J.R., and T. Jerzykiewicz. 1978. Cyclicity, tectonics and coal: some aspects of fluvial sedimentology in the Brazeau-Paskapoo formations, Coal Valley Area Alberta, Canada. Pages 441-468 *in* A.D. Miall, editor. Fluvial sedimentology. Canadian Society of Petroleum Geologists, Calgary, Alberta, Canada.

Meentemeyer, V., and E.O. Box. 1987. Scale effects in landscape studies. Pages 15-34 *in* M.G. Turner, editor. Landscape heterogeneity and disturbance. Springer-Verlag, New York, USA.

Mertes, L.A.K. 1985. Floodplain development and sediment transport in the Solimões-Amazon River, Brazil. Master's thesis. University of Washington, Seattle, Washington, USA.

Miall, A.D. 1978. Fluvial sedimentology: a historical review. Pages 1-47 *in* A.D. Miall, editor. Fluvial sedimentology. Canadian Society of Petroleum Geologists, Calgary, Alberta, Canada.

Mitchell, A.H.G., and H.G. Reading. 1978. Sedimentation and tectonics. Pages 439-476 *in* H.G. Reading, editor. Sedimentary environments and facies. Blackwell Scientific Publications, Oxford, England.

Morisawa, M. 1985. Rivers: form and process. Geomorphology Texts 7, Longman Group, Hong Kong.

Morrison, R.B. 1985. Pliocene/Quaternary geology, geomorphology and tectonics of Arizona. Geological Society of America, Special Paper 203:123-146.

Mosley, M.P. 1975. Channel changes on the River Bollin, Cheshire, 1872-1973. East Midlands Geographer 6:185-199.

Murphy, R.E. 1967. A spatial classification of landforms based on both genetic and empirical factors: a revision. Annals, Association of American Geographers 57:185-186.

Murphy R.E. 1968. Landforms of the world. Annals Map, Supplement 9. Annals, Association of American Geographers 58(1).

Naiman, R.J., H. Décamps, J. Pastor, and C.A. Johnston. 1988. The potential importance of boundaries to fluvial ecosystems. Journal of the North American Benthological Society 7:289-306.

Nanson, G.C., and H.B. Beach. 1977. Forest succession and sedimentation on a meandering-river floodplain, northeast British Columbia, Canada. Journal of Biogeography 4:229-251.

Neill, C., and L.A. Deegan. 1986. The effect of Mississippi River delta lobe development on the habitat composition and diversity of Louisiana coastal wetlands. American Midland Naturalist 116:296-303.

Nilsson, C. 1981. Riparian vegetation of northern Swedish rivers. Wahlenbergia 7:113-124.

Peltzer, G., P. Tapponnier, Z. Zhang, and Z.Q. Xu. 1985. Neogene and Quaternary faulting in and along the Qinling Shan. Nature 317:500-505.

Pflafker, G. 1964. Oriented lakes and linaments of northeastern Bolivia. Geological Society of America Bulletin 75:503-522.

Pickett, S.T.A., and P.S. White (editors). 1985. The ecology of natural disturbance and patch dynamics. Academic Press, Orlando, Florida, USA.

Pinay, G., H. Décamps, E. Chauvet, and E. Fustec. 1990. Functions of ecotones in fluvial systems, *this volume.*

Prance, G.T. (editor). 1982. Biological diversification in the tropics. Columbia University Press, New York, USA.

Pringle, C.M., R.J. Naiman, G. Bretschko, J.R. Karr, M.W. Oswood, J.R. Webster, R.L. Welcomme, and M.J. Winterbourn. 1988. Patch dynamics in lotic systems: the stream as a mosiac. Journal of the North American Benthological Society 7:503-524.

Putzer, H. 1984. The geological evolution of the Amazon basin and its mineral resources. Pages 15-46 *in* H. Sioli, editor. The Amazon: limnology and landscape ecology of a mighty tropical river and its basin. Dr. W. Junk, Dordrecht, The Netherlands; Boston, Massachusetts, USA; and Lancaster, England.

RADAMBRASIL 1977. Levantamento de recursos naturais. Volume 15. Folha S.B. 19 Juruá. Ministerio das Minas e Energia, Departamento Nacional da Producão Projeto Radambrasil, Rio de Janeiro, Brazil.

Räsänen, M.E., J.S. Salo, and R.J. Kalliola. 1987. Fluvial perturbance in the Western Amazon basin: regulation by long-term sub-Andean tectonics. Science 238:1398-1401.

Reading, H.G. (editor). 1978. Sedimentary environments and facies. Blackwell Scientific Publications, Oxford, England.

Reineck, H.E., and I.B. Singh. 1980. Depositional sedimentary environments with reference to terrigenous clastics. Second edition. Springer-Verlag, Berlin and Heidelberg, Germany.

Richards, K. 1987. Fluvial geomorphology. Progress in Physical Geography 11:432-459.

Risser, P.G. 1987. Landscape ecology: state of the art. Pages 3-14 *in* M.G. Turner, editor. Landscape heterogeneity and disturbance. Springer-Verlag, New York, USA.

Salo, J. 1988. Rain forest diversification in the western Amazon basin: the role of river dynamics. Reports from the Department of Biology 16, University of Turku, Turku, Finland.

Salo, J.S., and R.J. Kalliola. 1989. River dynamics and natural forest regeneration in Peruvian Amazonia. *In* J. Jeffers, editor. Rain forest regeneration and management. MAB (Unesco) Book Series, UNESCO and Cambridge University Press, Paris and Cambridge, *in press*.

Salo, J., R. Kalliola, I. Häkkinen, Y. Mäkinen, P. Niemelä, M. Puhakka, and P.D. Coley. 1986. River dynamics and the diversity of Amazon lowland forest. Nature 322:254-258.

Salo, J., and M. Räsänen. 1989. Hierarchy of landscape patterns in Western Amazon. Pages 35-45, *in* L.B. Holm-Nielsen, I. Nielsen, and H. Balslev, editors. Tropical forests: botanical dynamics, speciation and diversity. Academic Press, London, England, *in press*.

Schumm, S.A. 1977. The fluvial system. John Wiley and Sons, New York, USA.

Seidenschwartz, F. 1986. Vergleich von Flußuferkrautgesellschaften mit Wildkrautvegetation im tropischen Tiefland von Peru. Amazoniana 10:79-111.

Selley, R.C. 1982. An introduction to sedimentology. Second edition. Academic Press, London, England.

Sioli, H. 1984. The Amazon and its main affluents: hydrography, morphology of the river courses, and river types. Pages 127-173 *in* H. Sioli, editor. The Amazon: limnology and landscape ecology of a mighty tropical river and its basin. Dr. W. Junk, Dordrecht, The Netherlands; Boston, Massachusetts, USA; and Lancaster, England.

Sombroek, W.G. 1966. Amazon soils: a reconnaissance of the soils of the Brazilian Amazon region. Center for Agriculture Publications and Documents, Wageningen, The Netherlands.

Sternberg, H. O'R. 1960. Radiocarbon dating as applied to a problem of Amazonian morphology. Comptes Rendus du XVIII Congrès International de Géographie, Rio de Janeiro 1956:399-424.

Stoneley, R. 1969. Sedimentary thickness in orogenic belts. Pages 215-238 *in* Time and space in orogeny. Geological Society of London, London, England.

Summerfield, M.A. 1985. Plate tectonics and landscape development on the African continent. Pages 27-51 *in* M. Morisawa and J.T. Hack, editors. Tectonic geomorphology. Allen and Unwin, Boston, Massachusetts, USA.

Summerfield, M.A. 1986. Tectonic geomorphology: macroscale perspectives. Progress in Physical Geography 10:227-238.

Summerfield, M.A. 1987. Neotectonics and landform genesis. Progress in Physical Geography 11:384-397.

Teichert, C. 1958. Concepts of facies. Bulletin of American Association of Petroleum Geologists 42:2718-2744.

Terborgh, J. 1983. Five New World primates. Princeton University Press, Princeton, New Jersey, USA.

Thompson, J.N. 1978. Within-patch structure and dynamics in *Pastinaca sativa* and resource availability to a specialized herbivore. Ecology 59:443-448.

Tricart, J. 1975. Influence des oscillations climatiques resénts sur le modelé en Amazonie Orientale (Région de Santarém) d'après les images radar latéral. Zeitschrift für Geomorphologie 19:140-169.

Turnbull, W.J., E.S. Krinitzky, and L.J. Johnson. 1950. Sedimentary geology of the alluvial valley of the Mississippi River and its bearing on foundation problems. Pages 210-226 *in* P.D. Trask, editor. Applied sedimentation. John Wiley, New York, New York, USA.

Urban, D.L., R.V. O'Neill, and H.H. Shugart, Jr. 1987. Landscape ecology. BioScience 37:119-127.

Walker, L.R., J.C. Zasada, and F.S. Chapin III. 1986. The role of life history processes in primary successions on an Alaskan floodplain. Ecology 67:1243-1253.

Ware, G.H., and W.T. Penfound. 1949. The vegetation of the lower levels of the floodplain of the South Canadian River in central Oklahoma. Ecology 30:478-484.

West, D.C., H.H. Shugart, and D.B. Botkin (editors). 1981. Forest succession: concepts and application. Springer-Verlag, New York, USA.

Westoby, M. 1987. Soil erosion, as a landscape ecology phenomenon. Trends in Ecology and Evolution 2:321-322.

Whitmore, T.C., and G.T. Prance (editors). 1987. Biogeography and Quaternary history in tropical America. Clarendon Press, Oxford, England.

Wiens, J.A. 1976. Population responses to patchy environments. Annual Review of Ecology and Systematics 7:81-120.

Wiens, J.A., J.F. Addicott, T.J. Case, and J. Diamond. 1986. Overview: the importance of spatial and temporal scale in ecological investigations. Pages 145-153 *in* J. Diamond and T.J. Case, editors. Community ecology. Harper and Row, New York, USA.

Winkley, B.R. 1977. Manmade cutoffs on the lower Mississippi River: conception, construction and river response. United States Corps of Engineers, Vicksburg, Mississippi, USA.

Wolman, M.G., and L.B. Leopold. 1957. River flood plains: some observations on their formation. United States Geological Survey Professional Paper 282-C.

Key words: Amazon River, ecotone, landscape ecology, patch dynamics.

CHAPTER 5

LANDSCAPE DISTURBANCES AND LOTIC ECOTONES

Robert C. Wissmar and Frederick J. Swanson

ABSTRACT

This chapter discusses lotic ecotones of uplands and the importance of landscape disturbances in controlling ecotone function and stability. Lotic ecotones are described as zones of transition between adjacent ecological systems having characteristics uniquely defined by space and time scales and by the strength of interactions between systems. They are considered to be sensitive to gradients of limiting factors and landscape changes caused by physical and biological disturbances. In uplands or headwaters of mountain stream systems, physical disturbances, and interactions with landform conditions and hydrologic regimes, are of major importance in determining the structure and dynamics of ecotones. Lotic ecotones of high relief landscapes are viewed as being less stable than those of lowlands because they are subject to more frequent and diverse disturbances and complex topographic effects. Landform slopes, topographic aspects, edaphic gradients, and other geomorphic factors influence gravity-driven flow paths of materials and the availability of water and energy to transport materials. Disturbances such as landslides and floods, in narrow upland valleys, combine to exert lateral control on upland lotic ecotones. These controls on ecotone function and stability can be most evident in ecotones near lotic systems having steep channel slopes where fluvial and geomorphic processes strongly influence the development of riparian vegetation.

Field and modelling studies suggest several approaches for evaluating temporal and spatial effects of disturbance regimes and topographic factors on ecotonal riparian communities and their stability. Field studies include disturbance histories and changes in ages of riparian forest patches for two different types of mountain valleys (fluvial and glacially formed) in the Cascade Mountains of Oregon and Washington, USA. The determination of the relative physical stability of lotic ecotones is approached using geomorphic concepts

65

of phases of landform change and recovery following disturbance, and time intervals for disturbance recurrence. Recommendations are provided for additional descriptive and quantitative approaches that could be used in managing lotic ecotones.

INTRODUCTION

A major difficulty in defining the role of disturbances in ecological systems is the lack of sufficient paradigms coupling physical disturbance regimes with biological responses (Mooney and Gordon 1983, Sousa 1984, Pickett and White 1985, Forman and Godron 1986). Concepts concerning influences of different scales of disturbance on ecological functions and ecotones and ecosystems are needed in order to develop models at the landscape level (Risser *et al.* 1984, Wiens *et al.* 1985, Forman and Godron 1986, Naveh 1987, Turner 1987, Urban *et al.* 1987). Recent syntheses advancing new concepts for aquatic-terrestrial ecotones within a landscape mosaic give excellent examples of many of these shortcomings (Hansen *et al.* 1988 a, b; Holland 1988, Naiman *et al.* 1988, Resh *et al.* 1988, Reice *et al.* 1990, Pinay *et al.* 1990, Salo 1990).

This chapter examines the assertion that different types and scales of physical disturbances, along with major controls of landform conditions and hydrologic regimes, determine the structure and dynamics of lotic ecotones (lotic-land interfaces) in upland-mountainous landscapes. We focus on landscape disturbances in terms of the influences of fluvial and geomorphic processes on upland lotic ecotones. Other aspects of ecotone disturbance, such as the effects of large animals, fires, tree blowdown, and root rot infestations, on fragmentation of ecotone corridors and patches have been covered elsewhere (Forman and Godron 1981, Burgess and Sharpe 1981, Romme 1982, Dale *et al.* 1986, Turner 1987, Turner and Bratton 1987, Naiman 1988, Décamps *et al.* 1988, Odum 1990, Petts 1990).

We begin by providing definitions of the key terms, which are then treated in more detail in regard to emerging landscape perspectives. These definitions give rise to assertions about the influence of landscape disturbances on lotic ecotones. We examine these suppositions by first describing the role of disturbances within the array of influences on the structure and functioning of ecotones along longitudinal (upstream-downstream) and lateral (stream-landward) gradients. We focus on lotic ecotones that are interfaces of lotic and land systems, either sharp boundaries or gradients depending on position in a river basin and disturbance history. Examples are given of the effects of disturbance on the development of riparian vegetation gradients and patches of lotic ecotones in uplands familiar to us. Conceptual frameworks are presented that could be useful in coupling disturbance regimes with changes in stabilities of ecotones. We

66

conclude by suggesting approaches that might be used in the management of lotic ecotones.

DEFINITIONS

An *ecotone* can be defined according to a SCOPE/MAB working group definition (Holland 1988) as a zone of transition between adjacent ecological systems having a set of characteristics uniquely defined by space and time scales and by the strength of interactions between adjacent ecological systems.

Lotic ecotones can be defined, in the same manner, as fluvial boundaries (e.g. rivers and stream ecotones; Naiman *et al.* 1988). This definition follows that of Holland (1988) with the exception that resource patches are separated by both longitudinal (upstream-downstream) and lateral (landward) ecotones that operate over various spatial and temporal scales. The definition of Naiman *et al.* (1988) draws upon the river continuum concept (Vannote *et al.* 1980) and related inferences of processes of fluvial ecosystems involving downstream flows of water and materials (Elwood *et al.* 1983, Ward and Stanford 1983, Minshall *et al.* 1985, Statzner and Higler 1985, Naiman *et al.* 1987).

Patches adjacent to ecotones in fluvial systems can be defined as spatial units (e.g., biological communities and ecosystems) determined by patch characteristics and their interactions over various scales (Pringle *et al.* 1988). For example, riparian patches of lotic ecotones have relatively uniform vegetation composition and structure that contrast with neighbouring patches. Topography, substrate conditions, organisms, and disturbance influence patch composition, size, location, and shape (Forman and Godron 1981).

The term *landscapes* usually designates areas, on the scale of hectares to many square kilometres, that contain multiple patches. Landscapes are composed of landforms and ecological units such as patches (Forman and Godron 1986).

Landforms are land areas on a smaller scale than landscapes; they are individual elements of landscape topography, such as landforms created by landslides or gravel bars formed in streams by sediment deposition (Swanson *et al.* 1988).

A *disturbance*, from a landscape ecology perspective, is an event that causes a significant change from the 'normal pattern' in an ecological system (Forman and Godron 1986) – for example, an event creating an area of riparian vegetation distinctive in comparison to previous and neighbouring

67

patches. Another useful definition (Pickett and White 1985) that has recently been applied to stream ecosystems (Resh *et al.* 1988) considers a disturbance as any relatively discrete event in time that disrupts ecosystem, community, or population structure, and that changes resources, availability of substratum, or the physical environment. For ecotones, this definition needs to emphasise irregular events, over temporal and spatial scales, that cause abrupt structural alterations in biological communities and the physical environment. Attention should also be given to disturbances occurring under nonequilibrium conditions (Sousa 1984).

DISTURBANCE AND AQUATIC ECOTONES

Aquatic ecotones appear to be highly sensitive to landscape changes caused by physical and biological disturbances (Holland 1988, Naiman *et al.* 1988). Such landscape level conditions suggest that the stability of aquatic ecotones depends on disturbance events (e.g. landslides that dam lotic systems) and related interactions between hydrologic regimes and landform-edaphic features that form, maintain, and disrupt them. Examples of important responses of aquatic ecotones include alterations in surface water-groundwater exchanges and retention times, fragmentation of riparian zones, and woody debris accumulations (Peterjohn and Correll 1984, Pinay and Décamps 1988, Ward and Stanford 1989, Gibert *et al.* 1990). Aquatic ecotones where such disturbances are especially obvious include frequently disrupted (1) riparian areas and shallow waters of streams, rivers, floodplains, and lakes, and (2) landward portions of wetlands (Swanson and Lienkaemper 1982, Hupp and Osterkamp 1985, Wissmar 1986, Turner 1987, Agee 1988, Hook *et al.* 1988, Wissmar *et al.* 1988, Holland *et al.* 1990).

Lotic ecotones of uplands are the product of two interacting landscape functions: forest distribution patterns controlled by limiting factors, and the development of landforms, forest, and aquatic environments in various phases of recovery following disturbance. In uplands, where the mountains are steep and precipitation is high, we consider that periodic disturbances are more important than limiting factors in creating and maintaining lotic ecotones.

Disturbances may directly influence lotic ecotones at the landscape scale. Direct influences may be viewed as variations in ecotone and landscape configurations from 'normal conditions' for edaphic gradients, hydrologic regimes, and energy and material fluxes. Examples of direct influences of disturbances include removal of riparian vegetation by flash floods and landslides, and edaphic and vegetative modifications by large animals and man. Indirect influences, such as altered concentrations in gradients of various dissolved chemical constituents, and pathways of chemical reactions, may result from changes in edaphic and vegetative properties following direct impacts to a system.

LOTIC ECOTONES OF UPLANDS

We hypothesise that ecotones of upland streams of mountainous areas are less stable than those downstream because they are subject to more frequent, random, and diverse landscape disturbances and stronger landform controls. Topographic effects can be more complex because aspect and steepness of slopes influence gravity-driven flows of materials from hillslopes to valley floors and stream channels. Dissected, high relief landscapes focus surface and subsurface flows and consequently the availability of water and energy to transport sediment, large rocks, and organic debris. Water and material transport patterns are also influenced by interactions of landforms and the channel geomorphology of lotic systems. For example, variable sequences of constrained (e.g. landslides and canyons) and unconstrained channel reaches can alter erosional and depositional patterns of sediment. These features, when combined with hillslope disturbances and narrow valleys, exert lateral control on lotic ecotone functions. In contrast, downstream ecotones tend to be more stable because they are influenced less by frequent, random, and diverse disturbances. The broader topographic settings of lowlands allow longer periods for surface and subsurface water flows and patterns of soil development and movement. Persistent, nonrandom fluvial processes permit the development of more stable lotic ecotones. Lotic systems of lowland floodplains usually have low gradient channels and are affected, within fairly long time frames, by disturbances such as infrequent, large floods and modifications caused by agriculture, navigation, and urbanisation (Décamps *et al.* 1988).

Similar differences in lotic ecotones of upland terrains and lowland floodplains are noted by Pinay *et al.* (1990) in this chapter. They suggest that smaller floodplains reduce the development of riparian vegetation patches. These observations suggest that lotic ecotones of mountainous terrains can be expected to have smaller spatial features and reduced capacities to function because of lateral controls exerted by the surrounding topography and diverse disturbances (e.g. landslides and channel change). Effects of other disturbances on lotic ecotones, such as fire and wind, can be highly variable. This variability relates to the intensity and type of disturbance and to influences of topography. For example, steep slopes may favour the spread of fire while sharp, rocky ridges and wide, wet valley floors may retard the spread of fires.

The following sections discuss paradigms that couple disturbance regimes and biological responses at the landscape level. Important attributes include topographic scaling factors (e.g. channel slopes and landform shapes), disturbance regimes (temporal, spatial, and magnitude), and the stability of lotic ecotones. Examples show the roles played by stream channel slopes and fluvial and geomorphic disturbances in influencing lotic deposits and lateral gradients of riparian vegetation. The scale is then expanded to larger dimensions of the landscape by discussing concepts useful in modelling temporal and spatial influences of fluvial and geomorphic disturbances on the development of riparian patches and ecotone stability.

Channel slopes and colonisation by riparian vegetation

Geomorphic and vegetative characteristics of upland streams and ecotones can be influenced by abrupt changes in channel slope and associated hydraulics. Channel slope (the slope or gradient of the stream along a given reach) influences channel width and depth, water velocity, and discharge rates (Leopold *et al.* 1964). Flood events and movements of debris near slope discontinuities of narrow valleys can create morphometric adjustments at tributary confluences, alter main channel and floodplain geomorphologies, and stress animals and plants (Bull 1979, Statzner *et al.* 1988, Statzner and Higler 1985, Hupp 1982, Hickin 1984, Roy and Roy 1988).

In many steep, high-energy streams of uplands, spatiotemporal heterogeneity of lotic ecotones reflects fluvial patterns of erosion and deposition driven by variations in discharge and related debris inputs from landward disturbances (Benda 1985). During floods and debris flows, flow velocities can increase in reaches with increased slopes and cause considerable flood damage to adjacent riparian and floodplain vegetation. Such conditions may be especially apparent in narrow valleys above and below landform-constrained channels (e.g. gorges and canyons with steep slopes) where high flow velocity has most extensive contact with vegetated areas (Hupp 1982). The cumulative effect of channel shapes, valley floor widths, and disturbances in the narrow floodplains of upland valleys can be expected to increase the instability and ephemeral character of many lotic ecotones.

Insights about influences of channel disturbances on the stability of lotic ecotones have been gained from studies of the development of riparian vegetation along high energy streams (Smith 1976, Teversham and Slaymaker 1976, Hickin 1984). The magnitude, frequency, and duration of flooding and other disturbances in these systems provide excellent information on how disturbance events can influence most aspects of the vegetation life history patterns in lotic ecotones (Swanson and Lienkaemper 1982, Hupp 1982, 1983). Floods can affect vegetation patterns by destroying and subsequently excluding plants, by creating new areas for vegetation colonisation, and by forming elevational gradients where plants show varying tolerances to flows and sediment movements.

Recent studies of upland streams in northern California (USA) have attempted to define relations between sediment transport, colonisation by riparian trees of channel margins, and streambank recovery (Lisle 1989, Trush *et al.* 1989). The streams examined had experienced large floods that mobilised broad areas of valley floors, removed riparian vegetation, and widened channels. Trees such as alder (*Alnus* spp.) colonised at the low flow level in order to obtain adequate moisture during the dry season. However, these riparian stands became established only when the magnitude of flood-induced sediment transport declined and the width of the mobile channel bed was confined to low flow conditions. When such conditions occurred, the trees became established on the active-channel shelf and were thereafter resistant to typical annual high flows (Fig. 5.1). Lisle (1989) described the mobile bed as the channel area where bedload transport of sediment occurs and the active-channel shelf as the area between the active channel (bankfull discharge width) and mobile bed widths.

This information suggests a simple hypothesis that describes how channel slope influences fluvial and geomorphic processes and the development of riparian vegetation of lotic ecotones. The hypothesis is that the colonisation and density of riparian trees on the active-channel shelf increase with decreasing stream channel slope and corresponding decreases in bedload transport of sediment in the mobile bed (Fig. 5.2). A useful feature of this concept is that it may provide a means to identify the relative stabilities of different lotic ecotones. While studies of Lisle (1989) and Trush *et al.* (1989) suggest that this assertion might be testable at the landscape level, other factors in addition to channel slope need to be considered, such as threshold values of available stream power where channel deposits become subject to erosion and deposition (Bull 1979), the degree of channel curvature and constraint, and the rate of plant colonisation along lotic-riparian elevational gradients.

Lotic deposits and lateral gradients of riparian vegetation

Riparian vegetation of upland lotic ecotones can extend from the active-channel shelves (Fig. 5.1) to higher terrace deposits. Such riparian gradients and patches develop in response to frequent discharge and debris flow disturbances that alter channel and ecotone deposits. An excellent landscape

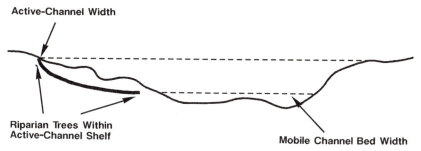

Figure 5.1 Diagram of a stream's mobile channel bed and active-channel width and shelf. The active-channel width is the area, largely unvegetated, where riparian stands can begin colonisation. The lower limit of plant endurance is the mobile channel bed width at low flow conditions

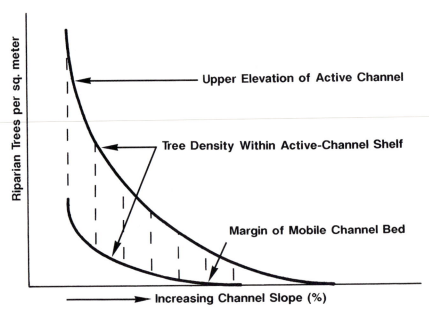

Figure 5.2 Concept of how channel slopes influence the development of riparian vegetation along streamsides. The hypothesis is that the colonisation and density of riparian trees on the active-channel shelf increase with decreasing stream channel slope and corresponding decreases in bedload transport of sediment in the mobile bed

Table 5.1 Fluvial geomorphic relations between valley floor vegetation and deposits. After Hupp and Osterkamp (1985)

Deposits*	Vegetation Type	%Time Inundated	Flood Frequency
Deposition bar	Herbaceous species	40%	—
Active-channel shelf	Riparian shrubs	0-25%	—
Floodplain	Floodplain forest	—	1-3 yr
Terrace	Terrace assemblages	—	3 yr

* Deposits include depositional bars within the main channel bed, the active-channel shelf, the floodplain above the active channel, and terraces. Terraces are at higher elevations and flooded less frequently than the floodplain. The active-channel shelf is the area between the floodplain and main channel bed that includes the steep bank slope and the lower limit of persistent woody vegetation

study that documents regionally consistent and discrete relations between deposits, flow regimes, and riparian vegetation types was conducted in northern Virginia, USA (Hupp and Osterkamp 1985). Examples of fluvial-geomorphic deposits, vegetation types, percentage of time inundated, and flood frequency are presented in Table 5.1. The depositional bars that experience inundation about 40% of the time were mainly covered with willow. The active-channel shelf, inundated 10 to 25% of the time, exhibited a riparian shrub forest – for example, red alder (*Alnus serrulata*), winterberry (*Ilex verticillata*), red willow (*Cornus amomum*), and black willow (*Salix nigra*). The floodplain, with a 1-3 yr flood frequency, was covered with a diverse forest dominated by black walnut (*Juglans nigra*), American elm (*Ulmus americana*), silver maple (*Acer saccharinum*), and hackberry (*Celtis occidentalis*). The terraces with 3-yr flood frequency were dominated by upland assemblages including oaks and hickories (Hupp and Osterkamp 1985).

Other investigations in British Columbia, Canada, and Oregon, USA (Teversham and Slaymaker 1976, Swanson and Lienkaemper 1982), demonstrate that certain vegetation types and distributions occur in ecotone patches that correspond with boundaries between geomorphic surfaces on gradients from the channel bed to the terraces. Such ecotones and contrasts in vegetation between patches were apparently controlled by variation in inundation frequency, substrate type, floods, and disturbances by bedload, ice, and debris movements (Yanosky 1983, Hupp 1983, Hupp and Osterkamp 1985).

Additional controls can be exerted by stabilising feedback of plants. Vegetation near channel margins can be very tolerant of channel disturbances, stabilising depositional bars and stream banks. Yanosky (1983) observed that many plant species near channels withstand a high duration of inundation and destructive flooding and exhibit a resilience through rapid sprouting of shrubs from damaged trunks and roots. Such features allow riparian vegetation to affect bank erodibility and lateral migration of channels (Smith 1976), thereby adding stability to lotic ecotones.

Disturbance regimes and developmental pathways of riparian patches

Once concepts of topographic scaling (channel slopes, fluvial deposits, landforms, and vegetative characteristics) have been formulated to describe influences of disturbances on lotic ecotones, attention needs to be given to evaluating temporal and spatial effects of disturbance regimes and biological responses at the landscape level. Perspectives can be examined by considering disturbance history (Décamps *et al.* 1988). Excellent examples are found by examining the role of past disturbances in the development of riparian forest patches in the Cascade Mountains of Oregon and Washington, USA. These studies provide historical information on changes in riparian and valley floor forest patches created by different types of disturbance and frequencies of recurrence. Major natural disturbances affecting the mountain forest include episodic floods, geomorphic changes in stream channels and landforms, fire, wind, and glacial activity (Fig. 5.3). Important landform disturbances include landslides and earthflows in glacial deposits on steep slopes. Human influences include clearcutting and road construction. Many of these events have recurrence intervals ranging from decades to a few

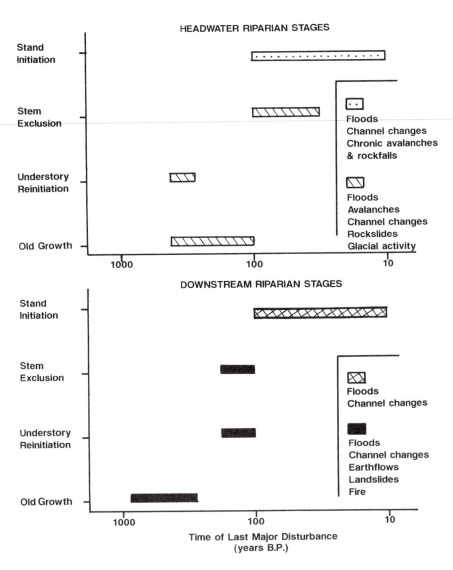

Figure 5.3 Major landscape disturbance and the development of riparian forest patches (successional stages) in downstream and headwater valleys of the Cascade Mountains of Oregon and Washington. The types of disturbance are indicated in the panel boxes. The bars show the length of time B.P. of the last major disturbance and subsequent successional stage. Disturbances that happened more than 1000 years ago include glaciation, volcanism, and tectonic uplift

centuries. Repeated volcanic eruptions also occur in these tectonically active coastal areas on time scales of centuries to millennia.

Examples of changes in the vegetative composition and ages of riparian forest patches in the Cascade Mountain valleys reflect the time of the last major disturbances (yr before present (B.P.)) and types of disturbances (Fig. 5.3). Disturbance regimes and the development of riparian forest patches (successional stages) are presented for an erosionally formed mountain valley in Oregon and a glaciated headwater valley in Washington. The physical and biological organisation of riparian forests in erosional valleys can be attributed mainly to the spatiotemporal characteristics of floods and changes in the geomorphology of stream channels. These alterations appear to affect the distribution, successional stages, and size of forest patches (S.V. Gregory, F.J. Swanson, and W.A. McKee, unpublished data, Forestry Sciences Laboratory and Oregon State University, Corvallis, Oregon, USA). Small patches (< 100 m²) may be reshaped several times annually by flow events. Larger patches (100-1000 m²) may be altered by high flows and channel changes (e.g. lateral movements) that recur on the time scale of years to several decades. Much larger landform areas (ha to km²) can be influenced by geomorphic processes, fire, and wind over hundreds to thousands of years. Large-scale alterations in the valley reflect more infrequent disturbances (10,000–100,000 yr) of volcanism, glaciation, and tectonic uplift. In contrast to erosional valleys, in steeper-headwater glaciated valleys more frequent and diverse types of disturbances are common (Oliver 1981, Oliver *et al.* 1985). The major changes in landforms and lotic ecotones reflect influences of frequent snow avalanches, rockslides, and episodic floods (Figs. 5.3 and 5.4).

Such retrospective information can be useful in designing studies that evaluate influences of frequent and infrequent disturbances on the temporal and spatial dynamics of lotic ecotones. Several biological studies of impacts of disturbances on forests have used transitional probability models of succession (Shugart *et al.* 1973, Romme 1982, Weinstein and Shugart 1983, Dale *et al.* 1986, DeAngelis *et al.* 1986). A diagram appropriate for the glaciated valleys shows how transitional probability models (e.g. Markov models) might be used to examine different developmental pathways of vegetative patches of ecotones in response to disturbances with different frequencies (Fig. 5.5). In mountain valleys, where disturbances are chronic to frequent, the riparian forest patches are commonly young, approaching 60 yr. In this case, Pathway 1 depicts vegetative patch development as being continually reset by disturbances and remaining in the stand initiation and exclusion successional stages during a system's physically disturbed phases (see definitions of reaction and recovery phases in the subsequent section on ecotone stability). Where disturbances are less frequent, development can proceed via Pathway 2. For Pathway 2, the developmental stages following stand initiation stage include stand exclusion (age 41-165 yr),

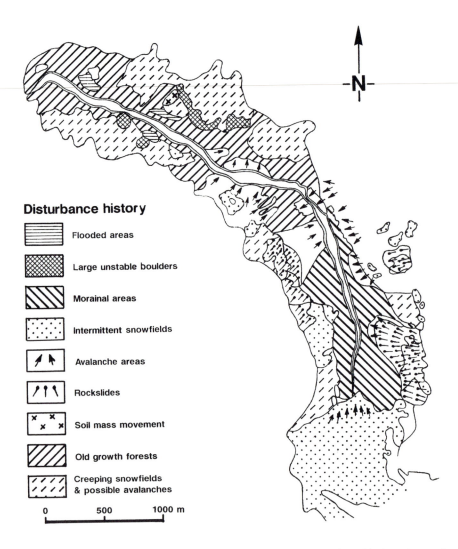

Disturbance history

	Flooded areas
	Large unstable boulders
	Morainal areas
	Intermittent snowfields
	Avalanche areas
	Rockslides
	Soil mass movement
	Old growth forests
	Creeping snowfields & possible avalanches

0   500   1000 m

Figure 5.4 Map of major disturbances influencing riparian vegetation of lotic ecotones of a glaciated valley located at the headwaters of the north fork of the Nooksack River in the North Cascade Mountains of Washington, USA. The north end of the valley is downstream. After Oliver *et al.* (1985)

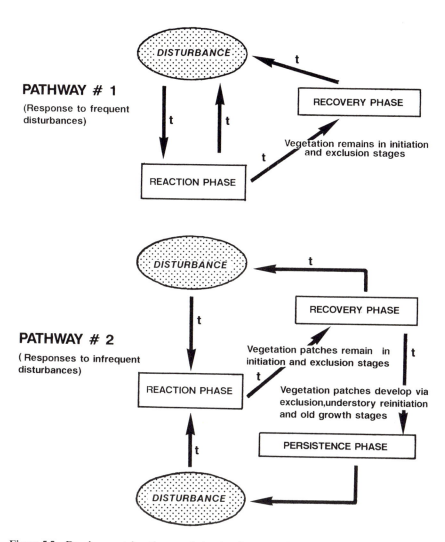

Figure 5.5 Developmental pathways of riparian forest patches in response to frequent and infrequent disturbances. Pathway 1 includes stand initiation and exclusion stages during reactive and recovery phases in ecotones following disturbances. Pathway 2 includes stand exclusion, understory reinitiation, and old growth stages after the recovery and during the persistence phases. See text and Fig. 5.7 for the definitions of reaction, recovery, and persistence phases in ecotones. The letter 't' indicates different transition times for riparian patches (successional stages)

understory reinitiation (age 144-480 yr), and old growth (age > 480 yr) (Fig. 5.5).

Spatial characteristics of disturbances may be considered along with evaluations of the effects of disturbance frequency and biotic responses (Fig. 5.5). One approach to spatially scaling disturbances in landscapes involves using probability models that contain functions describing the phasing of disturbances (Abugov 1982). For example, given the disturbance of a single riparian patch, the probability of that patch being disturbed during various time intervals is viewed as being independent of any probability of juxtaposed patches being disturbed during the same time interval (Fig. 5.6). In this case, biotic responses (Fig. 5.5) to a disturbance would be confined to single patches. Numerous and relatively frequent

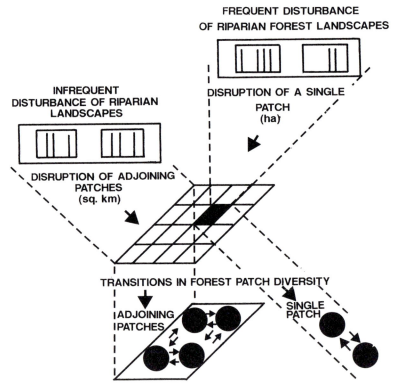

FREQUENT DISTURBANCE
OF RIPARIAN FOREST LANDSCAPES

INFREQUENT
DISTURBANCE OF RIPARIAN
LANDSCAPES

DISRUPTION OF A SINGLE
PATCH
(ha)

DISRUPTION OF ADJOINING
PATCHES
(sq. km)

TRANSITIONS IN FOREST PATCH DIVERSITY

ADJOINING
PATCHES

SINGLE
PATCH

Figure 5.6 Landscape perspective for lotic ecotones that describes disturbance impacts in terms of frequencies and two general spatial patterns. First, given a disturbance rate, the probability of an ecotone being disturbed during each time interval is viewed as being independent of the juxtaposed ecosystems being disturbed during the same time interval. Frequent disturbances are considered typical of this pattern. Second, the influence of patterning of disturbance is viewed as having landscape-wide ramification. Each time a disturbance occurs, the disruptions occur in ecotones and adjoining ecosystems. Infrequent and large disturbance events are considered typical of this pattern

disturbances like flooding, debris flows, and landslides, which can be common in uplands (Fig. 5.3 and 5.4), could be considered typical disturbances affecting single patches. In contrast to single-patch disturbance events, other disturbances may have more landscape-wide ramifications. In this situation, each time a disturbance affects a patch, the modification disrupts adjacent patches (Fig. 5.6). Infrequent and large-scale events such as storms and fires typify these landscape-wide disturbance patterns.

Disturbance regimes and the physical stability of lotic ecotones

Concepts concerning the influences of disturbance regimes in lotic ecotones need to be tested in different landscapes. In order to examine concepts like those presented here (Figs. 5.5 and 5.6), a general framework is needed to define the relative stability of different ecotones. We hypothesise that ecotones differ in physical stability or resistance to changes caused by disturbance. In contrast to other components or patches of a landscape, lotic ecotones might be recognised as transient and unsteady landscape components that appear and disappear in response to disturbances having great frequency. Consequently, ecotones are unstable, having spatial variations leading to transient features in terms of physical structure and biological organisation. Spatially and functionally, ecotones are highly sensitive to disturbances because of low resistance (e.g. steep channel slopes), low storage capacities (e.g. narrow valley floors and high sediment yield), and rapid reaction and recovery times (changes in channel geomorphology and biological recolonisation). Such characteristics would indicate that while the magnitude of disrupting forces that affect lotic ecotones may be less than in other patches of a landscape, the high frequency of disruption could cause greater change. As previously noted, we would expect such attributes to cause the stability of lotic ecotones to vary with respect to locations in a landscape (e.g. headwaters versus lowlands).

In contrast to lotic ecotones, juxtaposed land and water patches may be viewed as occupying 'more stable positions' in a landscape where disturbances are less frequent than the time for patch adjustment to them. As a result, the respective patches would be more insensitive to change than lotic ecotones. For example, in contrast to lotic ecotones, terrestrial patches may be the most stable because they exhibit more persistence of relief, higher resistance and storage capacities, and greater potential for superimposed vegetative patterns.

These concepts can be placed in a framework for use in evaluating the physical stability of ecotones. Here lotic ecotones are viewed as being subject to short-term or frequent disturbances while juxtapositioned patches display long-term responses to less frequent events. Patch structure and functions are considered to be more closely linked to widespread climatic-hydrologic and geomorphic changes. The framework draws upon geomorphic concepts of landform change and recovery (Brunsden and Thorns 1979, Chorley *et al.* 1984). The approach divides time into: *reaction phase* (A), the time taken for ecotones and other patches of landscapes to react to a disturbance; *recovery phase* (R), the time taken for a system to attain a characteristic equilibrium state; *persistence phase* (P), the period following R over which the characteristic state persists; and *disturbance recurrence* (D) time interval.

Within this framework, recovery (R) and disturbance recurrence (D) times have important roles to play in assessing ecotone stability and in determining ecotone adjustment to a wide range of disturbance time scales. The ratio of the recovery to disturbance recurrence (R:D) suggests differences in recovery characteristic of ecotones and ecosystems (Fig. 5.7). For unstable systems, the R:D ratios exceed one. The ratio is greater than one (> 1) because the mean recurrence time of disturbance events capable of producing changes is shorter than the time taken for the system to recover or equilibrate to a characteristic persistence state (P). Ratios greater than one indicate a minimal correspondence between processes of recovery and persistence. High R:D ratios might be viewed as common for predominantly transient systems, like many lotic ecotones in uplands.

For more stable systems, R:D ratios are commonly less than one (< 1). Here, adjustment to new conditions occurs before the next major disturbance. In this case, the characteristic persistent state (P) can exist after the initial recovery phase. The shortness of recovery times in relation to disturbance intervals suggests more predictable process-response relationships (Fig. 5.7).

Examples of apparent diagnostic power of the R:D ratio are shown in Table 5.2. Ratios of < 0.1 to 0.3 for riverine ecosystems suggest stable systems with longer disturbance intervals than recovery times. In contrast, ratios ranging from 0.5 to 10 for an array of small and large landslides in the Alps, Himalayas, and mountains of Japan imply unstable or transient systems with long recovery phases relative to short return periods for disturbance recurrence (Table 5.2). These transient systems can be viewed as having the ability to change but not the ability to always adjust before a new disturbance arrives.

These observations point to the need to view disturbance events and the stability of lotic ecotones as a series of adjustments between processes of disturbance recurrence and a system's responses during physical reactive, recovery, and persistence phases. At present, little is known about system characteristics that might be used to identify the states and pathways of systems during these time sequences. Numerous considerations need to be taken into account when comparing R and D characteristics like those in Table 5.2. For example, attention should be given to instances where disturbance events occur more frequently than recovery can take place. In another situation, the magnitude of a disturbance event might possibly play

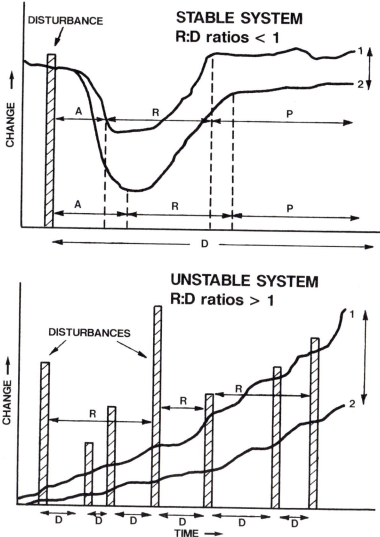

Figure 5.7 Concept of stable and unstable systems that divides time into phases for a system responding to a disturbance. Phases include reaction phase (A); recovery phase (R); persistence phase (P); and the time for disturbance recurrence (D). The stability of a system is recognised by ratios of recovery to disturbance recurrence (R:D). 1 and 2 indicate systems responding to disturbances of different magnitudes

a more important formative role in an ecotone's character than more frequent, smaller disturbance events.

Quantification of the magnitude of a disturbance event and its formative influences in ecotones and ecosystems is clearly an area of major future research. Potential approaches to estimating the magnitude of physical

Table 5.2 Representative disturbance recurrence times (D), recovery times (R), and R:D ratios for disturbed hillslopes and rivers

Disturbed System	Disturbance Recurrence Frequency (yr)	Recovery (yr)	R:D Ratio	Reference
RIVER CHANNELS AND BANKS				
Suspended sediments	50-100	5-10	0.1-0.2	Wolman and Gerson (1978)
Channel widths	3-200	1-15	0.01-0.3	Wolman and Gerson (1978)
HILLSLOPE LANDSLIDES				
Himalayas	10-20	10	0.4-1.0	Starkel (1972) Brunsden *et al.* (1989)
Japanese mountains	5	25	5	Wolman and Gerson (1978)
Alps	40-100	100-1000	1-10	Brunsden and Jones (1980)

disturbances have been described for fluvial systems (Wolman and Miller 1960, Chorley *et al.* 1984, Baker *et al.* 1987, Anderson 1988). In a seminal paper, Wolman and Miller (1960) maintain that despite flow variability, discharge of moderate frequency is responsible for determining channel capacity for transport of sediment. They describe the most significant discharge influencing channel capacity, through channel and bank morphologic adjustments, as the discharge that transported the most sediment for its given frequency of occurrence. They assert that the magnitude of the disturbance (the dominant stress or discharge) can be estimated as the product of the rate of sediment transport and the frequency of occurrences (Fig. 5.8). A recent study of different alluvial streams, where channels were both unconstrained (i.e. lateral migration of channels may occur) and constrained (i.e. lateral migration constrained by bedrock), suggests that Wolman and Miller's concept holds true for channel maintenance, recovery, and freedom to adjust boundaries (Carling 1988). These studies provide valuable paradigms for future investigations of disturbance frequency and magnitude in both aquatic and terrestrial ecosystems. Such information should prove useful in predicting influences of both natural and man-induced disturbance regimes on the stability of ecotones.

CONCLUSIONS AND RECOMMENDATIONS

We have recommended several possible approaches for obtaining better information about the effects of different disturbance regimes on lotic

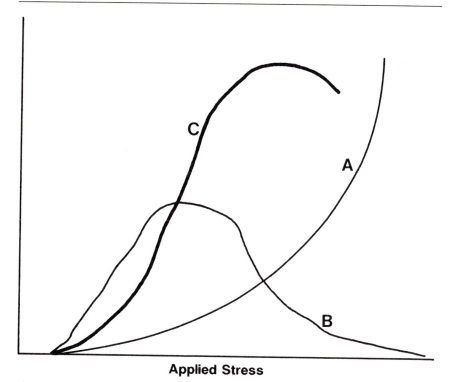

Applied Stress

Figure 5.8 Relationship between the rate of bedload movement (A) and the frequency of occurrence (B). The product (C) of the two curves (A and B) defines a maximum used to isolate a dominant stress or discharge. After Wolman and Miller (1960)

ecotones and juxtaposed ecosystems. The physical influences of disturbances on landform stability in natural systems have received much attention (Hack and Goodlett 1960, Swanson and Swanston 1977, Swanson 1981, Swanson *et al.* 1982), but few ecological studies have dealt with the effects of disturbance regimes on communities across regional landscapes (Romme 1982, Risser *et al.* 1984, Pickett and White 1985, Forman and Godron 1986, Turner 1987, Swanson *et al.* 1988). Much of the recent information on disturbance and the ecology of ecotones pertains to smaller-scale systems such as high energy streams and riparian zones (Teversham and Slaymaker 1976, Swanson and Lienkaemper 1982, Yanosky 1983, Hupp and Oster- kamp 1985, Lisle 1989, Trush *et al.* 1989).

In the context of landscapes, we have discussed how spatial and temporal information on geomorphic features can be essential to interpreting environ- mental disturbances and changes in system structure and dynamics. Examples of basic templates have been presented that could facilitate an understanding of natural background disturbance regimes and the sensitivities of ecotones and ecosystems. For instance, the effects of different

83

disturbance regimes, such as spatial patterning and rates of disturbance in hillslope and stream ecosystems, have major implications for understanding how biological communities develop in lotic ecotones of large landscapes (Smith 1976, Osterkamp and Hupp 1984, Hickin 1984, Agee 1988, Lisle 1989). Available information points to the need for studies at the regional landscape scale that facilitate predictions of the effects of disturbances on lotic ecotones and adjacent ecosystems of broad environmental gradients. Such information is fundamental to a better understanding of environmental changes at landscape and global scales.

Disturbance of aquatic ecosystems has been cited as one of the major topics having both fundamental and applied aspects in need of research during the next decade (Resh *et al.* 1988, Reice *et al.* 1990, Gore *et al.* 1990). A basic scientific problem in the evaluation of landscapes and their ecotones is the lack of testable models with short- and long-term predictive capabilities. The difficulty concerns not knowing the extent to which characteristic or repetitive changes in ecotones and ecosystems of a landscape are caused by disturbances of low frequency and high magnitude extremes. We understand that large disturbance events can dominate the main trends of change. Yet we do not know which events will be formative, or how to recognise temporal and spatial sequences of events and the ability of ecotones and ecosystems to recover to characteristic persistent states. Although we have presented information about representative disturbance recurrences and recovery phases for disturbed hillslopes and rivers, such landscape knowledge for both physical and biotic components of ecotones and ecosystems is generally lacking.

Many of the difficulties in studying landscapes arise from the need to acquire and interpret vast amounts of current and historical environmental information (e.g. dendrochronological and sedimentation records) in terms of their temporal variabilities and responses to episodic disturbance behaviour. Historical data are important because we must take into account the memory of systems. Memory is evaluated in terms of relative changes in a system caused by past disturbances and the ability of the system to adjust to new events. The wealth of information preserved in ecotones (e.g. dendrochronology, river alluvium, peat bogs, lake deposits, and other records) should play an important role in advancing our knowledge. Ecotones, which we have viewed as unstable system components and sensitive to frequent change, may exhibit distinct breaks in temporal and spatial records of a landscape mosaic. For example, ecotones may be important in the recognition of small spatial processes that operate on temporal scales of 10 to 100 yr. Time scales for both geomorphic and vegetative processes are important because they reflect controls on an ecotone's physical structure and patterns that can depend on landscapewide disturbances. In contrast, longer time scales that operate > 1000 yr for other landscape features, such as stable hard rock canyons and low relief energy plateaus, may have unrecognisable geomorphic processes. Nevertheless, perspectives at both scales have value in understanding ecotone and ecosystem dynamics across landscape gradients and for use in resource planning and management.

A prime example of the demands for landscape management information are those created by the passage in the United States of the National Environmental Policy Act of 1969 (Public Law 91-190; 42 U.S.C. 4321-4347). Federal resource managers must assess disturbances within the context of cumulative and long-term effects of proposed management actions on the environment. Cumulative effects amount to the incremental impact of an action when added to other past, present, and reasonably foreseeable future actions. The monitoring of effects of past and present activities has become an explicit policy requirement for forest and land managers. However, procedures and guidelines for implementing such directives remain vague and are not usually based on sound scientific information.

Considerable information useful for fundamental studies and management purposes can undoubtedly be obtained through evalution of concepts like those presented in this chapter and by development of landscape models that yield indices of landscape patterning. Useful measures for lotic ecotones might include fractal dimensions (O'Neill *et al.* 1988, Turner and Ruscher 1988) and indices of chaos (Naiman *et al.* 1988). Measures of fractals have made it possible to quantify complex boundaries or patch shapes and relate these pattens to the underlying processes (e.g. disturbances) that may affect pattern complexity. Indices depicting chaotic regimes have been shown to be useful where natural and human-induced perturbations push biological populations into chaos (Pool 1989).

Other research approaches could focus on ecological functions of landscapes and their ecotones by applying energy balance methods commonly used in evaluating agricultural landscapes. In agricultural cases, higher variabilities of energy flow and water cycling have been observed for individual ecosystems than for landscapes (Ryskowski and Kedziora 1988). Similar information on the variability of energy fluxes under different forest management and cutting practices (Franklin and Forman 1987) could be useful in pointing to differences in ecological stresses experienced by ecotones and ecosystems across the forest landscape. Many of the approaches advanced in this chapter could be used by resource managers in developing adaptive management programs. Such programs could include both the monitoring of disturbance regimes and their cumulative effects in land-water ecotones, and provisions for information feedback that improve long-term management plans.

ACKNOWLEDGEMENTS

The research was supported by the Center for Streamside Studies, College of Forest Resources, University of Washington, Seattle, Washington, USA, the United States Department of Agriculture Forest Service Agreement PNW-87-030, and Long Term Ecological Research and Riparian National Science Foundation grants (BSR 84-14325 and BSR 85-08356) to Oregon State University, Corvallis, Oregon, USA. The authors wish to thank Lee E. Benda, Stanley V. Gregory, and W. Arthur McKee for discussions and Robert J. Naiman for comments on the manuscript.

LITERATURE CITED

Abugov, R. 1982. Species diversity and phasing of disturbance. Ecology 63:289-293.

Agee, J.K. 1988. Successional dynamics in forest riparian zones. Pages 31-43 *in* K.J. Raedeke, editor. Streamside management: riparian wildlife and forestry interactions. Contribution 59, University of Washington, Institute of Forest Resources, Seattle, Washington, USA.

Anderson, M.G. 1988. Modelling geomorphological systems. John Wiley and Sons, New York, USA.

Baker, V.R., R.C. Kochel, and P.C. Patton. 1987. Flood geomorphology. John Wiley and Sons, New York, USA.

Benda, L.E. 1985. Delineation of channels susceptible to debris flows and debris floods. Pages 195-201 *in* International Symposium on Erosion, Debris Flow, and Disaster Prevention, Tsukuba, Japan.

Brunsden, D.D., and K.C. Jones. 1980. Relative time scales and formative events in coastal landslide systems. Zeitschrift für Geomorphologie, Supplement 34:1-19.

Brunsden, D.D., K.C. Jones, R.P. Martin, and J.C. Doornkamp. 1989. The geomorphological character of part of the Low Himalaya of eastern Nepal. Zeitschrift für Geomorphologie, *in press.*

Brunsden, D., and J.B. Thornes. 1979. Landscape sensitivity and change. Transactions of the Institute of British Geographers 4:463-484.

Bull, W.B. 1979. Threshold of critical stream power in streams. Bulletin of the Geological Society of America 90:453-464.

Burgess, R.L., and D.M. Sharpe. 1981. Forest island dynamics in man-dominated landscapes. Springer-Verlag, New York, USA.

Carling, P. 1988. The concept of dominant discharge applied to two gravel-bed streams in relation to channel stability thresholds. Earth Surface Processes and Landforms 13:355-367.

Chorley, R.J., S.A. Schumm, and D.E. Sudgen. 1984. Geomorphology. Methuen, London, England.

Dale, V.H., M. Hemstrom, and J. Franklin. 1986. Modeling the long-term effects of disturbances on forest succession, Olympic Peninsula, Washington. Canadian Journal of Forest Research 16:56-67.

DeAngelis, D.L., W.M. Post, and C.C. Travis. 1986. Positive feedback in natural systems. Springer-Verlag, New York, USA.

Décamps, H., M. Fortuné, F. Gazelle, and G. Pautou. 1988. Historical influence of man on the riparian dynamics of a fluvial landscape. Landscape Ecology 1:163-173.

Elwood, J.W., J.D. Newbold, R.V. O'Neill, and W. Van Winkle. 1983. Resource spiraling: an operational paradigm for analyzing lotic ecosystems. Pages 3-27 *in* T.D. Fontaine III and S.M. Bartell, editors. Dynamics of lotic ecosystems. Ann Arbor Science, Ann Arbor, Michigan, USA.

Forman, R.T.T., and M. Godron. 1981. Interaction among landscape elements: a core of landscape ecology. Pages 35-48 *in* S.P. Tjallingii and A.A. de Veer, editors. Perspectives in landscape ecology. Centre for Agricultural Publication and Documentation, Wageningen, The Netherlands.

Forman, R.T.T., and M. Godron. 1986. Landscape ecology. John Wiley and Sons, New York, USA.

Franklin, J.F., and R.T.T. Forman. 1987. Creating landscape patterns by forest cutting:

ecological consequences and principles. Landscape Ecology 1:5-18.

Gibert, J., M.J. Dole-Oliver, P. Marmonier, and P. Vervier. 1990. Surface groundwater ecotones, *this volume.*

Gore, J.A., J.R. Kelly, and J.D. Yount. 1990. Application of ecological theory to determining the recovery of disturbed lotic ecosystems: research needs and priorities. Environmental Management, *in press.*

Hack, J.T., and J.C. Goodlett. 1960. Geomorphology and forest ecology of a mountain region in the central Appalachians. United States Geological Survey Professional Paper 347, Renton, Virginia, USA.

Hansen, A.J., F. di Castri, and R.J. Naiman. 1988a. Ecotones: what and why? Biology International, Special Issue 17:9-46.

Hansen, A.J., F. di Castri, and P.G. Risser. 1988b. A new SCOPE project. Ecotones in a changing environment: the theory and management of landscape boundaries. Biology International, Special Issue 17:137-163.

Hickin, E.J. 1984. Vegetation and river channel dynamics. Canadian Geographer 28:111-126.

Holland, M.M. 1988. SCOPE/MAB technical consultations on landscape boundaries: report of a SCOPE/MAB workshop on ecotones. Biology International, Special Issue 17:47-106.

Holland, M.M., D.F. Whigham, and B. Gopal. 1990. The characteristics of wetland ecotones, *this volume.*

Hook, D.D., *et al.* (12 editors). 1988. The ecology and management of wetlands. Volume 1: Ecology of wetlands. Timber Press, Portland, Oregon, USA.

Hupp, C.R. 1982. Stream-grade variation and riparian forest ecology along Passage Creek, Virginia. Bulletin of the Torrey Botanical Club 109:488-499.

Hupp, C.R. 1983. Vegetation patterns in the Passage Creek gorge, Virginia. Castanea 48:62-72.

Hupp, C.R., and W.R. Osterkamp. 1985. Bottomland vegetation distribution along Passage Creek, Virginia, in relation to fluvial landforms. Ecology 66:670-681.

Leopold, L.B., M.G. Wolman, and J.P. Miller. 1964. Fluvial processes in geomorphology. W.H. Freeman, San Francisco, California, USA.

Lilse, T.E. 1989. Channel-dynamic control on the establishment of riparian trees after large floods in northern California. California Riparian Systems Conference, September 1988, Davis, California, USA.

Minshall, G.W., K.W. Cummins, R.C. Petersen, C.E. Cushing, D.A. Burns, J.R. Sedell, and R.L. Vannote. 1985. Developments in stream ecosystem theory. Canadian Journal of Fisheries and Aquatic Sciences 42:1045-1055.

Mooney, H.A., and M. Godron. 1983. Disturbance and ecosystems. Springer-Verlag, New York, USA.

Naiman, R.J. 1988. Animal influences on ecosystem dynamics. BioScience 38:750-752.

Naiman, R.J., H. Décamps, J. Pastor, and C.A. Johnston. 1988. The potential importance of boundaries to fluvial ecosystems. Journal of the North American Benthological Society 7:289-306.

Naiman, R.J., J.M. Melillo, M.A. Lock, T.E. Ford, and S.R. Reice. 1987. Longitudinal patterns of ecosystem processes and community structure in a subarctic river continuum. Ecology 68:1139-1156.

Naveh, Z. 1987. Biocybernetic and thermodynamic perspectives of landscape functions and land use patterns. Landscape Ecology 1:75-83.

Odum, W.E. 1990. Internal processes influencing the maintenance of ecotones: do they exist?, *this volume.*

Oliver, C.D. 1981. Forest development in North America following major disturbances. Forest Ecology and Management 3:153-168.

Oliver, C.D., A.B. Adams, and R.J. Zasoki. 1985. Disturbance patterns and forests development in a recently deglaciated valley in the northwestern Cascade Range of Washington, U.S.A. Canadian Journal of Forest Research 15:221-232.

O'Neill, R.V., *et al.* (11 authors) 1988. Indices of landscape pattern. Landscape Ecology 1:153-162.

Osterkamp, W.R., and C.R. Hupp. 1984. Geomorphic and vegetative characteristics along three northern Virginia streams. Bulletin of the Geological Society of America 95:1093-1101.

Peterjohn, W.T., and D.J. Correll. 1984. Nutrient dynamics in an agricultural watershed: observations on the role of a riparian forest. Ecology 65:1466-1475.

Petts, G.E. 1990. The role of ecotones in aquatic landscape management, *this volume.*

Pickett, S.T.A., and P.S. White (editors). 1985. The ecology of natural disturbance and patch dynamics. Academic Press, Orlando, Florida, USA.

Pinay, G., and H. Décamps. 1988. The role of riparian woods in regulating nitrogen fluxes between alluvial aquifer and surface water: a conceptual model. Regulated Rivers 2:507-516.

Pinay, G., H. Décamps, E. Chauvet, and E. Fustec. 1990. Functions of ecotones in fluvial systems, *this volume.*

Pool, R. 1989. Ecologists flirt with chaos. Science 243:310-313.

Pringle, C.M., R.J. Naiman, G. Bretschko, J.R. Karr, M.W. Oswood, J.R. Webster, R.L. Welcomme, and M.J. Winterbourn. 1988. Patch dynamics in lotic systems: the stream as a mosaic. Journal of the North American Benthological Society 7:503-524.

Reice, S.R., R.C. Wissmar, and R.J. Naiman. 1990. The influence of spatial and temporal heterogeneity and the background disturbance regime on the recovery of lotic ecosystems. Environmental Management, *in press.*

Resh, V.H., A.V. Brown, A.P. Covich, M.E. Gurtz, H.W. Li, G.W. Minshall, S.R. Reice, A.L. Sheldon, J.B. Wallace, and R.C. Wissmar. 1988. The role of disturbance in stream ecology. Journal of the North American Benthological Society 7:433-455.

Risser, P.G., J.R. Karr, and R.T. Forman. 1984. Landscape ecology: directions and approaches. Illinois Natural History Survey Special Publication Number 2, Champaign, Illinois, USA.

Romme, W.H. 1982. Fire and landscape diversity in subalpine forests of Yellowstone National Park. Ecological Monographs 52:199-221.

Roy, A.G., and R. Roy. 1988. Changes in channel size at river confluences with coarse bed materials. Earth Surface Processes and Landforms 13:77-84.

Ryszkowski, L., and A. Kedziora. 1988. Impact of agricultural landscape structure on energy flow and water cycling. Landscape Ecology 1:85-94.

Salo, J. 1990. External processes influencing origin and maintenance of inland water-land ecotones, *this volume.*

Shugart, H.H., T.R. Crow, and J.M. Hett. 1973. Forest succession models: a rationale and methodology for modelling forest succession over large regions. Forest Science 19:203-212.

Smith, D.G. 1976. Effect of vegetation on lateral migration of anastomosed channels of a glacier meltwater river. Bulletin of the Geological Society of America 87:857-860.

Sousa, W. 1984. The role of disturbance in natural communities. Annual Review of Ecology and Systematics 15:535-591.

Starkel, L. 1972. The role of catastrophic rainfall in the shaping of the relief of the lower Himalaya (Darjeeling Hills). Geographic Polon 21:103-147.

Statzner, B., J.A. Gore, and V.H. Resh. 1988. Hydraulic stream ecology: observed patterns and potential applications. Journal of the North American Benthological Society 7:307-360.

Statzner, B., and B. Higler. 1985. Questions and comments on the river continuum concept. Canadian Journal of Fisheries and Aquatic Sciences 42:1038-1044.

Swanson, F.J. 1981. Fire and geomorphic processes. Pages 401-420 *in* Proceedings of the Conference on Fire Regimes and Ecosystem Properties. USDA Forest Service General Technical Report WO-26, Washington, D.C.

Swanson, F.J., R.J. Janda, T. Dunne, and D.N. Swanston. 1982. Sediment budgets and routing in forested drainage basins. USDA Forest Service General Technical Report PNW-141, Portland, Oregon, USA.

Swanson, F.J., T.K. Kratz, N. Caine, and R.G. Woodmansee. 1988. Landform effects on ecosystem patterns and processes. BioScience 38:92-98.

Swanson, F.J., and G.W. Lienkaemper. 1982. Interaction among fluvial processes, forest vegetation, and aquatic ecosystems, South Fork Hoh River, Olympic National Park. Pages 30-34 *in* E.E. Starkey, J.F. Franklin, and J.W. Matthews, editors. Ecological research in National Parks of the Pacific Northwest. Forestry Sciences Laboratory, Corvallis, Oregon, USA.

Swanson, F.J., and D.W. Swanston. 1977. Complex mass-movement terrains in the western Cascade Range, Oregon. Engineering Geology, Geological Society of America 3:113-124.

Teversham, J.M., and J. Slaymaker. 1976. Vegetation composition in relation to flood frequency in Lillooet River Valley, British Columbia. Catena (Cremlingen-Destedt, Germany) 3:191-201.

Trush, W.J., E.C. Conner, and A.W. Knight. 1989. Alder establishment and channel dynamics in a South Fork Eel River tributary, Mendocino County, California. California Riparian Systems Conference, September 1988, Davis, California. USA.

Turner, M.G. (editor). 1987. Landscape heterogeneity and disturbance. Springer-Verlag, New York, USA.

Turner, M.G., and S.P. Bratton. 1987. Fire, grazing, and the landscape heterogeneity of a Georgia Barrier Island. Pages 85-101 in M.G. Turner, editor. Landscape heterogeneity and disturbance. Springer-Verlag, New York, USA.

Turner, M.G., and C.L. Ruscher. 1988. Changes in landscape patterns in Georgia, USA. Landscape Ecology 1:241-251.

Urban, D.L., R.V. O'Neill, and H.H. Shugart, Jr. 1987. Landscape ecology. BioScience 37:119-127.

Vannote, R.L., G.W. Minshall, K.W. Cummins, J.R. Sedell, and C.E. Cushing. 1980. The river continuum concept. Canadian Journal of Fisheries and Aquatic Sciences 37:130-137.

Ward, J.V., and J.A. Stanford. 1983. The serial discontinuity concept of lotic ecosystems. Pages 29-42 in T.D. Fontaine III and S.M. Bartell, editors. Dynamics of lotic systems. Ann Arbor Science, Ann Arbor, Michigan, USA.

Ward, J.V., and J.A. Stanford. 1989. Riverine ecosystems: the influence of man on catchment dynamics and fish ecology. Canadian Journal of Fisheries and Aquatic Sciences, in press.

Weinstein, D.A., and H.H. Shugart. 1983. Ecological modelling of landscape dynamics. Page 29-46 in H.A. Mooney and M. Godron, editors. Disturbance and ecosystems. Springer-Verlag, New York, USA.

Wiens, J.A., C.S. Crawford, and J.R. Gosz. 1985. Boundary dynamics: a conceptual framework for studying landscape ecosystems. Oikos 45:421-427.

Wissmar, R.C. 1986. Carbon, nitrogen, and phosphorus cycling in Pacific Northwest wetlands. Pages 51-69 in R.S. Strickland, editor. Wetland functions, rehabilitation, and creation in the Pacific Northwest: the state of our understanding. Washington Department of Ecology Publication 86-14, Lacey, Washington, USA.

Wissmar, R.C., J.A. Baross, M.D. Lilley, and C.N. Dahm. 1988. Nitrogen cycling in altered and newly created lakes near the Mount St. Helens volcano. Journal of Freshwater Ecology 4:551-568.

Wolman, M.G., and R. Gerson. 1978. Relative rates of time and effectiveness in watershed geomorphology. Earth Surface Processes 3:189-208.

Wolman, M.G., and J.P. Miller. 1960. Magnitude and frequency of forces in geomorphic processes. Journal of Geology 68:54-74.

Yanosky, T.M. 1983. Evidence of floods on the Potomac River from anatomical abnormalities in the wood of flood-plain trees. United States Geological Survey Professional Paper 1296. 1-42.

Key words: Disturbance, ecotone, geomorphic, landscape, lotic, riparian, streams, uplands.

CHAPTER 6

INTERNAL PROCESSES INFLUENCING THE MAINTENANCE OF ECOTONES: DO THEY EXIST?

William E. Odum

ABSTRACT

Ecotones typically appear to be created and maintained by large-scale, external processes causing sharp discontinuities in gradients of climate, nutrients, or hydrology. There are cases, however, where small-scale, 'internal' processes originating within the ecotone play an important role in ecotone persistence. In these situations, ecological succession is hypothesised to remain in a near steady state or disclimax condition for several reasons, such as (1) plant and microbial control of pore-water acidity and redox potential, (2) prolific plant root growth, (3) sediment and nutrient trapping by plants and microbes, and (4) selective grazing and seed predation by animals.

INTRODUCTION

The creation and maintenance of ecotones are, in general, thought to be controlled by extrinsic or external processes, originating outside or at a larger scale than the ecotone itself. (Fig. 6.1A). For example, ecotones such as forest-prairie edges appear to be created and maintained by discontinuities in gradients of climate (Webb et al. 1983), nutrients (Jordan 1985), and underlying bedrock and resultant soils (Williams and Colwell 1977). Wetland, floodplain, and lake edge ecotones are often formed by large-scale hydrological processes (e.g., river flooding, seasonal lake level changes) (Pieczynska 1990, Pinay *et al.* 1990, Salo 1990). Sustained human-induced disturbances such as forestry, farming, and urbanisation create ecotones by fragmenting the landscape into a complex mosaic of patches, corridors, and intervening ecotones.

If we assume that succession in ecotones is typically controlled by either external or human-caused processes, the question remains whether there are ecotones in which ecological succession is controlled by intrinsic

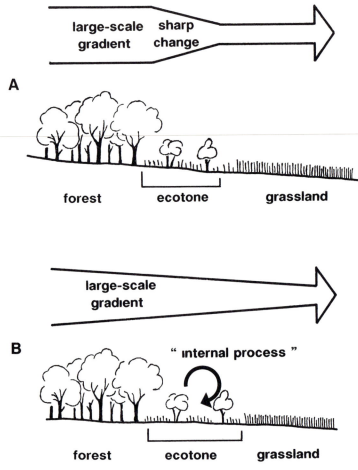

Figure 6.1 (A) Typical case in which an ecotone is created by discontinuity in a large-scale gradient (climate, geology, etc.). (B) Hypothetical case in which an ecotone results from a small-scale, internal process within the ecotone

processes originating *in situ* (Fig. 6.1B). Or, perhaps, are some ecotones the result of the interplay between internal and external processes?

It might be useful to review briefly the historical development of the ecotone concept. The ecotone was originally conceived as a spatial transition zone between two community types (Clements 1897, 1905). Subsequently, it was modified to include the *edge effect*, in which the numbers of individuals and species within ecotones often appeared to be greater than in the ecosystems on either side (Leopold 1933). The concept has recently been expanded to include temporal as well as spatial aspects (Grimm 1983), the ecotone as a *filter* of species and materials (Wiens *et al.* 1985), and the ecotone as a fluctuating border (Shugart 1984).

The definition of the ecotone has evolved to keep pace with these changes. A recent consultation between Unesco's Man and the Biosphere Programme (MAB) and the Scientific Committee on Problems of the Environment (SCOPE) has defined ecotone as 'a zone of transition between adjacent ecological systems, having a set of characteristics uniquely defined by space and time scales and by the strength of the interactions between adjacent ecological systems' (Holland 1988). With the expansion and maturation of this concept has come increasing realisation that ecotones may be more than spatial transition zones between communities. They may, in fact, be characterised by their own complex ecological processes and interactions.

INTERNAL PROCESSES THAT MAINTAIN ECOTONES

In the following sections, I review several cases in which there seems to be considerable internal control of ecotone persistence. In other words, these are presented as examples of small-scale processes apparently originating and occurring predominately within the boundaries of the ecotone. In each case, the net effect is to slow or prevent ecological succession so that an ecotone disclimax or steady state is maintained.

Control of pore-water acidity

The evidence for successional control of entire wetlands (e.g. bogs) and wetland ecotones (e.g. lake-terrestrial boundaries) through plant-mediated changes in pH of interstitial water is incomplete but compelling. As an example, the ability of *Sphagnum* mosses to lower the pH of wetland interstitial waters has been recognised for many years (Kurz 1928) and more recently traced to mechanisms of ion exchange (Clymo 1963) and organic acid excretion (Burgess 1975). If mosses can control interstitial pH for their own apparent benefit by excluding other plants, there should be aquatic-terrestrial ecotones dominated by mosses in more or less steady state conditions for long periods.

Glime *et al.* (1982) report a situation in which this appears to be the case (Fig. 6.2). They describe successional changes in a shallow, alkaline marsh ecotone surrounding Lawrence Lake, Michigan. The successional pattern consists of alkaline-tolerant mosses (bryophytes), such as species of *Drepanocladus*, which over time fill in the marsh and provide damp hummocks in which the interstitial pH gradually becomes less alkaline and eventually slighty acidic. Neutrophilic or nonacidophilic species of *Sphagnum* colonise the hummocks and gradually lower the pH of the interstitial waters further. Eventually the hummocks are colonised by acidophilic species of *Sphagnum* that lower the interstitial pH even further, exclude most other plants, and establish an acidic *Sphagnum*-dominated ecotone that may persist for many years.

Similar cases have been reported from other peat-forming environments.

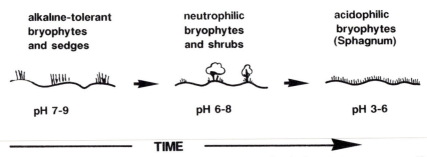

alkaline-tolerant
bryophytes
and sedges

neutrophilic
bryophytes
and shrubs

acidophilic
bryophytes
(Sphagnum)

pH 7-9   pH 6-8   pH 3-6

TIME

Figure 6.2 Successional changes due to bryophyte-mediated changes in pore-water pH.
Modified from Glime *et al.* (1982)

For instance, an example of ecotone expansion due largely to internal processes is provided by paludification, the process whereby blanket bogs grow beyond basin boundaries onto formerly dry land (Heinselman 1963) and may slowly advance up slopes as extreme as 18-20 degrees (Moore and Bellamy 1974). Although a favourable, damp climate must be present, paludification appears to occur largely as the result of peat-forming within the bog-upland ecotone.

Alterations of oxidation-reduction conditions

Although wetland plants grow in soils that lack oxygen and may be strongly reducing, they are able to transport atmospheric oxygen downward via diffusion through their aerenchyma system to the roots. Some of the oxygen may diffuse out of the roots, resulting in thinly oxidised rhizospheres in a predominantly reduced soil (Gambrell and Patrick 1978). If the root systems are sufficiently dense or highly efficient in transporting oxygen, the net effect may be to alter soil redox conditions in a more widespread fashion (e.g. oxidise a greater volume of soil than just the rhizosphere). This could lead to a competitive advantage for one plant species and ultimately result in a successional steady state condition in a wetland patch or ecotone.

While definitive examples are lacking, this hypothesis may not be as farfetched as it sounds. For example, Thibodeau and Nickerson (1986) have presented evidence suggesting that the black mangrove tree (*Avicennia germinans*), because of a more efficient root-aerating system, has a greater ability to alter the oxidation-reduction conditions and lower the concentration of hydrogen sulfide than does the red mangrove (*Rhizophora mangle*). This imples that black mangroves may flourish on soils that are stressful to red mangroves. It further suggests that, in mangrove ecotones where soil organic matter from the black mangroves has accumulated for long periods, black mangroves will dominate red mangroves, partly because of their superior root-aerating mechanism and partly because of soil changes they have helped to promote.

This is only a single, somewhat hypothetical example of plant-mediated changes in wetland soil redox conditions. It remains to be seen whether this is of general importance to plant interactions in wetlands and wetland-terrestrial ecotones.

Allelopathy

Negative chemical interaction between plants (allelopathy) is seen as a possible mechanism for establishing and maintaining ecotones. Muller (1965) and Muller and Chou (1972) suggested that the relatively bare ecotone that often separates certain shrubs in the California chaparral from surrounding grassland is the result of chemical inhibitors secreted by the shrubs. They identified terpines, phenols, and phenolic acids as instrumental in excluding grasses, forbs, and other shrubs. Bartholemew (1970) offered the alternate hypothesis that these ecotones result from the grazing of mice and rabbits. Whatever the cause, the end result is a relatively bare ring that may limit the spread of fire.

Other examples of allelopathy are reviewed by Putnam and Heisey (1983). In several cases, allelopathy appears to play a role in structuring the plant species composition within the transitional zone between communities such as forests and grasslands and shrubs and grasslands. However, without further experimental evidence, it is difficult to conclude that this is a major mechanism of ecotone successional control.

Control through prolific plant growth

Ecotones dominated by aggressive plant species commonly occur between wetlands and uplands and between open fields and forests. Other species are discouraged or excluded by the aggressive species through mechanisms such as canopy shading, dense root mats, or heavy litter production which prevents seedling establishment and growth.

Many plants utilise dense mats of roots and rhizomes to dominate and control ecotones. Examples include cattails (*Typha* spp.) and the common reed (*Phragmites communis*), which form dense bands in wetland areas between open water and drier uplands. Linde *et al.* (1976) attribute the success of *Typha* to its ability to spread aggressively and rapidly via its rhizome system, its ability to persist indefinitely once established, its high reproductive potential, and its ability to form dense mats of rhizomes which crowd out other wetland plants.

Other wetland plants, such as sedges (*Scirpus* spp.) and mangroves (*Rhizophora* spp.), utilise root and rhizome mats in combination with peat formation (Moore and Bellamy 1974) to exclude competing species and maintain an aquatic-terrestrial ecotone in a near steady state. Similar mechanisms are employed in terrestrial environments where grasses such as elephant grass (*Imperata cylindrica*), often in combination with periodic fires, form dense stands that persist indefinitely. Often the aggressive, dominant plants are exotic species; examples in the United States include Brazilian-pepper (*Shinus terebinthifolius*) in Florida (Myers 1983), the tree of heaven (*Ailanthus altissima*), and salt cedar (*Tamarix chinensis*).

Plants that trap sediments

Strips of vegetation can form effective traps for the retention of sediment particles (Novitzki 1978, MacCrimmon 1980). This occurs through interception and slowing of surface runoff or open-channel flow and simple, physical trapping of particles around roots and stems. This trapped sediment in combination with chemical and microbial processes may bind and sequester a variety of chemicals, ranging from heavy metals to nutrients such as nitrogen and phosphorus (reviewed by Mitsch and Gosselink 1986).

The combination of sediment and nutrient trapping can create elevated ecotones at the bottom of hillslopes or between upland and wetland communities (Fig. 6.3). For example, Eckblad *et al.* (1977) estimated that the wetland fringe along the edge of the upper Mississippi River, USA, traps enough sediment to raise the wetland ecotone surface 1.7 cm/yr. If these elevated, nutrient-enriched strips favour the continued dominance of the plants in the ecotone, this would appear to be an example of internal

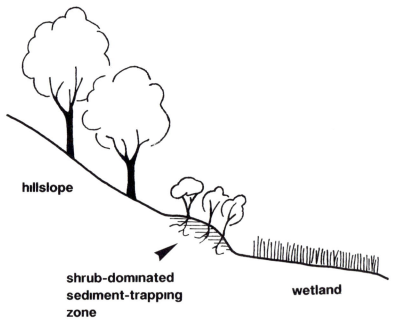

hillslope

shrub-dominated sediment-trapping zone

wetland

Figure 6.3 Sediment and nutrient trapping resulting from change in the slope of a hill and interception by a plant root and rhizome system

control.

A related example involves layers of accumulated plant litter that can immobilise nutrients, creating a within-system nutrient conservation mechanism that may contribute to the continuing dominance of certain plant species. Brinson (1977) showed that in alluvial swamp forests in the southeastern United States there was little or no net release of P, N, Ca, and Fe from autumn leaf fall until growth began the following spring. This was because of a net accumulation of these nutrients in the leaf litter on the forest floor for periods ranging from 16 to 56 weeks. Similar immobilisation or net accumulation of nutrients by leaf litter has been found in oak forests (Bocock 1963), streams (Kaushik and Hynes 1968), deciduous mountain forests (Gosz *et al.* 1973), mangrove forests (Twilley *et al.* 1986). and certain tropical forests (Vitousek 1984). Mechanisms that may produce similar effects on ecotone succession include nitrogen fixation, interception of nutrients in surface and shallow groundwater (Peterjohn and Correll 1984), fire recyling of scarce nutrients (Vogl 1970), and nutrient input from bird nesting and roosting (Onuf *et al.* 1977).

While many of these mechanisms of nutrient retention and interception are becoming better understood, the connection to ecotone maintenance is less clear. Tilman (1982) has argued that nutrient availability is a key factor in controlling the dynamics of plant succession. Carrying this one step further, one can hypothesise that efficient nutrient interception and recycling can contribute to the persistence of ecotone plant communities in an unchanged state.

Fire-adapted plants

The combination of fire-adapted plants and periodic fires can play a key role in maintaining the same successional state, or fire disclimax, in many communities (Odum 1971, Vogl 1977). It is not a difficult extrapolation to hypothesise the existence of ecotones maintained through the same process. This would require suitable climate (usually moderate rainfall with dry periods or seasons), periodic fires (often started by lightning), and plant species in the ecotone that become flammable during part of the year either by drying out, accumulating large amounts of flammable litter, or secreting flammable substances. This implies that the plants in the ecotone would differ from those in adjacent communities by being more likely to burn and burning much more frequently. In theory, this scenario would create a fire-maintained ecotone adjacent to communities in which succession proceeds with less dependence on fire.

As an example, Davison (1984) and Turner and Bratton (1987) report a case in which a shrub-dominated ecotone forms a transition between freshwater marshes and mature oak forests in the interior of coastal barrier islands. Both the freshwater marshes and the shrub ecotone accumulate organic fuels quickly and tend to burn during periodic coastal droughts (Webber 1935). However, these frequent fires usually do not get hot enough to extend far into the oak forests (Turner and Bratton 1987). Subsequently, the shrubs replace themselves (Veno 1976), as does the freshwater marsh. However, if the shrub ecotone becomes too wide or if the drought is particularly severe, fire may start in the wetlands or shrub ecotone and then invade and destroy the oak forest (Turner and Bratton 1987).

This is a single example of a fire-adapted ecotone remaining in a fire-controlled disclimax and buffering an adjacent fire-intolerant community from all but the most extreme conditions. Whether this is a common phenomenon and can be used in a pragmatic way by humans is not clear.

Maintenance by animal activities

Animals can have significant effects on plant community structure through activities such as grazing, nest and den construction, and seed predation. By extension, it seems possible that these activities might serve as a mechanism of internal maintenance within ecotones.

Grazing activities, particularly around patch bodies such as ponds and shrub clumps, offer the most obvious examples (Fig. 6.4). Earlier I mentioned the grazed and denuded zone between chaparral shrubs and adjacent grasslands (Bartholomew 1970). Remillard *et al.* (1987) have described a beaver (*Castor canadensis*) grazing-maintained ecotone of grasses without trees or shrubs located between the beaver pond and the surrounding forest. Randall (1965) described 'halos' of denunded substrate (bare sand) surrounding tropical patch reefs that lie in sea grass beds. These are apparently formed and maintained by the grazing activity of parrot fishes (family Scaridae), which range a few metres out from the reef and consume all sea grasses within this zone.

Animal impacts on ecotones are not limited to grazing. Termites have been shown to alter soil conditions to the extent that plants are affected and distinct zones are maintained around termite hills (Wood and Sands 1977). Turner (1985) has shown that while feral horses have a grazing impact on coastal wetlands, they also have a considerable effect through trampling and soil compaction. In some areas, this can be so great that no vegetation exists. In fact, trampled, compacted pathways from passage of large herbivores commonly form narrow ecotones between communities (e.g. between intertidal wetlands and adjacent dune ridges).

Another type of animal activity that may be of widespread importance involves the effects of selective seed predation. For example, Smith (1987) has hypothesised that the intertidal zonation of certain mangrove species may be affected by consumption of mangrove seeds (propagules) by crabs and other invertebrates. He demonstrated much higher seed predation of *Avicennia marina* in zones where it does not occur compared with low

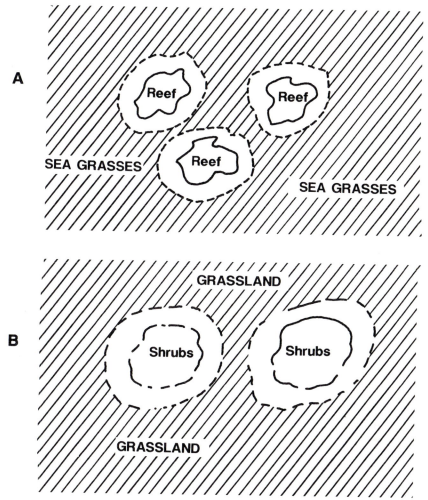

Figure 6.4 Grazing halos or bare rings around (A) patch reefs (Randall 1965) and (B) chaparral shrub patches (Bartholomew 1970)

predation in zones where it dominates. This process of effectively removing plant species and altering successional patterns through selective grazing and seed predation may be much more universal than previously recognised.

Synthesis of the preceding discussion suggests that the effects of animal activities have the potential to create and maintain ecotones. While some of these effects are obvious (heavy grazing, trampling), others such as seed predation are much more subtle. This suggests that other, less obvious effects of animals on ecotones may not have been adequately observed or described.

CONCLUSIONS

There is sufficient evidence to suggest that internal mechanisms are important and may often be a dominant means of maintaining certain types of ecotones. Processes such as moss-mediated control of pore-water acidity, expansion of blanket bogs, and development of extensive rhizome and root mats seem to be good examples of internal mechanisms dominating and, to a great extent, controlling the fate of ecotones over long periods.

In most cases, however, there appears to be an interplay between external and internal processes. Shrubs that burn frequently may dominate and control succession in an ecotone, but the burning frequency of the shrubs is ultimately controlled by regional climatology. Mosses may alter local pore-water pH conditions to their own advantage, but the presence or absence of mosses on a larger scale is determined by a combination of climate and local hydrology.

While the partitioning of processes into external and internal may seem artificial, it does help to generate hypotheses that can be tested and explored, possibly leading to a much better understanding of ecotone dynamics. Furthermore, there are potential applications for this knowledge that could lead to effective management tools.

Traditionally, highway medians, powerline right-of-ways, and fire containment trails are maintained at considerable expense through periodic mowing or ploughing. Would it be possible to design a self-maintaining median or right-of-way by establishing lower-growing plants, such as grasses and shrubs, that would exclude other plants through dense rhizome mats or allelopathy? In fact, some recent experimental highway median plantings in the United States have attempted to do this with some success.

Equally interesting is the possibility of establishing and maintaining runoff filter strips at the bottom of agricultural fields to trap both soil particles and nutrients and to protect bodies of water from accelerated eutrophication. Unfortunately, these usually consist of grasses that are re-established periodically at some expense. Future designs based on naturally occurring ecotones as described in this chapter might offer an equally effective but cheaper solution.

LITERATURE CITED

Bartholomew, B. 1970. Bare zone between California shrub and grassland communities: the role of animals. Science 170:1210-1212.

Bocock, K.L. 1963. Changes in the amount of nitrogen in decomposing leaf litter of sessile oak (*Quercus petraea*). Journal of Ecology 51:555-566.

Brinson, M.M. 1977. Decomposition and nutrient exchange of litter in an alluvial swamp forest. Ecology 58:601-609.

Burgess, J.A. 1975. Organic acid excretion and the impact of *Sphagnum* mosses on their environment. Proceedings of the Birmingham Natural History and Philosophy Society 23:21-24.

Clements, F.E. 1897. Peculiar zonal formations of the Great Plains. American Naturalist 31:968.

Clements, F.E. 1905. Research methods in ecology. University Publishing Company, Lincoln, Nebraska, USA.

Clymo, R.S. 1963. Ion exchange in *Sphagnum* and its relation to bog ecology. Annals of Botany (London) 27:309-324.

Davison, K.L. 1984. Vegetation response and regrowth after fire on Cumberland Island National Seashore, Georgia. Master's thesis. University of Georgia, Athens, Georgia, USA.

Eckblad, J.W., N.L. Peterson, and K. Ostlie. 1977. The morphometry, benthos and sedimentation rates of a floodplain lake in Pool 9 of the Upper Mississippi River. American Midland Naturalist 97:433-443.

Gambrell, R.P., and W.H. Patrick, Jr. 1978. Chemical and biological properties of anaerobic soils and sediments. Pages 375-423 *in* D.D. Hook and R.M.M. Crawford, editors. Plant life in anaerobic environments. Ann Arbor Science, Ann Arbor, Michigan, USA.

Glime, J.M., R.G. Wetzel, and B.J. Kennedy. 1982. The effects of bryophytes on succession from alkaline marsh to *Sphagnum* bog. American Midland Naturalist 108:209-223.

Gosz, J.R., G.E. Likens, and F.H. Bormann. 1973. Nutrient release from decomposing leaf and branch litter in the Hubbard Brook Forest, New Hampshire. Ecological Monographs 43:173-191.

Grimm, E.C. 1983. Chronology and dynamics of vegetation change in the prairie-woodland region of southern Minnesota. New Phytologist 93:311-350.

Heinselman, M.L. 1963. Forest sites, bog processes, and peatland types in the glacial Lake Agassiz region, Minnesota. Ecological Monographs 33:327-374.

Holland, M.M. (compiler). 1988. SCOPE/MAB technical consultations on landscape boundaries: report of a SCOPE/MAB workshop on ecotones. Biology International, Special Issue 17:47-106.

Jordan, C.F. 1985. Nutrient cycling in tropical forest ecosystems. John Wiley and Sons, New York, USA.

Kaushik, N.K., and H.B.H. Hynes. 1968. Experimental study on the role of autumn-shed leaves in aquatic environments. Journal of Ecology 56:299-243.

Kurz, H. 1928. Influence of *Sphagnum* and other mosses on bog reactions. Ecology 9:56-59.

Leopold, A. 1933. Game management. Charles Scribner's Sons, New York, USA.

Linde, A.F., T. Janisch, and D. Smith. 1976. Cattail: the significance of its growth, phenology and carbohydrate storage to its control and management. Technical Bulletin Number 94, Department of Natural Resources, Madison, Wisconsin, USA.

MacCrimmon, H.R. 1980. Nutrient and sediment retention in a temperate marsh ecosystem. International Revue der gesamten Hydrobiologie 65:719-744.

Mitsch, W.J., and J.G. Gosselink. 1986. Wetlands. Van Nostrand Reinhold, New York, USA.

Moore, P.D., and D.J. Bellamy. 1974. Peatlands, Springer-Verlag, New York, USA.

Muller, C.H. 1965. The role of chemical inhibition (allelopathy) in vegetational composition. Bulletin of the Torrey Botanical Club 93:332-351.

Muller, C.H., and C.L. Chou. 1972. Phytotoxins: an ecological phase of phytochemistry. Pages 201-216 *in* J.B. Harborne, editor. Phytochemical ecology. Academic Press, New York, USA.

Myers, R.L. 1983. Site susceptibility to invasion by the exotic tree *Melaleuca quinquenervia* in southern Florida. Journal of Applied Ecology 20:645-58.

Novitzki, R.P. 1978. Hydrology of the Nevin wetland near Madison, Wisconsin. United States Geological Survey Water Resources Investigations 78-48, Washington, D.C., USA.

Odum, E.P. 1971. Fundamentals of ecology. Second edition. Saunders, Philadelphia, Pennysylvania, USA.

Onuf, C.P., J.M. Teal, and I. Valiela. 1977. Interactions of nutrients, plant growth and herbivory in a mangrove ecosystem. Ecology 58:514-526.

Peterjohn, W.T., and D.L. Correll. 1984. Nutrient dynamics in an agricultural watershed: observations on the role of a riparian forest. Ecology 65:1466-1475.

Pieczyńska, E. 1990. Lentic aquatic-terrestrial ecotones, *this volume.*

Pinay, G., H. Décamps, E. Chauvet, and E. Fustic. 1990. Functions of ecotones in fluvial systems, *this volume.*

Putnam, A.R., and R.M. Heisey. 1983. Allelopathy: chemical interactions between plants. What's New in Plant Physiology 14:21-24.

Randall, J.E. 1965. Grazing effect on sea grasses by herbivorous reef fishes in the West Indies. Ecology 46:255-260.

Remillard, M.M., G.K. Gruendling, and D.J. Bogercki. 1987. Disturbance by beaver (*Castor canadensis* kuhl) and increased landscape heterogeneity. Pages 103-122 *in* M.G. Turner, editor. Landscape heterogeneity and disturbance. Springer-Verlag, New York, USA.

Salo, J. 1989. External processes influencing origin and maintenance of inland water-land ecotones, *this volume.*

Shugart, H.H. 1984. A theory of forest dynamics: the ecological implications of forest succession models. Springer-Verlag, New York, USA.

Smith, T.J., III. 1987. Seed predation in relation to tree dominance and distribution in mangrove forests. Ecology 68:266-273.

Thibodeau, F.R., and N.H. Nickerson. 1986. Differential oxidation of mangrove substrate by *Avicennia germinans* and *Rhizophora mangle.* American Journal of Botany 73:512-516.

Tilman, D. 1982. Resource competition and community structure. Princeton University Press, Princeton, New Jersey, USA.

Turner, M.G. 1985. Ecological effects of multiple perturbations on a Georgia salt marsh. Dissertation. University of Georgia, Athens, Georgia, USA.

Turner, M.G., and S.P. Bratton. 1987. Fire, grazing and the landscape heterogeneity of a Georgia Barrier Island. Pages 85-101 *in* M.G. Turner, editor. Landscape heterogeneity and disturbance. Springer-Verlag, New York, USA.

Twilley, R.R., A.E. Lugo, and C. Patterson-Zucca. 1986. Litter production and turnover in basin mangrove forests in southwest Florida. Ecology 67:670-683.

Veno, P.A. 1976. Successional relationships of five Florida plant communities. Ecology 57:498-508.

Vitousek, P.M. 1984. Litterfall, nutrient cycling, and nutrient limitation in tropical forests. Ecology 65:285-98.

Vogl, R.J. 1970. Fire and the northern Wisconsin pine barrens. Pages 175-209 *in* Proceedings 10th Annual Tall Timbers Fire Ecology Conference. Tallahassee, Forida, USA.

Vogl, R.J. 1977. Fire: destructive menace or natural process? Pages 261-289 *in* J. Cairns et al., editors. Recovery and restoration of damaged ecosystems. University Press of Virginia, Charlottesville, Virginia, USA.

Webb, W.L., W.K. Lauenroth, S.R. Szarek, and R.S. Kinerson. 1983. Primary production and abiotic controls in forests, grasslands, and desert ecosystems in the United States. Ecology 64:134-151.

Webber, H.J. 1935. The Florida scrub, a fire fighting association. American Journal of Botany 22:344-361.

Wiens, J.A., C.S. Crawford, and J.R. Gosz. 1985. Boundary dynamics: a conceptual framework for studying landscape ecosystems. Oikos 45:421-427.

Williams, C.H., and J.D. Colwell. 1977. Inorganic chemical properties. Pages 105-126 *in* J.S. Russell and E.L. Greacen, editors. Soil factors in crop production in a semi-arid environment. University of Queensland Press, Saint Lucia, Queensland, Australia.

Wood, T.G., and W.A. Sands. 1977. The role of termites in ecosystems. Pages 245-292 *in* M.V. Brian, editor. Production ecology of ants and termites. Cambridge University Press, Cambridge, England.

Key words: Ecotone, disclimax, successional control.

CHAPTER 7

LENTIC AQUATIC-TERRESTRIAL ECOTONES: THEIR STRUCTURE, FUNCTIONS, AND IMPORTANCE

Ewa Pieczyńska

ABSTRACT

Boundaries between water bodies and adjacent terrestrial patches (lentic ecotones) form extremely differentiated biotopes with respect to their spatial and temporal variability. Ecotone size and configuration depend on shore slope and water level fluctuations, as well as depositional and erosional processes. Lentic ecotones are colonised by diverse species of plants and animals, characterised by a shifting proportion of aquatic and terrestrial species. There are various sources of autochthonous and allochthonous organic matter in lentic ecotones. These materials vary considerably in decomposition dynamics; however, material resistant to decomposition (plant litter) dominates the standing stock of detritus. Macrophytes have a central position in nutrient cycling, determining most of the important physical and biological characteristics of lentic ecotones. Responses of lentic ecotones to pollution, as well as their protection and restoration, are also discussed, and specific suggestions are made for their management.

INTRODUCTION

Boundaries between water bodies (lakes, ponds, reservoirs) and adjacent terrestrial patches – lentic ecotones – play an important role in coupling terrestrial with aquatic ecosystems. Several specific ecotonal structures and processes are characteristic of areas bordering water bodies. These include specific physical and chemical characteristics, as well as the occurrence of unique plant and animal communities and their associated biological processes.

Lentic ecotones may be analysed from both theoretical and practical points of view. Ecotonal habitats, with their typically great heterogeneity, offer opportunities to test many important ecological concepts. On the other hand, they can be important in mitigating unfavourable changes in aquatic ecosystems. Ecotones are also important for the whole watershed in determining and controlling ecological processes in the landscape. They regulate landscape mosaic by influencing energy and nutrient flow between adjacent patches in the ecosystems. Important ecological processes may be readily observed in boundaries (Wiens *et al.* 1985, Naiman *et al.* 1988, Di Castri *et al.* 1988).

To illustrate a large-scale process within the landscape, ecotones in the 'wide sense' (Fig. 7.1A, I) are usually considered. This includes the whole aquatic littoral zone and the neighbouring terrestrial patches. Specific ecotonal structures and processes are analysed for boundaries in the 'narrow sense' (Fig. 7.1A, II), including the area between the highest and lowest season water levels as well as the neighbouring patches that are splashed or exposed during wave action.

There is limited information on the structure and functioning of ecotones at the terrestrial-aquatic interface compared with information for open waters of lakes, ponds, and reservoirs, on the one hand, and typical terrestrial habitats, on the other. The ecotonal studies usually concern physical and chemical features of environment, or particular plant or animal communities which are often analysed separately. Comprehensive investigations of lake littoral zones are scarce.

The objectives of this article are to summarise existing information on the structure and dynamics of lentic ecotones and to relate this information to the effective management of lakes, ponds, and reservoirs.

PHYSICAL, CHEMICAL, AND BIOLOGICAL PROCESSES

Size, physical, and chemical factors

Various terminologies have been proposed for the division of shorelines of water bodies into specific zones (Hutchinson 1967). The most common classifications and synonyms are presented in Fig. 7.2.

Spatial variation of the land-water ecotone depends on the periodic flooding and drying regime. The size of this ecotone depends on the configurations of shore terrace and terrestrial areas adjoining the lake, on water level fluctuations, and depositional and erosional processes which can change this configuration (Fig. 7.1B). It differs considerably among lakes and even within one lake (Table 7.1).

In many lentic ecotones, considerable amounts of plant remains accumulate, forming heaps of detritus. This detritus has different origins and forms ranging from macrophytes and leaf litter fragments to fine particles. Usually a great variability is observed in detritus distribution along the shores of water bodies, which is affected by littoral plant density and distribution characteristics of adjacent forests, and exposure to wave action. At some

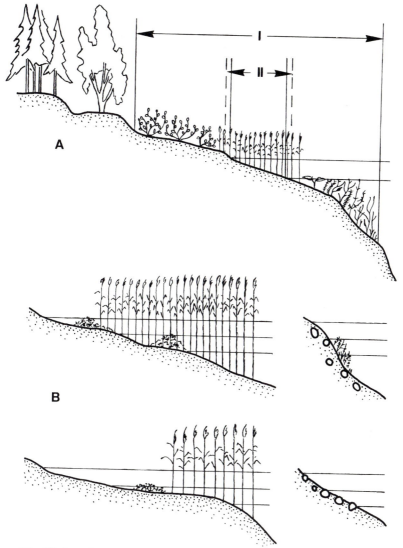

Figure 7.1 (A) Aquatic-terrestrial transition zone. (B) Influence of shore slope, water level fluctuations, and detritus deposition on the configuration of lentic ecotones

water levels, the detritus accumulating on the shore is sufficient to isolate near-shore shallows pools (Fig. 7.1B).

Environmental properties of lentic ecotones are determined, in general, by local climate, type of soils and rocks, and lake water chemistry. But this zone represents highly differentiated biotopes with respect to spatial and temporal variability in microclimate (light and temperature), structure and chemistry of sediments, and water chemistry within littoral plants, swamps,

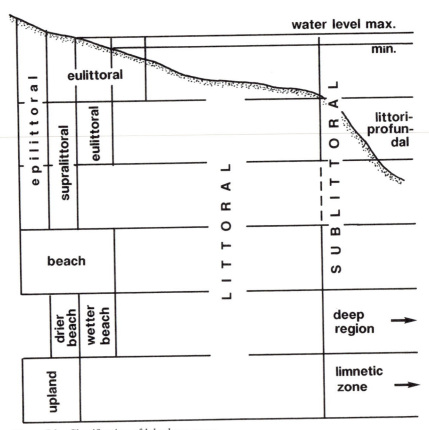

Figure 7.2 Classification of lakeshore zones

and marshes surrounding the ecotone (Björk 1967, Pieczyńska 1972, Zax 1973, Planter 1973, Dykyjová and Květ 1978, Carignan 1985, Gunatilaka 1985). Even on exposed stony and gravel shores, intersite heterogeneity is substantial, particularly in sediment structure (Dall *et al.* 1984).

Near-shore shallows and small lakeside water bodies partly separated from the main water body have special physicochemical conditions. Atmospheric precipitation, winds, ice cover, and other physical parameters are of greater importance here than in typical land and water habitats. These habitats are under a variable influence of detritus from land and lake origins which accumulate there. This, in addition to the small volume of water, causes higher concentrations of organic and mineral substances and more frequent oxygen deficits than in deeper parts of the lake (Pieczyńska 1972).

In general, among various types of lentic ecotones, exposed stony shores and sandy beaches are less heterogeneous compared with muddy, detritus-

Table 7.1 Area of the ecotonal zone between the highest and lowest water levels in four Masurian Lakes, Poland, in 1967. After Pieczyńska (1972)

Lake	*Yearly Difference in Water Level (cm)*	*Distance between Shorelines during the Highest and Lowest Water Levels (m)*		*Area between Shorelines during the Highest and Lowest Water Levels*	
		Average	*Range of variations*	*ha*	*% of total lake surface*
Mikołajskie	41	12	0.8–103	16	3.5
Śniardwy	41	53	1.9–296	441	4.0
Tałtowisko	41	15	1.1– 71	17	5.2
Warniak	28	8	1.2– 16	2	5.3

dominated shores with rich vegetation. In the latter, there are usually considerable differences in the chemistry of water and sediments along the transect from the shore towards open water, and also visible seasonal and diurnal changes in water chemistry.

Community structure of lentic ecotones

Plants. Most water bodies are bordered with habitats dominated by macrophytes. The zonal character of macrophyte distribution is very distinct (Hejný 1960, 1971; Segal 1971, Hutchinson 1975). The water level fluctuations determine the structual variation (both in space and time) of macrophytes in the border zone of many water bodies. Hejný (1971) presents the concepts of ecophases, ecoperiods, and ecocycles considering the dynamics of vegetation in standing waters in temperate zones. According to Hejný, ecophases are described by an 'actual environment' determined by water level and other specific ecological factors (Fig. 7.3). Ecoperiods are sequences of ecophases during one growing season in temperate regions, and ecocycles are determined by a sequence of ecoperiods over several years. An example is given in Table 7.2 of vegetation changes due to water level fluctuations in a pond described in terms of ecoperiods.

Numerous species of trees and shrubs are important components of vegetation in the terrestrial parts of lentic ecotones. Their distribution and dynamics are determined by shore gradient, climatic conditions, soil types, and various interactive biological factors. Jeník and Větvička (1973) show,

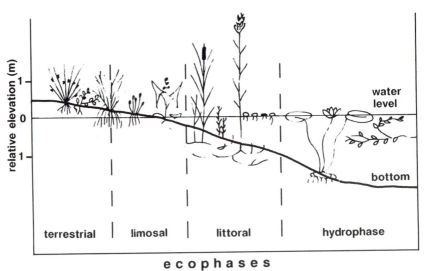

Figure 7.3 Simplified presentation of ecophases in a fishpond littoral. Vertical axis: the distance from actual water level in metres. From Hejný and Husák (1978)

Table 7.2 Changes in pond plant communities in years following summer drainage as the water level in a pond gradually returns to its normal position. Data from fishponds in Czechoslovakia. From Hejný and Husák (1978)

Years after Summer Drainage*	Central Part of Fishpond		
	Ecoperiod	Range of community types	Vegetation Dynamics in the Littoral (general trends)
0 (summer drainage)	Limosoterrestrial	Bidention – Nanocyperion – Litorellion – Agropyro-Rumicion	Onset of stenoecious ephemerous communities of bare bottoms greatly differing in production, followed by their full development and subsequent decay. Degradation of reed-swamp stands.
1	Limosolittoral	Oenanthion – Litorellion (+ nuclei of Potamogetonion pusilli) – Nanocyperion – Agropyro-Rumicion	Onset of stenoecious ephemerous littoral communities and of stenoecious forms of therophytes. Life of reed-swamp stands returning to normal; appearance of their regeneration phase in the sublittoral.
2	Littoralhydrophase	Lemnion – Potamogetonion pusilli – Oenanthion – regenerating Phragmition – Litorellion	Full development to disappearance of stenoecious littoral communities and of stenoecious cenoses of ephemers. Beginning of stabilisation of cenoses in the pond.
3	Hydrophase	Lemnion – Potamogetonion pussilli – Litorellion or Callitricho – Batrachion	Disappearance of stenoecious forms. Stabilisation of all cenoses in the pond.

*Each year corresponds to a certain ecoperiod and a range of plant community types in the central part of the pond and to a certain vegetative development in the littoral

for example, that the pattern and dynamic of marginal stands are affected by the way dominant species reproduce and by habitat properties (Fig. 7.4).

The vegetation of lentic-ecotones of tropical lakes differs from that of temperate lakes. The density of large, freely floating plants can become very great in the tropics. Also, in certain tropical situations, grasslands gradually become a grassy swamp covered by water during the rainy season. Papyrus swamps are typical of a number of tropical water bodies. As demonstrated by Thompson (1976), the interwoven roots and older buried portions of rhizomes of papyrus can form a compact floating mat up to 2 m thick covered by living vegetation (Fig. 7.5).

A great many factors that could determine the spatial extent and zonation of littoral macrophytes are suggested by the literature. However, some general relationships are emerging. Duarte *et al.* (1986), who analysed data for 139 lakes, found that biomass and the spatial extent of emergent macrophytes are, on the average, proportional to the lake area. Compared with submerged plants, which are controlled by underwater light, emergent plants are most affected by lake morphometry and particularly by the average shoreline gradient. Empirical models describing and predicting macrophyte biomass and spatial area on the basis of morphometric and

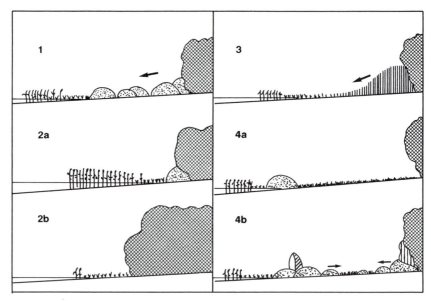

Figure 7.4 Schematic profiles across the littoral zone of a fishpond, showing the structure and dynamics of marginal stands of woody plants. (1) Flat shore with generative regeneration of *Salix cinerea*. (2a) Steep shore with a mantle of *Salix cinerea* bushes on the edge of the forest. (2b) Steep shore with spouting crowns of the marginal forest trees. (3) Flat shore with vegetative regeneration of *Populus tremula*. (4a) Flat shore with a gap between *Salix cinerea* and the forest margin caused by moving and grazing. (4b) Expansion of the woody plants after human interference has ceased. From Jeník and Větvička (1973)

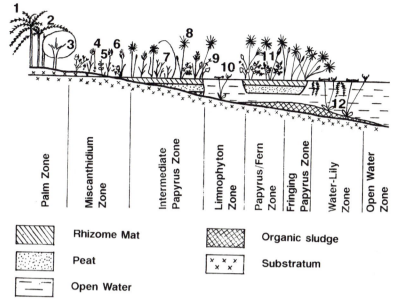

Figure 7.5 shows legend entries:
Rhizome Mat
Peat
Open Water
Organic sludge
Substratum

Figure 7.5 Vegetation of a Lake Victoria swamp. The species represented are (the list is not intended to be exhaustive, including only some of the most typical plants): (1) *Phoenix reclinata*. (2) *Raphia monbuttorum*. (3) *Mitragyna stipulosa*. (4) *Sphagnum* spp. (5) *Dissotis brazzei* and *Leersia hexandra*. (6) *Miscanthidium violaceum*. (7) *Ficus verruculosa*. (8) *Cyperus papyrus*. (9) *Limnophyton obtusifolium*. (10) *Nymphaea caerulea* and *Trapa natans*. (11) *Dryopteris striata*. (12) *Ceratophyllum demersum*, *Utricularia* spp. and *Potamogeton* spp. From Thompson (1976)

climatic factors are possible with some simple measurements.

Spence (1982) shows a great variety of plant zonation in various lakes depending on environmental variables. According to Spence, wave action, sediment, and light regime determine primarily the zonation of macrophytes in lakes. The relative importance of these factors depends on the relative amount of vegetation within or below the wave-mixed zone.

Algae colonise various types of substrates: stones (epilithic), bottom sediments (epipelic), animals (epizooic), higher plants (epiphytic). Planktonic algae and algae loosely connected with substrate can also become abundant. Shore boundaries differ as to the dominance of particular algal groups. At some sites there are mosaics of all these elements; at others one group dominates distinctly. Attached algae dominate in the shores with rocky or stony substrates. Their distribution is determined by the water level fluctuations, wave action, and grazing (Felföldy 1958, Stockner and Armstrong 1971, Schindler *et al.* 1973, and Kann 1982). The zonal character of their distribution is usually observed (Fig. 7.6).

Animals. Well known are the animals on sandy beaches and stony shores

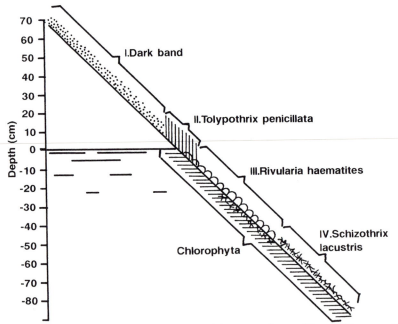

Figure 7.6   The zonal distribution of algae colonising stony shores of Lunzer Untersee. After Kann (1982)

(Moon 1935, Pennak 1940, Neel 1948, Brittain and Lillehammer 1978, Dall *et al.* 1984), as well as those colonising macrophytes (Soszka 1975, Dvořák and Best 1982). The seasonal changes of both community structure and density of macroinvertebrates vary at particular sites, reflecting the life cycle patterns of particular species.

Animal communities in lentic ecotones are distinctly affected by water level fluctuations resulting in a characteristic zonation. Stony shores are abundantly inhabited in the submerged zone, but not in the zone exposed to the atmosphere. On sandy beaches, there is rich fauna in the emergent zone associated with pore water. Yet, comparison of macroinvertebrates inhabiting various types of shores in Masurian Lakes (Poland) indicates that sandy shores are poorest in species abundance. Here the most abundant macrofauna is observed in small lakeside pools. Numerous animals occur also in fine detritus and reed heaps which accumulate in the lentic ecotone (Pieczyńska 1972).

'Edge effect' – an increase of animal abundance in ecotonal habitats (Di Castri *et al.* 1988) – is usually not observed on exposed sandy and stony shores. However, it can be observed on some isolated shores with muddy substrates and rich vegetation. In such habitats, semi-aquatic forms, which are typical for these shore zones, are extremely abundant. Such is the case in the Masurian Lakes, where Oligochaeta, Coleoptera, and particularly

Diptera, occur in very high densities. However, increased invertebrate abundance on these ecotones may not be a rule. For instance, Dvořák (1978) found that the quantity of macroinvertebrates was greater in the littoral section of fishponds affected by pelagic water than in the rather isolated biotopes. He indicated several factors responsible for this difference, including trophic conditions (accumulation of phytoplankton) and water chemistry (dystrophic character of isolated littoral).

Lentic ecotones are penetrated permanently or occasionally by many species of birds and mammals. For birds, seasonal differences in their numbers and community structure are determined by breeding seasons and migration periods, which vary in different geographic regions. Many birds are adapted to particular plant zones and use sites of various vegetative depths as nesting or feeding grounds (Dobrowolski 1973, Hudec and Šťastný 1978). Data collected by the International Waterfowl Research Bureau, which coordinated international activity in the field of waterfowl protection, have demonstrated the value of lakeshores for permanent bird populations as well as for migratory species.

Mammals in lentic ecotones have been less investigated than birds. Yet available data indicate the existence of rich populations in wetlands bordering water bodies. For example, Pelikán (1978) found 31 mammal species in reed swamps of Nesyt fishponds (herbivores, insectivores, and carnivores were represented). The muskrat (*Ondatra zibethica*) occurs in high densities in some lentic ecotones. It uses large quantities of macrophytes for both food and lodge building (Pelikán 1978, Toivonen and Meriläinen 1980). Kozakiewicz (1985) found that lakeside habitats (Masurian Lakeland, Poland) are constantly inhabited by a community of small mammals (rodents and insectivores, *Clethrionomys glareolus* dominate), and that the boundary between land and water is not a barrier to movement.

Shore zones of water bodies also form important habitats for many fish species. They use macrophyte stands as spawning and rearing grounds. Macrophytes also form important feeding habitats for young and adult fish of many species. For instance, Grash (1978; in de Nie 1987), on the basis of studies on North German lakes, has listed 17 adult fish species showing preference for various parts of the littoral as feeding habitats. Deufel (1978; in de Nie 1987) has shown that, for a number of fish populations in Lake Constance (Table 7.3), stands of *Phragmites* and other emergent plants are an important spawning and feeding habitat.

Ecosystem processes in lentic ecotones

Primary production and allochthonous inputs provide three sources of organic matter that can be distinguished in the lentic ecotone. These are (1) organic matter produced *in situ*, by a community of producers living there permanently or temporarily, (2) allochthonous matter of terrestrial

Table 7.3 Fish species in Lake Constance temporarily living in the zone of emergent vegetation. After Deufel (1978, from de Nie 1987)

Fish Species	Function of Emergent Vegetation	
	Feeding habitat	Spawning area
Anguilla anguilla (eel)	+	
Esox lucius (pike)		+
Abramis brama (bream)		+
Blicca bjoerkna (white bream)		+
Carassius carassius (crucian carp)		+
Cyprinus carpio (carp)		+
Gobio gobio (gudgeon)	+	+
Leuciscus cephalus (chub)		+
Leuciscus leuciscus (dace)		+
Phoxinus phoxinus (minnow)	+	
Rhodeus sericeus (bitterling)		+
Rutilus rutilus (roach)	+	+
Scardinius erythrophthalmus (rudd)	+	+
Tinca tinca (tench)	+	+
Misgurnus fossilis (weatherfish)	+	+
Noemacheilus barbatulus (stone loach)	+	+
Silurus glanis (wels or European catfish)		+
Gasterosteus aculeatus (stickleback)		+
Cottus gobio (bullhead)	+	

origin, supplied from the drainage basin of the lake, and (3) allochthonous matter of lake origin, produced in a deeper part of a lake but accumulated on the shore as a result of wave action.

Allochthonous and autochthonous matter can be distinguished in many ecosystems (lakes, ponds), and also in their different hydrologic zones (pelagial, profundal). However, the majority of aquatic and terrestrial systems have a constant prevalence of usually one type of organic matter. Lentic ecotones vary greatly in this respect. At the boundaries of many lakes there are habitats with allochthonous and autochthonous sources of similar significance. But there are also habitats constantly or temporarily under the dominant influence of allochthonous material of terrestrial or aquatic origin, and also some where *in situ* primary production is of decisive significance.

Primary production. Investigations on macrophyte biomass and production are numerous, but comparison of data for various sites is difficult because

Table 7.4 Annual net primary production of aquatic communities. After Westlake (1963) from Wetzel (1983)

Type of Ecosystem	Approximate Net Organic (dry) Production $(mt \cdot ha^{-1} \cdot yr^{-1})$	Range $(mt \cdot ha^{-1} \cdot yr^{-1})$
Marine phytoplankton	2	1–4.5
Lake phytoplankton	2	1–9
Freshwater submersed macrophytes		
Temperate	6	1–7
Tropical	17	12–20
Marine submersed macrophytes		
Temperate	29	25–35
Tropical	35	30–40
Marine emergent macrophytes (salt marsh)	30	25–85
Freshwater emergent macrophytes		
Temperate	38	30–45
Tropical	75	65–85 +

of different techniques applied, especially related to production. Generally, emergent machrophytes (most common in lentic ecotones) are among the most productive communities in the world. In temperate zones they attain an annual production of 30 to 45 mt/ha, and in tropical regions 65 to 85 mt/ha. Compared with emergents, submerged plants are less productive (Table 7.4).

Algal production varies greatly in the shore zone but periodically has a great intensity (Wetzel 1964, Pieczyńska 1972, Schindler *et al.* 1973, Komárková and Marvan 1978, Adams and Prentki 1982, Gons 1982, and others). Yet many influences limit algal primary production in ecotonal habitat: nutrient limitation, periodic drying of the environment, and shading by macrophytes and near-shore trees (Pieczyńska 1972).

Allochthonous input. Organic matter entering lentic ecotones from terrestrial patches has several origins (Fig. 7.7). However, most quantitative estimations deal mainly with litterfall from trees.

Leaf litter is a major source of energy in some lotic systems. Yet it is of minor importance in most lakes, except for some oligotrophic and small eutrophic lakes with heavily forested shorelines (Wetzel *et al.* 1972, Gasith and Hasler 1976, Odum and Prentki 1978, Le Cren and Lowe-McConnell 1980, Carpenter *et al.* 1983, Pieczyńska *et al.* 1984). Even when the role of litterfall is negligible on the scale of the whole water body, it can be an important source of organic matter and nutrients in ecotonal habitats.

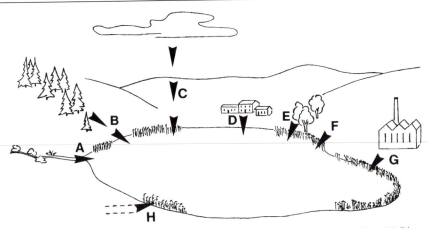

Figure 7.7   The main sources of allochthonous matter in the shore zone of lakes. (A) River tributaries. (B) Products of surface erosion. (C) Atmospheric precipitation. (D) Domestic sewage. (E) Litterfall. (F) Products of shore erosion. (G) Industrial sewage. (H) Underground inflows

Gasith and Hasler (1976), Pieczyńska *et al.* (1984), and others have shown that only a slight amount (usually < 10%) of leaf litter moves > 10 m from the shoreline. The main fall usually concentrates on the shoreline and up to 1 or 2 m from shore. This input of allochthonous detritus changes over time because of seasonal climate and phenologic cycles of near-shore vegetation. In the north temperate zone, maximum values are usually observed in October or November (Table 7.5) and the input begins to increase in August.

Allochthonous material of lake origin is also an important source of organic matter in many lentic ecotones. Accumulation of pelagic plankton on lakeshores is well known in limnologic literature as a 'shore effect.' Plankton accumulates mainly during algal blooms, combined with strong wave action. Besides pelagic algae, the littoral algae often accumulate on the shore due to wave action. They are mostly species that form large mats floating in the water or lying on the bottom. In Lake Mikołajskie, Poland, the amount of algae accumulated in the lentic ecotone is directly

Table 7.5   Terrestrial plant remains falling into the littoral zone of three Masurian Lakes, Poland. After Pieczyńska *et al.* (1984)

| Lake | Litter Input in Dry Weight (g/m^2) | | |
	Maximum per day	Mean per day	Total per year
Mikołajskie	4.7 (November)	0.6	221
Majcz Wielki	5.1 (October)	0.4	228
Głebokie	7.7 (October)	0.9	526

proportional to their biomass in the lake. For example, in 1967, when 20 shore sites were simultaneously analysed, the biomass of accumulated algae varied between < 1 and 5 g/m (fresh weight), whereas, in 1976 (after increased eutrophication), between < 1 and 105 g/m were found (Pieczyńska 1986).

It is also known that periphyton, detritus from various sources, and macrophytes accumulate on lakeshores (Sebestyén 1950, Björk 1967, Pieczynska 1972, Dykyjová and Květ 1978). However, the majority of accumulated material is from damaged macrophytes. In Lake Mikołajskie during one year, on 1 m of shoreline, a total of 8100 g dry weight of macrophytes accumulated, with > 90% being *Phragmites australis* (Pieczyńska 1972).

The remains of most submerged plant species recorded in Lake Mikołajskie are found on shore. Those species from shallow water that are exposed to waves dominate the standing stock. For reeds, it is usually standing dead plants that are destroyed by waves, whereas for submerged species even fragments of young healthy plants are found on shore.

A distinct seasonal periodicity is observed in the accumulation of leaves, panicles, and stalks of *Phragmites* (Fig. 7.8). About 90% of the annual accumulation of stalks takes place in early spring after ice thaw. Leaves and panicles normally accumulate in late autumn and spring (this year's and last year's production, respectively). In terms of biomass, stems dominate the standing stock of dead reeds that accumulate in the shoreline ecotone.

The seasonal variability of organic allochthonous inputs to shore habitats is high. Allochthonous detritus of terrestrial origin accumulates mainly in autumn (in temperate zones), whereas reeds accumulate in early spring (standing dead biomass after ice thaw), and submerged macrophytes appear there in summer and autumn. Algae occasionally accumulate over various periods of the vegetation season.

Decomposition. Organic matter produced or accumulated in lentic ecotones is decomposed *in situ* by organisms living in this zone, or is transported to neighbouring aquatic and terrestrial patches by wave action or by organisms occasionally penetrating these areas. Decomposition studies in lentic ecotones deal mostly with the disappearance of macrophytes (literature review: Dickinson and Pugh 1974, Úlehlová 1976, Le Cren and Lowe-McConnell 1980, Kulshreshtha and Gopal 1982a, b; Wetzel 1983, Polunin 1984) and allochthonous leaf litter (Dickinson and Pugh 1974, Hodkinson 1975, Gasith and Lawacz 1976, and Barnes *et al.* 1978).

Organic material in lentic ecotones varies considerably with respect to its susceptibility to decomposition. Studies in the reed belt of Lake Mikołajskie have shown that total disappearance of dead plants, animals, and their remains varies from < 10 days (algae and animal tissues) to about

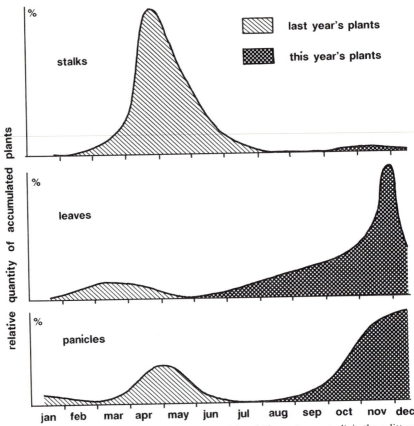

Figure 7.8 Accumulation of stalks, leaves, and panicles of *Phragmites australis* in the eulittoral of Lake Mikoƚajskie. Changed from Pieczyńska (1972)

1 month for some submerged plants, to > 2 yr for reed shoots and tree leaves (Pieczyńska et al. 1984). The great differences observed in decomposition rates (even within the same plant and animal species) may result from differences in the initial chemistry of decomposing material. Melillo *et al.* (1983, 1984) demonstrated that initial litter quality (e.g. nitrogen and lignin content) is the dominant factor influencing decomposition rate.

It is important to note that the slowest decomposition rates are associated with the most abundant organisms and litter in the littoral zone. This is one reason for the great detritus accumulations on the shore zone of lakes. Undoubtedly, the decomposition rate of animal tissue is faster than that of vascular plants, but body parts of many animals (mainly molluscs) resist decomposition for many years, contributing to the structure of bottom sediments.

Utilisation of organic matter by microorganisms is of basic significance in the shore zone, because little of the detrital matter can be directly eaten and assimilated by the fauna (e.g. macrophytes, tree leaves). Lentic ecotones are therefore colonised by a large and diverse microbial community. Úlehlová (1976) has shown differences in biomass of bacteria on various plant substrates and in the littoral mud of ponds. The lowest bacterial biomass was associated with the emergent parts of standing dead plants (e.g. reeds), the greatest biomass was associated with submerged plant material (Table 7.6).

The differences in the decomposition rates of various organisms are quite obvious considering differences in their body structure. But the decomposition rate of the same material may also be different in various environments. For example, Godshalk and Wetzel (1978) have found differences in the decomposition of particulate organic matter (POM) and dissolved organic matter (DOM) for several species of macrophytes under various environmental conditions. This may be significant in ecotonal habitats that are, even for small areas, heterogeneous in space and time. These differences are illustrated in Fig. 7.9, where decomposition is shown to be fastest in swampy shore areas with temporary pools low in the reed belt and even lower for the exposed shore. One may expect, however, that because of extensive detritus movements (due to wave action), organic matter goes through successive decomposition stages under different conditions. When the water level rises, materials produced or accumulated in the eulittoral (at different stages of decomposition) move by wave action to other parts of the lake, where they are utilised by organisms of various trophic levels. When the water level falls, these materials remain on land, thus fertilising ecotonal areas surrounding the lake.

Úlehlová (1976) demonstrated great differences in the rate of cellulose

Table 7.6 Ranges of bacterial biomass on different structural constituents of the littoral ecosystem in the Nesyt fishpond, Czechoslavakia. After Úlehlová (1976)

Habitat	Substrate	Biomass	
		mg/g (min.–max.)	*g/m² (min.–max.)*
Standing dead plants	*Phragmites communis*	0.06–0.17	0.001–0.033
	Typha angustifolia	0.02–0.60	0.0004–0.118
Floating plant litter	*Typha angustifolia*	0.02–10.40	—
Terrestrial litter	Upper layer	0.02–1.20	0.02–1.00
	Lower metamorphed layer (5 cm)	0.03–1.64	1.4–64.3
Aquatic litter	Upper layer	0.08–4.35	0.07–3.50
	Lower metamorphed layer (5 cm)	0.08–1.50	0.8–59.60
Sapropel	5 cm layer	0.01–0.47	0.4–16.3

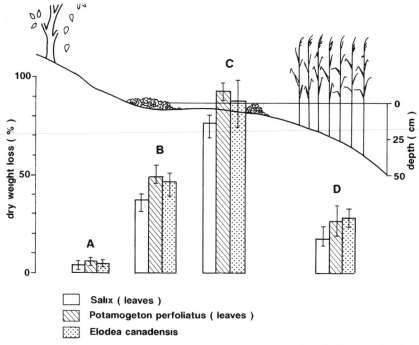

Figure 7.9 Disappearance rates of plant material exposed in various habitats of the shore zone of Lake Mikoɫajskie (July-August). Percentage losses of dry weight after 10 days of exposure

decomposition in several macrophyte stands. The highest rate of decomposition was on a substrate free of vegetation, whereas the slowest rate was in a *Glyceria* stand (in a terrestrial ecophase) (Table 7.7). Detritus at various

Table 7.7 Average rates of cellulose decomposition (CDR) on some bottom sites in the Nesyt fishpond, Czechoslovakia. After Úlehlová (1976)

Site	CDR $(g \cdot m^{-2} \cdot d^{-1})$	CDR $(g \cdot m^{-2} \cdot yr^{-1})$
1. Open water	3.74	1050
2. *Hippuris vulgaris*	3.15	882
3. *Phragmites communis* (organic layer)	2.26	640
4. *Phragmites communis* (rooting layer)	1.25	362
5. *Phragmites communis* with *Carex riparia*	1.60	460
6. *Glyceria maxima* (terrestrial ecophase)	0.82	300

stages of decomposition also vary in size, structure, chemical composition, and number and composition of associated microbes (Úlehlová 1976, Bastardo 1979). This further differentiates the fates of decomposing material. For example, feeding animals show a preference for different kinds of detritus (Bärlocher *et al.* 1978, Smock and Harlowe 1983, Arsuffi and Suberkropp 1984).

Nutrient cycling and energy flow. Organic matter produced in lentic ecotones or imported from adjacent patches has various fates. It may undergo consumption, autolysis, breakdown, and decomposition at different times and in different ways. Part of the organic matter may be released into the environment during the life of producers. A part may be buried at various stages of decomposition and a part may be exported out of the system. The importance of these pathways may be different in different lentic ecotones. Unfortunately, because of this complexity, only a few models of littoral metabolism or nutrient budgets can be found in the literature (Imhof and Burian 1972, Wetzel and Allen 1972, Dykyjová and Květ 1978, Adams and Prentki 1982, Sarvala *et al.* 1982, Gunatilaka 1985).

Macrophytes hold a central position in the nutrient cycling of shoreline ecotones. The rate of nutrient uptake by roots and shoots, translocation, and release by healthy and decaying plants strongly influences the nutrient cycling of the ecosystem. These processes may differ from lake to lake. The role of macrophytes in nutrient cyling differs in various lentic ecotones. This difference is determined mainly by species composition (proportion of emergent, submerged, and freely floating species), production-to-biomass ratio, and concentrations of nutrients in various littoral zones. For example, Prentki *et al.* (1979) and Adams and Prentki (1982), who demonstrated the role of macrophytes for the phosphorus budget in the littoral zone of Lake Wingra, Wisconsin, USA, showed that macrophytes (mostly *Myriophyllum spicatum*) intercepted only minor quantities of P from terrestrial runoff, sequestering phosphorus mainly from sediments (Fig. 7.10). These authors suggest that dissolved P released from these plants is used predominantly by pelagic biota. The Lake Wingra case is a specific one. This is an urban lake receiving large inputs of P from a storm sewer system and it has a high flushing rate. The dominant macrophyte species *Myriophyllum spicatum* has most of its biomass in a surface water canopy during the growing season, and the plants are poorly suited to extract nutrients from storm water flowing across the lake bottom.

The role of macrophytes in nutrient cycling is determined primarily by the site of nutrient uptake. It is obvious that for emergent plants sediment is the prime nutrient source. However, submerged macrophytes can absorb phosphorus from both water and sediments. Nevertheless, there are contradictory opinions on which factors regulate the proportion of nutrient uptake by shoots or roots (Boström *et al.* 1982, Carignan 1982). Denny

121

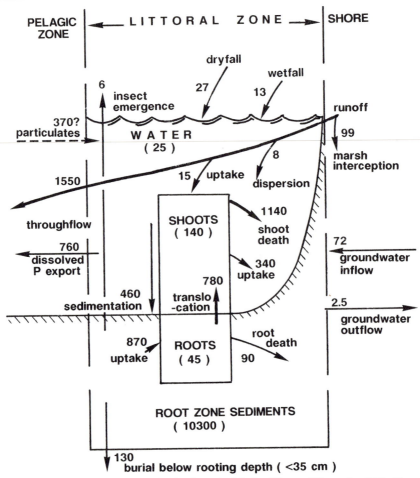

Figure 7.10 Phosphorus budget in the littoral of Lake Wingra, Wisconsin, USA. From Adams and Prentki (1982)

(1972) suggested that morphology, root-shoot biomass ratio, vascular differentiation, simplicity of anatomy, and degree of submergence may play an important role in determining the major site of nutrient absorption. Carignan (1982) shows the opposite: under similar phosphorus availability, different species of submerged plants behave similarly. Relative differences in phosphorus concentration in water and sediments determine the uptake site. The concentration of phosphorus is usually higher in interstitial water, suggesting that submerged macrophytes act to pump nutrients from sediments to the water column.

The exchange of material between lentic ecotones and adjacent land and water patches is determined by physical (i.e. wind, water flow, wave action)

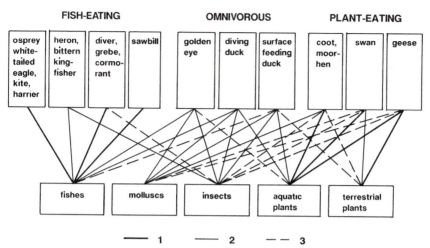

Figure 7.11 Trophic groups of waterfowl. (1) Food taken > 70%. (2) Food taken 20-70%. (3) Food taken < 20%. From Dobrowolski (1973)

and biological (i.e. migration) factors. Terrestrial animals (birds, mammals, reptiles, insects) feeding in lentic ecotones directly export ecotonal organic material. They use and export to neighbouring patches live or dead organisms and the detritus. Birds are an important group of consumers in lentic ecotones by feeding on a wide variety of organisms (Fig. 7.11). The density of birds may be very high (especially during seasonal migration), and they distinctly influence nutrient and energy movements between the shore zone of water bodies and their neighbouring patches. Fishes are particularly important for the movement of organic materials between water bodies and their margins. Also insects, which occur abundantly in transitional zones, are significant in the transfer of nutrients especially during mass emergence. Their role varies greatly over time because different species emerge at different periods of the vegetative season. In conclusion, the influence of animals in lentic ecotones on organic matter movements between adjacent ecological systems can vary widely depending on the trophic status of particular animal groups, their life cycles, and their ability to migrate (Naiman 1988).

Classification of lentic ecotones

Numerous classification systems for shore zones of water bodies have been proposed. They are usually based on criteria such as dominant macrophyte species, water depth, permanence, soil types, and bottom sediments. The majority of classifications deal with wetlands and the littoral zones of lakes (Hutchinson 1975, Gopal *et al.* 1982).

Cowardin *et al.* (1979) presented a hierarchical classification of wetlands and deep-water habitats in the United States which considered hydrologic, geomorphologic, chemical, and biological characteristics. Marine, estuarine, riverine, lacustrine, and palustrine systems were proposed. The latter two types are related to the shore zone of lakes and are useful in describing many lentic ecotones. The lacustrine system is divided into two subsystems: limnetic and littoral. Six classes are distinguished within the littoral zone (Fig. 7.12). The lacustrine systems include the permanently flooded lakes and reservoirs, intermittent lakes and reservoirs, and some tidal lakes. The palustrine system has eight classes, grouping the vegetated wetlands (marsh, swamps, bog, etc.) with the small shallow permanent or intermittent water

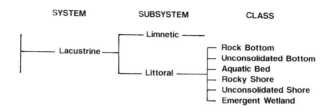

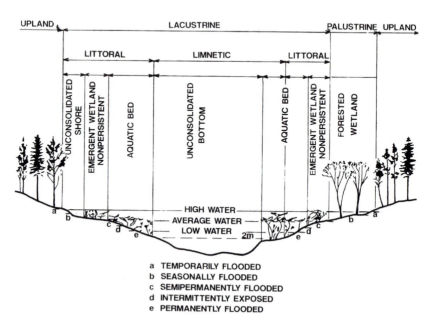

Figure 7.12 Distinguishing classes and examples of habitats in the lacustrine system. From Cowardin *et al.* (1979)

bodies (Fig. 7.13). These habitats may also occur as islands or on the shore of various water bodies.

One of the more complex classifications of littoral lake zones was proposed by Bernatowicz and Zachwieja (1966). Ten types of littoral habitats are distinguished on the basis of lake morphology and vegetation. This classification is based on observations of northeastern Polish lakes of primarily glacial origin, but it can be useful in characterising the littoral region of any lake. The following fundamental types of littoral zones have been identified: litholittoral (mostly rocky shores, either lacking vegetation or having poor vegetation), psammolittoral (sandy beaches, no emergent vegetation), psammolittoral with great-lake helophytes, and phytolittoral (the entire littoral zone is covered by macrophytes). There are seven types of phytolittoral which differ in distribution of macrophytes and in proportion

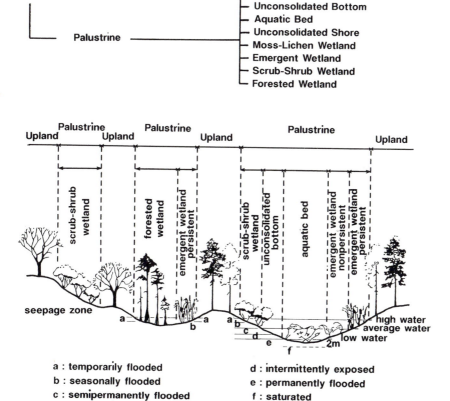

Figure 7.13 Distinguishing classes and examples of habitats in the palustrine system. From Cowardin *et al.* (1979)

of emergent, floating-leaved, and submerged vegetation. These are: large-lake phytolittoral, small-lake phytolittoral, pond phytolittoral, marsh phyto-littoral, midlake phytolittoral (islands in lakes covered by vegetation), atrophic phytolittoral, and artificial littoral (changed by man).

Different limnological types of lakes also have different types of ecotonal shore zones. Oligotrophic lakes with sandy and rocky shores usually have a small and poorly differentiated ecotonal zone; litholittoral and psammolittoral dominate. Large mesotrophic and eutrophic lakes with a wide shore terrace, a differentiated shoreline, and a considerable water level fluctuation possess a wide range of ecotonal shore zones; various littoral types are recorded. Small eutrophic lakes and ponds with slight water level changes have a small boundary range, but they can be greatly differentiated because of rich vegetation; pond and marsh phytolittoral is most frequently observed. Dystrophic (bog) lakes, despite the small fluctuations of water level, usually have a wide eulittoral because of their low shore gradient. Yet this zone is poorly differentiated in the majority of cases because of homogeneous vegetation occurring there; atrophic phytolittoral is the most typical.

MAN-MADE DISTURBANCES OF LENTIC BOUNDARIES: MANAGEMENT, PROTECTION, AND RESTORATION

Damaged ecotones

In most regions, areas bordering lakes, ponds, and reservoirs are under human influence. Domestic and industrial sewage, agricultural usage of drainage basins, recreational activities, airborne pollutants, water level control, and macrophyte exploitation visibly change lentic ecotones and, in many cases, cause disturbance and damage. Effects of increasing eutrophication and pollution are the best known. Biotic elements at boundaries respond, first of all, by a decrease in macrophyte biomass and cover (Eloranta 1970, Schiemer 1979, Lachavanne 1982, Schröder and Schröder 1982, Best *et al.* 1984, Ozimek and Kowalczewski 1984, Boar and Crook 1985, de Nie 1987).

Lachavanne (1985), who studied aquatic plants in Swiss lakes varying in productivity (ultraoligotrophic to hypereutrophic), has shown the relationship between macrophyte occurrence in deep lakes and eutrophic-ation (Fig. 7.14). At the mesoeutrophic stage of eutrophication, vegetation is very abundant, whereas in the hypereutrophic stage there is a visible regression of macrophytes. According to his observations and the literature data, one can identify several possible causes for the decline of submerged macrophytes: direct toxic effect of high phosphorus concentrations, decrease in light intensity due to phytoplankton blooms, the development of filamentous algae (floating and epibenthic), and substrate enrichment in organic matter.

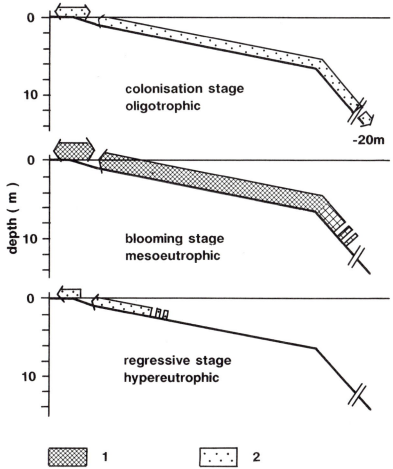

Figure 7.14   Colonisation of deep lakes by macrophytes in relation to eutrophication. (1) Highly abundant vegetation. (2) Poor vegetation. From Lachavanne (1985)

Phillips *et al.* (1978), who studied the Norfolk Lakeland, England, have shown that the mechanism for submerged macrophyte suppression in shallow lakes may be differentiated (Fig. 7.15). They suggest that, at relatively high nutrient loading, the loss of macrophytes is often due to increased growth of, and shading by, epiphytes and filamentous algae loosely associated with macrophytes. Thus, phytoplankton development is subsequent rather than causative. For moderate levels of nutrient input they showed a restriction of phytoplankton production by macrophyte competition for nutrients. The importance of filamentous algae in the decline of macrophytes is suggested not only for submerged macrophytes but also for emergent forms such as *Phragmites* (Schröder 1987).

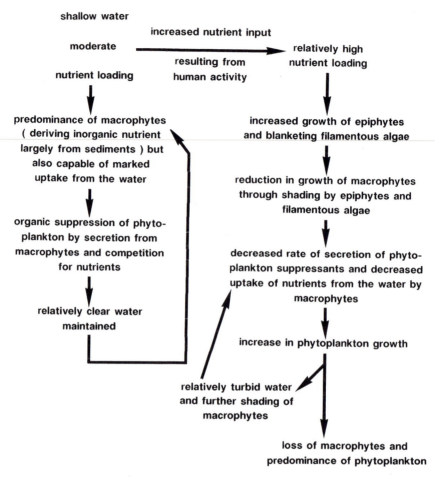

Figure 7.15 Hypothesis to account for decline in macrophyte populations when lakes are fertilised. From Phillips *et al.* (1978)

The majority of literature data on the decline of macrophytes deals with competition between algae and submerged plants. Only in some circumstances is an invasion of submerged plants noticed (e.g. *Elodea canadensis*, Rørslett *et al.* 1985). Yet, for emergent vegetation there has been an observed expansion of plants, mainly reeds in some shallow lakes (e.g. in Neusiedler Lake, Austria; Löffler 1979, Gunatilaka 1985), as well as distinct species dying out at different localities (de Nie 1987).

Inland water boundaries are increasingly affected by tourism and recreation. Shore zones of lakes are particularly vulnerable to increased tourist activity. Tourist centres, roads, swimming, and motorboats all produce deleterious effects when conducted on a massive scale. Shores can be damaged, changes may occur in the littoral water and sediments, and biological changes may occur in plant (primarily through mechanical damage of macrophytes) as well as animal communities. Other detrimental changes in the shore zone of water bodies, as found in the literature, include the effect of acidification (Roelofs and Schuurkes 1983), fishpond management (Dykyjová and Květ 1978), and water level regulation (Björk 1980, Toivonen 1983, Rørslett 1985). Most of the change to ecotonal systems is due to several influences acting simultaneously, making resolution of the issue very complex (de Nie 1987).

The role of macrophytes in nutrient entrapment

The accumulation of nutrients (mainly N and P) in macrophyte tissues determines to a great extent the ability of these plants to form a protective barrier. The amount of accumulated nutrients depends on the physiological capacity for nutrient uptake by particular species, as well as on the macrophyte biomass. Depending on the ecosystems, one may find evidence in the literature that macrophytes are important or insignificant for nutrient depletion from the water column. For example, Bernatowicz (1969) found that, in the small (38 ha) Lake Warniak in Poland, which is almost entirely overgrown by macrophytes in summer, the total amount of nutrients accumulated in macrophytes is much greater than the amount dissolved in water. Similar calculations for lakes with poor vegetation show very low quantities of nutrients accumulated in plant biomass (Loenen and Koridon 1978).

The literature provides examples where, under some conditions, an increase in nutrient concentrations in the environment is reflected in an increase in accumulation within the plants. Yet, as already demonstrated, a nutrient enrichment of lake water beyond certain limits results in a decrease in macrophyte biomass. Thus, nutrient accumulation per unit length of shore zone decreases as illustrated by Ozimek (1978) from Lake Mikołajskie. The amount of nitrogen and phosphorus accumulated in plant tissue (per unit weight) is greater at polluted sites (i.e. domestic sewage) compared with unpolluted sites. However, when comparing the accumulation per unit area of littoral surface, the results obviously depend on plant biomass. The accumulation of nutrients is very low at polluted sites close to the sewage outlet where vegetation is destroyed by the sewage. Yet the greatest values are found at polluted sites farther from the outlet, where diluted sewage fertilises the environment and the vegetation is dense. One may conclude that submerged macrophytes cannot play a significant role in nutrient entrapment in waters with high concentrations of pollutants (Fig. 7.16). Submerged plants are quickly destroyed and relatively small amounts of nutrients are assimilated. Submerged macrophytes may, however, be successful biological filters in slighty polluted habitats, where they

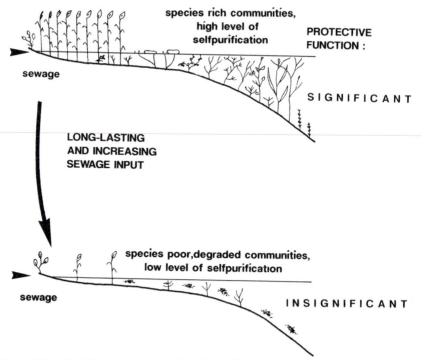

Figure 7.16 Simplified presentation of the effect of long-lasting sewage input on the littoral zone of lakes

grow abundantly. Emergent and submerged plants can then be harvested at the end of the vegetation season. Even if not, they still contribute to nutrient inactivation during the growing season and subsequent to the growing season when they form detritus in bottom sediments.

Management, protection, and restoration

Management practices in shore zones of water bodies include the control of excessive macrophyte growth, prevention of ecotonal habitats against disturbances, and restoration of degraded shore systems. Littoral and marginal plants are the main objects of these management practices. Available techniques for controlling the nuisance growth of macrophytes include: harvesting or burning of emergents, lake level regulation, use of chemicals (usually herbicides), light limitation (use of various shading materials), and biological control by herbivorous fishes, mainly grass carp, *Ctenopharyngodon idella* (Crisman 1986, de Nie 1987).

Littoral habitats are frequently protected and restored to retain natural habitat for fish and aquatic birds and to retain littoral vegetation for its potential importance in nutrient entrapment. Various techniques are

130

suitable for restoration of degraded macrophytes stands; artificial recolonisation by replanting, sediment removal, water level regulation, fencing, and construction of artificial littorals.

One of the best known examples in the literature for restoration is the recultivation of Lake Hornborga in Sweden (Björk 1980). As the water level dropped, the lake became overgrown with emergent vegetation. Aquatic birds no longer used the lake. The restoration programme for this lake consisted of raising the water level and reed cutting, and it was a success. Submerged plants began to dominate in place of emergent species, and the birds returned. Other Swedish management practices now consist of connecting wetlands to lakes in order to generate multiple uses and functions (macrophyte production; waterfowl, fish, and wildlife refuges; water reservoirs).

Grass carp are used for control of aquatic plants at many sites (van Zon 1978, Krzywosz *et al.* 1980, van der Zweerde 1983, Kucklentz 1985, de Nie 1987). Grass carp quickly eliminate macrophytes, but there are side effects related to water quality that must be considered. Grass carp may increase nutrient cycling, since they have a low food assimilation rate and high faeces production. Therefore, the macrophytes may disappear, but other environmental problems emerge in their place.

There are contradictory opinions of the role of vegetation bordering lakes in water quality and eutrophication processes. Both beneficial and detrimental effects can be found in the literature (Lee *et al.* 1975, Rich and Kowalczewski 1976, Kowalczewski 1978, Gaudet 1979). However, field observations and field and laboratory experiments show that pleustonic plants (Culley *et al.* 1981), emergent macrophyte stands (Gersberg *et al.* 1983, 1984, 1986), and submerged macrophyte-periphyton complexes (Mickle and Wetzel 1978a,b) can remove effectively various materials from water. This suggests that, under some conditions, macrophytes can form a protective barrier or a biological filter for nutrients and particulates.

These potential properties of aquatic communities were used successfully in the restoration programme for Lake Jackson, Florida, USA (Fernald and Cason 1986). An underdrain filter system in the retention area and an artificial marsh system were constructed. Several marsh compartments were used, each with different sets of planted macrophytes. Artificial marshes effectively removed organic and mineral substances from the water; bottom sediments also acted as a nutrient sink. Fernald and Cason (1986) believe that methods used at Lake Jackson are most effective in regions having a long growing season, with regular and moderate rainfall. The methods would be only marginally effective in temperate and cold climates.

Ecotonal macrophyte stands were also used to provide water quality protection practices for Lake Balaton, Hungary. This lake has been facing eutrophication from increasing external loads of nutrients (Herodek *et al.* 1988). After having removed most (80%) phosphorus of point source origin (effluents), management efforts were focussed on controlling inputs of nonpoint source origin, most of which were contributed by tributary water. Many of these tributaries had been, in historic times, connected to the lake through vast ecotonal marshlands, which act to filter external loads. One of these (i.e. Kis-Balaton) was reconstructed in the vicinity of the mouth of the Zala River, the largest tributary. The reconstructed system functioned as expected. Roughly, 70% of sediments and 50% of nutrients were removed by the ecotonal wetland (G. Jolankai, personal communication).

In the restoration and protection programme of shallow Lake Bikcze, Poland (Wojciechowski 1976), a system guarding against excessive runoff was used. An embankment and ditches, deeper than the groundwater level, were constructed surrounding the lake. These treatments, together with transformation of vegetation in the drainage basin, improved lake water quality.

The cultivation of macrophytes for the purpose of cleansing sewage water has often been suggested. Some macrophyte species (e.g. *Lemna*, *Glyceria*, *Schoenoplectus*, and *Eichhornia*) have been used in sewage ponds. Such studies and practices are not usually linked directly with the protection of natural lakes; however, information on the mechanisms of nutrient accumulation by various species of plants could be utilised in programmes of natural lake management.

The disappearance of shore and littoral vegetation in polluted water bodies is often a signal for restoration. The restoration programme for vegetation of Loch Leven, Scotland (Jupp and Spence 1977), included, among others, formation of near-shore lagoons where different plants species could be grown to form suitable habitat for aquatic birds. In Lake Constance, Germany, *Phragmites* was successfully replanted on specially prepared shores. Fences were constructed in Havel lakes (West Berlin) to prevent losses in reed stands (Markstein and Sukopp 1983; see de Nie 1987). Several other techniques have been developed (de Nie 1987). Yet, to be cautious, all these methods should be used carefully because of possible noncontrolled side effects.

The importance of ecotonal shore zones varies from locality to locality, and we are still far from a full understanding of their potential role in the interrelationship between water bodies and the surrounding areas. However, it is possible to suggest some physical and biological characteristics that are important for ecotonal systems, especially for their protective importance to lakes.

The physical characteristics are: (1) lake morphometry; (2) shore terrace development, which determines the area potentially overgrown by macrophytes (the slope of shore terrace influences the proportion of surface area colonised by emergent and submergent plants); (3) exposure to waves, which may have a destructive effect on macrophytes; (4) water level fluctuations, which influence the surface area of the littoral zone periodically emergent or isolated from the lake; and (5) structure and chemistry of sediment and interstitial water (phosphorus and nitrogen concentrations), which regulate nutrient uptake from the substrate by macrophytes.

The biological characteristics are: (1) diversity of producers, which determines the effectiveness of nutrient uptake; when the community consists of various morphological and physiological groups of plants (algae and macrophytes), the total primary production is usually higher; (2) production-to-decomposition ratio, which regulates the rate of nutrient cycling; dominance of organic material resistant to decomposition leads to accumulation of a large amount of detritus and isolation of some nutrient pools from circulation; and (3) species composition of macrophytes, which affects nutrient uptake from water and bottom sediments. Macrophyte species vary greatly in their life cycles, physiology, morphology, and anatomy. As to their protective functions, the phenology is one of the most important. For example, evergreen species (such as *Characeae, Elodea, Fontinalis*) are much more important than *Potamogeton* species growing only for several months each year.

All these environmental and community characteristics should be taken into account in ecotonal restoration and management programmes. Some of these parameters may be obtained easily (such as geomorphological characteristics) or even from literature data (such as morphophysiological properties of plants or their life cycle). On the basis of this information, it is then possible to predict to what extent the shore zone of a given lake may be effective for nutrient entrapment from throughflowing water and to what extent it is possible to change ecotone properties.

CONCLUSIONS

The ecotonal zone between uplands and lakes has its own unique environmental characteristics and specific biological processes:

1. Lentic ecotones form unusually differentiated habitats. Interactions between the uplands and the water body favour the formation of specific habitats. Various microenvironments are formed within the shore zone of a water body and, further, similar microenvironments occur in certain sections of water bodies contrasting in size, depth, productivity, and catchment area.

2. Lentic ecotones are colonised by rich plant and animal communities characterised by a shifting proportion of terrestrial and aquatic organisms, as well as unique flora and fauna. These habitats are important feeding, breeding, and rearing grounds for many animal species. An 'edge effect' (i.e. a greater number of species and greater density of organisms) is observed in many ecotonal habitats.

3. Different kinds of allochthonous and autochthonous material are the

sources of organic matter in ecotonal shore zones: primary production (organic matter produced in shore zones by macrophytes and algae living there), accumulated material produced in the deeper parts of the lake and brought onto the shore by wave action, and accumulated material of terrestrial origin supplied from the drainage basin.

4. Much of the organic matter produced or accumulated in lentic ecotones is utilised *in situ* by organisms inhabiting this zone. This material varies in food quality for macroconsumers and in susceptibility to decomposition by microbes. This influences the development and spatiotemporal arrangement of food chains. In most cases, lentic ecotones are detritus-dominated systems and a detrital food chain dominates.

5. Lentic ecotones often accumulate organic matter. Most is resistant to decomposition (tree leaves, macrophytes). A fast decomposition rate in several ecotonal habitats makes this material available to higher trophic levels much quicker than in typical land and water habitats.

6. Physical properties and biological processes in ecotones are influenced considerably by water level fluctuations. Periodic flooding or drying is responsible for the appearance or disappearance of habitat for terrestrial or aquatic organisms. Water level fluctuations also affect primary production and decomposition processes.

7. Differentiations in lake habitats and neighbouring terrestrial areas (due to configuration, types of soil and bottom, and vegetation) cause a variety of interactions to occur between terrestrial and aquatic patches, not only in different ecosystems but also in specific parts of the shore zone on a single lake. Associated with the ecotones of each water body there are several subsystems variously connected with the surrounding aquatic and terrestrial patches.

8. A majority of ecotonal habitats are under visible human impact. Lake eutrophication, airborne pollution, sewage input, agricultural practices, tourist activity, and other activities change lentic ecotones and often damage them. Disappearance of terrestrial and aquatic vegetation is the most common response to unfavourable conditions.

9. Lentic ecotones, because of their multiple ecological functions and their significance in the landscape and in water bodies, require special protection and management. Management practices in ecotonal habitats between terrestrial and aquatic ecosystems should include protection of natural shores, restoration of degraded sites, and creation of new habitats that can serve as a protective barrier for dissolved nutrients and particulates.

ACKNOWLEDGEMENTS

I thank R.J. Naiman and the two anonymous reviewers for their constructive comments and suggestions, and Unesco's Man and the Biosphere Programme for travel support.

LITERATURE CITED

Adams, M.S., and R.T. Prentki. 1982. Biology, metabolism and function of littoral submersed weedbeds of Lake Wingra, Wisconsin, USA: a summary and review. Archiv für Hydrobiologie, Supplement 62:333-409.

Arsuffi, T.L., and K. Suberkropp. 1984. Leaf processing capabilities of aquatic hyphomycetes: interspecific differences and influence on shredder feeding preferences. Oikos 42:144-154.

Barnes, J.R., R. Ovink, and K.W. Cummins. 1978. Leaf litter processing in Gull Lake, Michigan, USA. Verhandlungen Internationale Vereinigung Limnologie 20:475-479.

Bärlocher, F., R.J. Mackay, and G.B. Wiggins. 1978. Detritus processing in a temporary vernal pool in southern Ontario. Archiv für Hydrobiolgie 81:269-295.

Bastardo, H. 1979. Laboratory studies on decomposition of littoral plants. Polskie Archiwum Hydrobiologii 26:267-299.

Bernatowicz, S. 1969. Macrophytes in the lake Warniak and their chemical composition. Ekologia Polska, Seria A 17:447-467.

Bernatowicz, S., and J. Zachwieja. 1966. Types of littoral found in the lakes of the Masurian and Suwalki Lakelands. Ekologia Polska, Seria A 14:519-545.

Best, E.P.H., D. de Vries, and A. Reins. 1984. The macrophytes in the Loosdrecht Lakes: a story of their decline in the course of eutrophication. Verhandlungen Internationale Vereinigung Limnologie 22:868-875.

Björk, S. 1967. Ecologic investigations of *Phragmites communis*: studies in theoretic and applied limnology. Folia Limnologica Scandinavica 14:1-248.

Björk, S. 1980. Restoration of degraded lake ecosystems. Pages 196-219 *in* N. Duncan and J. Rzóska, editors. Land use impact on lake and reservoir ecosystems. Facultas-Verlag, Vienna, Austria.

Boar, R.R., and C.E. Crook. 1985. Investigations into the causes of reedswamp regression in the Norfolk Broads. Verhandlungen Internationale Vereinigung Limnologie 22:2916-2919.

Boström, B., M. Jansson, and C. Forsberg. 1982. Phosphorus release from lake sediments. Archiv für Hydrobiologie, Beiheft Ergebnisse der Limnologie 18:5-59.

Brittain, J.E., and A. Lillehammer. 1978. The fauna of the exposed zone of Øvre Heimdalsvatn: methods, sampling stations and general results. Holarctic Ecology 1:221-228.

Carignan, R. 1982. An empirical model to estimate the relative importance of roots in phosphorus uptake by aquatic macrophytes. Canadian Journal of Fisheries and Aquatic Sciences 39:243-247.

Carignan, R. 1985. Nutrient dynamics in a littoral sediment colonized by the submersed macrophyte *Myriophyllum spicatum*. Canadian Journal of Fisheries and Aquatic Sciences 42:1303-1311.

Carpenter, J.W., R.H. Green, and C.G. Paterson. 1983. A preliminary organic carbon budget for a small dystrophic lake in Maritime Canada. Hydrobiologia 106:275-282.

Cowardin, L.M., V. Carter, F.C. Golet, and E.T. LaRoe. 1979. Classification of wetlands and deepwater habitats of the United States. United States Fish and Wildlife Service FWS/OBS-79/31, Washington, D.C., USA.

Crisman, T.L. 1986. Eutrophication control with an emphasis on macrophytes and algae. Pages 200-239 *in* N. Polunin, editor. Ecosystem theory and application. John Wiley, Chichester, England.

Culley, D.D., Jr., E. Rejmánková, J. Kvet, and J.B. Frye. 1981. Production, chemical quality and use of duckweeds (Lemnaceae) in aquaculture, waste management, and animal feeds. Journal of the World Mariculture Society 12:27-49.

Dall, P.C., C. Lindegaard, E. Jonsson, G. Jonsson, and P.M. Jonasson. 1984. Invertebrate communities and their environment in the exposed littoral zone of Lake Esrom, Denmark, Archiv für Hydrobiologie, Supplement 69:477-524.

Denny, P. 1972. Sites of nutrient absorption in aquatic macrophytes. Journal of Ecology 60:819-829.

Di Castri, F., A.J. Hansen, and M.M. Holland (editors). 1988. A new look at ecotones: emerging international projects on landscape boundaries. Biology International, Special Issue 17:1-163.

Dickinson, C.H., and G.J.F. Pugh (editors). 1974. Biology and plant litter decomposition. Volume 2. Academic Press, London, England.

Dobrowolski, K.A. 1973. Role of birds in Polish wetland ecosystems. Polskie Archiwum Hydrobiologii 20:217-221.

Duarte, C.M., J. Kalff, and R.H. Peters. 1986. Patterns in biomass and cover of aquatic macrophytes in lakes. Canadian Journal of Fisheries and Aquatic Sciences 43:1900-1908.

Dvořák, J. 1978. Macrofauna of invertebrates in helophyte communities. Pages 389-395 *in* D. Dykyjová and J. Květ, editors. Pond littoral ecosystems: structure and functioning. Springer-Verlag, Berlin, Germany.

Dvořák, J., and E.P.H. Best. 1982. Macroinvertebrate communities associated with the macrophytes of Lake Vechten: structural and functional relationships. Pages 115-126 *in* R.D. Gulati and S. Parma, editors. Studies on Lake Vechten and Tjeukemeer, The Netherlands. Dr. W. Junk, The Hague, The Netherlands.

Dykyjová, D., and J. Květ (editors). 1978. Pond littoral ecosystems: structure and functioning. Springer-Verlag, Berlin, Germany.

Eloranta, P. 1970. Pollution and aquatic flora of waters by a sulphite cellulose factory at Mantta, Finnish Lake District. Annales Botanici Fennici 7:63-141.

Felföldy, L.J.M. 1958. A contribution to the ecology and biological productivity of the diatom mass-vegetation on the stony shores of Lake Balaton. Annales Instituti Biologici (Tihany) Hungaricae Academiae Scientiarum 25:331-342.

Fernald, E.A., and J.H. Cason. 1986. Development of an artifical marsh in Tallahassee, Florida: Lake Jackson, a case study. Page 229-241 *in* J. Lauga. H. Décamps, and M.M. Holland, editors. Land use impacts on aquatic ecosystems: the use of scientific information. MAB/Unesco, Toulouse, France.

Gasith, A., and A.D. Hasler. 1976. Airborne litterfall as a source of organic matter in lakes. Limnology and Oceanography 21:253-258.

Gasith, A., and W. Ławacz. 1976. Breakdown of leaf litter in the littoral zone of a eutrophic lake. Ekologia Polska 24:421-430.

Gaudet, J.J. 1979. Seasonal changes in nutrients in a tropical swamp: North Swamp, Lake Naivasha, Kenya. Journal of Ecology 67:953-981.

Gersberg, R.M., B.V. Elkins, and C.R. Goldman. 1983. Nitrogen removal in artificial wetlands. Water Research 17:1009-1014.

Gersberg, R.M., B.V. Elkins, and C.R. Goldman. 1984. Use of artificial wetlands to remove nitrogen from wastewater. Journal of the Water Pollution Control Federation 56:152-156.

Gersberg, R.M., B.V. Elkins, S.R. Lyon, and C.R. Goldman. 1986. Role of aquatic plants in wastewater treatment by artificial wetlands. Water Research 20:363-388.

Godshalk, G.L., and R.G. Wetzel. 1978. Decomposition in the littoral zone of lakes. Pages 131-143 *in* R.E. Good, D.F. Whigham, and R.L. Simpson, editors. Freshwater wetlands: ecological processes and management potential. Academic Press, New York, USA.

Gons, H.J. 1982. Structural and functional characteristics of epiphyton and epipelon in relation to their distribution in Lake Vechten. Hydrobiologia 95:79-114.

Gopal, B., R.E. Turner, R.G. Wetzel, and D.G. Whigham (editors). 1982. Wetlands: ecology and management. National Institute of Ecology, International Scientific Publications, Jaipur, India.

Gunatilaka, A. 1985. Nährstoffkreisläufe im Schilfgürtel des Neusiedler Sees. Auswirkungen des Grünschnittes. Wiss. Arb. Bgld. 72:225-310.

Hejný, S. 1960. Okologische Charakteristik der Wasser- und Sumpf-pflanzen in den Slowak-ischen Tiefbenen (Donau-und Theissgebiet). Vyd. SAV, Bratislava, Czechoslovakia.

Hejný, S. 1971. The dynamic characteristic of littoral vegetation with respect to changes of water level. Hidrobiologia (Bucharest) 12:71-85.

Hejný, S., and Š. Husák. 1978. Higher plant communities. Pages 23-64 *in* D. Dykyjová and

J. Květ, editors. Pond littoral ecosystems: structure and functioning. Springer-Verlag, Berlin, Germany.

Herodek, S., V. Istvanovics, and J. Zlinszky. 1988. Phosphorus metabolism and eutrophication control of Lake Balaton. Verhandlungen Internationale Vereinigung Limnologie 23:517-521.

Hodkinson, I.D. 1975. Dry weight loss and chemical changes in vascular plant litter of terrestrial origin, occurring in a beaver pond ecosystem. Journal of Ecology 63:131-142.

Hudec, K., and K. Šťastný. 1978. Birds in the reedswamp ecosystem. Pages 366-372 *in* D. Dykyjová and J. Květ, editors. Pond littoral ecosystems: structure and functioning. Springer-Verlag, Berlin, Germany.

Hutchinson, G.E. 1967. A treatise on limnology. Volume 2: Introduction to lake biology and the limnoplankton. John Wiley and Sons, New York, USA.

Hutchinson, G.E. 1975. A treatise on limnology. Volume 3: Limnological botany. John Wiley and Sons, New York, USA.

Imhof, G., and K. Burian. 1972. Energy-flow studies in a wetland ecosystem (reed belt of the lake Neusiedler See). Springer-Verlag, Vienna, Austria.

Jeník, J., and V. Větvička. 1973. Ecology and structure in stands of *Salix* spp. in the Třeboň Basin (a preliminary report). Pages 39-46 *in* S. Hejný, editor. Ecosystem study on wetland biome in Czechoslovakia. Czechoslowak IBP/PT-PP Report Number 3, Třeboň, Czechoslovakia.

Jupp, B.P., and D.H.N. Spence. 1977. Limitations of macrophytes in a eutrophic Lake Loch Leven [Scotland]. II. Wave action, sediments and waterfowl grazing. Journal of Ecology 65:431-446.

Kann, E. 1982. Qualitative Veranderungen der litoralen Algenbiocönose österreichischer Seen (Lunzer Untersee, Traunsee, Attersee) im Laufe der letzten Jahrzehnte. Archiv für Hydrobiologie, Supplement 62:440-490.

Komárková, J., and P. Marvan. 1978. Primary production and functioning of algae in the fishpond littoral. Pages 321-337 *in* D. Dykyjová and J. Květ, editors. Pond littoral ecosystems: structure and functioning. Springer-Verlag, Berlin, Germany.

Kowalczewski, A. 1978. Importance of bordering wetland for chemical properties of lake water. Verhandlungen Internationale Vereinigung Limnologie 20:2182-2185.

Kozakiewicz, A. 1985. Lakeside communities of small mammals. Acta Theriologica 30(9):171-191.

Krzywosz, T., W. Krzywosz, and J. Radziej. 1980. The effect of grass carp, *Ctenopharyngodon idella* (Val.), on aquatic vegetation and ichthyofauna of Lake Dgal Wielki. Ekologia Polska 28:433-450.

Kucklentz, V. 1985. Restoration of a small lake by combined mechanical and biological methods. Verhandlungen Internationale Vereinigung Limnologie 22:2314-2317.

Kulshreshtha, M., and B. Gopal. 1982a. Decomposition of freshwater wetland vegetation. I. Submerged and free-floating macrophytes. Pages 259-278 *in* B. Gopal, R.E. Turner, R.G. Wetzel, and D.F. Whigham, editors. Wetlands: ecology and management. National Institute of Ecology. International Scientific Publications, Jaipur, India.

Kulshreshtha, M., and B. Gopal. 1982b. Decomposition of freshwater wetland vegetation. II. Aboveground organs of emergent macrophytes. Pages 279-292 *in* B. Gopal, R.E. Turner, R.G. Wetzel, and D.F. Whigham, editors. Wetlands: ecology and management. National Institute of Ecology, International Scientific Publications, Jaipur, India.

Lachavanne, J.B. 1982. Influence de l'eutrophisation des eaux sur les macrophytes des lacs suisses: resultats preliminaires. Pages 333-339 *in* J.J. Symoens, S.S. Hooper, and P. Compere, editors. Studies on aquatic vascular plants. Royal Botanical Society of Belgium, Brussels, Belgium.

Lachavanne, J.B. 1985. The influence of accelerated eutrophication on the macrophytes of Swiss lakes: abundance and distribution. Verhandlungen Internationale Vereinigung Limnologie 22:2950-2955.

Le Cren, E.D., and R.H. Lowe-McConnell (editors). 1980. The functioning of freshwater ecosystems. Cambridge University Press, Cambridge, England.

Lee, G.F., E. Bentley, and R. Amundson. 1975. Effects of marshes on water quality. Pages 105-127 *in* A.D. Hasler, editor. Coupling of land and water systems. Springer-Verlag, Berlin, Germany.

Loenen, M., and A.H. Koridon. 1978. Role of the littoral vegetation in the phosphorus and nitrogen balance of the Lake Drontermeer. Verhandlungen Internationale Vereinigung Limnologie 20:935-938.

Löffler, H. (editor). 1979. Neusiedlersee: the limnology of a shallow lake in central Europe. Dr. W. Junk, The Hague, The Netherlands.

Melillo, J.M., R.J. Naiman, J.D. Aber, and K.N. Eshleman. 1983. The influence of substrate quality and stream size on wood decomposition dynamics. Oecologia (Berlin) 58:281-285.

Melillo, J.M., R.J. Naiman, J.D. Aber, and A.E. Linkins. 1984. Factors controlling mass loss and nitrogen dynamics of plant litter decaying in northern streams. Bulletin of Marine Science 35:341-356.

Mickle, A.M., and R.G. Wetzel. 1978a. Effectiveness of submersed angiosperm-epiphyte complexes on exchange of nutrients and organic carbon in littoral systems. I. Inorganic nutrients. Aquatic Botany 4:303-316.

Mickle, A.M., and R.G. Wetzel. 1978b. Effectiveness of submersed angiosperm-epiphyte complexes on exchange of nutrients and organic carbon in littoral systems. II. Dissolved organic carbon. Aquatic Botany 4:317-329.

Moon, H.P. 1935. Flood movements of the littoral fauna of Windermere. Journal of Animal Ecology 4:216-228.

Naiman, R.J. 1988. Animal influences on ecosystem dynamics. BioScience 38:750-752.

Naiman, R.J., H. Décamps, J. Pastor, and C.A. Johnston. 1988. The potential importance of boundaries to fluvial ecosystems. Journal of the North American Benthological Society 7:289-306.

Neel, J.K. 1948. A limnological investigation of the psammon in Douglas, Lake Michigan, with especial reference to shoal and shoreline dynamics. Transactions of the American Microscopical Society 67:1-53.

Nie, H.W. de. 1987. The decrease in aquatic vegetation in Europe and its consequences for fish populations. European Inland Fisheries Advisory Commission, Occasional Paper Number 19, FAO, Rome, Italy.

Odum, W.E., and R.T. Prentki. 1978. Analysis of Five North-American lake ecosystems. IV. Allochthonous carbon inputs. Verhandlungen Internationale Vereinigung Limnologie 20:574-580.

Ozimek, T. 1978. Effect of municipal sewage on the submerged macrophytes of a lake littoral. Ekologia Polska 26:3-39.

Ozimek, T., and A. Kowalczewski. 1984. Long-term changes of the submerged macrophytes in eutrophic Lake Mikolajskie (North Poland). Aquatic Botany 19:1-11.

Pelikán, J. 1978. Mammals in the reedswamp ecosystem. Pages 357-365 in D. Dykyjová and J. Květ, editors. Pond littoral ecosystems: structure and functioning. Springer-Verlag, Berlin, Germany.

Pennak, R.W. 1940. Ecology of the microscopic metazoa inhabiting the sandy beaches of some Wisconsin lakes. Ecological Monographs 10:537-615.

Phillips, G.L., D. Eminson, and B. Moss. 1978. A mechanism to account for macrophyte decline in progressively eutrophicated fresh-waters. Aquatic Botany 4:103-126.

Pieczyńsksa, E. 1972. Ecology of the eulittoral zone of lakes. Ekologia Polska 20:637-732.

Pieczyńsksa, E. 1986. Sources and fates of detritus in the shore zone of lakes. Aquatic Botany 25:153-166.

Pieczyńska, E., D. Balcerzak, A. Kolodziejczyk, Z. Olszewski, and J.I. Rybak. 1984. Detritus in the littoral of several Masurian lakes (sources and fates). Ekologia Polska 32:387-440.

Planter, M. 1973. Physical and chemical conditions in the helophytes zone of the lake littoral. Polskie Archiwum Hydrobiologii 20:1-7.

Polunin, N.V.C. 1984. The decomposition of emergent macrophytes in fresh water. Advances in Ecological Research 14:115-166.

Prentki, R.T., M.S. Adams, and S.R. Carpenter. 1979. The role of submersed weedbeds in the internal loading and interception of allochthonous materials in Lake Wingra, Wisconsin, USA. Archiv für Hydrobiologie, Supplement 57:221-250.

Rich, P.H., and A. Kowalczewski. 1976. Wetland metabolism. Pages 73-83 in M.W. Lefor, W.C. Kennard, and T.B. Helfgott, editors. Proceedings: Third Wetlands Conference. University of Connecticut, Institute of Water Resources, Report Number 26, Storrs, Connecticut, USA.

Roelofs, J.G.M., and J.A.A.R. Schuurkes. 1983. Impact of acidification and eutrophication on macrophyte communities in soft waters. Pages 197-202 *in* Proceedings of the International Symposium on Aquatic Macrophytes. Faculty of Science, Nijmegen, The Netherlands.

Rørslett, B. 1985. Regulation impact on submerged macrophytes in the oligotrophic lakes of Setesdal, South Norway. Verhandlungen Internationale Vereinigung Limnologie 22:2927-2936.

Rørslett, B., D. Berge, and S.W. Johansen. 1985. Mass invasion of *Elodea canadensis* in a mesotrophic, South Norwegian lake: impact on water quality. Verhandlungen Internationale Vereinigung Limnologie 22:-2920-2926.

Sarvala, J., T. Kairesalo, I. Koskimies, A. Lehtovaara, J. Ruuhijärvi, and I. Vähä-Piikkiö. 1982. Carbon, phosphorus and nitrogen budgets of the littoral *Equisetum* belt in an oligotrophic lake. Hydrobiologia 86:41-53.

Schiemer, F. 1979. Submerged macrophytes in the open lake: distribution pattern, production and long-term changes. Pages 235-250 *in* H. Löffler, editor. Neusiedlersee: the limnology of a shallow lake in central Europe. Dr. W. Junk, The Hague, The Netherlands.

Schindler, D.W., V.E. Frost, and R.V. Schmidt. 1973. Production of epilithiphyton in two lakes of the Experimental Lakes Area, northwestern Ontario. Journal of the Fisheries Research Board of Canada 30:1511-1524.

Schröder, R. 1987. Das Schilfsterben am Bodensee-Untersee. Beobachtungen, Untersuchungen und Gegenmassnahmen. Archiv für Hydrobiologie, Supplement 76:53-99.

Schröder, R., and H. Schröder. 1982. Changes in the composition of the submerged macrophyte community in Lake Constance: a multi-parameter analysis with various environmental factors. Memorie dell' Istituto Italiano di Idrobiologia 'Dott. Marco de Marchi' 40:25-53.

Sebestyén, O. 1950. Studies on detritus drifts in Lake Balaton. Annales Instituti Biologiae Pervestigandae Hungarici 19:49-64.

Segal, S. 1971. Principles on structure, zonation and succession of aquatic macrophytes. Hidrobiologia (Bucharest) 12:89-95.

Smock, L.A., and K.L. Harlowe. 1983. Utilization and processing of freshwater wetland macrophytes by the detrivore *Asellus forbesi*. Ecology 64:1556-1565.

Soszka, G. 1975. The invertebrates on submerged macrophytes in three Masurian lakes. Ekologia Polska 23:371-391.

Spence, D.H.N. 1982. The zonation of plants in freshwater lakes. Advances in Ecological Research 12:37-125.

Stockner, J.G., and F.A.J. Armstrong. 1971. Periphyton of the Experimental Lakes Area, northwestern Ontario. Journal of the Fisheries Research Board of Canada 28:215-229.

Thompson, K. 1976. Swamp development in the head waters of the White Nile. Pages 177-196 *in* J. Rzóska, editor. The Nile, biology of an ancient river. Dr. W. Junk, The Hague, The Netherlands.

Toivonen, H. 1983. Changes in dominant macrophytes of 54 small Finnish lakes in 30 years. Pages 220-224 *in* Proceedings of the International Symposium on Aquatic Macrophytes. Faculty of Science, Nijmegen, The Netherlands.

Toivonen, H., and J. Meriläinen. 1980. Impact of the muskrat (*Ondatra zibethica* L.) on aquatic vegetation in small Finnish lakes. Pages 131-138 *in* M. Dokulil, H. Metz, and D. Jewson, editors. Shallow lakes: contributions to their limnology. Dr. W. Junk, The Hague, The Netherlands.

Úlehlová, B. 1976. Microbial decomposers and decomposition processes in wetlands. Studie Ceskoslovenske Akademie Ved 17:1-112.

Wetzel, R.G. 1964. A comparative study of the primary productivity of higher aquatic plants, periphyton and phytoplankton in a large, shallow lake. Internationale Revue der gesamten Hydrobiologie 49:1-61.

Wetzel, R.G. 1983. Limnology. Saunders College Publishing, Philadelphia, Pennsylvania, USA.

Wetzel, R.G., and H.L. Allen. 1972. Functions and interactions of dissolved organic matter and the littoral zone in lake metabolism and eutrophication. Pages 333-347 *in* Z. Kajak and A. Hillbricht-Ilkowska, editors. Productivity problems of freshwaters. PWN, Polish Scientific Publishers, Warszawa-Krakow, Poland.

Wetzel, R.G., P.H. Rich, M.C. Miller, and H.L. Allen. 1972. Metabolism of dissolved and particulate detrital carbon in a temperate hardwater lake. Memorie dell' Istituto Italiano di Idrobiolgia, Supplement 29:185-243.

Wiens, J.A., C.S. Crawford, and J.R. Gosz. 1985. Boundary dynamics: a conceptual framework for studying landscape ecoystems. Oikos 45:421-427.

Wojciechowski, I. 1976. Influence of the drainage basin on the eutrophication of the amesotrophic Lake Piaseczno and diseutrophication of the pond Lake Bikcze. Acta Hydrobiologica 18:23-52.

Zax, M. 1973. Die Temperaturresistenz von *Phragmites communis* Trin. Polskie Archiwum Hydrobiologii 20:159-164.

Zon, J.C.J. van. 1978. The use of grass carp in comparison with other aquatic weed control methods. Pages 15-24 *in* Proceedings of the Grass Carp Conference, Gainesville, Florida, USA.

Zweerde, W. van der. 1983. The use of grass carp (*Ctenopharyngodon idella* Val.) in the management of watercourses in the Netherlands: effects and side effects. Pages 322-326 *in* Proceedings of the International Symposium on Aquatic Macrophytes. Faculty of Science, Nijmegen, The Netherlands.

Key words: Boundaries, decomposition, lakes, littoral habitats, management, production.

CHAPTER 8

FUNCTIONS OF ECOTONES IN FLUVIAL SYSTEMS

Gilles Pinay, Henri Décamps, Eric Chauvet and Eliane Fustec

ABSTRACT

Ecotones are important in regulating interactions in lotic systems. These interactions take place in the three-dimensional geometry of space: vertical, transversal, and longitudinal. This chapter emphasises transversal and longitudinal lotic ecotones. The objective is to illustrate the functions of terrestrial-aquatic as well as instream ecotones in fluvial systems. Considerations of ecotones within nonequilibrium fluvial landscapes are shown to provide improved management perspectives for lotic ecosystems.

INTRODUCTION

It is well known that the terrestrial environment strongly influences the ecological functions of running water (Hynes 1975). Theories elaborating this idea include the river continuum concept and its derivatives (Vannote *et al.* 1980, Minshall *et al.* 1983, 1985; Statzner and Higler 1985, Naiman *et al.* 1987), as well as the nutrient spiralling concept (Newbold *et al.* 1981, Elwood *et al.* 1983, Newbold 1987). The comprehension of interactive systems, such as fluvial valleys (Décamps 1984, Ward and Stanford 1987), obliges one to consider rivers in a landscape context (Risser *et al.* 1984, Urban *et al.* 1987).

The importance of ecotones has been emphasised in regulating landscape level interactions in lotic systems (Naiman *et al.* 1988a, b). We consider an ecotone to be a functional entity having a set of characteristics and interactions that depend on its transitional position between adjacent ecological systems uniquely defined by space and time scales (Holland 1988). A boundary constitutes a physical limit between two patches. The ecotone thus defined is not only a boundary but an area of interaction with two or more adjacent systems.

This interaction takes place in the three-dimensional geometry of space:

vertical, transversal, and longitudinal (Roux 1982, Amoros *et al.* 1987, Ward and Stanford 1989, Ward 1989). We refer here to transversal and longitudinal lotic ecotones (vertical ecotones are treated by Gibert *et al.* 1990). Transversal ecotones (mainly terrestrial-aquatic) relate rivers to their terrestrial surroundings; this aspect is especially important to the ecology of large alluvial rivers. Among terrestrial-aquatic ecotones existing within river corridors we have chosen to deal with riparian zones. These riverine areas often have woody growth in continuous ribbons along the fluvial corridor. They constitute an appropriate scale for investigation of terrestrial-aquatic ecotone functions along river segments. Longitudinal ecotones (mainly aquatic-aquatic) correspond to the various longitudinal sections succeeding each other along the hydrographic network.

The objective of this chapter is to illustrate the functions of terrestrial-aquatic as well as instream ecotones in fluvial systems. Consideration of their status within nonequilibrium fluvial landscapes is shown to lead to improved management perspectives.

TERRESTRIAL-AQUATIC ECOTONES

Instability of terrestrial-aquatic ecotones

A main feature of terrestrial-aquatic ecotones is their spatial and temporal instability. For instance, Braga and Gervasoni (1983) have shown the extent of lateral movements of the Po River, Italy, between the 16th and 20th centuries (Fig. 8.1). This focusses on several aspects of natural dynamics of river meanders: downstream movements, cutoffs, and the decrease of curve radius. In some situations these changes have been hampered by natural processes, such as northwest of Piacenza, where alluvial deposits of the Trebbia River (a tributary of the Po) limit the Po River from shifting its course. Today the course of the Po River is embanked with dikes. The dikes have been built to protect the valley against floods, and thus limit erosional processes. One consequence of diking is that rivers are no longer connected with their floodplains. Diking operations delete secondary channels and oxbows, thereby tremendously diminishing ecotone length.

Two case studies illustrate the spatial and temporal variability of terrestrial-aquatic ecotones: the Willamette River, Oregon, USA (Sedell and Froggatt 1984), and the Garonne River, France (Fortuné 1988a). Between 1854 and 1967, along a 25 km reach of the Willamette River near Harrisburg, Oregon, bank lengths decreased from 250 km to 64 km.

Similarly, man-made structures have greatly modified the flow pattern of the Garonne River at Toulouse, France, since at least the 12th century (Fortuné 1988b). Between 1680 and 1982, along a 2 km reach of the river in the city of Toulouse, bank length decreased from 11.4 to 7.2 km and the number of islands declined from 17 to 4. This decrease in ecotone length along river courses seems to be a constant tendency within the evolution

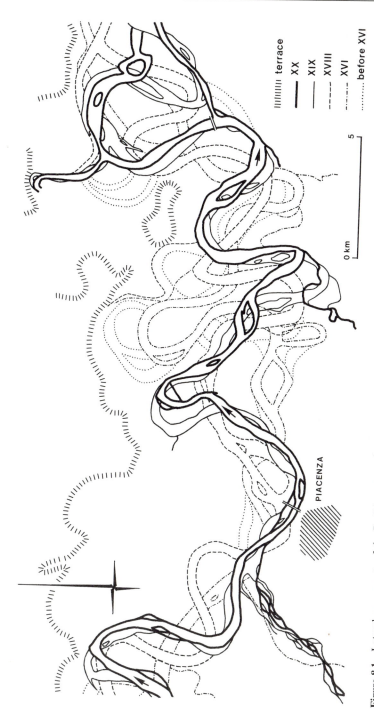

Figure 8.1 Lateral movements of the Po River, Italy, between the 16th and 20th centuries. Adapted from Braga and Gervasoni (1983)

of alluvial valleys of developed countries. This trend is noticeable in several large European rivers like the Rhine (Carbiener *et al.* 1987), the Danube (Bethemont and Bravard 1986), the Rhône (Bravard 1987), and the Loire (Maillard 1981).

Attempts to control the natural instability of these fluvial systems result in an artificial reduction of terrestrial-aquatic ecotones. These changes relate to socio-economic factors that modify the fluvial landscapes of developed countries: protection against floods, navigation needs, agriculture, industrialisation, and urbanisation. These same socio-economic pressures are beginning to be felt in developing countries. Among others one can cite flood problems in Bangladesh (Rasid and Paul 1987), the Zambezi River, Zimbabwe, impounded with huge dams (Pinay 1988), and the Nile River, Egypt (Davies 1979). In each case river impoundments have been realised to the detriment of ecotonal riparian forests, even though they are well known as reducers of flood effects.

Ecotones as reducers of flood effects

Terrestrial-aquatic ecotones absorb flood peaks in alluvial plains (Graf 1980, Schlosser and Karr 1981, Petersen *et al.* 1987). The importance of this function is shown by the effects of straightening and channelisation on the hydrology of the Rhine River between Bâle (Basel), Switzerland, and Mainz, West Germany (Fig. 8.2). At the turn of the 18th century, the 'pristine' Rhine River was divided into innumerable interconnected channels along four different geomorphologic sectors, from an upstream braided sector to a downstream meandering sector. Impoundments planned by engineer Tulla and realised between 1817 and 1876 confined the Rhine within an artificial channel. This channel, limited by straight banks, was navigable but has drastically altered the nature of the river. Initially, dikes situated 0.5 to 2 km from each side of the channel sustained gallery forest which could be flooded. Eventually, further channelisation and impoundments reduced or deleted even these flooded zones, resulting in an amplification of flood waves and an acceleration of their downstream transfer. Another consequence of the straightening of the Rhine is that its embankments have isolated the channel from its terrestrial environment, which in turn has isolated the river from its alluvial groundwater. The consideration of the great importance of ecotonal riparian forests has led to the reconnection of a stretch of the Rhine River, north of Karlsruhe, West Germany, with its floodplain (Schäffer 1973).

Ecotones as natural filters against diffuse pollution from the floodplain

Ecotonal riparian forests constitute natural filters against diffuse nutrient pollution (Lowrance *et al.* 1984, Peterjohn and Correll 1984, Jacobs and Gilliam 1985). Recent studies on the Garonne River, France, illustrate this

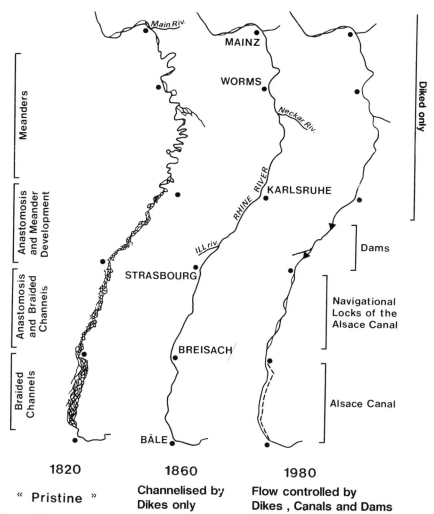

Figure 8.2 Straightening and channelisation of the Rhine River since 1820 between Bâle (Basel), Switzerland, and Mainz, West Germany

contention. The hypothesis that has been tested here is that these riparian woods eliminate nitrate as the groundwater passes from the agricultural fields to the river. The alluvial plain supports substantial agricultural production dominated by cereals, with an increase in intense cultivation of crops such as soya, colza, and sunflower. Peach and apple orchards are also important. Riparian woods have been reduced but are continuous along the river.

In 1986 more than 500 wells were sampled to study the quality of the groundwater in the floodplain (E. Fustec, unpublished data; Chauvet and

145

Décamps 1989). Three points are to be made from the results (Fig. 8.3): (1) there existed a large heterogeneity of nitrate levels, ranging from undetectable to nearly 300 mg NO_3/L with more than 63% of the samplings above 50 mg/l (the norm for potability); (2) nitrate concentration in the groundwater changed with land use, the best gradient being: woods, pastures, orchards, fallow lands, cereals, market gardening, urban areas; and (3) within the alluvial plain, the groundwater near the river had the lowest nitrate content compared with more distant zones. Moreover, nitrate was almost or totally eliminated before reaching the surface water of the river.

We examined how a riparian woodlot eliminated nitrate from groundwater along a transverse section near a tributary of the Garonne River (Pinay 1986, Pinay and Décamps 1988). In the upper reach of a transect perpendicular to the river (Fig. 8.4), the input of allochthonous nitrate from the groundwater diminished rapidly because of intense denitrification. At sites closer to the river, nitrates that are denitrified originated exclusively from the mineralisation of *in situ* accumulated organic matter. Consequently, about 30 m of flow of the groundwater under the woodlot is enough to remove its nitrate, and the lower reach provides the potential for further denitrification. Furthermore, the nitrate removal capacity of this riparian woodlot appears far more important than the removal actually realised. This result was confirmed by the constant presence of reduced manganese and iron in the aquifer in the lower reach (where they are utilised as terminal acceptors of electrons in absence of nitrate) and by denitrification rates of up to 50 mg $N_2 \cdot m^{-2} \cdot d^{-1}$ in the field compared with the potential denitrification rates of 350 $N_2 \cdot m^{-2} \cdot d^{-1}$ estimated experimentally with nitrate additions.

When considering a system like the Garonne River and its riparian forests, four questions deserve more attention: (1) How applicable is this conceptual model to other natural and artificial riparian forests? (2) What are the consequences of the fragmentation of the continuous forest along a river? (3) Is the role of this filter zone also important when the flow is from the river to fields and not from the fields to the river? (4) A major effect of river regulation is to suppress the extent and diversity of the buffer zone constituted by riparian forests: in this case, how efficient are the substituted ecotones for controlling nutrient pollution?

Ecotones as a source of organic carbon for rivers

Basically, organic carbon in rivers is either autochthonous or allochthonous. Autochthonous organic carbon derives from primary production within the river itself, while carbon of allochthonous origin is based on decomposed products of terrestrial organisms. The importance of exogenous organic matter in rivers was first recognised by Thienemann (1912). Following

146

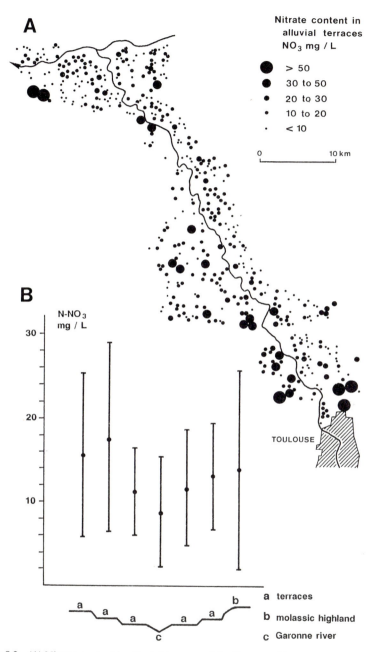

Figure 8.3 (A) Nitrate content in alluvial terraces of the Garonne River, France. (B) Average and standard deviation of nitrate content in the different geomorphologic formations of the Garonne River corridor

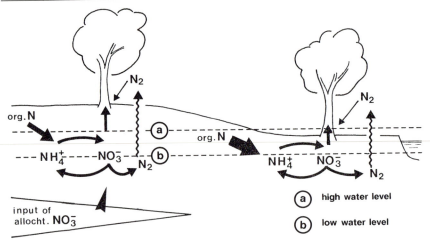

Figure 8.4 Spatial evolution of the nitrogen cycle across a transect perpendicular to the Louge River within the riparian wood. Adapted from Pinay and Décamps (1988)

Hynes (1963, 1975) several authors demonstrated that terrestrial litter constituted the main energy supply for forested headwater streams. Small forested creeks normally receive an average of 400 to 600 $g\cdot m^{-2}\cdot yr^{-1}$ of allochthonous carbon, in which dead leaves represent 350 $g\cdot m^{-2}\cdot yr^{-1}$ (Bird and Kaushik 1981). The river continuum concept proposed that, when the size of the river increases from its source to its mouth, the importance of allochthonous vegetation in the organic matter budget of the river decreases (Vannote *et al.* 1980). Annual direct litter inputs to large rivers usually range between 10 and 40 g/m^2 of water surface (Mathews and Kowalczewski 1969, Conners and Naiman 1984, Chauvet and Jean-Louis 1988, Karlström 1988). Yet large rivers have a greater surface water area than small creeks for the collection of allochthonous carbon.

Land-water ecotones are also influenced by lateral fluxes of terrestrial litter. Nevertheless, these lateral transfers towards aquatic ecosytems seem to represent a smaller proportion of allochthonous inputs to large rivers than to small ones. The importance of this contribution is a function of channel morphology and flood intensity (Conners and Naiman 1984).

Dissolved organic carbon inputs from terrestrial environments to rivers also have received some attention (Hynes 1983, Naiman *et al.* 1987, Ford and Naiman 1989). Humic substances are the major constituents of dissolved organic matter in rivers (Ishiwatari 1985, Malcolm 1985, Steinberg and Muenster 1985). Terrestrial vegetation is one source of humic material, as are autochthonous organisms and sewage. Among humic substances, lignin signatures in rivers have been reported by Ertel *et al.* (1984). Recently, Fustec *et al.* (1989) have experimentally shown that humification of lignin compounds generally occurred, but at low rates. It appears that these transformations are stimulated by the presence of a well-developed flooded zone, where primary production is high. It follows that the reduction of ecotones along rivers would lead to a substantial modification of dissolved organic carbon sources in lotic ecosystems.

Terrestrial-aquatic ecotones not only constitute transitional zones between upland and river regarding nutrient fluxes, they also act as connection lines for species fluxes along river corridors.

Ecotones as connection lines for special fluxes

Lotic ecotones constitute intermediary zones between aquatic and terrestrial ecosystems. Thus they contain species belonging to each distinct environment as well as species typical of humid zones. This entails a high biological diversity along terrestrial-aquatic ecotones. However, ecological conditions vary greatly between seasons as a function of hydrologic regime. For instance, active migration of fish species from rivers towards their floodplains has been well documented by Welcomme (1979, 1985). The different types of migration (i.e., trophic, reproductive) occur according to the hydrologic regime of rivers. The most spectacular example concerns the Amazon River (Sioli 1984). During the flood period (4 to 10 months), the water level rises 15 m above baseflow, allowing hundreds of fish species to enter the flooded riverine forests to feed on terrestrial arthropods, fruits, seeds, flowers, and leaves that have fallen into the water.

An important characteristic of natural ecotonal riparian forests is their connectivity. This feature has to be considered from the standpoint of both the aquatic environment and the riverine forest environment. Connectivity in the aquatic environment allows movements of materials and organisms between the main fluvial channel and its secondary channels and oxbows lakes. The role of these movements for fish population dynamics is critical. For instance, oxbow lakes constitute spawning and nursery areas for many fish species. These zones provide habitat for fishes during critical portions of their life history. Connectivity between riparian forests is also crucial for species fluxes. It allows, for instance, various exchanges among bird populations, as it has been demonstrated along the fluvial corridor of the Garonne River (Décamps *et al.* 1987, Joachim 1987).

Lastly, riparian forests seem to be a favourable environment for species invasions. Since at least the 18th century, several exotic species have colonised riverine areas along European fluvial corridors. Of 1100 plant species recorded in riparian habitats of the Adour River, France, 235 were alien species (A.M. Tabacchi and E. Tabacchi, unpublished data). This percentage of alien species is high when compared with other temperate terrestrial ecosystems, and could be related to the natural instability of riparian zones.

INSTREAM ECOTONES

Various physical and chemical discontinuities exist from the sources to the mouth of a river. The physical discontinuities consist of variations in temperature, slope, and the influence of tributaries on channel geomorphology. Chemical discontinuities may occur when, for instance, a river passes onto a different geologic substrate. These discontinuities constitute some of the instream ecotones. However, we will consider these instream ecotones in order to address the following questions, keeping in mind that gas exchanges also exist at the surface water-atmosphere ecotone (Johnston and Naiman 1987) and chemical exchanges exist at surface water-groundwater ecotones (treated by Gibert *et al.* 1990). What are the extent of these natural disruptions and how do they influence biological discontinuities? How do human activities interfere with natural discontinuities? What are the consequences of creating artificial disjunctions along river systems?

Complexity of the hydrographic network

Unidirectional water flow promotes mixing of materials from upstream towards downstream. It also entails longitudinal linkages with a dependence of downstream zones on upstream zones. These linkages are underlined in unifying concepts in lotic ecology, such as the river continuum (Vannote *et al.* 1980) and the nutrient spiralling concepts (Webster 1975, Newbold *et al.* 1981). This unidirectional water flow results in large spatiotemporal heterogeneities in lotic ecosystems, such as riffle-pool sequencing, as well as a dynamic substrate mosaic in any given stream sector. Changing discharge patterns alternately erode or deposit, and provide the existence of distinct yet more or less ephemeral habitats for running water fauna. These two contrasted tendencies, towards homogeneity and heterogeneity, create shifting mosaics typical of running water (Naiman *et al.* 1988a, Pringle *et al.* 1988). The resulting discontinuities produce a variety of ecotones along hydrographic networks. Some ecotones, at the entire system scale, appear to be stable in space and time (e.g. where a river changes slope as it exits the mountains and enters the plains), while other ecotones, at a smaller scale, appear less stable (e.g. shifting substrate mosaics that are reshaped during floods).

At the entire system scale, the complexity of the hydrographic network constitutes the first parameter of ecotone existence. Fish zones from Huet's typology – trout (*Salmo fario*), grayling (*Thymallus thymallus*), barbel (*Barbus barbus*), bream (*Abramis brama*) – are delineated by slope and stream width (Huet 1949). Moreover, distinctions made by Illies and Botosaneanu (1963) in deriving rhithron, crenon, and potamon zones depend on clear boundaries: main confluences that separate hydrographic networks into various stream orders (Strahler 1957). At confluences where stream order changes, so are there considerable changes in hydrologic conditions.

These changes in hydrologic conditions (a doubling of flow usually) are followed by biotic conditions displayed spatially. These changes create an ecotone where upstream and downstream communities mix: some species appear, while others disappear over some distance, depending on the stream order considered. For instance, ecotones at the confluence of 1st and 2nd order streams may traverse a distance of 100 m, while ecotones at the confluence of two 8th order streams can comprise several kilometres. This tendency corresponds to an adjustment to conditions created by increasing flow from upstream towards downstream.

Locations of abrupt slope changes constitute another important class of discontinuities. These zones, described by hydraulic stress, have a key role in benthic invertebrate distribution (Statzner and Higler 1986, Statzner 1987, Statzner *et al.* 1988). They can lie along the longitudinal profile of a river over several stream orders, and they can correspond to gradients of slope or depth, as well as temperature, and have repercussions on benthic and pelagic trophic dynamics.

At a given sector scale the patches and their boundaries differ along the hydrographic network (Naiman *et al.* 1988a, Pringle *et al.* 1988). On a large scale, heterotrophic processes dominate in the headwaters, where retention devices create distinct patches of organic detritus. Autotrophic processes dominate in the middle course, where light penetration creates patches of aquatic vegetation. Heterotrophic processes may again dominate in large turbid rivers, although plankton and littoral macrophytes may have an important role in nutrient dynamics. At a medium scale, riffles and pools differ in their substrata, particulate organic matter accumulation, and plant distribution. Yet the main difference between headwaters and middle and lower reaches is the density and the juxtaposition of the patches. This is important from a functional point of view. Significant variations were found by Meyer (1980) for the dynamics of phosphorus between pools and riffles. At a small scale, Pringle (1985a, b) has shown the existence of distinct dynamics at the level of chironomid tubes, leading to accumulation of ammonia-N, orthophosphate, and total phosphorus. This results in algal biomass being 12 times more elevated than in adjacent substrata.

Man-created discontinuities

Most rivers are impounded by dams, which constitute obstacles for longitudinal exchanges along fluvial systems. These obstacles are instream discontinuities that are particularly distinct because of their size. These man-created boundaries profoundly affect the structure and function of the rivers. Yet how do their effects differ from those of natural boundaries? Ward and Stanford (1983) have provided elements of a response to that question with the serial discontinuity concept. This concept was proposed to deal with the discontinuities in stream ecosystem structure and function engendered by stream regulation. It has already contributed to stream ecosystem theory (Cummins *et al.* 1984) in recognising the importance of dam position along the continuum and in proposing discontinuity distance as a measure of the upstream-downstream shifts resulting from impoundments (Ward and Stanford 1987).

This discontinuity distance (DD) is the downstream (positive) or upstream (negative) shift of a parameter at a given distance due to the presence of a dam (Fig. 8.5). It is accompanied by a measure of the difference in the parameter intensity (PI) attributed to the presence of the dam. Ward and Stanford (1983) give an example of the regulation of a river system causing the distribution pattern of typical lotic species to shift to conditions typical of three stream orders downstream and a shift in abundance from 3000 to 2000 organisms/m^2 (DD = +3 and PI = −1000 organisms/m^2). Such reasoning, including parameter intensity and stream order displacement, has been successfully adapted to natural conditions to explain the impact of a beaver dam on stream ecosystem dynamics (Naiman *et al.* 1986, 1988a).

The position of a dam (headwater, middle reach, lower reach) influences the ecological response, since parameters vary from headwaters to the river mouth. Ward and Stanford (1983) assume that these ecologic responses are a function of stream order for 16 physical, chemical, and biological parameters. In the example (Fig. 8.5) taken from Ward and Stanford (1983), they postulate that regulation of the headwaters will suppress the biotic diversity in the receiving stream primarily because of the disruption of detrital transport and the spiralling of nutrient and organic matter. They attribute the severe reduction of biotic diversity in impounded middle reaches to the altered thermal regime (Ward and Stanford 1979a), while enhanced environmental heterogeneity below dams would lead to an increase of biotic diversity (Ward and Stanford 1979b). Even if most of these predictions remain to be tested and explained, they suggest that the role of discontinuities, whether natural or artificial, varies greatly according to their position along the water course and what parameter is considered.

Clearly, the serial discontinuity concept is a useful approach in quantifying the effects of ecotones along river systems. Yet it still needs to be considered on a wide range of ecotones with attention to various degrees of artificiality, permanence in time, abruptness, and permeability of individual ecotones. Regarding ecotone permeability, an important aspect to consider is their role as key devices for retention of material along water courses.

Retention of matter and energy

Running waters constitute a vector for the transfer of material from elevated reaches to the bottom of drainage basins. This downhill movement of materials in lotic systems is restrained by retention devices, of which ecotones in general are probably the most important.

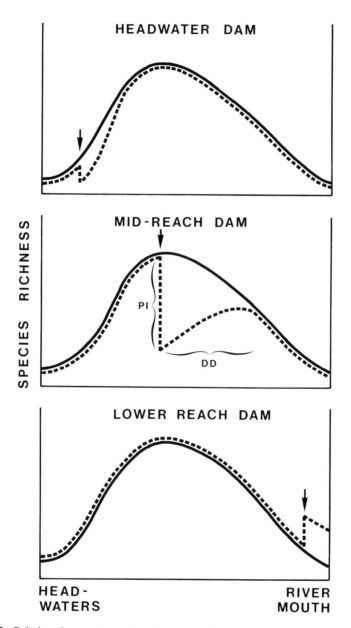

Figure 8.5 Relative changes in species richness as a function of stream order, based on interpretation of natural stream continuum theory (solid lines) and postulated effects (dashed lines) of damming (arrows) at the headwater, middle reach, and lower reach of a river system. Adapted from Ward and Stanford (1983). See text for definitions of DD (discontinuity distance) and PI (parameter intensity)

An analysis of this role of lotic ecotones is related to the concept of nutrient spiralling (Webster 1975, Webster and Patten 1979). During their displacement, downstream nutrients are absorbed, utilised, and released by organisms. Their downstream transport is coupled with transformations from organic to mineral matter. Elwood *et al.* (1983) defined spiralling length as the mean distance travelled downstream by a nutrient atom during its cycle; others (Newbold *et al.* 1983, Mulholland *et al.* 1985) have measured lengths of spiralling of about 100 m.

As shown by Minshall *et al.* (1983), the tightness of these spirals is linked to the number of times the same nutrient atom is utilised in a section of river, and therefore to the productivity of this section. Our point here is that terrestrial-aquatic ecotones play a major role in the retention of nutrients during displacement downstream (Fig. 8.6). Strong interactions between streams and the ecotonal riparian forest entail substantial exchanges of matter and energy within the floodplain. Changes in the characteristics of nutrient recycling processes in these terrestrial-aquatic ecotones (i.e. spiralling length and the amount of material recycled) play a role in the retention of energy and matter along the course of the river. Such a role may be seen at different scales, including a riparian zone along a river course, a riffle-pool sequence within a reach, and localised patches of substratum within the same riffle (Frissell *et al.* 1986). As an example, the substrate characteristics of the mosaic within one reach that may affect the retention of nutrients include patch size, distribution, density, juxtaposition, and diversity (e.g. sand, gravel, clay, previous organic accumulations). The stability of the mosaic is also an important factor to be considered when dealing with retention of material along water courses. When considering streams as dynamic ecosystems, some important questions arise regarding the role that ecotones play within this dynamic landscape. What is the impact of disturbances, like floods, on terrestrial-aquatic ecotones? What is the role of ecotones in the resistance or the resilience of lotic systems to such disturbances?

ECOTONES IN NON-EQUILIBRIUM FLUVIAL LANDSCAPES

Fluvial landscapes may qualify as nonequilibrium systems, considering the relative size of most of the disturbances and landscape units (Shugart and West 1981). Their dynamics depend on exchanges and interactions between the different elements of a mosaic that includes aquatic, semi-aquatic, and terrestrial patches. As suggested by the patch dynamics concept (Pickett and White 1985), ecotones between these patches play a major role in this process. To understand this role, it is first necessary to refer to the hierarchical nature of lotic systems (Allen and Starr 1982), and then to consider controls exerted by ecotones on the dynamics of lotic systems. The intrinsic dynamics of ecotones in lotic systems, and the concept of

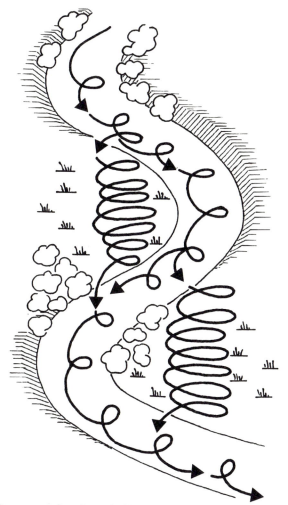

Figure 8.6 The concept of nutrient spiralling in a fluvial system. Strong interactions between a stream and its ecotonal riparian forest entail tremendous exchanges of matter and energy within the floodplain. These interactions should lead to changes in the characteristics of nutrient recycling processes in the terrestrial-aquatic ecotones (i.e. spiralling length and the amount of material recycled)

ecotone in time compared with the concept of ecotone in space in highly dynamic systems such as lotic systems, need to be considered as well.

Hierarchy of the scales in space and time

Scale problems constitute one of the key questions when studying the role of ecotones in the structure and dynamics of lotic ecosystems (Fig. 8.7). For

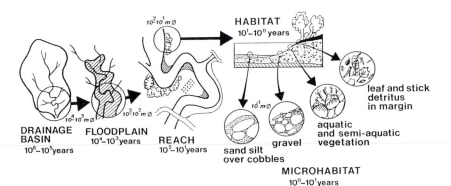

Figure 8.7 Hierarchical organisation of a stream system and its habitat subsystems. Adapted from Frissell *et al.* (1986)

instance, drainage basin scale is usually taken into account when dealing with diffuse pollution (Lauga *et al.* 1988), while floodplain scale is used to forecast fish yield of African rivers (Welcomme 1979), or the riffle and pool scale in order to study life cycles of invertebrates (Elliott 1973, Décamps and Lafont 1974). Moreover, each organism living in lotic systems has its own perception of patches and their limits. For instance, a terrestrial-aquatic boundary may be impermeable to fish, permeable to birds and mammals, and not really perceived by parasites of birds, mammals, or fish (Naiman *et al.* 1988b). Similarly, a riffle-pool ecotone may constitute a barrier to one species of invertebrate but not to another. An individual amphibian may alter its perception of a boundary during its life cycle. These observations suggest that the ecotone concept must not be dissociated from the concept of scale. Thus, four key factors (or issues) require a hierarchical perspective: lotic ecotone typology, adjustments to increasing flow downstream, imbricating of riparian ecotones, and persistence in time.

The typology of lotic ecotones depends on the typology of patches from which ecotones constitute their limits. These lotic patches were classified recently by Frissell *et al.* (1986) in a system organised in hierarchical levels, comprising stream sections, reach, riffle-pool, and microbial subsystems. Each hierarchical level develops within its own spatiotemporal scale; the next highest organisational level includes and controls the level below. At each hierarchical level ecotones limit patches or subsystems. These ecotones have attributes (Naiman *et al.* 1988b): contrasts in rates and processes, energetics, resilience, stability, biotic composition, shape, and size. One of the main questions, not yet solved, dealing with lotic ecotone typology would be the utilisation of these attributes in a hierarchical perspective.

This typology is important to consider, since it influences the dynamics of ecotones. Van der Maarel (1976) distinguished five types after considering the following characteristics: abruptness of the transition, degree of homogeneity within the adjacent patches, and the importance of the difference

156

between the patches. Another characteristic should be added, particularly for terrestrial-aquatic ecotones along rivers (Daubenmire 1968). It is the mosaic character of these ecotones, with peninsulas and islands from each community interpenetrating due to local topographic heterogeneities (Pinay *et al.* 1989).

Another factor of complexity in lotic ecotones is spatial and temporal adjustment to flow increases. Minshall *et al.* (1983) and Naiman *et al.* (1987) have shown, for instance, that recycling times of carbon increase several times over the course of a river. Do instream ecotones play a role in this phenomenon? Riparian ecotones seem to be very sensitive to variations in longitudinal conditions. In headwater streams the boundary with the stream edge is sharp, with an overlap of the vegetation characteristic of the riparian ecotone and of the slopes (Fig. 8.8). In middle order streams the distinction is easier between submerged aquatic vascular plants, emergent aquatic plants and sedges, and early successional woody plants such as willow (*Salix* spp.), alder (*Alnus* spp.), and hardwood species. In larger rivers with several channels and oxbow lakes, the riparian patches become most diversified and expand within the floodplain. The entire ecotonal zone is divided into numerous internal ecotones depending on the topographic heterogeneity of the riparian area.

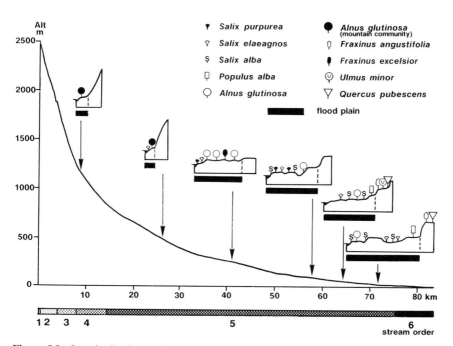

Figure 8.8 Longitudinal zonation of the ecotonal riparian forest along the Tech River, France (M. Izard, personal communication)

Imbricating of riparian ecotones comes from subsystem development within terrestrial-aquatic ecotones along rivers. As shown in the previous paragraph, this imbricating becomes more complicated from upstream to downstream. In upstream stretches terrestrial-aquatic limits seem relatively well defined. On the contrary, in downstream stretches these boundaries include several encased elements which develop and persist within specific scales (Pinay *et al.* 1989).

Two features characterise the persistence of large river ecotones. First, riparian ecotones are dependent on floods, which act to restructure alluvial forests on annual, decadal, or longer intervals. Second, subsystem instability maintains the metastability of the whole riparian ecotone. Thus exists a patch mosaic of different riparian plant communities, which maintains riparian ecotone persistence as well as its rejuvenation over time (Pautou and Décamps 1984). Yet, more research is needed on the influence of flood periodicity and intensity on the biotic richness of imbricating ecotones in riparian space.

Ecotonal control of the dynamics of lotic systems

Interactions between adjacent patches may be modified by ecotonal control of the movement of energy, materials, and organisms from one spatial unit of the landscape to another (Wiens *et al.* 1985). Therefore, the dynamics of lotic systems are very closely linked to the temporal heterogeneity of patches and their ecotones. These fluxes may be continuous and non-selective across some ecotones and periodic and selective across others (Naiman *et al.* 1988a, Pringle *et al.* 1988). Moreover, the status of a lotic ecotone is subjected to changes in its ability to control fluxes.

An example is the patch dynamics induced by beaver (*Castor canadensis*) in North America (Naiman *et al.* 1986, 1988c). Beaver create patches in two ways: foraging in the adjacent riparian zones and building dams in the stream channel. Foraging is selective (Jenkins 1979), and this changes the composition of riparian plant communities as well as allochthonous inputs to the aquatic environment (Conners and Naiman 1984). Dam building creates a patch body, the longevity of which is determined by the permeability of the ecotones with adjacent patch bodies (Johnston and Naiman 1987).

Beaver dams in a drainage network represent a shifting mosaic, changing the relative importance of ecosystem parameters along river channels. For example, primary production may be typical of a 3rd order stream in one pond and of a 9th order stream in another, and may be of the normal 2nd order in the riffle connecting these two ponds (Naiman *et al.* 1988c). Moreover, this situation varies as the beaver population fluctuates over time, causing alterations of the stream channels. Naiman *et al.* (1986, 1988a) have shown that this shifting mosaic induced by beaver has the potential to influence many biogeochemical budgets for North American watersheds. Moreover, cyclic changes in the density of patches can have long-term consequences to the drainage basin.

Another characteristic to be considered is that some ecotones are more or less ephemeral in fluvial landscapes. Certain ecotones (e.g. sediment deposits) may appear or disappear annually, and may be displaced in longitudinal or transversal directions. Variation in hydrologic regime is the main factor for this mobility in space and time. For example, erosional and depositional processes during floods may suppress ecotones or create new ones in the channel and in surrounding terrestrial patches. This phenomenon is well documented for the Rhine River in Germany (Schäffer 1973), where displacements of oxbow lakes along the fluvial corridor result from changes in sediment load and discharge (Fig. 8.9). Embankments have resulted in an isolation of the river from its floodplain, and consequently have arrested the mobility of ecotonal oxbow lakes in the corridor.

Dynamics of lotic ecotones

Ecotones control interactions between adjacent patches, influencing the dynamics of fluvial landscapes, but are particularly sensitive to hydrologic change. For example, a deepening of the water table in the Garonne River corridor in France led to the dehydration of the most sensitive species in the riparian vegetation (Décamps *et al.* 1988). Similar situations have been observed in several European fluvial corridors, but we still lack comprehensive studies to understand these effects at larger landscape or global scales. This is an important point, since some organisms living in ecotones may be near their limits of life conditions and theoretically would respond quickly to environmental change. Thus ecotones may be useful as early indicators of environmental change, not only in the floodplain but also for the surrounding landscape.

Under normal conditions, the dynamics of riparian ecotones are mostly influenced by the fluvial hydrologic regime. Along European rivers, riparian vegetation evolves from a pioneer forest of willow to an oak hardwood forest in response to changing flood regimes that affect erosional and depositional processes. Multisuccessional vegetative pathways operate over a temporal scale ranging up to several centuries along the Garonne River (Décamps *et al.* 1988). Deposition and erosion interact at varying intensities and frequencies with the riparian vegetation over 100-yr cycles with the fluvial corridor. Normally, these interactions keep riparian communities in early stages of succession. The pioneer communities are dominated by sedge (*Carex* spp.), willow (*Salix alba*), and alder (*Alnus glutinosa*), with occasional oak (*Quercus* spp.) on the terrestrial edge of the riparian zone. A decrease in seasonal flooding of the riparian community results in changes via several possible successional pathways leading, in this example, to a

159

Figure 8.9 The Rhine River, north of Karlsruhe, West Germany, within its floodplain. Arrows show the relationships between the river and its old meanders. Adapted from Schäffer (1973)

Quercus robur community when the system, no longer influenced by flooding, becomes a purely terrestrial system. Similar situations have been described for riparian forests associated with the Rhine River (Carbiener 1983), the Rhône River (Pautou and Décamps 1984), and the upper Amazon River (Salo *et al.* 1986).

Another example of the dynamics of riparian ecotones concerns the production of willow. Neither the river itself nor the most elevated areas in the floodplain are favourable to the willow community, due to the depth of the water table, but there are favourable places in the ecotone depending on the topographic heterogeneity.

These two examples concerning the dynamics of ecotonal riparian forests support the assertion of Naiman *et al.* (1988a) emphasising that a paradox of modelling boundaries is predicting when and where ecosystem parameters become unpredictable relative to adjacent homogeneous patches. One approach to overcoming this problem is to use models dealing with uncertainty. Naiman *et al.* (1988a) proposed using chaos theory to deal with the uncertainty of changes in resource patch properties. The premise of chaos theory is that chaotic, or seemingly unpredictable, behaviour is in reality a special manifestation of an underlying structure. Furthermore, Naiman *et al.* (1988a) believe that ecotones behave in ways such that they are not simple averages of adjacent resources patches: the spatial patterning of environmental factors and the interactions between patches are as important in determining ecotone dynamics as are the characteristics of the adjacent patches.

The concept of the ecotone in time

As boundaries more or less sharp and frequent in space separate homogeneous patches, catastrophic events more or less rapid and frequent in time separate periods of homogeneity. This concept of the ecotone in time seems to be particularly useful in describing the chaotic dynamics of fluvial landscapes (Wiens *et al.* 1985).

Alluvial forests have adjusted to floods and are now dependent on them. This situation is similar to the impact of fire on plant communities in the prairies of North America (O'Neill *et al.* 1986). Moreover, floods influence the spatial organisation of resource patches within the riparian ecotones. They also create a large variety of local instabilities that in turn allow a metastability for the riparian ecotone.

Human activities have substantially changed the time scale of these natural events. For instance, embankments along the Loire River, France, resulted in less frequent but more catastrophic floods when the level of the river was higher than the level of the artificial banks (Dion 1961). Similarly, the channelisation of the Garonne River at Toulouse has led to a simplification of the substrata and a diminution of the terrestrial-aquatic ecotones (Fortuné 1988b). This reduction of ecotonal riparian forests, coupled with the construction of a mill dam downstream, led to a poor resistance of the system to disturbances and to increasing economic effects of catastrophic floods in the city of Toulouse.

Change is occurring in all natural systems, especially in fluvial systems where rivers can be considered as nonequilibrium systems. Consideration of the concept of ecotones in time and space seems to be appropriate for a better understanding of the functioning of highly dynamic landscapes such as fluvial corridors. These dynamic considerations will improve fluvial system management.

MANAGEMENT

Fluvial ecotones, particularly those at the terrestrial-aquatic interface (i.e. riparian zones), constitute areas of high interest in the management of river systems. Budd *et al.* (1987) stress the aesthetic and recreational values of such areas as well as the role of riparian zones in preserving water quality and controlling erosion. Other authors have emphasised the buffering capacities of ecotonal riparian forests, in relation to nutrient runoff from agricultural lands towards surface waters, and their ability to act as wildlife refuges (Petersen *et al.* 1987). However, management of fluvial ecotones has to face three main challenges.

The first challenge stems from the fact that, most of the time, management decisions concern particular habitats rather than their boundaries (Risser 1990). This has led to a disappearance of ecotonal zones that were considered useless areas.

The second challenge arises because most management decisions consider, as a goal, the creation of stable conditions when dealing with ecosystem regulation. In fact, ecotones exist only through the variability of the forces that create them. It becomes necessary to take into account natural processes such as floods (White 1979). Flood-created disturbances provoke rejuvenation of riparian zones with patches coexisting at different degrees of maturity, thus resulting in a metastability of plant and animal communities. Fluvial ecotone management cannot be dissociated from flood management.

The third challenge comes from the human perceptions of riparian zones. Areas subjected to frequent and regular flooding have been either coveted or avoided for a long time. They have been considerably reduced in surface area by agricultural activities, facilitated by the natural fertility of alluvial soils, and by forest exploitation, which is simplified by log transportation on rivers.

Among the most important decisions regarding management of riparian areas are the types of ecotones to be considered and what areas require management. For instance, what is the size (i.e. surface) of ecotonal riparian forest that we must maintain along rivers in order to maintain fluvial landscape functioning? We have some information on the buffering capacities of riparian zones in regard to nitrate runoff from agricultural soils (Peterjohn and Correll 1984, Jacobs and Gilliam 1985, Pinay and Décamps 1988). These authors have found that nitrate in the groundwater was eliminated with about 30 m of flow beneath a riparian wood. To what extent can these results be extrapolated for groundwater areas heavily loaded in nitrate? Are these sizes large enough to express the ecotonal effect of riparian forests for bird communities (Décamps *et al.* 1987, Joachim and Lauga 1990)? The difficulty of applying the available research results to specific circumstances shows that management of fluvial ecotones obliges one to consider very carefully the processes one really wants to manage.

Management of riparian zones is essential for fluvial systems management because of their interface position between the terrestrial and stream ecosystem. Although watershed management is the goal, riparian control measures constitute an effective starting point, because most processes governing fluvial landscape dynamics are controlled by riparian areas.

CONCLUSION

In recent times we have had to face many emerging questions concerning river ecology. They might be synthesised into three main challenges. The integration of fluvial systems as a functional landscape entity constitutes one of these challenges. It prompts one to seek an understanding of how landscape patches are organised and how they interact with aquatic systems. Examination of the role of ecotones in influencing biodiversity, resistance and resilience to disturbances will help provide a fluvial perspective within landscapes.

Another challenge concerns the effects of cumulative impacts on river systems. Although it is possible to predict the direct effects of phosphorus loading, increase of temperature, and decrease of discharge or toxic emissions on a river ecosystem over a short period, we still do not know how complex aquatic systems react to repetitive disturbances of different intensities or to the synergetic effects of combined disturbances. Consideration of reversible and irreversible tendencies, disruptions, and discontinuities will allow more accurate forecasts at the decadal time scale.

A third important challenge is related to river management and restoration of damaged ecosystems. This point entails several questions: What is a damaged system? What is meant by restoration? What are the methods and how can results be predicted? In fact, historically, human activities have influenced the dynamics of aquatic ecosystems so deeply that even the definition of a natural environment poses a problem. Traditionally, management of aquatic ecosystems has consisted of trying to stabilise river systems that are intrinsically unstable. River system dynamics are characterised by a wide range of events that occur over different space and time scales and sustain the variability of the entire system.

Recently, particular attention has focussed on the functions of ecotones in fluvial systems. Today we have a better understanding of the importance of riparian areas along river systems as reducers of flood effects, natural filters against diffuse pollution from the floodplain, sources of organic carbon for rivers, and connection lines for species fluxes. Moreover, one can now estimate more precisely the role of terrestrial-aquatic and instream ecotones in the retention of matter and energy along rivers.

It prompts one to consider other time and space scales in order to understand the role of lotic ecotones in fluvial landscapes. This scale is related to hydrographic networks as well as variability of lotic ecotone structure from headwaters towards river mouths. Such scales of perception imply comparison of different river systems regarding climatic and geomorphic characteristics. Comparative studies of ecotones along fluvial systems will offer an original contribution in response to emerging questions in river ecology.

ACKNOWLEDGEMENTS

We thank the anonymous reviewers for constructive comments on the manuscript. Research support was provided by the Centre National de la Recherche Scientifique (France).

LITERATURE CITED

Allen, T.F.H., and T.B. Starr. 1982. Hierarchy: perspectives for ecological complexity. University of Chicago Press, Chicago, Illinois, USA.

Amoros, C., A.L. Roux, A.L. Reygrobellet, J.P. Bravard, and C. Pautou. 1987. A method for applied ecological studies of fluvial hydrosystems. Regulated Rivers 1: 17-36.

Bethemont, J., and J.P. Bravard. 1986. Gabcikovo: un grand projet et une controverse. Revue Géographique de Lyon 25:19-41.

Bird, G.A., and N.K. Kaushik. 1981. Coarse particulate organic matter in streams. Pages 41-58 *in* M.A. Lock and D.D. Williams, editors. Perspectives in running water ecology. Plenum, New York, USA.

Braga, G., and S. Gervasoni. 1983. Evoluzióne stòrica dell'àlveo del fiume Po nel territòrio Lodigiano. Piacentino: rischi iderogeòlogici connessi. Atti Convegno Naz. Il suòlo come risórsa 60:59-69.

Bravard, J.P. 1987. Le Rhône de Genève à Lyon. La Manufacture, Lyon, France.

Budd, W.W., P.L. Cohen, P.R. Saunders, and F.R. Steiner. 1987. Stream corridor management in the Pacific Northwest, I. Determination of stream corridor widths. Environmental Management 11:587-597.

Carbiener, R. 1983. Le grand ried central d'Alsace: écologie et évolution d'une zone humide d'origine fluviale rhénane. Bulletin Ecologie 14:249-277.

Carbiener, R., E. Dillman, E. Dister, and A. Schnitzler. 1987. Crues et inondations. Colloque CEREG, Strasbourg, France.

Chauvet, E., and H. Décamps. 1989. Lateral interactions in a fluvial landscape: the River Garonne, France. Journal of the North American Benthological Society, 8:9-17.

Chauvet, E., and A.M. Jean-Louis. 1988. Production de litière de la ripisylve de la Garonne et apport au fleuve. Acta Oecologica 9:265-279.

Conners, M.E., and R.J. Naiman. 1984. Particulate allochthonous inputs: relationships with stream size in an undisturbed watershed. Canadian Journal of Fisheries and Aquatic Sciences 41:1473-1484.

Cummins, K.W., G.W. Minshall, J.R. Sedell, C.E. Cushing, and R.C. Petersen. 1984. Stream ecosystem theory. Verhandlungen Internationale Vereinigung Limnologie 22:1818-1827.

Daubenmire, R. 1968. Plant communities. Harper and Row, New York, USA.

Davies, B.R. 1979. Stream regulation in Africa: a review. Pages 113-142 *in* J.V. Ward and J.A. Stanford, editors. The ecology of regulated streams. Plenum, New York, USA.

Décamps, H. 1984. Towards a landscape ecology of river valleys. Pages 163-178 *in* J.H. Cooley and F.B. Golley, editors. Trends in ecological research for the nineteen eighties. Plenum, New York, USA.

Décamps, H,., M. Fortuné, F. Gazelle, and G. Pautou. 1988. Historical influence of man on the riparian dynamics of a fluvial landscape. Landscape Ecology 1:163-173.

Décamps, H., J. Joachim, and J. Lauga. 1987. The importance for birds of the riparian woodlands within the alluvial corridor of the river Garonne. S.W. France. Regulated Rivers 1:301-316.

Décamps, H., and M. Lafont. 1974. Cycles vitaux et production des *Micrasema* pyrénénnes dans les mousses d'eau courante (Trichoptera, Brachycentridae). Annales de Limnologie 10:1-32.

Dion, R. 1961. Histoire des levées en Val de Loire. Paris, France.

Elliott, J.M. 1973. The life cycle and production of the leech *Erpobdella octoculata* (L.) (Hirudinea: Erpobdellidae) in a Lake District stream. Journal of Animal Ecology 42:435-448.

Elwood, J.W., J.D. Newbold, R.V. O'Neill, and W. Van Winkle. 1983. Resource spiraling: an operational paradigm for analyzing lotic ecosystems. Pages 3-27 *in* T.D. Fontaine III and S.M. Bartell, editors. Dynamics of lotic ecosystems. Ann Arbor Science, Ann Arbor Michigan, USA.

Ertel, J.R., J.I. Hedges, and E.M. Perdue. 1984. Lignin signature of aquatic humic substances. Science 223:485-487.

Ford, T.E., and R.J. Naiman. 1989. Groundwater-surface water relationships in boreal forest watersheds: dissolved organic carbon and inorganic nutrient dynamics. Canadian Journal of Fisheries and Aquatic Sciences 46:41-49.

Fortuné, M. 1988*a*. Usages passés et écologie de la Garonne. Dissertation. Université de Toulouse, Toulouse, France.

Fortuné M. 1988*b*. Historical changes of a large river in an urban area: the Garonne River, Toulouse, France. Regulated Rivers 2:179-186.

Frissell, C.A., W.J. Liss, C.E. Warren, and M.D. Hurley. 1986. A hierarchical framework for stream habitat classification: viewing streams in a watershed context. Environmental Management 10:199-214.

Fustec, E., E. Chauvet, and G. Gas. 1989. Lignin degradation and humus formation in alluvial soils and sediments. Applied Environmental Microbiology, 55:922-926.

Gibert, J., M.J. Dole-Olivier, P. Marmonier, and P. Vervier. 1990. Surface water-groundwater ecotones, *this volume*.

Graf, W.L. 1980. Riparian management: a flood control perspective. Journal of Soil and Water Conservation 35:158-161.

Holland, M.M. (compiler). 1988. SCOPE/MAB technical consultations on landscape boundaries: report of a SCOPE/MAB workshop on ecotones. Biology International, Special Issue 17:47-106.

Huet, M. 1949. Aperçu de relations entre la pente et les populations piscicoles des eaux courantes. Schweizerische Zeitschrift für Hydrologie 11:333-351.

Hynes, H.B.N. 1963. Imported organic matter and secondary productivity in streams. International Congress of Zoology 16:324-329.

Hynes, H.B.N. 1975. The stream and its valley. Verhandlungen Internationale Vereinigung Limnologie 19:1-15.

165

Hynes, H.B.N. 1983. Groundwater and stream ecology. Hydrobiologia 100:93-99.

Illies, J., and L. Botosaneanu. 1963. Problèmes et méthodes de la classification et de la zonation écologique des eaux courantes considérées surtout du point de vue faunistique. Mitteilungen Internationale Vereinigung Limnologie 12:1-57.

Ishiwatari, R. 1985. Geochemistry of humic substances in lake sediments. Pages ·147-180 *in* G.R. Aiken, D.M. McKnight, R.L. Wershaw, and P. MacCarthy, editors. Humic substances in soil, sediment, and water: geochemistry, isolation, and characterization. John Wiley and Sons, New York, USA.

Jacobs, T.C., and J.W. Gilliam. 1985. Riparian losses of nitrate from agricultural drainage waters. Journal of Environmental Quality 14:472-478.

Jenkins, S.H. 1979. Seasonal and year-to-year differences in food selection by beavers. Oecologica 44:112-116.

Joachim. J. 1987. La mésange nonnette *Parus palustris* dans les ripisylves garonnaises. Alauda 55:63-66.

Joachim, J., and J. Lauga. 1990. Influence of climatic hazards on woodland bird communities along an alluvial corridor. Journal of Biogeography, *in press*.

Johnston, C.A., and R.J. Naiman. 1987. Boundary dynamics at the aquatic-terrestrial interface: the influence of beaver and geomorphology. Landscape Ecology 1:47-57.

Karlström, V. 1988. Environmental factors, detritus and bottom fauna in the Ricklean, a north Swedish forest river. Report of the Institute of Limnology, University of Uppsala, Sweden.

Lauga, J., H. Décamps, and M.M. Holland, editors. 1988. Land use impacts on aquatic ecosystems: the use of scientific information. Académie de Toulouse, Toulouse, France.

Lowrance, R.R., R.L. Todd, and L.E. Asmussen. 1984. Nutrient cycling in an agricultural watershed. II. Streamflow and artificial drainage. Journal of Environmental Quality 13:27-32.

Maillard, P. 1981. Observations sur l'enfoncement du lit de la Loire. Pages 1-13 *in* L'écologie et l'aménagement de la Loire. Ministére de l'Environnement, Mission des études et recherches, Paris, France.

Malcolm, R.L. 1985. Geochemistry of stream fulvic and humic substances. Pages 181-209 *in* G.R. Aiken, D.M. McKnight, R.L. Wershaw, and P. MacCarthy, editors. Humic substances in soil, sediment, and water: geochemistry, isolation, and characterization. John Wiley and Sons, New York, USA.

Mathews, C.P., and A. Kowalczewski. 1969. The disappearance of leaf litter and its contribution to production in the River Thames. Journal of Ecology 57:543-552.

Meyer, J.L. 1980. Dynamics of phosphorus and organic matter during leaf decomposition in a forest stream. Oikos 34:44-53.

Minshall, G.W., K.W. Cummins, R.C. Petersen, C.E. Cushing, D.A. Bruns, J.R. Sedell, and R.L. Vannote. 1985. Developments in stream ecosystem theory. Canadian Journal of Fisheries and Aquatic Sciences 42:1045-1055.

Minshall, G.W., R.C. Petersen, K.W. Cummins, T.L. Bott, J.R. Sedell, C.E. Cushing, and R.L. Vannote. 1983. Interbiome comparison of stream ecosystem dynamics. Ecological Monographs 53:1-25.

Mulholland, P.J., J.D. Newbold, J.W. Elwood, L.A. Ferren, and J.R. Webster. 1985. Phosphorus spiralling in a woodland stream: seasonal variations. Ecology 66:1012-1023.

Naiman, R.J., H. Décamps, J. Pastor, and C.A. Johnston. 1988a. The potential importance of boundaries to fluvial ecosystems. Journal of the North American Benthological Society 7:289-306.

Naiman, R.J., M.M. Holland, H. Décamps, and P.G. Risser. 1988b. A new UNESCO programme: research and management of land/inland water ecotones. Biology International, Special Issue 17:107-136.

Naiman, R.J., C.A. Johnston, and J.C. Kelley. 1988c. Alteration of North American streams by beaver. BioScience 38:753-762.

Naiman, R.J., J.M. Melillo, and J.E. Hobbie. 1986. Ecosystem alteration of boreal forest streams by beaver (*Castor canadensis*). Ecology 67:1254-1269.

166

Naiman, R.J., J.M. Melillo, M.A. Lock, T.E. Ford, and S.R. Reice. 1987. Longitudinal patterns of ecosystem processes and community structure in a subarctic river continuum. Ecology 68:1139-1156.

Newbold, J.D. 1987. Phosphorus spiralling in rivers and river-reservoir systems: implications of a model. Pages 303-327 *in* J.F. Craig and J.B. Kemper, editors. Regulated streams: advances in ecology. Plenum, New York, USA.

Newbold, J.D., J.W. Elwood, R.V. O'Neill, and A.L. Sheldon. 1983. Phosphorus dynamics in a woodland stream ecosystem: a study of nutrient spiralling. Ecology 64:1249-1265.

Newbold, J.D., J.W. Elwood, R.V. O'Neill, and W. Van Winkle. 1981. Measuring nutrient spiralling in streams. Canadian Journal of Fisheries and Aquatic Sciences 38:860-863.

O'Neill, R.V., D.L. DeAngelis, J.B. Waide, and T.F.H. Allen. 1986. A hierarchical concept of ecosystems. Princeton University Press, Princeton, New Jersey, USA.

Pautou, G., and H. Décamps. 1984. Ecological interactions between the alluvial forests and hydrology of the Upper Rhône. Archiv für Hydrobiologie 104:13-37.

Peterjohn, W.T., and D.L. Correll. 1984. Nutrient dynamics in an agricultural watershed: observations on the role of a riparian forest. Ecology 65:1466-1475.

Petersen, R.C., B.L. Madsen, M.A. Wizbach, C.H.D. Magadza, A. Paarlberg, A. Kullberg, and K.W. Cummins. 1987. Stream management: emerging global similarities. Ambio 16:165-179.

Pickett, S.T.A., and P.S. White (editors). 1985. The ecology of natural disturbance and patch dynamics. Academic Press, Orlando, Florida, USA.

Pinay, G. 1986. Relations sol-nappe dans les bois riverains de la Garonne. Etude de la dénitrification. Dissertation. Université de Lyon I, Lyon, France.

Pinay, G. 1988. Hydrobiological assessment of the Zambezi river system: a review. WP88-089, International Institute for Applied Systems Analysis, Laxenburg, Austria.

Pinay, G., and H. Décamps. 1988. The role of riparian woods in regulating nitrogen fluxes between the alluvial aquifer and surface water: a conceptual model. Regulated Rivers 2:507-516.

Pinay, G., H. Décamps, C. Arlès, and M. Lacassin-Sères. 1989. Topographic influence on carbon and nitrogen dynamics in riverine woods. Archiv für Hydrobiologie, 114:401-414.

Pringle, C.M. 1985*a*. Effects of chironomid (Insecta: Diptera) tube-building activities on stream diatom communities. Journal of Phycology 21:185-194.

Pringle, C.M. 1985*b*. Nutrient heterogeneity and the maintenance of species diversity: periphyton response to substratum and water enrichment in a nutrient-poor stream. Dissertation. University of Michigan, Ann Arbor, Michigan, USA.

Pringle, C.M., R.J. Naiman, G. Bretschko, J.R. Karr, M.W. Oswood, J.R. Webster, R.L. Welcomme, and M.J. Winterbourn. 1988. Patch dynamics in lotic systems: the stream as a mosaic. Journal of the North American Benthological Society 7:503-524.

Rasid, H., and B.K. Paul. 1987. Flood problems in Bangladesh: is there an indigenous solution? Environmental Management 11:155-173.

Risser, P.G. 1990. The ecological importance of land-water ecotones, *this volume.*

Risser, P.G., J.R. Karr, and R.T. Forman. 1984. Landscape ecology: directions and approaches. Illinois Natural History Survey, Special Publication Number 2, Champaign, Illinois, USA.

Roux, A.L. (editor). 1982. Cartographie polythématique appliquée à la gestion écologique des eaux; étude d'un hydrosystème fluvial: le Haut Rhône. Centre National de la Recherche Scientifique, Centre Régional de Publication, Lyon, France.

Salo, J., R. Kalliola, I. Häkkinen, Y. Mäkinen, P. Niemelä, M. Puhakka, and P.D. Coley. 1986. River dynamics and the diversity of Amazon lowland forest. Nature 322:254-258.

Schäffer, W. 1973. Altrhein verbund am nördlichen Oberrhein. Courier Forschungsinstitut Senckenberg 7:1-63.

Schlosser, I.J., and J.R. Karr. 1981. Water quality in agricultural watersheds: impact of riparian vegetation during base flow. Water Resource Bulletin 17:233-240.

Sedell, J.R., and J.L. Froggatt. 1984. Importance of streamside forests to large rivers: the isolation of the Willamette River, Oregon, USA, from its floodplain by snagging and streamside forest removal. Verhandlungen Internationale Vereinigung Limnologie 22:1828-

1834.

Shugart, H.H., Jr., and D.C. West. 1981. Long-term dynamics of forest systems. American Scientist 69:647-652.

Sioli, H. 1984. The Amazon: limnology and landscape ecology of a mighty tropical river and its basin. Dr. W. Junk, Dordrecht, The Netherlands; Boston, Massachusetts, USA; and Lancaster, England.

Statzner, 1987. Characteristics of lotic ecosystems and consequences for future research directions. Pages 366-390 *in* E.D. Schulze and H. Zwölfer, editors. Potentials and limitations of ecosystem analysis. Springer-Verlag, New York, USA.

Statzner, B., J.A. Gore, and V.H. Resh. 1988. Hydraulic stream ecology: observed patterns and potential applications. Journal of the North American Benthological Society 7:307-360.

Statzner, B., and B. Higler. 1985. Questions and comments on the river continuum concept. Canadian Journal of Fisheries and Aquatic Sciences 42:1038-1044.

Statzner, B., and B. Higler. 1986. Stream hydraulics as a major determinant of benthic invertebrate zonation patterns. Freshwater Biology 16:127-139.

Steinberg, C., and U. Muenster. 1985. Geochemistry and ecological role of humic substances in lakewater. Pages 105-145 *in* G.R. Aiken, D.M. McKnight, R.L. Wershaw, and P. MacCarthy, editors. Humic substances in soil, sediment, and water: geochemistry, isolation, and characterization. John Wiley and Sons, New York, USA.

Strahler, A.N. 1957. Quantitative analysis of watershed geomorphology. Transactions of the American Geophysical Union 38:913-920.

Thienemann, A. 1912. Der Bergbach des Sauerland. International Revue der gesamten Hydrobiologie, Hydrographic Supplement 4:1-125.

Urban, D.L., R.V. O'Neill, and H.H. Shugart, Jr. 1987. Landscape ecology. BioScience 37:119-127.

Van der Maarel, E. 1976. On the establishment of plant community boundaries. Berichte der Deutschen Botanischen Gesellschaft 89:415-443.

Vannote, R.L., G.W. Minshall, K.W. Cummins, J.R. Sedell, and C.E. Cushing. 1980. The river continuum concept. Canadian Journal of Fisheries and Aquatic Sciences 37:130-137.

Ward, J.V. 1989. The four-dimensional nature of lotic ecosystems. Journal of the North American Benthological Society, 8:2-18.

Ward, J.V., and J.A. Stanford (editors). 1979*a*. The ecology of regulated streams. Plenum, New York, USA.

Ward, J.V., and J.A. Stanford (editors). 1979*b*. Ecological factors controlling stream zoobenthos with emphasis on thermal modification of regulated streams. Pages 35-55 *in* J.V. Ward and J.A. Stanford, editors. The ecology of regulated streams. Plenum, New York, USA.

Ward, J.V., and J.A. Stanford (editors). 1983. The serial discontinuity concept of lotic ecosystems. Pages 29-42 *in* T.D. Fontaine III and S.M. Bartell, editors. Dynamics of lotic ecosystems. Ann Arbor Science, Ann Arbor, Michigan, USA.

Ward, J.V., and J.A. Stanford (editors). 1987. The ecology of regulated streams: past accomplishments and directions for future research. Pages 391-409 *in* J.F. Craig and J.B. Kemper, editors. Regulated streams: advances in ecology. Plenum, New York, USA.

Ward, J.V., and J.A. Stanford (editors). 1989. Riverine ecosystems: the influence of man on catchment dynamics and fish ecology. Canadian Special Publications of Fisheries and Aquatic Sciences, 106:56-64.

Webster, J.R. 1975. Analysis of potassium and calcium dynamics in stream ecosystems on three southern Appalachian watersheds of contrasting vegetation. Dissertation. University of Georgia, Athens, Georgia, USA.

Webster, J.R., and B.C. Patten. 1979. Effects of watershed perturbation on stream potassium and calcium dynamics. Ecological Monographs 49:51-72.

Welcomme, R.L. 1979. Fisheries ecology of floodplain rivers. Longman, London, England.

Welcomme, R.L. 1985. River Fisheries. FAO Fisheries Technical Paper, Rome, Italy.

White, P.S. 1979. Pattern, process, and natural disturbance in vegetation. Botanical Review 45:229-299.

Wiens, J.A., C.S. Crawford, and J.R. Gosz. 1985. Boundary dynamics: a conceptual framework for studying landscape ecosystems. Oikos 45:421-427.

Key words: Boundary, ecotone, fluvial corridor, management, riparian forest, river.

CHAPTER 9

THE CHARACTERISTICS OF WETLAND ECOTONES

Marjorie M. Holland, Dennis F. Whigham and Brij Gopal

ABSTRACT

Wetlands occur in almost every type of landscape, providing a wide range of natural functions of value to humanity. They are among the earth's most productive ecosystems and are absolutely essential to many plant and animal species, especially migratory birds. More specifically, there is evidence to suggest that the boundaries between wetlands and other ecosystems are among the most important components of wetlands. In a landscape context, wetlands and wetland ecotones are important transition zones between uplands and aquatic ecosystems. They are sites where nutrient concentrations change as water flows between terrestrial and aquatic ecosystems, and are thus important buffers between uplands and open waters. Research questions are suggested in two categories: (1) issues related to both wetland patches and ecotones, and (2) issues related specifically to wetland ecotones.

INTRODUCTION

Wetlands provide a wide range of valuable functions for humans (Mitsch and Gosselink 1986, Bedford and Preston 1988). They have local and international significance as regulators of the hydrologic cycle and they improve water quality. Wetlands also provide important habitat for freshwater and marine organisms, and are critical to many bird species as breeding sites and staging areas during migration. It is, in part, the importance of wetlands for bird migration and for essential faunal habitat that has led to a variety of international agreements addressing wetland conservation and management (Maltby 1986, Hollis *et al.* 1989). Yet, in a landscape context, wetlands are also important regulators of nutrient and sediment fluxes between terrestrial and aquatic ecosystems (Forman and Godron 1986, Mitsch and Gosselink 1986).

Little is known, however, about the ecotones between wetlands and other types of ecosystems. In this chapter we focus on the characteristics of wetland ecotones, especially ecological processes occurring in them. Finally, we identify research areas requiring attention in responsible management plans for wetland patches and ecotones.

DEFINITION OF WETLANDS AND WETLAND ECOTONES

Wetlands are defined as lands transitional between terrestrial and aquatic systems where the water table is at or near the surface or the land is covered by shallow water (Cowardin *et al.* 1979). Wetland ecosystems have one or more of the following three attributes: (1) they support, at least periodically, hydrophytes, (2) the substrate is classified predominantly as an undrained hydric soil, and (3) the substrate is saturated with water or covered by shallow water at some time during the growing season each year.

Wetlands occur over a wide range of hydrologic conditions, and the common terms used to describe them have a long history (Denny 1985, Mitsch and Gosselink 1986, Symoens 1988). It is necessary, therefore, to go beyond the wetland definition to consider wetlands and wetland ecotones in the context of an accepted classification system. The system we chose is the one adopted in the United States (Cowardin *et al.* 1979). However, we have chosen to divide the six major categories listed in that system into two types: tidal wetlands and inland wetlands (Table 9.1).

Tidal wetlands. Exchanges of material between open water ecosystems and tidal wetlands occur once or twice daily in response to tidal cycles. Salinity is an important driving factor in coastal tidal wetlands, but its importance decreases upstream where wetlands influenced by salt water are gradually replaced by freshwater tidal wetlands (Odum *et al.* 1984).

Inland wetlands. Most wetlands are not along coastlines but in interior regions. Frayer *et al.* (1983) estimate that 38×10^6ha, or about 95% of the total wetlands of the conterminous United States, are inland. Exchanges of materials between the three types of inland wetlands (Table 9.1) and adjacent ecosystems are likely to change on a seasonal basis in response

Table 9.1 Types of tidal and inland wetland ecosystems. From Mitsch and Gosselink (1986)

1. Tidal Wetland Ecosystems
   Tidal salt marshes
   Tidal freshwater marshes
   Brackish tidal wetlands

2. Inland Wetland Ecosystems
   Inland freshwater marshes
   Northern peatlands
   Swamps

to precipitation patterns. There are many types of inland wetlands. The categories listed in Table 9.1 are three of the most widespread types in North America. Readers are referred to chapters in this volume by Pinay *et al.* and Pieczyńska for discussions of riverine wetlands and lake edge wetlands, respectively.

Inland freshwater wetlands are usually characterised by (1) soft-stemmed emergent species including cattail (*Typha*), arrowhead (*Sagittaria*), pickerelweed (*Pontederia*), phragmites (*Phragmites australis*), manna grass (*Glyceria*), and sedges (*Carex*), (2) a shallow water regime, and (3) generally shallow peat deposits. These wetlands are ubiquitous in North America. Examples of regions where marshes dominate include the prairie pothole region of the Dakotas (USA) and Canada, and the Everglade region of Florida (Mitsch and Gosselink 1986).

Northern peatlands are associated with the deep peat deposits of the north temperate regions of North America, such as areas found in the states of Wisconsin, Michigan, and Minnesota and most of the Canadian provinces. Bogs and fens, the two major types of northern peatlands, occur over a wide range of conditions. The thick peat deposits develop in old lake basins or form as blanket bogs, which expand across the landscape.

Swamps, according to a United States definition, are wetlands dominated by trees or shrubs. They often have standing water for most if not all of the growing season (Mistch and Gosselink 1986). Swamps occur in a variety of nutrient and hydrologic conditions and, in southeastern United States, are often dominated by various species of cypress (*Taxodium*), ash (*Fraxinus*), maple (*Acer*), and sour gum (*Nyssa*).

Ecotones. Wetlands, like all ecosystems, have internal and external boundaries separating distinct vegetation patches. Some wetland ecotones are clearly delineated, while for others it is difficult to distinguish where one patch ends and the other begins. In this paper we accept the working definition of a MAB/SCOPE working group (Holland 1988): An ecotone is a zone of transition between adjacent ecological systems, having a set of characteristics uniquely defined by space and time scales and by the strength of the interactions between adjacent ecological systems. The use of *ecological system* here is analogous to that of *patch*, and may refer to wetland patches and contiguous upland or open water patches. Throughout this chapter the term *wetland ecotone* is analogous to *landscape boundary*, *transition zone*, or *wetland boundary*. Although we recognise that wetland patches are heterogeneous internally, we present little information on ecotones within wetlands because of the lack of published papers on their characteristics.

We can categorise wetland ecotones into four types (Table 9.2). Most coastal and inland wetlands, referred to as patch bodies by Johnston and Naiman (1987), have lateral boundaries connecting them to adjacent upland and open water ecosystems. Johnston and Naiman (1987) use the phrase

Table 9.2 Comparison of the types of flows that dominate ecotones in tidal and inland environments

Type of Wetland (patch body)	Type of Ecotone	
	Upland-wetland	Wetland-open water
Tidal	Ecotone dominated by flows from wetland. Variations in flow generally small and predictable.	Ecotone dominated by flows from estuarine area. Variations in flow may be large or small but usually predictable.
Inland	Ecotone dominated by flows from upland. Large variations with high unpredictability.	Ecotone dominated by flows from open water. Large variations but mostly predictable.

patch body to describe volumetric landscape units, which have boundaries with upper and lower strata in addition to boundaries with adjacent patches. The connections across ecotones can be through either lateral or surficial boundaries. Surficial boundaries separate overlying patch bodies, while lateral boundaries separate patch bodies that are adjacent to each other on the same plane. Transfers across surficial boundaries have a vertical direction, while transfers across lateral boundaries are primarily horizontal (Johnston and Naiman 1987).

In both tidal and inland wetlands, vertical transfers may occur across at least five surficial boundaries (Figs. 9.1 and 9.2), while horizontal transfers may occur across at least five lateral boundaries. Transfers across surficial boundaries include transfers from aerobic to anaerobic soils, from aerobic soils to surficial vegetation and litter, from vegetation and litter to aerobic soils, from open water to the atmosphere, and from open water to aerobic soils. Transfers across lateral boundaries include transfers from the upland to the wetland (upland-wetland ecotone), or from the wetland into open water (wetland-open water ecotone), from groundwater aquifers into soils, or across vegetation zones with each zone dominated by different species (wetland-wetland ecotones).

WETLAND PATCHES AND ECOTONES AS LANDSCAPE FEATURES

Most landscapes contain wetland ecosystems that often form transitions (ecotones) between upland and open water ecosystems, and water flowing through the landscape will usually cross several wetland ecotones (Fig. 9.3). The example given in Fig. 9.3 demonstrates that most landscapes contain more than one wetland and that wetlands often form a continuum between the uplands and downstream tidal ecosystems. The figure illustrates three common types of ecotones in the landscape: upland-wetland, wetland-wetland, and wetland-open water. In this example, surface water and

174

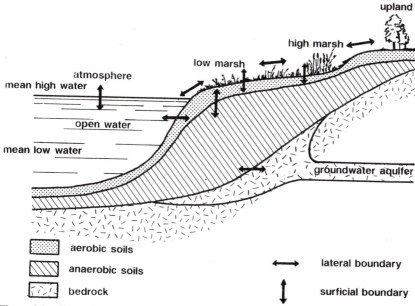

Figure 9.1 Generalised diagram showing ecotones between tidal wetlands and adjacent systems. Refer to Johnston and Naiman (1987) for discussion of lateral and surficial boundaries

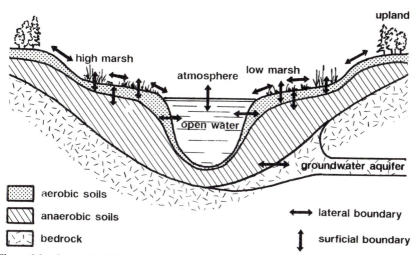

Figure 9.2 Generalised diagram showing ecotones between inland wetlands and adjacent systems. Refer to Johnston and Naiman (1987) for discussion of lateral and surficial boundaries

groundwater would first flow from upland habitats (forests and cultivated fields) across the upland-wetland ecotone into the riparian forest. The second ecotone would be the wetland-open water ecotone between the

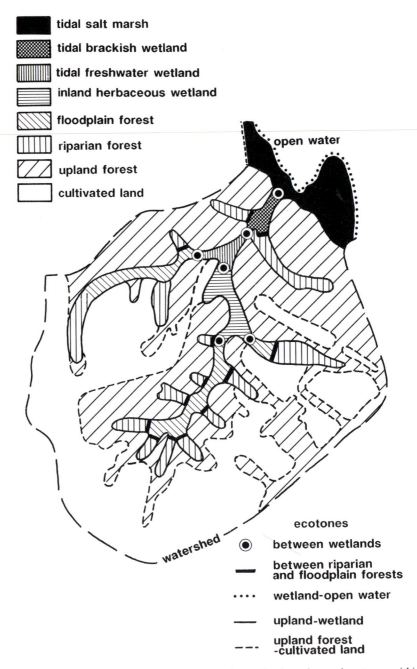

tidal salt marsh

tidal brackish wetland

tidal freshwater wetland

inland herbaceous wetland

floodplain forest

riparian forest

upland forest

cultivated land

open water

ecotones

● between wetlands

— between riparian and floodplain forests

•••• wetland-open water

— upland-wetland

--- upland forest -cultivated land

watershed

Figure 9.3 Generalised diagram of representative wetland patches and ecotones within a drainage basin. Adapted from Whigham *et al.* (1988)

176

riparian forest and the first order stream. Once in the stream channel, water would move along the wetland continuum, passing from riparian forests into floodplain forests. Changes in water quality parameters would occur *in situ* in the stream channels except during flooding events when water in the streams would cross the open water-wetland ecotone and come into contact with the wetland surface.

Water leaving the floodplain forests would, in some situations, pass through wetland-wetland ecotones formed where floodplain forests meet inland herbaceous wetlands. Water passing through inland herbaceous wetlands often moves as sheet flow across the surface rather than in distinct stream channels. The next downstream ecotone would be the wetland-wetland ecotone at the transition between the inland herbaceous wetland and the floodplain forest. Except during flooding periods, water would remain in the streams as it moved through floodplain forests. After the water had flowed through the wetland-wetland ecotone between the floodplain forest and the tidal freshwater wetland, interactions between the streams and the wetland would occur twice daily in response to tidal flooding. The topographically lowest ecotone in the landscape is formed between the salt marsh and the open water ecosystem. In addition to the ecotones described, all of the wetlands also have an upland/wetland ecotone at the border between the uplands and the wetlands. Overall, water moving through this typical coastal plain (USA) landscape would pass through 7 different types of wetlands and across 10 ecotones. As will be shown later in this chapter, important changes in water quality occur as water moves across ecotones, and the changes may be more dramatic in some ecotones than in others.

Upland-wetland and wetland-open water ecotones (Fig. 9.3) may be rather static, but more often they are dynamic in both space and time (Johnston and Naiman 1987). Wetland-open water ecotones can change in space as wetlands expand into open water areas (ponds, lakes, and impoundments) or as wetlands erode. For example, high velocity current will often scour away sediments and vegetation, causing erosion (Johnston and Bell 1976, Shure and Gottschalk 1985). On the other hand, low velocity currents will allow sediment deposition, thus increasing wetland vegetation (Holland and Burk 1982, 1984).

Longer-term shifts in the position of ecotones within coastal landscapes are common and often result from variations in sea level (DeLaune *et al.* 1987). In climates where blanket bogs are formed, upland-wetland ecotones shift towards the uplands as wetlands expand over the landscape (Richardson 1981). Humans also influence the position of ecotones (Hackney and Yelverton 1990), as do animals (Naiman *et al.* 1986, 1988). Changes in the position of ecotones may also occur over shorter periods and may be reversible (Brinson *et al.* 1985, Zedler and Beare 1986).

STRUCTURAL AND FUNCTIONAL DYNAMICS

Physical characteristics

Structural and functional characteristics of wetland ecotones are influenced primarily by hydrologic regimes, but other factors may at times be important (Johnston and Naiman 1987). Hydrologic conditions affect many abiotic factors, including salinity, soil anaerobiosis, and nutrient availability. Since hydrology is the primary forcing function in wetlands, the biotic characteristics of wetlands and wetland boundaries are almost always controlled by hydrologic changes (Niering 1987). Differences in the magnitude (depth of submergence by tides and waves), frequency, and duration of the hydrologic interactions between ecosystems result in a variety of conditions within ecotones over different spatial and temporal scales.

Physical features of the environment play an important role in determining the biotic characteristics of ecotones in tidal wetlands. Tides, patterns of sediment movement, freshwater inputs, geological history, geographical location, and shoreline structure, combined with human land use and animal activities, all influence the development and extent of ecotones in tidal wetlands. The interaction of tides, sediments, and geological history in determining changes in wetland ecotones has been well documented for the northeastern USA (Bloom 1964, Bloom and Ellis 1965, Redfield 1972, Orson *et al.* 1987), but is less well known for other regions.

Orson *et al.* (1987) demonstrated the importance of the interaction between physical characteristics in a study of tidal wetland development in the Pataguanset River estuary, Connecticut, USA. They showed that as coastal submergence progressed over 3500 yr, salt marsh-upland ecotones replaced upland-freshwater marsh ecotones and, once established, were able to extend landward over submerging uplands and seaward over emerging mud flats. The acceleration in the relative rates of eustatic sea level rise over the last few centuries may have significant effects on future development of coastal wetlands (Flessa *et al.* 1977, Harrison and Bloom 1977, McCaffrey 1977, Boesch *et al.* 1983), and the study of this phenomenon will have implications for predicting the locations of future wetland-upland ecotones.

The same physical features, except for tides, are also important in determining the development of inland wetlands and associated ecotones. The interaction of climate and geology in determining changes in wetland ecotones has been well documented for lake-sedge and fen-*Sphagnum* peatland ecotones in extreme northern and southern regions of the northern hemisphere (Pigott and Pigott 1959, 1963; Heinselman 1970, Moore and Bellamy 1974, Moss 1980, Mitsch and Gosselink 1986).

Shallow basins only a few meters deep fill in by sedimentation, by peat accumulation at the margins, and by encroachment of vegetation from upland towards open water (Moss 1980). Pigott and Pigott of the northern

178

hemisphere (1959, 1963) demonstrated the developmental complexities of inland wetland ecotones in studies of Malham Tarn, Yorkshire, England. About 12-13,000 yr B.P., just after the lake formed, tundra vegetation predominated in the adjacent upland. During ensuing years, emergent plants, including various species of Poaceae and Cyperaceae, colonised the wetland-open water ecotone, and peat developed. A few thousand years ago the peat mat built up above the level of groundwater. At that point rain became the main water source, and through leaching the peat became acidic enough to allow *Sphagnum* to dominate. In recent centuries a general drying has allowed cotton grass (*Eriophorum vaginatum*) to invade. Cotton grass peat now forms the most recent peat layer (Pigott and Pigott 1959, 1963). Thus the interaction of climate and substrate has caused lake-sedge and fen-*Sphagnum* ecotones to change dramatically over time. Recent initiatives to understand global environmental change (Risser 1985, Holland 1988) may recast the importance of these and similar studies in predicting future locations of upland-inland wetland boundaries should major climatic shifts occur.

Functional characteristics: ecotones of tidal wetlands

Ecotones are important and dynamic components of landscapes and are active sites for retention and transformation of nutrients (Peterjohn and Correll 1984). The term *retention* implies that materials are retained within the ecotone. Retention is usually accomplished when nutrients are assimilated into and stored in plant biomass or buried in the substrate. Transformation refers to a change in form and, in this instance, the transformation of nitrogen into NO_2 by denitrification.

Wetland-open water ecotones (surface water). Many studies of tidal wetlands have focussed on import-export characteristics (Nixon and Lee 1985), and in some investigations ecotones were considered (Bertness 1984, 1985; Hopkinson and Schubauer 1984, Mitsch and Gosselink 1986). In general, ecotones receive high nutrient and sediment inputs, especially in particulate form. Sediments near the lateral ecotone between the wetland and the tidal creek are better oxidised, and concentrations of toxic compounds are lower than those of sediments in the surficial ecotone between the tidal wetland and flooding tidal waters (Mendelssohn *et al.* 1982).

The study of Wolaver *et al.* (1983) in a Virginia (USA) salt marsh is probably representative of changes occurring in the surface water ecotone between tidal wetlands and open water ecosystems. Using an experimental flume, they were able to show significant exchanges between the flooding water on the incoming tide and the wetland surface. It should be noted, however, that the pattern was not the same for all nutrients examined or for all seasons. Nitrite was the only nutrient to show a net export across the surficial ecotone between the wetland surface and the open water. There was a net uptake of NH_4-N, NO_3, PO_4, dissolved organic N, dissolved organic P, particulate N, and particulate P from the surface water by the wetland surface. Seasonal uptake patterns were associated with vegetative metabolism as well as with microbial activities at the substrate surface.

There is less known about interaction occurring across wetland-wetland ecotones between tidal wetlands and upstream inland wetlands. The location of the ecotone, usually based on salinity (Brinson *et al.* 1985), can vary in both space and time. During periods of high freshwater discharge, the ecotone occurs further downstream than it does during periods of low freshwater discharge. Brinson *et al.* (1985) conducted a study of a coastal estuarine system in North Carolina where a brackish tidal wetland was contiguous to a forested inland freshwater wetland. During the course of the study there was a regional drought, and brackish water intrusion into the forested wetland resulted in increased mortality of trees, lower production rates, and changes in the patterns of nutrient-cycling. All these changes occurred at the boundary between the tidal and inland wetlands.

Wetland-open water ecotones (groundwater). Exchanges of groundwater with surface water occur slowly in tidal wetlands except at the ecotone between the wetland and the adjacent open water ecosystem (Agosta 1985, Jordan and Correll 1985, Yelverton and Hackney 1986, Harvey *et al.* 1987). Between floods the sediments drain more completely in this narrow zone than in high marsh areas, because of differences in sediment grain size and because the area also contains numerous animal burrows. The exchange of nutrients between marsh and open water is much greater than between open water and aerobic or anaerobic soils (Jordan and Correll 1985, Harvey *et al.* 1987). Most groundwater leaving tidal wetlands comes from surface water infiltrating the sediments, which moves back towards open water. The slow movement of groundwater from interior areas of tidal wetlands can affect the nutrient composition of groundwater flowing across the lateral boundary from the substrate to open water (Agosta 1985). In a few situations, however, there is significant mixing between true groundwater and open water (Valiela *et al.* 1978).

Exchanges across ecotones similar to those just described for saltwater tidal wetlands also occur in freshwater and estuarine tidal wetlands. Whigham and Simpson (1978) studied a tidal freshwater wetland in New Jersey, USA, finding significant changes in the nutrient composition of tidal water when it flowed over the surficial ecotone between the wetland surface and the overlying water. In another study in the same ecosystem, Simpson *et al.* (1981) studied distribution patterns of heavy metals discharged into the wetland from a storm drain. Most metals (lead, mercury, and others) were removed from the water column within a few metres of where the discharge pipe entered the wetland ecotone. The authors attributed the reduction in concentrations of heavy metals to deposition and sedimentation within the marginal (ecotonal) areas of the wetland.

Functional characteristics: ecotones of inland wetlands

The flow of surface and subsurface water through inland wetlands is also variable (Cowardin *et al.* 1979, Mitsch and Gosselink 1986), but unlike that of tidal wetlands, it is almost always in one direction (Table 9.2). Like tidal wetlands, inland wetland groundwater is usually anaerobic. Aerobic conditions may be present only in a shallow surface layer. In many nontidal wetlands, periods of low hydrologic inputs are characterised by a lowering of the water table, draining of sediments, and an increase in the depth of the aerobic zone. These wetting and drying cycles play an important role in the nutrient dynamics of inland wetlands (Howard-Williams 1985).

Processes occurring in inland wetlands are also strongly influenced by their drainage basins (Livingston and Loucks 1979, Porter 1981), the chemical composition of waters flowing into the basins (Richardson *et al.* 1978), and the sediment load of the surface water (Jaworski and Raphael 1978, Stuckey 1978). Jaworski *et al.* (1979), for example, attributed declines in the abundance of floating-leaved and submerged aquatic plants in undiked wetlands along western Lake Erie (USA) to a local surface runoff across upland-wetland ecotones. They recommended a wetland management strategy that included a corridor of terrestrial vegetation to protect the wetlands from excessive turbidity and nutrient loading from upland runoff.

The amount of surface water available to most inland wetlands depends on hydrologic inputs from precipitation or from upstream ecosystems (Howard-Williams 1985). In some inland wetlands, surface flow occurs in distinct drainage channels and there appears to be little exchange of materials across the wetland-open water ecotone between streams and adjacent wetlands except during floods (Kuenzler *et al.* 1977, Mitsch *et al.* 1979, Brinson *et al.* 1984, Brinson 1988, Whigham *et al.* 1986). In some inland wetlands, streams are not present and water moves as sheet flow over the surface. In those instances, there are clear patterns of interaction between the water column and the wetland across the ecotone (Verry and Timmons 1982, Richardson and Marshall 1986).

Wetland-open water ecotones (surface water). Vitt *et al.* (1975) and Vitt and Bayley (1984) studied peat systems in Canada and characterised nutrient movement across the ecotone between the wetland and open water. The concentration of calcium in surface water decreased as water flowed across the wetland, with greatest changes at the ecotone between the wetland and open water (Vitt *et al.* 1975). In Manitoba, Vitt and Bayley (1984) examined the relations between vegetation and water chemistry in four bogs where changes in pH and concentrations of Na$^+$, K$^+$, Ca^{++}, and Mg^{++} were greatest at the wetland-open water ecotone.

Verhoeven *et al.* (1988) studied nutrient relations between wetlands and adjacent open water ecosystems in the Netherlands. Changes in electrical conductivity (a measure of the overall nutrient content) of surface water decreased most rapidly in the ecotone when the wetland surface was flooded from an adjacent ditch. The authors suggested that changes were due to active plant nutrient uptake in the ecotone. Vermeer (1985), working in the same areas as Verhoeven *et al.*, found similar conductivity patterns. He also showed that changes in concentrations of nutrients were greater near the ecotone between ditches and the wetland (Fig. 9.4).

Verhoeven *et al.* (1988) further demonstrated the conditions under which this ecotone effect may be important. When the vegetation in contact with open water is a floating mat (i.e. typical of earlier stages of fen succession), mat elevation will adjust to water level changes in the adjacent ditch or pond. Therefore, water flooding the wetland from the ditches will always be in contact with the floating mat, and it can be expected that significant interactions will occur at the surficial ecotone. When vegetation becomes anchored to the bottom (i.e. characteristic of later stages of succession), the mat does not adjust to changing water levels. Floodwaters then have little contact with vegetation, resulting in less nutrient uptake at the surficial ecotone.

Wetland-open water ecotones (groundwater). There have been fewer studies of nutrient transformations occurring as groundwater moves across wet-

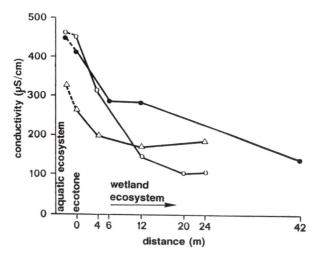

Figure 9.4 Differences in conductivity measured in the ground and ditch water along three wet grassland transects (means of 10 samples). Adapted from Vermeer (1985)

182

land-open water ecotones. Verhoeven *et al.* (1988) compared conductivity changes occurring in groundwater moving from open water to adjacent wetlands in the Netherlands. Similar to patterns they found for surface water (see section above), the greatest changes occurred at the wetland ecotone for metals and nutrients in subsurface water (Fig. 9.5). The ability of peat systems to retain nutrients, especially P, has been demonstrated clearly by Richardson and Marshall (1986), and it would be expected that many of the chemical transformations occur as groundwater crosses wetland-open water ecotones of peat systems. Richardson and Marshall (1986) have also shown that the peat substrate can become saturated with P, losing its uptake capacity. This suggests that under conditions of high nutrient loading, ecotones may have a limited ability to retain phosphorus and other nutrients.

McKnight *et al.* (1985) studied the distribution and characteristics of humic substances in Thoreau's Bog, Massachusetts, USA, where the upper moss (*Sphagnum*) layer was the primary site of dissolved organic carbon (DOC; <0.5 μm diameter) production. They showed the greatest changes in interstitial DOC concentrations at the ecotone between the bog and a central area of open water. Similar results were found by Gaudet (1979), who demonstrated that nutrients from upstream sources were more effectively retained when passing through a floating mat of vegetation in an African lake compared with periods when water from upstream areas was transported directly under the vegetative mat and into the lake.

Verhoeven *et al.* (1988) give an interesting example of how blockage of a surficial boundary between wetland vegetation and the underlying stratum can have an important impact on nutrient exchanges. In groundwater discharge areas there is a net movement of water out of the aquifer, across the ecotone, and into the substratum of the wetland. Although the groundwater is often polluted from nearby agricultural areas, most nutrients are adsorbed by the wetland substrate and do not reach the substrate surface where vegetation assimilation would occur. This situation is, however, limited to a few decades, since the adsorptive ability of the peat layer will ultimately be exceeded (Richardson and Marshall 1986).

Seischab (1987) sampled interstitial and subsurface water along a transect crossing several vegetative ecotones ranging from deciduous and evergreen wetland forests to herbaceous and open water areas. We compared the percentage change in nutrient concentrations (positive or negative) as water moved across ecotones between the eight different wetland types with the percentage change as water moved within homogeneous patches (Table 9.3). The greatest change occurred across the ecotones, demonstrating the importance of ecotones in regions with multiple wetlands.

Upland-wetland ecotones (surface water). Upland-wetland ecotones have been shown to be important for surface water and groundwater quality

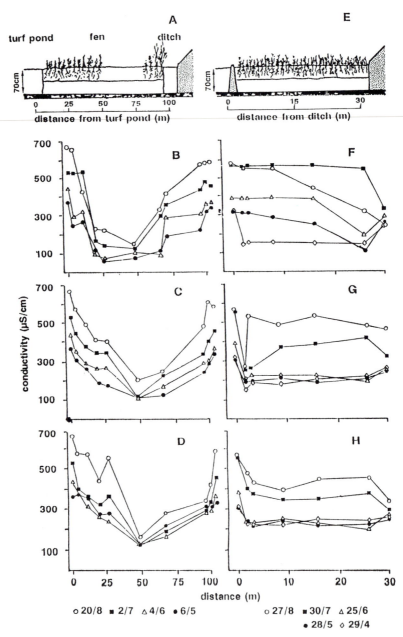

Figure 9.5   Electric conductivity of water samples along transects in the Molenpolder fen (A-D) and the Westbroek I fen (E-H). A and E: Schematic representation of the transects. B and F: Conductivity at the soil surface. C and G: Conductivity 20 cm below soil surface. D and H: Conductivity 60 cm below soil surface. Adapted from Verhoeven *et al.* (1988)

Table 9.3 Percentage change in water quality parameters for pairs of sampling sites within and between different zones of vegetation. Values are means, independent of whether the changes were positive or negative. From Seischab (1987)

Parameter	Within Zone	Between Vegetation Zones
pH	1.68	5.25
Conductivity	5.96	37.69
Calcium	6.66	32.61
Magnesium	6.77	21.93
Nitrate	56.48	78.75

(Peterjohn and Correll 1984, 1986; Cooper *et al.* 1986, Schnabel 1986). This is particularly true where the upland areas are dominated by agricultural practices, which export large amounts of sediments and nutrients.

Sediments eroded from uplands primarily move in surface water. This is also the primary pathway for phosphorus movement in agricultural landscapes, since most phosphorus is attached to sediment particles (Lowrance *et al.* 1984, Pionke *et al.* 1986). Nitrogen moves primarily in subsurface water as dissolved nitrate, ammonium, and organic nitrogen (Peterjohn and Correll 1984, 1986).

Surface water containing sediment and nutrients passes through the upland-wetland ecotone as overland flow. When overland flow is not channelised, there is ample opportunity for water to come into contact with the surface litter layer. As the intensity of runoff increases, overland flow often becomes channelised flow, there is less contact between the water and the litter, and there is less retention of sediments and nutrients. This has been shown by Jordan *et al.* (1986), who found that sediment transport through a coastal plain landscape occurred primarily during large storms when the retention ability of upland-wetland ecotones in riparian forests was bypassed.

The velocity of surface water slows as it passes through the surface litter layer in the ecotone, trapping sediments and adhering nutrients. Whigham *et al.* (1986) found that the litter layer within riparian forests retained large amounts of sediment and that some phosphorus was trapped along with the sediment. Most phosphorus, however, passed through the riparian zone, since deposited sediments had low phosphorus concentrations compared with the finer sediments (clays) passing through to the adjacent aquatic ecosystem. Much of the phosphorus attached to the fine sediments was retained by wetlands further down the hydrologic gradient (Whigham *et al.* 1988). Compared with phosphorus, most nitrogen is removed from subsurface water at the upland-wetland ecotone (Peterjohn and Correll 1984). The primary mechanism for nitrogen removal in the ecotone appears to be denitrification driven by inputs of nitrate-nitrogen in groundwater from the upland, the presence of reduced sediments in the ecotone, and the high organic matter content of the soil.

Upland-wetland ecotones (*groundwater*). In contrast, the movement of groundwater across upland-wetland ecotones is even more dynamic and potentially important as a landscape feature. Schnabel (1986) showed that more nitrate was removed from groundwater during periods of low hydrologic discharge than during periods of high discharge across an upland-wetland ecotone. During periods of high discharge, more water moves across the ecotone as overland flow, and there is less contact time for vegetative uptake and microbial transformation of nutrients (Pionke *et al.* 1986). Schnabel (1986) found nitrate concentrations decreased by more than 50% within 16 m of the upland-wetland ecotone when those conditions prevailed. Peterjohn and Correll (1984, 1986) and Lowrance *et al.* (1984) report similar results. Gilliam *et al.* (1986) found high rates of denitrification also occurred near the wetland-open water ecotone when surface aerobic and subsurface anaerobic zones were present.

Subsurface processes discussed so far are primarily mediated by microbial metabolism (Lowrence *et al.* 1984, Peterjohn and Correll 1984). The role of vegetation in nutrient retention at ecotones is less clear. Fail *et al.* (1986) conducted one of the few ecotone studies where measurements of plant nutrient uptake were made. These authors tested the hypothesis that vegetation in a wetland (riparian forest) was important in retaining nutrients transported from adjacent upland agricultural areas. They found primary production and nutrient uptake rates were higher in the upland-wetland ecotone receiving high nutrient inputs from the uplands. This suggests that vegetation at the upland-wetland ecotone is responsive to changes in nutrient availability. While they did not indicate spatial patterns in rates of biomass and nutrient accumulation, high rates of root production within the first 8 m of the ecotone suggest that the ecotonal areas are important for nutrient retention.

Lateral and longitudinal exchanges across ecotones

Examples given in the previous section allow us to formulate some general statements about the importance of wetland ecotones in landscapes: (1) Hydrologic characteristics probably have the greatest role in determining the fate of materials moving across wetland ecotones. With few exceptions, hydrologic and nutrient inputs across wetland ecotones vary temporally, and the ability of nutrients to be retained or transformed within an ecotone is negatively related to how quickly water moves across the ecotone as surface water or groundwater. (2) The movement of material across ecotones in tidal wetlands is more predictable than in inland wetlands (Table 9.2). (3) Interactions across wetland-open water ecotones dominate patterns of nutrient exchange within tidal wetlands (Wolaver *et al.* 1983). (4) Exchanges across the upland-wetland ecotone are not important in estuarine areas unless significant amounts of groundwater from upland areas discharge into the tidal wetlands (Valiela *et al.* 1978). (5) During periods of extreme tidal events (spring and storm tides), coastal ecotones are probably not important as sites for sediment and nutrient exchange. (6) The movement of materials across wetland-open water ecotones in inland environments is probably more variable and less predictable than in tidal areas (Table 9.2). When surface and groundwater flows through riparian zones into first order streams across a lateral wetland-open water boundary, important nutrient transformations occur (Schnabel 1986, Ford and Naiman 1989). Once the water has entered the aquatic system, it moves downstream to higher order streams. Compared with streams, however, there is much greater retention and transformation capacity where water from the stream flows across wetland ecotones (e.g. in impounded areas), as shown by Naiman *et al.* (1986) for landscapes containing beaver-created impoundments. (7) When the capacity of upland-wetland ecotones is exceeded (e.g. during storms), downstream wetlands and wetland ecotones become important (Whigham *et al.* 1988). (8) Wetland ecotones provide an important buffering capacity within landscapes.

Biotic characteristics of wetland ecotones

Biotic diversity. It has been suggested that ecotones support relatively high biological diversity (Patten *et al.* 1985). Wetland ecotones can have a high species diversity, but species diversity for a particular wetland boundary may be affected by a variety of factors (van der Maarel 1976), and thus may be difficult to predict. In a New England (USA) inland freshwater marsh complex, Burk (1977) found vascular plant species diversity to be lowest at the wetland-open water ecotone, higher in the middle of the marsh, and highest at the upland-wetland ecotone. Similarly, in several tidal marshes sampled in northeastern United States, vascular plant species diversity was generally lowest at the wetland-open water ecotone, higher in the wetland center, and highest at the upland-wetland ecotone (Senerchia-Nardone and Holland 1985, Senerchia-Nardone *et al.* 1986). However, in other instances, upland-wetland ecotones may be sharp and have few species, if any. We believe that the answer to the question about higher biodiversity in wetland ecotones needs to be addressed with additional lateral transect studies crossing from uplands to wetlands to open water patches, and focussing on species richness in the wetland-upland or wetland-open water ecotones.

Primary production. Conditions stressful in other environments may increase primary production in plants adapted to wetland ecotones. For example, Sharma and Gopal (1977) studied biomass structure in the cattail (*Typha elephantina*) along a gradient from open water through wetland to upland. In the dry upland stand, flooded occasionally for a short period, aboveground biomass was small, maximum biomass was obtained in the middle stand which was flooded frequently, and the permanently flooded stand had intermediate values (Sharma and Gopal 1977). It seems important for future studies to focus on analyses of productivity at wetland-upland or wetland-open water ecotones.

Community structure. Historic names for different kinds of wetlands (e.g. marshes, fens, bogs, swamps) imply general recognition of distinctive associations of plants that are readily recognised and, at least loosely, comprise a community. One reason these associations have been so clearly identified is that zonation patterns in wetlands are often thought to be sharp, with abrupt boundaries that call attention to vegetation change, and by implication to the uniqueness of each zone (Mitsch and Gosselink 1986).

Recent evidence suggests that in at least one wetland species, several phenotypes have evolved (Keeley 1979). Phenotypes may allow different populations within the same species to tolerate different environmental conditions, and thus to survive not only within a wetland, but also at the wetland-open water and upland-wetland ecotones. Keeley (1979) has reported population differentiation in tupelo (*Nyssa sylvatica*) along a soil moisture gradient from upland sites, which are never flooded, to floodplain wetlands, which are periodically flooded and drained, to permanently flooded swamps. Upland plants were very intolerant of flooded soils. In contrast, swamp plants were quite tolerant of flooded soils. The floodplain population produced a distinctly flood-tolerant phenotype, but not nearly as tolerant of flooded conditions as the swamp phenotype. Keeley (1979) concluded that floodplain plants apparently have been selected to be similar to upland plants under drained conditions and swamp plants under flooding, and one consequence of this is that their tolerance of flooded conditions is intermediate. Thus selection may have preserved genotypes capable of acclimating to either drained or flooded conditions, with the result that the phenotypes are optimally adapted to neither. It appears at least in the case of *Nyssa sylvatica* that phenotypic gradients have developed across wetland ecotones. Similar work on other wetland transition zone species would help in understanding their physiological and genetic survival strategies.

Community development. Much thought has been devoted to the question whether wetlands always develop into drier terrestrial habitats, and thus if wetland ecotones are invaded by upland species, or if open water is invaded by wetland plants, or both (Odum 1971, Livingston and Loucks 1979, Holland and Burk 1984, Niering 1987). Certain species are especially likely to invade other communities because of life history traits such as arrival time, growth rates, and longevity patterns (Glenn-Lewin 1980, Noble and Slatyer 1980, Hibbs 1983). Van der Valk (1981) presents an approach to wetland succession where the presence and abundance of each species depends on its life history and its adaptation to the environment of a site. Traditional theories of the relation of wetland succession and the climax state to diversity, stability, and resilience might well be reconsidered (Livingston and Loucks 1979, van der Valk 1981, Niering 1987). There is growing evidence that continuous disequilibrium due to periodic physical disruption is necessary for the continued high productivity of wetlands and associated systems. As long as fluctuating hydrologic conditions persist, a wetland ecotone will remain in a state of *pulse stability* (Odum 1971). In low energy situations, Welling *et al.* (1988) have shown that ecotones between different vegetation types change very little once species have become established. It would thus appear that many wetland ecotones are influenced by biotic interactions and that physical conditions are only important under certain conditions.

Anthropogenic stabilisation of such systems often reduces productivity. Wetland ecotone management goals based solely on concepts of homeostasis and stability could be disruptive to the functioning of the wetland itself, as well as to adjacent systems (Livingston and Loucks 1979). To assist present wetland ecotone managers, research is needed to identify traditional, low-intensity management techniques that have successfully maintained or enhanced the functions of ecotones in the past, and thus have promoted sustainable utilisation of wetland patches and ecotones (Clark and Holling 1984, Hollis *et al.* 1988).

Recognition of the importance of wetland ecotones

The importance of upland-wetland ecotones has been recognised by some state governments in the United States, and legislation has been passed to ensure that they are maintained (Holland and Balco 1985). New Jersey now requires a 50 m buffer zone between uplands and wetlands (Tubman 1988); this legislation was based in part on a scientific wetland-upland buffer delineation model (Roman and Good 1986). How variable can that width be at different locations in the landscape to reach desired water quality goals? Is the maintenance of the upland-wetland ecotone more important at some locations in the landscape than others? We believe that upland-wetland ecotones are most efficient in areas that are topographically lower in the landscape where soils have both aerobic and anaerobic layers, important requirements for denitrification (Peterjohn and Correll 1984, Whigham *et al.* 1988). Ecotones topographically higher on the landscape might efficiently intercept sediments and nutrients in surface water but would be less efficient at intercepting nutrients in groundwater, because the shallow groundwater would most often be aerobic.

In the highly managed landscape of the Netherlands, the length of wetland-open water ecotone is high compared to the area of wetland. During dry periods, there is a net movement of water into wetlands from the extensive ditch systems. Polluted river water is the hydrologic source for those exchanges, and wetland-open water ecotones play an important role in intercepting nutrients before they reach the interior of wetlands (Verhoeven *et al.* 1988). Thus, in the Netherlands, wetland-open water ecotones have an important assimilative capacity for aquatic pollutants.

CONCLUSION

We summarise this chapter by presenting a list of significant research questions. They are divided into two categories: (1) issues related to both wetland patches and ecotones, and (2) issues related specifically to wetland ecotones.

Issues related to wetland patches and ecotones

1. What role does vegetation play in nutrient uptake, especially in upland-wetland ecotones during the growing season? There is evidence to demonstrate that vegetation can play an important role in removing nutrients from the substrate and groundwater (Peterjohn and Correll 1984, Fail *et al.* 1986). We do not know, however, how variable this characteristic is among different types of wetlands nor the importance of the ecotone itself. This last issue is of particular importance because the little data available suggest that upland-wetland ecotones may be important landscape features for the interception of nutrients, especially nitrogen.

2. How does the assimilative capacity of the wetland ecotone compare with the assimilative capacity of the wetland patch? Most investigations have focussed on wetland patches, but not on ecotones. However, evidence given in this chapter suggests that the wetland boundary may be the most important part of the wetland. Is this observation true, and is it true for all types of wetlands?

3. Can the assimilative capacity of wetland patches and ecotones be enhanced or maintained through management? This question is obviously important, yet there is little information directly addressing it.

4. At what temporal or spatial scale are research results most useful for decision making and management? Wetland research takes time, can be expensive, and usually considers only one wetland at a time. Most questions asked of wetlands ecologists, however, deal with issues at several scales, many of which focus on landscape issues (Di Castri and Hadley 1988, Holland 1988). It would be productive to consider several

190

hierarchical levels, including both wetland patches and ecotones. An example would be to consider all wetlands in a drainage basin (Fig. 9.3). The goal would be to determine which types of wetlands and ecotones are most important in intercepting nutrients and sediments. This approach has the potential to identify emergent processes by moving from a single wetland boundary to a wetland and then to a series of wetlands in a drainage system.

Issues related specifically to wetland ecotones

1. At what level of human investment have ecotones been maintained and restored in the past, and is there any evidence of positive benefits from those actions?

2. Does the nutrient retention efficiency of wetland ecotones, particularly in tidal wetlands, change when the edge-to-area ratio is altered? If boundaries are important to wetland function, there should be a relation between nutrient retention capacity and the size (area) of the boundary or the ratio of ecotone length to patch volume (patch body).

3. How does the assimilative capacity of upland-wetland ecotones vary under different topographic and geologic settings, and between different types of upland and wetland ecosystems?

4. Along definable hydrologic gradients, are wetland ecotones topographically higher in the landscape more important in retaining and transforming nutrients than ecotones lower in the landscape?

5. How important are wetland-open water ecotones, especially in landscapes where a high percentage of the surface water volume occurs in lakes and ponds? In those situations, is the ratio of wetland area to open water more important than the length of wetland ecotone?

6. Do wetland ecotones support high biological diversity? This question needs to be addressed with additional lateral transect studies crossing from uplands to wetlands to open water ecosystems, and focussing on species richness in the wetland-upland or wetland-open water ecotone.

7. Is primary production higher in wetland-upland or wetland-open water ecotones than in the wetland patches themselves?

8. Have wetland plants evolved several phenotypes to allow the coexistence of different populations of the same species within a wetland, as well as at the wetland-open water and upland-wetland ecotones?

Strategies for future research

Research provides valuable information to decision makers. Yet, for scientists, perhaps the most difficult question to answer is what research should be done when the information base is small and the need for information is great. We believe that field research and simulation modelling both need to be accomplished and coordinated so that the results will be useful to both scientists and resource managers. Based on our review, we suggest the following priority areas:

- Study the importance of upland-wetland ecotones in a variety of landscapes simultaneously.

- Characterise the relationship between wetland size, hydrologic characteristics, and dimensions of the ecotone on the assimilative capacity of the wetland patches and ecotones.

- Use existing management questions to develop a series of experiments that will test our ability to maintain or enhance the functions of wetland ecotones.

- Identify traditional, low-intensity management techniques that have successfully maintained or enhanced the functions of wetland ecotones in the past.

- Utilise existing descriptive and predictive models to identify parameters of wetland patches and ecotones that need to be better understood.

- Establish lateral transects crossing from uplands to wetlands to open water ecosystems and assess biological diversity in wetland-upland and wetland-open water ecotones.

Towards a management of wetland patches and ecotones

Wise use of wetland patches and ecotones requires action on a broad scale, giving consideration to all factors affecting wetlands and the drainage basins of which they are a part. A fundamental understanding of ecosystem and hydrological processes is necessary for good management (Hollis *et al.* 1989). Careful synthesis and integration should ultimately result in national wetland policies that include consideration of upland-wetland and wetland-open water ecotones. Major items for developing such policies may include:

- A national inventory of wetland patches and ecotones

- Identification of the benefit and values of these wetland patches and ecotones (Simpson 1985)

- Definition of the priorities for each site in accordance with the needs of, and socio-economic conditions in, each country

- Proper assessment of environmental impact before development projects are approved, continuing evaluation during the execution of projects, and full implementation of environmental conservation measures that take full account of the recommendations of this process of environmental assessment and evaluation

● Use of development funds for projects that permit conservation and sustainable utilisation of wetland resources

Realisation that wetland patches and ecotones cannot be managed in isolation from upstream inputs and downstream impacts has led to the development of wetland legislation and policies at the local and national level in many developed countries (Holland and Balco 1985, Roman and Good 1986, Tubman 1988). In addition to the creation of parks and reserves, legislation may require that alteration of wetlands and stream courses tributary to, and downstream from, the protected site be subject to regulation (Verhoeven *et al.* 1988). Most wetland patches and ecotones in developing countries retain a wide range of their natural functions (Gaudet 1979). Many rural economies in Africa and in Southeast Asia depend on the utilisation of these wetland patches and ecotones. Accordingly, it is neither practical nor desirable that all extractive activity be precluded from all wetland systems (Hollis *et al.* 1988). Rather, mechanisms for sustainable utilisation of wetland patch and ecotone resources need to be developed and promoted (Clark and Holling 1984), and this can be accomplished through solid interdisciplinary research that has vision for the future.

ACKNOWLEDGEMENTS

We thank John O'Neil and Joe Magnone for making electronic communication between the authors possible. The paper was written while DFW was on sabbatical leave at the University of Utrecht (The Netherlands). The financial support of Nederlandse Organisatie voor Wetenschappelijk Onderzoek (NWO) and NSF grants DEB-79-11563, CEE-82-19615 and BFR83-16948 for DFW and USA Man and the Biosphere Program (MAB) for MMH is appreciated. We are grateful for constructive comments on various drafts of the manuscript by Y.L. Grossman, R.J. Naiman, W.E. Odum, R.W. Prach, and an anonymous reviewer. Jos Verhoeven and Willem Kroerselman provided valuable discussions on various aspects of the chapter.

LITERATURE CITED

Agosta, K. 1985. The effect of tidally induced changes in the creekbank water table on pore water chemistry. Estuarine and Coastal Shelf Science 21:389-400.

Bedford, B.L., and E.M. Preston. 1988. Developing the scientific basis for assessing cumulative effects of wetland loss and degradation on landscape functions: status, perspectives and prospects. Environmental Management 12:751-771.

Bertness, M.D. 1984. Ribbed muscles and *Spartina alterniflora* production in a New England salt marsh. Ecology 65:1794-1807.

Bertness, M.D. 1985. Fiddler crab regulation of *Spartina alterniflora* production on a New England salt marsh. Ecology 66:1042-1055.

Bloom, A.L. 1964. Peat accumulation and compaction in a Connecticut coastal marsh. Journal of Sedimentary Petrology 34:599-603.

Bloom, A.L., and C.W. Ellis, Jr. 1965. Postglacial stratigraphy and morphology of coastal Connecticut. Connecticut Geological and Natural History Survey Guidebook 1. Hartford, Connecticut, USA.

Boesch, D.F., D. Levin, D. Nummedal, and K. Bowles. 1983. Subsidence in coastal Louisiana: causes, rates and effects on wetlands. United States Fish and Wildlife Service FWS/OBS 83-26, Newton Corner, Massachusetts, USA.

Brinson, M.M. 1988. Strategies for assessing the cumulative effects of wetland alteration on water quality. Environmental Management 12:655-662.

Brinson, M.M., H.D. Bradshaw, and M.N. Jones. 1985. Transitions in forested wetlands along gradients of salinity and hydroperiod. Journal of the Elisha Mitchell Scientific Society 101:76-94.

Brinson, M.M., H.D. Bradshaw, and E.S. Kane. 1984. Nutrient assimilative capacity of an alluvial floodplain swamp. Journal of Applied Ecology 21:1041-1057.

Burk, C.J. 1977. A four year analysis of vegetation following an oil spill in a freshwater marsh. Journal of Applied Ecology 14:515-522.

Clark, W.C., and C.S. Holling. 1984. Sustainable development of the biosphere: human activities and global change. Pages 283-299 in T.F. Malone and J.G. Roederer, editors. Global change. The International Council of Scientific Unions Press, Paris, France.

Cooper, J.R., J.W. Gilliam, and T.C. Jacobs. 1986. Riparian areas as a control of nonpoint pollutants. Pages 166-192 in D.L. Correll, editor. Watershed research perspectives. Smithsonian Institution Press, Washington, D.C., USA.

Cowardin, L.M., V. Carter, F.C. Golet, and E.T. LaRoe. 1979. Classification of wetlands and deepwater habitats of the United States. United States Fish and Wildlife Service FWS/OBS-79/31, Washington, D.C., USA.

DeLaune, R.D., W.H. Patrick, and S.R. Pezeshki. 1987. Foreseeable flooding and death of coastal wetland forests. Environmental Conservation 14:129-133.

Denny, P. (editor). 1985. Ecology and management of African wetland vegetation. Dr. W. Junk, Dordrecht, The Netherlands.

Di Castri, F., and M. Hadley. 1988. Enhancing the credibility of ecology: interacting along and across hierarchical scales. GeoJournal 17:5-35.

Fail, J.L., M.N. Hamzah, B.L. Haines, and R.L. Todd. 1986. Above and belowground biomass, production, and element accumulation in riparian forests of an agricultural watershed. Pages 193-224 in D.L. Correll, editor. Watershed research perspectives. Smithsonian Institution Press, Washington, D.C., USA.

Flessa, K.W., K.J. Constantine, and M.K. Cushman. 1977. Sedimentation rates in a coastal marsh determined from historical records. Chesapeake Science 18:172-176.

Ford, T.E., and R.J. Naiman. 1989. Groundwater-surface water relationships in boreal forest watersheds: dissolved organic carbon and inorganic nutrient dynamics. Canadian Journal of Fisheries and Aquatic Sciences 46:41-49.

Forman, R.T.T., and M. Godron. 1986. Landscape ecology. John Wiley and Sons, New York, USA.

Frayer, W.E., T.J. Monahan, D.C. Bowden, and F.A. Graybill. 1983. Status and trends of wetlands and deepwater habitat in the conterminous United States, 1950s to 1970s. Department of Forest and Wood Sciences, Colorado State University, Fort Collins, Colorado, USA.

Gaudet, J.J. 1979. Seasonal changes in nutrients in a tropical swamp: North Swamp, Lake Naivasha, Kenya. Journal of Ecology 67:953-981.

Gilliam, J.W., R.W. Skaggs, and C.W. Doty. 1986. Controlled agricultural drainage: an alternative to riparian vegetation. Pages 225-243 in D.L. Correll, editor. Watershed research perspectives. Smithsonian Institution Press, Washington, D.C., USA.

Glenn-Lewin, D.C. 1980. The individualistic nature of plant community development. Vegetatio 43:141-146.

Hackney, C.T., and G.F. Yelverton. 1990. Effects of human activities and sea level rise on wetland ecosystems in the Cape Fear River estuary, North Carolina, USA. In D.F. Whigham,

R.E. Good, and J. Kvet, editors. Wetland case studies. Tasks for Vegetation Science Series. Dr. W. Junk, Dordrecht, The Netherlands, *in press*.

Harrison, E.Z., and A.H. Bloom. 1977. Sedimentation rates on tidal salt marshes in Connecticut. Journal of Sedimentary Petrology 47:1484-1490.

Harvey, J.W., P.F. Germann, and W.E. Odum. 1987. Geomorphological controls of subsurface hydrology in the creekbank zone of tidal marshes. Estuarine and Coastal Shelf Science 25:677-691.

Heinselman, M.L. 1970. Landscape evolution and peatland types, and the Lake Agassiz Peatland Natural Area, Minnesota. Ecological Monographs 40:235-261.

Hibbs, D.E. 1983. Forty years of forest succession in central New England. Ecology 64:1394-1401.

Holland, M.M. (compiler). 1988. SCOPE/MAB technical consultations on landscape boundaries: report of a SCOPE/MAB workshop on ecotones. Biology International, Special Issue 17:47-106.

Holland, M.M., and J. Balco. 1985. Management of fresh waters: input of scientific data into policy formulation in the United States. Verhandlungen Internationale Vereinigung Limnologie 22:2221-2225.

Holland, M.M., and C.J. Burk. 1982. Relative ages of western Massachusetts oxbow lakes. Northeastern Geology 4:23-32.

Holland, M.M., and C.J. Burk. 1984. The herb strata of three Connecticut River oxbow swamp forests. Rhodora 86(848):397-415.

Hollis, G.E., M.M. Holland, J. Larson, and E. Maltby. 1989. Wise use of wetlands. Nature and Resources, 24:2-13.

Hopkinson, C.S., and J.P. Schubauer. 1984. Static and dynamic aspects of nitrogen cycling in the salt marsh graminoid *Spartina alterniflora*. Ecology 65:961-969.

Howard-Williams, C. 1985. Cycling and retention of nitrogen and phosphorus in wetlands: A theoretical and applied perspective. Freshwater Biology 15:391-431.

Jaworski, E., and C.N. Raphael. 1978. Fish, wildlife and recreational values of Michigan's coastal wetlands, wetland value study phase I. United States Fish and Wildlife Service Region II, Twin Cities, Minnesota, USA.

Jaworski, E., C.N. Raphael, P.J. Mansfield, and B.B. Williamson. 1979. Impact of Great Lakes level fluctuations on coastal wetlands. National Technical Information Services Publication 296403, Washington, D.C., USA.

Johnson, F.L., and D.T. Bell. 1976. Plant biomass and net primary production along a flood-frequency gradient in the streamside forest. Castanea 41:156-165.

Johnston, C.A., and R.J. Naiman. 1987. Boundary dynamics at the aquatic-terrestrial interface: the influence of beaver and geomorphology. Landscape Ecology 1:47-57.

Jordan, T.E., and D.L. Correll. 1985. Nutrient chemistry and hydrology of interstitial water in brackish tidal marshes of Chesapeake Bay. Estuarine and Coastal Shelf Science 21:45-55.

Jordan, T.E., D.L. Correll, W.T. Peterjohn, and D.E. Weller. 1986. Nutrient flux in a landscape: The Rhode River watershed and receiving waters. Pages 57-76 *in* D.L. Correll, editor. Watershed research perspectives. Smithsonian Institution Press, Washington, D.C., USA.

Keeley, J.E. 1979. Population differentiation along a flood frequency gradient: physiological adaptations to flooding in *Nyssa sylvatica*. Ecological Monographs 49:89-108.

Kuenzler, E.J., P.J. Mulholland, L.A. Ruley, and R.P. Sniffen. 1977. Water quality in North Carolina Coastal Plain streams and effects of channelisation. Report Number 13-27. Water Resources Research Institute of University of North Carolina, Raleigh, North Carolina, USA.

Livingston, R.J., and O.L. Loucks. 1979. Productivity, trophic interactions and food-web relationships in wetlands and associated systems. Pages 101-119 *in* P.E. Greeson, J.R. Clark, and J.E. Clark. Wetland functions and values: the state of our understanding. Proceedings of the National Symposium on Wetlands. American Water Resources Association, Minneapolis, Minnesota, USA.

Lowrance, R., R. Todd, J. Fail, Jr., O. Hendrickson, Jr., R. Leonard, and L. Asmussen. 1984. Riparian forests as nutrient filters in agricultural watersheds. BioScience 34:374-377.

Maltby, E. 1986. Waterlogged wealth. Earthscan Press, London, England.

McCaffrey, R.J. 1977. A record of accumulation of sediments and trace metals in a Connecticut,

USA salt marsh. Dissertation. Department of Geology and Geophysics, Yale University, New Haven, Connecticut, USA.

McKnight, D., E.M. Thurman, R.L. Wershaw, and H. Hemond. 1985. Biogeochemistry of aquatic humic substances in Thoreau's Bog, Concord, Massachusetts. Ecology 66: 1339-1352.

Mendelssohn, I.A., K.L. McKee, and M.L. Postek. 1982. Sublethal stress controlling *Spartina alterniflora* productivity. Pages 223-242 *in* B. Gopal, R.E. Turner, R.G. Wetzel, and D.F. Whigham, editors. Wetlands: ecology and management. International Science Publications, Jaipur, India.

Mitsch, W.J., and J.G. Gosselink. 1986. Wetlands. Van Nostrand Reinhold, New York, USA.

Mitsch, W.J., C.L. Dorge, and J.R. Wiemhoff. 1979. Ecosystem dynamics and a phosphorus budget of an alluvial cypress swamp in southern Illinois. Ecology 60:1116-1124.

Moore, P.D., and D.J. Bellamy. 1974. Peatlands. Springer-Verlag, New York, USA.

Moss, B. 1980. Ecology of fresh waters. John Wiley and Sons, New York, USA.

Naiman, R.J., C.A. Johnston, and J.C. Kelley. 1988. Alteration of North American streams by beaver. BioScience 38:753-762.

Naiman, R.J., J.M. Melillo, and J.E. Hobbie. 1986. Ecosystem alteration of boreal forest streams by beaver (*Castor canadensis*). Ecology 67:1254-1269.

Niering, W.A. 1987. Wetlands hydrology and vegetation dynamics. National Wetlands Newsletter 9:10-11.

Nixon, S.W., and V. Lee. 1985. Wetlands and water quality: a regional review of recent research in the United States on the role of fresh and saltwater wetlands as sources, sinks, and transformers of nitrogen, phosphorus, and various heavy metals. Waterways Experiment Station, United States Army Corps of Engineers, Vicksburg, Mississippi, USA.

Noble, I.R., and R.O. Slatyer. 1980. The use of vital attributes to predict successional changes in plant communities subject to recurrent disturbances. Vegetatio 43:5-21.

Odum, E.P. 1971. Fundamentals of ecology. Second edition. Saunders, Philadelphia, Pennsylvania, USA.

Odum, W.E., T.J. Smith III, J.K. Hoover, and C.C. McIvor. 1984. The ecology of tidal freshwater marshes of the United States east coast: a community profile. United States Fish and Wildlife Service FWS/OBS-83/17, Washington, D.C., USA.

Orson, R.A., R.S. Warren, and W.A. Niering. 1987. Development of a tidal marsh in a New England River valley. Estuaries 10:20-27.

Patten, B.C., S.E. Jorgensen, B. Gopal, J. Kvet, H. Loeffler, Y. Svirezhav, and J. Tundisi. 1985. Ecotones: an edge approach to gene pool preservation and management in the biosphere. Prospectus for a new SCOPE programme from the Scientific Advisory Committee for wetlands and shallow continental water bodies. Athens, Georgia, USA.

Peterjohn, W.T., and D.L. Correll. 1984. Nutrient dynamics in an agricultural watershed: observations on the role of a riparian forest. Ecology 65:1466-1475.

Peterjohn, W.T., and D.L. Correll. 1986. The effect of riparian forest on the volume and chemical composition of base flow in an agricultural watershed. Pages 244-262 *in* D.L. Correll, editor. Watershed research perspectives. Smithsonian Institution Press, Washington, D.C., USA.

Pieczyńska, E. 1990. Lentic aquatic-terrestrial ecotones, *this volume*.

Pigott, C.D., and M.E. Pigott. 1963. Late-glacial and post-glacial deposits at Malham, Yorkshire. New Phytologist 62:317-334.

Pigott, M.E., and C.D. Pigott. 1959. Stratigraphy and pollen analysis of Malham Tarn and Tarn Moss. Field Studies 1(1):1-17.

Pinay, G., H. Décamps, E. Chauvet, and E. Fustec. 1990. Functions of ecotones in fluvial systems, *this volume*.

Pionke, H.B., R.R. Schnabel, J.R. Hoover, W.J. Gburek, J.B. Urban, and A.S. Rogowski. 1986. Mahantango Creek watershed: fate and transport of water and nutrients. Pages 108-134 *in* D.L. Correll, editor. Watershed research perspectives. Smithsonian Institution Press, Washington, D.C., USA.

Porter, B.W. 1981. The wetland edge as a community and its value to wildlife. Pages 15-24 *in* Brandt Richardson, editor. Selected Proceedings of the Midwest Conference on Wetland Values and Management. Fresh Water Society, Saint Paul, Minnesota, USA.

Redfield, A.C. 1972. Development of a New England salt marsh. Ecological Monographs

42:201-237.

Richardson, C.J. 1981. Pocosin wetlands. Hutchinson Ross, Stroudsburg, Pennsylvania, USA.

Richardson, C.J., and P.E. Marshall. 1986. Processes controlling movement, storage, and export of phosphorus in a fen peatland. Ecological Monographs 56:279-302.

Richardson, C.J., T.L. Tilton, J.A. Kadlec, J.P.M. Chamie, and W.A. Wentz. 1978. Nutrient dynamics of northern wetland ecosystems. Pages 217-242 in R.E. Good, D.F. Whigham, and R.L. Simpson, editors. Freshwater wetlands: ecological processes and management potential. Academic Press, New York, USA.

Risser, P.G. (compiler). 1985. Spatial and temporal variability of biospheric and geospheric processes: research needed to determine interactions with global environmental change. The International Council of Scientific Unions Press, Paris, France.

Roman, C.T., and R.E. Good. 1986. Wetlands of the New Jersey Pinelands: values, functions, and impacts. Division of Pinelands Research Center for Coastal and Environmental Studies, Rutgers, the State University, New Brunswick, New Jersey, USA.

Schnabel, R.R. 1986. Nitrate concentrations in a small stream as affected by chemical and hydrological interactions in the riparian zone. Pages 263-282 in D.L. Correll, editor. Watershed research perspectives. Smithsonian Institution Press, Washington, D.C., USA.

Seischab, F.K. 1987. Succession in a *Thuja occidentalis* wetland in western New York. Pages 211-214 in A.D. Laderman, editor. Atlantic white cedar wetlands. Westview Press, Boulder, Colorado, USA.

Senerchia-Nardone, P., and M.M. Holland. 1985. Floristic comparison of two tidal wetlands in the Connecticut River estuary. Newsletter of the Connecticut Botanical Society 13(3): 1-6.

Senerchia-Nardone, P., A. Reilly, and M.M. Holland. 1986. Comparison of vascular plant zonation at Iona Island Marsh (Hudson River estuary) and Lord's Cove Marsh (Connecticut River estuary). Pages 1-35 in J.C. Cooper, editor. Polgar Fellowship Reports of the Hudson River Estuarine Sanctuary Program, 1985. New York State Department of Environmental Conservation, Hudson River Foundation, United States Department of Commerce, New York, USA.

Sharma, K.P., and B. Gopal. 1977. Studies on stand structure and primary production in *Typha* species. International Journal of Ecology and Environmental Sciences 3:45-66.

Shure, D.J., and M.R. Gottschalk. 1985. Litter-fall patterns within a floodplain forest. American Midland Naturalist 114:98-111.

Simpson, P. 1985. WERI: A plug for protection. The Landscape 25:5-9.

Simpson, R.L., R.E. Good, and B.R. Frasco. 1981. Dynamics of nitrogen, phosphorus, and heavy metals in Delaware River freshwater tidal wetlands. Final Technical Completion Report. Corvallis Environmental Research Laboratory, United States Environmental Protection Agency, Corvallis, Oregon, USA.

Stuckey, R.L. 1978. The decline of lake plants. Natural History 87(7):66-69.

Symoens, J.J., editor. 1988. Vegetation of inland waters. Kluwer Academic Publishers, Dordrecht, The Netherlands.

Tubman, L.H. 1988. New Jersey's freshwater wetlands protection act. Journal of the Water Pollution Control Federation 60:176-179.

Valiela, I., J.M. Teal, S. Volkmann, D. Shafer, and E.J. Carpenter. 1978. Nutrient and particulate fluxes in a salt marsh ecosystem: tidal exchanges and inputs by precipitation and groundwater. Limnology and Oceanography 23:798-812.

Van der Maarel, E. 1976. On the establishment of plant community boundaries. Berichte der Deutschen Botanischen Gessellschaft 89:415-443.

Van der Valk, A.G. 1981. Succession in wetlands: a Gleasonian approach. Ecology 62:688-696.

Verhoeven, J.T.A., W. Koerselman, and B. Beltman. 1988. The vegetation of fens in relation to their hydrology and nutrient dynamics. Pages 249-282 in J.J. Symoens, editor. Vegetation in inland waters. Dr. W. Junk, Dordrecht, The Netherlands.

Vermeer, H. 1985. Effects of nutrient availability and groundwater level on shoot biomass and species composition of mesotrophic plant communities. Dissertation. University of Utrecht, Utrecht, The Netherlands.

Verry, E.S., and D.R. Timmons. 1982. Waterbone nutrient flow through an upland-peatland watershed in Minnesota. Ecology 63:1456-1467.

Vitt, D.H., P. Achuff, and R.E. Andrus. 1975. The vegetation and chemical properties of patterned fens in the Swan Hills, north central Alberta. Canadian Journal of Botany 53:2776-2795.

Vitt, D.H., and S.E. Bayley. 1984. The vegetation and water chemistry of four oligotrophic basin mires in northwestern Ontario. Canadian Journal of Botany 62:1485-1500.

Welling, C.H., R.L. Pederson, and A.G. van der Valk. 1988. Recruitment from the seed bank and the development of zonation of emergent vegetation during a drawdown in a prairie wetland. Journal of Ecology 76:483-496.

Whigham, D.F., C. Chitterling, and B. Palmer. 1988. Impacts of freshwater wetlands on water quality: a landscape perspective. Environmental Management 12:663-671.

Whigham, D.F., C. Chitterling, B. Palmer, and J. O'Neill. 1986. Modification of runoff from upland watersheds: the influence of a diverse riparian ecosystem. Pages 283-304 *in* D.L. Correll, editor. Watershed research perspectives. Smithsonian Institution Press, Washington, D.C., USA.

Whigham, D.F., and R.L. Simpson. 1978. Nitrogen and phosphorus movement in a freshwater tidal wetland receiving sewage effluent. Pages 2189-2203 *in* Coastal Zone 78. Proceedings of the Symposium on Technical, Environmental, Socio-economic, and Regulatory Aspects of Coastal Zone Management. American Society of Civil Engineers, Minneapolis, Minnesota, USA.

Wolaver, T.G., J.C. Zieman, R. Wetzel, and K.L. Wolf. 1983. Tidal exchange of nitrogen and phosphorus between a mesohaline vegetated marsh and the surrounding estuary in the lower Chesapeake Bay. Estuarine and Coastal Shelf Science 16:321-332.

Yelverton, G.F., and C.T. Hackney. 1986. Flux of dissolved organic carbon and pore water through the substrate of a *Spartina alterniflora* marsh in North Carolina. Estuarine and Coastal Shelf Science 22:252-267.

Zedler, J.B., and P.A. Beare. 1986. Temporal variability of salt marsh vegetation: the role of low-salinity gaps and environmental stress. Pages 295-306 *in* D. Wolfe, editor. Estuarine variability. Academic Press, New York, USA.

Key words: Ecotone, gradients, hydrology, landscape, management, wetlands.

CHAPTER 10

SURFACE WATER-GROUNDWATER ECOTONES

Janine Gilbert, Marie-José Dole-Olivier, Pierre Marmonier
and Philippe Vervier

ABSTRACT

Groundwater ecotones are interaction zones occurring between various surface water resource patches of the watershed and the groundwater localised under them. They influence the landscape mosaic by regulating energy and water flow between adjacent systems. This article gives some examples of vertical and horizontal ecotones and proposes a classification for groundwater-surface ecotones based on hydrologic dynamics and patch dominance. Five major types of ecotones can be identified by various examples. The chapter then focusses on the unique functions of groundwater ecotones related to processes occurring in these contact zones: elasticity, permeability, biodiversity, and connectivity. Considering the ecotone concept over the different space and time scales found inside the underground environment, the authors discuss whether internal underground ecotones exist or not. Finally, some gaps in knowledge and areas for future research are identified.

INTRODUCTION

Most of the water in rivers and lakes comes from subsurface aquifers and underground runoff (Castany 1985, Vanek 1987). This underground continental water represents 40% of the volume of fresh water. Russian hydrologists estimate it at $24 \times 10^6 \, \text{km}^3$ (including islands) in a depth ranging from 0 to 2000 m. This estimation was reduced to $16 \times 10^6 \, \text{km}^3$ taking geological structures into account (Castany 1982). Whatever the estimates, this underground reservoir represents a considerable quantity of fresh water distributed evenly from a geographic standpoint, and far exceeds the amount found on the surface in lakes (0.22% of the volume of fresh water) and rivers (0.005%) (Unesco 1978).

Aquifers can be classified into three main groups according to the structure of the voids and the spatial heterogeneity: porous or interstitial aquifers (e.g. floodplain or ocean shore), karstic aquifers (limestone areas), and subsurface aquifers (Freeze and Cherry 1979, Unesco 1980). Groundwater links the more-or-less isolated surface aquatic systems (Holland *et al.* 1990, Pieczyńska 1990, Pinay *et al.* 1990). Groundwater functions as a link between various ecological systems. All of these systems are connected, exchanging energy and matter at their dynamic limits, or at their ecotones.

The general definition of an ecotone (Holland 1988) is applicable to groundwater ecotones. Initially, one may consider that these boundaries are those separating surface systems from underground patch bodies along the drainage network. At this scale, the contrast between the surface and underground environment is very strong. The physical environment, the quality, density, and structure of the biotic communities, the biotic interactions, the stability of the system, and the general functioning of the two systems are very different; and these interactions change according to the type of groundwater.

The underground environment is heterotrophic. It receives its organic matter from upstream almost exclusively from the surface ecosystem via the vegetation. The underground environment then transforms, stores, and exports this organic matter downstream. What roles do ecotones play in this phenomenon? This is the question that we deal with in this chapter.

Our purpose is to focus on the unique features of groundwater ecotones. First, we propose a classification of groundwater-surface ecotones based on hydrologic dynamics and patch dominance. Second, we consider elasticity, permeability, biodiversity, and connectivity in these contact zones. Third, we discuss the ecotone concept and expand it to include various discontinuities at the different space and time scales of the underground environment. Finally, we identify research areas that require further attention.

MAJOR TYPES OF GROUNDWATER-SURFACE WATER ECOTONES

Using the *patch dynamic* concept (Pickett and White 1985), ecotones occur on a variety of spatiotemporal scales and have properties that are scale dependent (Hansen *et al.* 1988, Holland 1988, Meentemeyer and Box 1987). Thus the surface-underground ecotone can be examined on several spatial scales. For example, on a habitat scale, the ecotones are the various river-aquifer junctions related to the habitat heterogeneity, occurring either close to the bank or to the substrate. On a patch scale, ecotones are the spring, the sinkstream, or the subsurface flow. On a landscape scale, the floodplain is the transition zone between the karst and the river.

The classification of groundwater-surface water ecotones that we propose relates to the patch scale (i.e. the intermediate type of scale) illustrated in

Fig. 10.1. It is functional, based on hydrologic dynamics, on the direction of material fluxes, and thus on dominant relations between underground and surface water flow. Several parameters are involved, such as substrate grain size, quantity of organic matter, physicochemistry of the water, and faunal distribution. Thus hydrologic dynamics constitute a key synthetic component for the functioning of aquatic ecosystems, acting as an organising factor for the whole system both in space (heterogeneity) and time

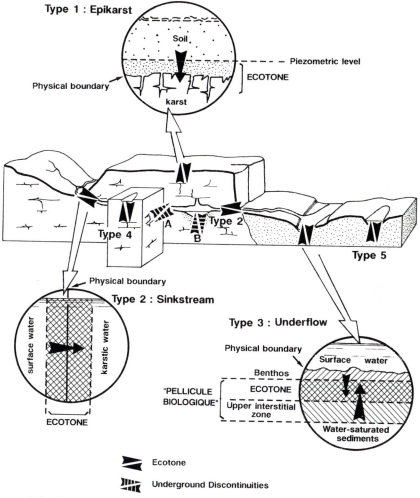

Figure 10.1 Main types of groundwater-surface water ecotones (vertical and horizontal types). Type 1: soil-karstic aquifer interface (epikarst). Type 2: sinkstream or spring. Type 3: stream underflow. Type 4: sinkstream of lake bottom. Type 5: infiltrating lentic water. Examples of discontinuities inside underground environment: (A) instream discontinuities (confluence). (B) underground water-water saturated sediment interface

(instability). Consequently, we consider ecotones as forming discontinuities in space which develop in three dimensions (Johnston and Naiman 1987, Naiman *et al.* 1988a, b). In this chapter we refer to vertical and horizontal ecotones related to hydrologic dynamics and the nature of the patch. The vertical type of ecotone concerns the transition zone between surface systems such as rivers and lakes and the groundwater under them. The horizontal type corresponds to springs and sinkstreams (Fig. 10.1).

Classification can be based on a hierarchy of hydrologic processes and exchanges (Fig. 10.2): (I) Hydrologic dynamics are directly or indirectly linked to runoff water. (II) There are strong or weak hydrologic dynamics. (III) Hydrologic dynamics are modified by a change in the matrix at the boundary. (IV) There are several variations in the direction of water flows and dominance.

First level: links between hydrologic dynamics and runoff water

Indirect links: land-water ecotones. In terrestrial ecosystems, water from rainfall percolates down (by force of gravity, in a vertical direction) through the soil. Capillary rise of water from the saturated zone into the unsaturated zone occurs, especially when the water table is fairly shallow. This happens when dynamic exchanges take place between the soil and the upper layer of the underground aquifer (soil-epikarst or soil-phreatic water; Figs. 10.1 and 10.2, Type 1). Hydrologic instability results from the vertical oscillations in the groundwater (seasonal fluctuations).

Direct links: water-water ecotones. These ecotones occur in all surface and groundwater systems where there are zones of interaction between the same general types of environment (i.e. water-water ecotones). Temporal variations in flux rates can be measured by three independent parameters: amplitude (high or low), general tendency to change (increase, decrease, stationary), and rhythm (regular or irregular, slow or fast). In reality, these parameters are closely linked. They make it possible to identify ecotones having large or small temporal variations in flux rates (i.e. related to the degree of instability of exchanges on the scale of the hydrologic cycle).

Second level: types of hydrologic dynamics

Large changes in intensity of water fluxes: lotic ecotones (Fig. 10.2). Water, with its dominating role as a vector, acts mainly by setting in motion large quantities of materials and organisms. The size of the ecotone varies considerably during the hydrologic cycle.

Small changes in intensity of water fluxes: lentic ecotones (Fig. 10.2). The role of water is confined to that of a medium enabling exchanges to take place. Only slight quantities of organic matter and animals are transported.

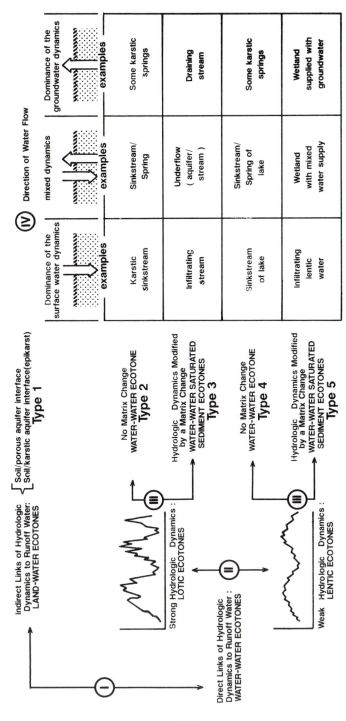

Figure 10.2 Functional classification of ecotones based on the water dynamics: I Links of hydrologic dynamics to runoff water. II Types of hydrologic dynamics. III Hydrologic dynamics modified by a moderate change at the boundary. IV Dominant water dynamics

203

There is little drift, and dispersal phenomena (physicochemical and biological) are dominant within the ecotone. The shifting of the ecotone in space and in time is weak. For instance, an alluvial plain, with its well-developed vascular system stemming from the drainage axis formed by the river, provides a high diversity of ecotones. It has a wide range of connections between surface and underground water flows, ranging from lotic systems to stagnant pools, to uplands (Bravard *et al.* 1986, Amoros *et al.* 1987a, b). These ecotones are established by the relative position of the piezometric surface and the degree of clogging of the sediment.

Third level: hydrologic dynamics modified by a change in the matrix at the boundary

One kind of hydrologic dynamics only (water-water ecotones). The ecotone develops at the physical boundary separating groundwater and surface environment in lotic systems (Fig. 10.2, Type 2) and in lentic systems (Fig. 10.2, Type 4). The physical boundary consists of differences in the light regime; on one side of the ecotone there are daily rhythms, whereas on the other side there is permanent darkness. Hydrologic dynamics do not change.

Two different hydrologic dynamics (water-water saturated sediment ecotones). The ecotone develops between free-flowing water and water saturated sediment. This creates a filter for water flow, with the ecotone being influenced by two hydrologic regimes in both lotic (Fig. 10.2, Type 3) and lentic systems (Fig. 10.2, Type 5). The physical boundary is formed by light limitation and the water-sediment boundary.

Fourth level: direction and dominant dynamics of the water flow

Surface water dynamics are dominant. The flow is unidirectional towards the underground environment. The water characteristics and animal communities in this type of ecotone are similar to those of the surface environment. The ecotone is situated almost completely in the underground environment, such as a sinkstream or an infiltrating stream (Fig. 10.2).

Neither environment dominates. The direction of the water flow can reverse. This situation is often due to variability of surface water levels, with intermittent inputs of organic matter (in the form of detritus and living organisms) to the groundwater. Examples include junctions between subsurface flow and rivers, karstic areas that function alternately as a spring and as a sinkstream during the annual hydrologic cycle, secondary channels separated from the river upstream, and marshes. The ecotone may be subject to spatial movements, depending on river discharge or, for marshes, recharge by variable surface runoff (Fig. 10.2).

Groundwater dynamics are dominant. The direction of the water flux is towards the surface environment; water and animal community characteristics are similar to those of the groundwater environment. The ecotone is situated almost completely in the surface environment. The situation is found quite frequently in springs and oxbow lakes fed and maintained by groundwater inputs or in flow-through lakes (Fig. 10.2).

UNIQUE FEATURES OF GROUNDWATER-SURFACE WATER ECOTONES

In groundwater ecotones, water functions as a medium (sustaining the ecotone), as a flow (discharge), and as a vector (transporting and stimulating). As for living organisms, they are both fluxes (quantities of animals circulating per unit of time) and vectors affecting the spatial distribution of resources by transporting materials (Wiens *et al.* 1985, Forman and Godron 1986) or by maintaining the free flow of water and organic matter in the sediments (i.e. the anticlogging process by pelletisation; Danielpol 1984). These groundwater ecotones are more than just the spatial volume of their physical boundary between two adjacent systems (the boundary layer between light and permanent darkness, or a change of matrix). In most cases groundwater ecotones are wide and develop on either side of substrates, often asymmetrically.

The ecotone classification that we propose implies the existence of distinct structural and functional types of ecotones. Contrasting functional types of ecotones reveals the unique features of different groundwater ecotones.

Elasticity

Elasticity is defined by variations in the spatial limits of the ecotone. Characteristic differences between the ecotone and its two adjacent patches make it possible to identify the boundaries of the ecotone from its biotic and abiotic features. Normally, indicators or functional groups (Bournaud and Amoros 1984, Blandin 1986) are useful for this, with biotic ones integrating far more information than abiotic ones.

External parameters characterise each of the two adjacent environments. For example, in the interstitial system of the active channel of the Rhône River, France, *Hydropsyche* (Trichoptera) and *Heptagenia* (Ephemeroptera) are indicators of surface water and hence reflect the upper boundary of the ecotone (Fig. 10.3). In contrast, the *Bathynella* (Crustacea) and *Microcharon* (Isopoda) are strict phreatobites which indicate a highly stable hydrology. They are indicators of the deep groundwater layer. Hence they reflect the lower boundary of the ecotone. Biotic and abiotic indicators also exist within the ecotone. For example, there are physicochemical characteristics that indicate mixing between two types of water (i.e. temperature, conductivity, silica or nitrate content; Dole 1983, Marmonier 1988), and characteris-

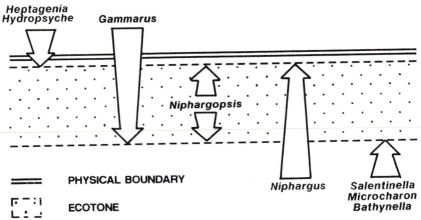

Figure 10.3 Example of animal distribution within the ecotone in the underflow of the Rhône River (France)

tic species found only inside the ecotone (i.e. the Amphipod *Niphargopsis casparyi* and the Ostracod *Fabaeformiscandona wegelini*; Marmonier 1988). The ecotone is also biotically characterised by a blend of epigean and hypogean fauna which, by their composition and spatial arrangement, may describe the principal functional features of the ecotone and its limits with adjacent patches.

At a given time, spatial elasticity varies according to the nature of the hydrologic flows and the environmental components (i.e. biotic or abiotic). Indeed each hydrologic flow and each environmental component defines its unique boundaries for the ecotone. The flow hierarchy can be based on active width of each type of flow (Fig. 10.4). Generally the physicochemical flows, such as temperature (White *et al.* 1987) and ionic charge, create the widest ecotones. The flows of dissolved organic matter (DOM) can also establish the boundaries of the ecotone far beyond the physical boundary.

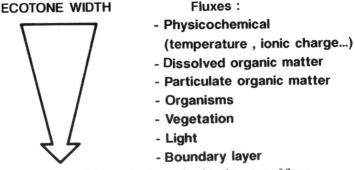

Figure 10.4 Boundary variability of ecotone related to the nature of fluxes

Ecotone width decreases when one considers only particulate organic matter (POM), which is less labile than the DOM. These abiotic flows are often closely linked to the hydrology. The same does not apply to organisms that also bring about numerous biological processes (adaptations, behaviour phenomena). The ecotone they define is often much narrower than the one defined by the abiotic flows. Lastly, the ecotone delimited by vegetation is very narrow, since it is directly linked to the availability of light, which is essentially the physical boundary separating surface and subsurface sediments. All these flows define contact zones and unique areas (overlapping or separate), which together form the ecotone. Separately, they do not describe the same phenomena, and several fundamental questions arise as to which flows and components are to be chosen for a specific program along with the appropriate spatial and temporal scales.

Spatiotemporal elasticity can be defined for a given flux (temperature, ionic charge, organisms). It depends on the hydrology, and, more generally, on disturbance regime (e.g. flooding). In temperate regions, floods may occur throughout the hydrologic cycle, or they may be concentrated within a given season.

In karstic aquifers where circulation is rapid, floods are brief and violent. They act on the elasticity of underground aquatic ecotones by two possible pathways (Fig. 10.5). In the first example the disturbance passes from patch A to patch B through the water-water ecotone; the disturbance is transmitted directly, since the ecotone has developed with the direction of flow (e.g.

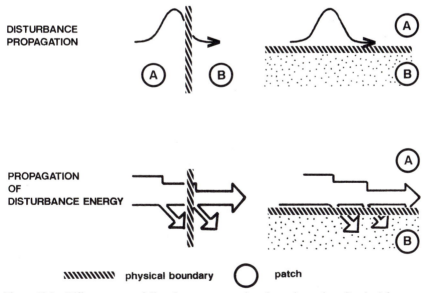

Figure 10.5 Different types of disturbance propagation through patches. On the left: water-water ecotone. On the right: water-water saturated sediment ecotone

207

springs or sinkstreams). the karstic system of Foussoubie (Ardèche, France) is a specific example (Fig. 10.6, Vervier 1988). During floods, underground water fluxes near the outlet are mainly of surface origin (low HCO_3/Ca^{++} ratio and an abundance of epigean insects). During baseflow, there is a phase during which the influence of surface water gradually decreases until it is nonexistent (the HCO_3/Ca^{++} ratio increases) and the environmental

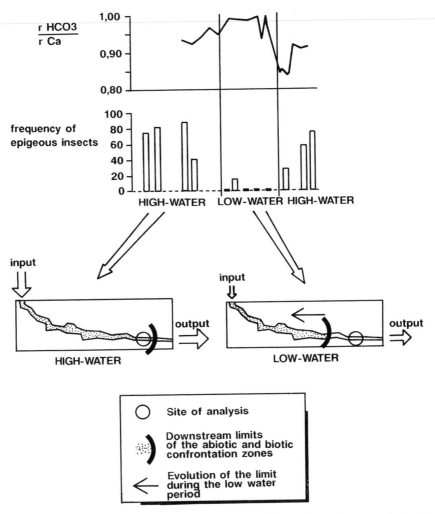

Figure 10.6 Fluctuations of the downstream limits of the confrontation zone during the hydrologic cycle: example of an interaction between the surface stream, La Planche, and the karstic system of La Foussoubie (Ardèche, France). Biotic and abiotic confrontation zone is identified using the HCO_3^-/Ca^{++} ratio and the percentage of epigean insects. The fluctuations of the downstream limits during high water and low water periods are represented at the bottom of the figure

gradient no longer exists (Fig. 10.6). Thus, during the hydrologic cycle, the interaction zone of abiotic fluxes may be nonexistent (low water) or it may reach from the entrance of the subterranean system to its outlet (high water). In karstic springs the thermal fluxes are considerable, since the surface environment receives water at a relatively constant temperature. The spring acts as a 'microthermal power station', especially at periods of high water during winter. Its influence can be felt 500 m beyond the physical boundary, especially if the surface stream is made up mostly ($> 50\%$) of groundwater, as in the Dorvan-Cleyzieu karstic system (Gibert 1986). Thus, in a karstic environment, the ecotone can extend over several hundreds of metres and even several kilometres during a flood.

In the second case the disturbance is transmitted by patch A (Fig. 10.5). Its propagation is maximum in A and somewhat reduced from A to B, depending on the permeability of the ecotone (water-water saturated sediment). The ecotone develops perpendicular to the unidirectional force of the current. The boundary modifies the disturbance, acting as a stabiliser for the disturbed system (Naiman *et al.* 1988a, b). This can be illustrated by the spatial distribution of interstitial fauna after a flood. In a channel of the Rhône River, the spatiotemporal distribution of organisms was studied during the summer low water period (Fig. 10.7). The influence of the hydrologic flux is shown by the succession of amphipods in space and time (Marmonier and Dole 1986). After a flood, *Gammarus* (an indicator of surface water) sinks into the sediments (either through passive drift, carried along by the hydrologic flux, or through active migration; see Rouch and Danielopol 1987). The boundaries of the ecotone are pushed deeper into the sediment. During low water, the habitat of *Gammarus* is gradually confined to superficial water infiltration zones and to upper layers of the sediment. On the other hand, *Salentinella* comes from the deep zones of the substrate (i.e. groundwater) and rises gradually between each flood period. The ecotone diminishes in depth during low water periods: in the upper infiltration zone its lower boundary may be situated at -1 m below the surface of the sediments; whereas in zones where groundwater emerges, it is situated < -0.5 m below the sediment surface.

Identical results have been obtained in other rivers where both epigeous and hypogeous organisms readjust their vertical distribution in the sediments according to the surface discharge (Williams and Hynes 1974, Poole and Stewart 1976, Danielopol 1976). Moreover, depending on the disturbance regime (Dole and Chessel 1986) and hydrologic cycle (Mathieu *et al.* 1987), some populations change their distribution strategy. In these river-aquifer ecotones the elasticity is less than in springs or sinkstreams; it concerns a distance of only a few metres. However, hundreds of riverine invertebrates have been collected from a grid of wells 10 m deep, located on the floodplain up to 2 km from the channel of the Flathead River, Montana, USA (Stanford and Ward 1988).

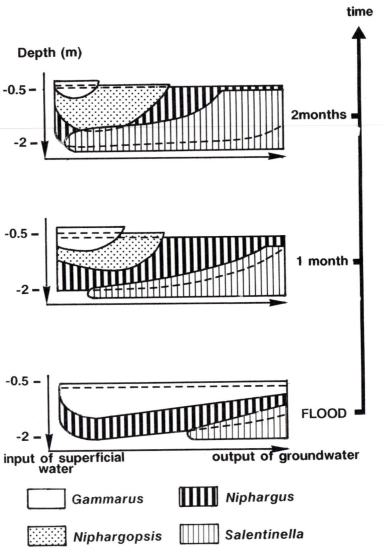

Figure 10.7 Dynamic of spatial distribution of amphipods after a flood in the underflow of the Rhône River (France). Horizontal: surface water-groundwater gradient. Vertical: depth in the sediments. Adapted from Marmonier and Dole (1986)

Permeability

Exchanges and transfers between the surface and groundwater are linked to the dynamics of water through ecotones. Matter and energy move from the surface towards the hypogeous environment, including the input of drainage erosion, litterfall, sewage, and waste. When underground water arrives in surface ecosystems, it carries nutrients to the surface environment.

Various kinds of flux permeability may be found depending on the porosity of the physical boundary which acts as a selective filter. We examine two types of permeability: almost complete transmission of fluxes through a physical boundary with a large mesh (spring or sinkstream ecotone) and nearly complete retention of fluxes by a fine-meshed boundary (interstitial ecotone).

Spring or sinkstream ecotone. Fluxes, such as the constant export of organic matter, take place in one direction only. Consequently, we can speak of adjacent ecological systems where one is the donor and the other the recipient. In karstic springs most fluxes are examples of direct passage from one patch to another because the physical boundary is very open.

From a qualitative point of view, organic matter does not enter and leave the underground environment in the same form. Décamps and Laville (1975) have shown that in a karst the infiltrating water contained POM that was 300 times more concentrated than in the water leaving the system (Table 10.1). However, the quantity of DOM was more or less the same (10 mg/L). In ecotones there is no selective filtration, since biotic and abiotic fluxes are conveyed through a single medium, water.

Table 10.1 Transport of organic matter from the sinkstream to the spring during one day. Adapted from Décamps and Laville (1975)

| | Particulate Organic Matter (mg/L) | | | |
Time of Day	Coarse	Fine	Very Fine	Dissolved Organic Matter (mg/L)
SINKSTREAM				
0930	438.29	16.10	1.54	10.75
1100	424.05	17.08	2.50	11.52
1300	384.18	14.07	2.25	19.35
1500	220.85	12.55	1.34	22.18
1700	215.79	11.67	1.61	20.16
SPRING				
0930			2.10	11.59
1100			0.80	13.67
1300			0.70	7.73
1500			1.30	5.19
1700			1.50	12.45

Interstitial ecotone. The sediments of rivers, lakes, wetlands, estuaries, and coastal waters are biologically active zones, affecting the hydrology and the chemical content of water moving through them. In many situations processes occurring in these zones generate substantial nutrients and energy resources for adjacent systems. Various solutes present different concentrations in groundwater and in surface water. This implies that passage through the ecotone is often accompanied by transformation and degradation of complex organic inputs by a variety of processes (e.g. physical, chemical, or biological) which are often coupled with oxidation-reduction reactions. For example, oxygen may serve as the major terminal electron sink in the oxygenated layer. In the profundal strata, where oxygen is rapidly depleted, decomposition of organic matter continues by fermentation. This yields small molecules, the breakdown of which involves denitrification-sulfate reduction and methane production (Stenbergen and Verdouw 1984).

These ecotones are retentive areas which are frequently a rich source of soluble, chemically reduced elements such as ammonia, methane, hydrogen sulfide, organic carbon, organic nitrogen, organic phosphorus, and trace metals. They can serve as sources of energy for chemosynthetic microbial populations (such as nitrifiers, methane oxidisers, sulfur oxidisers, manganese-iron oxidisers) (Dahm *et al.* 1988). They serve also as a source of nutrients for rich and diversified animal communities (benthos and biological layer – the 'pellicule biologique' described by Dole 1983). Animal distribution is often linked to the organic matter content of sediments (Bretschko and Leichtfried 1988). Thus organic matter, animal communities, biochemical and biological activities, and sediments – separately and together – affect the permeability of fluxes in these ecotones.

Sediment deposits can function either as a source or a sink for many essential nutrients, depending on whether the surface or the underground environment is considered. The ecotone serves as a sink for POM from surface ecosystems. The retention process is important, especially in the running water where a large part of POM is adsorbed to the sediments (Danielopol 1976, Bretschko 1983, Leichtfried 1985). For example, Fontvieille (1987) calculated the carbon budget of a river polluted by waste from pig farms (Albenche, France). He estimated that in autumn the quantity of carbon retained was $4.25\,g \cdot m^{-2} \cdot d^{-1}$, most of which was stored in the sediments.

Contradictory hypotheses may be found regarding C, N, and P fluxes through the ecotone. Sometimes groundwater is thought to dilute organic carbon in river systems (Fisher and Likens 1973, Kaplan *et al.* 1980). A consequence of this would be the oligotrophisation phenomenon that can be observed in certain European alluvial plains where ecological succession stops and oxbow lakes are rejuvenated (Carbiener and Kapp 1981, Castella and Amoros 1984, Castella 1987). In other systems the opposite occurs. Hynes (1983) suggested that the hyporheic zone serves as a sink for organic matter, stripping dissolved organic carbon (DOC) from inflowing groundwater and from water flushed by storms from bank storage in unsaturated zones. Some results suggested that DOC from groundwater can contribute significantly to the carbon budget of rivers. For example, Wallis *et al.* (1981), who studied the Marmot Basin (Alberta, Canada), found that DOC averaged 21.2 mg/L in the unsaturated zone (under the soil), 5.9 mg/L in the saturated zone (groundwater), and only 2.2 mg/L in surface waters. These authors suggested that half of the DOC in groundwater appears to be lost as it passes into the stream, presumably because of exposure to benthic bacteria as it seeps through the sediments. Naiman *et al.* (1987) showed that annual fluvial transport of DOC in a boreal forest stream (First Choice Creek, Quebec, Canada) was higher in groundwater (2.7×10^6 g/yr) than in throughflow (6.3×10^5 g/yr). The same results were obtained by Ford and Naiman (1989). However, comparing the DOC of groundwater at different vertical levels within the streambed with the DOC in water flowing freely in the channel, Rutherford and Hynes (1987) concluded that, on the whole, water from the streambed neither diluted nor augmented DOC concentration of the free-flowing streamwater in either summer or fall, or day or night. DOC content in the ecotone appears to be much more heterogenous than either the dilution or stripping hypotheses would suggest.

The ecotone could be an important source of nitrogen for the surface water. Capone and Bautista (1985) suggest that groundwater nitrate may be an important factor in the eutrophication of nitrogen-limited surface water. However, denitrification processes are very common in ecotones. They have been observed in wetlands where the aquifer is on an even level with the soil (Odum 1990, Holland *et al.* 1990) and in lake sediments (Chen and Keeney 1974, Priscu and Downes 1987). Similarly, inputs of allochthonous nitrate from groundwater rapidly disappear as phreatic water passes through riparian woods (Peterjohn and Correll 1984, Pinay and Décamps 1988). Yet Wissmar *et al.* (1987) show high nitrification rates in aerobic riverine deposits, and Jansson (1980) points out that inorganic nitrogen flux from sediment to lake water may affect the productivity of the lake. This flux is minimised by the uptake of NH_4^+ by the benthic blue-green algae at the sediment surface. Jansson observed transformation of mineral NH_4^+ (present in interstitial water) to dissolved organic nitrogen in lake water. This transformation is the result of excretion of dissolved organic compounds from living algae, or degradation of dying organisms.

Concentrations of phosphorus are usually higher in the interstitial waters (Carignan 1982, Adams and Prentki 1982). Phosphorus may be retained in the sediments by an oxidised microzone at the sediment-water interface, but may still be available to benthic organisms (Ford and Naiman 1989). Yet there are contradictory opinions. According to Wetzel (1983), low levels of phosphorus are to be expected in groundwater because of the low solubility of phosphate-containing minerals. Likewise, according to Liechfried (1985), dissolved organic matter in the interstitial water plays a minor role in the stream budget. In mountains with gravel streams, total phosphorus amounts to about 0.01 mg/L. Thus standing stock is low, but the turnover may be rapid.

During pollutant transport by surface waters, there is some permanent or temporary storage taking place in the sediments and groundwater. For example, the concentrations of inorganic pollutants in the Glatt River in Switzerland influence, up to a distance of at least 110 m from the channel, the concentrations of heavy metals and anions in the groundwater (Von Gunten and Kull 1986). The ecotone acts as a sink for pollutants but also as a source long after the pollution of waterways has abated (Salomons *et al.* 1987). Interstitial fauna and the biofilm in the ecotone intervene in the purification of the surface water during infiltration to the sediments and groundwater (Danielopol 1976).

Exact mechanisms of transformation of matter at the boundary between groundwater and surface water require further research. Although the existence of fluxes of organic matter through the ecotone is well known, the role of the ecotone and its effectiveness seem to vary greatly from one system to another, and from one site to another. Moreover, it is important to remember that the groundwater has different origins (e.g. soil water, deep groundwater, underflow) with different nutrient compositions. These change with the geologic strata, vegetative cover, latitudinal and altitudinal gradients, and sampling depth.

Biodiversity

The colonisation of deep river sediments by benthic organisms has been studied by numerous authors (e.g. Bishop 1973, Williams and Hynes 1974, Bretschko 1981, Pennak and Ward 1986, and Stanford and Ward 1988). At the same time, phreatobiologists have noticed that river sediments contain many stygobiont organisms, which come from the deep underground environment and colonise these biotopes (Husmann 1975, Danielopol 1976, Mestrov and Lattinger-Penko 1977–78, Gibert *et al.* 1977, Dole 1985). This dual source for organisms colonising groundwater ecotones poses the issue of the biodiversity of ecotone communities.

It is generally admitted that the biodiversity of an ecotone is higher than the biodiversity of the two adjacent communities. This is called the *edge effect* (Leopold 1933, Naiman *et al.* 1988a, b). The case of groundwater ecotones seems to be rather different. Density and biodiversity are usually much higher in surface environments than in underground ones. Consequently, the surface-underground ecotone does not correspond to a richer zone, but to a zone of *intermediate biodiversity* between two adjacent patches. For example, in a Jurassic karstic spring (Vervier *et al.* 1986) (Fig. 10.8), biodiversity is greatest in the surface environment (13 species) and low in the underground environment (2 or 3 stygobiont species). In the transition zone, near the physical boundary (permanent darkness and day-

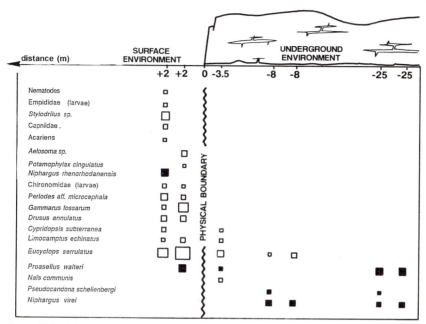

Figure 10.8 Biotic interaction zone in a karstic spring (adapted from Vervier *et al.* 1986). The abundance of each taxon is transformed in abundance class (geometric progression of ratio 2) and represented by squares. Size of squares: smallest, 1 individual; largest, more than 128 individuals. Grey squares: hypogean animals; white squares; epigean animals

night regime), diversity is intermediate, ranging between 5 and 9 species. Similarly, in an oxbow lake on the Rhône River (lône du Grand Gravier) 11 species of Coleoptera can be found in the surface water (Castella 1987), only 4 species in the interstitial habitats (Dole 1983), and only one stygobiont species in the deep phreatic water (Richoux and Reygrobellet 1986).

Equivalent results can be cited for other groups of insects. However, this intermediate biodiversity is not always found for all systematic groups. Certain groups can be more diversified in the ecotone. For example, in an oxbow lake of the Danube River, Austria, there are 17 species of Ostracoda Candoninae at a depth of 50 cm and only 15 species in the surface water (Danielopol 1983).

What are the biotic factors that explain this intermediate biodiversity? The first reason that can be suggested is the decrease in the quantity of organic matter and oxygen (Dole 1983, Bretschko and Leichtfried 1988), which limits colonisation of benthic sediments by organisms. For example, in the oxbow lake of the Danube River there was almost 30 to 50% O_2 saturation at a depth of 50 cm, but $< 10\%$ at 2 m (Danielopol 1983). Further, the environmental variability in the superficial layer of sediments limits colonisation of these sediments by stygobiont organisms, which are adapted to more constant environments.

Another reason is the lack of light and vegetation in the groundwater environment. Most grazers and algae scrapers (Ephemeroptera, Heptageniidae, for example; Fig. 10.3) are seldom found in deep interstitial environments. Similarly, the decrease in water current in the sediment explains why net-spinning carnivorous organisms (e.g. Trichoptera, Hydropsychidae) never form stable populations in the interstices. A more omnivorous diet makes it possible for other epigeous species to colonise the ecotone. Detritivores (e.g. Crustacea Gammaridae, Fig. 10.3) settle and even proliferate in those zones where the sediment is regularly supplied with organic matter from surface water (Marmonier and Dole 1986).

The last reason proposed relates to the low number of organisms strictly adapted to this ecotone. For example, in Rhône River sediments only two species have a spatial distribution that is more or less limited to the ecotone (see below). Hypogeous organisms cannot survive beyond the physical boundary, which thus forms a barrier because of their numerous morphological, physiological, and ethological adaptations. *Niphargus rhenorhodanensis*, the most abundant hypogeous Crustacean in the underflow of the Rhône River channel, was found only five times (10%) in samples of benthic fauna taken over one year from an active river channel (Gaschignard-Fossati 1986). *Niphargopsis casparyi*, which is very common in the interstitial environment of wetlands in the Ain River floodplain (France), was found in only 2.3% of the samples of benthic fauna (Castella 1987).

Connectivity

Ecotones are important for the whole watershed in influencing and controlling landscape processes. They regulate the landscape mosaic, affect energy flow between adjacent systems, and intervene in the landscape connectivity (Wiens *et al.* 1985). Connectivity measures the process by which the subpopulations of a metapopulation in a mosaic landscape are interconnected to form a demographic functional unit (Merriam 1984). Connectivity is the primary measure of corridor structure and also a measure of how connected or spatially continuous a corridor or a matrix may be (Forman and Godron 1986). But the connectivity between the landscape elements can also be seen in a more diffuse way. The ecotone can play a preponderant role in this process. In a spatial sense, connectivity depends on the number of connections between elements and how information-filtering properties influence the quality of the connections.

In surface environments, exchanges take place mainly along corridors (or the matrix). This represents the easiest way for information to circulate (e.g. circulation is rapid and the corridors protect moving biological elements; Merriam 1984). The connections between one or more systems through ecotones are probably much less efficient. The ecotones would then play a secondary role in the connectivity of the system.

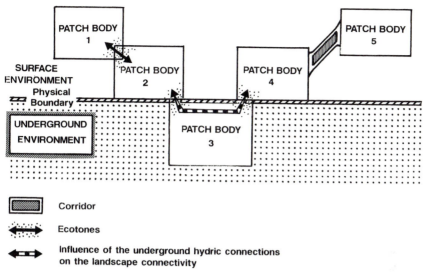

Figure 10.9 Diagram showing the role of surface water-groundwater ecotones in landscape connectivity

In underground environments where corridors and the matrix are sometimes nonexistent (interstitial aquifer), ecotones become an important means of establishing connectivity. The degree of connectivity between surface and underground systems depends directly on the properties of the ecotone between the two systems, and in particular on those properties related to the circulation of information. Ecotones may modify or even increase the connectivity of the whole landscape (Fig. 10.9). Through the medium of an underground patch body, two surface patches, originally isolated, can be linked. For example, the temporary outflow of lake water into the karst of the Neuchâtel Jura (Switzerland) carries some of its fauna (such as Cladocera) with it. At the basin exit, which gives birth to a surface stream 6.5 km from the lake, the various populations reappear to colonise the surface environment (Moeschler 1982). Comparable results have been found with bacteriophages (Aragno and Müller 1982), Copepoda (Rouch 1980), and epigeous insects (Décamps and Laville 1975, Décamps and Rouch 1973). Moreover, connectivity can play a role in the longevity of subsystems (Merriam 1984, Amoros and Roux 1988) and, thus, in the stability of the whole system.

CONCERNING THE EXISTENCE OF INTERNAL UNDERGROUND ECOTONES

A quantitative and dynamic functional approach to the underground environment has been applied only in the last 20 years. Likewise, ecosystems have not been fully defined, and consequently their limits are not precise in most cases.

On the scale of the whole karstic system, hydrogeologic study has revealed the existence of an organised hierarchical system following the progressive drainage of water carried towards a small number of outlets. It cannot be reduced to a single aspect such as the unidirectional gravitational flow (vertical dimension) of water. The horizontal dimension is conferred by the geologic structure and the layering of different aquifers. For example, consider the three interdependent circumscribed levels that interdigitate to form three subsystems: subsurface aquifer, epikarstic aquifer, and deep aquifer in the French Jurassic karst (Gibert 1988). The different aquifers are separated by boundaries, and different discontinuities occur along the drainage network.

Discontinuities inside underground aquifers

In karstic underground water, the network is similar to surface hydrographic networks, not in two dimensions but in a three-dimensional volume. Like a surface drainage network, an underground network has main confluences between secondary channels and the primary channel. Although it is not possible to define stream orders in subterranean environments because of inaccessibility, it is important to underline the existence of real underground rivers with large tributaries. In the giant underground system of the Nakanai Mountains (New Britain, Papua New Guinea) above the confluence of the tributary Luse River, the average discharge of the Matali River is about 90 m^3/s. During a flood the flow has been estimated at 1000 m^3/s for a 350 km^2 drainage basin (Maire 1981). A unique aspect of the subterranean environment is the functional absence of land-water ecotones. There are no inputs from either of the banks or from a forest canopy. This fact is related to the absence of vegetation and the absence of soil development.

In the different permeability zones occurring at different levels, the drainage network forms discontinuities inside the aquifer, thus isolating sectors with various permeabilities. Important discontinuities correspond to flow direction and change in slope. For example, these include falls, cascades, shafts, and the passage of water between a vertical flow and a horizontal flow (such as water percolation inside a cave forming a subhorizontal stream).

On the scale of a given sector (e.g. patch or microhabitat), discontinuities are found along the streams and are linked to different flow velocities, which form riffles and pools. These discontinuities play a major role in niche separation. A qualitative view of the niche organisation of Amphipoda and Isopoda in Greenbrier Valley (West Virginia, USA) streams has been presented by Culver (1982). Sometimes important silt deposits occur in many parts of the underground system and the rivers run above the alluvium like surface rivers on the floodplain. The confrontation zones between water and saturated sediment act to structure communities and the spatial distribution of populations (Magniez 1974, Gibert 1986).

In the porous aquifer, as in the karstic aquifer, vegetation is absent but the variety of habitats is reduced to a minimum, since there is only one type of physical habitat, the pore space. In addition, it is considerably reduced in size and the community structure is strongly linked to the abiotic environmental factors (Bretschko 1983, Danielopol 1983, Dole 1983). Sediment size is often considered to be a principal habitat factor in the interstitial environment. However, the drainage system is not homogeneous in this respect. It presents privileged axes of flow that create discontinuities between erosional and depositional zones (Fogg 1986). As yet there are few data concerning discontinuities inside the porous aquifers. Since we do not really know the mosaic of the different ecotones, we do not know much about the structural and dynamic aspects of the boundaries.

Functions of these discontinuities

Discontinuities such as channel confluences disperse matter and energy and decrease heterogeneities along the groundwater network. However, at the microhabitat scale (e.g. riffle-pool) the water-water saturated sediment ecotones retain POM and animals from the surface environment inside the groundwater aquifer. This is demonstrated by the annual accumulation of organic matter at such an interface in a French karstic system (Gibert 1986). In free-flowing water there are 600 mg/m^3 of DOC, 40-300 μg/m^3 of POC, 33 μg/m^3 aquatic fauna and 4 μg/m^3 terrestrial fauna (drowned organisms). In the sediment (mud) the POM quantity is 14 mg/g, several orders of magnitude larger than that found in the water column. Thus most of the POM is trapped by the sediment and released with high waters.

Are discontinuities ecotones or not?

A key question is whether some or all of these underground discontinuities can be considered ecotones. If we apply Holland's definition (1988), which is very general, to the underground environment, it can be examined over different spatial and temporal scales.

If we consider an ecotone to be of type 3 (underflow, water-water saturated sediment; Fig. 10.1), why not do so in the case of type B (underground underflow, water-water saturated sediment; Fig. 10.1)? Similarly, if we consider a surface confluence to be an ecotone (Pinay *et al.* 1989), why not the example. given for type A (underground confluence; Fig. 10.1)? These are situations where interactions and functioning are different in adjacent systems, and they possess boundaries or edges. Basically, the same processes occur above and below ground, but they are simplified in the underground environment. Holland's definition, like any definition if

219

taken to extremes, makes it possible to find ecotones everywhere, and the whole concept loses its meaning in such a case. It is perhaps better to relate the concept of ecotones to the nature of the question being asked.

CONCLUSION

Underground aquatic ecotones have been defined as the interaction zone between surface and underground systems. They are connected with various surface systems, such as lotic, lentic, and wetland, and thus it is difficult to establish a general model for all types of underground ecotones. Basically, the water dynamics strongly influence the functioning of the ecotone. Major fluxes of water and materials may be either unidirectional or bidirectional, and may originate either at the surface or in the underground environment. Considering this diversity, we have identified four fundamental types of ecotone which, from a functional standpoint, provide new and original data for the ecotone concept.

First, the notion of elasticity addresses both the spatial dimension of the ecotone (weak in ecotones linked to systems with weak hydrologic dynamics and strong for ecotones linked to systems with strong hydrologic dynamics) and the spatiotemporal dimension (which depends on the hydrology, biology, and nutrient cycling). Elasticity is related to permeability of the ecotone to fluxes. It is obvious that if the ecotone occurs in a single medium (e.g. water), its permeability will be greater than if it occurs between two different media. The more elastic an ecotone, the more permeable it is. Moreover, if it is highly permeable, it transmits disturbances more easily. This is one reason why in the first case ecotones may be very sensitive to disturbance. However, in the second case (different media) ecotones contribute to the stability of the adjacent patches after disturbance. In subsurface ecotones we find a wide range of elasticity, permeability, and sensitivity to disturbances. These concepts are linked, responding in the same manner along the continuum from the clogged interstitial ecotone to the completely open spring ecotone.

As for communities, the ecotone is situated between two highly contrasted systems. On the surface the habitats are numerous and varied, and linked to the vegetation. In the underground environment the role of vegetation disappears, and the biodiversity and number of habitats decrease sharply. Thus, in general, the biodiversity of the groundwater ecotone is intermediate between that of each of the two systems. Moreover, the ecotone is not simply a passage between two systems. It forms a hidden link connecting surface and subsurface systems that have been too often neglected. It plays an important role in the organisation of landscape connectivity. It may even intervene in the regulation of gene flow between isolated patches.

These basic characteristics, and the questions raised in this chapter, justify our continuing research into ecotones along two main lines of investigation: the structure and functioning of groundwater ecotones at different scales of perception, and the effects of human activities on this functioning and thus on ecotone management policies.

International literature refers to the great diversity of data concerning nutrient fluxes between underground and surface systems. Most are contradictory, probably because of the geoclimatic area in which each ecotone is situated. We must seek a general theory that takes into account these factors, together with some others. As for animals, studies that have described the density and diversity occurring in these ecotones are still relatively recent, and many questions remain to be answered concerning influences that act to determine the community structure and dynamics.

Finally, studies of these ecotones must also focus on the impact of human activity (e.g. dams, recreational areas, irrigation) on the surface environment and, to a lesser degree, on the underground environment. These activities lead to modifications, which may or may not be permanent, of the corresponding ecotone. How then are we to protect ecotones, especially those that play a role in the homeostasis of surface ecosystems or those that contribute to the quality of the underground water used for domestic consumption by acting as barriers to pollutants? This research should lead to a policy for the restoration and management of ecotones.

ACKNOWLEDGEMENTS

We thank our friends and colleagues of the Underground Hydrobiology and Ecology Laboratory: J. Carrillo, M. Creuze des Chatelliers, R. Ginet, D. Martin, J. Mathieu, R. Laurent, J.L. Reygrobellet, and M.J. Turquin for contributing their time and discussions, and G. Thoiron for editing the English text. We are grateful to D. Danielopol (Austria), H. Décamps (France), R.J. Naiman (USA), and J.A. Stanford (USA) for critical review of this manuscript.

LITERATURE CITED

Adams, M.S., and R.T. Prentki. 1982. Biology, metabolism and function of littoral submersed weedbeds of Lake Wingra, Wisconsin, USA: a summary and review. Archiv für Hydrobiologie, Supplement 62:334-409.

Amoros, C., J.C. Rostan, G. Pautou, and J.P. Bravard. 1987a. The reversible process concept applied to the environmental management of large river systems. Environmental Management 11:607-617.

Amoros, C., and A.L. Roux. 1988. Interactions between water bodies within the floodplains of large rivers: function and development of connectivity. Munstersche Geogr. Arbeiten 29:125-130.

Amoros, C., A.L. Roux, J.L. Reygrobellet, J.P. Bravard, and G. Pautou. 1987b. A method for applied ecological studies of fluvial hydrosystems. Regulated Rivers 1:17-36.

Aragno, M., and I. Müller. 1982. Premières expériences de traçages des eaux souterraines dans le karst du jura neuchâtelois (Suisse) à l'aide de bactériophages. Bulletin du Centre d'Hydrogéologie, Neuchâtel 4:41-58.

Bishop, J.E. 1973. Observations on the vertical distribution of the benthos in a Malaysian stream. Freshwater Biology 3:147-156.

Blandin, P. 1986. Bioindicateurs et diagnostic des systèmes écologiques. Bulletin d'Ecologie 17:215-307.

Bournaud, M., and C. Amoros. 1984. Des indicateurs biologiques aux descripteurs de fonctionnement: quelques exemples dans un système fluvial. Bulletin d'Ecologie 15:57-66.

Bravard, J.P., C. Amoros, and G. Pautou. 1986. Impact of civil engineering works on the succession of communities in a fluvial system: a methodological and predictive approach applied to a section of the upper Rhône River, France. Oikos 47:92-111.

Bretschko, G. 1981. Vertical distribution of zoobenthos in an Alpine brook of the Ritrodat-Lunz study area. Verhandlungen Internationale Vereinigung Limnologie 21:873-876.

Bretschko, G. 1983. Die Biozönosen der Bettsedimente von Fließgewassern ein Beitrag der Limnologie zur naturnahen Gewässerregulierung. Wasserwirtschaft, Wasservorsorge, Forschungsarbeiten Bundesministerium für Land und Forestwirtschaften, Vienna, Austria.

Bretschko, G., and M. Leichtfried. 1988. Distribution of organic matter and fauna in a second order, alpine gravel stream (Ritrodat-Lunz study area, Austria). Verhandlungen Internationale Vereinigung Limnologie, 23:1333-1339.

Capone, D.G., and M.F. Baustista. 1985. A groundwater source of nitrate in nearshore marine sediments. Nature 313:214-216.

Carbiener, R., and E. Kapp. 1981. La végétation à *Potamogeton coloratus* Vahl, phytocénose oligotrophe très menacée des rivières phréatiques du Ried d'Alsace. Bericht International Symposium Cramer, Vaduz 585-600.

Carignan, R. 1982. An empirical model to estimate the relative importance of roots in phosphorus uptake by aquatic macrophytes. Canadian Journal of Fisheries and Aquatic Sciences 39:243-247.

Castany, G. 1982. Principes et méthodes de l'hydrogéologie. Editeur Dunod Université, Paris, France.

Castany, G. 1985. Liaisons hydrauliques entre les aquifères et les cours d'eau. Système global aquifère-rivière. Stygologia 1:1-25.

Castella, C., and C. Amoros. 1984. Répartition des Characées dans les bras morts du Haut-Rhône et de l'Ain et signification écologique. Cryptogamie, Algologie 2-3:127-139.

Castella, E. 1987. Apport des macroinvertébrés aquatiques au diagnostic écologique des écosystèmes abandonnés par les fleuves. Recherche méthodologique sur le Haut-Rhône français. Dissertation. Université Lyon I, Lyon, France. Volume 1 (2 volumes).

Chen, R.L., and D.R. Keeney. 1974. The fate of nitrate in lake sediment columns. Water Resources Bulletin 10:1162-1172.

Culver, D.C. 1982. Cave life: evolution and ecology. Harvard University Press, Cambridge, Massachusetts, USA, and London, England.

Dahm, C.N., D.L. Carr, and R.L. Coleman. 1988. Interactions between anaerobic hyporheic zones and processes and benthic microbial activity. Summary in Bulletin of the North American Benthological Society 5:79.

Danielopol, D.L. 1976. The distribution of the fauna in the interstitial habitats of riverine sediments of the Danube and the Piesting (Austria). International Journal of Speleology 8:23-51.

Danielopol, D.L. 1983. Der Einfluß Organischer Verschmutzung auf das Grundwasser-okosystem der Donau im raum Wien und Niederosterreich. Bundesministerium für Gesumdheit und Umweltschutz. Wein, Forschungberichte 5:5-160.

Danielopol, D.L. 1984. Ecological investigations on the alluvial sediments of the Danube in the Vienna area: a phreatobiological project. Verhandlungen Internationale Vereinigung Limnologie 22:1755-1761.

Décamps, H., and H. Laville. 1975. Invertébrés et matières organiques entraînés lors des crues à l'entrée et à la sortie du système karstique du Baget. Annales de Limnologie 11:287-296.

Décamps, H., and R. Rouch. 1973. Recherches sur les eaux souterraines. Le système karstique du Baget. I. Premières estimations sur la dérive des invertébrés aquatiques d'origine épigée. Annales de Spéléologie 28:89-110.

Dole, M.J. 1983. Le domaine aquatique souterrain de la plaine alluviale du Rhône à l'est de Lyon: écologie des niveaux supérieurs de la nappe. Dissertation. Université Lyon I, Lyon, France.

Dole, M.J. 1985. Le domaine aquatique souterrain de la plaine alluviale du Rhône à l'est de

Lyon. 2. Structure verticale des peuplements des niveaux supérieurs de la nappe. Stygologia 1:270-291.

Dole, M.J., and D. Chessel. 1986. Stabilité physique et biologique des milieux interstitiels: cas de deux stations du Haut-Rhône. Annales de Limnologie 22:69-81.

Fisher, S.G., and G.E. Likens. 1973. Energy flow in Bear Brook, New Hampshire: an integrative approach to stream ecosystem metabolism. Ecological Monographs 43:421-439.

Fogg, G.E. 1986. Groundwater flow and sand body interconnectedness in a thick multiple-aquifer system. Water Resources Research 22:679-694.

Fontvieille, D. 1987. La circulation du carbone organique dans les écosystèmes lotiques: cas du phénomène d'autoépuration. Dissertation. Université Lyon I, Lyon, France.

Ford, T.E., and R.J. Naiman. 1989. Groundwater-surface water relationships in boreal forest watersheds: dissolved organic carbon and inorganic nutrient dynamics. Canadian Journal of Fisheries and Aquatic Sciences 46:41-49.

Forman, R.T.T., and M. Godron. 1986. Landscape ecology. John Wiley and Sons, New York, USA.

Freeze, R.A., and J.A. Cherry. 1979. Groundwater. Prentice-Hall, Englewood Cliffs, New Jersey, USA.

Gaschignard-Fossati, O. 1986. Répartition spatiale des macroinvertébrés benthiques d'un bras vif du Rhône: rôle des crues et dynamique saisonnière. Dissertation. Université Lyon I, Lyon, France.

Gibert, J. 1986. Ecologie d'un système karstique jurassien: hydrogéologie, dérive animale, transits de matières, dynamique de la population de *Niphargus* (Crustacé Amphipode). Mémoires de Biospéologie, Moulis 13:379.

Gibert, J. 1988. Functional sub-units of an exsurgence karstic system, and exchanges with the surface environment: reflections on the characterization of natural aquatic groundwater ecosytems. Verhandlungen Internationale Vereinigung Limnologie, 23:1090-1096.

Gibert, J., R. Ginet, J. Mathieu, J.L. Reygrobellet, and A. Seyed-Reihani. 1977. Structure et fonctionnement des écosystèmes du Haut-Rhône français. IV. Le peuplement des eaux phréatiques: premiers résultats. Annales de Limnologie 13:83-97.

Hansen, A.J., F. di Castri, and R.J. Naiman. 1988. Ecotones: what and why? Biology International, Special Issue 17:9-46.

Holland, M.M. 1988. SCOPE/MAB technical consultations on landscape boundaries: report of a SCOPE/MAB workshop on ecotones. Biology International, Special Issue 17:47-106.

Holland, M.M., D.F. Whigham, and B. Gopal. 1990. The characteristics of wetland ecotones, *this volume*.

Husmann, S. 1975. The boreoalpine distribution of groundwater organisms in Europe. Verhandlungen Internationale Vereinigung Limnologie 19:2983-2988.

Hynes, H.B.N. 1983. Groundwater and stream ecology. Hydrobiologia 100:93-99.

Jansson, M. 1980. Role of benthic algae in transport of nitrogen from sediment to lake water in a shallow clear water lake. Archiv für Hydrobiologie 89:101-109.

Johnston, C.A., and R.J. Naiman. 1987. Boundary dynamics at the aquatic-terrestrial interface: the influence of beaver and geomorphology. Landscape Ecology 1:47-57.

Kaplan, L.A., R.A. Larson, and T.L. Bott. 1980. Patterns of dissolved organic carbon in transport. Limnology and Oceanography 25:1035-1043.

Leichtfried, M. 1985. Organic matter in gravel-streams. Verhandlungen Internationale Vereinigung Limnologie 22:2058-2062.

Leopold, A. 1933. Game management. Charles Scribner's Sons, New York, USA.

Magniez, G. 1974. Observations sur *Stenasellus virei* dans ses biotopes naturels (Crustacea, Isopoda, Asellota des eaux souterraines). International Journal of Speleology 6:115-172.

Maire, R. 1981. Giant shafts and underground rivers of the Nakanai mountains (New Britain). Spelunca, Supplément 3:8-9.

Marmonier, P. 1988. Biocénoses interstitielles et circulation des eaux dans le sous-écoulement d'un chenal aménagé du Haut-Rhône français. Dissertation. Université Lyon I, Lyon, France.

Marmonier, P., and M.J. Dole. 1986. Les Amphipodes des sédiments d'un bras court-circuité du Rhône: logique de répartition et réaction aux crues. Sciences de l'Eau 5:461-486.

Mathieu, J., D. Debouzie, and D. Martin. 1987. Influence des conditions hydrologiques sur la dynamique d'une population phréatique de *Niphargus rhenorhodanensis* (Amphipode

223

Gammaridé souterrain). Vie et Milieu 37:193-200.

Meentemeyer, V., and E.O. Box. 1987. Scale effects in landscape studies. Pages 15-34 *in* M.G. Turner, editor. Landscape heterogeneity and disturbance. Springer-Verlag, New York, USA.

Merriam, G. 1984. Connectivity: a fundamental ecological characteristic of landscape pattern. Proceedings of the International Association of Landscape Ecology 1:5-15.

Mestrov, M., and R. Lattinger-Penko. 1977-78. Ecological investigations of the influence of a polluted river on surrounding interstitial underground waters. International Journal of Speleology 9:331-335.

Moeschler, P. 1982. Traçage des eaux souterraines dans le karst Neuchâtelois à l'aide d'éléments aquatiques d'origine épigée. Bulletin du Centre d'Hydrogéologie, Neuchâtel 4:41-58.

Naiman, R.J., H. Décamps, J. Pastor, and C.A. Johnston. 1988*a*. The potential importance of boundaries to fluvial ecosystems. Journal of the North American Benthological Society 7:289-306.

Naiman, R.J., M.M. Holland, H. Décamps, and P.G. Risser. 1988*b*. A new Unesco programme: research and management of land/inland water ecotones. Biology International, Special Issue 17:107-136.

Naiman, R.J., J.M. Melillo, M.A. Lock, T.E. Ford, and S.R. Reice. 1987. Longitudinal patterns of ecosystem processes and community structure in a subarctic river continuum. Ecology 68:1139-1156.

Odum, W.E. 1990. Internal processes influencing the maintenance of ecotones: do they exist?, *this volume*.

Pennak, R., and J. Ward. 1986. Interstitial fauna communities of the hyporheic and adjacent groundwater biotopes of a Colorado mountain stream. Archiv für Hydrobiologie, Supplement 74:356-396.

Peterjohn, W.T., and D.L. Correll. 1984. Nutrient dynamics in an agricultural watershed: observations on the role of a riparian forest. Ecology 65:1466-1475.

Pickett, S.T.A., and P.S. White. 1985. Patch dynamics: a synthesis. Pages 371-384 *in* S.T.A. Pickett and P.S. White, editors. The ecology of natural disturbance and patch dynamics. Academic Press, Orlando, Florida, USA.

Pieczyńska, E. 1990. Lentic aquatic-terrestrial ecotones, *this volume*.

Pinay, G., and H. Décamps. 1988. The role of riparian woods in regulating nitrogen fluxes between the alluvial aquifer and surface water: a conceptual model. Regulated Rivers 2:507-516.

Pinay, G., Décamps, E. Chauvet, and E. Fustec. 1990. Functions of ecotones in fluvial systems, *this volume*.

Poole, W.C., and K.W. Stewart. 1976. The vertical distribution of macrobenthos within the substratum of the Brazos River, Texas. Hydrobiologia 50:151-160.

Priscu, J.C., and M.T. Downes. 1987. Microbial activity in the surficial sediments of an oligotrophic and eutrophic lake, with particular reference to dissimilatory nitrate reduction. Archiv für Hydrobiologie 108:151-160.

Richoux, P., and J.L. Reygrobellet. 1986. First report on the ecology of the phreatic water beetle *Siettitia avenionensis* Guignot (Coleoptera, Dytiscidae). Entomologica Basiliensia 11:371-384.

Rouch, R. 1980. Le système karstique du Baget. X. La communauté des Harpacticides: richesse spécifique, diversité et structures d'abondances de la nomocénose hypogée. Annales de Limnologie 16:1-20.

Rouch, R., and D.L. Danielopol. 1987. L'origine de la faune aquatique souterraine, entre le paradigme du refuge et le modèle de la colonisation active. Stygologia 3:345-372.

Rutherford, J.E., and H.B.N. Hynes. 1987. Dissolved organic carbon in streams and groundwater. Hydrobiologia 154:33-48.

Salomons, W., N.M. de Rooij, H. Kerdijk, and J. Bril. 1987. Sediments as a source for contaminants? Hydrobiologia 149:13-30.

Stanford, J.A., and J.V. Ward. 1988. The hyporheic habitat of river ecosystems. Nature 335:64-66.

Stenbergen, C.L.M., and H. Verdouw. 1984. Carbon mineralization in microaerobic and anaerobic strata of Lake Vechten (The Netherlands): diffusion flux calculations and sedimentation measurements. Archiv für Hydrobiologie 19:183-190.

Unesco. 1978. World water balance and water resources of the earth. U.S.S.R. Communication for the International Hydrological Decade. Studies and Report in Hydrology 25, Paris, France.

Unesco. 1980. Surface water and groundwater interaction. Studies and Report in Hydrology 29, Paris, France.

Vanek, V. 1987. The interactions between lake and groundwater and their ecological significance. Stygologia 3:1-23.

Vervier, P. 1988. Hydrologie et dynamique des peuplements aquatiques souterrains: comparaison de deux systèmes karstiques des gorges de l'Ardèche. Dissertation. Université Lyon I, Lyon, France.

Vervier, P., J. Gibert, R. Laurent, and A. Couturaud. 1986. Plongée souterraine et hydrobiologie dans la Source Bleue, Montperreux, Doubs: utilisation de substrats artificiels pour étudier la faune des réseaux noyés. Spelunca 22:37-42.

Von Gunten, H.R., and T.P. Kull. 1986. Infiltration of inorganic compounds from the Glatt River, Switzerland, into a groundwater aquifer. Water, Air and Soil Pollution 29:333-346.

Wallis, P.M., H.B.N. Hynes, and S.A. Telang. 1981. The importance of groundwater in the transportation of allochthonous dissolved organic matter to the streams draining a small mountain basin. Hydrobiologia 79:77-90.

Wetzel, R.G. 1983. Limnology. Saunders College Publishing, Philadelphia, Pennsylvania, USA.

White, P.S., C. Elzinga, and S. Hendricks. 1987. Temperature patterns within the hyporheic zone of a northern Michigan river. Journal of the North American Benthological Society 6:85-91.

Wiens, J.A., C.S. Crawford, and J.R. Gosz. 1985. Boundary dynamics: a conceptual framework for studying landscape ecosystems. Oikos 45:421-427.

Williams, D.D., and H.B.N. Hynes. 1974. The occurrence of benthos deep in the substratum of a stream. Freshwater Biology 4:233-256.

Wissmar, R.C., M.D. Lilley, and M. de Angelis. 1987. Nitrous oxide release from aerobic riverine deposits. Journal of Freshwater Ecology 4:209-218.

Key words: Biodiversity, connectivity, ecotone, elasticity, groundwater-surface water interaction, permeability.

CHAPTER 11

THE ROLE OF ECOTONES IN AQUATIC LANDSCAPE MANAGEMENT

Geoffrey E. Petts

ABSTRACT

Ecotones at the land-water interface are fundamental components of aquatic landscapes, varying from narrow strips to broad wetlands. They have been classified according to the determining hydrological and geomorphological processes. Each has a diverse fauna and flora, playing important roles in the functioning of the adjacent terrestrial and aquatic systems. An ecotone is in quasi-equilibrium with the adjacent systems and is adjusted to a particular pattern of disturbance. Over the past 300 years, man has destroyed these ecotones to 'improve' aquatic systems for navigation and flood control, and terrestrial systems for agriculture. Ecotones have been modified indirectly by land use change and river regulation. This destruction is continuing today in developing countries.

This chapter proposes that aquatic landscape management will benefit from maintaining and restoring land-water ecotones because of their value for conserving biota, their visual quality, and their potential values for water quality control and as early indicators of environmental change. The approach, based on the 'best practicable environmental option,' focusses on two scales. First, management should seek to provide the magnitude, frequency, and duration of flows necessary to sustain the ecotone. Secondly engineering works, controls on human activities, and controls on biota are also advocated, particularly to manage patches within the ecotone. However, a number of needs are identified for management to be effective. The most important of these is to specify the minimum sizes of sustainable ecotones and their critical hydrogeomorphological processes. These would also facilitate the development of vulnerability maps to improve the scientific basis of impact assessment and management.

227

INTRODUCTION

'If landscape boundaries are important in influencing ecological flows and biodiversity, and human actions are dramatically altering these boundaries, then management actions are clearly desirable,' wrote Hansen *et al.* (1988:25). The landscape boundaries, especially the land-water interface have been the focus for the socio-economic development of civilisations. For 5000 years, man has sought to confine the spatial dimensions of this interface and to control its hydrogeomorphological dynamics. The great ancient civilisations of Egypt, Mesopotamia, and Indo-China were all founded here. Rivers and lakes supply water and provide routeways for navigation, their freshwater fisheries are a traditional resource, and their floodplains and lake deltas provide soils for agriculture. Rivers also provide for power production. Increasingly, aquatic landscapes are seen as social and ecological resources providing for recreation and conservation.

The structure and function of the dynamic boundary between terrestrial and aquatic systems are determined by hydrological, geomorphological, and biogeochemical processes – processes that are conditioned by the catchment ecobiome (Petts and Foster 1985). Thus the land-water interface has been modified in two ways. Direct modifications relate to flood control, navigation improvement, and land reclamation. Indirect changes have resulted from land-use changes and discharges of waste products within the drainage basin.

In aquatic landscape management, this decade has witnessed two important developments. First, it is now clear that sustainable economic development is *dependent* on sound environmental management (Sewell and Biswas 1986). During the past 10 years, there has evolved a greater awareness of the problems of water and land resource development for freshwater ecosystems (Welcomme 1979, Petts 1984, Davies and Walker 1986). With this has come a recognition of the urgency needed in managing the land-water interface. Secondly, it is now recognised that abiotic factors must be managed if biota are to be conserved (Petts 1984).

As noted by Legendre and Demers (1984), this decade has been characterised by the recognition that biological processes within aquatic systems are driven by hydrodynamic forces. Certain developments have served to direct attention to the need for management to focus in the first instance on these hydrodynamic forces rather than on their biological effects: the application of hierarchical frameworks in assessing impacts (Petts 1980, 1984) and evaluating management options (Petts 1989), and the recognition that transient states are an intrinsic component of natural and man-impacted systems (Petts 1987).

Aquatic landscape management involves the maintenance and enhancement of natural systems and the restoration of man-modified systems to their natural state. This article has three objectives: to discuss how

228

an improved knowledge of ecotones can advance aquatic landscape management, to review the effects of past and present management practices on land-water ecotones, and to discuss environmentally sound alternatives for managing ecotones in the context of sustainable water resource development.

ECOTONES IN AQUATIC LANDSCAPES

A landscape may be viewed as a mosaic of patches. Each patch has particular composition with peculiar origin and dynamics, size, and shape, and spatial continuity or connectivity (Forman and Godron 1981). Every landscape contains a recognisable and repeated size hierarchy of patches. Patch dynamics are measured by the flux of energy, sediments and nutrients, and biological populations. These fluxes are influenced by, and to a large degree determine, the character of the dynamic interpatch boundary or *ecotone*. The definition of ecotone used in this article is that given by Holland (1988:60): 'An ecotone is a zone of transition between adjacent ecological systems, having a set of characteristics uniquely defined by space and time scales and by the strength of the interactions between adjacent ecological systems.'

Distinguishing between ecotone and patch has caused much debate. At the microscale it is easy to conceive of an ecotone as a membrane of a little thickness acting as a regulator of energy and nutrient fluxes. The distinction between ecotones and patches becomes less clear as the boundary becomes wider. Furthermore, the definition of a patch changes relative to the size of organisms living within it. Many patches, such as floating vegetation or a floodplain pool, have considerable gradients across themselves, as well as at their margins. Nevertheless, the definition of an ecotone may be clarified by specification of appropriate scales of observation.

Hydrodynamic controls of land-water ecotones

For aquatic landscape management, the above definition may be elaborated by considering the determining hydrodynamic forces, rather than structural or biological characteristics. Consider that the land-water ecotone is the transitional zone between primary lotic or lentic systems and the adjacent terrestrial system. Within the ecotone, allogenic processes dominate. This contrasts with most autogenic process-dominated terrestrial systems (Décamps *et al.* 1988).

Land-water ecotones are influenced to a greater or lesser degree by four types of disturbance: inundation, desiccation, sedimentation, and erosion. The interaction of these processes creates heterogeneity within the ecotone and its structure relates to the magnitude and frequency distribution of fluvial processes. These reflect the hydrological regime and geomorphological dynamics of the river, which are determined fundamentally by climate, geology, drainage basin size, and valley slope.

Most ecotones are adjusted to hydrogeomorphic events with frequencies of up to about once in 10 or 20 years. However, rarer, higher magnitude events may be important also. The long-term significance of such extreme events varies with geographical region (Wolman and Gerson 1978) and with the stage of landscape evolution (Schumm 1977). Beyond the limits of the ecotone, the terrestrial or aquatic systems may be perturbed by a flood or drought, but in either case the system recovery period is usually shorter than the return period of the event and the perturbation has no long-term effect on the system.

This defines the land-water ecotone in a condition of quasi-equilibrium. Dynamic hydrochemical gradients exist across the ecotone. Patches within the ecotone evolve and succeed at different rates from terrestrial ones. The distribution of patches within the ecotone changes and the boundaries of the ecotone move. Parts of the ecotone are destroyed more or less frequently by fluvial processes, but these are replaced by the new, 'juvenile' forms. Consequently, the overall patch diversity remains unchanged over a time scale of 10^2 yr and a dynamic balance is maintained.

Classification of land-water ecotones

At the macroscale, each ecotone is characterised by a vertical zonation related to flow variability. An excellent example of this, for the Garonne River, France, is given by Décamps *et al.* (1988). This zonation is superimposed on a mosaic of substrate patches of different ages and sediment composition which reflect the historic pattern of erosion and deposition. Around a lake the ecotone forms a fringing zone expanding to cover several 1000 km^2 in deltaic areas. Lake morphometry and water level variability are controlling factors. Along a river the ecotone forms a dynamic corridor of variable width. In its most restricted form the ecotone equates with a narrow riparian zone. The ecotone bordering alluvial rivers is the active, seasonally inundated floodplain, which, for tropical rivers in particular, may extend for 10 km or more on either side of the channel. A classification of land-river ecotones is presented in Fig. 11.1.

The geomorphological dynamics of land-river ecotones reflect both the upstream-downstream gradient of fluvial processes and the geographical setting (Naiman *et al.* 1988a, Pinay *et al.* 1990). In the headwaters, the ecotone forms a narrow riparian zone determined by both hillslope hydrology and channel flow variability. Along streams greater than 4th order, valley widening weakens the relationship between hillslope and channel. Downstream, the ecotone, manifested by the active floodplain, becomes increasingly dominated by fluvial processes and reflects the balance between stream power and sediment load. Canyon rivers are a special case. Three general types of alluvial river may be defined (Petts and Foster 1985).

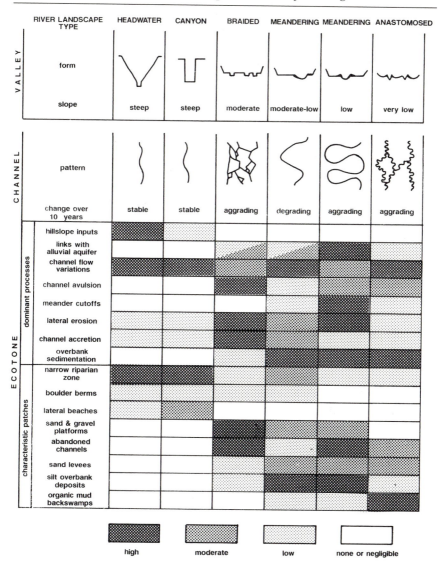

Figure 11.1 A classification of river-land ecotones. (A) General scheme based on geomorpho-logical setting. (B) Hydrogeomorphological characteristics of the ecotones

Land-river ecotones of high-energy braided rivers are particularly dynamic, being affected by rapid lateral erosion and frequent channel avulsion (Salo 1990). Multi-thread anastomosed rivers, associated with very low energy environments, are characterised by lateral stability, but channel avulsion is common. However, their ecotones are determined by the frequency and duration of inundation; 60 to 90% of the ecotone can be backswamp. Meandering channels form intermediate types of ecotone

231

which may be dominated by channel migration and avulsion, lateral floodplain accretion, overbank sedimentation, or the character of floodplain inundation. Along very active rivers, the ecotone may incorporate many abandoned channels filled to a greater or lesser degree with fine sediments. In reality, of course, land-river ecotones represent a continuum of morphological types.

An ecotone's characteristics reflect not only the present-day process dynamics of the adjacent aquatic and terrestrial systems but also their long-term evolution over time scales measured in 10^2-10^5 years. The influence of the Pleistocene glaciations, for example, is clearly seen in the latitudinal gradient of ecotones (Naiman *et al.* 1988a). Thus land-water ecotones today are determined by hydrology and geomorphology, constrained by the historic legacy of former conditions and modified by biological interactions.

Role of ecotones in aquatic landscapes

Managers react cautiously to expanding terminologies and multiplication of jargon. Therefore, it is pertinent here to examine in more detail how advances in specific knowledge of ecotones might contribute to the development of management strategies for aquatic landscapes. Traditionally, management has focussed on patches. Conservation has been concerned primarily with the preservation of species within patches by defining more or less artificial boundaries around them. Scientists have sought to define laws related to intrapatch dynamics emphasising genetic, structural, and functional similarities between patches, and often reinforcing the need for reductionist studies. This focus has hindered scientific advance towards understanding water management problems.

The role of the ecotone concept in management is to focus attention on the transitional zone, or dynamic boundary, at the land-water interface. This is important for two reasons. First, the ecotone concept emphasises the ways in which patch management will affect ecotones and adjacent patches, because impacts may be buffered or magnified by the ecotone. Secondly, the concept is holistic and requires for its understanding multidisciplinary and long-term perspectives. Ecotones are especially important in aquatic landscapes (Table 11.1) and should receive particular attention in management plans.

Biological diversity

Ecotones have an environment significantly different from the interior of the adjacent patches, with a different species composition and abundance. Typically the ecotone has a high biological diversity and may provide favourable sites for species dispersion, enabling the rapid colonisation of patches created by disturbance (Risser 1990). Consequently, ecotones have a great importance for maintaining biological diversity and the global gene pool.

232

Table 11.1 Characteristics of ecotones that may have significance for aquatic landscape management

ECOTONES PROVIDE UNIQUE HABITATS FOR BIOTA

High Biological Diversity
    Alluvial forests (Robertson *et al.* 1978, Salo *et al.* 1986, Amoros *et al.* 1987)
    Fish (Welcomme 1979, Bailey 1986, Petrere 1988)
    Animals (Attwell 1970, Davies 1986, Rosenberg 1988)
    Birds (Kellerhals and Gill 1973, Frith 1977, Décamps *et al.* 1987)

High Biological Productivity
    Wetland forests (Mitsch *et al.* 1979, Bren 1989)
    Fisheries (Welcomme 1979, Lowe-McConnell 1986, Petrere 1989)
    Birds (Frith 1977, Welcomme 1979)

Sources for Species Dispersal to New Patches (Ecotones)
    (Naiman *et al.* 1988a, b)

ECOTONES REGULATE INTERPATCH DYNAMICS

Contribute organic matter to aquatic system (Cuffney 1988, Karr and Schlosser 1978, Sedell and Froggatt 1984, Triska 1984, Stanford and Ward 1986, Lowe-McConnell 1986)

Provide nutrients sinks for agricultural runoff (Karr and Schlosser 1978, Omernik *et al.* 1981, Peterjohn and Correll 1984, Yates and Sheridan 1983, Pinay and Décamps 1988)

Influence movement and migration of birds and mammals (Johnston and Naiman 1987, Décamps *et al.* 1988)

ECOTONES MAY PROVIDE INDICATORS OF HYDROCLIMATIC CHANGE

Interface systems between process domains are particularly sensitive to external controls and may be useful indicators of environmental impacts (Stockton and Fritts 1973, Johnson and Bell 1976a, Mitsch *et al.* 1979, Williams 1978, Turner and Karpiscak 1980, Reilly and Johnson 1982, Grelsson 1988)

ECOTONES HAVE STRONG VISUAL QUALITY

Create colour, variety, and distinctive images (Shuttleworth 1983, Dearden 1987)
Create both prospect and refuge images (Appleton 1975)
Provide wilderness experience (Martin and Inglis 1984)

Land-water ecotones contain a particularly diverse range of habitats. These reflect the mosaic of resource and disturbance patches of different age and successional stages. Over time, the botanical character of an ecotone evolves to reflect the regional vegetation type, site characteristics, and the activity of herbivores (Ranney *et al.* 1981).

Floods and droughts are fundamental components of the system to which many biological populations are adapted and on which some are dependent. In semi-arid regions, tree growth, for example, is intimately related to the hydrological regime (Everitt 1968); and in humid environments, flooding may be responsible for the distribution of species according to their flood tolerance (Robertson *et al.* 1978). Flooding is necessary to maintain adequate growth and regeneration of red gum (*Eucalyptus camaldulensis*) forests along the Murray River, Australia (Bren 1988), and cypress (*Taxodium* spp). wetlands in the central and southeastern USA (Mitsch *et al.* 1979, Mitsch and Ewel 1979, Brown 1981). Mitsch and Rust (1984) emphasise that flooding reduces competition from less water-tolerant species, while Bren (1988) demonstrates that a secondary effect of flooding in the Murray River floodplain is to keep populations of leaf-defoliating moths at low densities and to prevent the invasion of introduced species.

Topographic differences determining local variations in flood frequency and duration produce vegetation zones. The lower limit of lichens (Gregory 1976), herbs and forbs (Leopold and Skibitzke 1967), and trees (Sigafoos 1964) have been related to water level. Vegetation zones form a continuum of patches within the riparian forest; the boundary between each patch may be transitional or abrupt, reflecting species tolerances for moisture conditions. Furthermore, the maintenance of critical soil moisture levels during the growing season gives rise to high productivity in alluvial forests; higher or lower moisture values inhibit growth. This applies also to lake margins (Kozlowski 1982, Grelsson 1988).

Resource patches are defined not only by inundation characteristics (i.e. elevation) but also by the permeability of the sediments and soils. Thus, Robertson *et al.* (1978) defined three resource patches that characterise the ecotone of the southern Mississippi River, USA (Table 11.2). Décamps *et al.* (1988) describe a similar structure for the Garonne River ecotone, France. Soil fertility is a secondary factor (Johnson and Bell 1976a, b). Inputs of nutrients or nutrient-laden sediments in floodwaters are also important. However, the role of the soil may be related to the chemical changes that occur in flooded soils, notably the availability of micronutrients, including N, Fe, Mn, and Cu.

It has long been established that habitat diversity within land-water ecotones is related to the regular and repeated rejuvenation of successions associated with disturbance. Channel migration, avulsion, and deposition

Table 11.2 Resource patches of a natural bottomland forest ecotone of the southern Mississippi River, USA. After Robertson *et al.* (1978)

Characteristic	Patch A	Patch B	Patch C
Relative elevation	Highest	Intermediate	Lowest
Flooding	Infrequent	Short duration each year	Several months each year
Soil texture	Sandy	Silty-clayey	Clayey
Soil drainage	Good	Poor	Very poor
Vegetation	*Acer saccharum*	*Quercus michauxii*	*Acer rubrum*
	Ulmus rubra	*Q. muhlenhergii*	*Fraximus pennsylvanica*
	Quercus rubra	*Q. pagodaefolia*	
	Tilia americana	*Q. shumardii*	
	Asimina triloba	*Asimina triloba*	
	Liquidambar	*Liquidambar*	*Liquidambar*
	styraciflora	*styraciflora*	*styraciflora*
		Ulmus americana	*Ulmus americana*

are clearly important in this context. For example, fluvial erosion causing trees to fall into the river exposes an interior patch rejuvenating the 'edge' (Shugart 1990). The mobility of the river channel is reflected in the age structure of trees (Everitt 1968) and biological diversity (Amoros *et al.* 1987) of the alluvial plain. Thus, Salo (1990) and Salo *et al.* (1986) showed that along the upper Amazon River in Peru, channel dynamics play a major role in creating and maintaining high biological diversity within the ecotone.

Fisheries

Most natural floodplain rivers have diverse and abundant fish faunas supporting rich inland fisheries (Welcomme 1979). Seasonally inundated alluvial plains provide a rich mosaic of habitats for fish. In any one year recruitment, growth, and survival are correlated with the flooded area. Fringing vegetation and floating islands of vegetation shelter juvenile fish or small, characteristically vegetation-dwelling species. Many species are adapted to spawn in this ecotone during the flood season while others are dependent on the annual inundation for food. Within the ecotone, abandoned channels have high primary production and, when remaining in permanent contact with the main river, provide important shelters for fishes from the main stream during floods.

In tropical rain forests, a wide variety of fish depend on the annual inundation of the floodplain forest ecotone. Bailey (1986) stresses the value of inundation zones in maintaining the fish diversity and productivity of the Zaire River, central Africa. In the lower Mekong River, Southeast Asia, a number of species of carp and catfish spawn and rear young in the inundated zones (Pantulu 1986). Here also the annual flooding of lakes within the ecotonal alluvial forest provides an important allochthonous organic matter input, maintaining highly productive freshwater fisheries. Within the central basin of the Amazon River, Brazil, allochthonous forest foods are the main diet for fish, enabling these rivers to carry much higher fish populations than might be expected from their lack of autochthonous primary production (Lowe-McConnell 1986).

Flooded meadows, such as those that seasonally cover many of the world's savanna areas, also contain a variety of habitats related to subtle variations of relief, and provide important fish habitats (Welcomme 1979). The margins of the ecotone are usually colonised by young fish, but the floodplain pools provide both seasonal and permanent habitats for many species. In scrubland, the submerged branches and roots provide additional feeding substrates and shelter.

Vertebrates other than fish

Seasonally inundated grassland floodplains provide valuable habitat to many herbivores (and their predators) which utilise these areas in large numbers, their grazing being facilitated by the slow but continuous uncovering of nutritious herbage as floodwaters retreat during the dry season. Thus, along the Zambezi River in Zimbabwe, before flow regulation, the floodplain with its residual pools was inundated each year to a depth of 5 m; silts and nutrients were deposited; and stagnant pools were flushed. At the same time, herbivores were driven off, so that aided by waterborne seed disperal, the vegetation could recover from the intense grazing pressure to which it was subjected during the dry season (Attwell 1970).

Ecotones are especially important for amphibians, which are usually abundant along rivers and on natural floodplains, especially around floodplain lakes and pools, as are several reptile groups – crocodiles, monitors, iguanas, and turtles. Along the Murray River, Australia, for example, the long-necked tortoise (*Chelodina longicollis*) prefers swampland and floodplain environments, and several species of frog are restricted to the river corridors (Walker 1986). Of the mammals that depend on the land-water interface, the otter (*Lutra lutra*) and *Hippopotamus* have received greatest attention, being widespread along natural river systems. The water buffalo (*Syncerus caffer*) once thrived on the floodplain areas along the Zambezi River (Davies 1986). In the MacKenzie River delta, Canada, aquatic fur-bearing mammals depend on the spring flood, which maintains high biological productivity in alluvial habitats (Rosenberg 1986). Here, the beaver (*Castor canadensis*) feed on willow (*Salix*), balsam poplar (*Populus balsamifera*), and alder (*Alnus crispa*). In the absence of normal flooding and siltation these communities would be replaced by white spruce (*Picea glauca*), which is not used by beaver.

Birds are a particularly conspicuous feature of the land-water interface. The life cycle of many species is closely linked to floods (Welcomme 1979). Fledgelings are often reared at the time when small fish are most abundant during the receding flood, for example. In inland Australia, the billabongs (oxbow lakes) are of extreme importance to many waterfowl, as is the annual flood regime with which breeding is synchronised (Frith 1977). Riparian habitats in northern Canada are especially important for waterfowl during drought years, when they provide sanctuary and breeding ground for large numbers of birds from the prairies to the south (Kellerhals and Gill 1973).

In confined rivers the riparian corridor is very narrow but the land-water interface is nonetheless important for wildlife. Indeed, Stanford and Ward (1986) consider that although limited in area, the longitudinally and locally variable riverbank and lakeshore vegetation is an important part of the biophysiography of the American Southwest. Along the Colorado River, for example, the ecotone provides organic matter for the river communities and cover and forage area for birds and other wildlife in an otherwise arid area. Indeed, Décamps *et al.* (1987) demonstrate that even a narrow woodland corridor can have considerable value for both sedentary and migratory birds, not least by providing access routes for new colonisers to island woods on the hillslopes.

Nutrient regulation

Ecotones appear to regulate patch dynamics by controlling the import of energy and matter from adjacent patches. During the past decade, the importance of the land-water interface in regulating water quality in agricultural watersheds has been demonstrated. Karr and Schlosser (1978) suggested that riparian woods could reduce diffuse source pollution in rivers and lakes. Subsequent research (e.g. Yates and Sheridan 1983, Peterjohn and Correll 1984, and Pinay and Décamps 1988) has shown that riparian woods are effective water quality filters and nutrient sinks for runoff from agricultural areas. About 90% of the nitrogen and 80% of the phosphorus in shallow and deep throughflow can be retained, utilised, and transformed in riparian woods. This is 10 times and double the efficiency of cropland for removing and transforming nitrogen and phosphorus, respectively (Peterjohn and Correll 1984). However, Pinay and Décamps (1988) emphasise that the frequency and duration of flooding have an important influence on the functioning of the riparian woods as nutrient sinks. They demonstrated that waterlogging of soils within the ecotone is necessary to sustain the buffering capacity for nitrogen transfer between the terrestrial and aquatic systems.

Environmental monitoring

Ecotones are transitional zones and usually contain several organisms that are near their tolerance limits. Consequently, natural and human-induced process changes may be expressed first by changes in ecotones and not the aquatic or terrestrial systems themselves. Thus it has been suggested that ecotones may show early indications of climatic change (Di Castri *et al.* 1988).

There is no doubt that interface systems are generally the most sensitive to process changes. This is no less true of the land-water interface, which may be easily disrupted by climatic and human-caused hydrological changes (Stockton and Fritts 1973, Johnson and Bell 1976a, Mitsch *et al.* 1979) and by changes in water and sediment quality. The loss or significant decline of sensitive species in a land-water ecotone may be an early warning signal of system stress. Just as through functional redundancies, changes in the compositional structure of an ecosystem usually show up before the effects on functions become manifest (Kimball and Levin 1985). Species with short generation times respond to variations in the environment more precisely than those with long generation times (Southwood 1977). Thus landscapes frequently rejuvenated by channel migration and avulsion may be particularly sensitive to change.

Environmental monitoring may benefit from focussing on land-water ecotones, especially where problems of catchment management are concerned. They may be of less use for studies of climatic change because of the buffering capacity of the catchment ecobiome. However, land-water ecotones in small catchments within transitional climatic regions warrant further investigation in this context.

Visual quality

Ecotones have visual qualities that make an important contribution to value assessments. This is especially true for landscape preservation where they can positively influence social and political perspectives.

In judgements based on subjective values involving comparative appraisals of landscapes, consensus is clearly important (Dearden 1987). Most landscape evaluation techniques are based on the general assumption that there is a broad consensus within society about which landscapes are more attractive than others (Jacques 1980). Shuttleworth (1983) defined two fundamental levels of consensus. First is the response to landscape quality on a continuum from beautiful to ugly. That water enhances landscape quality is now accepted as axiomatic (Dearden 1987). Landform and relief, and complexity of the visual image, are also significant. The land-water interface is particularly important within lowland agricultural landscapes (Shuttleworth 1983). These are generally characterised by smoothness, tidiness, flatness, and passiveness; the land-water interface creates strong and distinctive images, variety, and colour.

The second level of consensus is the response to landscape character on a gradient from untouched wilderness to completely man-made. Many studies on landscape evaluation have concluded that the degree of naturalness is of universal appeal. However, perception of 'naturalness' involves observed interaction with the landscape. As Appleton (1975:69) stated: 'aesthetic satisfaction, experienced in the contemplation of landscape, stems from the spontaneous perception of landscape features which, in their shapes, colours, spatial arrangement and other visible attributes, act as sign-stimuli indicative of environmental conditions favourable to survival, whether they really are favourable or not.'

Appleton simplified his description of habitat theory to one in which the capacity of an environment to provide unimpeded opportunities to see (the prospect) and to hide (the refuge) determines the landscape value. As Appleton notes (p. 217), an 'edge' can be a 'zone of compromise in which the participant can achieve the advantages of good visibility and effective concealment at the same time.' Water surfaces are strongly prospect oriented, while marginal reeds and rushes can provide striking refuge elements. Riparian woods are important refuges by the very nature of their fabric, providing numerous entry points, concealment from view, and shelter. Yet their internal openness also permits a measure of prospect. In contrast, the stark linear margins of cleaned and channelised rivers and streams provide negligible refuge and subdued prospect within a uniform artificial landscape.

Tuan (1973) argues that environmental evaluation should be pursued at the level of social and moral philosophy and of ecological principles, and not merely at the level of aesthetics. Clearly, evaluations of landscape must do more than reveal a critic's own sensitivity and uniqueness. Moreover, the concept of naturalness is itself problematic given the long history of land use change and water management. Modern approaches to landscape design have their roots in the 18th century landscape designs of Capability Brown and André Le Nôtre. Although the geometric regularity of Le Nôtre's work contrasted with the curvilinear features and informality of Brown's, both exploited the potentialities of water and open space. However, their neat, well-organised landscapes composed of uniform patches within a homogeneous matrix differed radically not only from the earlier 17th century Picturesque School but also from the natural environment.

Nevertheless, the acceptability of the 'panoramic' landscapes of Brown is manifested in the replacement of ecologically diverse floodplain forests and wetlands by arable fields or pastures with grass to the river's, or lake's, edge. For many, the Brownian style landscapes are 'natural'; few have personal experience of truly natural ecotones. Thus methods devised to assess landscapes according to the degree of naturalness (e.g. Leopold 1969), a positive factor, and evidence of human influence, a negative factor, may be difficult to apply. Indeed, the introduction of a reservoir or canal into an otherwise man-made landscape can greatly enhance environmental quality (Shuttleworth 1983). Today, natural rivers with overhanging and fallen trees, debris jams, and wetland areas along their banks are often seen as untidy, unhealthy waste areas that are damp, difficult, and dangerous – characteristics of a hazard and not a resource.

Although somewhat removed from the scientific basis of both this chapter and book, the above paragraphs review some fundamental factors influencing the decision-making process. It is important that scientists recognise why conflicts arise in landscape evaluation. There is no doubt that in many cases, arguments for landscape conservation or restoration are justified on the basis of subjective assessments, focussing on the views of users and not on objective ecological grounds. Conflicts arise when objective and subjective evaluations yield contrasting and opposing conclusions. Policy makers with little environmental expertise often have considerable difficulty distinguishing between rational and irrational advice. Science must address management problems in an holistic way, giving due consideration to all management needs. Scientists must be prepared to communicate their knowledge and advice to decision makers in a way appropriate to the specific problem under consideration. For example, with regard to a new dam project, a strongly qualified yes, giving guidance as to how the scheme should be planned and operated to enhance or at least maintain the ecology, will receive greater respect than an emotional no. Furthermore, such an approach would strengthen the conservation argument when a negative response can be justified because the affected area is of ecological importance.

HISTORICAL MANAGEMENT OF LAND-WATER ECOTONES

Traditionally, centres of populations developed near water sources. Wetlands were drained and floodplain woods removed for agriculture, to provide timber, and to fight diseases such as malaria. Rivers were channelised for flood control and maintained for navigation. As a result, natural ecotones have been drastically reduced in spatial extent and their ecological character has been markedly altered. Man has also created new ecotones along extensive canal, irrigation, and drainage systems, and around reservoirs.

Ecotones of forest zone rivers

Throughout the forest zones of the world, large rivers were once characterised by wooded alluvial plains, and many large rivers were influenced by debris from the forests. For example, log jams characterised the Colorado River in Texas (USA) until 'river management' was introduced (Kaynes 1970). Many of the early expeditions exploring North America recorded their primeval character (Hind 1860).

Alluvial forests clearly had a major impact on the river, introducing large quantities of timber and other organic debris. In the 19th century on the Red River in Louisiana, USA, debris jams of tree trunks up to 36 m long and 1.75 m diameter reduced the channel width from 185 m to 40 m. This induced bed aggradation of up to 7 m and created backswamp lakes, many over 30 km long (Triska 1984). Moreover, downed trees created patches for vegetation succession on the forest margin. They also provided sites for sediment and leaf litter storage; nitrogen fixation; oviposition, pupation, and emergence of invertebrates; and fish refugia and rearing sites. Beaver (*Castor canadensis*) in North American rivers made significant contributions to the maintenance of this diverse hydrosystem by cutting riparian trees and building dams. Where beaver have increased after near extinction at the turn of the century, they have markedly increased water area, the length of the land-water interface, and the width of the ecotone (Naiman *et al.* 1986, 1988b; Johnston and Naiman 1987).

Under natural conditions, the ecotone and lotic system interacted strongly. However, many ecotones have a long history of human modification. On the Red River, Triska (1984) reports that large timber rafts were removed between 1830 and 1875, and between 1880 and 1920 over 300,000 snags (downed trees) were removed. Similarly, on a 1600 km reach of the lower Mississippi, during a 50-year period from 1870, 800,000 snags were removed (Sedell *et al.* 1982). Typically, data indicate that along large natural rivers with alluvial forests one downed tree occurred for every 3 m of riverbank (Sedell and Froggatt 1984). There is no doubt that the impact of downed trees on the habitat diversity of large rivers was considerable. However, their role in large rivers will probably remain uncertain, as many rivers were 'improved' and have subsequently been maintained as such for more than 100 years.

In Europe, virtually all major rivers had been channelised by 1900 (Petts 1987, Petts *et al.* 1989b). Records of early schemes reporting the systematic building of embankments for flood control and land reclamation date prior to the 11th century, and the technology of river control and land drainage was well advanced by 1700. In 1817, Tulla initiated the channelisation of the braided section of the Alsatian Rhine, and his often quoted statement that 'As a rule, no stream or river needs more than one bed!' became general policy for engineers. Possibly the greatest single work of the 19th century was the regulation of the Tisza (Theisz) River, which drains the southern and western Carpathians. Beginning in 1845, 12.5×10^6 ha of floodplain marsh were drained and the river course shortened by 340 km.

Engineering works spread so rapidly during the 19th century for two main reasons: the need to combat malaria by eliminating the mosquito habitat, and the concern over increased flooding along many European rivers, which was perceived to have been caused by deforestation and land drainage. Hermann *et al.* (1890) reported that during the late 19th century, floods and dangerous inundations were on the increase among the rivers flowing through the cultivated lands of central Europe. The alluvial forest had been cleared to such an extent that the central and lower part of the streams were flowing through long stretches of treeless country.

During the 20th century, river regulation by dams has further contributed to the isolation of rivers from their riparian zones and alluvial plains. Today, most rivers are channelised and their floodplains have been drained for agriculture or plantation forestry. The ecotone has been reduced to a narrow, relatively simple riparian zone. Isolation of the main river from its alluvial plain – thus eliminating access to backwaters, floodplain lakes, and marshes – has had a major effect in changing the ecological diversity of the highly productive alluvial corridor (Pautou and Décamps 1984). Concomitant lowering of groundwater levels and the elimination of the flood season have resulted in a less diverse and dynamic system (Bravard *et al.* 1986, Amoros *et al.* 1987). Fish stocks have also been severely affected (Welcomme 1979, Petts 1984). On the Rhine, for example, Lelek (1989) noted that the decline of the artisanal fishery coincided with river channelisation in the 19th century.

Ecotones of rivers in grassland and semi-arid zones

River regulation in semi-arid areas can lead to a marked increase in the width and diversity of land-water ecotones along confined and floodplain rivers. In xeric regions, lotic environments tend to be autotrophic but the riparian system acts as an important corridor, providing a vital source of organic matter, and habitat for birds and animals. Along the Colorado River in the Grand Canyon, USA, the effect of river regulation has been to diversify the ecotone (Turner and Karpiscak 1980). Two new geomorphological and botanical zones have been created (Fig. 11.2), and this has been advantageous for animals and birds.

Although the two rivers are geomorphologically different, a similar response to river regulation has been described along the North Platte and Platte in Nebraska, USA (Williams 1978). During the 19th century, explorers' reports generally agree, the riverbanks rarely had any trees. Today the channel has adjusted to the regulated flow regime, and the channel width is between 10 and 70% of the 1865 channel. Vegetation encroachment and sedimentation have created a new alluvial plain charac- terised by a range of trees of all sizes, including willow (*Salix*), cottonwood (*Populus*), elm (*Ulmus*), and maple (*Acer*), and flowering plants. This new ecologically diverse corridor is about 300 m wide and extends for 480 km along the river.

Reilly and Johnson (1982), however, suggest that whether a flora typical of a particular geographical region is maintained will depend on the precise nature of the hydrological changes. Thus, below Garrison Dam on the Missouri River, USA, a larger proportion of the annual flow is now released in the nongrowing season. This has had a severe impact, manifested by declining annual tree growth, on those species at or near the edge of their geographical distribution, such as American elm (*Ulmus americana*). Trees

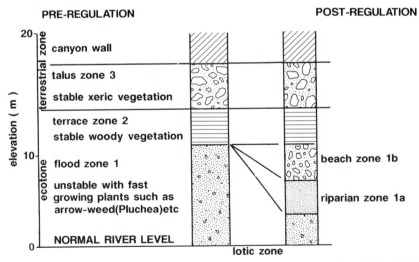

Figure 11.2 Changes of ecotone structure following regulation of the Colorado River in the Grand Canyon, USA. After Carothers *et al.* (1979) and Turner and Karpiscak (1980)

242

with deep root systems such as the cottonwood (*Populus deltoides*) were least affected, although the year-to-year growth increment showed a distinct change. Cottonwood growth was correlated with spring streamflow in the pre-dam period and with rainfall in the post-dam period. Greatest changes were found where fine-grained, relatively impermeable soils dominated (Reilly and Johnson 1982, Mitsch and Rust 1984). Species associated with more permeable sites were more tolerant of the regulated flow conditions.

Reservoirs

The creation of man-made lakes has markedly increased the length of shoreline and littoral habitats in most countries. In the United Kingdom alone there are some 450 major reservoirs. These have created about 2500 km of new ecotone between the lentic environment and the land – approximately double that of the ecotone between the lotic environment and the land, which it replaced. These man-made ecotones can be important for conservation. In the Anglian Water Authority and Thames Water Authority regions alone, 10 water supply reservoirs and adjacent land areas were designated Sites of Special Interest between 1955 and 1986. All are of international or national importance for several bird species (Moore and Driver 1989).

The ecological value of reservoir margins depends on the magnitude and frequency of lake level fluctuations, the rate of water level change, and the morphometry of the lake. Furthermore, within open, treeless valleys, wave action may be significant, with waves up to 3 m high being reported (Petts 1984). Davies (1986) reviews studies of the ecology of the Lake Kariba, Zimbabwe, shoreline, which acts as a man-made floodplain, in part replacing that lost by river regulation below the dam. Lake level fluctuations add to the nutrient pools of both the terrestrial and aquatic systems. During drawdown, aquatic animals and plants decompose or are consumed by birds and migratory herbivores attracted by the development of lush vegetation. During inundation, decomposing vegetation and dung supply nutrients to the aquatic environment. Furthermore, the need to maintain the ecotone is illustrated particularly by the *Hippopotamus*, which feeds on land at night and defaecates in water by day, providing an important nutrient source for the aquatic system.

The impact of reservoir filling on forest species along the shoreline depends on the frequency, depth, duration, and timing of inundation (Kozlowski 1982), although the response of different species varies markedly. Butorin *et al.* (1973) indicated that subsequent to the filling of the Rybinsk Reservoir in the Soviet Union, groundwater levels rose in the surrounding hillsides, and this caused a decrease of tree growth within a narrow zone around the reservoir. In contrast, Mickievicz (1973) found no effect on *Pinus* growth in permeable, sandy soils, along the shores of a reservoir in

Poland. Grelsson (1988) similarly found no measurable changes in growth of spruce (*Picea abies*) on permeable gravel and detected only minor changes in the growth of *Pinus sylvestris* along the shore of a daily fluctuating hydropower reservoir in Sweden.

Artificial channels

Like reservoirs, the canals constructed for navigation, irrigation channels, and land-drainage ditches make up thousands of kilometres of new land-water ecotone. In many areas such features are important components of landscape, especially in semi-arid regions. Thus Yousef and Sheikh (1981) reported that the effect of a canal at Al-Kharj in Saudi Arabia led to the appearance of mesophytes, hydrophytes, and swamp plants in an area formerly dominated by halophytes and xerophytes. *Phoenix, Tamarix*, and *Ziziphus* dominate the riparian zone and swamp plants form a continuous belt fringing the canal. Along navigation canals the abundance of marginal aquatic plants is inversely related to boat traffic (e.g. Murphy and Eaton 1983), and the ecotone is narrow, reflecting the stable water level. Nevertheless, canal corridors often provide refuge for some species typical of ecotones along natural rivers which are now channelised and devoid of riparian vegetation.

MANAGEMENT ALTERNATIVES

Natural resources must be conserved if economic and social development is to take place in a sustainable manner. Investment in good environmental practice can make good business sense by enhancing a company's reputation and by reducing costs through increased efficiency and avoidance of wastes. The need for sound environmental management is no less urgent in developing countries where resource abuse enforced by poverty is the fundamental cause of environmental degradation (Barbier 1987). The argument is that poor people often have no choice but to seek immediate economic benefits at the expense of the long-term sustainability of their livelihoods. Sustainable development requires improvement of the material standards of living of the poor. Equally important is the need for environmentally sound approaches to development and for incentives to induce economic behaviour that is environmentally sound.

The best practicable environmental option

An approach to environmental management that seeks to reduce impacts to a minimum while having the benefit of a case-by-case view of specific problems is the concept of the best practicable environmental option (BPEO). BPEO was first used in Britain by the Royal Commission on Environmental Pollution (1976). In that report the significance of the concept is highlighted by considering its elements in reverse word order (Table 11.3). Option selection emphasises the diligent and imaginative search for alternatives. Environmental evaluations should seek to discover the unusual and improbable impacts of a scheme as well as the familiar and likely, in both the short and long term. Such evaluations must also consider local, national, and international perspectives. The assessment of practicability recognises that complete evaluations in monetary terms are seldom possible and experience has to be used in arriving at a decision. The choice of the best practicable option will not necessarily be the cheapest, and if environmental considerations are compromised by socio-economic factors, this should be openly acknowledged.

The selection of a BPEO requires a systematic approach to decision making in which the practicability of all reasonable options is examined and in which maintenance and enhancement of the environment are key themes. In aquatic landscape management, land-water ecotones justify particular considerations because (1) they have special ecological, recreational, and aesthetic values, and (2) the functions of the ecotone have implications for the management of the adjacent terrestrial and aquatic sytems. Indeed, restoration of ecotones along European rivers, for example, might not only provide for recreation and conservation but also help reduce nutrient inputs.

For practical purposes, management of land-water ecotones requires consideration of two spatial scales:

1. At the large scale, management must seek to sustain the hydrological and geomorphological processes that determine the ecotone between major terrestrial and aquatic systems.

2. At a smaller scale, management should seek to maintain the diversity of patches *within* this ecotone (and then indirectly the ecotones between the

Table 11.3 Components of the best practicable environmental option. Based on Royal Commission of Environmental Pollution, 12th Report (1988)

OPTION: The procedure for selecting a BPEO should include a diligent and imaginative search for alternative ways of achieving the desired result.

ENVIRONMENTAL: The evaluation of options for their environmental effects is undertaken early in the decision-making process. Local and remote, short- and long-term effects must be considered, and the possibility of improving the environment should always be explored. Plans should be developed to monitor environmental effects.

PRACTICABLE: 'Reasonably practicable' means having regard, among other things, for local conditions and circumstances, the financial implications, and the current state of technical knowledge.

BEST: There is probably never an absolute best. The option chosen as best, based on the interpretation and evaluation of predicted impacts, is unlikely to be best for all time. Flexibility in management is important, and a BPEO must be kept under review.

patches) by managing the patches themselves. However, this should be considered only once the optimum solution (given all economic, social, and ecological considerations) for large-scale management is determined.

Four general options have been proposed for river management (Petts 1989), and these provide a useful framework for considering aquatic ecotones: secondary regulation; biological controls, including controls on human activities; preservation; and compensation. The four options can be organised in a decision-making framework (Fig. 11.3).

Management decisions should be based upon a scientific survey. This should provide information for landscape evaluation and define areas that are more or less vulnerable to particular changes. The significance of landscape may be related to a range of quantifiable and objective criteria (Table 11.4) as well as qualitative ones such as 'naturalness,' 'typicalness,' and 'intrinsic appeal.' The potential value should also be considered, since through appropriate management or natural change, a site may develop an ecological or recreational value greater than currently exists.

The most useful criterion is 'vulnerability.' This reflects the sensitivity of habitats, communities, and species to environmental change. It also includes fragile components that are often difficult to restore. The assessment of vulnerability depends on information gained from analyses of historical changes (Petts *et al.* 1989b), yet knowledge transferred from one system to another remains to be evaluated. Nevertheless, vulnerability maps are useful in planning and in communicating ecological needs to decision makers and the public.

At the first management level, options for modifying and managing developments aim to maintain the hydrological and geomorphological characteristics of the ecotone. The economic and environmental effectiveness of first-order management proposals should then be evaluated in relation to second-order options. Finally, and only if a combination of first and second-order management options cannot provide the best practicable solution, third-order options should be assessed. Often conflicts between developers and conservationists have arisen because of a failure by both parties to consider secondary regulation measures, provided by the first and second-order options. Petts (1989) has argued that to achieve sustainable development of water resources in the context of river projects, the immediate emphasis must be the development of such measures.

Secondary regulation measures

Flow control. The influence of hydrology on land-water ecotones should be divided into two components (Table 11.5): water level (frequency and duration of inundation) and water volume (discharge and/or groundwater). The fundamental objective in the management of riparian and littoral ecotones is to maintain the natural flooding regime. This includes not only

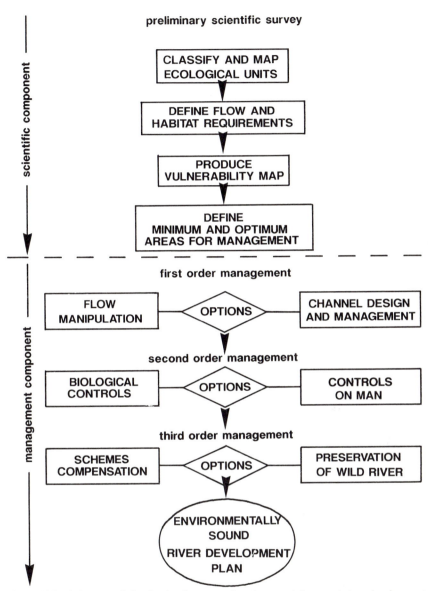

Figure 11.3 A framework for the development of environmentally sound river development. Based in part on Petts (1989)

the magnitude of water level variation but also the timing of high and low flows; for example, flooding during the growing season may decrease tree growth (Bell and Johnson 1974).

The hydraulic conditions necessary to maintain the morphological

Table 11.4 Objective criteria for the assessment of conservation value. After Radcliffe (1977)

SIZE: Larger sites are often more highly valued than smaller ones, but other factors to consider are relative size of the site compared with sites of similar type and whether the site is of sufficient size that small changes within will not lead to the loss of the site's interest.

DIVERSITY: One of the most important site attributes is the variety of both communities and species, which depends largely on habitat diversity.

RARITY: The presence of one or more species, communities, or habitats on a site, from a national or international standpoint, gives it higher value than a comparable site with no rarities.

RECORDED HISTORY: The existence of a scientific record of long standing adds considerably to the value of a site.

POSITION IN ECOLOGICAL UNIT: In the event that two sites of equal intrinsic value represent a certain formation or succession, the close proximity of one site to a highly rated example of another type increases the value of the site.

Table 11.5 Guidelines for flow management in conservation

With reference to vulnerability map and information on minimum and optimum areas for conservation or restoration:

1. Alter the hydrological regime as little as possible.

2. Allocate water and define operational rules for regulating the flow and water level regime: (a) allocate water to meet ecotone needs; (b) provide water when needed by ecotone.

3. Maintain discharges by using reservoir releases, interbasin transfers, and, for small rivers, groundwater abstractions.

4. Maintain water levels by using weirs, embankments, and sluices.

5. Ensure that the management plan for the ecotone does not cause unacceptable changes to the lotic system (e.g. vary flow-water level at a rate that mimics natural flow variations).

6. Initiate a monitoring programme to evaluate the effectiveness of flow and water level control measures.

7. Have a flexible management scheme to be able to respond to problems identified in item 6 and to new scientific knowledge.

dynamics of the ecotone must also be considered. For rivers, dams, and reservoirs, interbasin transfers and even groundwater abstractions can be used to maintain minimum flows and to mimic natural discharge patterns. However, action must be taken to prevent excessive reduction of low water levels. This may arise as a result of lowering the channel bed by degradation caused, for example, by an interruption to the downstream transfer of sediment below a dam (Petts 1984). Lowering water levels during the dry season could increase floodplain drainage, possibly leading to desiccation.

One example of the successful application of flow regulation for conservation is the utilisation by fishes of an artificial flood release from Lake Kariba, on the Zambezi River, for spawning the Mana Pools floodplain (Kenmuir 1976). Thus, Davies (1979) proposed that careful management of reservoir releases could sustain high levels of fish productivity in two ways: (1) by inducing adult fish migration, and (2) by filling the pools above supply level so that discharge back to the river as the flood recedes attracts fish into the pools for spawning.

As long as the natural seasonal flow pattern is retained, weirs can be used to maintain water levels in the main river and to control flow into floodplain backwaters. These, together with embankments, can be used to divert, constrict, or impound flow on the floodplain to maintain adequate water depths. Bren (1988) discusses the possible application of these tools to the management of the red gum forests along the Murray River, Australia. However, here the problem is to define the flood regime given that marked year-to-year variability is a characteristic of the river. Nevertheless, the controlled 'irrigation' of floodplain forests may prove to be an important conservation measure, although little is known about precisely how much water is needed and when. The solution of such questions would lead to the formulation of simple operational rules for conservation and to help rationalise water regulation. In an environment of competing water uses, the control rules would define conservation water levels and discharges for different hydrological scenarios, including drought years. An example is given by Lambert (1988).

In reservoirs the controlled lake level fluctuations can be used to maintain a 'floodplain' system. For Lake Kariba, for example, Bowmaker (1973; cited in Davies 1986) recommended that half-cycle fluctuations in lake level should not exceed 2 m and that the rate of change should be less than 0.6 m/month. However, where the regime of natural lakes is to provide relatively stable water levels, excessive reservoir drawdown during the dry season may cause problems. Under such circumstances, the land-water ecotone may be maintained by creating marginal lagoons. Controlled outlets in the embankments of these lagoons allow water levels to be maintained independently of the reservoir, especially where the lagoons are fed by inlet streams. In some United Kingdom reservoirs, artificial lagoons and artificial floating islands have been used successfully for the conservation of wildfowl habitat (Moore and Driver 1989).

Structural design and maintenance. Recently, the traditional river engineering objectives of river regulation, land drainage, and erosion control have been supplemented by conservation. Physical habitat management requires the recognition of critical habitats for biological communities or at least target species (Petts *et al.* 1989a). The emphasis is on ecotone morphologies that determine the hydrological and hydraulic characteristics, and floodplain dispersion of floodwaters (Table 11.6). Along the Rhine, channels and

Table 11.6 Guidelines for channel restoration. Based on McConnell *et al.* (1980), Brookes (1989), and Welcomme (1989)

1. Alter channel and ecotone only when necessary, keep alterations to a minimum, and incorporate natural features into the scheme.
2. Retain the majority of trees.
3. Retain small debris accumulations and only clear snags (rooted or downed trees and logs) where major blockage problems arise.
4. Undertake channel maintenance from one bank, leaving one bank intact, and use manual techniques wherever possible; alternatively, work from a boat if mechanical devices are necessary, or in small streams from alternate banks.
5. Retain floodplain lakes and channel backwaters, or create new ones, and provide for seasonal connection with the main river.
6. Set embankments well back from the riverbank, and create flood channels or utilise existing floodplain lakes for storage during extreme events to provide wetland and backwater habitats.
7. Initiate a monitoring programme to evaluate the effectiveness of restoration measures.
8. Have a flexible management scheme to be able to respond to problems identified in item 7.

floodplain lakes isolated by channelisation have been reconnected to improve habitat; new ponds have been excavated along the Danube for fish production; and in areas of inundated floodplains along the Missouri and Mississippi dredged sand has been used to create islands to reduce wind fetch, reduce erosion, and enhance habitat (LARS 1989).

The morphological dynamics of an ecotone may be sustained to a greater or lesser degree by appropriate flow regulation. Thereby habitat diversity and quality may be maintained. Erosion may be required to rejuvenate disturbance patches, while channel cutoffs and deposition may be needed to create resource patches. However, flow regulation may be supplemented by periodic introductions of sands or gravels to construct artificial bars and engineering works to control the rate and location of channel erosion. For example, wing dikes have been used successfully to diversify marginal habitats (Lelek 1989). More dramatic works, such as the artificial cutoff of a meander (Brookes 1985, 1987), may be advantageous in rejuvenating the dynamics of the ecotone. Such works may be required with a frequency 1:20 < 50 years depending on the natural frequency of channel cutoffs within the natural system.

The components of ecologically sympathetic engineering practices are shown in Fig. 11.4. The practices are based on the concept of the two-stage channel, confining the normal range of flows to the original channel while flood flows are contained within a larger channel excavated from the floodplain. To this may be added embankments set well back from the riverbank to provide seasonal high flood storage and even to contain flood channels of floodplain lakes that may be used to store floodwater during

Figure 11.4 Cross-profile of a river and the river-land ecotone identifying the components of environmentally sound management: (1) natural channel with submerged and marginal vegetation; (2) natural riparian zone; (3) flood berm excavated and planted to create new wetlands; (4) flood embankments set well back from river's edge and sown with wildflowers; (5) additional embankments set away from river to create (6) emergency flood control channel and/or floodplain lake with link to main river controlled by sluices, weirs, or gated ducts

extreme events. The flood channels and storage lakes are connected to the main river by a simple weir or grated sluice. At all times, it is desirable to maintain or emulate the characteristics of the natural system, both in terms of spatial structure and temporal dynamics. Examples of the successful application of such practices are given by Brookes (1989) and Gardiner (1988). Morphologically diverse designs for channelised rivers have been shown, in some situations, to have hydraulic as well as ecological advantages (Jaeggi 1989).

Biological control. Seibert (1968) stratified the riparian system into four zones: (1) aquatic plants to reduce bed erosion at the base of the bank; (2) reed bank zone at channel margin to provide bank protection from currents and waves; (3) softwood zone of riparian tree communities for bank stabilisation and to provide shading; and (4) hardwood zones set back from the channel.

In recent years there has been a return to the use of living vegetation rather than artificial materials for erosion control (Brookes 1985). Some plant species have considerable potential for bank protection (e.g. Conchou and Pautou 1987), but erosion problems can inhibit the planting of riverbanks or lakeshores because the plants are physically broken by wave action and river currents or the root mats are undercut. The development of geotextiles is providing significant opportunities for riparian conservation. Matting or netting is used to protect the bank and roots from erosion while allowing shoots to grow through the holes (Fig. 11.5). In the Norfolk Broads, UK, experiments with various types of asphalt matting and plastic netting, with reed rhizomes (*Phragmites australis*) or pond sedge (*Carex*) placed on the bank before laying the geotextile, suggest the method has

251

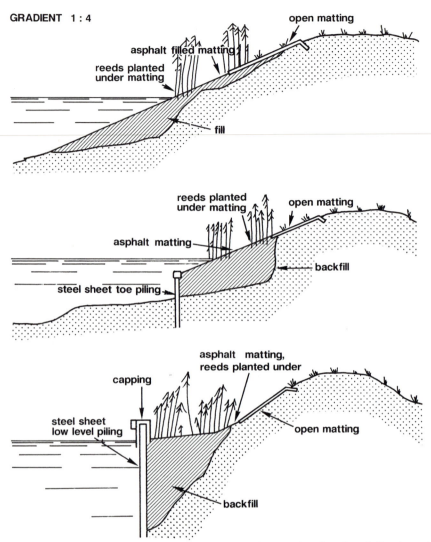

GRADIENT 1 : 4

open matting

asphalt filled matting

reeds planted
under matting

fill

reeds planted
under matting

open matting

asphalt matting

backfill

steel sheet toe piling

asphalt matting,
reeds planted under

capping

steel sheet
low level piling

open matting

backfill

Figure 11.5 Application of geotextiles in channel bank protection. Based on J. Brooke and J. Ash, unpublished data

considerable potential (J. Brooke and J. Ash, unpublished data).

Planting trees in a floodplain has ecological and engineering advantages as well as hydraulic disadvantages (Rankin 1980). However, the hydraulic disadvantages can be mitigated in several ways: by planting new vegetation and removing unwanted species or controlling where trees are allowed; or by controlling over what area and in what configuration they grow. For a stream in lowland England with an east-west orientation, Dawson (1978) recommended that 50 m stands of trees should be planted every 70 m along the south bank to provide shading and to prevent excessive aquatic weed growth. The unshaded sections would be maintained by occasional tree cutting to allow controlled aquatic plant growth.

This category of options also includes controls on animals. Culling may be justified to prevent problems of overpopulation or to control bank erosion. In the Norfolk Broads, UK, considerable problems were caused by the coypu (*Myocaster coypu*), resulting from its grazing of bankside vegetation, especially reed beds, and burrowing into embankments (Brooke and Ash, unpublished data). Alternatively, where self-reproducing populations are no longer viable, stocking can be undertaken either using cultivated species or species transferred from one area to another.

Controls on man. Man-induced erosion and degradation of riparian zones can arise in several ways. Careless trampling and cutting of vegetation by tourists, walkers, and fisherman may have adverse impacts, but excessive boat traffic and boat speeds can also cause severe erosion problems. The creation of closed areas for all or part of the year has been a fundamental tool of conservation and has been widely successful, especially in the establishment of bird sanctuaries on parts of reservoirs (Moore and Driver 1989). However, controls on hunting, fishing, and boating by licensing are also important as a management tool.

This concept also extends to land use. Fencing off bankside areas from livestock can accelerate the recovery of bankside vegetation in cleared areas (Platts 1984). Turner (1985) reports an experimental scheme to encourage the continuation of traditional livestock grazing practices so as to conserve the unique character of marsh landscape in part of the Norfolk Broads, UK. During the previous 25 years in England, declining livestock profits, together with stable and generally high arable profits, have led to the ploughing of former grassland marshes. The scheme involves annual payments of £125/ha to farmers as an incentive to keep land in grass while imposing conditions to ensure that the grazing lands are managed in ways compatible with conservation. The conditions are not onerous: stocking rates must be about 5 beasts to 2 ha; nitrogen fertiliser applications are limited to about 370 kg/ha; and herbicidal use is strictly controlled. In 1988 nearly 3600 ha were managed in this way.

Compensation schemes and the nonuse alternative. New environments cannot support old communities, and it would be naive to believe that secondary regulation can be used in every case to maintain or restore *complete* biological communities. In most cases the BPEO necessitates acceptance of at least some impacts, and in such cases compensation schemes may be used to minimise their consequences. Such schemes include, for example, the provision of alternative fisheries, such as aquaculture, or new recreational facilities.

Alternatively, the ecological value of an ecotone – based on international, national, or local criteria – may necessitate the prohibition of development. In such cases, the ecotone (and its adjacent terrestrial and aquatic systems) could be designated a conservation area. Nicholson (1961) argued that such nonuse is justifiable in three ways. First, there is a need to protect genetic resources (especially for the future restoration and maintenance of heavily developed rivers). Secondly, there is a probability that an economic use of unknown value will be found in the future. Thirdly, there are aesthetic, educational, or scientific values that, if not apparent now, may arise in the future.

Recognition that non-development is an acceptable use has been a major constraint to the development of rational environmental management. Yet it would be irrational for society to destroy ecotones that have a key role in sustaining land and water resources, especially if society accepts responsibility for future generations. The debate concerning development or conservation has invariably led to conflict in part because of a failure to consider these as *final* options in a structured evaluation process. The underlying objective of management must be to facilitate resource development while providing for ecological conservation. The BPEO in most cases involves positive and integrated management based on first and second level options.

Problem of scale. In all the above options a major problem arises concerning the zoning of landscape for management purposes. The economic costs and the environmental effectiveness of all options relate to the size of the area being managed. Walther (1986) defined *zoning* as a growth control and planning technique that is applied to establish territorial structures by denominating areal units for specific purposes. This includes the protection of conservation and wilderness areas as well as satisfying the economic need to allocate resources in space, and the management need to define and organise responsibilities and operations. It is important to note that zoning clarifies long-term planning goals and policies in spatial terms. Vulnerability maps could provide a useful tool for assessing the spatial dimensions and intensity of impacts, but as yet science is unable to define the optimum and minimum sizes of different ecotones for conservation to be effective. 'Size' must include shape and connectivity in order to incorporate Southwood's (1977) concept of heterogeneous space being composed of the trivial ranges (food gathering range) and migratory ranges of different species.

Despite the debate that arose during the mid-1970s concerning the size of nature reserves (Simberloff and Abele 1976), the subsequent discussions of the minimum critical size of ecosystems (Lovejoy and Oren 1978), and renewed discussion of patch definition (Pringle *et al.* 1988), remarkably little is known about the scale necessary for sustaining functioning ecosystems. A riparian wood 20 m wide may be adequate to effectively reduce nitrate losses to rivers from intensively cultivated land (Pinay and Décamps 1988); that is 2 ha of land for every kilometre of riverbank. Yet how effective is this size for wildlife conservation? Brown and Dinsmore (1986) showed that bird species richness is greater for moderate sized 'islands' and less for large isolated 'islands.' Clearly, connectivity and shape are also fundamental variables that need evaluation and quantification.

PROSPECTS

Natural systems present most probable long-term average states. Their responses to changes of the control variables involve many degrees of freedom, and there can be no simple solution to the prediction of impacts (Petts 1984, 1987). A degree of uncertainty exists in any option evaluation. Science thrives on uncertainty, but managers usually demand a level of certainty greater than science can provide at the current state of knowledge. Nevertheless, it is imperative that science makes a major contribution to the development of protocols to manage environmental resources while continuing to gain fundamental scientific information.

There is already a body of evidence to suggest that ecotones could play a major role in aquatic landscape management, influencing the philosophy, approaches, methods, and tools. The 'best practicable environmental option' approach is advocated for the management of aquatic landscapes, utilising a hierarchical framework for the appraisal of new and existing projects. Three separate actions can lead to the establishment, maintenance, or even enhancement of some biological populations: (1) the prudent application of management tools; (2) monitoring of management performance; and (3) flexibility in management to respond to new scientific knowledge and the development of improved tools. Openness and accountability are central to BPEO, and the grounds for a particular decision must be clearly defined so that the chosen management option can be reviewed as scientific knowledge and socio-economic needs change.

Management requires an institutional framework, appropriate legislation and regulation, and the social and political will to pay. Scientific tools and methods represent only a relatively small part of management. Nevertheless, scientists can make important contributions to management by addressing four important problems:

1. The hydrological and hydraulic controls of ecotones at the land-water interface must be quantified. This must include duration, frequency, and timing of inundation in relation to ecotone topography and soil-sediment characteristics. Moreover, the morphological dynamics must be defined. This may involve such variables as rate of channel migration and frequency of avulsion or channel cutoff based on historical data.

2. The critical size of sustainable ecotones must be specified giving due regard to connectivity with adjacent land-water ecotones and patches within the drainage basin.

3. Predictive models of ecotone responses to stresses must be developed if the full value of ecotone management is to be realised. Moreover, such models would embrace not only the limiting conditions required to maintain ecotones but also the definition of environmental performance indicators (Duinker and Baskerville 1986). These are features that decision makers can use to gauge the performance of a BPEO.

4. While there is no completely scientific and objective means of striking a balance between environmental and other considerations, ecological criteria must be established for the classification and comparative appraisal of aquatic landscapes.

Today, many aquatic landscapes reflect human values and life-styles. Conservation will benefit from the management of man-modified and man-made ecotones as well as natural ones. Conservation issues have become important for some societies, but many nations are too near the borderline of hunger and poverty to feel able, politically, to invest in environmental protection. One view in resource development is that society should accept that flora and fauna must change towards that capable of tolerating the new conditions (Ackers and Thompson 1987). However, sound environmental management is a prerequisite for sustainable economic growth. The assumption that conservation is a luxury reserved for those countries with the highest standards of living has hindered the development of appropriate management strategies for sustainable resource development in developing countries. On the other hand, claims by some 'conservationists' that all development schemes are inevitably destructive have delayed the integration of rational ecological argument in aquatic landscape management.

Ecological rationality does not involve preservation per se. It does require a concern for the conservation and enhancement of the natural environment in relation to societal needs or desires. In a review of river regulation in the United Kingdom (Petts and Wood 1988), three factors have been preeminent in the development of successful river management: consultation, cooperation, and flexibility. These are also important factors for the successful application of BPEO to aquatic landscape management within which the management of ecotones may play a key role.

ACKNOWLEDGEMENTS

I am grateful to many colleagues for informed discussions especially concerning the question 'When is an ecotone not an ecotone?' In particular, I am pleased to acknowledge valuable comments by Robin Welcomme,

Malcolm Greenwood, Henri Décamps, Robert J. Naiman, and an anonymous reviewer.

LITERATURE CITED

Ackers, P., and G. Thompson. 1987. Reservoir sedimentation and influence of flushing. Pages 845-868 *in* C.R. Thorne, J.C. Bathurst, and R.D. Hey, editors. Sediment transport in gravel-bed rivers. Wiley, Chichester, England.

Amoros, C., A.L. Roux, A.L. Reygrobellet, J.P. Bravard, and G. Pautou. 1987. A method for applied ecological studies of fluvial hydrosystems. Regulated Rivers 1:17-36.

Appleton, J. 1975. The experience of landscape. Wiley, London, England.

Attwell, R.I.G. 1970. Some effects of Lake Kariba on the ecology of a floodplain of the mid-Zambezi valley of Rhodesia. Biological Conservation 2:189-196.

Bailey, R.G. 1986. The Zaire system. Pages 201-214 *in* B.R. Davies and K.F. Walker, editors. The ecology of river systems. Dr. W. Junk, Dordrecht, The Netherlands.

Barbier, E.B. 1987. The concept of sustainable development. Environment Conservation 14:101-110.

Bell, D.T., and F.L. Johnson. 1974. Flood-caused tree mortality around Illinois reservoirs. Transactions of the Illinois State Academy of Science 67:28-37.

Bravard, J.P., C. Amoros, and G. Pautou. 1986. Impacts of civil engineering works on the succession of communities in a fluvial system: a methodological and predictive approach applied to a section of the Upper Rhône River. Oikos 47:92-111.

Bren, L.J. 1988. Effects of river regulation on flooding of a riparian red gum forest on the River Murray, Australia. Regulated Rivers 2:65-77.

Brookes, A. 1985. River channelisation: traditional engineering methods, physical consequences and alternative practices. Progress in Physical Geography 9:44-73.

Brookes, A. 1987. The distribution and management of channelised streams in Denmark. Regulated Rivers 1:3-16.

Brookes, A. 1989. Alternatives for channel modification. Pages 139-162 *in* J.A. Gore and G.E. Petts, editors. Alternatives in regulated river management. CRC Press, Boca Raton, Florida.

Brown, M., and J.J. Dinsmore. 1986. Implications of marsh size and isolation for marsh bird management. Journal of Wildlife Management 50:392-397.

Brown, S. 1981. A comparison of the structure, primary productivity, and transpiration of cypress ecosystems in Florida. Ecological Monographs 51:403-427.

Butorin, N.V., S.L. Vendrov, K.N. Dyakonov, A. Reteyum, Yu and V.I. Romanenko. 1973. Effect of Rybinsk Reservoir on the surrounding area. Pages 242-250 *in* W.C. Ackerman, G.F. White, and E.B. Worthington, editors. Man-made lakes: their problems and environmental effects. Geophysical Monograph 17, American Geophysical Union, Washington, D.C.

Carothers, S.W., S.W. Aitchison, and R.R. Johnson. 1979. Natural resources, white water recreation and river management alternatives on the Colorado River, Grand Canyon National Park, Arizona. Pages 253-259 *in* R.M. Linn, editor. Proceedings, First Conference on Scientific Research in National Parks. United States Department of the Interior, Washington, D.C., USA.

Conchou, O., and G. Pautou. 1987. Modes of colonisation of an heterogenous alluvial area on the edge of the Garonne River *Phalaris arundinacea L* Regulated Rivers 1:37-48.

Cuffney, T.F. 1988. Input, movement and exchange of organic matter within a sub-tropical coastal blackwater river-floodplain system. Freshwater Biology 19:305-320.

Davies, B.R. 1979. Stream regulation in Africa: a review. Pages 113-142 *in* J.V. Ward and J.A. Stanford, editors. The ecology of regulated streams. Plenum, New York, New York, USA.

Davies, B.R. 1986. The Zambesi River system. Pages 225-268 *in* B.R. Davies and K.F. Walker, editors. The ecology of river systems. Dr. W. Junk, Dordrecht, The Netherlands.

Davies, B.R., and K.F. Walker, editors. 1986. The ecology of river systems. Dr. W. Junk, Dordrecht, The Netherlands.

Dawson, F.H. 1978. Aquatic plant management in semi-natural streams: the role of marginal vegetation. Journal of Environmental Management 6:213-221.

Dearden, P. 1987. Consensus and a theoretical framework for landscape evaluation. Journal of Environmental Management 24:267-278.

Décamps, H., M. Fortuné, F. Gazelle, and G. Pautou. 1988. Historical influence of man on the riparian dynamics of a fluvial landscape. Landscape Ecology 1:163-173.

Décamps, H., J. Joachim, and J. Lauga. 1987. The importance for birds of the riparian woodlands within the alluvial corridor of the river Garonne, S.W. France. Regulated Rivers 1:301-316.

Di Castri, F., A.J. Hansen, and M.M. Holland (editors). 1988. A new look at ecotones: emerging international projects on landscape boundaries. Biology International, Special Issue 17:1-163.

Duinker, P.N., and G.L. Baskerville. 1986. A systematic approach to forecasting in environmental impact assessment. Journal of Environmental Management 23:271-290.

Everitt, B.L. 1968. Use of the cottonwood in an investigation of the recent history of a floodplain. American Journal of Science 266:417-439.

Forman, R.T.T., and M. Gordon. 1981. Patches and structural components for a landscape ecology. BioScience 31:733-740.

Frith, H.J. 1977. Water fowl in Australia. Reed, Sydney, Australia.

Gardiner, J.L. 1988. Environmentally sound river engineering: examples from the Thames catchment. Regulated Rivers 2:445-469.

Gregory, K.J. 1976. Lichens and the determination of river channel capacity. Earth Surface Processes 1:273-285.

Grelsson, G. 1988. Radial stem growth of coniferous trees near Swedish reservoirs. Regulated Rivers 2:535-545.

Hansen, A.J., F. di Castri, and R.J. Naiman. 1988. Ecotones: what and why? Biology International, Special Issue 17:9-46.

Hermann, Dr., J. Klein, and Dr. Thome. 1890. Land, sea and sky. Translated by J. Minshull et al., 1979. Ward, Lock and Company, London, England.

Hind, H.Y. 1860. Narrative of the Canadian Red River Exploring Expedition of 1857. Reprinted in 1971 by Charles E. Tuttle, Tokyo, Japan.

Holland, M.M. (compiler). 1988. SCOPE/MAB technical consultations on landscape boundaries: report of a SCOPE/MAB workshop on ecotones. Biology International, Special Issue 17:47-106.

Jacques, D.L. 1980. Landscape appraisal: the case for a subjective theory. Journal of Environmental Management 10:107-113.

Jaeggi, M.N.R. 1989. Channel engineering and erosion control. Pages 163-189 in J.A. Gore and G.E. Petts, editors. Alternatives in regulated river management. CRC Press, Boca Raton, Florida.

Johnson, F.L., and D.T. Bell. 1976a. Tree growth and mortality in the streamside forest. Castanea 41:34-41.

Johnson, F.L. and D.T. Bell. 1976b. Plant biomass and net primary production along a flood-frequency gradient in the streamside forest. Castanea 41:156-165,.

Johnston, C.A., and R.J. Naiman. 1987. Boundary dynamics at the aquatic-terrestrial interface: the influence of beaver and geomorphology. Landscape Ecology 1:47-57.

Karr, J.R., and I.J. Schlosser. 1978. Water resources and the land-water interface. Science 201:229-234.

Kaynes, W.H. 1970. Facies and development of the Colorado River delta in Texas. In J.P. Morgan, editor. Deltaic sedimentation and erosion. Society of Modern Economic Palaeontologists and Mineralogists, Special Publication 15:78-108.

Kellerhals, R., and D. Gill. 1973. Observations on the potential downstream effects of large storage projects in northern Canada. Transactions of the Eleventh International Congress of Large Dams 1:731-754.

Kenmuir, D.H.S. 1976. Fish spawning under artificial flood conditions on the Mana floodplain, Zambezi River. Kariba Studies 6:86-97.

Kimball, K.D., and S.A. Levin. 1985. Limitations of laboratory bioassays: the need for ecosystem-level testing. BioScience 35:165-171.

Kozlowski, T.T. 1982. Water supply and tree growth. Part II: Flooding. Forestry Abstracts 43:145-161.

Lambert, A. 1988. Regulation of the River Dee. Regulated Rivers 2:293-308.

LARS. 1989. Proceedings of the International Large River Symposium. Canadian Journal of Fisheries and Aquatic Sciences, Special Publication 106.

258

Legendre, L., and S. Demers. 1984. Towards dynamic biological oceanography and limnology. Canadian Journal of Fisheries and Aquatic Sciences 41:2-19.

Lelek, A. 1989. The Rhine and some of its tributaries under human impact in the last two centuries. Canadian Journal of Fisheries and Aquatic Sciences, *in press*.

Leopold, L.B. 1969. Quantitative comparison of some aesthetic factors among rivers. United States Geological Survey Circular 620.

Leopold, L.B., and H.E. Skibitzke. 1967. Observations on unmeasured rivers. Geographiska Annaler 494:247-255.

Lovejoy, T.E., and D.C. Oren. 1978. The minimum critical size of ecosystems. Pages 7-12 *in* R.L. Burgess and D.M. Sharpe, editors. Forest island dynamics in man-dominated landscapes. Springer-Verlag, New York, USA.

Lowe-McConnell, R.H. 1986. The fish of the Amazon system. Pages 339-352 *in* B.R. Davies and K.F. Walker, editors. The ecology of river systems. Dr. W. Junk, Dordrecht,The Netherlands.

Martin, V., and M. Inglis. 1984. Wilderness: the way ahead. Findorn Press, Forres, Scotland.

McConnell, C.A., D.R. Parsons, G.L. Montgomery, and W.L. Gainer. 1980. Stream renovation alternatives: the Wolf River story. Journal of Soil and Water Conservation 35:17-20.

Mickievicz, G. 1973. Improvement of forest biotope conditions on the adjoining areas of low land reservoirs. Transactions of the Eleventh International Congress on Large Dams 1:237-256.

Mitsch, W.J., C.L. Dorge, and J.R. Wiemhoff. 1979. Ecosystem dynamics and a phosphorus budget of an alluvial cypress swamp in southern Illinois. Ecology 60:1116-1124.

Mitsch, W.J., and K.C. Ewel. 1979. Comparative biomass and growth of cypress in Florida wetlands. American Midland Naturalist 101:417-426.

Mitsch, W.J., and W.G. Rust. 1984. Tree growth responses to flooding in a bottomland forest in northeastern Illinois. Forest Science 30:499-510.

Moore, D.E., and A. Driver. 1989. The conservation value of water supply reservoirs. Regulated Rivers, 4(2):203-212.

Murphy, K.J., and J.W. Eaton. 1983. Effects of pleasure-boat traffic on macrophyte growth in canals. Journal of Applied Ecology 20:713-729.

Naiman, R.J., H. Décamps, J. Pastor, and C.A. Johnston. 1988a. The potential importance of boundaries to fluvial ecosystems. Journal of the North American Benthological Society 7:289-306.

Naiman, R.J., C.A. Johnston, and J.C. Kelley. 1988b. Alteration of North American streams by beaver. BioScience 38:753-762.

Naiman, R.J., J.M. Melillo, and J.E. Hobbie. 1986. Ecosystem alteration of boreal forest streams by beaver (*Castor canadensis*). Ecology 67:1254-1269.

Nicholson, M. 1961. The environmental revolution. Penguin, Harmondsworth, England.

Omernik, J.M., A.R. Abernathy, and L.M. Male. 1981. Stream nutrient levels and proximity of agricultural and forest land to streams: some relationships. Journal of Soil and Water Conservation 36:227-231.

Pantulu, V.R. 1986. The Mekong River system. Pages 695-720 *in* B.R. Davies and K.F. Walker, editors. The ecology of river systems. Dr. W. Junk, Dordrecht, The Netherlands.

Pautou, G., and H. Décamps. 1984. Ecological interactions between the alluvial forests and hydrology of the Upper Rhöne. Archiv für Hydrobiologie 104:13-37.

Peterjohn, W.T., and D.L. Correll. 1984. Nutrient dynamics in an agricultural watershed: observations on the role of a riparian forest. Ecology 65:1466-1475.

Petrere, M. 1989. River fisheries in Brazil: a review. Regulated Rivers, 4(1):1-16.

Petts, G.E. 1980. Long-term consequences of upstream impoundment. Environmental Conservation 7:325-332.

Petts, G.E. 1984. Impounded rivers: perspectives for ecological management. Wiley, Chichester, England.

Petts, G.E. 1987. Timescales for ecological change in regulated rivers. Pages 257-266 *in* J.E. Craig and J.B. Kemper, editors. Regulated streams: advances in ecology. Plenum, New York, USA.

Petts, G.E. 1989. Perspectives for ecological management of regulated rivers. Pages 3-24 *in* J.A. Gore and G.E. Petts, editors. Alternatives in regulated river management. CRC Press, Boca Raton, Florida, USA.

Petts, G.E., and I.D.L. Foster. 1985. Rivers and landscape. Edward Arnold, London, England.

Petts, G.E., J.G. Imhof, B.A. Manny, J.F.B. Maher, and S.B. Weisberg. 1989a. Management of fish populations in large rivers: a review of tools and approaches. Canadian Journal of Fisheries and Aquatic Sciences. Special Publication 106:578-588.

Petts, G.E., A.L. Roux, and H. Moller (editors). 1989b. Historical changes of large alluvial rivers in Western Europe. Wiley, Chichester, England.

Petts, G.E., and R. Wood (editors). 1988. River regulation in the United Kingdom. Special Issue, Regulated Rivers 2(3).

Pinay, G., and H. Décamps. 1988. The role of riparian woods in regulating nitrogen fluxes between the alluvial aquifer and surface water: a conceptual model. Regulated Rivers 2:507-516.

Pinay, G., H. Décamps, E. Chauvet, and E. Fustec. 1990. Functions of ecotones in fluvial systems, *this volume*.

Platts, W.S. 1984. Fencing to control livestock grazing on riparian habitats along streams: is it a viable alternative? North American Fisheries Management 4:266.

Pringle, C.M., R.J. Naiman, G. Bretschko, J.R. Karr, M.W. Oswood, J.R. Webster, R.L. Welcomme, and M.J. Winterbourn. 1988. Patch dynamics on lotic systems: the stream as a mosaic. Journal of the North American Benthological Society 7:503-524.

Rankin, D. 1980. Trees and rivers. Journal of the Soil Conservation Service of New South Wales 36:129-133.

Ranney, J.W., M.C. Bruner, and J.B. Levenson. 1981. The importance of edge in the structure and dynamics of forest islands. Pages 67-96 *in* R.L. Burgess and D.M. Sharpe, editors. Forest island dynamics in man-dominated landscapes. Springer-Verlag, New York, USA.

Ratcliffe, D.A. (editor). 1977. A nature conservation review: the selection of biological sites of national importance to nature conservation in Britain. 2 volumes. Cambridge University Press, Cambridge, England.

Reilly, P.W., and W.C. Johnson. 1982. The effects of altered hydrologic regime on tree growth along the Missouri River in North Dakota. Canadian Journal of Botany 60:2410-2423.

Risser, P.G. 1990. The ecological importance of land-water ecotones, *this volume*.

Robertson, P.A., G.T. Weaver, and J.A. Cavanaugh. 1978. Vegetation and tree species patterns near the northern terminus of the southern floodplain forest. Ecological Monographs 48:249-267.

Rosenberg, D.M. 1986. Resources and development of the Mackenzie system. Pages 517-540 *in* B.R. Davies and K.F. Walker, editors. The ecology of river systems. Dr. W. Junk, Dordrecht, The Netherlands.

Royal Commission. 1976. Air pollution control: an integrated approach. Royal Commission on Environmental Pollution, 5th Report. Her Majesty's Stationery Office, London, England.

Royal Commission. 1988. Best practicable environmental option. Royal Commission on Environmental Pollution, 12th Report. Her Majesty's Stationery Office, London, England.

Salo, J. 1990. External processes influencing origin and maintenance of inland water-land ecotones, *this volume*.

Salo, J., R. Kalliola, I. Häkkinen, Y. Mäkinen, P. Niemelä, M. Puhakka, and P.D. Coley. 1986. River dynamics and the diversity of Amazon lowland forest. Nature 322:254-258.

Schumm, S.A. 1977. The fluvial system. Wiley, New York, USA.

Sedell, J.R., F.H. Everest, and F.J. Swanson. 1982. Fish habitat and streamside management: past and present. Pages 244-255 *in* Proceedings of the Society of American Foresters, Annual Meeting. Society of American Foresters, Bethesda, Maryland, USA.

Sedell, J.R., and J.L. Froggatt. 1984. Importance of streamside forests to large rivers: the isolation of the Willamette River, Oregon, USA, from its floodplain by snagging and streamside forest removal. Verhandlungen Internationale Vereinigung Limnologie 22:1828-1834.

Seibert, P. 1968. Naturnahe Querprofilgestaltung bei Anbau von Wasserlaufen. Natur und Landschaft 35:12-13.

Sewell, W.R.D., and A.K. Biswas. 1986. Implementing environmentally sound management of inland waters. Resources Policy 12:293.

Shugart, H.H. 1990. Ecological models and the ecotone, *this volume*.

Shuttleworth, S. 1983. Upland landscapes and the landscape image. Landscape Research 8:7-14.

Sigafoos, R.S. 1964. Botanical evidence of floods and floodplain depositions. U.S. Geological Survey Professional Paper 485-A:1-35.

Simberloff, D.S., and L.G. Abele. 1976. Island biogeography theory and conservation practice. Science 191:285-286.

Southwood, T.R.E. 1977. Habitat, the templet for ecological strategies? Journal of Animal Ecology 46:337-365.

Stanford, J.A., and J.V. Ward. 1986. The Colorado River System. Pages 353-374 *in* B.R. Davies and K.F. Walker, editors. The ecology of river systems. Dr. W. Junk, Dordrecht, The Netherlands.

Stockton, C.W., and H.W. Fritts. 1973. Long-term reconstruction of water level changes for Lake Athabasca by analysis of tree rings. Water Resources Bulletin 9:1006-1027.

Triska, F.J. 1984. Role of wood debris in modifying channel geomorphology and riparian areas of a large lowland river under pristine conditions: a historical case study. Verhandlungen Internationale Vereinigung Limnologie 22:1876-1892.

Tuan, Y.F. 1973. Visual blight: exercises in interpretation. Pages 23-27 *in* P.F. Lewis, D. Lowenthal, and Y.F. Tuan, editors. Visual blight in America. College Resource Paper 23, American Association of Geographers, Washington, D.C., USA.

Turner, K. 1985. The Broads grazing marshes conservation scheme. Landscape Research 10:28-39.

Turner, R.M., and M.M. Karpiscak. 1980. Recent vegetation changes along the Colorado River between Glen Canyon Dam and Lake Mead. United States Geological Survey, Professional Paper 1132.

Walker, K.F. 1986. The Murray-Darling river system. Pages 631-660 *in* B.R. Davies and K.F. Walker, editors. The ecology of river systems. Dr. W. Junk, Dordrecht, The Netherlands.

Walther, P. 1986. The meaning of zoning in the management of natural resource lands. Journal of Environmental Management 22:331-343.

Welcomme, R.L. 1979. Fisheries ecology of floodplain rivers. Longman, London, England.

Welcomme, R.L. 1989. Floodplain fisheries management. Pages 209-234 *in* J.A. Gore and G.E. Petts, editors. Alternatives in regulated river management. CRC Press, Boca Raton Florida, USA.

Williams, G.P. 1978. The case of the shrinking channels: the North Platte and Platte Rivers Nebraska. United States Geological Survey, Circular 781.

Wolman, M.G., and R. Gerson. 1978. Relative scales of time in watershed geomorphology. Earth Surface Process 3:189-208.

Yates, P., and J.M. Sheridan. 1983. Estimating the effectiveness of vegetated floodplains/wetlands as nitrate-nitrite and orthophosphorous filters. Agricultural Ecosystems and Environment 9:303-314.

Yousef, M.M., and A.M. El-Sheikh. 1981. The vegetation alongside a running water canal at Al-Kharj. Journal of the College of Science, Riyard University 12:23-51.

Key words: Applied ecology, boundary, ecotone, management, terrestrial-aquatic.

CHAPTER 12

THE SOCIO-ECONOMIC VALUE OF ECOTONES

Brigitte Desaigues

ABSTRACT

The conflicts between different uses of ecotones are highlighted with examples from the Renaissance to the present. As a first step towards the resolution of such conflicts, one needs to develop methodologies for obtaining quantitative estimates of the socio-economic values of ecotones. The economic theory of measuring environmental benefits is reviewed, and the principal tools are described and illustrated with examples: the travel cost method, the hedonic price method, and contingent valuation. Complications, due to uncertainty and irrational behaviour, are also discussed. The last part of the chapter addresses the management of ecotones. The major threats to ecotones involve questions of land use. The experiences with various regulatory approaches in different countries are reviewed.

CONFLICTS BETWEEN DIFFERENT USES OF ECOTONES

The interest of ecotones

Ecotones can be envisioned as transition zones between land and water (banks of rivers, lakes, ponds, swamps, and estuaries) as well as regions where exchanges between surface and underground water occur. Thanks to the interaction between different ecosystems, ecotones are especially rich in flora and fauna, forming a genetic pool for microevolution. They play a role as regulator and stabiliser of landscapes, by controlling the flow of water and other matter between adjacent areas, by filtering nutrients (phosphorus and nitrogen), and by maintaining diversity. They also contribute to the formation of microclimates. For a more detailed description of the characteristics of ecotones we refer to the other articles in this volume, in particular the one by Petts.

A consumer values an ecotone for its potential uses, and these are highly dependent on his or her profession, income, and culture. A farmer raises fish in the ponds of an ecotone, a hunter benefits from its rich fauna, the local environment protection agency counts on the purifying effect of its forests, a hiker is charmed by a beautiful landscape that brings relief from the stress of city life. But the farmer may also prefer to drain ponds and swamps to increase grain production, and the government may decide to straighten a river for navigation or dam it for flood control.

Let us illustrate the relativity of preferences with an example that may appear extreme but whose basic pattern is typical: the wetlands of Bharatpur, India (Purseglove 1986). These wetlands serve as wintering habitat for the Siberian crane, which is threatened by extinction. For the farmers of Bharatpur the protection of the wetlands presents a very negative value, interfering as it does with the collection of fuelwood and the grazing of cattle. But for the Indian government and for the international scientific community these wetlands embody a reserve of great value. Not surprisingly, the farmers rebelled when the government prohibited the traditional uses; six people were killed during the confrontation. It is not always possible to satisfy all the diverging interests. History shows that man has sometimes, for reasons of economic welfare or public health, destroyed ecotones after having patiently built, preserved, and utilised them over centuries. The ecological imperative cannot always stand up to other, more urgent claims, especially when it is often poorly understood or appreciated.

Evolution of conflicts: a historical perspective

Since the beginning of history man has exploited the richness offered by ecotones, as evidenced by the earliest settlements on lakes and riverbanks. With the evolution of agriculture and increased population densities, he has further learned to drain wetlands and make them habitable (e.g. marshes in Holland and in the southwest of France). He began to create new ecotones, well aware of the diverse fauna they could provide, and he learned to manage them for his greatest benefit. But this benefit cannot be appreciated in the same manner today as 500 years ago. As standards of living and culture rise, novel uses become more desirable, and one cannot condemn them in the name of some mythical 'good old days.' Some examples will illustrate such socio-economic changes of 'best use' and the emergence of new conflicts over the course of history.

Management of wetlands. To begin, we mention the ponds of Dombes (Berard 1982). The region of Dombes (Department de l'Ain, France) is a plain of 900 km², 250 to 300 m above sea level, more or less inclined in the southeast-northwest direction, and with shallow valleys. The soil is clay, almost impermeable, and moist because of abundant rainfall. This has allowed the inhabitants to create, since the 13th century, artificial ponds, simply by raising shallow dams and flooding low-lying areas. In the 15th century these ponds were considered 'in the public interest.' The carp (*Cyprinus carpio*) raised in these ponds brought good money, and the activity was declared tax exempt. By the 18th century more than 200 km² were covered by water. Today the ponds account for only 110 km², after having been almost completely dried up during the second half of the 19th century; 60 km² of ponds in the Dombes region were eliminated to make room for the construction of the Bourg-Santonay railway. In addition, a lively debate arose around 1850 between those who depended on the carp and those who wanted to drain the ponds for public health. The ponds were blamed for fever epidemics that raged in the region. For similar reasons the swamps of the Landes (southwest France) have been drained, and their disappearance was considered at the time as social progress. Paradoxically, what saved the ponds of Dombes was the criterion of profitability, while those of the Landes were eliminated because there was no economic interest (low population density).

Even today the production of carp (mostly for export) continues to be profitable in the Dombes, and this unique system of man-made ponds is being maintained. However, new activities are beginning to encroach upon this old practice, partly complementary to, partly in competition with it: hunting and tourism. The ecotone is not destroyed, but its uses are being reconsidered as the society that created it evolves.

In developed countries, especially of northern Europe, the principal threat to wetlands arises from the pressure to drain them to make more land available for agriculture. But such drainage has been going on for centuries: while in France only 10% of the total agricultural land has been obtained by draining, this percentage is 37% in the Federal Republic of Germany and 65% in the Netherlands (Baldock 1984). This development has been supported directly by the governments of Europe, especially since the Second World War, to increase agricultural output.

Management of water flow. In order to improve the flow of rivers to avoid floods, to better drain the land, and to facilitate navigation, rivers have been straightened or dammed (Décamps and Naiman 1989). Thus the area of riparian zones has been reduced along with the diversity of flora and fauna in a region. But one must recall the damage that used to be inflicted by floods; once a natural process has been brought under permanent control, people tend to forget its ravages and begin to criticise the measures taken because of their secondary effects. This latter example illustrates a classical conflict between managers and protectors of the environment, or between farmers and protectors of the environment.

Current trends. Today these conflicts appear more acute because of increased population density and the associated intensification of the use of natural resources and environments. The conflicts evolve along with the society that produces them. Ours differ from those of the past because of conditions peculiar to our time: (1) the search for ever more efficient exploitation of ecotones in the course of the rapid growth since the Second World War; (2) the increased population density (the world population has just passed the 5 billion mark, with projections of around 10 billion by the middle of the next century); and (3) changes in individual preferences, tied to improved standards of living and increasing appreciation of environmental goods.

Extrapolating the tendencies apparent today, one might expect that in developed countries the old conflicts with or between commercial uses of ecotones may partly be replaced by conflicts with housing and with or between leisure activities: hunting, fishing, tourism, and nature preserves.

Towards a solution

To resolve these conflicts it is necessary, first of all, to determine the value of what is to be protected, in accordance with the preferences of society. This forms the subject of the next section, where we survey the methods available for estimating the socio-economic value of ecotones (these techniques are equally valid for any environmental good). The basic problem is that ecotones do not have a price that adequately expresses their value, whereas a market economy requires the translation of values into prices. Economists have made great progress in this direction, and today the theory of the valuation of nonmarket goods is well developed. Once the question of the value of an ecotone has been settled, one can proceed to the thorny problem of management. There are many conflicts, mostly linked to rights of property. Frequently the latter are not clearly defined. Who owns the river? The farmer whose land is flooded periodically, the tourist who likes to picnic in the shade of a willow, or the engineer in charge of preventing natural catastrophes? Environmentalists, taking themselves in effect to be legitimate proprietors of certain attributes of ecotones such as biological diversity, accuse farmers of destroying these attributes in the name of a narrow and egotistic property right that legitimises the maximisation of agricultural output (and with it their standard of living). How can one explain to the farmers that their property rights are now reduced by certain restrictions, while they continue to be subject to full payment of the property taxes?

To an increasing extent farmers are being asked to become the guardians of the landscape. But we must not forget the cost: wetlands suffer from reduced productivity and increased incidence of cattle disease. If drainage is not sufficiently profitable or if the restrictions on the use of the land become too stringent without adequate compensation, the farmer may prefer to abandon the land, as has happened in parts of Normandy, France (Mermet and Mustin 1983). Thus it becomes necessary to find new management modes that can take such goods into account and that can adapt themselves to growing demands for environmental protection. These modes could be of a regulatory or of a decentralised nature; for instance, a farmer could learn to place a value on a new good for which a demand is developing. Such values will not always be easy to implement, because of conflicts with preexisting property rights. Whenever there is change, there is conflict. And those who demand protection of the environment must also expect to bear some of the cost. One is faced with a problem of adjustments over time and space for which the solution is not obvious. These questions form the subject of the section below on management of ecotones. The chapter closes with some recommendations for future research.

THE VALUATION OF SOCIAL BENEFITS OF ECOTONES

Economists have developed tools that enable a public decision maker to include in his economic evaluation both nonmarket goods and uncertainties (Johanson 1987). In this section we describe cost-benefit analysis (CBA), a method of choice currently used in developed marked economies, and we add a discussion of the techniques used to quantify the value of certain functions of ecotones.

Theoretical postulates of CBA (a brief summary)

CBA is a single-criterion selection method that identifies and measures costs and benefits associated with alternative projects (Layard 1974). The benefits are measured by the increase in the production of goods and services, including those provided by the environment. Costs are measured by the increase of resources used by the project. Costs and benefits are summed over time, with correction factors that reduce them to equivalent present values. The utility of money is assumed to be the same for all individuals: the utility of avoiding a loss of $1 equals the utility of a gain of $1. This is an approximation, because the relation between money and utility is not necessarily linear, as we shall see later.

The aim of CBA is to extend the domain of economic rationality to public decisions. The allocation of resources according to CBA is consistent with that of the market, because it respects the economic efficiency criterion. This concept is used to rank social states on the basis of two main value judgements:

1. Social ranking ought to be based on individual preferences, where it is implicitly assumed that each individual is the best judge of his preferences and acts rationally – that is to say in a consistent manner. Changes in individual utilities are equated with changes in consumer surplus (defined below).

2. The Pareto principle says that state A is better than state B if it improves the well-being of a person without diminishing the well-being of another person. But to compare two states characterised by gainers and losers we must have recourse to the generalised Pareto principle: the choice of a project can be justified if it offers a net benefit to society as a whole, even if it is not followed by compensation of the loser by the gainers.

CBA uses the market prices to calculate costs and benefits, and assumes that the project is sufficiently small not to modify the relative price structure. CBA is used to evaluate and rank a small number of alternative projects, not to find the optimum.

While there is no organised market for environmental goods, consumers do express their preferences implicitly. The economist must quantify these preferences by observing how consumers allocate their resources. The analysis of consumer behaviour permits the calculation of values as if a market existed, at least in principle.

Measuring environmental benefits

One can distinguish two categories of environmental benefits: those that pass through the market and those that do not. For the former, one or several attributes of the environment enter into the production function of market goods such as forest products, commercial fish, or water. An improvement of environmental quality entrains enhanced productivity or reduced production costs for such goods. Based on prices and revenues seen by individuals, these effects can be measured using simple models that integrate supply and demand functions. In the same way, direct costs or damage functions are used to measure the benefit of pollution control.

Among the benefits that do not pass through the market, one can distinguish between those that can be measured by observing the behaviour of consumers, and those, when consumer behaviour is too difficult to observe, that can be evaluated by direct interrogation.

What is measured? In the case of market goods, the price measures the willingness to pay for the last unit that is consumed. The relation between price P and quantity Q is called the demand function; it is shown schematically in Fig. 12.1, where the area P'ABP" represents a change in consumer surplus if price changes from P' to P".

If the price is P', the consumer purchases all Q' units at the same price P', even though he would be willing to pay more than P' for the initial units. The difference between the amount he actually pays and the total amount he would be willing to pay is called the consumer surplus. It is a monetary approximation of his individual utility. To illustrate this important concept, consider a price drop from P' to P"; then the consumer surplus increases by the area P'ABP". Analogously, an improvement in environmen-

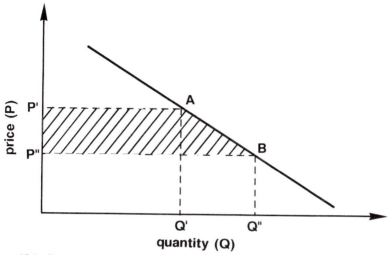

Figure 12.1 Demand function and consumer surplus

tal quality expresses itself as a change in consumer surplus, corresponding to a change of his well-being.

However, this measure of consumer surplus is controversial. It is not strictly a measure of the change in well-being, because when moving along the demand curve, it is the income that is held constant and not the utility; a price change implies a change in utility. To arrive at an ideal monetary measure of changes in well-being one should use the compensated demand curves of Hicks (1943); they allow the well-being to be held constant, either at the initial or at the final level. Thus one obtains two measures of surplus: (1) compensating surplus, measured relative to the initial state, and (2) equivalent surplus, measured relative to the final state.

To illustrate, let us compare the three measures of surplus in Fig. 12.2, where the Hicksian demand functions have been superimposed on the ordinary demand function of Fig. 12.1. Since the Hicksian demand function is defined with respect to a particular price, two such functions are shown: H' for price P' and H" for price P". The ordinary surplus is seen to lie between the two Hicksian measures: the compensating surplus (area P'ADP") and the equivalent surplus (P'CBP") (Smith 1986). In practice, Hicksian demand curves are difficult to determine. The problem is further complicated by the psychological factors discussed later.

In environmental matters one is faced with changes in quality rather than price, hence we define the following measures of surplus: (1) the compensating surplus is the amount an individual is willing to pay for an improvement of the environment (i.e. willingness to pay); and (2) the equivalent surplus is the amount an individual would have to receive in the absence of an improvement if he is to have the same satisfaction as if

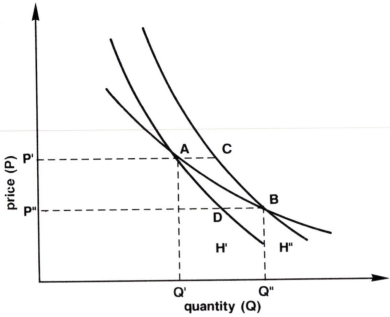

Figure 12.2 Hicksian demand curves H' and H", compensating surplus and equivalent surplus

the improvement were implemented (i.e. willingness to receive).

Determination of the demand function for environmental goods. Widely used in the estimation of recreational benefits, the *travel cost method* was introduced by Clawson and Knetsch (1966). The idea is simple: people express their demand for a recreational site through their travel expenditures (and possibly entrance fees) necessary to reach the site. The demand function is constructed from the relation between the travel cost (price) and number of visits (demand), considering a number of suitably chosen geographic regions. In the simplest case one looks at travel cost proportional to distance, one assumes that the site is the only goal of the trip, and one does not distinguish between different activities at the site.

The surplus provided by the site is measured by the area under the demand curve and the horizontal line corresponding to the actual travel cost, as shown in Fig. 12.3. If travel cost or entrance fee increases relative to income, the demand (i.e. the number of visits) drops. The value associated with the improvement of a site is approximated by the increase in the frequency of visits, at this or at comparable sites.

Since its introduction, this method has been developed and refined, taking into account such items as sociodemographic variables (income, age, etc.), existence of substitute sites (Krutilla and Fisher 1975), and value of the time spent in transit to or at the site (Mendelsohn 1984, Smith and

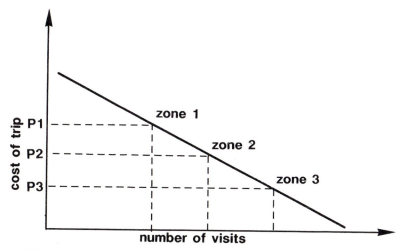

Figure 12.3 Demand curve for recreational site

Desvouges 1986).

To estimate the value of a single attribute of a site, one starts by estimating the demand for a number of comparable sites, aggregating all attributes except the one of interest (e.g. the density of game). Then one regresses the differences in demand for a site against the difference in this attribute (Mendelsohn 1984). In the United States, where the travel cost method has been used routinely to evaluate the benefits of recreation, roughly half of the total benefits from improvements in water quality are due to recreational benefits (Freeman 1986).

With certain goods the market price reflects the demand for environmental attributes. The price of a house, for example, depends on the air quality of the site. Correlating the price of houses with air quality, one can derive the demand function for clean air. The *hedonic price method* has been used successfully for the region of Los Angeles, USA (Brookshire *et al.* 1981). One assumes that, all else being equal, a difference in price captures the entire willingness to pay for better air quality. The collection and analysis of data require not only much effort but extreme care to ensure scientific validity. In this study the authors have identified pairs of regions that are as identical as possible in all aspects (especially socio-economic variables) except air quality. Thus the difference in price reflects the difference in the value of air quality as perceived by the inhabitants, assuming they are properly informed. Another interesting application of this method is the evaluation of the impact of zoning on the price of houses in the Chesapeake Bay area, USA (Beaton 1988).

The consensus is that this method yields a lower bound on the willingness to pay, because people find it difficult to express a preference for air quality (or protected shorelines) when buying a house: since it is only one among a large number of competing criteria, air quality may be overwhelmed by other criteria. The difficulty and thus the high cost to implement this method explain why it has remained relatively undeveloped.

One of the potential benefits of environmental improvement lies in the reduction of defensive expenditures (e.g. reduced need to repaint buildings if there is less acid rain). However, it has been found that the value of such effects is generally small compared with recreational benefits (Courant and Porter 1981). The household production function is sometimes used to understand the relation between market goods and the value associated with environmental improvements. But the requirement for extensive data bases and sophisticated econometric analyses has considerably limited their application.

Contingent valuation methods. When behaviour is difficult to interpret, one can ask people directly how much they would be willing to pay for an environmental improvement, as if a market did exist. This method supposes that the answers given when presented with a hypothetical situation correspond to what one could have observed in a market. In recent years much important research on the CBA has focussed on this approach (Cummings *et al.* 1986), since it is the only one that can account for intangible benefits.

One proposes to the interviewee a change in environmental quality and asks two questions: (1) What is the largest amount you would be willing to pay for it (compensating surplus)? (2) For a reduction in quality, what is the lowest amount you would be willing to accept as compensation for this loss (equivalent surplus)? In addition, the questionnaire includes socio-economic variables such as income, age, and profession.

As long as income effects are weak (i.e. account for small changes), economic theory considers willingness to pay and equivalent surplus as equivalent measures. In practice, however, one finds great differences: the equivalent surplus is larger, sometimes by as much as a factor of 10. For that reason one usually chooses the willingness to pay: it seems to correspond more closely to the type of market transactions with which people are familiar.

Some weaknesses of the method remain, in particular because of bias due to the payment vehicle or due to the choice of initial bid. The respondent may lack the experience to express his preferences correctly. And often the outcome depends on the quality of the questionnaire and the skill of the interviewer. Moreover, one assumes that people are adequately informed, that they are capable of rank ordering their preferences, that they are consistent in their choices, and that their responses are without bias.

Let us compare the results of this method with those obtained by the travel cost method and by the hedonic price method, for three examples.

Comparison of different valuation methods. Smith and Desvouges (1986) estimated, for the year 1981, the recreational value of a change in water quality along the Monongahela River in Pennsylvania (USA). They used two methods: contingent valuation and travel cost method. For the purpose of the study they divided the region into 13 sites, considered comparable in all aspects except water quality. The conclusions are based on a sample of 69 persons who use these sites. Three possible changes in water quality are considered: (1) a deterioration that would eliminate all recreational activities, (2) an amelioration that would allow fishing, and (3) an amelioration that would allow swimming. The results are shown, as annual values (1981, U.S.$), in Table 12.1.

Theoretically the travel cost method, as a measure of consumer surplus, should be higher than the willingness to pay and lower than the willingness to receive. The different contingent valuations depend on the question that was asked: direct question; payment vehicle such as annual tax or bill; or an offer of bids (would you pay $...? increasing from a starting value of $25 or decreasing from a starting value of $125). Part of the discrepancy between the different results is attributed to the existence of substitute sites, implicitly taken into account by people when they choose the destination of their trip. Their choices have evolved through experience, and this is implicitly reflected in the travel cost method. The latter is thus more reliable than contingent valuation, which confronts people with a question they are not accustomed to answering.

Duffield (1984) has estimated, for the year 1981, the benefit of preserving the Kootenai Falls (Montana, USA), for which a hydroelectric development has been proposed. He used the travel cost method and contingent valuation, and compared the results, as summarised here in Table 12.2. The travel cost method is based on a sample of 462 persons, and the contingent valuation on 281 persons, with extrapolation to 63,700 visits per year. Two models are considered: log-linear and semilogarithmic. The

Table 12.1 Results obtained by the travel cost method and by contingent valuation, for improvement of water quality of the Monongahela River. From Smith and Desvouges (1986)

Approach	Sample size	*Water Quality Change (annual values, 1981 U.S.$)*		
		Loss of area	*Boatable to fishing*	*Boatable to swimming*
Contingent valuation				
Direction question	17	19.71	21.18	31.18
Payment card	17	19.71	30.88	51.18
Iterative bidding ($25)	19	6.58	4.21	10.53
Iterative bidding ($125)	16	36.25	20.13	48.75
Simple travel cost method	69	3.53	7.16	28.86

Table 12.2 Travel cost method and contingent valuation. Adapted from Duffield (1984)

Category	Annual Value (1981 U.S.$1000)
Travel cost estimate log-linear	243
Semilog	420
Willingness to pay	
Entrance fee	91
Utility bill	1002
Willingness to drive	536
Compensation survey estimate	
1981	6359
1982	4995
Compensation survey direct only	
1981	700
1982	550

latter is better for the subgroup for whom the falls are only a stopover.

More interesting is the difference that appears between the willingness to pay and the equivalent surplus (or compensation), for which the current literature finds a ratio in the range of 1 to 6. In Duffield's study, when people are asked what fraction of the compensation they attribute to the loss of direct use, they do not indicate more than 11% of the willingness to receive (or equivalent surplus). We shall come back to the question of direct and indirect use when we discuss option value later. Finally, we note the dependence on payment vehicle. For a fictitious entrance fee people answer by analogy to entrance fees that exist in the region; for a utility bill their valuation corresponds to the maximal willingness to pay. The willingness to drive, another form of contingent valuation, corresponds to the additional distance that people say they would be willing to drive to visit the falls. The travel time is not counted, because most people state that they consider it a pleasure rather than a cost.

The contingent valuation and hedonic price methods are compared in a study by Brookshire *et al.* (1981) to evaluate the social benefit of an air quality improvement in the region of Los Angeles (California, USA). This region was chosen for two reasons: statistical data are available, and the population is quite aware of local differences in air quality. These methods could be applied to ecotones as well, such as the valuation of land or houses along a river (Beaton 1988).

In order to be able to attribute a difference of house prices to a difference of air quality, the authors arranged the data in six pairs of sites that are approximately equivalent in all socio-economic variables except air quality.

Simple correlation between prices and air quality suggests that 25% of the price difference is associated with a move from poor to intermediate air quality (defined as 17% difference in suspended particulates and 26% difference in NOx), and 28% of the price difference is associated with a move from intermediate to good air quality (additional 24% reduction in suspended particulates and 32% in NOx). At a second stage the authors have refined their results by correcting the price differences according to income, quality of neighbourhood, and so forth. Now the corresponding price differences are only 6.5%. That implies a willingness to pay approximately $43 per month.

For the contingent valuation, the term *air quality* has been divided into three characteristics: aesthetic effects, acute health effects, and chronic health effects. Photographs were shown to illustrate the difference between poor, intermediate, and good air quality. Different payment vehicles were employed to test the sensitivity of the responses. The results indicated an average value of $26 to $29 per month. That contingent values are less than the implicit willingness to pay is to be expected, because the former is limited by the demand function of the individual whereas the latter takes into account differences in demand functions between low and high income individuals.

Valuation of the natural production functions. In cases where certain functions of an ecotone provide direct commercial benefits, one obtains a lower bound for the value of the ecotone by measuring the cost of substitutes that would be necessary if the ecotone were to disappear (Batie and Shabman 1982). Four examples illustrate this approach.

1. Marshland has a certain capacity of wastewater cleanup, estimated at 21.7 kg of BOD (biological oxygen demand) per ha per day (Gosselink *et al.* 1974, as cited by Point 1986). Given that the alternative cost of eliminating a kg of BOD is $0.088, such a marsh is therefore worth $700 per ha per year as a secondary water treatment plant. This economic value exists only if there is a social demand for water treatment.

2. The Gulf Coast of the United States provides an example where marshes can have a certain economic value as a buffer zone against hurricanes. Taking into account the magnitudes and probabilities of property damage due to hurricanes, as a function of the depth of the coastal buffer zone, Farber (1987, 1988) derives an estimate for the resulting social value of marshland. In his study, the value of hurricane protection turns out to be an order of magnitude smaller than the value of mineral and hunting rights.

3. The value of marshland for the production of crabs has been estimated by Lynne *et al.* (1981), using a bioeconomic model. The authors consider

that the price of crabs rewards two production factors, labour and land. The productivity off these marshes is low, and so is the resulting estimate for the value of the land: about $7/ha. If the demand for crabs were to go up, the production mode would change from simple collection with traps to intensive cultivation, and the value of the marsh would increase.

4. Brown and Hammack (1974), in a famous study of the demand for hunting, determined the value of wetlands near the American-Canadian border for the reproduction of migratory waterfowl. As this value turns out to be higher than that of producing grain, it would be preferable for society to preserve these wetlands for the reproduction of waterfowl. However, the implementation of this conclusion faces a serious practical difficulty: the wetlands are located in Canada, the hunters in the United States.

While these examples show the progress that has been made in the valuation of environmental goods, they also highlight how difficult (and thus expensive) it is to carry out a good study and how much the results can depend on the method. Furthermore, without a social demand, no value could be assigned to the production function of an ecotone.

Decision under uncertainty and irreversibility

Until now we have assumed that people are well informed, certain of their choices, and understand the consequences. But uncertainty is large for environmental issues. People do not know the exact probability of becoming sick as a result of air pollution; they do not know whether an environmental good will be available tomorrow, or whether they will actually use it at some time in the future. Furthermore, some choices may be difficult or impossible to reverse.

The concept of option value has been developed to account for the value that a person assigns to the elimination of uncertainty regarding availability or use of a future resource. Another way of dealing with uncertainty is to postpone the decision until better information becomes available. Some theoretical literature has sprung up around the study of this process (the quasi-option value of Henry 1974, Arrow and Fisher 1974) which we do not discuss because it does not yet seem to have found much practical application.

Definition of option value. The benefits associated with environmental improvements are generally considered to be of two types: those linked to its direct use (recreation, irrigation, etc.), and those linked to its mere existence. The latter are grouped under the term *option value*. This classification is not always clearcut; aesthetic values, for example, are often included among the latter. In any case, the option value has been found to play a very significant role. For instance, some people are willing to pay a substantial amount of money for the creation of wildlife preserves in central Africa, even if they are not sure of ever visiting them; they want to ensure the option of having these sites in case the opportunity of a visit arises, or they simply treasure their existence as part of our natural heritage. The option value is defined as the amount an individual is willing to pay, in addition to the expected value of his or her direct use, in order to reduce the uncertainty or ensure the existence of future use (Weisbrod 1964, and many others).

Theoretical measure of option value. Let us take a hypothetical example, adapted from Bishop (1986). Suppose a certain remote site, the habitat of an endangered reindeer, is threatened by a proposed mining development. Mr. Citizen is asked how much the preservation of this site is worth to him. He is not a current user of the site, but he esimates his probability of wanting to visit this site at some time in the future as 50%; furthermore he states that the present value of his consumer surplus, in case of a visit, would be $175 (ex post value, discounted to the present). If the visit never takes place, his surplus is zero. Thus the expectation value of his surplus is $87.50 ($=\$175*0.50 + \$0*0.50$). However, he is willing to pay $100 now if that ensures the preservation of the site (economists use the term *option price* to designate willingness to pay in the presence of uncertainty). The difference between the expectation value of his surplus and what he is willing to pay now is his option value; it is $100 - \$87.50 = \$12.50$.

Option value in practice. This kind of precision is difficult to achieve in practice, as most individuals have only a vague idea of the monetary value of their well-being. An attempt to measure option value has been made by Smith and Desvouges (1986) as part of their study mentioned earlier. In their contingent valuation survey they took great care to explain, to each of the 301 families in the study, the concepts of use value and option value. Users and nonusers were interviewed and four different payment vehicles were considered. Faced with a potential loss, people stated an option value amounting to 60 to 76% of their willingness to pay. For an improvement of water quality the option value represents 30 to 60% of the willingness to pay (the percentages depend on payment vehicle and on starting value of the bids). Generally, option values appear to be comparable to use values (Fisher and Raucher 1984). However, one should beware that the results are highly dependent on the quality of the questionnaires and the skill of the interviewers.

Limits of the applicability of cost–benefit analysis

It would be a grave error to believe that CBA could be employed in all situations. Because of such errors, CBA is often rejected out of hand, even if there is no better alternative. The economist must be careful to consider the limitations and weaknesses of CBA.

Implicit hypotheses about individual behaviour. The assumption of rational behaviour may be fairly valid for routine transactions, where people benefit from extensive learning experience. But when one comes to infrequent or unusual occurrences, experience and intuition are lacking. The resulting behaviour frequently appears irrational. The valuation of environmental benefits often falls outside the realm of everyday experience. There is no established price system to hone our intuition about values, and often the effects of our actions are very uncertain.

The work of Kahneman and Tversky (1986) can shed some light on these questions. These authors, in a series of classic experiments, have attempted to measure the value that individuals assign to potential gains and losses. They found: (1) a loss of $100 appears more negative than a gain of $100 appears positive; (2) people are risk adverse when faced with an uncertain gain: they tend to prefer a small but certain gain to one that is larger (in expectation value) but uncertain; and (3) people are risk seekers when faced with a certain loss: they tend to prefer an uncertain loss to one that is certain even if the resulting expectation value is more negative.

These preferences can be understood if the relation between money and utility is not linear but rather of the type sketched in Fig. 12.4. These

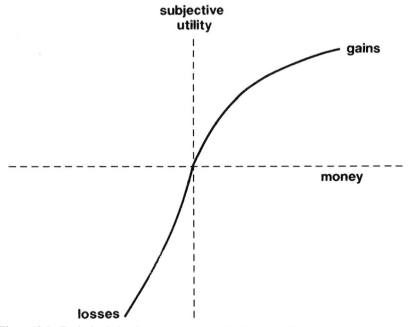

Figure 12.4 Typical relation between money and subjective utility

deviations from rationality (in the sense of the economist) depend very much on the circumstances. They are substantial: their magnitude can easily exceed 30%. Rationality is greatest in routine transactions, for example the buying and selling carried out by merchants. Some of these phenomena have already been studied more than two centuries ago by Bernoulli (1738), who explained the aversion risk in terms of decreasing marginal utility of money. In addition, choices can be influenced by the context in which they are made: if a choice can be phrased in two logically equivalent ways, one involving an apparent gain, the other an apparent loss, the decision is likely to depend on the phrasing of the choice – a phenomenon known as framing. Finally, there is a bias in subjective probabilities. Gains with intermediate probabilities are underestimated, gains with small probabilities are overestimated, and gains with very small probabilities are either neglected or overestimated. In any case, the subjective perception of probabilities can introduce large errors in the valuation of environmental benefits. These effects do not mean that one should reject the principle of maximising the expectation value of utility. But as long as people have not learned the principles of rationality, the peculiarities of behaviour should be taken into account (Arrow 1983). The World Bank (Yudelman 1985) has found that in the poorest countries risk aversion leads peasants to minimise their losses rather than maximise their gains. This fact has prevented the attainment of the goals of certain development projects.

Aggregation of costs and benefits over time. Future costs and benefits must be expressed as equivalent present values, since $1 next year does not have the same utility as $1 today (the latter could be spent, yielding immediate gratification, or it could be invested, yielding income). The equations are analogous to the calculation of compound interest, with a rate that is called social discount rate. We do not want to join the debate about the appropriate choice of this rate, referring instead to the review by Lind (1982). At this point we address two related problems.

First, what is the present value of goods whose value increases over time? Environmental goods do not benefit from technological progress, and their supply does not increase. Their demand, on the other hand, will grow under the pressure of increasing population and increasing standard of living (Desaigues and Toutain 1978). Thus their value is likely to grow, as has indeed been observed in developed countries. In the discounting of future values, the growth of environmental values must be taken into account – for example, by using an escalation rate. For the choice of this rate there is an interesting model by Henry (Organisation for Economic Cooperation and Development 1986), who shows how, for an optimal utilisation, the price escalation rate should depend on the renewal rate of the resource.

Second, what should be the time span on the analysis? It should be limited by the time scale over which personal preferences change. Such change is rapid during periods of strong technological growth, as we are experiencing now. Thus it may be risky to extend the analysis more than 5 or 10 years into the future. And even when preferences remain invariant, the willingness to pay for the protection of the environment increases with increasing income.

Valuation of ecological damage. The valuation of ecological damage is very difficult to realise when there is no direct impact on human activities. And even when there is a direct impact, one should not forget that the reactions to this kind of damage (loss of biological diversity, changes in productivity, alteration of natural processes such as filtering of nutrients, etc.) are very different for people of different cultural background. One of the fundamental difficulties lies in the long time lag between cause and effect. Our actions today will slowly degrade the environment, and the negative effects will take a long time to become fully apparent. Thus it is difficult to imagine an optimal allocation of resources over space and time. We are condemned to err and to bear the cost of these errors. Let us, more modestly, try to limit this cost, especially in developing countries, by recognising the limits of valuation, by seeking other means of managing natural resources when economic calculation becomes insufficient, and by avoiding, whenever possible, irreversible actions (difficult though this may be, especially in the poorest countries with their rapidly growing population).

Note that the concept of irreversibility is not always clearcut in practice. Natural systems have a strong resilience, although with different time constants for different effects. A change that may appear irreversible on the scale of a decade may correct itself over the course of centuries. For instance, in certain rivers of France where salmon had completely disappeared around 1900 because of pollution, they have since returned. Further research in ecological risk assessment will certainly help to clarify this concept.

Domain of applicability of CBA. To sum up, cost-benefit analysis should be limited to those projects where (1) people are capable of assigning monetary values to their preferences, (2) people have learned from experience to be consistent in their choices, and (3) the pertinent information is readily available.

It is not surprising that this method has been applied in the most developed countries. Could it be used in developing countries as well? The answer is yes, with precautions and, as necessary, supplemented by nonmonetary measures of costs and benefits – a solution that seems to be followed by the World Bank for the evaluation of the profitability of projects.

How about centrally planned economies? In theory the allocation of resources in these countries is already at the social optimum. But in practice the protection of the environment faces problems similar to those of market countries. Also there is a trend towards decentralised decision making. An adaptation of CBA could easily be imagined, and it would certainly be interesting to see how these economies might manage their environmental goods.

CBA and the search for optimal solutions. In the past, most applications of CBA have been rather narrow in scope, simply comparing a proposed project with the status quo or a reference project. For example, one would ask: should a swamp area be drained for corn production or left as it is? If left undeveloped, the area would have, say, a certain recreational benefit to hunters. The decision would thus depend on whether the net benefit of development (profit from corn production minus cost of draining) exceeds the recreational benefit. However, the tools of CBA could also be employed in the search for optimal projects. For the example of the swamp area, one could consider any degree of partial development, as well as a mix of several different types of development (e.g. cattle production, biomass plantation, and nature preserve). Such an analysis is more complex, and consequently more expensive than a simple yes or no decision. But we benefit from the learning experience, and with time, gain more and more experience in the evaluation of environmental projects; and thus the cost of information decreases.

MANAGEMENT OF ECOTONES

Good management of ecotones requires decision tools that can identify the 'good choice', based on the agreed upon criteria, and a social organisation that allows the efficient implementation of the decisions.

The role of organisation is crucial. We know from experience that some types of organisation are more costly and less efficient than others. One would like to be able to identify those that are most efficient. The problem is complex, and our understanding is still very incomplete. Instead of trying to develop a general theoretical framework, we discuss several examples, bad ones and good ones, from which important lessons can be drawn. What follows concerns essentially the developed countries, with particular reference to France.

Sources of failure

Even if the tools for good decision making exist, quite a few decisions that have been made cast doubt on the rationality of public choices. Such failures can be explained mainly by erroneous economic analysis, a decision process ill suited for current problems, inefficient regulatory instruments, and gaps in scientific knowledge.

Erroneous economic analysis. In his review of wetland drainage in Europe, Baldock (1984) concludes that cost-benefit analysis is an excellent tool but has frequenlty been carried out in a careless or misleading manner. Underestimation of environmental costs and overly optimistic assessment of profits from development are typical.

As an example of inadequate or unrealistic economic analysis we cite the Port of Saint Nazaire, France (Henry 1983). In 1977 the Port of Nantes-Saint Nazaire and the Ministry of Transportation proposed a large public works project to make the port accessible to large ships, with the goal of stimulating the regional economy. This would require deepening the estuary and filling 500 ha of marshes. The Ministry of the Environment pointed out the harmful effects on the environment: reduced water quality, and interference with the reproduction of fish and the migration of birds. Negotiations, studies, and hasty decisions followed. Three years later the swamps have disappeared, but industrial and commercial entrepreneurs show little interest in joining the development; navigation in the estuary has actually become more difficult than in the past. The Court des Comptes (controller for public expenditures) castigated the project and found that the initial assessment of the economic situation had been done very poorly. One source of error, apparently not uncommon, came from the fact that the government subsidised part of the cost, and this cost component was not included in the CBA because the study was done within the narrow perspective of the Port Administration. Furthermore, the estimates of profitability were too optimistic, assuming certainty instead of considering different possibilities of development. Had environmental constraints been taken into account correctly, one would have been forced to be more careful in the economic analysis. Possible solutions would have been a modified development with sufficient profits to pay for environmental costs or abandonment of the project.

A similar instance of distortion by government subsidies can be found in the drainage of wetlands, which in France represents the principal threat to ecotones. Drainage would certainly be more limited if the government would not subsidise 50% of its costs, with the goal of stimulating agricultural output.

The case of Nantes-Saint Nazaire highlights the value of revisiting a project after it has been completed and seeing to what extent the original expectations have been met. Much could be learned from such post facto evaluation of public projects, especially about the realism of the underlying economic analyses. The importance of post facto evaluation has been emphasised, in a somewhat different context (social policies), by the interesting study of Monnier (1987). Unfortunately, the practice of post facto evaluation has been rare until now.

The decision process. When the responsibility for the environmental management is shared by different institutions, each in the pursuit of its own goals, with diverging interests, one can hardly talk of decision making. Rather, decisions emerge out of a dynamic process between institutional actors (Henry 1983), and results may be better explained by the theory of games than by the search for a social optimum. As each institution pursues its goals (e.g. construction of port facilities, expansion of the road network, increase of cultivated land), environmental goods are only an input; and when a problem arises (such as the destruction of a rare ecosystem), it is first of all viewed as an obstacle to the realisation of that institution's plans. In reality, there is not one single general interest, but many different interests, often with a local rather than national perspective.

In fact, these public institutions function like monopolies, not constrained by the rules of the market. How does one know if their choices are justified by adequate studies that integrate economic and ecological constraints and evaluate alternatives? Comparing countries of the same economic development points out disparities in the analysis. In Bavaria, rivers are managed in a way that combines improvement in water flow successfully with preservation of fauna and flora (Binder 1986). In England and Japan, high tension lines are placed underground. The same actions have not been taken in France. It appears that minimisation of total cost (i.e. monetary and environmental) does not occur spontaneously. Lacking strictly defined constraints, institutions prefer technical optimisation to economic optimisation. More examples can be found in Henry (1983) and in Montgolfier and Natali (1987).

The multiplication of actors in the administration of land, with divergent or competing objectives, often poses more problems than it can resolve. This is shown by the example of France, where formal responsibility for the protection of wetlands rests with the Ministry of the Environment while drainage is controlled by agricultural interests, in particular the Departmental Direction of Agriculture. The results are highly variable, depending on the attitudes of the chief engineer and of the various local forces. By contrast, in the Netherlands there is better integration of agricultural and environmental decision making within a single ministry, the Ministry of Agriculture and Fishing.

Regulatory instruments. The basic problem lies in the lack of a signal, analogous to prices, that can transmit information on environmental values to the various actors. In order to induce organisations to integrate environmental considerations into their decision making, different countries have developed different approaches: environmental impact studies, taxes, restrictions of use, and so forth. Environmental impact studies now seem to be required for all major projects in developed countries; but they are only a first step, and further measures are needed.

The theory and practice of regulatory instruments are best developed with regard to water pollution. It is easy to show (Baumol and Oates 1975) that a policy of effluent taxes minimises the total cost of pollution control, and organisations that are charged with the implementation (for instance the Agences de Bassin in France) bear witness to the progress made in this field. But while pollution from a point source is relatively easy to regulate by means of effluent taxes or strict limits, nonpoint sources (e.g. nitrates from agriculture) pose a more difficult problem. Even more challenging is the problem of land use. In fact, the major threats to ecotones involve problems of land use, such as drainage, industrial development, and flood control. Some lessons from various experiments are beginning to emerge, but much remains to be learned. What management tools are most effective? At what level should they be organised: local, regional, or national?

There are decentralised instruments, like taxes and subsidies, that can induce certain desired activities. One could, for instance, subsidise special types of cultivation (Baldock 1984), or one could tax land according to its actual use rather than its market value, thus providing an incentive to retain low intensity utilisation (Feitelson 1987). An interesting approach is the system of land trusts in the USA (Hocker 1987). These are private or governmental organisations that buy land when it is threatened, to resell it with restrictions on future uses (conservation easements). Another possibility is the system of transferable development rights that has been tried in the Chesapeake Bay Critical Area Program (Bowen 1987). Then there are regulatory instruments such as zoning, the traditional tool for the control of land use. It could be coupled with land purchase by the government. For the sake of equity it is necessary to adequately assess the impact and set up compensation schemes for those whose rights of land use are restricted. But zoning is often considered too rigid and too costly for situations of rapid development. In France this approach has not been very successful for the protection of ecotones, as zoning decisions are not subjected to an environmental impact study.

We see that there is no unique solution, rather the best approach depends on the administrative organisations and on the mentality in each country. It is important not to attempt to go against the fundamental structures of a country.

Lack of scientific understanding. The problem is complex. One remarks that at the scale of decision making the knowledge of the natural environment (hydrology, soil science, fauna, flora) is most often lacking or in the hands of organisations or academic scientists who do not sufficiently disseminate their knowledge (Falque 1987). Rivalries between administrators further impede the flow of information. But what information do the administrators need? Simple quantitative data about a site, or indicators about the fate of ecosystems when subjected to a certain use? Both types of information, certainly. An informal inquiry of French managers was carried out by the

Ministry of the Environment in 1985, concerning the needs for applied ecological reseach; 146 different responses were received, illustrating the problems, the uncertainties, and the questions that the administrators have to face.

With regard to the current state of knowledge, we quote some observations by people who have to make decisions. One, by the Regional Administration for Architecture and Environment of the Bretagne (France): 'In this field only a tiny fraction of decision makers are even aware of the lack of knowledge. The vast majority are content to enlighten their decisions with personal impressions or with a sense of the power play between the various pressure groups.' And another response by the Departmental Direction of Agriculture and Forests of Haute-Savoie (France): 'Lacking sufficient knowledge, the protection (of the environment) is not practised in an ideal fashion and according to scientific principles. The fact is that to advance in this field one has to exploit opportunity and power play; that's how far behind one is with the protection of the environment.' The need for valuation of natural goods in monetary terms is also emphasised.

There is a great need for information that is clearly organised and directly applicable. But often it is poorly formulated in relation to the complex problem of economic, ecological, and social constraints. The functions of choice and of administration are frequently mixed, illustrating the difficulty of operating in a world full of interaction and change. The criterion 'of ecological interest' remains too vague to serve as guide in practice. For example, during the 1970s the swamps of Lavour, in the above mentioned Dombes region, with a surface of 22 km², were designated to be of 'great ecological interest' according to the Prefecture and the Departmental Direction of Agriculture. Ten years later only 2.5 km² of these swamps remain, the rest having been drained by local farmers. Today the question of turning the remaining swamps into a nature reserve is being discussed.

We need a better understanding of threshold effects, cumulative impacts, and irreversibilities. Long-term ecological effects are poorly known. Much could be learned in this regard by studying the history of the interaction of man and environment over the course of centuries. A very promising approach that could provide decision makers with quantified impacts of human activities is ecological risk assessment. It is a process of identifying and quantifying probabilities of adverse changes in the environment resulting from a particular technology. The assessment of risk must be based on objective estimates of ecological damage: probabilities of population extinction or reductions in the abundance of plants and animals. The end points, or adverse effects, to be quantified must be relevant for society to influence decision making. The predictions about future states of nature are inevitably uncertain, so it is necessary to quantify uncertainty and to incorporate uncertainty into decision making. This would reduce the irrationality surrounding the management of environment. This method has been successfully applied to estimate the risks of synfuel-derived contaminants to fish populations (Barnthouse and Suter 1984, Barnthouse *et al.* 1987).

Examples of integrated economic and ecological management

Based on these observations, it seems that the following conditions are necessary for an integrated management: (1) sufficient scientific knowledge to forecast ecological and economic consequences, (2) a decision process that permits the exploration of alternatives and the emergence of negotiated solutions, and (3) regulatory instruments or economic policies that ensure correct implementation (compensating payments, subsidies, taxes).

There is nothing utopian about these proposals: examples show that they have been used successfully. I will discuss three of them below. Besides, the state of knowledge is improving; in the European Community this is happening with the development of ecological cartography, and in France with the program of Compatibilité Patrimoniale (i.e. accounting for the natural heritage). Such systems of ecological accounting, analogous in spirit to the accounting of the national economy, are being developed and refined, and they will allow the construction of better forecasting models. Finally, there is the need for negotiation when several different groups are involved. Much about the art of negotiation or environmental mediation has been learned by practice, as summarised in works such as Raiffa (1982).

The Chesapeake Bay Critical Area Program. The Chesapeake Bay in the United States provides a very instructive example of a strategy to improve the environment. The hierarchy of the organisation and the administrative instruments merit a detailed presentation. In 1984 the General Assembly of Maryland created a commission of 25 members, representing concerned interests (agriculture, industry, land developers, local governments, environmental groups), to coordinate a program of protecting the Chesapeake Bay. A critical zone is declared, consisting of the waters of the bay and the adjacent land up to a distance of 300 m inland. The General Assembly defined the principal objectives as: (1) limiting the negative impacts of pollution, (2) conserving fish, wildlife, and flora, and (3) defining zoning policies that permit economic development while protecting the environment. The commission then develops more detailed criteria to implement these objectives, and passes these criteria on to the local authorities, thus enabling the latter to develop local programmes for environmental protection. This scheme is summarised graphically in Fig. 12.5.

Integration of economic and ecological objectives. As a good example we discuss the management of the swamps of Sillingy (Haute-Savoie, France) (Fischesser and Dupuis 1987). In 1982, at the occasion of land redistribution

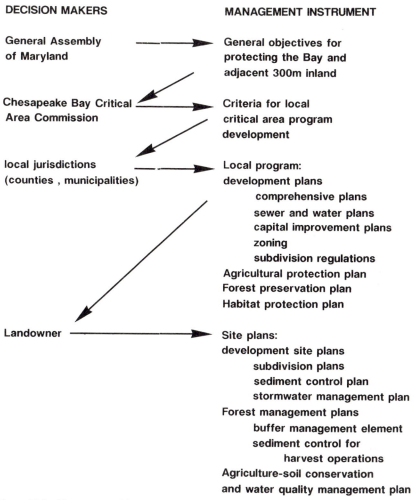

DECISION MAKERS

MANAGEMENT INSTRUMENT

General Assembly
of Maryland

General objectives for
protecting the Bay and
adjacent 300m inland

Chesapeake Bay Critical
Area Commission

Criteria for local
critical area program
development

local jurisdictions
(counties , municipalities)

Local program:
development plans
 comprehensive plans
 sewer and water plans
 capital improvement plans
 zoning
 subdivision regulations
Agricultural protection plan
Forest preservation plan
Habitat protection plan

Landowner

Site plans:
development site plans
 subdivision plans
 sediment control plan
 stormwater management plan
Forest management plans
 buffer management element
 sediment control for
  harvest operations
Agriculture-soil conservation
and water quality management plan

Figure 12.5 Management hierarchy for protection of Chesapeake Bay. The arrows indicate how decisions are passed on from one level to the next. Adapted from Davis (1987)

in the communities of Sillingy and Nonglard (a process needed for the intensification of agriculture), the question of the future of the swamps arose. The options were: draining (to make room for grain production), abandoning (in which case the forest would take over rapidly), and a nature preserve.

The swamps covered 220 ha, the useful agricultural surface 1350 ha. The case was debated even within the Departmental Direction of Agriculture and Forests, because it involved two of its divisions with conflicting interests. The division of ground and water management wanted to improve the standard of living of the local farmers while the division of nature protection wanted to protect the swamps for their ecological interest (including 60 species of birds, 10 species of birds of prey, and 200 species of plants specific to the region). Further interest groups were local governments, farmers and agricultural organisations, and associations for hunting, fishing, beekeeping, tourism, and nature protection.

A process of mediation was set in motion to resolve this conflict in 1983. The mediator had the task of structuring and leading the negotiations forward by using techniques of integrating the data and of presenting and explaining them in simple form. Gradually, alternative solutions were explored. Evolutionary scenarios allowed the forecasting of economic and ecological consequences. The scenarios were organised around two extreme solutions: the swamp disappears, or the swamp is completely protected.

In 1985, at last, a compromise was adopted, after evaluation of costs and benefits (some stated in financial terms, some not):

- The redistribution involves 80 ha, of which 30 ha were wet prairies to be drained by repairing an old network of water pipes. The drained areas are arranged in groups, surrounded by swamps. The owners of the swamps promise to maintain them by mowing.

- Two water reservoirs were created at the two ends of the swamps.

- Owners who did not want to drain their land (since only 50% of that cost will be subsidised, not much in view of the expected productivity) were regrouped by land exchange. Part of the land could be sold to hunters.

- Special contracts ensured that certain farmers could mow 5 ha/yr (cost approximately $1000/yr, paid by the community).

- A nature trail across the swamp would be open to visitors.

- New types of agriculture were to be explored, such as production of vegetables.

This solution offered the following advantages: (1) the drainage was less costly than for other alternatives; (2) the natural environment was better preserved; and (3) the farmers were encouraged to try products with higher value.

The choice of regulatory instruments. While the benefit of environmental protection accrues to society, the cost often falls disproportionately on certain individuals, especially farmers. Gradually, arrangements are being developed to compensate the affected individuals for restrictions of their property rights. (Such compensation is analogous to subsidies that have been paid to farmers in Western Europe for the last 30 years to improve their standard of living.) That alternative can turn out less costly than if the state were to purchase outright the land of greatest ecological interest.

This approach is practised more and more in Holland, where a policy of contracts is used to integrate the protection of the environment into the practice of agriculture (Hesse 1986). For this purpose special 'regulated zones' were defined by the Dutch governments in 1977, comprising 8% of the total agricultural land and consisting mostly of wetland prairies used for pasture and hay production; they are the nesting site of avian waders. One of the first places for trying out this policy is the island of Terschelling in Frisia, where the following rules have been administered by the Ministry of Agriculture and Fishing since 1980. Four types of constraints are imposed: preserving the existing surface water level; not using pesticides; not ploughing or levelling the prairies; mowing from the centre towards the edge. In some zones certain additional restrictions apply between 12 April and 22 June on at least 15% of the area: no fertilising; no mowing; no grazing; and so forth. Contracts are signed for the duration of three years, and farmers have the option of proposing only a portion of the land for utilisation.

The compensation consists of two components. The first, compensation for current expenses, is based on the difference in fodder production (per ha of land and per kg of milk) between the regulated zones and the zones of normal agriculture in the region. Differences in labour or of fertiliser cost are accounted for. The second component, compensation for adjustment, is a payment, decreasing to zero over 18 years, to help amortise any overinvestment in equipment that the farmer may have made before this policy was in place.

The total amount of the compensation ranges from $135 to $100 per ha annually (1981), depending on local circumstances. This compensation represents the price paid by society for the preservation of the landscape. The scheme has been criticised for lack of flexibility, but it will certainly be further developed and improved. It will be interesting to follow this experiment further.

CONCLUSION

What can one conclude about the state of the art of managing ecotones? The basic economic valuation and decision tools are fairly well developed (in particular cost-benefit analysis and the valuation of nonmarket goods), and they have been used extensively and successfully for many projects. But they are only a first step in the process, and they need to be followed by negotiation of acceptable solutions and by implementation in a management program. In these latter areas much progress remains to be made. Several interesting approaches are being explored in different countries, and the lessons are worth paying attention to. Important gaps remain also on the scientific side, to better understand the ecological consequences of our decisions.

To improve the management ecotones, further research is needed especially on the following questions:

1. Identify compatible uses of ecotones. The lack of precise knowledge in this field often impedes the successful negotiation of solutions. Furthermore, such knowledge would allow cost-benefit analysis to be used more effectively.

2. Improve the understanding of irreversibilities and of uncertainties. This is crucial for improving the process of decision making. The development of research in ecological risk assessment holds much promise.

3. Refine system analysis, linking economic and ecological models. Which are the economic parameters relevant for ecological modelling? Which ecological variables can be translated into economic terms? This group of questions suggests where most work seems needed.

4. Develop global indices to express the essential results of economic and ecological modelling in terms that decision makers can understand.

5. Improve valuation techniques for ecotones:

- Systematise the social value of certain functions assured by ecotones. For example, the value of riparian forests in their role as filter of nutrients could be expressed as a function of local pollution in terms of dollars per kg per year. Similarly, the value of a river for fishing can be stated in these units, as has been done in effect by the National Office of Forests in France when it leases riverbanks to local fishing clubs, for approximately $150 per km annually.

- Frequent polling of individual preferences (as is done in Germany, for instance, but not in France). That is an important indicator for the decision, more important than any other scientific index.

- Learn to take better advantage of the role that touristic, cultural, and recreational activities can play in the protection of the environment; frequently that is the most effective strategy available, because organisations for hunting, fishing, and so forth, have a strong interest in maintaining the environment.

6. Identify good management tools, best suited for each particular problem and well adapted to the administrative structures and mentalities in each country.

7. Reflect on methods of compensation that are not too costly, that are sufficiently equitable, and that could even pass across national borders.

8. Adapt the methods to developing countries.

9. Perform post facto evaluations of projects to learn from experience.

ACKNOWLEDGEMENTS

I am grateful to A. Rabl of Princeton University for many valuable suggestions and discussions. I would also like to acknowledge helpful comments by R. Barre of the Conservatoire National des Arts et Metiers, C.A. Davis and E. Feitelson of the Chesapeake Bay Critical Area Commission, P. Point of the Université de Bordeaux I, and two anonymous referees.

LITERATURE CITED

Arrow, K.J. 1983. Behaviour under uncertainty and its implications for policy. Pages 19-32 *in* B.P. Stigum and F. Wenstøp, editors. Foundations of utility and risk theory with applications. D. Reidel, Dordrecht, The Netherlands.

Arrow, K.J., and A.C. Fisher. 1974. Environmental preservation, uncertainty and irreversibility. Quarterly Journal of Economics 88:312-319.

Baldock, D. 1984. Wetland drainage in Europe. The Institute for European Environmental Policy, the International Institute for Environment and Development, Russel Press Ltd., Nottingham, England.

Barnthouse, L.W., and G.W. Suter. 1984. Risk assessment: ecology, Mechanical Engineering 106:36-39.

Barnthouse, L.W., G.W. Suter, and R.V. O'Neill. 1987. Treatment of risk in environmental impact assessment. Environmental Management 11:295-303.

Batie, S.S., and L.A. Shabman. 1982. Estimating the economic value of wetlands: principles, methods and limitations. Journal of Coastal Zone Management 10:225-278.

Baumol, W.J., and W.E. Oates. 1975. The theory of environmental policy. Prentice-Hall, Englewood Cliffs, New Jersey, USA.

Beaton, P. 1988. The impact of zoning on the price of houses in the Chesapeake Bay Area. Center for Urban Policy Research, Rutgers University, New Brunswick, New Jersey, USA.

Berard, L. 1982. Terres et eaux en Dombes. Presses Universitaires de Lyon, Editions de la Maison des Sciences de l'Homme, Lyon, France.

Bernoulli, D. 1738. Exposition of a new theory on the measurement of risk. Translated and reprinted in Econometrica (1954) 22:23-36.

Binder, W. 1986. Ouvrages hydrauliques et entretien des cours d'eau, l'expérience bavaroise [Water projects and management of water flow: the case of Bavaria]. Pages 87-108 *in* C. Henry and J.C. Toutain, editors. Milieux naturels: illustration de quelques réussites. Editions du Centre National de la Recherche Scientifique, Paris, France.

Bishop, R.C. 1986. Resource valuation under uncertainty: theoretical principles for empirical research. Pages 133-152 *in* V.K. Smith, editor. Advances in applied micro-economics. Volume 4. Jai Press, London, England.

Bowen, G.A. 1987. The Calvert County experience. Workshop: Prospects and Problems of Economic Instruments as Complements to the Chesapeake Bay Critical Area Program. The Chesapeake Bay Critical Area Commission, Annapolis, Maryland, USA.

Brookshire, D.S., R.C. d'Arge, W.D. Schulze, and M.A. Thayer. 1981. Experiments in valuing public goods. Pages 123-171 *in* V.K. Smith, editor. Advances in applied micro-economics. Volume 1. Jai Press, London, England.

Brown, G.M., and J. Hammack. 1974. Waterfowl and wetlands: toward a bioeconomic analysis. Johns Hopkins University Press, Baltimore, Maryland, USA.

Clawson, M., and J.L. Knetsch. 1966. Economics of outdoor recreation. Johns Hopkins University Press, Baltimore, Maryland, USA.

Courant, P.N., and R. Porter. 1981. Averting expenditure and the cost of pollution. Journal of Environmental Economic and Management 8:321-329.

Cummings, R.G., D.S. Brookshire, and W.D. Schulze. 1986. Valuing environmental goods: an assessment of the contingent valuation method. Rowman and Allanheld, Division of Littlefield, Adams & Co., Totowa, New Jersey, USA.

Davis, C.A. 1987. A strategy to save the Chesapeake shoreline. Journal of Soil and Water Conservation 42:72-75.

Décamps, H., and R.J. Naiman. 1989. L'ecologie des fleuves. La Recherche 20:310-319.

Desaigues, B., and J.C. Toutain. 1978. Gérer l'environnement [Managing the environment]. Economica, Paris, France.

Duffield, J. 1984. Travel cost and contingent valuation: a comparative analysis. Pages 67-87 *in* V.K. Smith, editor. Advances in applied micro-economics. Volume 3. Jai Press, London, England.

Falque, M. 1987. Analyse critique et prospective des études d'impact [Critical analysis and future of impact studies]. Cahiers du Groupe d'Exploration et de Recherches Multidisciplinaires sur l'Environnement et la Société 12:521-538.

Farber, S. 1987. The value of coastal wetlands for the protection of property against hurricane wind damage. Journal of Environmental Economics and Management 14:143-151.

Farber, S. 1988. The value of coastal wetlands for recreation: an application of travel cost and contingent valuation methodologies. Journal of Environmental Management 26:299-312.

Feitelson, E. 1987. The promise and problems of economic instruments for local jurisdictions around the Chesapeake Bay. Workshop: Prospects and Problems of Economic Instruments as Complements to the Chesapeake Bay Critical Area Program. The Chesapeake Bay Critical Area Commission, Annapolis, Maryland, USA.

Fischesser, B., and M.F. Dupuis. 1987. Un processus de mediation au service d'un remembrement en zone sensible [A process of negotiation for redistribution of sensitive land areas]. Cahiers du Groupe d'Exploration et de Recherches Multidisciplinaires sur l'Environnement et la Société 12:433-468.

Fisher, A., and. R. Raucher. 1984. Intrinsic benefits of improved water quality: conceptual and empirical perspective. Pages 37-65 *in* V.K. Smith, editor. Advances in applied micro-economics. Volume 3. Jai Press, London, England.

Freeman, A.M. 1986. Estimating the benefits of environmental regulations. Pages 211-230 *in* J.D. Bentkover, V.T. Covello, and J. Mumpower, editors. Benefits assessment: the state of the art. D. Reidel, Dordrecht, The Netherlands.

Gosselink, J.G., R.M. Odum, and R.M. Pope. 1974. The value of tidal marsh. Center for Wetland Resources, Baton Rouge, Louisiana, USA.

Henry, C. 1974. Investment decisions under uncertainty: the irreversibility effect. American Economic Review 64:1006-1012.

Henry, C. 1983. Economics and the conservation of natural environments. Publications du Laboratoire d'Econometrie de l'Ecole Polytechnique, Paris, France.

Hesse, J. 1986. Les mécanismes contractuels appliques à la conservation de la nature [Contractual arrangements applied to the conservation of nature]. Pages 69-86 *in* C. Henry and J.C. Toutain, editors. Milieux naturels: illustration de quelques reussites. Editions du Centre National de la Recherche Scientifique, Paris, France.

Hicks, J.R. 1943. The four consumer's surpluses. Review of Economic Studies 11:31-41.

Hocker, J. 1987. Land trust innovations: the national view. Workshop on the Prospects and Problems of Economic Instruments as Complements to the Chesapeake Bay Critical Area Program. The Chesapeake Bay Critical Area Commission, Annapolis, Maryland, USA.

Johanson, P.O. 1987. The economic theory and measurement of environmental benefits. Cambridge University Press, Cambridge, England.

Kahneman, D., and A. Tversky. 1986. Choices, values and frames. Pages 194-210 *in* H.R. Arkes and K.R. Hammond, editors. Judgement and decision making. Cambridge University Press, Cambridge, England.

Krutilla, J.V., and A.C. Fisher. 1975. The economics of natural environments: studies in the valuation of commodity and amenity resources. Johns Hopkins University Press, Baltimore, Maryland, USA.

Layard, R. 1974. Cost-benefit analysis. Penguin Books, Harmondsworth, Middlesex, England, and Baltimore, Maryland, USA.

Lind, R.C. 1982. Discounting for time and risk in energy flow. Resources for the Future, Johns Hopkins University Press, Baltimore, Maryland, USA.

Lynne, G.D., P. Conroy, and F.J. Prohaska. 1981. Economic valuation of marsh areas for marine production processes. Journal of Environmental Economics and Management 8:175-186.

Mendelsohn, R. 1984. An application of the hedonic travel cost framework for recreation modelling to the valuation of deer. Pages 89-101 *in* V.K. Smith, editor. Advances in applied micro-economics. Volume 3. Jai Press, London, England.

Mermet, L., and M. Mustin. 1983. Assainissement agricole et régression des zones humides en France [Agricultural drainage and reduction of wetlands in France]. International Institute for Environment and Development, London, England.

Monnier, E. 1987. Evaluations de l'action des pouvoirs publics. Economica, Paris, France.

Montgolfier, J. de, and J.M. Natali. 1987. Le patrimoine du futur. Economica, Paris, France.

Organisation for Economic Cooperation and Development. 1986. Public management of forest projects. Annexe 2. Paris, France.

Point, P. 1986. Elements pour une approche économique du patrimoine naturel. Pages 137-138 *in* Les comptes du patrimoine naturel. Collections de l'Institut National de la Statistique et des Etudes Economiques. Série C. Paris, France.

Purseglove, J.J. 1986. Protection de la nature et ménagement des cours d'eau en Angleterre et Pays de Galles [Protection of the nature and water flow management in England and Wales]. Pages 131-146 *in* C. Henry and J.C. Toutain, editors. Milieux naturels: illustration de quelques réussites. Editions du Centre National de la Recherche Scientifique, Paris, France.

Raiffa, H. 1982. The art and science of negotiation. Harvard University Press, Cambridge, Massachussetts, USA.

Smith, V.K. 1986. A conceptual overview of the foundations of benefit-cost analysis. Pages 13–34 *in* J.D. Bentkover, V.T. Covello, and J. Mumpower, editors. Benefit assessment: the state of the art. D. Reidel, Dordrecht, The Netherlands.

Smith, V.K., and W.H. Desvouges. 1986. Measuring water quality benefits. Kluwer-Nijhoff, Boston, Massachusetts, USA, and Dordrecht, The Netherlands.

Weisbrod, B.A. 1964. Collective consumption services of individual consumption goods. Quarterly Journal of Economics 78:471-477.

Yudelman, M. 1985. World Bank and agricultural development: an insider's view. World Resources Institute, Washington, D.C., USA.

Key words: Cost-benefit analysis, ecotones, environmental economics, environmental management, land use.

CHAPTER 13

AQUATIC-TERRESTRIAL ECOTONES: SUMMARY AND RECOMMENDATIONS

Robert J. Naiman and Henri Décamps

ABSTRACT

Significant points and issues identified at the Sopron symposium relate to a diverse array of ecotone characteristics. These include the origin and maintenance of aquatic-terrestrial ecotones, fundamental ecotone behaviour, development of a central body of theory, the usefulness of ecotones for detecting global change and influencing biodiversity, and ecotone classification. These points highlight the principal challenges facing aquatic ecologists and managers now and in the future. Informational needs are multiple and complex in a rapidly changing world where ecotones are becoming increasingly important in the regulation of ecosystem and landscape level processes.

INTRODUCTION

There are compelling reasons for examining aquatic and terrestrial ecosystems as a series of discrete patches or communities with reasonably distinct ecotones, rather than as gradual gradients or continua. Most populations and processes in nature are arranged in discrete patches (Pickett and White 1985); boundaries between these patches are readily detected on various spatial and temporal scales (Forman and Godron 1986); and the landscape is being increasingly divided into patches with clearly defined boundaries (Naiman *et al.* 1988). It is difficult to apply gradient or continuum concepts to ecosystems where sharply defined zones exist naturally, or to systems experiencing sustained anthropogenic alterations.

The authors in this volume suggest that it may be informative to view ecosystems as a collection of resource patches separated by ecotones. This approach is not proposed as a replacement for continuum or gradient concepts but rather as complementary to them, providing a perspective that operates over various spatial and temporal scales. It is a perspective that appears to be especially pertinent in today's world: as civilisation expands, there are substantial changes in the ratios of ecotone length to patch area and to patch volume. These alterations are seen in the changing proportion of riparian forests to agricultural fields and river channels over the past several centuries (Sedell and Froggatt 1984, Décamps and Naiman 1989, Petts *et al.* 1989,). An important but still unanswered question is whether human-created ecotones have the same properties as natural ecotones. Alarmingly, changes in the ecotone-to-surface and ecotone-to-area ratios of the landscape are proceeding without sufficient information on the long-term environmental implications of these anthropogenic alterations.

FUNDAMENTAL ISSUES

This volume treats only aquatic-terrestrial ecotones. Yet a thorough understanding of ecotones concerns a complex domain requiring a broad environmental and social perspective. Despite their restricted scope, these symposium proceedings provide an initial introduction to the broader subject and express a diversity of opinions and perspectives. A key point of the symposium has been to realise the diversity of fundamental issues posed by aquatic-terrestrial ecotones in a world increasingly divided and modified.

Mankind faces unprecedented environmental issues in the next decades as exploitation and modification of the earth's natural resources increase. As natural resources become scarce, their economic and societal value increases, creating the potential for national and international conflicts. At the same time, extraction and processing of resources create environmental problems with global implications (Di Castri *et al.* 1984, Di Castri and Hadley 1988). Yet there are positive approaches to this seemingly pessimistic scenario. One approach is better management of existing resources through understanding and utilisation of the natural properties of ecosystems over the long term. The authors in this volume are suggesting that an 'ecotone perspective' may be one of several appropriate avenues to pursue.

We believe that in the next decades there are at least six main challenges facing aquatic ecologists at the ecosystem or landscape level:

- Creation of a landscape perspective for aquatic systems

- Determining the cumulative effects of land use practices

- Rehabilitating damaged ecosystems

- Management of natural variability

- Prudent conservation of natural systems

- Clarifying relations between resource economics and the environment

These challenges can be partly met with an ecotone-patch dynamics approach. A landscape perspective requires an approach that treats large areas as a system of interacting patches partly regulated by their ecotones. Cumulative effects result from perturbations being transmitted through the system along pathways that are often unpredictable and irreversible. Ecotones act to modify, or even control, transmission of disturbances between patches. Ecotones can also be used to assist the recovery of patches from disturbance by using their natural properties for adaptive silvicultural and engineering solutions. Ecotones, patches, and ecosystems are naturally variable in time and space. Yet most aquatic systems are managed for stability. An ecotone approach would require a new, and needed, perspective for the management of uncertainty. The difficult issues related to the conservation of natural systems could be made easier if key ecotonal features were preserved and protected. Finally, many of the environmental issues we face are directly driven by global resource economics and international monetary exchange rates. Their effects on land use patterns and environmental quality require a patch-ecotone perspective.

These challenges become increasingly pertinent when one considers that fresh water represents an essential element for the social, economic, and ecological well-being of every country on earth. Fresh water is a resource with multiple uses for agriculture, industry, recreation, transport, fisheries, environmental functioning, and human health. Groundwater, lakes, wetlands, streams, and rivers constitute the natural freshwater environment increasingly in need of better protection and management. Aquatic-terrestrial ecotones have been identified as a key component affecting, and perhaps regulating, the quality of these waters.

In the remainder of this chapter we want to consider three interrelated issues that can be used to evaluate advances presented in this volume towards a better understanding of the ecology and management of aquatic-terrestrial ecotones: (1) What did we learn from this experience? (2) How do these advances relate to management? (3) What are the needs for the future?

LESSONS FROM THIS EXPERIENCE

Most ecotones are created and maintained by external environment forces. Internal mechanisms contribute to their maintenance but are relatively weak when compared with external influences. It follows that the creation of ecotones eventually depends on the variability of forcing functions (i.e. disturbance, edaphic factors, climate, geomorphology) operating on spatial and temporal scales that may be different for each major type of ecotone. The biological characteristics of the ecotones are closely related to, or even determined by, these spatiotemporal forcing functions. This essential coherence of spatial and temporal scales obliges a careful characterisation of specific ecotones proposed for study.

Another lesson from the comparisons made at Sopron is that ecotones differ in their ability to modify materials moving through them. This variability of the functional role of ecotones depends on the spatiotemporal variability of the external forces that create and maintain the ecotones, and the structure of the ecotones themselves. For example, mature riparian forests will probably have functional chracteristics different from riparian forests at earlier successional stages.

The central body of theory related to aquatic-terrestrial ecotones is still rudimentary. But perhaps this is not a major shortcoming while researchers are developing an 'ecotone perspective.' It is recognised, however, that the spatial and temporal arrangements of resource patches and their ecotones are important in the functioning of the landscape. Patch resource character-istics and their associated ecotones exhibit considerable contrast across biomes, providing a potentially rewarding perspective for comparative studies. Yet there are several techniques that can be adapted to provide insights into ecotonal characteristics (e.g. percolation theory, neutral models, and chaos theory).

Researchers have different responses concerning relationships between ecotones, global change, and biodiversity. From a conceptual standpoint it is possible to argue, quite convincingly, that global change can be detected early in ecotonal areas, but the exact response from the ecotone is not known. Likewise, it is possible to argue that biodiversity may be either increased or decreased in ecotones. Quite simply, the answers are not known. They may be different for different types of ecotones, and resolution requires more information, including field experiments.

It is important to understand that *identification of what is, or is not, an ecotone depends on the nature of the question being asked.* This is an important point since ecotones (and patches) occur over a wide variety of spatial and temporal scales. At present, researchers are conducting ecological studies over scales ranging spatially from 10^{-8} to 10^7 m and temporally from 10^{-7} to 10^8 yr; this represents 16 orders of magnitude (Minshall 1988). It is therefore essential to appreciate that different questions and perspectives (i.e. microbial, macrofauna, and global) will result in different ways of identifying ecotones.

Perhaps the most important lesson has to do with the complexity of the environmental issues and their relation to social and economic issues. These latter forces are great, yet as ecologists we are often unable to anticipate how social and economic concerns will affect the environment. There is an urgent need for better linkages between sociologists, economists, and ecologists in order to provide this vision. Perhaps an ecotone or patch perspective can provide a common theme for useful discussions.

RELATIONSHIP TO MANAGEMENT

The management of variable systems is difficult because of their inherent complexity and unpredictability. This is why certain management processes

298

(e.g. BPMO) have been developed (Petts 1990). However, actual management offers relatively little to natural systems. One fundamental reason is that management is often based, either implicitly or explicitly, on the concept of environmental stability. Yet, particularly when one considers aquatic-terrestrial ecotones, one must learn to manage *for* environmental variability. This requires new perspectives, tools, and techniques in order to place management at a level where decisions are based on a sound understanding of natural systems. The challenge is formidable but the potential environmental and economic rewards are enormous.

This latter point is especially pertinent. The level of managerial effort expended on ecotones depends on their perceived value to society – a fact that should be incorporated into our scientific consciousness. One must realise that the aesthetic and economic values of many aquatic-terrestrial ecotones can be used to improve societal awareness of ecotonal functions.

Finally, management must assure a coherent connection between fundamental knowledge of ecotonal structure and function and the restoration of damaged systems. This will require an interdisciplinary effort demanding that engineers, ecologists, hydrologists, economists, and specialists from other disciplines work together closely towards a common goal. The results will be obvious.

NEEDS FOR THE FUTURE

There are two major categories of needs for the advancement of an 'ecotone perspective': an improved knowledge base and new tools and techniques. Each represents a major challenge for effective implementation.

The major improvements needed in the knowledge base are:

- Synthetic models of complex phenomena and complex systems

- A classification scheme based on appropriate spatial and temporal scales

- Better understanding of ecotonal relationships between surface waters and groundwaters

- Greater comprehension of ecotones as natural systems that can speed the recovery process of damaged systems

- Mechanisms and processes for efficient managerial implementation of ecotonal information and improved societal awareness of ecotonal values

Addressing these knowledge gaps can be partly accomplished with existing tools and techniques. However, symposium participants also stressed the need to advance quickly in developing new techniques or in adapting existing methods from other disciplines. The major tools and techniques needed include:

- Improved training and use of high speed computers for evaluating connectivity, variability, and cumulative effects in complex systems

- Development of spatial and temporal statistical methods for the quantitative evaluation of patch and boundary dynamics

- Continual development of techniques associated with Geographic Information Systems (GIS), nuclear magnetic resonance (NMR), and remote sensing (SPOT, Landsat, EOS) that have direct relevance to ecotone identification and processes

- Development of long-term demonstration sites that can be used for interdisciplinary and cross-cultural education at all levels (e.g. societal, scientific, and managerial)

Many of these needs are being addressed independently for other programs concerned with the environmental issues in the next decade. A major task will be to adapt the knowledge, tools, and techniques to an 'ecotonal perspective' in order to provide a solid conceptual and practical framework for improving environmental understanding and the human condition.

CONCLUSION

The main challenge for mankind is not to develop systems based on natural resource exploitation, as has been done for the past several centuries. Rather it is to maintain (or even enhance) economic strength through wise and efficient use of existing resources, while maintaining (or enhancing) the quality of life and the quality of the environment. An 'ecotone perspective' can help meet that challenge.

The positive aspects of an 'ecotone perspective' for the management of aquatic systems include improved water quality, improved fish and wildlife production, enhanced recreational opportunities, an aesthetically pleasing environment, and a human population in better harmony with nature for the long term. In combination, these aspects present a strong argument for considering an ecotone perspective for ecological systems.

The proceedings of this symposium synthesise only part of a large and complex informational base about aquatic-terrestrial ecotones. This publication signals the early stages of a programme, and a perspective, promising to develop quickly in a rapidly changing world – a programme and perspective that should have a positive impact on the quality of human life.

ACKNOWLEDGEMENTS

We thank P.G. Risser, J.F. Franklin, and G. Pinay for comments on the manuscript. Financial support was provided by the United States National Science Foundation (BSR 87-22852), the Centre National de la Recherche Scientifique, the United States Man and the Biosphere Program (Department of State), and the Unesco Man and the Biosphere Programme.

LITERATURE CITED

Décamps, H., and R.J. Naiman. 1989. L'ecologie des fleuves. La Recherche 20:310-319.

Di Castri, F., F.W.G. Baker, and M. Hadley (editors). 1984. Ecology in practice. Tycooly International Publishing, Dublin, Ireland.

Di Castri, F., and M. Hadley. 1988. Enhancing the credibility of ecology: interacting along and across heirarchical scales. Geo Journal 17:5-35

Forman, R.T.T., and M. Godron. 1986. Landscape ecology. John Wiley and Sons, New York, USA.

Minshall, G.W. 1988. Stream ecosystem theory: a global perspective. Journal of the North American Benthological Society 7:263-288.

Naiman, R.J., H. Décamps, J. Pastor, and C.A. Johnston. 1988. The potential importance of boundaries to fluvial ecosystems. Journal of the North American Benthological Society 7:289-306.

Petts, G.E. 1990. The role of ecotones in aquatic landscape management, *this volume.*

Petts, G.E., A.L. Roux, and H. Moller (editors). 1989. Historical changes of large alluvial rivers in Western Europe. Wiley, Chichester, England.

Pickett, S.T.A. and P.S. White (editors). 1985. The ecology of natural disturbance and patch dynamics. Academic Press, Orlando, Florida, USA.

Sedell, J.R., and J.L. Froggatt. 1984. Importance of streamside forests to large river: the isolation of the Willamette River, Oregon, USA, from its floodplain by snagging and streamside forest removal. Verhandlungen Internationale Vereinigung Limnologie 22:1828-1834.

Key words: Aquatic, boundary, ecotone, landscape, terrestrial.

INDEX

Acer, 173
Acer saccharinum, 73
acidity (pH)
  effect on ecotones, 93–94, 129
  in wetlands, 182, 195
Acre Province, Brazil, 46, 54
active-channel shelf, 71, 72
active-channel width, 71
Adour River, 149
aerobic conditions, 175, 181, 186, 189, 213
Africa, 45, 156, 183, 193, 235, 277
Agences de Bassin, 284
aggradation, 231
  Amazon, 54
agriculture, 8
  and bird species, 10
  buffering of runoff from, 163, 183, 186, 233, 237
  drainage for, 265, 266
  Dutch regulated zones, 289
  experiments, 100
  nutrient content of streams, 15–16
  restrictions on, 266–267
  uplands, 185
  watersheds, 237
Ailanthus altissima, 96
Ain River, 216
Albenche, France, 212
Alberta, Canada, 213
alder, 70, 73, 157, 159, 236
algae, 111, 112, 127, 128, 133
  blue-green, 213
  production, 115, 116–117, 151
Al-Kharj, Saudi Arabia, 244
allelopathy, 95
allochthonous inputs
  in lentic ecotones, 113–114, 115–117
  in lotic ecotones, 146, 148
  in tropics, 235
  into streams, 10
  nitrate from groundwater, 213
alluvium
  ecosystem functions, 204, 230, 233, 241

fans, 45, 46, 47, 49
floods, 144, 158, 161, 162, 234
Garonne River, 144–146, 147
oligotrophisation, 212
Po River, 142
Quaternary, 48
research, 82
underground, 219
Alnus spp., 70, 73, 157, 159, 236
Alps, 44, 80, 82
Alto Madre de Dios River, 56
Amazon River, 38, 235
  Amazon basin, 44, 52–58
  biodiversity, 52, 55, 56
  environments of equilibrium, 40
  erosional bank, 47
  fish species, 149
  flooding, 161
  megaform border zones, 40
  mesoform fluvial changes, 43
  Quaternary fluctuations, 48
  várzea-terra firme ecotone, 40, 53–54, 55–56
amphibians, 236
amphipods, 206, 209, 210, 218
anaerobic conditions, 174, 175, 181, 186, 189
  See also Oxidation-reduction conditions
anastomosing channels, 49, 53, 56
Andes, 43, 54, 56
angiosperms, 55
Anglian Water Authority, 243
animals
  amphibians, 236
  and flooded areas, 235
  and organic matter in sediments, 212
  culling, 253
  ecotone functions of, 233
  effects on plant communities, 98–99
  herbivores, 235–236
anions in groundwater, 214
aquaculture, 253
aquatic ecotones

303